Historical Geography of the United States

BY RALPH H. BROWN

PROFESSOR OF GEOGRAPHY

UNIVERSITY OF MINNESOTA

UNDER THE EDITORSHIP OF

J. RUSSELL WHITAKER

HARCOURT, BRACE & WORLD, INC.

NEW YORK   CHICAGO   BURLINGAME

PRINTED IN THE UNITED STATES OF AMERICA

Preface

THE HISTORICAL geographer of so vast and varied a land as the United States assumes many responsibilities. To begin with, there is the necessity of preparing a factual record which will be something more than a bare listing of places and peoples and industries. Over and above this is the problem of interpretation. For example, southern New England early became a manufacturing region; of this one can entertain no reasonable doubt — but the answer to the question Why? is open to various possibilities. No phase of historical geography is more important, moreover, than that of weighing the effectiveness of beliefs as distinct from actual knowledge in the occupancy and settlement of regions. The classic example is the " Great American Desert " idea of the first half of the nineteenth century, but there were many others.

The past geography of a region is only partly told when account has been taken of the cultural landscape. The picture must be extended to include the natural setting — land surface, vegetation, soils, climate — not as we know it today but as it was known or understood during the period under consideration. The very processes of settlement have greatly altered some of these natural circumstances and if they have not changed in fact, there is always the possibility, even the probability, that beliefs concerning them have changed. To cite a few instances, the Ohio River of 1800 was not the Ohio River as we know it today, and the environs of Detroit are certainly not a morass of lakes and swamps barely worth the cost of surveying, as they were considered in the 1820's. Gone are the Big Woods of southeast Minnesota as known to the pioneers, although efforts are being made to preserve the remaining few acres which have escaped the ax and the plow; and the tidal swamps of the lower Sacramento have yielded to the drainage and irrigation projects of the past century. Just as the producer is careful to avoid anachronisms in the staging and costuming of a historical play, so in this book the picture of the environment is, so far as possible, related in time with the events which are recorded.

This interpretation of the functions of historical geography, which has long been defined but rarely exemplified as simply " the geography of the past," depends on original, eyewitness accounts and contemporary maps. The availability of such material has mainly prescribed the space and time limits of this regional study. In general, regions are considered at the earliest period for which there is reliable and adequate source material. Some regions have been omitted, or are treated briefly or incidentally, because search has failed to yield a sufficient body of trustworthy matter basic to a geographical inquiry. The book pretends to be no more exhaustive within its field than one-volume works on the present-day geography of North America. Because of the inaccessibility to the reader of perhaps nine-tenths of the source material, quotations are often more lengthy than would normally be expected.

This is a survey of the character of American regions in earlier times. "American" identifies mainly the United States, but the eastern provinces of Canada form integral parts of the preliminary chapters. Although present-day conditions are not wholly neglected, the chief emphasis is on past periods within time limits varying with the region considered. Thus the earlier sections embrace the Colonial period, sufficiently so, at least, to provide a background for understanding national development. No attempt is made to reconstruct the original landscape of the coastal regions previous to the colonization period; for here the only eyewitnesses were the aborigines, who, it may be observed, were an uncommunicative people. The development of the Atlantic slope of the continent is sketched, in Part Two, through the opening decade of the nineteenth century. Limitations of space set by a moderate-sized book prohibit a study of the same region in later times.

Advancing westward with the tide of settlement, attention is next turned upon the Ohio country. To prevent a general survey from becoming a volume in itself, descriptions of this significant inland region are limited to the beginning or formative period of its occupancy; that is, to about 1830. All other Western regions — the Upper Great Lakes and Interior Northwest, and the Far West — are of such character as to permit consideration to the decade of the 1870's. Slavish adherence to certain limiting years, however, would seem to be undesirable in a study of this nature. Occasionally, therefore, textual and illustrative matter relates to more recent times just as, in the reverse sense, standard North American texts of recent years occasionally and rightly reach back into the past. Such excellent works as *North America* by J. Russell Smith and M. Ogden Phillips (Harcourt, Brace, 1940), *The Geography of North America* by George J. Miller and Almon E. Parkins (Wiley, 1934), *Regional Geography of Anglo-America* by Charles Langdon White and Edwin J. Foscue (Prentice-Hall, 1943), and *The Geographic Basis of American Economic Life* by Harold H. McCarty (Harper, 1940) will inform the reader concerning the present character of the regions discussed in these pages.

Each chapter is provided with a brief bibliographical list, placed at the end of the complete text. The lists are no more than suggestive, and they may be considered quite inadequate by the thorough student of history. In that view the author concurs. However, it seemed unwise to prepare a text in which every page would be pock-marked with footnote citations to rare or unavailable works. It is hoped that the greater ease of reading thus permitted will compensate for the absence of traditional footnotes.

In the years of preparation for this work the author has assumed heavy, though pleasant, obligations which cannot be discharged in one paragraph. Many who have rendered aid through publications are mentioned in the text and listed in the bibliographies or the index. Material has been gathered in a large number of institutions. Gratitude is hereby extended not only to these libraries and academies, but to their staffs, without whose expert aid little could have been accomplished. Special mention is hereby made of the assistance given by Dr. G. M. Wrigley and Dr. John K. Wright of the American Geographical Society; Mrs. Margaret Dempster Gidney of the Connecticut Reserve Historical Society; Miss Lois Fawcett and Miss Bertha Heilbron of the Minnesota Historical Society; and Mrs. Clara Egli Le Gear of the Division of Maps of the Library of Congress. Valuable directions in the discovery and selection of illustrative matter were given by Mr. Hirst Milhollen of the Prints and Photos Division of the Library of Congress. Personal inspection of records in various parts of the country was made possible by several grants from the Graduate School of the University of Minnesota and a grant-in-aid from the Social Science Research Council. A number of publications resulted from these grants before a book of this character was contemplated. Special tribute is due my colleague, Professor Darrell H. Davis, whose vision of a course of study in historical geography which would be representative of the field led to a dozen-year research program culminating in this book. I have been particularly fortunate in my editor, Professor J. R. Whitaker; his handiwork appears on every page, although the reader may not be aware of it. Last, but by no means least, I am indebted to my typist and unofficial editor — my wife, Eunice R. Brown, who in making these contributions found herself also a pioneer student in this presentation of the historical geography of a great country.

RALPH H. BROWN

University of Minnesota
July, 1946

Contents

Part One

THE COLONIZATION PERIOD

CHAPTER I

Early Geography: Fact and Fancy

IT is related that the general use in America of the cast-iron plow was somewhat delayed beyond the year of its invention by prevailing beliefs of the time. Some people felt that the new plow had a poisoning effect on the soil. Equally significant was the belief that it encouraged a more profuse growth of weeds than had its wooden predecessor. Two other reasons for the delay in the use of the iron plow have been advanced: it cost more, and if the brittle landside or moldboard should snap, only by a major operation could either be repaired. We now recognize the latter two reasons as valid, and can easily appreciate their importance in retarding the adoption of a useful tool by an intelligent people. There was also some real basis for the belief that the new plow induced greater weed growth, for in doing a superior job of turning the soil, it gave the weeds a better chance to grow. The belief that the iron plow poisoned the soil had no basis in fact, but we are not justified in discarding this belief as a reason for the delay in the use of the implement. We cannot, to be sure, assess the relative importance of this belief, which now appears so utterly strange, but we must give it some weight.

Men at all times have been influenced quite as much by beliefs as by facts, and of this there is no better illustration than the early colonization activities along the Atlantic seaboard. The first colonies which proved to be permanent were started in the early years of the seventeenth century, at a time when little was actually known about the geographical conditions of the region. True, explorers had visited the western shores of the North Atlantic over a century before the colonization period — plenty of time, one would think, for the accumulation of essential information. However, the long years intervening between the arrival of the adventurous explorers and the no less courageous colonists had been curiously unproductive of new geographical knowledge. The causes of this long gap during which beliefs about America were dominant over facts have been the subject of many learned treatises, with less agreement among the various authorities than might be expected. We can at least identify two distinct periods: (1) the early exploratory period from 1497 to 1535, and (2) the colonization period beginning, as a permanent development within what is now the United States, in 1607.

The motives which drew the explorers to this side of the Atlantic were mixed and many: They sought the fabled Northwest Passage, new fishing grounds and related land bases, and territories to claim for their respective countries; personal ambitions or love of adventure, too, may well have played dominant roles. The Cabots, John and Sebastian, came to the coasts of the St. Lawrence in 1497; two years later, a Portuguese expedition under Gaspar Corte Real ranged over the western Atlantic waters; in 1524 Giovanni Verrazano led a French expedition to the New World, with a landfall at Cape Fear, North Carolina, and possibly entering Delaware Bay. Most notable of all, perhaps, were the voyages of Jacques Cartier — especially his voyage of 1535 when he penetrated the St. Lawrence, with French flags and soldiery, to the site of present-day Montreal. And then, for two generations or more, no further advance, as far as North America's east coast was concerned. It was the end of an era.

The beginning of the new era later in the same century was marked by the planting of colonies. It was, in fact, a burst of colonization of international scope. Spain established St. Augustine in 1565, and two decades later the British were represented in the short-lived venture of the Raleigh colonists on Roanoke Island. The first permanent English colony was made at Jamestown, Virginia, in the early summer of 1607, and in the next year the French occupied Quebec. These were the beginnings, enough to suggest the character of the new order. It would seem that political, economic, and intellectual conditions in Europe, especially in England, were now more favorable to actual colonization than they had been at earlier times. The " right of discovery," which had remained for so long an empty title, was now to be made effective by " entering upon and taking possession of the land." Expansionism was the order of the new day.

We have, therefore, the spectacle of a major colonization effort that was ill supported by funds of geographical knowledge. This deficiency, however, was not to last long. The founding of the colonies in the New World was accompanied by floods of reports and maps which, like all floods, gathered up indiscriminately the harmful and the helpful. It will pay us to consider the nature of these contemporary reports so that we may judge the extent of their reliability and their possible effects on continued colonization.

The reports first to come out of the colonization period were in narrative form. They related day-by-day events or presented observations, along with comments on personalities, pausing briefly at times to reflect on the trials and triumphs of the colonists. As sources of geographical information, the narratives are far from ideal. The diary-like reports of the Pilgrim Fathers may be taken as examples. They contain many references to the soil, natural products, and Indian peoples and their ways of life, but there is an evident tendency on the part of the writers to enlarge on the blessings of Nature and to minimize her deficiencies. In using the Pilgrim reports for reconstructing the conditions under which they lived, we must constantly bear in mind that their writings reflect the hopes and aspirations of a people.

The colonial geographical descriptions that were most effective in developing thought in Britain are now classed under the broad and unexalted heading of

"Colonization or Promotion Tracts." Published in England, and sometimes written there, these pamphlets or small books usually carried somewhere in their encyclopedic titles such phrases as " true relation," " brief and true chronicle," or " true and historical narrative." It is not too much to say that the majority of these publications were propagandist in effect if not in intent. As in the narratives, their geographical content was limited in space and restricted in breadth of view; more likely than not, too, it was blemished with error or poor judgment.

Commonly, each tract pertained to only one colony of the many in existence before 1650. By devices more or less skillfully concealed, the author usually attempted to divert at least a part of the immigration stream toward the particular colony under review. Favorite devices included a large emphasis on its opportunities and resources, a correspondingly brief reference to unfavorable items in the environment (unless, indeed, such unpleasant subjects were omitted altogether), and a tendency to suggest comparisons favorable to itself and invidious to neighboring colonies. The geography in the tracts cannot, therefore, be taken at face value, but they were powerful agencies in developing *ideas* about America and in encouraging prejudices for or against a part of the whole colonial area. The British colonization tracts, in brief, occupy the twilight zone between fact and fancy. The French, in contrast to the British, were much more realistic about their colony of New France, as we shall presently learn.

The general geographies were another class of writings that were mightily influential in developing concepts of America in European minds, and were thus a part of the whole colonizing movement. The geographies were written largely at second hand, either by professional geographers or by gifted amateurs. These " armchair geographers " fitted the new American world into books which theretofore had dealt primarily with other lands, books already a quarter of a century old that could be revived by new editions. Accordingly, the treatment of the new land tended to be a stereotyped version of the older sections, and also to be far behind the events that moved so swiftly on the other side of the Atlantic. A similar lag related to the maps which sometimes accompanied these volumes. But by the 1640's, books were issued in England which were devoted entirely to the new land. Some of these new geographies were concerned with all of England's colonies from Guiana to Newfoundland, while others described more limited areas, such as New England or Virginia.

Many of these geographers professed to be completely detached from any special interest that might influence the accuracy of their contents. It seems, however, that some of the authors, too many for the satisfaction of present-day investigators, were agents of one or more of the colonizing companies or, to say the least, were predisposed in favor of the expansionist movement. Such writers were not above twisting truth to support a cause they considered worthy. A present-day authority in this field, Fulmer Mood, has recently announced the astonishing fact that a half-century of British colonial enterprise had elapsed before there was available to British readers a usable and trustworthy geographic account of the American colonies. This first reliable account was published in

London in 1651 under the title of *A Description of the New World or America, Islands and Continents . . . as They Were All in the Year 1649*. The author was a George Gardyner who was personally experienced in American affairs and who states, in good tradition, " I have related nothing but what my own knowledge or good intelligence persuades me is certainly true." And this also may be taken as the keynote of the present book.

CHAPTER 2

Taking Possession of the Land

R EADING history and chronicles," says Struthers Burt in his book *Philadelphia:
Holy Experiment* (Doubleday, Doran, 1945), " one wonders how any country was ever settled " — especially the eastern coast of North America. He calls
attention to the inadequacy of preparations in the homelands and to the general
ignorance of conditions to be encountered in the New World. Human inadequacy and physical difficulties were indeed profound, yet there were compensating factors that enabled the colonies to take root in American soil. Among these
factors none was more important than the over-all similarities with the homelands in climate and natural vegetation. As Professor Carl O. Sauer has said, " It
would be impossible, indeed, to cross an ocean anywhere else and find so little
that is unfamiliar on the opposite side." Moreover, it is well to be reminded that
the Atlantic coast was inhabited before the arrival of European colonists. Not
only had the Indians opened innumerable clearings in the forest, but their crops
and methods of culture, supplementing the natural foods of the new land, made
the transition from Europe all the less severe. One other favoring condition — a
coastal environment affording safe anchorages and additional food resources —
helps a reader of " history and chronicles " to understand how the eastern coast
became settled. Each of these factors will be considered at some length.

SIMILARITIES IN CLIMATE, REAL OR ASSUMED

The British people, to whom the colonization tracts were mainly directed,
needed little urging to accept the idea that the American coast northward from the
James River was somewhat like the homeland. On the general principles known
at the time, this seemed reasonable enough. Maps for nearly a century had represented the western shore of the Atlantic with fair exactness, in latitudes suggesting a temperate climate. True, there had been some sobering experiences in
colonization, particularly in Newfoundland and in the North Carolina locale of
Raleigh's " lost " colony. But perhaps between the northern and southern ex-
tremities lay a land more suited to English peoples. Over a period of nine or ten
decades, proponents of colonization enlarged upon the attractiveness of the climates between the far north and the far south.

Plymouth was scarcely a dozen years old before it was proclaimed that New

England's latitude placed it in the " golden meane," a region " by all judicious men accounted the principal part of all America, for habitation, and the commodiousness of the Sea." Others placed that " golden meane," that happy medium between heat and cold, farther south — which meant in Virginia or Maryland. Then when Georgia completed the family of thirteen colonies in 1732, the " golden meane " shifted, according to some writers, to that quarter. It is easily seen how this kind of specious reasoning, necessarily unsupported by factual data, was applicable to almost any colony. From Virginia it was reported as early as 1610 that " Our transported Cattell, Horses, Kine, Hogs, and Goats, do thrive most happily," and Bermuda was recommended as a land " suited to the English temper."

Captain John Smith on New England. Perhaps the first man to endorse publicly a specific part of the Atlantic coast as a future home for Englishmen, and to do so without ulterior motive, was the famous Captain John Smith.

During the years 1614 and 1615, Captain (or " Admirall ") Smith voyaged along the coast of the area soon to be partitioned into Rhode Island and Providence Plantations, Connecticut, Plymouth, and Massachusetts Bay — which was also to include the Province of Maine. The region was called " New England " in his reports and on the map he issued in 1616, presumably because of outward resemblances to old England, or because it corresponded in latitude with " New Albion " (California) of the " South " (Pacific) Ocean. Since this was only a coasting voyage not permitting inspection of the interior, he was uncertain as to the " true substances of the Land " but, as if to ensure its continued existence as a *new* England, English names were bestowed upon many a cape, peninsula, island, and harbor. Much of the nomenclature, according to the map, was suggested by Prince Charles, elder son of King James I. His " Plimouth " actually became Plymouth four years later; " Cape Anna " is Cape Ann of today, and his " River Charles " has also retained its name since that time. Easily recognized as Cape Cod is " Cape James." (See Fig. 3.)

" I would rather live here than any where," Smith said of New England. Its excellence for habitation was evidenced in the " greatness " of the timber and the abundance of fish in near-by waters, as well as by the numerous gardens of the Indian peoples. Four years before the founding of Plymouth, Smith said that if he were the leader of a colony, New England should be the place for it; and should such a colony fail to maintain itself in a land evidently so provident, then, he stoutly declared, " let us starve."

Criticism of contemporary thought. The writers of this time did not stray far from essential truth in holding out to colonists the expectation of finding congenial coastal climates from Virginia to Maine. Without asserting that the climate was in all respects the same on both sides of the Atlantic, they did suggest *general* similarities. Frequently mentioned were the long summers in New England, their increasing span toward the south, and the mild winters of Virginia. Those who complained of the hot Southern summer were urged to wear clothes more suited to the climate than the kind they had been accustomed to wear in another (and cooler) part of the world. Advocates of Virginia settlement correctly pointed to its comparability in latitude with Palestine, thereby, however, encouraging false belief in climatic similarities. As early as this time, the beneficial effects of cooling sea breezes were mentioned; to use a favorite word of the time, they " assuaged " the summer heat. This was of course true only for limited areas within reach of local sea breezes.

Various writers during the early Colonial period recognized differences of climate between the Old World and the New and yet, by direct statement or implication, belittled the differences. They anticipated no barriers to the transference of familiar English grains and livestock. A bothersome point, not to be explained for many generations, was the apparent contradiction presented by the more severe seasons in America. All of Britain lay poleward of all its American colonies except Newfoundland, and yet the homeland experienced the milder winter seasons.

Fully to appreciate the assumption of the similarity of climate on opposite sides of the Atlantic, the student must ignore temporarily much that he may have learned about climatic differences from modern data and classifications. Such differences as there were gradually became apparent to the colonists, probably with but little dismay on their part. " This was a lustier land to which the settlers had come," says Professor Sauer, " a land of hotter summers and colder winters, of brighter and hotter sun and more tempestuous rain, a land suited to and provided with a greater variety of vegetation than the homelands of Europe."

RESEMBLANCES IN NATURAL VEGETATION

English colonial areas. Similarities between the colonial area and the British homelands were further pointed up in the pamphlets by reference to the vegetation. This was not always done in a wholly enlightening manner; rather, the " descriptions " amounted to little more than long and tedious lists of trees and their shrubby undergrowth. Possibly the writers felt they could assume that prospective readers in England and elsewhere were familiar with the species referred to; there was no need, therefore, for elaboration. The common tree names constantly mentioned indicates this: elm, oak, maple, beech, and so on.

It is clear from various colonial reports that by 1630 " foure sorts of Oke " of the many actually present in the Northern forests had been identified. Ash, willow, poplar, and birch are also mentioned. Farther north, cedar, spruce, and pines were said to predominate, while along the sandy Southern coasts other pines and " cypress," in the swamps, were listed. There was much understandable misnaming of the needle-leaved trees, which were often assumed to be allied to somewhat similar species in Europe. The " cypress " of the Southern swamps, for example, was incorrectly assumed to be a counterpart of the Old World cypress. Nut-bearing trees, because of their food-producing capacities as well as their value as timber, received special mention. Chestnut, walnut, and many types of pines were recommended for shipbuilding and other construction purposes.

Scarcely less important in the colonial mind, if we may judge from the amount of descriptive space they occupy, were the small plants and herbs of the forest floor. Here again, common names are employed in contemporary writings: penny-royal, sorrel, liverwort, angelica, thyme, anise, and watercress — all presumably familiar to Old World readers.

Realistic descriptions of New France. If we glance into the early French descriptions of the coast of Maine and of its northward extension into Acadia (Nova Scotia), a similar emphasis will be found. The narrative of Samuel de Champlain, telling in great detail of his surveys from 1604 to 1607, is replete with references to the " fine trees " and the variety of vegetation. However, he warned specifically, as most of the British writers did not, against inferring climatic similarities with the homeland from the resemblances of vegetation. For instance, referring to the vicinity of present-day Saco, Maine, Champlain found the inland forests " very open, but nevertheless [they] abound in oaks, beeches, ashes, and elms, and in wet places there are numbers of willows " — tree types familiar to his readers. " Not that I am of opinion," he adds, " that it is not cold here, although the place lies in latitude 43° 45′ " — nine degrees farther south than Paris. The Indians, however, " remain permanently in this place."

Champlain's realistic descriptions in the opening of the seventeenth century of what is now Maritime Canada marked a turning point in French thinking about the American possessions. Up to that time it had been popular to consider them quite literally as comprising a new France, and thus altogether suitable for occupancy by Frenchmen.

It cannot be said that this idea — that the new France duplicated the environment of the old — was derived directly from Jacques Cartier, but he seems to have been the first to encourage such belief. Cartier's second voyage up the St. Lawrence River in 1535–36 penetrated to the site of present-day Montreal, then occupied by a large Indian town named Hochelaga. The preamble to his classic report to King Francis I contains the following: " And now through the present exploration undertaken at your royal command for the discovery of the lands in the west formerly unknown to you and to us, lying in the same climates and parallels as your territories and kingdoms, you will learn of their fertility and richness, of the immense numbers of peoples living there, of their kindness and peacefulness, and likewise of the richness of the great river, which flows through and waters the midst of these lands of yours, which is without comparison the largest river that is known ever to have been seen."

This statement, as well as assurances in the report itself that trees well known to Frenchmen thrived in New France, must have been welcome news to royal authorities. But Cartier's optimistic account was not followed by French settlement in the St. Lawrence Valley. An experimental venture occurred in 1604 on the small island of St. Croix, but it is said that " all returned to France, bringing back no greater spoils than the Topography and descriptions of Seas, Capes,

Coasts, and Rivers which they had traversed." The first seigniorial grants in the valley, contemporary with the beginnings of Massachusetts Bay Colony, led to no influx of people. In fact, of the first sixty grants during the years from 1632 to 1663, not more than six were made to genuine settlers. The picture of a New France still empty in 1635 led two missionaries, Fathers Paul Le Jeune and Jean de Brébeuf, to say: " Geographers, Historians, and experience show us that every year a great many people leave France who go to enroll themselves elsewhere, for, although the Soil of our country is very fertile, the French women have this blessing, that they are still more so. . . . Would it not be better to empty Old France into New, by means of colonies, than to people Foreign countries? "

Beginning with Champlain's accounts, geographical reports coming out of New France during these early years told of a land very different from France. Granted that the possessions were actually farther south than Paris, said one missionary in 1626, yet " the Winter generally lasts here 5 months and a half; the snow is 3 or 4 feet deep." As if in an endeavor to counteract discouraging pictures of interminable wildernesses of frigid winters, emphasis shifted to riches of copper, pelts and fur, and fisheries. Experience had shown, by 1650 at least, that New France was indeed very unlike the homeland.

INDIAN CLEARINGS, INDIAN OLD FIELDS, AND BURNINGS

Until recently, it has been customary to picture the Atlantic coast as " an uninterrupted forest " at the time of first colonization. This false supposition, says Professor Sauer, resulted from a misunderstanding of the numbers of Indians resident along the coast and immediate interior in the early 1600's and " an underestimation of the extent to which the Indians had been engaged in agriculture." Modern writers have also underestimated the total effect of fires set by the Indians, an ancient practice regularly followed in their hunting activities. One need not delve very deeply into the original records to realize that the Indians had altered the forest cover to an extent far out of proportion to their numbers. To correct the prevailing misinterpretations, it will be necessary to consider the distribution of the Eastern Indians and their methods of making a living.

Distribution and mode of life. Recent estimates by Alfred L. Kroeber, James Mooney, and Herbert J. Spinden lead to the conclusion that about 125,000 Indians were resident along the Atlantic seaboard from the St. Lawrence River to Florida at the opening of the seventeenth century. According to Spinden, for example, the Indian population of the Northeast — that is, the area now included in New England, New York, Pennsylvania, and New Jersey — was 55,600, while 52,200 lived along the seaboard from Maryland to Georgia. Estimates of the native population of the Canadian maritime region at a comparable time vary from 25,000 to 50,000. The over-all density of population was about one person to 4 square miles, but there were great variations from place to place. Density of Indian population reached its maximum in the Chesapeake Bay region and was least in the interior. Southern New England perhaps ranked next in aboriginal population; according to Charles C. Willoughby, this region had a total population of 24,000 at the beginning of the seventeenth century despite the plague which had swept through the villages just before the arrival of Europeans. Kroeber's analysis of tribal data " leaves little doubt that as a whole the population density in the farming parts of the Atlantic and Gulf region was perhaps twice as heavy on the coast, including habitats on tidewater or within a day's travel of salt water, as immediately inland thereof."

The majority of the Eastern Woodland Indians (a general grouping of several linguistic stocks) carried on agriculture, but their dependence on this economy was highly variable. Nearly every native household practiced farming, not wholly from necessity, but partly to gain luxuries not obtainable from the gathering of wild products, hunting, and fishing. In the view of Kroeber, " Agriculture . . . was not basic to life in the East; it was auxiliary." A correct view of the Eastern Indians places them in villages varying in size from 50 to 200 inhabitants, with clearings of considerable extent round about. William Strachey's early description of Virginia presents this picture of a typical aboriginal village in its oasislike setting within the forest:

Theire habitations or townes are for the most part by rivers, or not far distant from fresh springs, commonly upon a rise of a hill that they may overlooke the river, and take every small thing into view which sturrs upon the same. Theire houses are not many in one towne, and those that are stand dessite [dispersed] and scattered without forme of a street, farr and wyde asunder. . . . About theire houses they have commonly square plotts of cleared grownd, which serve them for gardens, some one hundred, some two hundred foote square, wherein they sowe their tobacco, pumpons, and a fruit like unto a musk millino . . . in the tyme of theire huntings they leave their habitations, and gather themselves into companyes . . . where they passe the tyme with hunting and fowling up towards the mountaines, by the heads of their rivers, wher indeed there is plentye of game.

Indian clearings for farming. Indians usually started a clearing by burning the undergrowth and " deadening " the larger trees by making incisions into the sapwood. This caused the trees gradually to die, and as the sunlight penetrated through the withering branches, planting began. Seeds were generally planted in " hills " dug by crude implements, such as half an oyster shell bound to a stick, and fertilized with fish or seaweed. The common Indian crops of maize, pumpkins, squash, and beans were often planted intermixed in the same field, or even in the same hill. The stumps of the larger trees would usually remain throughout the life of the clearing as a planting field. The Indians apparently had no tool comparable to the plow, not even the Creeks of the Southern interior, who possessed horses at least by the time they were first visited by traders. Attempts to teach the Creeks the use of the plow during the eighteenth century were futile; they said, not without primitive humor, that the white's man plow was nothing less than a horse trap.

The diminishing yield of clearings after several years of use naturally led to the making of new openings within easy reach of the villages. Replacement of worn-out fields through unknown centuries of time explains why the number of clearings, or "Indian old fields," as they became known to the colonists, were much more extensive than the total Indian population would suggest. In short, the Indians practiced "shifting agriculture" in much the same manner as do certain tropical peoples at the present time. And as with primitive peoples today, the villages were often removed to wholly new sites within the same general territory. This was done not merely to secure virgin ground for planting, but also in order to have access to new supplies of game, fruits, berries, roots, and herbs. It is believed also that new village sites were selected after a dozen or more years as a means of escaping the filth that inevitably accumulated in the near vicinity of a village long inhabited. These customs and practices explain why references to Indian old fields are a part of nearly every contemporary description of the early Colonial period.

Indian-set fires. The Eastern Indians, as already observed, combined farming with hunting or, perhaps more truly, supplemented their hunting of birds and game with farming and fishing. As experienced woodsmen, they had of course learned that deer and other browsing animals sought grassy glades or areas of small growth with tender leaves and shoots. It was also observed that both grass and shrubby undergrowth advanced rapidly in burnt-over tracts, whence the practice of firing the woods to attract game. In some areas, as in New England, the woods were regularly burned in the fall and spring, a practice followed in later times by the American pioneer. There is some evidence to suggest that the Indians fired woods as a means of rounding up game within enclosures for easy slaughter with arrows. They may also have burned woods around their villages to protect them from chance fires of natural origin. There was some restraint in these latter practices, however, because any advantages were secured at the heavy price of destruction of fruits and berries and the driving away of birds, squirrels, and other small game.

Extent and significance of clearings and burnings. Firsthand observations on Indian clearings and burnings and their significance in pioneer settlement are so numerous as to prohibit full citation, but it is advisable to present a few excerpts from records of undoubted accuracy. The following descriptions relate to various sections of the Atlantic seaboard from Canada to Virginia.

Comment on Clearings — Champlain and Others. The eminent explorer Champlain was perhaps the first to survey that part of the Massachusetts coast now known as Gloucester Harbor; certainly he was the first to describe it in terms intelligible to us, in reports based on personal observations from 1604 to 1607. Attracted by the landscape, already somewhat tamed by man, he named it " Beautiful Port " and judged its natural advantages to be comparable with those farther north. But more important for present purposes, he observed that " Some of the land is cleared and they are constantly clearing more. . . . There are also fine meadows for supporting numbers of cattle." (See Figs. 1a and 1b.)

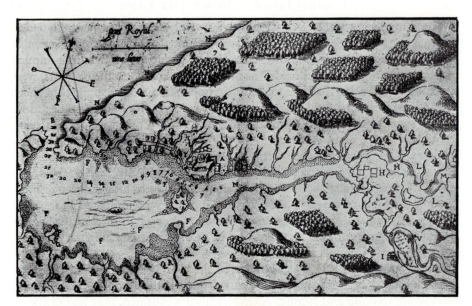

1a Port Royal, harbor and environs, sketched by Champlain in 1602. Like all Champlain maps, this was drawn from a single point and thus presents some distortions. The cartographer resided two years at this place (see A on the sketch), making possible a rather extensive survey. The modern town of Annapolis Royal occupies the site marked H. This map and the three that follow are taken from *The Works of Samuel de Champlain,* 1922, edited by H. P. Biggar, and used here with permission of the Champlain Society, Toronto.

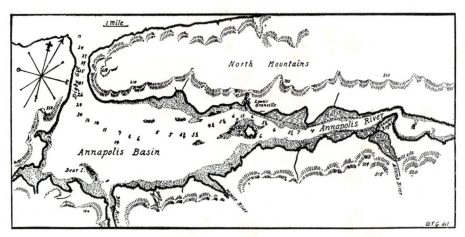

1b Port Royal according to modern charts, for comparison with Champlain's sketch of the same harbor. (Courtesy of the Champlain Society)

Original records of Plymouth Plantation contain a number of references to the existence of cleared land and fields recently planted with corn. The inference is inescapable that these clearings were of some importance in determining the site of the original settlement. Furthermore, the site was not merely chanced upon, as many have been led to believe. The Pilgrims originally touched land on Cape Cod, not too favorable a place for settlement, but even in that sandy waste were found " a pond of clear fresh water and shortly after a quantitie of clear land wher the Indians had formerly set corne, and some of their graves." Three separate parties were dispatched to search for a more favorable site; one of these found a good harbor (Plymouth) about 25 miles from the *Mayflower's* original landing. (See Figs. 2a and 2b.) " On Munday they sounded the harbour and founde it fitt for shipping, and marched onto the land, and founde diverse cornfields and little running brooks, a place (as they supposed) fitt for situation, at least it was the best they could find." It appears that they had to go some distance from the settlement, possibly a quarter-mile, to find timber suitable for their varied needs. Lack of adequate cutting tools was a further handicap in starting a new life.

Other Coastal Clearings of New England. Many of the early Massachusetts Bay records comment on the original presence of clearings, and on the desolation of the surrounding woods caused by repeated Indian burnings.

In a number of coastal settlements, good timber was to be found only in swampy areas or along streams where stands were protected, to some degree, from repeated fires. Large and useful trees, it was said in one record, could not be found " on the upland ground, but must be sought in the lower grounds, where the woods are wett when the country is fired, by reason of the snow water that remains there for a time." Cedars were reported as extinct from the higher lands, " for the Salvages by this Custom of theirs, have spoiled all the rest; for this Custom hath been continued from the beginnings."

An account written from Salem in 1630 seems to foreshadow the literature issued in promotion of more southern localities at a later period. Possibly the amount of timber-free land is exaggerated in stating that most of the land was

fit for Pasture, or for Plow or Meddow ground, as men please to employ it; though all the Countrey be as it were a thicke wood for the generall, yet in diverse places there is much ground cleared by the Indians, and especially about the Plantations; and I am told that about three miles from us a man may stand on a little hilly place and see diverse thousands of acres of ground as good as need to be, and not a Tree on the same.

One could wish that the author of this account, identified by bibliographers as Francis H. Higginson, had devoted two or three hours to personal verification of the concluding passage of his report.

It is generally agreed, from available evidence, that many of the clearings on the borders of Massachusetts Bay were unoccupied at the time of the first settlements because of the epidemic mentioned above that had swept through the Indian villages. This conclusion is suggested by John White, writing in 1630 as follows:

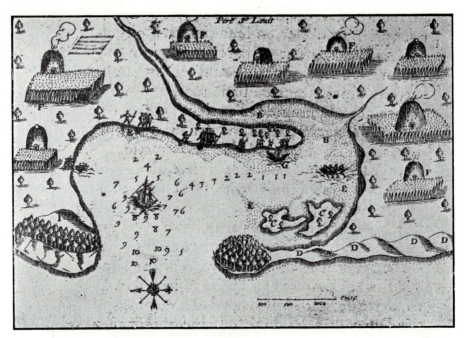

2a Champlain's map of Plymouth Harbor, drawn in 1607, emphasizes Indian habitations and cultivated land. Compare with the following map drawn according to recent surveys. (Courtesy of the Champlain Society, Toronto)

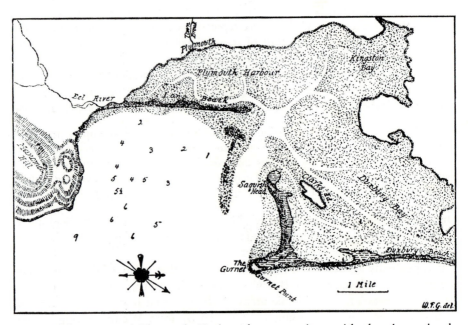

2b Modern map of Plymouth Harbor, for comparison with the above sketch. (Courtesy of the Champlain Society, Toronto)

The land affords void ground enough to receive more people than this State can spare, and that not only wood grounds, and others, which are unfit for present use; but in many places much cleared Land for tillage, and large marshes for hay and feeding cattle, which comes to pass by the desolate hapening through the three years' plague, about twelve or sixteen yeeres past, which swept away most of the inhabitants all along the Sea coast, so that there was no person left to lay claime to the soyle which they possessed; in most parts of the rest, the Contagion hath left alive one person of one hundred.

The vacated Indian fields along the southern New England coast at the time of its settlement are further confirmed by reports of the journey of Edward Winslow and Stephen Hopkins of Pokanoket, near the present site of Bristol, Rhode Island, to visit the chief Massasoit. They journeyed along the banks of the Taunton River, where, they said, " are and have been many towns. The ground is very good upon both sides, it being for the most part cleared. Thousands of men have lived here which died in the great plague not long since, and pity it was and is to see so many goodly fields so well seated without men to dress and manure the same."

Openings in New France, the St. Lawrence Valley, and near Lake Champlain. The dependable reports of Champlain, covering his surveys up the St. Lawrence River to the site of Montreal and into and beyond the lake which bears his name, are eloquent with respect to original clearings in the forest.

The span of three-fourths of a century that separated the visits of Cartier (1535) and Champlain (before 1610) had seen many changes in the Indian population. Cartier, perhaps with the exaggeration permitted an original explorer, told of the large numbers of River Indians, peaceful and agricultural. So many and large were the villages at the time of Cartier that it has often been suggested, among other explanations, that originally the name " Canada " signified a place of large Indian lodges. Sometime after Cartier's visit, a series of intertribal wars occurred which had greatly reduced the native population by the time of Champlain's arrival. Gone was the great Indian village of Hochelaga that had been described by Cartier. But the clearings remained there and in many another place where the natives had formerly resided in peace. Near Mount Royal, later to share its name with Montreal, were " more than 60 arpents [about 50 acres] of land which have been cleared and are now like meadows, where one might sow grain and do gardening. Formerly Indians cultivated these lands, but they have abandoned them on account of the frequent wars which they carried on there. And there are many other fine meadows which would feed as many cattle as one could wish, and there are also the varieties of woods which we have in our forests."

Champlain's route took him up the Richelieu River, which from its mouth to the first rapids, " a distance of fifteen leagues, is very level and bordered with woods, as are all the other places mentioned above, and with the same varieties of woods "; but near the rapids " are meadows where no Indians live, by reason of the wars." Coming out upon the broad surface of Lake Champlain, he inspected several islands formerly inhabited by Indians but now abandoned, and from here could be seen the Eastern (Green) Mountains "on the tops of which there was snow. I enquired of the natives whether these parts were inhabited. They said they were, and by the Iroquois, and that in those parts there were

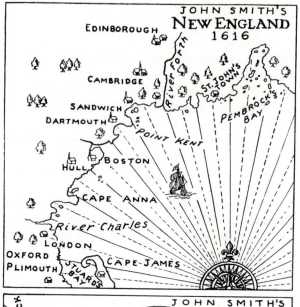

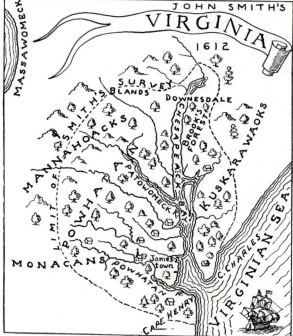

3

Simplified copies of maps by Captain John Smith. Originals can be seen in C. O. Paullin's *Atlas of the Historical Geography of the United States,* published jointly by the Carnegie Institution of Washington and the American Geographical Society of New York, 1932.

beautiful valleys and fields rich in corn such as I have eaten in that country, along with other products of abundance."

Clearings in the South: Virginia. The forests of tidewater Virginia, when first beheld by the settlers, were luxuriant and lofty, properly bringing forth exclamations of awe. They were not, however, uninhabited, and could be termed primeval only in a poetical sense. Beyond the swamps, the floor beneath the towering trees was at that time relatively free from undergrowth. Far beyond the clearings of the village-living Indians, of whom there were probably 17,000 east of the mountains in Virginia at the time Jamestown was founded, forests were open enough to permit easy passage on foot or on horseback, and from ground level objects could be distinguished at some distance. The general absence of undergrowth was understood at the time to have resulted from repeated Indian-set fires that were not severe enough to kill the larger trees.

John Smith calculated that there were 5,000 Indians within 60 miles of Jamestown at the time of settlement, living in villages varying in size from 30 to 200 persons. Some of the villages were palisaded, containing a score of separate dwellings. Each village was a tiny island of cultivation within a sea of forest which itself had been burnt thin roundabout. Philip A. Bruce, Virginia historian, suggests that there were as many as 3,000 acres of cleared land within the vicinity of present-day Hampton, where Ke-cough-tan was located in presettlement days. Figure 3 (*lower*) represents this area according to a very early map.

Generally speaking, the Virginia Indians had shown much shrewdness in selecting the better soils and more sightly places for their villages. Apparently, the natives were still largely in possession of their clearings, not having been decimated by war or disease as in Northerly areas. This state of affairs hindered the progress of occupying the land by incoming Europeans. Also it possibly accounts for the known inferiority of some of the sites chosen for the first white settlements. Abandoned clearings soon became known in Virginia, as in New England and Spanish Florida, as " Indian old fields."

Following an exhaustive study of Virginia records, Hu Maxwell, a specialist in forestry, concluded that " no explorers of any extensive region failed to report openings in the forest, made, or supposed to have been made, by natives for the purpose of agriculture." He estimated that there were from 30 to 40 acres of treeless land per capita of Indian population at the beginning of Virginian settlement. This estimate provides a convenient quantitative measure of the modification of the natural environment wrought by the farming-hunting-fishing Indian peoples who, to some degree (and to a degree now often not appreciated), prepared the stage for the European settler.

TIDEWATER ADVANTAGES

The excellent harbors around which settlements inevitably collected were given much emphasis in early colonial reports. " Commodious " was the adjective most frequently used to describe them.

Protected sites. To accommodate the tiny vessels of the time, a harbor need not be very large or deep. Hence, harbors which today are relegated to minor or incidental use had at that time advantages equal to those of greater capacity; Salem's harbor, for example, was important until it was superseded by Boston's. More important than size or depth, actually, was protection — not only from wind and wave but also from possible enemy attack. Many harbors were praised, if not originally selected, because of inherent defensive properties.

St. Augustine Harbor, in Spanish Florida, the first haven to have been thoughtfully selected for occupancy, offered protection as its chief, if not sole, advantage. The most conspicuous defensive feature of St. Augustine soon came to be the man-made Fort St. Marks above the town and overlooking the shallow inlets to the Matanzas River. Offshore lay Anastasia Island, which afforded natural protection to vessels lying behind it. The harbor, with entrances only 8 feet in depth, was notoriously difficult of navigation; hence unfriendly visitors unfamiliar with the approaches were under a special handicap. In other respects St. Augustine's harbor, already having been used a half-century by the time the British colonies were founded, was quite inferior. The surrounding country was relatively unproductive, and no large river led back into the interior. (See Fig. 4.)

Harbors of Cape Ann, Massachusetts. The harbors northward of Boston, on the minor peninsula called Cape Ann from the earliest days, as we have seen, were recommended for their all-year availability, their depth, and their " commodiousness," and it was also held to be important that they were comparatively difficult of access. In a characteristic comment in 1630, these harbors, such as

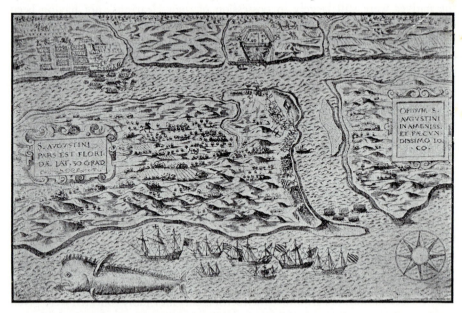

4 St. Augustine, Florida, as mapped about 1586. (Courtesy of the Carnegie Institution.)

Salem's, were declared to be all the better because there was a " verie difficult and dangerous passage into them for strangers." The early sounding of Plymouth Harbor resulting in the discovery that it was suitable for shipping has already been mentioned.

Properties of the Jamestown site. Some of the mystery that has attached to the selection of the Jamestown site disappears when the foregoing comments are considered. The choice of that particular spot on the James River was deliberate. It is stated that as many as eleven days were spent in searching the lower 40 miles of the river for a site conforming to certain Orders in Council, framed with little knowledge of local geography, that listed theoretically desirable features. Many likely places were already occupied by Indian villages; other possibilities were discarded for one reason or another. The site chosen confirmed the Orders in but one main respect: it was safe. Virtually an island in 1607 because it was separated from the land at high tide, this bit of low land afforded protection from weather and also from possible attack. Swampy roundabout, with no open fields — the Indians, apparently, having avoided this islandlike peninsula — the Jamestown site won little praise even from the more enthusiastic writers. Lest conclusions unfavorable to all of Virginia be drawn from the unsuitability of Jamestown's location, as early as 1610 pamphleteers hastened to assure their readers that many tidal basins were not swampy.

Other advantages of tidewater location. Desire to maintain connections with the homeland was implicit in the almost universal settlement around harbors and along tidal rivers. The growth of the colonies was dependent upon continued arrivals of people and their equipment, and it was not long before return loads were on the way. Sassafras and tobacco were sent from Virginia to England at least as early as 1619; wood ashes and fish products soon came from the Northern colonies and islands.

The shipment of fish, in the form of heavily salted " green " cod and dried salt cod, was relatively an old story by 1626, when Champlain wrote: " Along the whole southern coast of the said island of Newfoundland there are many good ports, anchorages, and harbours, amongst them Placentia, Trespassy Bay, and All Saints' Bay, as also on the . . . St. Pierre Islands, where many vessels go to fish, and where they dry the fish." Newfoundland's northeast and southwest coasts were at this time frequented by French, Basque, and English fishermen, but the coast facing the Gulf of St. Lawrence was but little known in Champlain's day.

Coastal residents were also ensured of supplies of salt, fish, and oyster shells for fertilizing the land, as well as edible sea foods of astounding variety. Salt-making by the simple process of evaporating sea water, sometimes hastened by application of heat, was one of the first industries, retaining its importance throughout the Colonial period and even beyond.

Descriptions of the early days and later were filled with lists of sea foods and related commentary. Said to be " verie numerous " were cod, bass, haddock, herring, lobster, mullet, crab, oysters, and clams. The annual salmon run was a dependable source of food, and a perennial mystery, too. In 1630 it was related that " the season of their coming was begun when we came first to New England in June, and so continued for about three months apace." Even at this early date, salmon and shad, running up the New England rivers as well as the Hudson and the Delaware, were caught with nets. Much of the fish catch had to be thrown back, however, for lack of salt and storage facilities.

NATIVE PLANT FOODS AND INDIAN CROPS

The first few years were obviously the critical ones in the development of a colony. The ships in which the people came also carried many supplies, but not nearly enough to sustain the new settlements for any length of time. Fortunate it was that the new environment contributed many edible wild products; and still more fortunate that Indian agriculture made large contributions toward meeting the need for food.

Under the stimulus of necessity much was learned in a very short time about native fruits, nuts, berries, and roots. Of this we are certain when we see long lists of such products promptly recorded in the first descriptions.

Chestnuts and walnuts of the more Northern forests were much prized for the table, as were acorns for animal food. The cherry and the grape were abundant and widely distributed. From the presence of native grapes in the Southern forests, an early assumption that imported vines would " agree exceeding well with the Soyle and Climate " eventually led to experiments in wine-making.

Among the berries of the Northern forests — blackberries, blueberries, raspberries, and strawberries — the last-named were most often mentioned with enthusiasm, possibly because they were familiar in England. It was soon learned that strawberries were most abundant in tracts recently burned over or in Indian old fields. The famous Roger Williams held them to be the best of the native fruits of Rhode Island, where they were most prevalent in areas formerly tilled by the aborigines. " I have seen as many as would fill a ship within a few miles compasse," he boasted. Others were content to mention merely that strawberries were " plentie in their time." Mulberries, a favorite food of the Virginia Indian, were adopted by the colonists. Among the roots available for human food and prepared for the table in a variety of ways, none was more important than the bulbous root of the common Eastern sunflower — Jerusalem artichoke as it was then called, apparently for no very good reason.

Not to extend the list of wild foods in an encyclopedic manner, mention may be made of gooseberries, cranberries, plums, and crab apples. Their importance might easily be overemphasized; however, they were good talking points for the promoters of colonization, who appeared on the scene in increasing numbers following the 1630's.

No foods were more vital during the early years of trial in the colonies than the Indian products; scarcely less important were the native methods of agriculture which were adopted by the newcomers. Indian corn (maize) was possessed by the Indians wherever colonists came in contact with them and yet, strangely enough, it was never found growing wild. Kidney beans, pumpkins, and squash developed by Indian peoples also became known to the settlers. None of these products, it is believed, originated with the Eastern Woodland Indians. Presumably they had spread from remote centers of development, perhaps in the Southwest or Mexico and possibly as far away as South America. Remarkable as the agriculture of the Eastern Indian in the early 1600's may be considered, however, it was nevertheless deficient in many respects. Most notable of these deficiencies was the lack of animal husbandry; the rearing of cattle, horses, and sheep was among the major contributions of Europeans to early American agriculture.

In recent times it has been popular to minimize the positive contributions of the native Indian peoples to white settlement. We need not go very far back in literature, however, to find a more just and tolerant view of the significant place occupied by the Eastern Woodland Indian. Speaking of the value of one of his products, Nathaniel Southgate Shaler observed in 1894: " The progress of our conquest of this continent would have been relatively slow had it not been for the good fortune which put this admirable food plant in the possession of our people." Not only did the Indian contribute corn, but also a method of growing it and other crops; later on we shall have occasion to point to still further aboriginal aids to white settlement.

CHAPTER 3

Making Land and Sea Productive

FISHERIES OF THE NORTH ATLANTIC

THE transference of European peoples and their material cultures to the New World — in short, the process of colonization — commenced with the fisheries of the North Atlantic. To consider this earliest and simplest form of colonization we must go back to the opening years of the sixteenth century. When Cartier achieved his discovery of the St. Lawrence River in 1534, he found fishing ships already there. In fact, it is altogether likely that European fishermen had been coming to these waters for a generation earlier than Cartier. Thus the Northern fisheries were a forerunner of the voyages of discovery, as they were also, and more obviously, a step in the direction of land settlement overseas from Europe. But the step between the fishery as conducted in the time of Cartier and the permanent occupancy of North American lands near the fishing grounds was a very long one.

For many years, the fleets were land-based on Europe; for, in effect, the fishermen shifted their enterprises westward from Old World waters while still operating from home ports. The shift of operations to new sources of supply involved no necessary readjustments in other practices. The distances were not much greater: look at a globe and notice the narrowing of Atlantic reaches toward the north. The catch was brought home for drying, just as it was from the nearer fishing grounds. Beheaded and partly cleaned, the cod were laid down on shipboard, heavily salted for preservation. This was the " wet fishery " in an almost unmodified form, yielding a crude product, but one highly marketable in Mediterranean Europe, where it was known as " green cod " or " core fish."

Fishing vessels, after a month or six weeks of buffeting by North Atlantic storms — which must have been as severe then as they are now — often landed near the fishing grounds to secure shelter, to make repairs, or to replenish supplies of food and fresh water. These connections were vital but nevertheless tenuous, at least until the industry was expanded to include the drying of cod on beaches. With this expansion the industry was at last attached to the land and the " shore fishery " was added to the continuing wet fishery. To prosecute the shore fishery various kinds of equipment were needed: wharves for landing; " factories " for dressing fish; "flakes" for drying them; also a temporary shelter for crews, which consisted of a dozen or more men per vessel. The equipment of the shore fishery might well have been labeled "made in Europe," so slight was the dependence upon local materials. Suitable sites were available within the sheltering harbors of Newfoundland, of other islands such as the Miquelons, of Nova Scotia (Acadia), and elsewhere. Little was known about the lands near the fishing grounds, and the glimpses from vessels or narrow beaches of forest-clad mountain slopes were not reassuring. Newfoundland then had an undeservedly bad reputation for permanent settlement. With the approach of winter, the fishermen evacuated their coastal strips, storing some of the equipment (though this was a risky business) but returning most of it to the waiting vessel. For example, sailcloth was refitted to the rigging after having served for tenting during the fishing season. Inevitably, attachment to the land became more intimate, finally resulting in actual settlement as the industry advanced from the transitory or seasonal fishery to the sedentary type (called by the French *la pêche sédentaire*). The procedure here, then, will be to discuss first the early phases of the banks fishery and then take up the shore fishery, which both led to and grew out of permanent settlement of near-by lands.

The banks fishery — early phases. The name "Newfoundland" today of course identifies the great island near the Grand Banks; but when these grounds first became of interest to Europeans, "New-founde-lande" was a word of general coverage for all of the north-coast country. Equally general in map nomenclature was "Baccalaos" — "Land of the Dried Codfish."

The Spanish and Portuguese, and their near neighbors the Basques, were leading figures in the early-day Grand Banks fisheries, although we are likely to place more emphasis on fishermen from France and Britain. Spanish fishermen first appeared in the Northern waters about 1540, some twenty years later than the fleets hailing from Bayonne in France. As one of their chief weapons of competition the Spanish had large supplies of salt, especially important in the wet fishery, which required so much of this product.

Possibly as many as 200 fishing vessels from European ports annually appeared on the banks at the opening of the season. In 1578, according to Hakluyt, no less than 400 vessels of all descriptions were engaged in fishing — though this may have been an exaggeration. Of whatever country of origin, the vessels were similarly equipped. Each ship, operating with a crew of a dozen men, could expect a cargo of from 20,000 to 25,000 fish after a month or six weeks of fishing. Fish were taken with a hempen hand line, the hook of which was baited with the entrails of cod, or occasionally with herring. In this world of high seas and bleak skies, the fishermen sometimes disported themselves by catching birds as well as fish with hook and line, so numerous were flocks of fulmars, petrels, guillemots, and great auks hovering over the schools of fish. To experienced fishermen, flocks of birds seen from afar were a welcome promise of good fishing ahead. Oil was sometimes made from the livers of the birds.

Land bases and equipment for shore fishery. With the realization that near-by land bases were advantageous, the competition for possession of the more favorable beaches began. The vessels reaching the scene first had their choice of the available beaches. The winner of a race for a beach proclaimed himself Shore Admiral, and assumed local authority over the inhabitants and the property found there.

Method in the shore fishery was brought to a high efficiency by the skillful Basques. Once the beach had been selected and admiralty over it established, equipment was stripped from the vessels to be used for lodgings on land. The size of the mainsail, it is said, determined the proportions of the main dwelling. Landing stages were contrived, perhaps equipped with a house at one end for dressing the fish as they were delivered. (See Fig. 5.) The staging, or " fish flakes," on which the flesh of the fish was to be dried was also prepared in advance of the catch. Small boats, sometimes assembled from parts that came as cargo from the

5   Shore operations in the codfishery at the opening of the eighteenth century, from a contemporary map:

A — Clothing of fishermen
B — Fishing line
C — Manner of fishing
D — Dressing of fish
E — Trough into which they throw cod when dressed
F — Salt boxes

G — Manner of carrying cod
H — Cleaning of cod
I — A press to recover cod liver oil
K — Casks to receive water and blood that comes from livers
L — Another cask to receive the oil
M — Manner of drying cod

home country, were made ready to serve a number of purposes. They were used for catching bait fish, although mackerel and herring were sometimes caught in nets from shore. They were also used for communicating with the main vessel offshore, or for searching out near-by fishing grounds — a local operation known among the French as a *dégrat*.

Shore fisheries and settlement: Cape Breton and Gaspé. The Grand Banks and other similar but less extensive banks in the same general area first attracted deep-sea fishermen to the New World, but it was not until the activity was extended toward the North American mainland that effort at actual settlement was displayed. Cape Breton and the Gaspé Peninsula illustrate the relation between shore fishing and land occupancy.

" Cape Breton," in its original usage, identified the northeast tip only of the island to which the name now applies. According to a description of Cape Breton in 1672, " the margin and the interior contain almost nothing but mountains of rocks. But that which makes it valued are the ports and roadsteads which the ships use to make the fishery. Mackerel and Herring are very abundant around the island, and the Fishermen make their bait of them for catching the Cod." Search of the island revealed good supplies of wood, essential for many purposes, and also of coal, but the latter resource was not to assume importance for several generations to come.

The first settlement of the Gaspé Peninsula was the result of the wide-spreading fishing industry. When it was observed that the cod was predatory on other fish, such as the capelin of coastal waters, the fishermen learned to follow the movements of the smaller species to find the cod. Apparently the waters off Gaspé were a favorite habitat of capelin and cod, and fishermen thus were early brought to that picturesque region. Gaspé is mainly a rugged land, but its coast offered numerous beaches, and beyond them lay meadows suitable for erecting flakes. The meadows were not all natural ones, but were made, it is said, " by the great quantities of Fir which the fishermen have cut down there to make their stages, and which they continue to cut down every day." Deforestation had proceeded to such an extent that even in 1672 only a few scrubs remained near at hand, and if useful logs were needed, the fishermen had to go " to the mountain, which is two musket shots from the coast, and bring them upon their shoulders, which is very fatiguing."

Sable Island, an early fishing and supply depot. In modern geographical accounts, Sable Island is scarcely mentioned, for it is but 20 miles long and 1 mile wide — a minute speck in the North Atlantic. This island, which has long borne as its name the French word for sand, *sable,* lies, as the map shows (Fig. 6), about 200 miles off Nova Scotia. During the late eighteenth century, when Sable first appeared on reliable maps, the island was nearly twice its present size, and what is even more important, was of marked significance in the fishing industry. Powerful forces of erosion during a century and a half have evidently swept away much of the lower land, and winds have spread sand dunes over meadows formerly useful for grazing; even the general altitude is believed to have been

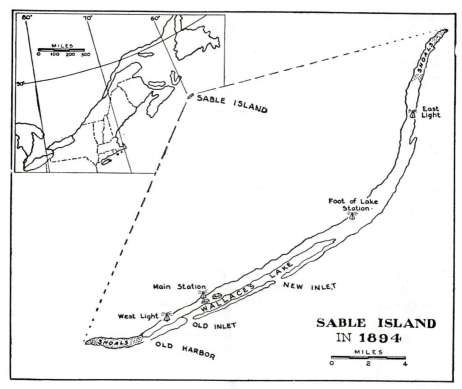

6   Sable Island in 1894. Adapted from a map in *Proceedings and Transactions, Royal Society of Canada,* Vol. 12 (1894), Sec. 2, p. 49.

lowered. Possibly, too, the original coast line offered more favorable anchorages than does the coast line of today. It seems, however, that Sable Island was more of a hazard than an aid to navigation, and certainly that is its position today. The reduction of the visible parts of the island increased the possibilities of shipwreck, for the Sable Banks, which were its roots, remained as extensive as ever, and only slightly submerged. Heavy fogs often concealed the island and the shoals and their 50-mile-long line of breakers, which on clear days gave warning of danger ahead. To some extent, Sable Island was the Cape Hatteras of the North, because, like the cape of North Carolina, Sable Island and Banks were danger points for navigators.

The limited natural advantages of Sable Island were enhanced by the introduction of cattle at an early, but not definitely known, date. The year of introduction is placed by one authority in 1518, thus antedating by far similar introduction in Florida. Whatever the date, it is known that the cattle multiplied and that for more than a century they furnished food supplies for fishermen, who were doubtless in great need of such food. The cattle, probably from lack of care and through wanton destruction, eventually disappeared, but they were remembered as late as 1760. when it was said: "Formerly some persons of humanity put cattle ashore to breed for the relief of the shipwrecked, and by multiplying, they answered that benevolent charitable end; until some wicked, mean, rascally people from the continent destroyed them to make gain . . . of their hides and tallow."

AGRICULTURAL READJUSTMENTS IN THE ENGLISH COLONIES

" Bringing European cattle in the sixteenth century to Sable Island, of all places! " one might be led to exclaim at this point. But other importations no less strange are known to have occurred, and it is suspected that if the whole story could be told it would prove once again that truth may be stranger than fiction. It should be recalled that at the beginnings of colonization, little was known about the climate and soils of the Atlantic seaboard. Understanding of these ventures is furthered, too, by the knowledge that even after the formation of the chartered companies, such as the Massachusetts Bay Company, free and individual enterprise was the rule. *Planning* was certainly not a characteristic feature of early colonization; indeed, in the sense of comprehending the possibilities and limitations of the environment, it was then impossible. Moreover, the majority of the colonists, coming from the lower economic ranks of society, could scarcely have brought with them all the material they wanted, or even the best samples of either livestock or any other kind of equipment needed. Probably most of them wished not so much to " start life anew," as we are prone to see it, but rather to continue in the new land the more familiar ways of gaining a livelihood. Through all of these circumstances, strange equipment was often brought to strange places.

We have fairly good accounts of the colonists who first came to America, but only scattered records of the equipment — tools, livestock, food plants — which they brought with them. Something more is known of the importations that arrived after the earliest colonies were established, for by then colonial leaders had some basis for judging the needs of the people and the capacities of the land for yielding those needs. Further material for interesting study comes from the many attempts to develop special products, such as silk and wine, in the new Anglo-American frontier. These ventures, inspired by authorities to further the then-current mercantilistic policy of Britain, were often ill adapted to the environment and social life of the colonies and thus were short-lived. Some of these economic experiments will be discussed later, but it seems desirable first to trace the more universal adaptations of European agricultural crops and practices to the American environment.

Colonial " native cattle." By the year 1650 there were perhaps 50,000 " native cattle " in the British colonies, somewhat less than half the human population. These cattle sprang from a stock as varied as can well be imagined, all from Europe, because there were no strictly native cattle in America. Although we are at a loss to describe the colorations of these beasts, it is at least known that they were small in size. The gross weight of average cattle on the Rhode Island market did not exceed 350 pounds, and even the best oxen were slender and ill-shaped. By 1650, importation of new stock from Europe was dwindling, and there was much interchange of young bulls and heifers among the colonies. By slow degrees, a "native cattle" was in the process of evolution from hetero-geneous sources.

The first animals to be imported into the British colonies were those which arrived on the James River some time before 1609 — possibly in 1607 with the first adventurers. A few additions of British cattle were made in 1610, but the 100 or so that arrived in Virginia in 1611 came from the West Indies and possibly bore the traits of the early Spanish cattle. Natural increase, new importations from the West Indies and Europe, and wise regulations governing the slaughter-ing of cattle resulted in rapid growth of Virginia cattle herds to 500 head in 1620, and as many as 30,000 in 1639. By the latter date Virginia was supplying live-stock to Maryland and perhaps to other colonies, with a resulting decline in the Virginia cattle population until the year 1648. Thereafter the gains were steady.

There was no room for cattle on the *Mayflower,* it would seem, for the first specimens — three heifers and a bull — arrived at Plymouth on the ship *Charity* in 1624. Other importations during the next few years provided cows for the Cape Ann settlements, but it was not until the financially strong Massachusetts Bay Company was formed that importations came on a larger scale from Devonshire. Between the years 1620 and 1633, livestock were brought to Massachusetts in nearly every ship, but losses on board were undoubtedly heavy. It is reported that of the 200 cattle ordered for the Massachusetts Bay Colony on one voyage, 70 died on the long transatlantic crossing.

Variety in original cattle breeds was the colonial rule. New York, in good Dutch tradition, received its first cows from Texel, Holland, and from other localities in 1625 came more than 100 head of livestock, including stallions, mares, and sheep. Similarly, the settlements along the Delaware, Scandinavian in ori-gin, were supplied by the Swedish West India Company. Large yellow cattle from Denmark were the original breed of New Hampshire, brought there in 1631 by Captain John Mason. Elsewhere, English and French varieties pre-dominated.

The transfer of these many breeds into environments generally resembling those of the homelands involved no great difficulties. Nevertheless, the colonists were not prepared to maintain the stock in such a manner as would lead to its improvement. It was said in 1749 by Per Kalm, a Swedish traveler, that the "cat-tle are allowed to wander through the woods and uncultivated grounds, where they are half-starved, having long ago extirpated the annual grasses by cropping them too closely in the Spring, before they have time to form their flowers and to shed their seeds." As a matter of fact, the seaboard environment was deficient in nutritious grasses. Great was the dependence upon swale hay, coarse in tex-ture and difficult to store for winter use. Salt-marsh hay was even worse, though it gave an outward appearance of luxuriance; according to an observant traveler, "this hay is rank and sour." The shrewd Captain John Smith, referring to New

England, said in his meandering style: "There is grasse plenty, though very long and thicke stalked, which being neither mowne nor eaten, is very ranke, yet all their cattell like and prosper well therewith, but indeed it is weeds, herbs, and grasse growing together, which, although they be good and sweet in Summer, they will deceive your cattell in Winter."

Furthermore, the practice of sowing grasses for hay and pasture had not developed in England at the time the colonies were established. This becomes clear from the following table:

ENGLISH GRASSES

Type of Grass	Year of Introduction of Seeds into British Isles
Red clover	1633
Sainfoin	1651
Yellow clover	1659
Perennial rye	1677
White or Dutch clover	1700
Timothy (from America)	1760

The background of the colonists, therefore, did not include the efficient care and control of cattle. Moreover, the pioneering nature of settlement in America delayed the adoption of practices leading to improvement of livestock. In all probability, quality was depreciated rather than improved until sometime after the Revolution.

Narragansett planters, first colonial stockmen. The majority of colonial farmers kept livestock, at least by the end of the seventeenth century, but the first region to assume pre-eminence in this capacity was the Narragansett country. Many people today associate this bit of Rhode Island with racing horses — an incidence carrying the suggestion of historical background.

The emergence of Narragansett as a grazing country, with supplementary agriculture, resulted from a combination of many factors. The ancient limits of the region as expressed in Indian treaties are somewhat vague, and there seems to be no contemporary map suitable for reproduction. Apparently, however, the colonial area of grazing and farming extended along the west shore of Narragansett Bay southward through Kingston, with an inland reach of some 15 miles, or very close to the Connecticut line. A lowland of gentle relief, this soon became a region of much individuality, retained through the Colonial period and into the present. Economically and socially, this famous region includes several off-lying islands, the largest of which was known in earlier times as Rhode Island. The Blaskowitz map of the Revolutionary period, simplified in Figure 7, gives a correct view of the settled areas of Rhode Island and the mainland at that time. Newport, on Rhode Island, was the leading city of earlier times, with Providence of secondary importance.

An impetus to the early settlement of Narragansett, patents to which were issued between 1631 and 1643, was its freedom from woods. We are not surprised to learn that Indians, in this instance the Narragansetts, were held largely re-

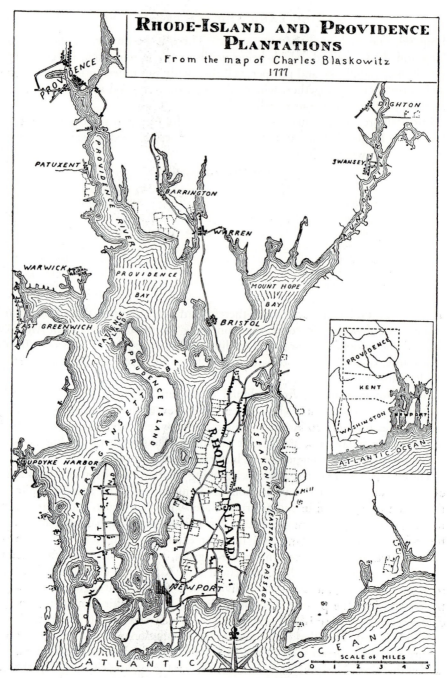

7 Rhode Island and Providence Plantations in 1777. This is a simplified redrawing of the elaborate and beautiful map of Blaskowitz. It emphasizes, among other things, the insular character of Rhode Island.

sponsible for this unnatural condition. With an elemental shrewdness that the aborigines often displayed, they had selected this exceptional area for village residence and agriculture, with which they combined, as did their white successors, much fishing in the bay.

The surface of Narragansett presents a smoother contour than do most New England areas, though much of the soil was then, as it is now, thin and boulder-strewn. Other positive attractions in early days were tidewater location, real or assumed climatic benefits from position on the sheltered side of the bay, and fishing opportunities. Particularly important were the extensive areas of natural pasture, not wet meadow but upland grazing country. This coincidence of factors appealed to the imagination of many colonial enthusiasts, who were not slow to advocate wine industries and the importation of silkworms. But regional economy did not proceed along those visionary lines; instead, the people prosaically raised grains and tended livestock.

In its large landholdings the Narragansett country was an anomaly in New England. According to tradition, the " Smith Tract " of over 17,000 acres was enclosed within boundaries 9 miles in length by 3 miles in breadth. The " Champlin Tract," more certainly known, contained 2,000 acres, and other farms included 5 or 6 square miles. These were princely estates, suitable for a master-slave association, and so it is not surprising to learn that here was one of the larger Negro populations of the Northern colonies. It is impossible to say just how many slaves were held by the planters (for so they were called), because data are given by counties and states, but it is known that most of Rhode Island's slaves were owned by Newport and Narragansett persons. There were probably more than 3,000 slaves in Narragansett in 1750. A few Indians were also held as servants.

In this unusual natural and social setting, the planters developed a pastoral-agricultural aristocracy which gravitated toward the breeding of stock — cattle, sheep, horses. The famed Narragansett pacer originated here. Horses were sold on foreign markets — in the West Indies and Dutch Guiana — and were extensively advertised in Charleston, South Carolina, between 1734 and 1740. It was said in 1675 that here " there are more sheep than anywhere in New England." Next in importance were dairy products, particularly cheese, which was largely exported. Hides were sent to local tanneries. The planters also raised corn, rye and other small grains, hemp, flax, and tobacco. A pre-Revolutionary visitor to Narragansett wrote appreciatively: " After dinner we took a walk to see their cattle grazing in the pastures; and were led into some as fine meadows as ever I saw in Old England."

Introduction of the common field crops.   Within a generation after the founding of the first British colonies, nearly all the common crops of northern Europe had been introduced — " for keeps " we might say informally — into America. Agricultural economy at first was primarily a subsistence economy, so limited were the opportunities for exchange of produce among the colonies. The day of agricultural specialization was far in the future, to follow a long period of trial and error in the raising of various crops. The immediate needs of the colonists required the local production of a wide range of crops, both for food and as raw material. Granted an environment not definitely intolerant, many plants yielded well enough to justify their retention in the subsistence economy.

So many were the variables and unknowns that much more than one year of crop failure was required to prove further trials useless. Successive years of wheat-crop failures in Massachusetts, for example, were not completely discouraging. The chances were fairly good that any field crop acclimated to western Europe would find a habitat well suited to it here, and apparently the seeds of all the crop plants of Europe were brought to each of the seaboard colonies. Exact records, however, are lacking for most of the common food plants.

The hardy cereals. During the exploration period immediately preceding settlement, wheat was grown successfully in a number of Northern seaboard localities. The explorer Bartholomew Gosnold, for example, harvested a crop of wheat which he had planted in 1602 on one of the Elizabeth Islands in Buzzards Bay, off the south coast of Massachusetts. This experience in practical agriculture was probably of little historical significance, scarcely an adequate presettlement test of the possibilities of cereal culture. The first Virginia wheat is said to have been grown in the year 1611; from that date the acreage increased slowly until about 1650, when tobacco culture took precedence over all other crops. Wheat was being raised in New Netherland (New York) as early as 1626 and probably also at the same time in New England. The years of introduction of wheat into colonies founded later — for example, Maryland and Pennsylvania — are not certainly known, but the crop is generally mentioned in their earliest descriptions. Its growth appears to have been most successful in the middle colonies, where in the eighteenth century it became the principal crop and from whose ports flour was a leading export.

Wheat stalks grew tall and rank in coastal Virginia and southward, but yielded disappointingly few kernels. Proponents of Southern colonization often attributed this circumstance to the soils, presenting it as a recommendation as to their richness; but subsequent world-wide experience with wheat suggests that climatic warmth and moisture were more directly responsible. The wheat of Massachusetts and Connecticut was subject to what the colonists called late-season " blasting " or " mildew." This disease, whose causes are now well understood by plant pathologists, mystified Connecticut farmers of the seventeenth and eighteenth centuries. They attributed the " blast " to all sorts of causes that seem fantastic to us in a more technically enlightened age. It was seriously held, for example, that the salt-bearing breezes from the near-by Atlantic somehow poisoned the plant. Faith in this explanation was apparently not shaken by similar difficulties reported by farmers in the Connecticut Valley in Massachusetts, which was too far distant from the ocean to be affected by " salty " sea breezes. George Washington, in commenting upon the general excellence of New England farming, spoke of the " blight or mildew " that unfortunately destroyed the wheat stands. In spite of the " mildew," New England farmers doggedly sowed wheat in their irregularly shaped fields throughout the Colonial and Revolutionary periods.

Of some benefit was an early Massachusetts law requiring the eradication of barberry found in woods near wheat fields. This law was passed, of course, generations in advance of pathological knowledge which recognizes the barberry as a host plant for wheat rusts. A critical German traveler during the Revolution, Dr. Johann David Schoepf, was moved to speak disdainfully of the law that " was passed against the poor barberry "; but he added, by way of explanation, that " New Englanders are known for their strange beliefs and practices as well." Until after the Revolution, experiments in wheat-growing were entirely with the winter variety. The first spring wheat, later so important in the Dakotas, was introduced into Long Island in the 1780's, but it proved ill suited to the seaboard environment.

Wheat was not the popular source of flour that it later became. Native corn (maize), ground into meal, was a substantial item in the diet, the more so because corn could be raised successfully in various types of climate and soils. Rye was introduced at an early time in many of the colonies, and its flour was often mixed with that of corn in breadmaking. The two plants were often sown together in the same field.

There is some doubt as to when and where oats was introduced from the Old World, because from the context of some early reports it appears possible that wild varieties growing naturally in many coastal areas may have been mistaken for cultivated oats.

Introduction of European fruits. Among the supplies brought over in the first waves of settlement were seeds of all kinds of common fruits, particularly apple, pear, and quince. Since fruit trees require some years to mature when started from seed, accounts of them are comparatively rare until well along in the seventeenth century. One Connecticut farmer, notable for his integrity, wrote in 1635 of making " five hundred hogsheads of cider out of my orchard in one year." Since this quantity would have been an impossibility if the orchard (supposedly a very extensive one) had been raised from seed, some authorities have concluded that a form of apple, perhaps a crab apple, was possessed by the Indians, to the roots of which graftings could be made. That the Indians had apples is confirmed but not proved by some exploratory journals which refer to the apple as an indigenous fruit. Also it is further confirmed by the Algonkian word *mish-i-min*, identified as "apple." Governors Island in Boston Harbor appears to have been the first site of apple production from European seed. We learn that on October 10, 1639, " ten fair pippins were brought, there being not one apple or pear tree planted in any part of the country but upon that island." A nursery for young trees was started in Danvers, near Salem, in 1640.

Contributions from the lower latitudes. It has sometimes been said, and not wholly in jest, that the only immediate and practical effect of the Cabot discovery voyages of 1497–98 was the introduction of the turkey into western Europe. By the time of permanent settlement in America this prized bird had become

domesticated in Europe and actually made the American-bound voyage with
some of the first colonists. The turkey was but one of many useful native products
that were "introduced" in this roundabout fashion at the time of colonization.

Cotton, Upland and Sea-island. Upland cotton was first grown in the James
River settlements in 1621, from seeds brought in from Mediterranean Europe,
where it had been grown for nearly a century. Before that, this variety of cotton
had been a domesticated plant in Mexico, and thus was presumably indigenous
to the Americas. In its new development on the Southern seaboard, upland cotton remained of minor significance until the middle of the eighteenth century,
supplying limited domestic needs but nothing for export. The cause of this inferior position of the crop which ultimately dominated the plantation South was,
as is well known, the difficulty of removing the seeds from a tight meshing of
fibers. Removal of seeds was a hand process until the invention of a cleaning
machine by Alphonse du Breuil, a New Orleans planter. The Du Breuil machine, dating from 1742, caused a minor flurry in cotton production in Louisiana;
but it was not a complete success, nor were several other similar inventions which
were put forward during the next half-century. The invention and promotion of
the cotton gin in 1794 by Eli Whitney initiated the new era in American cotton
culture.

A measure of the unimportance of cotton in pre-Revolutionary days is suggested in the exportation of but seven bags of it from Charleston in 1748. Following the Revolution, sea-island or blackseed cotton was brought to the Georgia
mainland from the off-lying islands, where it had been produced for some years
commercially on plantations. The original sea-island cotton was brought to the
so-called Golden Isles of Georgia from the West Indies, presumably the Bahamas.
It was never raised extensively beyond the lower coastal lands of Georgia, South
Carolina, and Spanish Florida.

Tobacco. An error frequently repeated is that tobacco, which so early and
for so long a time reigned supreme among Virginia products, was one of the
plants inherited from the Indians there. The Indians did raise tobacco, to be
sure, but the plantation variety was not a native one, but a migrant from the
American tropics, possibly Trinidad. It was first grown on the James River in
1612 as an experimental venture. At this time the market for tobacco was just
opening up in England, and Virginia, the first permanent British North American colony with climatic conditions permitting its growth, became the chief early
source. (See Fig. 8.) Here was a climate with tropical characteristics in a summer
long enough between frosts to permit the completion of all the time-consuming
operations, from the setting out of the seedlings to the stripping of the leaves.
That there were other tobacco climates at least the equal to that of coastal Virginia is obvious in the many areas, widely dispersed in latitude, since invaded by
this tropical plant.

Rice from Madagascar, the Orient, and Northern Italy. Perhaps the first
major crop plant in the plantation scheme to be brought to America with deliberate forethought was rice. This could only have happened fairly late in the

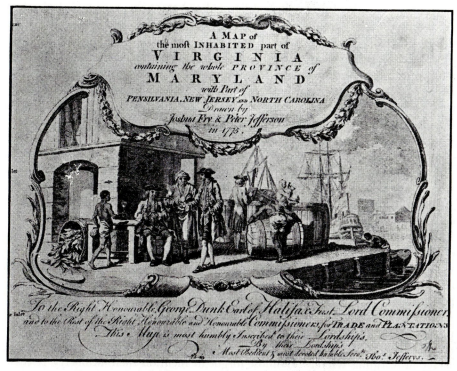

8 This elaborate map title of 1775 is a composite view of tobacco, tobacco hogs-heads, sailing vessel, and costuming of people, at a Virginia landing. Peter Jefferson, coauthor of the map, was the father of Thomas Jefferson.

Colonial period, when considerable knowledge of climatic possibilities had been amassed. There is rather direct evidence that rice culture near Charleston was begun before 1690 and was part of the plan of an official of the East India Company, who considered " from the situation, nature of the soil, and climate, that rice may be produced to great advantage in Carolina." Portuguese vessels trading to the Orient and including Charleston in their voyages brought additional rice seeds from the East Indies. New varieties came from Egypt and Madagascar in 1712 and 1713. Thomas Jefferson, who was always interested in agricultural improvements, arranged for the sending of seeds from the northern regions of Italy — Piedmont and Lombardy — through the port of Leghorn. For nearly a century, rice remained a principal plantation product of the Southern seaboard from South Carolina to Florida.

PRODUCTION SCHEMES MORE OR LESS FANCIFUL AND IMPRACTICAL

A certain degree of fanciful thinking about the possibilities of the Atlantic seaboard is noticeable throughout the Colonial period, from the founding of Jamestown at least to the 1740's, when indigo culture was encouraged, with fleeting success, in South Carolina. This expanse of time included the origin of the Georgia Colony, classic example of philanthropic colonial planning by the British. " Anything can happen there " might have been an expression familiar to many English financiers during these many years. Mercantilistic plans to free Britain of dependence upon foreign lands for valuable commodities found expression in the outright encouragement of the production in the American colonies of raw silk and wine and the manufacturing of glass, and in perennial attempts to develop plantations of ginger, pineapples, indigo, oranges, and many other crops. The failure of any of these plans in one colony did not prevent similar attempts elsewhere, or even in the same place at a later time. Intermixed with true vision in colonial progress there was much that was visionary.

Silk industry encouraged, particularly in Georgia. Advocacy of raw-silk production in the Southern British colonies began in 1623 in Virginia and reached its culmination in the settlement of Georgia in 1732. Early Virginia descriptions, especially those found in the Colonization Tracts, contain many references to white-mulberry trees growing naturally in the woods; hence, according to these advertisers, the fundamental basis of a silk industry was already provided. Experience of course proved otherwise, for this industry was ill suited to conditions in the New World at the time. Through lack of skill and labor, and the unexpected rise of tobacco as an export product, attempts to make raw silk were sporadic, and within three-fourths of a century almost forgotten. In 1676 an observer in Virginia wrote, " I almost forgot to mention their Mulberry [trees], whereof they have a great store about their houses; these were planted at first to feed Silkworms, but that design failing, they are now of little use amongst them."

With the beginning of settlement in Georgia, which was the most elaborate colonization project on the seaboard, the possibilities of silk and other unusual products were again brought to the front. This was good grist for the mills of Georgia enthusiasts who would create a Utopia of small landholdings on the Savannah River, without Negro slavery or spirituous liquors, specializing in tropical and semitropical produce which would not be competitive with that of other Southern colonies.

Chief among the advocates of Georgia settlement was the leader, General James Edward Oglethorpe, whose various declarations in support of the plans of the Trustees show a curious blending of fact and fancy. In one of his papers, first pointing out that Georgia lay in the same latitude as China, Persia, Palestine, and Madeira, he presented the plausible conclusion that, provided " Georgia becomes well peopled . . . it is highly probable that England may be supplied with raw Silk, Wine, Oil, Dyes, Drugs, and many other materials for manufacture, which she is obliged to purchase from Southern countries."

Georgia lands were granted on condition that the patentee plant 100 white-mulberry trees for each 10-acre clearing. The Trustees provided trees and silkworms, and also sent as instructors men familiar with the Italian silk industry. This determined effort was not wholly without result, for although as early as 1735 only 8 pounds of raw silk were exported from Savannah, hundreds of pounds were shipped out in 1759. But other activities, more suited to the environment and social life, ultimately triumphed. The last pound of raw silk was sold in Savannah in the year 1790.

South Carolina's indigo industry. The original intention on the part of South Carolina's proprietors to produce for the British market such items as wine, silk, ginger, sugar, cotton, and indigo has been indicated. Many of these products were subjects of perennial experiment during the early years, but only cotton and indigo proved successful. The discovery of indigo growing naturally in the coastal forests of South Carolina stimulated an effort to develop it as a plantation product. Two other varieties, the French or Hispaniola and the Guatemala or " true " indigo, were imported; and to encourage its culture Parliament in 1748 granted a bounty of 6d a pound on all indigo imported into Great Britain from America. Such being the stimulus, indigo accounted for one-tenth of the total value of exports from South Carolina in 1748. By the year 1756, when 200,000 pounds of the dye were shipped from Charleston, this plantation industry seemed in a fair way to fulfilling the wishes and promises of the planners. But only five years later, as will be shown in a later chapter, the industry was on a steep downgrade in the face of rapidly declining prices as a result of Oriental competition. Indigo-growing lingered for some years, longest in the Orangeburg district. With its passage from the economic scene about 1850, the final curtain was rung down on the visionary plans with which many of the colonies came into being.

FRENCH CONTRIBUTIONS TO COLONIAL ECONOMY

The activities of the French in colonial times have been associated in the popular mind, it would seem to an unfortunate degree, with martial exploits, with far-ranging explorations to gain territories for their King, and with Indian fur-trading. That there were many of these activities can scarcely be denied, because while the British colonists were engaged in the dull business above partly related, the French had laid claim to half a continent. The historians' account of their adventures is a romance. Plumed helmets gleamed in the shade of the forests, and priestly vestments were to be seen in the fitful light around the campfires of Indians, a people whom the French had learned to understand much better than had the British. But there are also the more prosaic but no less significant aspects of the French occupancy of the vast regions over which they had temporary political control and in which they made lasting cultural changes.

General farming in the St. Lawrence Valley. The French economy of the St. Lawrence Valley was genetically independent of that of the British colonies. The cattle were French-bred, some with the West Indies black strain. With shorter growing seasons, the range of crops in French Canada was more limited, but the settlers there had their hardy cereals, and they grew tobacco for home

9   Sugar-making in Louisiana in 1751. From *Report of the Commissioner of Agriculture for the Year 1867*, opposite p. 511.

use. They adopted the agricultural products of the Indians and, even more closely than did the English colonists, followed their methods of cultivation.

Sugar cane in Louisiana.   Special attention was paid to agriculture in Louisiana — that is, what comprises the state of that name today, not the Louisiana Purchase country — although there was some fur-trading as well. In the effort to develop a cash staple product many plants were tried, but none proved so remunerative as sugar cane.

The history of sugar cane previous to its arrival in the lowlands of Louisiana is most complicated, and some gaps have been left unfilled. It seems to have been taken from India to Spain by the Saracens, thence to Madeira and — in the early stages of Western Hemisphere settlement — to the West Indies, there coming at last within the French sphere of interest. We find that in the year 1751 a French troop transport bound for Louisiana touched at Port-au-Prince, Haiti, where Jesuit priests were permitted to send to New Orleans not only a supply of cane, but a few Negroes familiar with the growing of the cane and the manufacture of sugar.

When the culture of sugar cane was attempted in Louisiana, it was at first unsuccessful despite these favoring circumstances. Discouraged with the venture, the French abandoned its cultivation in 1769, temporarily turning their attention to indigo, cotton, and rice. Cane cultivation was later resumed, and in 1791 was declared successful. At that time there were two varieties of cane, the Malabar or Bengal and the Otaheite, but both of these have long since disappeared. The later history of cane in the Deep South need not be related here at length. It was introduced into Georgia on an American schooner in 1814, and a new variety of red-ribbon cane was brought in 1817 to New Orleans, where it was tested in the garden of one John J. Coiron at Terre aux Bœufs, and then commercially produced on Plantation Ste. Sophie in 1825. The operations in sugar manufacture in 1751 (Fig. 9) included the stripping of leaves, the chopping and grinding of the stalks, and the boiling in caldrons of the juice, which after being ladled into stone jars was exposed to the sun to secure more rapid concentration.

French agriculture in Kaskaskia, Illinois, 1682. Agriculture made a beginning in the American bottoms of the Mississippi River south of St. Louis in 1682, the year when Philadelphia was laid out by Penn's commissioners, a century before permanent settlement in Kentucky or Tennessee and twenty-eight years before New Orleans was founded. Kaskaskia is an old place, and so also are near-by Cahokia, Prairie du Rocher, Fort de Chartres, and Prairie du Pont. The French people lived at peace with the Indians they knew so well and whose women they freely married, and remained thus at peace for more than a century and a half.

About half the people of the small Kaskaskia village depended on Indian trade; the remainder were farmers. They were not good farmers. By comparison with the more advanced stage of agriculture on the seaboard in the same year, theirs represented a primitive stage. Being re-enacted here on a small scale were the processes of land use which had largely disappeared from the older settlements. It will be advantageous to spend a little time with this small-scale sample of American frontier culture.

The Kaskaskia French found their agricultural implements defective, just as had the Puritans, who had brought with them some tools suitable for English farms. The wooden plows of the French, sometimes called hog plows because of their rooting effect, had iron-plated shares and upright handles requiring a strong guiding hand. These French plows of Kaskaskia were not much inferior to the colonial plows of Massachusetts and Virginia at the same time. Until 1797 they remained basically of wood, and there were few improvements in the meantime.

Oxen, light in weight and poorly formed, provided the motive power. The French had no horses, differing greatly in this respect from the contemporary Spanish in the region that is now Texas and New Mexico. Flinty Indian corn was the chief crop. The seeds were dropped into the shallow furrow as the plow broke ground, to be covered by another furrow slice. This was the method of culture on land free of trees. If the plot were in the " deadening " stage, corn was planted in hills — as earlier it had been planted by the Indians on other frontiers. The shrinking leaves of the deadened trees admitted increasing light until eventually the limbs and trunk fell, to be burned for wood ashes on the ground. On such plots, the plow was of no use. Among the hills of corn were often planted Indian pumpkins, which would be strange-looking today, so greatly have they been improved.

In addition to corn, the Kaskaskia farmers raised wheat, which they cut with sickles and threshed in winter; also buckwheat, rye, and barley. Their small and hardy cattle with short black horns were French-bred; immigrants from Canada, these animals were well adapted to winters of the continental climate. Chickens and turkeys were attached to the household. The neat homes with their well-kept gardens fronting on the Kaskaskia River won praise from early visitors to this region.

The farms of the Kaskaskia French were plotted in the characteristic ribbon-like manner which the French adopted wherever they laid hold upon the land — Quebec, Detroit, Louisiana. They extended in narrow, parallel strips between the lower Kaskaskia River and the Mississippi. Beyond the farms, where lived families named Prévost, Bienvenue, Faggot, and the like, was a " common field " of some 8,000 acres for community use, as well as a separate " common " reserved for grazing purposes. In 1857 a close observer could still see in the bottom lands for 20 or 30 miles above Kaskaskia village the scars of furrows left by the industrious French farmers many years before.

CHAPTER 4

Filling Up the Land: French and English Settlements

CASUAL glances at maps sometimes lead to erroneous conclusions. For example, on the political map of North America in 1700 (Fig. 20A, page 77) the British colonial area shows to poor advantage. If we judge solely by extent of area explored and claimed, France had displayed far more vigor and enterprise than had its chief competitor. " New France " was of continental size, spreading over the vast interior and controlling the East coast's best natural route from the Atlantic — the St. Lawrence-Great Lakes waterway. " If the French had succeeded in discovering and controlling the mouth of the Mississippi," observed the geographer Nathaniel Shaler, " the fate of their settlements in the valley of that river might have been more fortunate."

In comparison with France's great domain, Britain's territory was small indeed. The British colonies were hemmed in between the French possessions and the seacoast, and not even all of the seacoast was theirs. On the north, French colonies extended into the present State of Maine; at the other extreme, Spanish territories extended to south of the Savannah River. Not until 1763 did Britain control the entire coast line from the St. Lawrence to Key West, and then only for twenty years. The War of Independence, as we know, freed the thirteen colonies, and Britain withdrew still further by re-ceding Florida to Spain.

INHABITED AREA MORE IMPORTANT THAN TERRITORIAL CLAIMS

The occupance map for 1700, however (Fig. 20B, page 77), gives a very different and more important picture of the relative dominance of the three chief colonizing powers. *Inhabited* New France consisted of a thin and discontinuous line of occupied territory around the shores of the Bay of Fundy and Acadia (Nova Scotia), and along the St. Lawrence River. In the interior there were scattered spots of settlement at Detroit and a few other Great Lakes fur-trading and missionary outposts, besides some half military, half agricultural villages near the Mississippi and the lower Ohio River. Spain's Florida was mostly unknown Indian country, with a handful of Spanish colonists living in St. Augustine and westward along a strip in north Florida extending to the Gulf of Mexico.

British settlements, in contrast, had expanded to nearly one-third of the claimed territory. Along the strategic coast line from the Penobscot in Maine to the southern boundary of Virginia, British-promoted colonies had absorbed, or rather engulfed, the settlements of other European countries earlier on the scene. Hardly more than place names on the map remained to identify " New Netherland " and " New Sweden." The inland outpost of New Netherland was Fort Orange, site of present-day Albany, but the more important nuclei of Dutch settlement had been New Amsterdam (on Manhattan Island) and Breuckelen (Brooklyn). On Delaware Bay the commercial-minded Dutch also maintained Fort Nassau (1623-51), but the lower Delaware River region in the present State of Delaware was originally New Sweden, with its Forts Christina and New Korsholm in addition to a few small villages. By 1700, however, the coast was partitioned into British colonies as far southward as Albemarle Sound, far below which was the settlement of Charleston, South Carolina, separate from all the rest.

The foregoing considerations show the importance of *sustained* emigration in the support of overseas colonies, just as the volume of a main river depends on the contributions of its tributaries. After the faltering opening years the flow of British emigration was strong and steady. Not only did Britons come, but people from other countries also found sanctuary within the English area. This was in sharp contrast to the early drying-up of the stream of Swedish settlement which briefly fed life into the so-called New Sweden.

A study of " filling up the land " is more than a dull recounting of the growth of population, for it includes as well the spreading of people over the land — their patterns of occupancy. These patterns varied according to two main factors: (1) the Old World backgrounds of the emigrating peoples and (2) the extent of adaptation to New World conditions. It is apparent that the French, British, and Spanish peoples brought with them different ideas and ideals concerning forms of rural land tenure; the original Spanish villa or town was very unlike the English village and those of northern Europe. Attempts to transplant any of these types outright to the frontierlike environment of the Atlantic coastal area generally met with failure, hence modification and adaptation in some degree was inevitable.

This dual study of population growth and forms of land occupancy on American soil will begin with the French colonial area, notably the St. Lawrence Valley, which presented a pattern remarkable for its simplicity and persistence. This will be followed by an inquiry, necessarily more complicated, into the varied settlement types of the many British colonies. A similar study of the Spanish colonial area, both on the Atlantic coast and in the Far West, is reserved for the following chapter.

THE FRENCH COLONIES OF THE NORTH

The French people were slow to rise to the bait offered them in the acquisition of new colonial territory, which had been recommended for its alleged similarities to the homeland. This lack of interest, deplored by governmental and religious authorities alike, was attributed to many causes, the relative importance of which it is difficult to measure. Some learned Frenchmen, writing in reference to comparatively unsuccessful French settlements in the Ohio Valley at a later time, felt that the average French rustic was less suited to frontier farm life than the Englishman or the German. It may at least be reasoned that the natural environment of the Northern lands available for French occupancy imposed limitations on commercial agriculture. The short growing season prohibited the staple crops which spelled success in Virginia, and much of the land was rough and thin-soiled. Subsistence farming was possible, but perhaps no more attractive than other occupations ready at hand. To many Frenchmen, the already existent fishing and fur-trading industries offered greater attractions, financial or otherwise, than did the plodding routine of a subsistence farm.

Land grants on Isle Saint-Jean (Prince Edward Island). An easy illustration of this early conflict of interests is provided by the island north of Nova Scotia known to us as Prince Edward Island. Under the French, who claimed it by right of discovery, it was called Isle Saint-Jean. During the seventeenth century the entire island was included in a number of grants made to individuals or companies. The grants were intended to serve two primary purposes: (1) the control of the fur trade and (2) the development of the sedentary fishery in Acadia and in the Gulf of St. Lawrence.

At that early time, the shores of Isle Saint-Jean and other islands in the gulf (for example, Percé) were frequented by walrus and seal, in the catching of

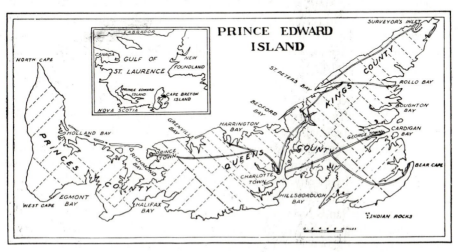

10 Prince Edward Island. A simplified version of a map published about 1800.

which the resident Micmac Indians were adept. The prospects of developing trade in walrus teeth and sealskins induced various companies to request grants on this strategically located island which, though largely rugged, presented some attractions to farmers. The " sedentary " fishery, however, proved not so lucrative as was anticipated; and the island, possessing as it did so limited an area, failed to develop as the center of a fur trade. Actual settlement did not occur until 1719, and then only on a small scale. According to a careful estimate by Thomas Pichon, a French visitor in 1760, the population had grown by that time to 1,354, with new arrivals daily coming from Acadia.

After Isle Saint-Jean became Prince Edward Island under the British a resurvey was ordered, this time into 67 townships. (See Fig. 10.) The British Board of Trade and Plantations offered these blocks of land by lottery in an apparent desire to have the land actually occupied, but at the same time set up provisions so stringent that few cared to accept. The terms demanded of each proprietor that one-third of his grant be settled within ten years from the date of the grant, to the proportion of 200 acres for each person. Penalty for failure to bring about this seemingly herculean task was forfeiture of the land to the Crown. Within a decade after the announcement of this curiously mixed plan only 19 of the 67 townships were partly settled. It was not until the opening of the nineteenth century that Prince Edward Island became appreciably occupied.

Seigniorial grants in the St. Lawrence Valley.   One of the more distinctive culture patterns of eastern North America took form in Lower Canada, especially within the 200 miles of river country between Quebec and Montreal. The seigniorial type of land tenure, of which the most conspicuous present-day features are the narrow " ribbon " farms stretching back from the St. Lawrence River, was in the beginning not tailor-made for that special environment. Feudalism still prevailed in old France when the new colony was undergoing settlement; hence it was not unnatural for French officials to assume that society in New France should rest on a similar basis. Overlordship and vassalage being the accepted social order, it was an easy step to create " seigniories " along the river, with eventual settlement to be accomplished by " habitants " who would be analogous to vassals in the homeland.

The process of awarding tracts of land began in the 1630's, but gathered little force for a quarter-century. There was, indeed, little occasion for haste in granting lands. Voluntary emigration was very slow. From 1633 to 1663 colonists came, as a rule, individually or in groups of three or four related families. During the next few years, more concerted action in centers like Paris, Rouen, and Rochelle succeeded in recruiting from their surrounding rural districts some 4,000 persons for the colony. By 1712 nearly all the territory on both shores of the St. Lawrence from Quebec to Montreal had been parceled out, and similar grants covered the lands bordering many tributaries, such as the Chaudière, the St. Francis, and the Richelieu. It was in the year 1712 that an official surveyor and cartographer, Gideon de Catalogne, commenced a two-year job of mapping

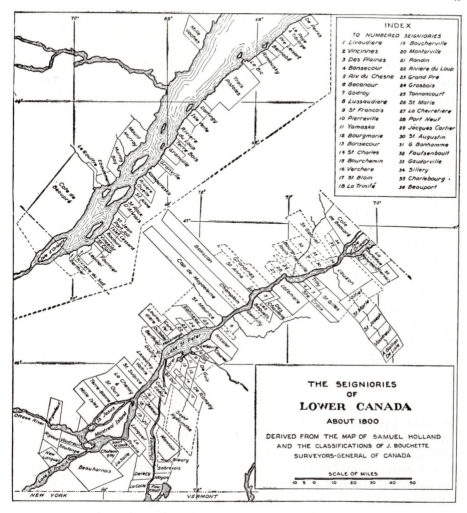

INDEX

TO NUMBERED SEIGNIORIES

1 Livaudiere	19 Boucherville
2 Vincinnes	20 Montarville
3 Des Plaines	21 Randin
4 Bonsecour	22 Riviere du Loup
5 Riv du Chesne	23 Grand Pre
6 Becanour	24 Grosbois
7 Godroy	25 Tonnancourt
8 Lussaudiere	26 St. Marie
9 St Francois	27 La Chevretiere
10 Pierreville	28 Port Neuf
11 Yamaska	29 Jacques Cartier
12 Bourgmarie	30 St. Augustin
13 Bonsecour	31 G Bonhomme
14 St Charles	32 Faufsenbault
15 Bourchemin	33 Gaudarville
16 Verchere	34 Sillery
17 St Blain	35 Charlebourg .
18 La Trinité	36 Beauport

THE SEIGNIORIES
OF
LOWER CANADA
ABOUT 1800

DERIVED FROM THE MAP OF SAMUEL HOLLAND
AND THE CLASSIFICATIONS OF J. BOUCHETTE
SURVEYORS-GENERAL OF CANADA

SCALE OF MILES
10 5 0   10   20   30   40   50

11   Seigniories of Lower Canada about the year 1800

the location, extent, ownership, and production of each seigniory. The map appearing here (Fig. 11) is not a copy of the Catalogne map, but derives from a similar survey made by Samuel Holland in 1783, after New France had been acquired by Great Britain. From this map you will note the general parallelogram form of the seigniories, as well as their variable extent. Cap La Magdeleine, for example, was at that time more than 60 miles in depth (measured away from the river), while many land grants had a depth of only 2 or 3 miles.

Isle d'Orléans as an Example.   Islands within the river were subdivided in a similar manner — the Island of Montreal, for example. A simpler case is provided, however, by Isle d'Orléans, near Quebec. This island, 20 miles long and 6 wide, was named in 1536 by Cartier, who reported: " The island . . . is rich with woods of all sorts, such as we find in France; it is very fine, edged with natural prairies on the north side that are flooded twice a day." The flooding is of course due to the tides, which are felt even as far as this up the St. Lawrence River. First settled by the French in 1650, several seigniors in turn owned Isle d'Orléans and subdivided it into small tracts for tenants, called *arrière-fiefs*. Within a decade the island was well peopled throughout its whole length, and compared with other similar areas of New France was one of the most densely inhabited. The island had a population of 4,312 in 1667, or nearly one-half the estimated population of all Lower Canada at that time. According to the best calculations, New France had 20,000 people in 1714 and 70,000 in 1759, the year of Quebec's surrender to General Wolfe.

Adaptations of Feudal Tenure to the Environment of Lower Canada. Seigniories were awarded at first to members of the nobility or to other persons of high distinction, but in the course of time grants were made to individuals from lower ranks of society and to institutions, especially the Church. A seigniorial " grant," it should be noted, did not signify a gift from the Crown, but rather certified that the recipient of the award was made trustee of the property and, as later interpreted, of only the surface of the areas involved, without mineral rights. The practice in Canada was to parcel the large grants into smaller tracts, the latter to be subject to freehold lease by the habitants. The partitioning process was hastened by the French tradition of equal inheritance rights to sons. The original areas of the seigniories were successively divided into smaller tracts, resulting in narrow strips like those of Kaskaskia. To prevent the continued subdivision of fields until they had become useless threads, an ordinance was passed in 1745 prohibiting habitants from building houses and stables upon land " less than one arpent and a half in front, by a depth of thirty or forty arpents." Like many statutes, this one was not strictly adhered to, but it probably prevented extreme subdivision. The standard tract appears to have been about one-ninth mile along the river and perhaps a mile in depth. For these tracts, called " concessions," seigniors received rent in money or produce.

Desire for frontage on the St. Lawrence River and its navigable tributaries obviously brought about this modification of the feudal system. The rivers furnished travel by water in summer and by ice in winter at a period and in an environment where other means of travel were either costly or wholly unobtainable. The natural result was a distribution of habitations like beads on a string, each one of which was within easy reach of the river or, to use habitant terminology, on the first côte. Village life, a characteristic of the feudal system in France, was thus eliminated. Occasional small agglomerations developed around a parish church, but few trading communities evolved other than the larger ones of Quebec, Montreal, and Trois Rivières. This situation distressed the authorities, who felt that such a dispersal of people subjected them more easily to surprise Indian attack. It seemed impossible, attractions of the river being what they were, to legislate villages into existence. Thus in transferring feudal life to New France, modifications were introduced. The chief of these resulted in the scattering of habitants, who lived on their farms rather than in a village as was the feudal custom. The peasants also achieved some independence of the seignior. Joseph Bouchette, an early authority, said in 1831: "These modifications have given to the feudal tenure of Lower Canada peculiarities that belong to itself and which seem singularly well adapted to the local circumstances of the country."

BRITISH COLONIAL SETTLEMENTS:
GENERAL CONSIDERATIONS

Types of rural and town settlement reached the maximum of variety within the British colonial area. One cause for the greater variety is to be found in the diverse natural environment in the long stretch of coast line and hinterland from Maine to Georgia. Four other factors, possibly less apparent but nonetheless fundamental, need more careful attention before the presentation of examples. These are (1) the pressure of population on the land, (2) the varied origins of the settlers, (3) the effect of the time-spread of the period of colonization, and (4) freedom from centralized authority.

Pressure of population on the land. The British colonies soon outstripped both the French and the Spanish colonies in numbers of people. Even as early as 1630 the centers of population in the Boston region were overspreading their original limits, leading a thoughtful observer of the time to liken the area to " an hive overstocked with bees." The term Lebensraum was not in the public mind at this early time; living space had to be provided, but there was plenty of it. It was necessary, however, to make orderly provision for incoming numbers of settlers. Moreover, natural increment was rapid, for this was a period of high birth rates which more than offset the comparatively heavy death rates. To take a single case, the population of Massachusetts was 2,000 in 1632, 16,000 in 1643, and 30,000 in 1665. A similar story for Virginia is told by the cartogram of population growth (Fig. 12) — a halting start, followed by rapid increments during the closing years of the seventeenth century. The graph compresses into a small space about all that is known concerning population growths before the time of accurate censuses.

People of many nationalities settled within the British colonial area. A false impression is sometimes created by the term " British colonies." The great bulk of the immigrants did come from the British Isles, but it is well to know that many other peoples contributed to the stream of settlement. For example, there were many German immigrants, although no unified country of Germany existed during the Colonial period. We shall find the settlers of German origin being referred to variously as " Salzburgers " or " Palatinates " or, at a later time, " Pennsylvania Dutch." There are no statistics covering the proportions of the racial or national groups in the British colonies, but probably the data below are fairly representative.

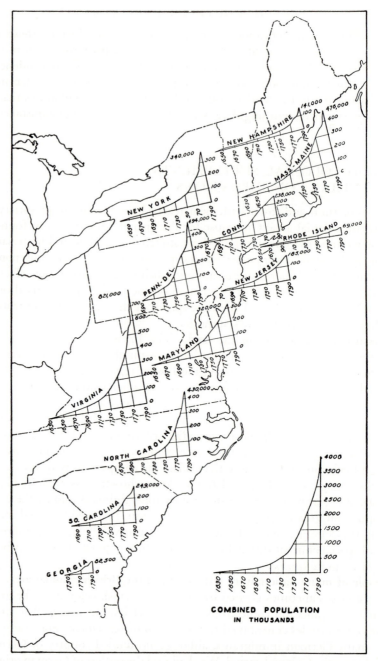

12 Population growth during the Colonial period and the beginnings of statehood to 1790. Adapted from a series of graphs by Franklin B. Dexter, " Estimates of Population in the American Colonies," *Proceedings of the American Antiquarian Society*, N. S., Vol. 5 (1889), pp. 22–50.

CLASSIFICATION OF WHITE POPULATION IN 1790 *

Stock	Percentage of Total
English	60.1
Scotch, incl. Ulster	8.1
Irish Free State	3.6
German	8.6
Dutch	3.1
French	2.3
Swedish	0.7
Spanish	0.8
Unassigned	6.8

* From *Report of the Committee of Linguistic Stocks,* American Council of Learned Societies, 1931.

Effect of time-spread of colonization.   More than a century elapsed between the first colonial activities in Virginia and New England and their concluding phases in eastern Georgia. As settlement progressed, experience gained from earlier successes or failures was turned to good advantage. Considerably more was known about the opportunities and limitations of the environment in 1720 than in 1620, and still more rapid progress was made in accumulating geographical knowledge. These gains were reflected, though not always immediately, in all aspects of social organization. The long time-interval also gave opportunity for theorists in colonization to come forward with the results of their labors. When the later colonies came into existence, ready-made plans for settlement, many of them idealistic, were presented for consideration. The more imaginative products of the theorists, it should be added, found little permanent expression in the land.

Freedom from centralized authority.   Characteristically British was the attitude which permitted much freedom of enterprise in colonial developments. Few " blueprints " of settlement processes were handed down from high places in the Government. Parliament largely delegated to lesser authorities the responsibility of land distribution among the colonists. That Georgia, the thirteenth among the colonies, was the first to receive significant financial aid from the Crown is one reason for its frequent selection by modern investigators for study as a laboratory of experiments in land settlement.

Details of colonization were left to the varied designs of proprietors, the chartered companies, and the general courts; British political leaders concerned themselves with the larger issues of colonization. For instance, the need for " buffer " settlements adjacent to the Florida frontier was of great concern until 1763, when Britain acquired Florida from Spain and thus attained its long-sought control of the entire Atlantic seaboard southward from Nova Scotia.

NEW ENGLAND'S COMPACT VILLAGES

The compactness of settlement which the French colonial authorities hoped for, but never achieved, early characterized the settlements of New England. No special planning seems to have been involved. The first settlers on Massachusetts Bay clustered about the meadows and Indian old fields, usually near the water's edge. "Plantations" in the original, Northern sense — that is, plantations of villages — included Dorchester, Cambridge, Salem, Roxbury, and Watertown. It is not surprising that settlement took this form in the New England area, just as it did, in the beginning, south of the Potomac. Many of the people came from English villages, often bestowing the old village name upon the new, and perhaps adapting, if not adopting, its ground plan as well. Rural and village life could be combined by providing for outlying fields along with common lands and town lots.

There were added incentives to village life in the new environment: the greater sense of security, the closeness to institutions such as the church. As a direct result both of overpopulation in the Boston area and of favorable reports received from Pequot Indians, "plantations" were also established in the Connecticut Valley in the 1630's, then comparatively more remote from Boston than Chicago is today. Another instance of the original usage of the term "plantation" is found in "Providence Plantations," part of the official title of the colony of Rhode Island.

Villages within towns. With the granting of land beyond the original coastal communities to "proprietors," a new phase of New England settlement was introduced. The grants were sometimes extensive, far greater than the immediate needs, their territory being commonly subdivided into "townships" varying in size and shape. In the usage of the time (continued to the present day), the township became known as the "town"; hence "town" is not synonymous with "village," as in other parts of the country. Within the town one or more clusters of people often developed, let us say at some sightly place selected for the location of the first church or, as in later times, near a useful waterfall.

Often a new village became the nucleus of a new town, which upon separation from the mother town began a corporate existence of its own. For instance, the Town of Groton in northeastern Massachusetts was incorporated at an early date. Within its large area several separate villages grew — Groton Center, West Groton, and others. During the 1870's the Boston and Maine Railroad established a junction of its lines in the southeastern part of the town area, resulting in a new village which soon had its own local government and was incorporated under the name of Town of Ayer.

Common lands and outlying fields. The method of disposition of town lands and of lands within the villages bore many resemblances to practices in the homeland. It has been said that the most characteristic feature of the New England town was its land system, a combination of individually owned land and that held in common by the villagers. Under this system, proprietors and villagers usually owned, in addition to house lots, planting fields at some distance from the village center. Sizes of house lots varied greatly, tending to become larger as newer villages were established. The house lots of North Field, Salem, represent a fairly typical case arising about the year 1700. (See Fig. 13.) Like many commu-

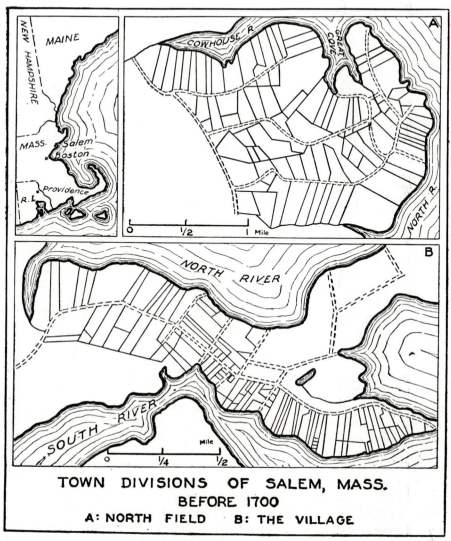

TOWN DIVISIONS OF SALEM, MASS.
BEFORE 1700
A: NORTH FIELD   B: THE VILLAGE

13   Early town divisions as exemplified by Salem, Mass. Adapted from S. Perley, *History of Salem, Massachusetts*, Vol. 1, pp. 312 and 314.

nities of early origin, Salem originally had a large common meadow known as Great Pasture, but as population increased this open space of some 4,000 acres was divided into lots for village families.

Reference to outlying common fields should not divert attention from the central " common " around which settlement often began within the older New England villages. Of varying shapes and dimensions, but usually not larger than an acre or two, the central commons have often been preserved, and still serve for public gatherings, band concerts, and general aesthetic purposes. Well known

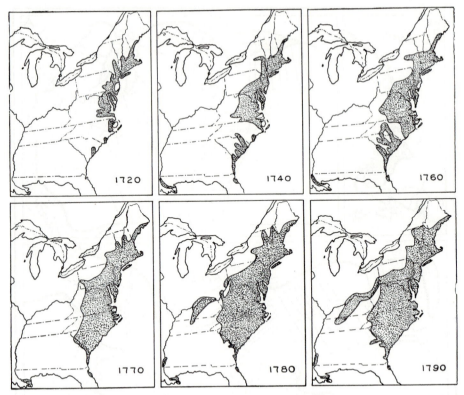

14   Seventy years of population expansion. Adapted from " A Series of Population
    Maps of the Colonies and the United States, 1625–1790," by Herman R. Friis,
    published in *Geographical Review,* Vol. 30 (1940), facing p. 464.

is Boston Common, within the heart of the city. In the smaller outlying towns, it
is often found that the common is a feature of the older villages within the
township limits, whereas villages originating at a later period have none.

    New England frontier villages, early eighteenth century. By 1720 the ad-
vancing frontier included an area sufficiently large to show up on a small-scale
map (Fig. 14). The frontier " line " in New England, starting near Portland,
Maine, slanted inland to include eastern New Hampshire, the greater part of
Massachusetts, all of Rhode Island, and most of Connecticut; it also extended
fingerlike up the valley of the Connecticut River. Settlement had spread toward
this frontier through the multiplication of towns and villages, planned in many
cases before the people arrived to take up the land, or growing haphazardly. The
more orderly pattern of villages established in the eighteenth century was in
part a measure of the experience gained during the earlier period, combined
with natural factors of site and the background of the people.

    Londonderry, New Hampshire, a Planned Frontier Community, 1720. As
the name suggests, Londonderry, New Hampshire, was founded by a group of

Irish immigrants, who had made some search of possible locations before choosing one a few miles southeast of Manchester. Among the reasons for its selection was the presence of a good water supply from a small stream (poetically named West Running Brook), a large extent of open land for pasture, and groves of nut-bearing trees — chestnut, walnut, butternut — which, in the thinking of the period, were uniformly taken as indicators of a superior soil. An earlier name for the site had been " Nutfield," suggesting superiority over " piny land," and " post-oak land." The Londonderry colonists marked out their house lots on either side of West Running Brook, allowing a frontage of 30 rods along its banks and extending therefrom until each comprised 60 acres. The dwellings were thus brought reasonably close together in what was known for a half-century thereafter as the Double Range. This plan served the interests of neighborliness and of defense against surprise attack, but at the same time led to a multiplicity of roads, expensive to maintain and to keep open in the winter. Favorable accounts of the colony sent to friends and relatives in Ireland brought about much emigration from that country to southeastern New Hampshire.

Street Villages of the Connecticut Valley. The advantages to be gained from laying out the street pattern of a proposed village in advance of its actual settlement (instead of later providing roads to connect straggling houses) are seen in a number of Connecticut Valley communities. The present tense is used advisedly, for many of these early-formed villages are today little larger than they were a century or two ago, and have retained their original features. The flat-to-rolling surface of the lowland favored a more orderly pattern than that permitted by the hilly surface of adjacent upland areas; moreover, by this time some lessons in planning had been learned. The Town Fathers found no difficulty in laying out, on the fairly level terrace surface, main north-south streets roughly paralleling the river.

To gain a picture of the early river-town patterns, we must consider briefly the terraced surface which was so influential in the town planning. Above the present Connecticut River flood plain is a series of three or four levels separated from one another (less conspicuously today than in early times because of the many changes brought about by man) by declivities of from 25 to 50 feet in height. These terraces are the result of the downcutting of the Connecticut River and its tributaries through superficial deposits, some of which were laid down during the glacial period. As described by an early-day French traveler, the first terrace above the flood plain

is naturally dry. This plain is bounded by another abrupt elevation of the surface, which has the appearance of having been executed by art in some period of remote antiquity. Beyond it, is another similar work, apparently still more ancient. There are, in some places, four alternations of these plains and perpendicular rises, one behind another, which ascend with the regularity of terraces in a garden, to the summits of the hills. Where the hills descend to the very brink of the river, these terraced plains are to be seen [on] only one side [of the stream]. More commonly, however, they appear on both sides: And in this case, the corresponding terraces, on the opposite sides, are of the same level. Contemplating these wonderful appearances, one is naturally led to conjecture, that these heights were once the immediate banks of the river, which in descending to its present channel gradually formed the successive flats and perpendicular elevations that we now see.

The foregoing description by the Duke de la Rochefoucauld-Liancourt in 1799 must rank among the minor classics in early land-surface interpretation.

The second terrace above the river was preferred for the village core; it was supposedly above flood level (though disastrous inundations have since occurred there), and this higher land had a reputation for greater healthfulness or " salubrity " than the lowlands nearer river level. In the language of the time, the still higher terrace, or rather the rising edge of it, was the " meadow hill."

In such a setting and in the year 1714, the village of Sunderland, Massachusetts, took form. The proprietors surveyed a wide main street along which house lots 14 rods wide were regularly spaced. The result was a closely knit community fronting upon its boulevard-like street, with planting fields and pastures near at hand in the background, stretching to the river on the west and toward the hills on the east. As population spread, the main street was extended, but reduced in width, making occasional bends, ultimately to join similarly advancing streets from contiguous villages. The long and slender " street village " of which Sunderland is a good example represents, as Edna Scofield has expressed it, " a transitional form between the compact village communities of the earlier colonial period and the scattered isolated farmsteads of the later period."

DEVELOPMENTS IN THE MIDDLE COLONIES

Expansion of settlement by single farmsteads rather than by closely knit villages was more characteristic of the middle colonies than elsewhere. The predominance in colonial Pennsylvania and New York of settlers from continental Europe, men who were themselves tillers of the soil, has been discussed by Professor Carl O. Sauer.

A complex history played a major role in determining the more cosmopolitan nature of the middle-colonies population. Before the arrival of Penn's settlers in 1681 there were 500 white settlers — mainly Swedes — on the banks of the Delaware, and when New Netherland was wrested from the Dutch in 1664 some 7,000 of their people were settled in the lower Hudson River Valley. The colonies of New York and Pennsylvania, which in this manner had inherited a varied population, continued to attract immigrants from continental Europe as well as from Ireland. The first wave of the Scotch-Irish (Scottish people who for some time had lived in Ireland) arrived in the 1720's and a second, according to Samuel S. Greene, from 1771 to 1773, " although there was a general current westward between these two eras." The Scotch-Irish in the middle colonies, as elsewhere, tended to move with the frontier or in advance of it; in fact, they were typical frontiersmen. The Germans (Dutch) became more or less fixed in their original areas of settlement — that is, eastern Pennsylvania and the Hudson

River Valley — and did not move with the frontier of this period. Doubtless this is the origin of the frequently repeated but untenable generalization that the German was not a frontiersman. On the contrary, it is indeed remarkable how numerous were first- and second-generation Germans on the very rim of the frontier in the North Central states, not to mention the classic example, to be studied in due time, of the German settlements west of Austin, Texas, in the 1830's.

The map (Fig. 14, page 54) shows better than words can tell the advancing frontiers of the middle colonies from 1720 to 1790. Note how the western point of white settlement in central New York remained stationary at the head of the Mohawk Valley, a point marked by Fort Stanwix (now Rome), from the 1740's on. Also observe that the more mountainous sections of the Appalachians in Pennsylvania remained beyond the frontier, although population spilled over into the valleys of the parallel-ridge-and-valley section of that great highland area. The valleys abounded in natural advantages for a pioneering people.

The middle colonies, originating a half-century later than those of New England, could have profited more than they actually did from the experiences of others. Although full advantage was not taken of past errors and successes, colonization procedures, in Pennsylvania especially, followed upon some forethought and planning. Community planning then had a beginning which has since become classic: the selection of the site of Philadelphia, and the laying-out of the street plan for Penn's " greate towne." The site was chosen by Penn's commissioners, who were dispatched from England to find a good harbor, necessarily on the Delaware River and particularly at its junction with a tributary. They were also to locate the intended city on a well-drained site so as to avoid the much-feared diseases attributed to swamp " effluvia." The commissioners found a place complying with these and other requirements at the junction of the Delaware with a river afterward to be named the Schuylkill. Philadelphia was the first American city to be laid out with the " checkerboard " street and block pattern, an innovation on this side of the Atlantic possibly deriving from lessons learned in the rebuilding of London following its great fire in 1666. Other Pennsylvania towns grew according to similar orderly plans. An observant visitor in Gettysburg or Harrisburg today can hardly fail to detect general resemblances between them.

The rapid dispersal of settlement, a characteristic of new countries, was particularly well developed in the middle-colony area. In fact, a moving picture rather than a static one is required to do justice to the spreading of settlement along the natural and man-made highways into previously unoccupied country. The adventurous attitude of the people, combined with natural attractions of the hinterland, led to the beginning of new settlements even before the earlier ones were firmly established.

PLANTATIONS OF MARYLAND AND VIRGINIA

The Southern plantation, about which so much has been written, was the product of a long and not-too-orderly evolution. It seems important, therefore, to consider briefly some of the forms of land tenure preceding that of the plantation.

The first centers of coastal population below the Potomac were compact communities differing in no essential respect from the early hamlets of New England. Jamestown was a compact residential-military village; St. Marys, the original point of settlement in Maryland, never outgrew its original village character. Charleston, South Carolina, originally walled for protection, was an urbanized center from the time it was formed. Indeed, there seems to have been a deliberate effort in the Southern lands, as elsewhere, both to form communities of commercial importance and to ensure means of defense. These attempts were only partially successful.

Plans for manors and baronies.   There were also attempts, at least in Maryland and South Carolina, to develop a manorial type of settlement; but, as Lewis C. Gray has remarked, " It was found impossible . . . to establish this relic of the past amidst the primitive conditions of the frontier." The royal charter of Maryland endowed Lord Baltimore and his heirs with feudal powers, but the manors that would have made these powers effective did not survive in the face of practical conditions. Lands were granted to proprietors according to the number of settlers transported; at one time, this amounted to 50 acres a person. This method of acquiring land by " headright " was sanctioned by the home Government and succeeded in promoting immigration in a region where otherwise it might have lagged. It is noteworthy that for no other colony was the promotional literature so loud in its claims of opportunity as were the pamphlets " describing " Maryland. Although estates of thousands of acres were not uncommon, nevertheless Maryland seemed not to be the place for the transplantation of a feudal manor system cut to an Old World pattern. Instead, a more modern variant of that system, the plantation, gradually evolved.

Similar attempts to carry Old World social life to the Southern seaboard occurred in South Carolina, where " baronies " were envisioned. A barony was to be the estate of a " Landgrave " and to consist of some 12,000 acres. The idea seems to have been to lay out the colony in squares of this size, somewhat analogous except in ground plan to the seigniories of the St. Lawrence country. One of these estates, named Wadboo Barony, was granted to a James Colleton in 1683, and it is said that the land remained in the same family until 1782, when a Confiscation Act divided it into twenty-eight parcels which were sold at public auction. According to Henry A. M. Smith, there are definite records of fifteen South Carolina baronies.

Beginnings of subsistence agriculture.   Grandiose schemes such as those reflected in the baronies were set aside, to be replaced by more practical plans better adapted to the needs and conditions of the settlers. Subsistence agriculture, involving the raising of such common crops as wheat and maize and the rearing of livestock, dominated both Maryland and Virginia during these early years. Further subsistence was gained from the fisheries, and the forests supplied many needs as well. There is no need to explore subsistence agriculture further here, since its development will be discussed later, alongside commercial tobacco production, which gradually forced other ways of making a living into the background.

The rise of commercial plantations. The production of tobacco was, and is, a time-consuming process. It started with the original clearing of land (extending to the continual clearing of other land to replace worn-out fields), and ended with the rolling or boating of the finished product to the inspection stations — steps to be discussed in a later section. The many and various operations between these extremes were performed by indentured white and Negro slave labor, resulting in a two-storied social life that required the control of large acreages by a single management. Although the Virginia-Maryland environment presented no particular advantage for raising West Indian tobacco not possessed by other coastal areas farther south, these settlements did have the advantage of being established at the time markets for tobacco were opening in western Europe and, once begun, tended to monopolize commercial production.

Although not anticipated at its inception, the land system accommodated itself to this type of exploitation. Planters established themselves on the many tidewater peninsulas which form the shores of Chesapeake Bay, each one's boat landing providing sufficient commercial access to the outside world. In such an environment, natural and social, commercial towns had little place. Remember, however, that subsistence and commercial farming based on free labor formed part of the regional economy.

In early colonial times the term " plantation " as used in the Chesapeake country seems to have applied to the clearings within a tract of wooded land, the outer legal boundaries of which may have been somewhat vague. Consequently, it is difficult for us to know how extensive the holdings were in early times. Colonial documents give very few precise figures, because — hard as it may seem to comprehend — our present-day definition of " plantation " did not exist at the time. It is believed that few plantations were smaller than 250 acres or larger than 500. Many planters owned or rented scattered parcels of land, perhaps not even in the same county, and this fact also complicates the answer to any questions as to size. We may be sure that the term " plantation " mainly identified a way of life — which we are apt to romanticize — and a manner of controlling land; only secondarily was greatness of area implied.

Population growth in Virginia. The growth curve of Virginia's population (see Fig. 12, page 50) was similar to that of the Northern colonies. Virginia made a feeble start, claiming only 351 inhabitants in its tenth year of existence, but experienced a rapid increase to 2,400 by the time Plymouth was founded. A massacre by Indians in 1633 reduced the numbers cruelly, but recovery was rapid and by 1650 Virginia had a population of nearly 10,000. Many of the data on

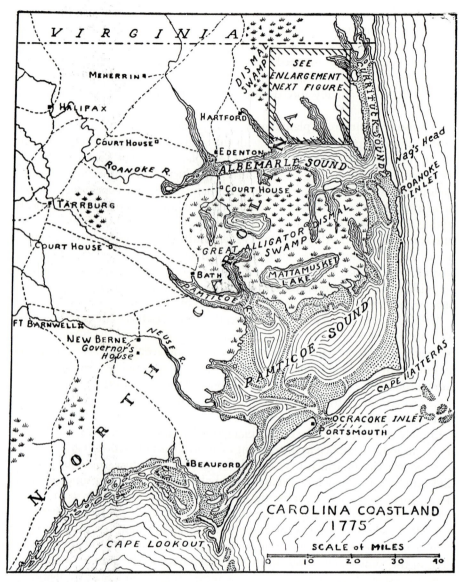

15a This representation of the North Carolina coast in 1775 is a simplified version of a map in the Arrowsmith *Atlas of North America* published in London in that year. Original spelling of names has been retained; for example "Pamticoe" is now Pamlico, "Beauford" has become Beaufort, and "New Berne" is now spelled without the final "e."

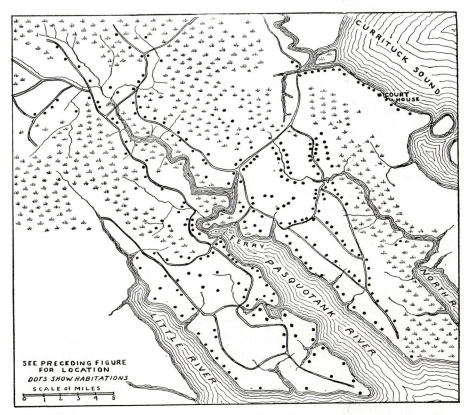

15b This figure, enlarging a portion of the foregoing map, is a greatly modified redrawing of an original map of the same scale found among the rare items in the map division of the William L. Clements Library, and used here with special permission. On the original map, the names of individual proprietors are written in the approximate positions of their lands; in this version, dots replace the names in the inferred location of their estates.

which the graphs in Figure 12 are based are conjectural, because there was no real census of the population until 1790. Some estimates made earlier than the first Federal census are vague as to whether the figures include both white and Negro population. In 1790, some 40 per cent of Virginia's 821,000 people were Negro. Maryland's population had a similar growth, and was similarly proportioned.

SMALL FARMS OF NORTH CAROLINA, BETWEEN CAPES HENRY AND FEAR

We are warned by an eminent authority, Charles C. Crittenden, against indulging in the treacherous term "Carolina," or still worse, "the Carolinas," because either may convey the impression that North Carolina and South Carolina were essentially alike. On the contrary, they were and are significantly different. (See Figs. 15a, 15b.)

The early cultural development of coastal North Carolina offers a sharp contrast to that of the regions to the north and south. Although there were some early plantations in eastern North Carolina, the dominant rural feature was the small farm with a minimum of Negro population.

From Cape Henry, Virginia, to Cape Fear (once called " Fare " through some confusion in pronunciation) is a distance of more than 300 miles. This stretch presents an almost continuous barrier of sandy reef hemming in the great sounds of Albemarle and Pamlico, into which flow rivers such as Cape Fear, Neuse, Tar, Roanoke, and Chowan. The surface of these sandy ramparts, which extend in a point at Cape Hatteras, has probably been changed less by man's action and more by natural forces than any similar stretch of Atlantic coast. Inlets are perennially appearing and disappearing, and we can only guess as to the depth and location of the inlets used by the small ships in colonial times. We are sure only that the reefs were different in that distant day, although but three inlets appear to have attained great commercial use — Cape Fear River, Old Topsail, and Ocracoke. Of these entrances, only the Cape Fear River provided a route to the interior, but its importance was lessened by hazardous shoals and sand bars. An intimate view of this strange setting is provided by a French traveler in 1765 who recorded informally that " the soil all along [is] very sandy and indifferent, the land Extremely level and Even, not the least appearance of a Small hill, nor a stone to be seen, but sea shells in plenty, which would seem to intimate that great part of Carolina was risen by the sands, thrown up by the Sea to a Certain height and then obliged itself to retire."

Through failure to success in settlement.   It is not surprising that early settlements failed to thrive in an environment of the character thus described. Between the time of Raleigh's disastrous venture on Roanoke Island (1587) and the first enduring settlements of the 1690's, at least two attempts to establish colonies ended in failure. One of these attempts had its inception in the minds of colonial promoters who knew little more about this part of the Atlantic coast than its latitude position, which was supposedly ideal for olive and grape culture and perhaps also for the mulberry tree, upon which a silk industry might be based. In 1680, this led to the transportation to the coast of North Carolina of about 50 French Huguenot families who were presumably skilled in these occupations. The colony soon disintegrated. The other early trial at settlement was made by a group of New Englanders who established themselves on Oldtown Creek and the lower Clarendon River. They also had disappeared before 1690. According to an early writer, Charles Williamson: " The barrenness of the soil in that vicinity was not overcome by flattering promises to adventurers. By numerous migrations to the southward, the colony was greatly reduced, and the whole country was again surrendered to the original Savage."

More successful were individual settlements that were based on regional opportunities, not upon promotional schemes developed by the theorists in colonization. By 1694, the colony had an estimated population of 2,000, largely white. With the extension of subsistence farming, livestock-raising, and forest-product industries, the number increased rapidly to 30,000 whites and 6,000 Negroes in 1732. These inhabitants were distributed mainly along the watercourses, occupying small farms and occasional plantations. The absence of village clusters and the sparsity of population along the public roads, which mainly followed the higher and drier land, often deceived strangers then, as today, concerning the numbers of people and the fundamental wealth of their land.

PLANTATIONS AND RIVER SWAMPS OF COASTAL SOUTH CAROLINA

The population-distribution maps showing the entirely separate development of North and South Carolina lend support to the caution against identifying "the Carolinas" in the historical sense. Although permanent settlement began at about the same time in North Carolina as in South Carolina, there was little connection between these two centers.

For some time after settlement, "Charleston" and "South Carolina" were fairly synonymous, so few were the settlements beyond the lower Ashley and Cooper rivers which unite to form Charleston's famous harbor. (See Fig. 16.) The population maps (Fig. 14, page 54) give the main outlines of the story: In 1720, a settlement cluster limited to the Charleston area; in 1740, fingerlike projections up the main rivers—PeeDee, Santee, Saltkehatchie, and Savannah; in later decades, further extension along the rivers and eventual spreading of the frontier on a wide front in the hilly Piedmont country.

The early relationship of the population to the rivers is explained by the dominance of rice production during the eighteenth century. Plantations developed in close proximity to the river swamps, and as long as this economy was dominant the higher interstream areas remained essentially unoccupied. The reclamation of the swampland required large expenditures of labor, a problem finding temporary solution in slavery. Data for 1708, when lowland rice production had made a good start, show 4,000 white people and 5,500 Negroes, a disproportion that increased in later decades as the rice economy became more firmly established. Alexander Hewatt, an early writer, estimated the population in 1765 as 40,000 whites and from 80,000 to 90,000 Negroes.

Rice economy thus explains why South Carolina's early plantations were tied to the swampy margins of rivers, with the habitations usually located on the inner margin of the swamp and not, as in Virginia, overlooking broad expanses of navigable water. With the decline of rice production during the opening decades of the nineteenth century, settlement advanced into the formerly avoided "pine barrens" between the rivers and toward the more distant higher Piedmont country. Also it should not be forgotten that Charleston continued to grow, and until the 1820's ranked among the first half-dozen cities in the country in size.

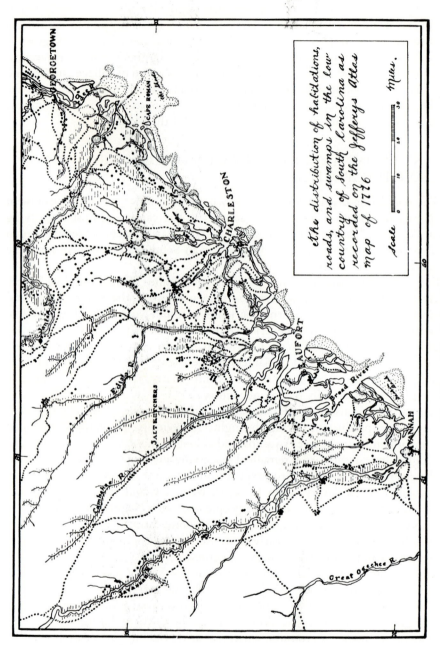

The distribution of habitations, roads, and swamps in the low country of South Carolina as recorded on the Jefferys Atlas map of 1776

Scale

Miles.

16　Coastal South Carolina, 1776

COLONIZATION, THEORETICAL AND PRACTICAL, IN GEORGIA

The Georgia of the early Colonial period was the region southward from the Savannah River to the Altamaha River. The name of the colony — and later state, which of course includes a larger territory — came into use in 1732, when it was named for King George II. Actual settlement occurred in that year according to a corporation or company plan which had received the support of the Crown.

Many years before the formation of the Georgia Colony, visionary plans for settlement within the Midway District — as the region between the Savannah and Altamaha rivers was familiarly known — had reached the "blueprint" stage. Owing to their fanciful character, the schemes expired before bringing about definite results. Insufficient account seems to have been taken not only of the natural environment, but also of the capabilities of the people — not an unusual error, as readers will have noticed. One of the known plans related to the development of a fancifully conceived community to be known as Azilia.

Idyllic Azilia. In the year 1717, a Sir Robert Montgomery secured from the South Carolina authorities a grant to the land of the Midway District. His idea was to create a province there to be known as the Margravate of Azilia. No statement concerning Azilia — its climate, soils, wealth, and so on — appears to have been too extravagant. "The most suitable country in the universe," it was said of Azilia more than once.

The published plan for a district in the proposed margravate was most elaborate (Fig. 17). In its rectangular outline the plan had something in common with others contemporary with it, but there the similarity stopped. The fortified outer limits of the district were to surround a woodland, within which there were to be 116 squares of 640 acres each. Separate houses were to occupy each of these 640-acre plots. At the convergence of the streets at the center of the district, the Margrave's mansion, doubtless like a gem in a diadem, was to be built. Planned also were four parklike forests of 16 square miles each, useful for recreation and the grazing of deer. Optimistically, Sir Robert bound himself to complete the settlement of the district within three years, else the land would revert to the Proprietors of South Carolina. It hardly needs saying that at the expiration of the allotted time there were no colonists, and the land did actually revert.

Growth of population. With the arrival of about 100 persons in October 1732, under Oglethorpe, the permanent settlement of Georgia began. Various motives, philanthropic, commercial, and political, led to the beginning stage of the thirteenth American colony. According to a pamphlet published in 1742, it was intended "to provide for poor People incapable of subsisting themselves at Home, and to settle a Frontier to South Carolina, which was much exposed by the small number of Inhabitants."

Three provisions of the Georgia settlement plan help to explain the relatively slow growth of the colony during the first two decades. In the first place, encouragement was given to the ownership of relatively small tracts of land, on the theory that this was beneficial to social life. As an instance of this policy, an original provision required the clearing and fencing of the land within eighteen years, else it would revert to the Trustees. Obviously, this limited the amount that one person could acquire. Secondly, trade with the Indians was prohibited, with the idea that this would restrict the possibilities of quarrel and conflict with the more powerful native peoples. The third provision excluded slavery, for on the one hand it was felt that there would be no place for slaves in a society whose main activities were the production of wine and silk, and on the other hand the managers regarded the purchase of slaves as a general cause for financial difficulties among colonists in other regions. Furthermore, since the Georgia colony was to serve the purpose of a buffer against the Spanish settlements to

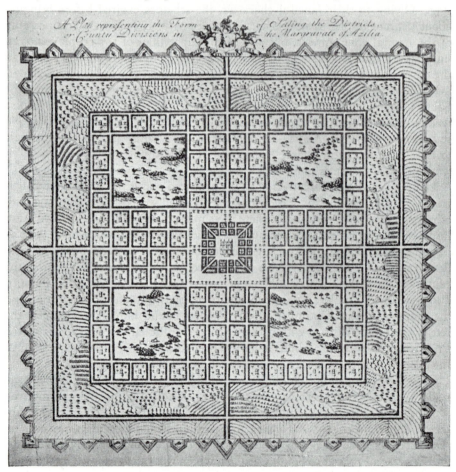

17   The elaborate plan of the proposed settlement between the Savannah and Altamaha rivers in colonial Georgia. This was published in many Colonization Tracts, and in Charles C. Jones, *The History of Georgia*, Boston, 1883, facing p. 72 of Vol. 1.

the south, it was presumed that slaveownership would tend to weaken rather than to strengthen this function.

The theoretical planning which brought Georgia into being may well have delayed settlement. Silk-making and wine culture were supported by the promoters to the extent of importing people from abroad skilled in these industries, but these activities were not wholly practical in terms of the environment and the people. Gradually the colonists turned to subsistence farming and plantation crops suited to the climate, the soil, and the abilities of the people. In its distribution, the population clung rather closely to the Savannah River and its principal tributaries. The town of Savannah boasted 130 houses in 1742; they were widely spaced, in order, it was said, to guard against the spreading of fires and to ensure the health of the people.

CHAPTER 5

Filling Up the Land: Spanish
Settlement in Florida and the Far West

BY TRADITION, "Colonial America" has come to mean the thirteen Atlantic seaboard colonies — in short, the beginnings of Anglo-America. This is certainly an arbitrary limitation of the geographical space within which colonizing activities were carried on, for all of eastern North America, and a considerable share of the present Southwest of the United States and California, at one time constituted colonial territory. Florida, for example, was controlled by Spain for nearly two and a quarter centuries. The following discussion of colonial Florida, however, will not be proportional to the time-expanse. Not only are there great and apparently unfillable gaps in the knowledge of Florida under Spain, but much that is known is not of present-day interest. It is recognized that many of Spain's developments in Florida were of short duration and had little carry-over into the present. Not so, however, with the Far Western portions of the Spanish colonial realm. Consequently, following the study of Florida (which during the early Spanish mission period included the Georgia coast), attention will be directed to the very different colonial territory of the Southwest and California.

SPANISH EXPANSION FROM ST. AUGUSTINE

The arrival of British colonists under Oglethorpe in 1732 marked the beginning of the *second* cycle of settlement on the Georgia coast, the first cycle, under the Spanish, having ended fifty years before their arrival. This half-century between the two occupations is one of the "silent periods" of the past. Although little is known about it, some reasonable inferences may be drawn. For instance, it is presumed that there was a general withdrawal or expulsion of the Indian groups which originally occupied the islands and coastlands of Georgia, and whose presence had drawn missionaries, soldiers, and some few settlers from St. Augustine. The English colonists have little to say about coastal Indians, but their frequent references to Indian old fields indicate that there had been a considerable native population.

Moreover, the British colonists of 1732 did not settle in the same sites as had their Spanish predecessors. The Spanish missions and related presidios (forts) had been established on the coastal islands, in our times romanticized under the general name of " Golden Isles." Although for nearly a century the Spanish had occupied some of the many islands not only in Georgia but northward into Port Royal Sound, South Carolina, there were few conspicuous evidences of their occupation by the beginning of British settlement. The " silent " half-century between the withdrawal of the Spanish and the arrival of the English colonists was sufficient, in that soil and climate, to efface most of the frail structures erected by soldiers and priests. In modern times archaeologists, both professional and amateur, have identified a few relics of the past and thus have added tangible evidence (and sometimes confusion) to the written records which have come down to us.

The enormous time-expanse with which we are now concerned may escape us if we do not realize that the Georgia coastal islands formed the first mission field invaded by the Spanish within the present limits of the United States. This endeavor was initiated in 1566, more than two hundred years before the renowned and more enduring California mission settlements were established.

Expansion: motives and periods. The two centuries (or to be exact, 197 years) of the first Spanish occupation in Florida and contiguous areas ended in 1763. Periods of expansion from St. Augustine, the only place continuously held, alternated with intervals of contraction and terminated, of course, in complete withdrawal. During these periods of expansion, the desire for land was always secondary and usually incidental. The most lasting motive for expansion was the desire of certain religious orders within the Roman Catholic Church to Christianize the infidel Indian. We are not surprised, therefore, to learn that the course of Spain's empire-building from the St. Augustine base led to regions poor in resources and wanting in self-sustaining properties.

The Christianizing motive often worked in co-ordination with political and military motives. North Florida and present-day Georgia composed a territory that was prized by England, France, and Spain — by the latter particularly because, through control of the coast line, trade lanes from Spain to the West Indies could be protected. Furthermore, the missionaries rarely carried their altars into the expanding frontier unaccompanied by soldiers, at least not after a few trials in a savage land had ended in tragedy for them. Religious and military operations were a united effort until late in the eighteenth century, when the Spanish Government abandoned its policy of financing garrisons merely for the protection of missions.

It is most convenient, although not wholly accurate, to limit our consideration to three periods of Spanish expansion from St. Augustine between the years 1566 and 1763. 1. During the first period, expansion was northward along the coast to Port Royal Sound, South Carolina. This period will be identified with the Salt-Water Mission Field, or the District of Guale (pronounced wah'le). 2. During the second period the expansion covered the regions inland from St. Augustine and along the St. Johns River, variously known as the Fresh-Water

District, the Patano country, and Timucua — the latter name deriving from the Timucuan Indians, who originally inhabited much of central Florida. 3. During the third and greatest period the expansion extended across northern Florida through the site of present-day Tallahassee, to Apalachee Bay and inland to central Alabama, the homeland of the Creek Indians. This area is sometimes referred to as Apalachee or the Apalachee Mission Field. The latter designation, however, is somewhat misleading, because military and commercial motives were by this time dominant over the theological. Then came the great collapse of Spanish control, resulting in the contraction of military, political, and commercial interests into an area scarcely reaching beyond the outer defenses of the city of St. Augustine.

First period: northward through the " Golden Isles."   Although St. Augustine was selected in 1565 as Spain's chief military, political, and commercial center northward of Havana, Cuba, the location was far from ideal. The port had defensive properties of site, and was near the trade lanes through the Bahama Channel leading to the Gulf of Mexico, but the city was unsupported by a productive or an accessible hinterland. " Northward the Course of Empire " might have been the slogan that led Spanish vessels on errands of discovery and commerce past the mouth of the St. Johns River, where Jacksonville is now located, past also the St. Marys River, which forms the nublike present boundary of southeastern Georgia, and into a maze of low coastal islands that are sufficiently close together to enclose an " inland sea." (Fig. 18.)

The island-studded coast and its narrow, shallow sea became known as Guale, or Lengua de Guale — the land or region of Gualean speech. After several unsuccessful attempts, missions were finally established on several of the islands which then bore names as follows:

SPANISH ISLAND MISSIONS

Present name	Indian name	Spanish name
Cumberland	Missoe	San Pedro
Jekyl	Ospo	Ospo or Oparavanos
St. Simons	Asao	San Simon
Sapelo		Zapala
St. Catherines		Santa Catalina or Guale
Ossabaw	Obispa	Asopo

In many respects, Guale offered an attractive mission field. The islands had sandy soil, it is true, but they were at least terra firma, which the swampy coast was not. The stations could be visited by easy trips in small boats or *perriaugers* made of split cypress logs. The Indians were less mobile than elsewhere, living in houses with palm-thatched roofs. They were essentially agricultural. It is reported that they were familiar with corn and more successful in its growth than were their priestly mentors. The somewhat precarious diet of the Gualeans was supplemented by wild products, including acorns, alligator meat, and a swamp potato from which a kind of bread was made. According to John T. Lanning, the Indian hunted deer " by disguising himself either with the head

18 The coast and islands of Georgia in 1780. The spelling of the names of the "Golden Isles" is that of the original map, which was drawn by William Bull, William Gerard de Brahm, and others, and is generally known as the John Stuart map. The illustration is a simplified redrawing of a small portion of the original in the John Carter Brown Library, Brown University.

or the whole skin of a deer, thus being able to get near enough to his prey to stab it."

The missionaries evidently introduced new crop plants, and attempted to develop among their charges more orderly economic ways as well as a new spiritual life. In 1567 José de Zapala introduced the orange, the olive, and the fig to the island doubtless named for him, but now known as Sapelo. An English visitor to St. Catherines in 1670 remarked on the number of "brave plantations" on which Indians, "wanting nothing in the world," were working.

Attempts to expand northward and to Christianize the Guales ended about 1700.

Second period: expansion inland. Spain's Indian policy in Florida largely worked against the spreading of colonial populations, even into the more favored areas. A wholesome fear of the Indians who roamed over the country beyond the St. Johns River is reflected in many ways, and not least in the elaborate defense system of St. Augustine. The massive forts and walls of the town can be taken as a truer index of Indian policy than the mission stations and chapels that were established during the seventeenth century. Chief element in St. Augustine's defense was the most formidable fortress north of Cuba — Castilla de San Marcos — which, says Verne E. Chatelaine, "even in its present state of ruin [is] impressive and forbidding." The St. Augustine of the Spanish period must be regarded as a walled city defended from possible attack no less by land than by sea. That the fear of the Indian was not misplaced was proved in the aboriginal uprising in the middle of the eighteenth century which sent the few Spanish colonists who had ventured beyond the coastal towns reeling back to the safety of their walls and forts.

The land policy restricted farm settlement. Distrust of what the Indians might do if antagonized guided the authorities in their land policy also. The attitude at the beginning was to regard the soil as the property of the native people, not to be taken from them either by treaty or by force. Prohibitions were thus placed on the ownership of land by individuals. This policy of complete restriction was sometimes relaxed as different governors assumed control, but regulations were generally unfavorable to widespread settlement. The country about St. Augustine remained unoccupied partly because of the inferior nature of the soil and partly because private land grants never gained a secure foothold in Florida under Spain. This policy, it will be seen, was the reverse of that country's attitude in other parts of its colonial empire in the New World.

Florida, it has been said with only slight exaggeration, was a colony without colonists. The greater number of the colonists lived in St. Augustine, which at the peak of its growth may have had 3,000 inhabitants. There were also some settlements along the St. Johns River, the Fresh-Water District; other town settlements were located on the far side of the peninsula on Apalachee Bay and near present-day Pensacola. The population of Spanish Florida, exclusive of soldiers and slaves, may have risen to 6,000, but hardly more than that. Far from being self-sustaining, Florida received direct financial aid from the Crown, and occasional delays in the receipt of annual installments of the subsidy caused distress and anxiety in St. Augustine.

The Central-Florida Indian. The two centuries of Spanish occupation in Florida witnessed many changes in the Indian population. Throughout the period, however, the central regions remained essentially Indian. The natives of the earlier periods are known to ethnologists as Timucuan, but very little is recorded of their manner of life. According to David Bushnell: "When they became known to Europeans, through the discoveries of Ponce de León, who landed near the present city of St. Augustine in the year 1513, they occupied many villages scattered across the northern part of the peninsula from the

Atlantic to the Gulf." Descriptions of granaries and storehouses made of coquina (otherwise known as tapia, or tabby — a weak cement composed of oyster shells and sand), with roofs thatched with palmetto, indicate that the Timucuans were no mere primitive farmers. They inhabited large lodges capable of housing many families — buildings " made much like a great barne," according to one explorer. Although the Timucuans were the kind of people with whom the priests were eager to work, they lacked strength and a warlike spirit, and were overrun by enemies at least twice during the opening years of the eighteenth century. Thereafter, little is heard about them, but according to Professor Verner W. Crane, the Timucuans shared the fate of the Gualeans — dispersal and amalgamation with other tribes.

The Timucuans were replaced in central Florida by the Seminole Indians, who originally came from the Lower Creek country, now known as southern Alabama and Georgia. In our day the Seminoles are associated with the Everglades of southern Florida. The name " Seminole " is said to mean " wild or wandering people," in distinction from the sedentary Creeks, who inhabited villages and lived mainly by agriculture. According to an early Indian agent in the Creek Nations, the Lower Creeks looked disapprovingly upon the wandering and disowned Seminoles. Gradually the wanderers pushed out of western Florida toward the south, maintaining their migratory habits; hence they were not promising material for missionary work. A strong people, jealous of their rights, the Seminoles remained a "problem " well into the period of American occupation. Their resistance in a country with which they had the advantage of familiarity made the Seminole War of 1816 memorable among Indian-white conflicts.

At the conclusion of the second period of expansion, it could not be claimed that the colonizers had succeeded in making the region an integral part of the Florida colony.

Expansion toward West Florida: third phase. Spanish expansion in Florida reached its height during the seventeenth century, when a string of widely spaced forts and mission stations was completed from St. Augustine to Apalachee Bay. (See Fig. 19.) The road that at one time — but only for a brief period — connected them has been called the Camino Real. The literal meaning of this grand name should not mislead anyone into imagining this mark on the land was a well-made highway, for " Royal Road " was in those days often applied to well-known trading or Indian paths such as this one undoubtedly was. The trans-Florida road or trail, with occasional branches, was apparently not mapped in detail until the British assumed control of Florida following its cession in 1763.

The Path from St. Marks to St. Marks. The original map drawn on the ground in 1778 (now in the Public Records Office, London, with copies in Washington) is over 8 feet long and 2 feet wide, permitting plenty of space for written comment: the character of the way, topographic features, Indian towns, savannas or Indian old fields (of which there were many), and forts or the ruins of them. By the time this map was made, the " road " had become a disconnected

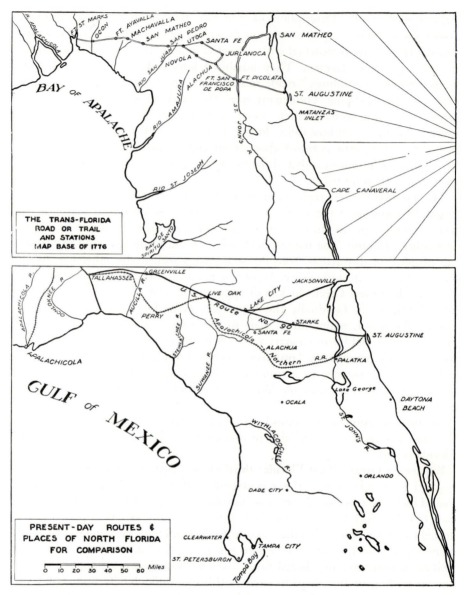

THE TRANS-FLORIDA
ROAD OR TRAIL
AND STATIONS
MAP BASE OF 1776

PRESENT-DAY ROUTES &
PLACES OF NORTH FLORIDA
FOR COMPARISON

0 10 20 30 40 50 60 Miles

19   (*Above*) The trans-Florida road or trail, the Camino Real of the Spanish period,
as shown on a map base of 1776. (*Below*) A modern map for purposes of comparison.

line of trails, with some portions impassable through lack of upkeep. The map commentary on that portion between Fort Picolata, on the east bank of the St. Johns River, and St. Augustine, is as follows: " The path is chiefly throe low Pine lands, part of which is wet and boggy after great Rains, is plain and well trod. Crosses many small creeks and branches which have low swamps, that are full of water in wet weather, but fordable. Range or Food middling good."

Opposite Picolata on the west bank of St. Johns River was Fort San Fran- cisco de Pupo, which when visited by the botanist William Bartram in 1774 was completely in ruins. Pupo protected for the time being a small Spanish village and mission station. At unequal intervals on the way across Florida were places bearing Spanish or Indian names, corrupted in map nomenclature: Jurla Noca, Alochua (Alachua of today), Nuovolla, San Pedro (identified as Tallahassee), San Matheo, Machavalla, Fort Ayavalla, and Ocon. Sante Fe, an Indian town with an " old field " much marveled at by some travelers, was on a branch of the main trail. At the end of the path on Apalachee Bay stood Fort San Marcos de Apalachee. The repetition of the name St. Marks on both termini of this ancient and now extinct path has been the source of some confusion to genera- tions of history students.

Trade with the Creek Nations.   The two Creek Nations, known as the Upper and Lower Creeks, did not form an effective mission field. Their combined population was large and the villages, though restricted in area, lay beyond the bounds of Spanish Florida. The Lower Creeks were nearer, on the lower Chat- tahoochee and Flint rivers beyond the present Florida-Georgia border; Fort Gaines, Georgia, and Eufaula, Alabama, are in the region as we know it today — the latter easily recognizable as the Creek Eufaulee. The Upper Creeks lived on the Coosa and Tallapoosa branches of the Alabama River and the upper Ocmulgee in Georgia. Present-day towns and cities in this area are Tallassee, Tuskegee, and Montgomery. After Spain's relinquishment of Florida to the British and about the time of the American Revolution, an explorer listed fifty- five towns of the Creek Nations. Allowing 200 persons to a village, probably a liberal figure, this gave an estimated population of 11,000. By that time the Creeks had absorbed the remnants of various tribes which had withdrawn from coastal Georgia, and peoples of many unlike tongues had found refuge in the Creek Confederacy, which was perhaps the most powerful assemblage the Ameri- can Indian had ever succeeded in organizing. Such a group was too formidable to be defied by a handful of Spanish soldiers and a few missionaries, however devoted to a cause.

Though the Creeks extended no welcome to missionaries, they were at least a source of trade. They were essentially a farming people, with hunting and trap- ping as side lines. Skins of deer, wildcat, fox, and muskrat came out of the Creek country, along with occasional cattle hides. But even if the trade in peltry and hides had gone exclusively to the Spaniards, the profits would not have justified their retention of all Florida. Attacks by enemies on the outlying set- tlements became more frequent, and the support of Florida was a constant burden on the Spanish treasury. By the middle of the eighteenth century St. Augustine was about all that remained of the colony. Its transfer to the British in 1763, by an item in the Treaty of Paris, did not greatly impair Spain's standing among the family of nations.

Considering the amount of energy expended and the long time-expanse involved, Spain had made no great gains in the colonizing of Florida. Possibly the experience was of some value to the authorities in shaping colonial policies for other parts of the New World. At least, expansion northward from Mexico yielded greater success.

LATIN–AMERICAN EXPANSION NORTHWARD
FROM OLD MEXICO

Alexander von Humboldt, renowned nineteenth-century geographer, remarked in 1811: " The national vanity of the Spaniards loves to magnify the spaces, and to remove, if not in reality, at least in imagination, the limits of the country occupied by them to as great a distance as possible."

Von Humboldt had reference to the disparity between the Spanish claims to vast territory in America north of the Rio Grande and the small areas in which they had made settlements. A study of the generalized occupance map (Fig. 20) bears out the truth of Von Humboldt's statement. Before the year 1800 there were essentially four main centers of Mexican colonial settlement — parts of two river valleys, and two separate coastal districts. The river valleys of the Gila (pronounced " hee'la ") and the Rio Grande (then known sometimes as Rio Bravo or Rio del Norte) were the areas earliest occupied. Spanish settlements were made along these rivers and some of their tributaries at a time roughly contemporary with the founding of Jamestown and Plymouth. Next in chronology was the occupation of parts of the Texas coast, with its inland center of San Antonio. Last, and perhaps best known today, was the spread of settlement northward along the California coast, then known as Alta (Upper) California, by extension of missions from Baja (Lower) California.

The same motives which led to expansion from St. Augustine operated in the Southwest and on the Pacific coast, but with varying intensity. Fears of foreign aggression, says Professor Herbert E. Bolton, largely inspired the activities of the Spanish Government in Texas; when such fears slept, " Texas was left pretty much to itself." Missionary activity held sway in the Rio Grande Valley north of El Paso, and also in Alta California, although on the coast there was perhaps half an eye toward the possibility of Russian intrusion. Settlements on the lower Gila River resulted at first from early explorations, but soon centered about Indian villages there and near present-day Tucson.

In pushing into these areas contiguous to Old Mexico, the Latin Americans were invading familiar territory. They met with difficulties, to be sure, but in a number of ways their colonizing procedures were facilitated; except for the Texas coast, the climate bore the stamp of aridity, similar in that respect to Mexico's.

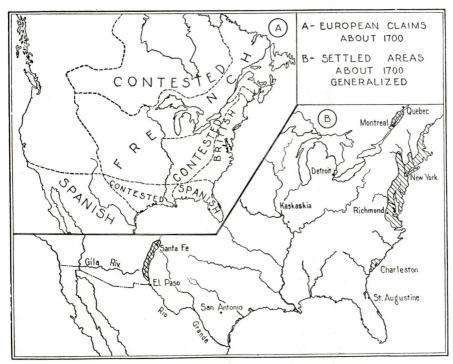

A- EUROPEAN CLAIMS ABOUT 1700

B- SETTLED AREAS ABOUT 1700 GENERALIZED

20   A generalized view of political claims and settled areas at the opening of the eighteenth century. Possessions or claims not actively disputed were largely confined to the Atlantic seaboard, or to regions contiguous to Old Mexico in the Southwest. Elsewhere, as along the Texas coast and in the interior, claims and counter-claims were the rule. Note particularly that the control of the Mississippi River was contested by the rival countries. Part A is a simplification of a corresponding map in *Harper's Atlas of American History* by Dixon Ryan Fox. (Courtesy of Harper and Brothers, publishers.)

The southern California coastal climate with its winter rains and hot summer sun was a counterpart of the climate of Spain's Mediterranean coast. Irrigation, a requirement for successful agriculture, was a familiar practice with the Mexican and Spanish peoples. The rearing of livestock under the special conditions of short grass and mild winters was pretty much the same in New Mexico as in Old Mexico. Adobe bricks, made of mud dried in the sun, provided the basic building material north as well as south of the "Rio Bravo." The introduction of crop plants and orchard trees from Spain by way of Mexico proved less exacting than similar importations from western Europe to the Atlantic coast. In short, colonization within the present area of the southwestern United States involved relatively few breaks with the past. Orderly procedures in settlement might well be expected in such a land and by these people.

Early outposts in East Texas. The planting of missions and forts in East Texas early in the eighteenth century was preceded, as this step was in other parts of the Southwest, by a period of exploration and planning. As early as 1676 (about a century before the outbreak of the American Revolution), favorable geographical reports of the Texas east coast and hinterlands were delivered to the authorities of Church and State in Mexico. Many of these leaders had their headquarters in El Paso, or more properly the El Paso District, a 20-mile stretch of the Rio Grande above and below the town. (The El Paso of that early day was located on the right bank of the river near the present town of Ciudad Juárez, Mexico; the United States El Paso came into being during the 1820's with the so-called Santa Fe trade — see Chapter 23.) At the beginning of the seventeenth century there were in the El Paso District as many as six missions, four Spanish *villas* or villages, and the presidio of El Paso — altogether comprising an important string of settlements with a population totaling between 2,000 and 3,000.

Threats of Louisiana-French aggression into East Texas were countered by the planting of missions and military stations along the coast in the early years of the eighteenth century. Selected for this purpose were Matagorda Bay and the lower Neches and Trinity rivers (near present-day Houston). One of these missions, bearing the name of St. Augustine, was located near the present Chambers City, with others 8 or 10 miles upstream. The inland site now familiarly known as San Antonio was also selected at this time. Within a few years ten missions and four presidios (not indicated on the map) were established along the Gulf coast, in the general neighborhood of San Antonio.

After nearly a half-century of occupation, all the missions and forts except San Antonio were abandoned. The causes of the withdrawal from these distant outposts in the 1720's have been the subject of much speculation. It has been suggested that the fear of French aggression had by that time subsided, especially with the shifting of the Franco-Spanish boundary eastward to the Sabine River, the present Texas-Louisiana state line. It has also been said that the priests who were stationed at these missions recommended their removal on the ground that they were climatically unhealthful. This latter consideration may well have played some part in the shifting Spanish interests in East Texas, for the environment was essentially different from that of the homeland and the country about El Paso. Other authorities believe that the Indians of the Texas coast were at that time few in number and intractable in nature, thus proving to be poor mission material.

By far the most significant of these remote group settlements — remote, that is to say, from El Paso — was San Antonio. Unlike the coastal settlements, San Antonio was reoccupied after a brief period of abandonment, and the town which then developed became the provincial capital and the first large city of Texas. When the Spanish explorers arrived there, an Indian village occupied a site near a spring in what is now San Pedro Park in the north-central part of the city.

The selection of San Antonio as a mission site was a happy one, for the San Antonio River, although not one of the large Texas rivers, provided sufficient water for irrigation and domestic needs; moreover, a natural focusing of routes gave the town regional importance. Not one mission but four were established within the San Antonio District, and a degree of safety was provided by a presidio, the Alamo, now memorable through its defense by Texans during the revolt against Mexico. The San Antonio District soon become famous for its varied agriculture, including the growing of sweet potatoes and cotton.

New Mexico. Latin-American settlement clung rather closely to the Rio Grande Valley, which seems to have had two distinct sections in relation to the administrative center of Santa Fe. "Rio Arriba," meaning literally "the river above," identified the upper basin and included Santa Fe, Taos, and other northern pueblos and Mexican towns. "Rio Abajo" ("the river from the top down") comprehended that part of the basin extending downstream for some 150 miles, thus including Bernalillo, Albuquerque, Socorro, and numerous other communities. It should be noted that Rio Abajo ended near the site of present-day Elephant Butte Dam and Reservoir, for farther south lay the Jornado del Muerto — the Journey of Death. The Jornado, as it is still known, was notoriously difficult of travel not only because of its rugged terrain but because of the absence of water inland from the Rio Grande. It is customary at the present time to refer to the upper and lower sections of the Rio Grande, but not with the same division of territory.

Rio Abajo presented a combination of geographical and cultural features well suited to the Spanish type of settlement. Geographically it was an extension of the El Paso District, with the degree of likeness fading as one progressed into the Rio Arriba country. Not only was the Santa Fe-Taos region 300 miles away from the older settled areas, but it was nearly a mile above sea level. Von Humboldt found the climate of northern New Mexico "remarkably cold" despite its location in the latitude of Syria. Perhaps having reference to seasons of unusual severity, he writes of freezing temperatures in the middle of May, and tells of finding the winter ice cover of the Rio Grande thick enough to bear the weight of horses and carriages. On the whole, however, it was a climate into which familiar crops, to be aided by irrigation, could be and were brought. The Spanish thought the region to be good, too, because of the possibilities of mineral wealth in the maze of mountains on either hand.

Indian Peoples of the Rio Grande Basin in New Mexico. From the cultural standpoint, the Rio Grande offered attractions in the presence of the Pueblo Indians, a sedentary people advanced in various arts, who inhabited about twenty-five apartmentlike pueblo dwellings on both sides of the Rio Grande and widely spaced among its tributaries. We have no reliable estimates of the pueblo population until 1760, when there were just over 9,000 persons all told. In the same year the Mexican-Spanish population was nearly 8,000, not including the inhabitants of the El Paso District.

The pueblos have changed but little during the two and a half centuries since they were finally conquered by the determined Spaniards. There were, in fact, two historic conquests of New Mexico; the first ended as early as 1680 when the would-be invaders with their women and children were driven back to El Paso by a concerted revolt of the Pueblo Indians. This revolt is pictured as a particularly vicious affair, resulting in the withdrawal of as many as 2,500 persons from the upper river country, including some Indians who had struck up an alliance with the Spaniards, or who could tolerate no longer the frequent raids of Apaches from the east. It was during the first conquest of New Mexico that the *villa* or town of Santa Fe was established, perhaps as early as 1605 and possibly as late as 1616.

The "reconquest" of New Mexico, involving no great conflict, took place in the 1690's, after which the population grew slowly but steadily. New *villas* were established, among them Albuquerque, founded in 1706 and destined to become a half-century later the largest New Mexican town (as it is today). Populations varied considerably, as is shown in the following table:

NEW MEXICO POPULATION, 1760

(Selected list of larger or more important Spanish villas and Indian pueblos)

	Spanish	Indian
Albuquerque	1,814	
Santa Fe	1,285	
La Cañada	1,515	316
Taos	160	505
San Juan	575	316
Santa Clara	277	257
San Ildefonso	30	484
Nambé	118	204
Santo Domingo		424
Jemez		373
Santa Ana		404
Sandia	222	291
Isleta, Belén	620	304
Acoma		1,052
Laguna	85	600
Zuñi		664

It will be noticed that by 1760 no Spanish town had as yet been established near Acoma, the largest pueblo in New Mexico, or near certain others. Some of the pueblos were on the downgrade, a few were already in a state of ruin. An example of the declining Indian town was the pueblo of Pecos, whose ruins in more recent times have been the subject of much popular and scientific interest. It is found from the studies of Alfred V. Kidder that the Pecos Pueblo was probably the largest Indian town in the Southwest when described by the chronicler of Coronado's expedition as " a large quadrangular structure of terrace form, on whose balconies one could make a circuit of the entire village without setting foot on the ground." Pecos Pueblo was made the site of an adobe mission which served the town for more than a century. Situated on the eastern border of the Pueblo country (approximately, present-day eastern New Mexico), the great Pecos town was exposed to Comanche raids, which in time were severe enough to reduce and discourage a peace-loving people. In the year 1797, says Kidder, only 189 remained within the crumbling walls, and in 1840 the handful of Pecos

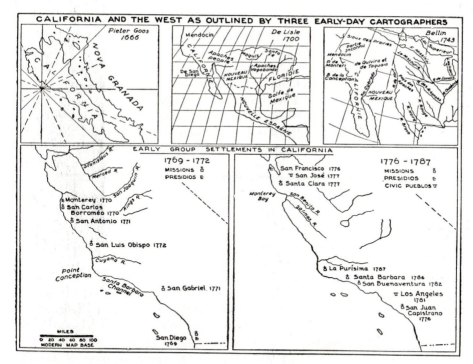

21 (*Above*) Early representations of Alta California by Pieter Goos, De Lisle, and Bellin. (*Below*) Group settlements and forts in California from 1769 to 1787.

Indians then remaining left their home to join the Jemez, with whom they were allied in language and by tradition.

Lower Colorado and Gila rivers. The lower Colorado River Valley was also the theater of early Spanish colonial enterprise. How early this was may be gathered from a brief review of the explorations which preceded settlement within the present limits of the State of Arizona.

The first explorations of the lower reaches of the Colorado River were made in 1542, although still earlier navigators had sailed up the Gulf of California, into which that mighty stream flows. Among other things, these earliest explorers found that Lower California was a peninsula, not an island as had been assumed before their time. New truths as well as commodities circulated slowly, however, with the result that the belief in California's insularity persisted for long thereafter; the common seventeenth-century maps, in fact, still represented the coast as an island of indefinite shape and size (Fig. 21, *top, left*). Through the discoveries (1698 to 1701) of Jesuit missionaries, including the famed Father Kino, " California " was at last shown as part of the continent.

The missionaries who followed the early explorers, far from being repelled by the desert landscape, judged the country to be good for their purposes, and established two missions. One of these, near the mouth of the Colorado River —

its site is not definitely known — was short-lived. The other, built at the mouth of the Gila River near the present-day city of Yuma, served the Indians in its vicinity for more than three-quarters of a century. We know that the Yuma mission was in existence in 1776, when priests rested there en route from Sonora, Mexico, to the then newly established missions in southern California. Its life ended sometime thereafter, but its physical remains were visible to the American parties which in 1846 explored this region as a preliminary to the Gadsden Purchase. The walls of the church were later demolished and their materials were put to practical use in the making of barracks for soldiers stationed at Fort Yuma.

The corridors of human time are very long in this arid Southwest country and their beginning is dimly lighted. The Federal exploring parties (1846 to 1855) came uniformly to the conclusion that settlement had long antedated the Spaniards who arrived there early in the eighteenth century. John Russell Bartlett, for example, felt that the "large trees, both erect and fallen, which now cover the bottom, even where the ditches appear," provided evidences of cultivation by Indians at a time long before the missionaries arrived.

San Xavier del Bac, Tumacacori, Casa Grande ruins.   Many generations have marveled at the extraordinary monuments of the past, now preserved from further molestation, within the vicinity of present-day Tucson and along the intermittent southern tributaries of the Gila. Nine miles south of Tucson is the restored San Xavier del Bac mission, which entered upon its slow decline as a functioning mission about the year 1810, after a century or more of activity. The ruins of San José de Tumacacori, near Tubac, Arizona, are preserved as a national monument. The date of origin is not clear, but Tumacacori was destroyed and rebuilt a number of times before entering upon its final desolation. Also ancient, and perhaps most mysterious of all, are the ruins of Casa Grande (Great House). We know from the reports of missionaries written in the 1780's that this ancient structure has been in ruins for nearly two centuries. Early American explorers suggested the probability of its having been erected by a race of Indians who had vanished before the coming of the first Spanish settlers. The scientists of the present generation seem still unable to solve the mystery.

California mission-presidio settlement to 1800.   Von Humboldt pointed out in 1811 that "although the whole coast of New California was carefully examined by the great navigator Sebastian Vizcaino (as is proved by plans drawn up by himself in 1602), this fine country was only, however, occupied by the Spaniards 167 years afterward." Could it have been that after two centuries of mixed success and failure elsewhere, they had become cautious of advances into new territory?

Coastal California northward to the Golden Gate was a "fine country" as Von Humboldt described it; poverty in good harbors was its only detriment. A condensed list of advantages would include the following: The climate was like that of Spain; the land was good for grazing; irrigation water was available; large numbers of Indians lived here; and the mountains bordering the coastal valleys were believed to contain minerals.

By the 1750's, governmental centers in Mexico — Mexico City and San Blas — stirred with talk of British designs on California. With this urge to activity, packet boats were dispatched from San Blas, touching ground at what is now San Diego in April, 1763 — the year that Spain was ceding Florida to the British. The resident Indians may be presumed to have been astonished; that they were resentful is indicated by Von Humboldt's statement that the surviving members of the party " were employed in digging graves for the bodies of their companions."

San Diego and the Mission Chain. In 1769, six years after the original trial, a fort and mission were established on the shores of San Diego Bay. A village arose in the vicinity of the adobe structures, later to become known as Old San Diego when the modern city grew from a new center a few miles distant. During the next quarter-century the Franciscan Fathers and their military aides worked with unprecedented speed, and by the time Von Humboldt conducted his survey (1811) the following missions had been established:

CALIFORNIA MISSION SETTLEMENTS TO 1811

(Named from south to north)

Name	Attached Indian Population
San Diego	1,559
San Luis Rey de Francia	532
San Juan Capistrano	1,013
San Gabriel	1,042
San Fernando	614
San Buenaventura	938
Santa Barbara	1,093
La Purísima Concepción	1,028
San Luis Obispo	699
San Miguel	614
Soledad	563
San Antonio de Padua	1,052
San Carlos de Monterey	638
San Juan Batista	958
Santa Cruz	437
Santa Clara	1,291
San José	622
San Francisco	814
TOTAL	15,507

It will be apparent from Figure 21 that the missions were not established in regular order from south to north. During the first four years — from 1769 to 1772 — missions or presidios were planted at irregular intervals from San Diego to Monterey, both in sheltered coastal valleys and directly on the coast. Between 1776 and 1787, the second period of mission activity, other stations were added to both the northern and the southern clusters, and a new type of settlement, the civic pueblo, came into being. Thus Los Angeles originated in 1781 as a town with no special religious or military functions. The various types of settlement formed until the year 1798 are recorded in Figure 22.

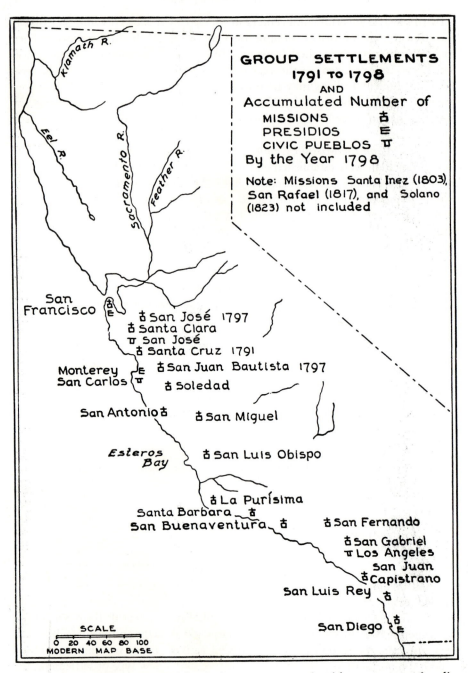

GROUP SETTLEMENTS 1791 TO 1798

AND

Accumulated Number of

MISSIONS ☩
PRESIDIOS E
CIVIC PUEBLOS ⊔

By the Year 1798

Note: Missions Santa Inez (1803), San Rafael (1817), and Solano (1823) not included

Klamath R.

Eel R.

Sacramento R.

Feather R.

San Francisco

☩ San José 1797
☩ Santa Clara
⊔ San José
☩ Santa Cruz 1791

Monterey
San Carlos

☩ San Juan Bautista 1797

☩ Soledad

San Antonio ☩   ☩ San Miguel

Esteros Bay   ☩ San Luis Obispo

☩ La Purísima

Santa Barbara ☩
San Buenaventura ☩   ☩ San Fernando

☩ San Gabriel
⊔ Los Angeles
San Juan ☩ Capistrano

San Luis Rey ☩

San Diego ☩ E

SCALE
0 20 40 60 80 100
MODERN MAP BASE

22   Group settlements in California from 1791 to 1798, with a summary of earlier settlements

The site of each mission was carefully selected with regard to natural advantages, such as soil and slope for irrigation, adequacy of water supply, accessibility and distance from other missions or forts, and the prospects of serving an Indian population. The natives of California's coast and interior Great Valley tended toward semimigratory habits. Not all were converted either to the religious faith which the padres taught or to the sedentary existence enforced by mission life. The larger proportion appear to have resumed their more carefree existence when the missions became less influential in the 1820's.

Introduction of Crops and Farming Practices. Longhorn cattle were brought into San Diego by the first settlers; it is said that in 1769 there were 200 cattle and 100 sheep within what is now San Diego County. Livestock production became a basic industry at all the missions, as is suggested by the following "census" taken in 1811:

CALIFORNIA MISSION LIVESTOCK, 1811

Cows and oxen	67,782
Sheep	107,177
Horses	19,429
Mules	877

All likely crops were introduced by the padres, who taught their charges how to grow them. Although the first trials at raising wheat in San Diego were unsuccessful, it soon became a universal crop. The "channel missions," that is, those along the coast near the "Santa Barbara canal" formed by the islands lying off the mainland, soon won a reputation for the excellence of their olives. The sheltered valley of Santa Clara, it was found, yielded better fruit than could be expected from the mission gardens directly on the coast. Wine grapes, often grafted to the roots of native varieties, were introduced during the first years, and wine-making became an important industry.

Growth and Decline of the Missions. Generally speaking, the California missions reached the height of their prosperity some ten to twenty years later than the period which we are considering. Some of the missions existed for only a few years: Santa Cruz, for example, whose ruins were never restored. The majority of the mission buildings went through periods of new construction or reconstruction, perhaps as a consequence of normal growth, or sometimes following disasters of fire or earthquake. An earthquake occurred on December 8, 1812, that affected the whole length of the mission chain, requiring much new masonry, as at San Juan Capistrano. Fire was particularly troublesome, especially in these early missions, which had roofs covered with a locally derived, tarlike bituminous material known as tule. This material, though serviceable for shedding rain, was highly inflammable; this the residents of San Luis Obispo realized fully in 1776, when the mission was fired from burning arrows shot by unbelievers. Soon, however, tile was substituted for tule, adding to the safety as well as improving the appearance of the buildings. Disaster of flood, fire, or earthquake occasionally caused a local change in the site of a mission. The present site of Santa Clara, for instance, is its third. After a flood of the Guadalupe River had washed out the original mission nearly 3 miles distant from the present location, a new one was built near the spot where the Southern Pacific Railroad station now stands. These buildings suffered in the earthquake shock of 1812 and were finally demolished by another, six years later.

Later developments of the missions.   Political shocks, however, were more damaging to the mission world than were the tremors caused by Nature. Mexico's declaration of independence from Spain in 1821 marked the beginning of mission decline. The trend toward secularization (separation of the missions from churchly authority) began with Mexico's independence and became final by legislative act on August 17, 1833. Unrest and turmoil held sway for more than a dozen years, not ceasing when California became territory of the United States. All was chaos when California was made a theater of the Mexican War, with 20,000 Indians dislodged from their mission residences, and church property occupied by ranchers or by the military. It was into this scene of confusion, made still worse by many indefinite or indefinable land grants with which Mexico had previously rewarded its citizens, that the tide of Anglo-American gold-seekers and settlers swept in 1848. Confusing though it be, the scene must remain in statu quo until our studies have followed the spread of Anglo-American settlement from the Atlantic to the Pacific.

Part Two

THE ATLANTIC SEABOARD AT THE OPENING

OF THE NINETEENTH CENTURY

Part Two

THE ATLANTIC SEABOARD AT THE OPENING
OF THE NINETEENTH CENTURY

CHAPTER 6

The Land: A General View

DURING the twenty years following the first session of the Congress in New York City in 1789, the United States expanded with unexampled rapidity. With a solid footing on the Atlantic coast, the territorial area was extended two-thirds of the way across the continent. Thirteen states with Atlantic coast lines had grown out of the same number of colonies, with boundaries similar to those of today. Maine was politically a district of Massachusetts and remained such until it became a state in 1820. Prelude of events to occur on a grander scale was the addition in 1792 of Vermont, the first inland area to achieve statehood, but in this case without a preliminary trial period as a Territory. Settlers west of the mountains in Virginia commonly referred to their land as the Western District of Virginia. This district was tacitly recognized by the United States in its Federal censuses of population until the 1860's, when, under the stress of disunion, this natural division was at last legalized by its admission to the Union as the State of West Virginia. State-making had gone on apace in the area between the Appalachians and the Mississippi River, with successive changes that are shown graphically in Figures 23 and 24.

These kaleidoscopic changes on the frontier of a country whose form of government was still on trial were viewed by political leaders with mingled apprehension and confidence. Not a few held to the belief that the strength of a country was measured less by the extent of its area than by the numbers of its people and their effective occupation of territory. People could be spread too thin in such a land, it was said. The idea that the population would become "thinly diffused" was advanced many times before the Louisiana Purchase was acquired and often during the decades that saw the country expanding to the Pacific Ocean. If ruin did not quickly follow, said a French geographer in 1804, at least "we shall discover nothing but a prolific source of present weakness and future disunion."

Many of the headshakers were European visitors who had seen countries totter and collapse, just as we have in our own time. The only comfort that these prophets of doom could salvage came from their assumption that the country west of the Mississippi River was a desert. They considered it providential that the uninhabitable West would counteract the will of the expansionists.

Others who thought about these matters were of a contrary opinion. They pointed to the unusual rate of population increase as shown by the Federal

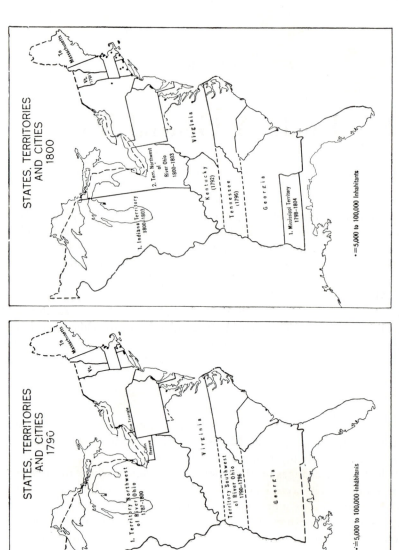

STATES, TERRITORIES
AND CITIES
1790

1. Territory Northwest
of River Ohio
1787–1800

Virginia

Territory Southwest
of River Ohio
1790–1796

Georgia

.∴= 5,000 to 100,000 Inhabitants

STATES, TERRITORIES
AND CITIES
1800

1. Indiana Territory
1800–1803

2. Terr. Northwest
of
River Ohio
1800–1803

Kentucky
(1792)

Virginia

Tennessee
(1796)

Georgia

1. Mississippi Territory
1798–1804

.∴= 5,000 to 100,000 Inhabitants

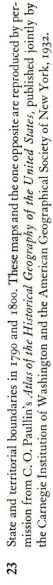

23 State and territorial boundaries in 1790 and 1800. These maps and the one opposite are reproduced by permission from C. O. Paullin's *Atlas of the Historical Geography of the United States*, published jointly by the Carnegie Institution of Washington and the American Geographical Society of New York, 1932.

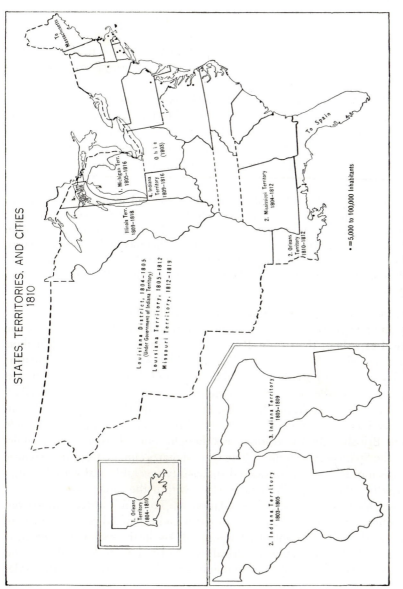

STATES, TERRITORIES, AND CITIES
1810

O h i o
(1803)

1. Michigan Terr.
1805–1816

4. Indiana
Territory
1809–1816

Illinois Terr.,
1809–1818

2. Mississippi Territory
1804–1812

2. Orleans
Territory
1810–1812

To Spain

Louisiana District, 1804–1805
(Under Government of Indiana Territory)
Louisiana Territory, 1805–1812
Missouri Territory, 1812–1819

•=5,000 to 100,000 Inhabitants

1. Orleans
Territory
1804–1810

3. Indiana Territory
1805–1809

2. Indiana Territory
1803–1805

24   States, Territories, and cities in 1810

censuses, starting in 1790 with about 4,000,000, rising to over 5,000,000 in 1800, and to over 7,000,000 in 1810. If this rate continued, and they saw no reason for believing otherwise, then the population would reach 80,000,000 in 1876 and over 800,000,000 in 1946. (The actual population in 1870 was 38,558,371, and it was estimated at 140,840,000 in 1946.)

The optimists were not sure that the trans-Mississippi country was uninhabitable, and were convinced from apparently reliable reports that in population capacity the Territory Northwest of the Ohio River was the equal of the Atlantic seaboard states. Besides, there were great resources, and the natural means of communication needed but little improvement. As a popular magazine announced in 1807:

This country possesses physical capabilities of greatness and wealth, without limits, and beyond all bounds; she has a territory, which is spread out to an interminable extent, and fertile in every production, conducing to the necessities and gratification of animal nature; her navigable rivers, her capacious harbors and convenient ports, and the broad bosom of the Atlantic main, which connects her with the kingdoms of Europe, all give to her the means and the facilities of acquiring the most ample and the most permanent strength.

You will recognize here all the elements of a Fourth-of-July oration.

Soberer and longer were the views of the men who from 1800 to 1810 were the geographical experts of their time. Perhaps best known today, because of their attainments in other directions, are Thomas Jefferson and Albert Gallatin; famed today among geographers for their maps and descriptions are such less well-known figures as Jedidiah Morse, Benjamin Smith Barton, Abraham Bradley, the French travelers André Michaux the elder and the younger, and Benjamin Henry Latrobe, to mention but a few. From their writings we conclude that: 1. The British-American frontier was thought more likely to prove troublesome than the Spanish-American. 2. The United States climate from the Atlantic to the Mississippi River was considered sufficiently favorable and varied to support a large population. 3. The land surface within the same area offered no serious obstacles to the spread of population. 4. The land surface, moreover, would permit the further development of roads and canalized rivers to form an efficient network. 5. The extent of resources still lay in the realm of conjecture, but some, such as the forests, were already so depleted as to demand care and conservation in use. These observations will be briefly discussed in the order mentioned.

BOUNDARY PROBLEMS

The British-American frontier. The people of the United States in 1810 did not look upon the boundary between their country and Canada with the sense of security that we enjoy today. The boundary perhaps seemed longer then than it does now, and in the Great Lakes region it failed to follow easily definable natural features. More important, the majority of the Canadian people were within a short distance of the United States — a troublemaking situation, in the view of the time. It seemed likely that the spread of the Canadian people in the immediate future would lead to further concentrations along the border.

In 1810 there was no Dominion of Canada, but rather the British Possessions of Upper and Lower Canada. The Ottawa River was the dividing line between these provinces. Upper Canada, with its ample areas in southern Ontario (now often called the Ontario Peninsula), was the principal section undergoing settlement, for under conditions then obtaining the lands of Lower or French Canada had nearly reached the saturation point of population. To some degree, Upper Canada had become a refuge for persons who had become dissatisfied with conditions in the United States. For example, considerable numbers of Germans who had not found Pennsylvania to their liking had recently taken up residence in what they thought was a freer land.

Politicians and military men of the United States viewed Upper Canada with more than a little anxiety, and considered the advisability of boundary fortifications. In a report to headquarters in 1799, Major Ebenezer Denny informed General Josiah Harmar that the British had their shore of Lake Erie " settled from one end to the other," and that a new town [Amherstburg?] at the entrance to the Detroit River was "very strong; it commands the river." Fears of international trouble were not unfounded, as we know from the operations of the War of 1812, which involved the Detroit River and Lake Erie as well as northern Vermont.

The Spanish-American boundary. The geographers of this period had much less to say about the Spanish-American boundary from Florida to the Mississippi River, and west of the Louisiana Purchase. Perhaps their comparative silence was owing more to a dearth of information than to an actual lack of importance. Florida was again a Spanish possession and still a colony without colonists, as it had been before the twenty years of British occupation from 1763 to 1783. The Louisiana Purchase had opened the Mississippi River for navigation, but Florida did not become American territory until its cession by Spain in 1821.

THE CLIMATIC ENVIRONMENT AS IT WAS VIEWED IN 1810

The essential features of the Atlantic coastal climate, about which there had been so much speculation in Colonial times, were fairly well known in 1810. There was still plenty of theory and misinformation, especially in popular circles, because "the weather " has always been a favorite topic of discussion. Even the experts were misled into some major errors about the temperature seasons of the Ohio country, although some facts at least were available. Instrumental readings at a dozen places along the coast from Charleston, South Carolina, to Nova Scotia had been sufficiently long and detailed to permit geographers to base their descriptions on facts rather than wholly on theory.

General approval of the Atlantic climate. The geographers inspected their instruments or the records made by others and pronounced the climate to be favorable — if one did not demand too much. The land was " well watered "; that is, the rainfall was generally adequate and dependable, distributed season- ally so as to favor the growth of crops. It was pointed out that along the south- ern coast the annual rainfall was more concentrated in the summer months than it was farther north. New England had about the same amount of moisture winter and summer, with nearly half the annual total falling in the solid form of snow. A century and a half of weather observation has not altered that general and important conclusion. The southern limit of a snow cover sufficiently deep to warrant the use of sleighs was, according to the experts, the Patapsco River, at the mouth of which the city of Baltimore is located.

One who thoughtfully reviews the contemporary descriptions of the Ameri- can environment, to be found not only in the geographies, but also in learned journals, popular magazines, and newspapers, cannot fail to conclude that the climate was made to appear more favorable than was justified by the facts then known. The reasons for this overcomplimentary cast are many and varied, and only a few can be explored here. Easily explained are the highly colored, almost lyrical climatic descriptions of restricted areas, say of a state, for which the author, with prospective settlement in view, wished to make out a good case. To some degree, the overfavorable climatic views of larger coverage are traceable to national pride, which was particularly evident in the early years of the Republic.

It was a subtle kind of propaganda, directed in part to European authors who had recorded their beliefs that the American environment was inferior to the European. The Abbé W. J. Reynal, the Count Georges L. L. de Buffon, and the poet Thomas Moore, more than any other Old World writers, had antago- nized American scientists by their long treatises or essays attempting to show that life forms in America were inferior to those of Europe: the Indian, for example, was held to be of a lower order than the peoples in Europe. When American writers took up the cudgels in defense of their land, they were likely to expatiate most on the climate. It was a relatively intangible element of the total environ- ment, and thus allowed the greatest opportunity for stretching the truth beyond demonstrable error. Perhaps the most forthright of America's academic de- fenders was Thomas Jefferson. The various editions of his long-lived *Notes on the State of Virginia* contain lengthy passages in refutation of the assertions of European philosophers who broadcast such intolerable views of America.

The majority of the lay public as well as most of the experts entertained a supreme faith in the belief that the American climate had changed, usually for the better, as a consequence of settlement. In most cases the belief was genuine enough, however ill-supported by evidence, but some of the bulky literature on this subject may safely be ticketed as propaganda in another form. It was said in effect: Perhaps the anti-American philosophers are correct in their un- favorable accounts of the *original* climate, but they do not realize that conditions have changed.

The " evidences " advanced by the many who wrote on the subject have a familiar ring to readers of this or any past generation, for the theme is timeless.

Accounts of earlier days, it was said, pictured the winters as being much more severe than they were between 1800 and 1810. It did not seem to matter that such accounts were largely impressionistic and noninstrumental, possibly recorded by travelers or explorers who were rarely stationed long at one place and who may have encountered winter weather in savage doses while on the march.

None of the actual weather records had been kept long enough by 1810 to tell anything important about changes of temperature or rainfall, but they were sometimes cited when they seemed to indicate trends in either or both. Reasoning that seemed plausible to these early-day scientists was more important than data. The conversion of forest land to the improved state over so wide an area was presumed somehow to modify the original controls of climate, and inevitably in the direction most likely to improve conditions. Charles Williamson of North Carolina put it thus, in abstract: With the clearing of forests, the land itself becomes more heated from the sun's rays. This results in more onshore winds, hence the tempering effect of the ocean is increased to the extent of reducing seasonal extremes and encouraging greater rainfall.

Modern research into climatic cycles as shown by long-time weather records at stations in the Eastern states enables us to understand better why there was so much insistence on the occurrence of a change during the early 1800's. According to Joseph B. Kincer, the period from 1801 to 1812 was marked by higher-than-average temperatures, and "for the summer, the highest points for the New Haven curve appear for the 20 years ending with 1807 [and that ending with 1881]." It would seem likely from the above conclusion, and also from the abnormally low temperatures along the Atlantic coast in 1816 (sometimes known as "eighteen hundred and froze-to-death"), that part of a cycle of climate was then mistaken for a progressive change of climate.

Logical explanations of contrasts with Europe. With climatic records available for coastal localities widely spaced in latitude, it was possible for the experts to make direct comparisons with similar if longer records maintained in European cities. A number of hypotheses for the differences had been advanced throughout the Colonial period, some of them so far-fetched as to appear ridiculous when repeated today. For example, the more severe winters of New England were attributed to "immense forests" which retained snow late in summer; or again, to the great heights of mountains at some vague point in the interior of the continent. A German traveler recorded his impression that in the United States "cold has the upper hand. The land is exposed to all the discomforts of the torrid and frigid zones, yet does not enjoy the advantages of either."

By the 1790's, however, the better-informed had reached the conclusion that the differences were largely owing to nothing more mysterious than the direction of prevailing winds. A physician in Salem, Massachusetts, who had maintained a detailed weather record since 1754, pointed out that the United States lay in the belt of prevailing westerlies, and "Since America lies to the westward of the Atlantic Ocean, we therefore feel less of the warming effect of the sea air in winter, as well as its cooling effects in summer." The student will recognize in this the essentials of the explanation as advanced in modern texts. This theory based on logical reasoning gradually won adherents, and by 1810 was so generally held that it was contained in widely used American geographies.

Belief in the warmer climate of the Ohio country. Corresponding climatic records for the trans-Appalachian country were not available by 1810, but that did not prevent the circulation of beliefs regarding the Northwest Territory. One belief in particular requires attention, because it played a part in attracting settlers to the Ohio country. Thomas Jefferson appears to have been the first to give popularity and authenticity to the idea that the temperatures of Ohio were significantly warmer than those in similar latitudes on the Alantic coast. This he announced in his *Notes on the State of Virginia,* which because of its wide reading by the American public was influential during the settlement period. As evidence for the supposedly warmer interior climate, Jefferson pointed to certain species of birds (for example, the parakeet) and vegetation (the catalpa) which explorers had reported finding farther north in the interior than on the Atlantic coast. This conclusion might well have been buried had it occurred in works of lesser popularity, but coming as it did from an author of high esteem, the idea was taken up and made even more of a certainty.

By the time Constantin F. Volney, the French geographer, wrote his treatise on the United States in 1804, there was said to be no doubt that the difference in climate was the equivalent of three degrees of latitude. Still later, in 1807, Benjamin Smith Barton held that " the point is put beyond any manner of doubt," because "the southern trees and shrubs . . . are in general found much farther north in the western than in the eastern parts of our country." Without exploring here all of its ramifications, we may conclude that this belief, which was later found untenable, was an effective element in encouraging Western settlement. We shall come upon it again later in this study.

EXPANSION NOT SERIOUSLY OBSTRUCTED BY
TOPOGRAPHIC FEATURES

Early maps of North America showed high mountain ranges occupying much of the interior. These fancied mountains gradually disappeared from the maps, and were replaced by the various " chains " of the Appalachians. At first, the Appalachians were thought to be so formidable as to prohibit easy communication across them, but this belief too was abandoned in the light of exploratory accounts. In fact, the spirit of optimism reached so high a pitch that by the 1790's many of the country's leaders thought it reasonable to consider connecting the headwaters of the Atlantic-flowing rivers with those of others joining the Ohio. Gaps or " saddles " in the Alleghenies, as for example toward the head of the Potomac, were presumed to offer possibilities for cross-country water transportation. All that was needed, it was felt, was the magic of initiative. Mistaken as these ideas surely were, they did not prevent attempts from being made. This is a good time to reread the story of the plow.

The "back country" was somewhere beyond the coastal towns and cities — a considerable distance, in fact — but with limits so indefinite and shifting as to defy representation on a map. Settlement had penetrated far beyond the eastern base of the Appalachians, fanning out into mountain "coves" and fertile limestone valleys, constantly pressing on through river-cut gaps in successive ridges to real or assumed opportunities beyond. Men of the Daniel Boone type, and a few women, had taken up land in the great valleys such as the Watauga, and far beyond the last Appalachian ridge. In fact, the mountain country appears to have been much less of a barrier to the expansion process than is commonly assumed. It is truer to say that settlement and routes of transportation conformed to the natural surface features, which by the early 1800's were reasonably well understood. We find that modern physiographic terms applicable to the Atlantic-seaboard states need only slight revision to furnish a suitable background for a study of the land surface as related to routes of travel.

The Eastern mountains. Essentially, three topographic units were then considered as forming the Appalachian country: (1) the Dividing or Allegheny Ridge on the west — identifiable as the summits of the maturely dissected Allegheny or Cumberland Mountains; (2) the Endless Mountains and their intervening valleys — the Parallel-Ridge-and-Valley Province, as it is known today; and (3) still farther east, the Blue Mountains or Blue Ridge, constituting the high country now known as the Blue Ridge Province. The term Blue Mountain (or Ridge) applied then to the heights southward of Virginia; a northward extension of these heights formed the first ridge to which one came in traveling westward; for example, from Philadelphia.

First in position from that approach was South Mountain, which many thought too inconsequential to deserve that term. "These mountains are not lofty," said a trustworthy recorder, speaking of South Mountain; "they are not seen till you come within a very few miles of them, and the ascent is so gradual that you get upon their top without perceiving it." Beyond lay the section of parallel valleys and ridges, the latter bearing such names as North Mountain and Kittatinny Ridge. One cannot but feel that in naming these various features the early observers had developed a useful terminology, derived in part from frontiersmen and Indians. The term "Endless Mountains," for example, is said by William Morris Davis to have derived from the native peoples, many of whose trails and hunting paths followed the twistings and turnings of the mountains for miles on end.

The Upper Country, later the Piedmont. The transition country between the outliers of the Blue Ridge and the low coastal plain, most extensive from Virginia southward to Georgia, was customarily referred to as the "Upper Country"; it was not until recent times that the term "Piedmont" became attached to it for identification. According to one French visitor, the hilly face of this transition belt is "distinguished by its risings, sometimes into long waves, and sometimes into round and insulated eminences." Another said: "Just at the point where the maritime part is terminated the soil rises gradually till it reaches the

Alleghany Mountains, and presents, upon the whole, a ground more irregular than mountainous, and interspersed with little hills as far as the mountains." This upland surface was seen to have many resemblances to the interior of southern New England, but its soils were better than those of the Northern area. Some of the better Upper Country soils were described as " mulatto," in reference to the top humus layer (then called " black mold ") resting on red earth, a high-class soil, as was indicated by the black-walnut trees growing there. No higher compliment could be paid a soil at this time, as well as earlier, than to identify it with groves of nut-bearing trees.

The Sea Sand Region: the Coastal Plain. Between the eastern margin of the Upper Country and the Atlantic, southward from Cape Cod, lay the " Region of Sea Sand " — the Coastal Plain in modern terminology. It was understood that this belt of country, widening inland toward the south, was originally sea bottom, and that the " line of the falls," formed by eastward-flowing rivers as they descended from the Upper Country, was the coast line in past geological times. Such interpretations were not popular in the early 1800's because they seemed to conflict seriously with Biblical teachings; nevertheless the scientists courageously held to their theories. As one of them said in 1807: " Long Island and the adjacent continent were, in former days, contiguous, or only separated by a small river, and the strait which now divides them was formed by successive inroads of the sea, from the eastward to the westward, in the course of ages." The Region of Sea Sand was often referred to as a low champaign (plain) presenting little topographic variety and covered with light to sandy soils in which fragments of stone were rarely seen. This region was not considered to be well suited to agriculture; nevertheless, because of its coastal position, it was the first to be settled. By 1810 there were, within the southern Coastal Plain, many desolated areas which had passed through the forest-to-forest cycle. That is, these areas had been originally cleared for agricultural use; with the impoverishment of the soil they had reverted to a wooded condition.

The Granite Region. New England, often referred to as the Granite Region, was considered a separate physiographic unit, not a northward extension of the Appalachian country. Geographers of that time were no more successful than those of more recent years have been in their attempts to present orderly descriptions of that complex part of the East. All kinds of surface were to be found, even, for full measure, a bit of the Sea Sand Region on Cape Cod. The surface of New England was pictured as varying from rough to rugged, occasionally surmounted by rounded heights such as Wachusett and Monadnock, and interrupted by river lowlands, most extensively along the Connecticut and the Hoosatonic. The culminating altitudes, however, were known to be in New Hampshire's White Mountains, with heights not exceeding 7,000 feet, lower by a half-mile than had been assumed before the 1790's.

DEVELOPMENT OF LINES OF CIRCULATION

Even the most patriotic citizen could not have claimed that the existing roads formed a " system," or that river improvement was anything more than a local undertaking. The roads of that time had grown as expediency demanded and without over-all planning. They were called " natural roads," to distinguish them conveniently from the few military roads which had been constructed during the Revolution and the earlier Indian wars. By 1810, however, a well-informed citizen could have told a thrilling story of transportation improvements already completed or under way. To the " natural roads " had been added a few turnpikes, whose crowned and graded surfaces were a new and welcome element in the American landscape. These first turnpikes, as we shall see, linked seaboard cities already connected after a fashion by country roads, but other turnpikes were being built toward the thinly occupied frontier and would soon outdistance the advancing columns of settlement.

Many rivers had been dredged or cleared of snags, and canals and locks enabled cumbersome arks and flatboats to slip by rapids which had formerly impeded traffic. Although expediency had largely dominated river improvements, there was some thought of connecting different rivers to form long-distance waterways. To cap it all, in 1807 the Congress had ordered a survey of the whole transportation problem, thus initiating a long line of the public-works projects for which this country has been distinguished. The survey was conducted by Secretary of the Treasury Albert Gallatin, whose reports and recommendations formed the basis for national policy and private undertakings for many years thereafter.

United States roads in 1810.   The basic roads of the country about the time of the Gallatin survey are most easily shown in map form. Figure 25 shows stage roads suitable for coach travel, and post roads over which mail was delivered. Since contracts were sometimes let for the delivery of mail on horseback in the more remote localities, a post road could vary much in its character from one end to the other. Hence many post roads were scarcely more than bridle paths while others, such as the Boston Post Road out of New York through coastal Connecticut, were heavily traveled by coach and post riders, as well as by animals driven on the hoof to market.

Road travel at this time was both slow and costly. The average number of days consumed in going from New York to various parts of the country (Fig. 26) is striking when compared to known rates today. For example, a southward-bound traveler favored by good roads and prompt stage connections could reach Philadelphia in one day, Baltimore in two, Washington in from three to four, Norfolk perhaps in five and, presumably well tired-out and reduced in ready cash, might reach Charleston, South Carolina, in ten or twelve days. Some of the slowness in travel was due to the necessity of ferrying the bridgeless rivers. A westward journey from New York for a corresponding distance was even slower,

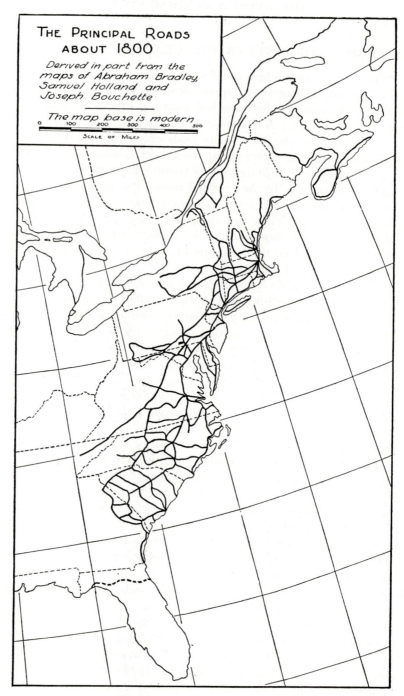

THE PRINCIPAL ROADS
ABOUT 1800

Derived in part from the
maps of Abraham Bradley,
Samuel Holland and
Jôseph Bouchette

The map base is modern

0   100   200   300   400   500

SCALE OF MILES

25   The principal roads about 1800

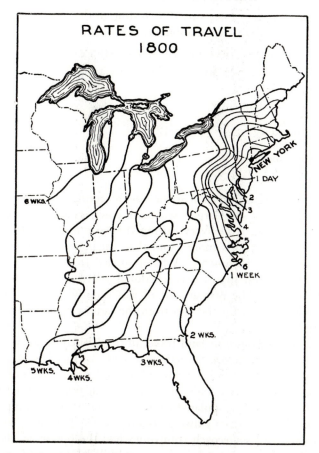

RATES OF TRAVEL
1800

6 WKS.

NEW YORK
1 DAY
2
3
4
5
6
1 WEEK

2 WKS.

3 WKS.

5 WKS.
4 WKS.

26   Rates of travel from New York in 1800. Reproduced by permission from C. O. Paullin's *Atlas of the Historical Geography of the United States,* published jointly by the Carnegie Institution of Washington and the American Geographical Society of New York, 1932.

because of the resistance offered to wheeled traffic by the Appalachian ridges. Going downhill, as well as up, was slow business.

Costs of passenger travel were relatively higher than today's, partly because of the necessity of overnight stops at taverns and roadhouses. Visitors from foreign countries, where the means of travel were in a more advanced state, often complained bitterly of the bad roads, the slow and uncomfortable stagecoaches, and the high rates charged for these very poor services. Not uncommon was the remark that apparently all Americans who were not lawyers or land agents were innkeepers, and that the members of each of these occupations had become adept at separating money from the public.

In the cost of mail service, a function early assumed by the Federal Government, we also find a measure of transportation difficulties. There were no postage stamps in those days, and rates varied according to the type of mail, its weight, and the number of miles to destination. An example of the rates follows:

COST OF DELIVERY OF SINGLE–SHEET LETTERS

(by Act of Congress, March 2, 1799)

Miles Carried	Cost in Cents
Not exceeding forty	.08
40 to 90	.10
90 to 150	.12½
150 to 300	.17
300 to 500	.20
Over 500	.25

Perhaps the best-organized mail service in the country was over the so-called Main Line connecting the larger seaboard cities, roughly corresponding to present-day U.S. Route 1. Delivery during the " summer establishment," from April 15 to October 15, was more rapid than during the remaining half-year, called the " winter establishment." A letter mailed from Machias, Maine, near the Canadian border, on June 1 was scheduled to arrive in Washington on the afternoon of June 20. The greater part of this time was taken up on the way from Machias to Boston, for the trip from the latter city to Washington was a matter of only five days.

The first notable advance in land travel in the United States was made with the development of turnpikes. Sometimes called " artificial roads " in the days of their origin, turnpikes were constructed by companies which obtained funds by selling shares to investors. The turnpikes were at first projected between the larger cities, or in heavily populated country where the road company felt that traffic could be diverted from existing country roads. Travelers, drivers of live-stock, post riders, and stagecoach companies had the option of keeping to the narrow, unballasted country road, say between Philadelphia and Lancaster, Pennsylvania, or turning onto the " pike," where tolls were paid for the use of an all-weather road. Americans early showed a preference for speedy travel, as is shown by the financial success of the majority of turnpike companies and the heavy tolls paid for the use of their roads.

The Capital Turnpike, from Philadelphia to Lancaster, completed in 1795 when the former city was still the nation's capital, fixed the standard for some time thereafter. Twenty-four feet wide, this pike was arched to shed water and substantially made by covering the graded surface with over a foot of rock and gravel. Small drainage lines were culverted; large streams such as the Schuylkill, the Great Brandywine, and the Conestoga were provided with bridges. (See Fig. 27.) Another great highway, in central New York, was known as the Rome-Geneva Turnpike. Opened for traffic in the year 1800, it was constantly extended into newly settled country and became a factor in the location of villages.

There was much activity in the buying of shares of newly formed turnpike companies. Typical was a letter which in 1797 forecast financial yields of 6 per cent on a new turnpike to Northampton in western Massachusetts, because it

AUTHORIZED TOLL RATES IN CONNECTICUT, ABOUT 1800

	Rate for Every 2 miles, in Cents
Four-wheeled pleasure carriage	.25
Chaise or sulky	.12½
Loaded cart or sled	.08
Empty cart or sled	.06¼
Loaded wagon	.12½
Empty wagon	.06¼
Horses, cattle, and mules (each)	.01
Pleasure sleighs, loaded	.06¼
Pleasure sleighs, empty	.03
Man and horse	.04
Mail stage	.06¼
Every other stage	.25
Single horse cart, loaded	.06¼
Single horse cart, empty	.04
Sheep and hogs	.00½

was "over a Country almost level," and travelers using it would "avoid those dreadful miles by the Swift River which have been so long and so justly a terror."

River improvements along the seaboard. The first canal-building projects in the seaboard states were devised primarily to serve local needs. It was not until the 1820's that far-seeing projects which envisioned linking up separate rivers into "systems" were actually commenced and completed. The earlier projects, now briefly to be considered, were the natural predecessors of the schemes we have come to associate with the so-called canal-building period.

Similar in purpose, though far separate in space, were the Middlesex Canal of Massachusetts, completed in 1804, and the Santee Canal in South Carolina, opened for use in July of 1800. Both were intended to add to or retain the commercial importance of the largest cities of those two states — Boston and Charleston. Each city was located near the mouth of a short river, the Charles and the Ashley-Cooper respectively, neither of which commanded a large tributary area.

27   An American landscape as illustrated in a popular magazine. The Schuylkill River near Philadelphia, from the *Columbian Magazine,* February, 1789.

In both cases a larger river entered the sea a few miles northward of the city site — the Merrimack in Massachusetts and the Santee in South Carolina. In an attempt to make each city the commercial mouth of the nearest large river, the Middlesex and Santee canals were undertaken. (See Fig. 28.)

The Middlesex Canal, about 30 miles long and 30 feet wide, struck across

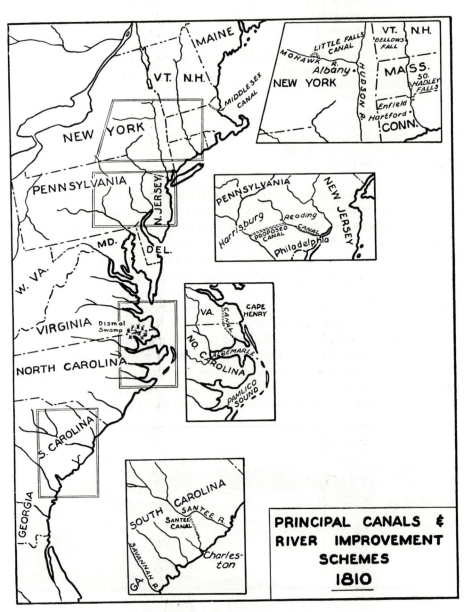

28   Principal canals and river improvement schemes, 1810

country to the site of present-day Chelmsford, making necessary the construction of 20 locks and a half-dozen aqueducts over rivers lying between. The canal permitted the floating of boats up to 75 feet in length, drawn by horses at 3 miles an hour; logs were also floated to market from the forest lands in New Hampshire. In later years other canals upstream on the Merrimack were constructed, at a reported cost of £28,000.

The Santee Canal, some ten years in the building, connected the Santee with the Cooper River, whose headwaters rise in lowlands very near the "elbow" of the Santee. About 20 miles long, the Santee Canal was capable of floating boats carrying 20 tons, mostly of cotton and lumber. Both Middlesex and Santee canals passed out of use with the coming of more efficient means of transportation, but portions of their original routes can still be traced.

Through the construction of a half-dozen canals and locks at various Connecticut River falls, including Enfield Falls, Connecticut, South Hadley and Millers Falls in Massachusetts, and Bellows Falls, Vermont, navigation had been opened by 1810 from Long Island Sound to White River, a distance of some 300 miles. This was no small undertaking, considering the period. The work, begun in 1792, was interrupted by floods at various times. Portions of these obsolescent canals can now be seen alongside the Connecticut River, where they continue to be used as millraces for manufacturing plants.

The Mohawk River was improved many years before work began on the Erie Canal. The first improvements of the Mohawk River looking toward its increased navigability were undertaken without reference to unified canal projects. The Mohawk River freighter in early days was known as the Schenectady boat, about 50 feet long and capable of carrying 10 tons of produce when the river was at high stage. Shallows and snags and seasonal changes of depth made for difficult transportation. In a mood of generosity the New York Legislature appropriated the sum of $600 for clearing the lower river and for financing surveys which would decide whether canals were necessary. Eventually the Western Inland Lock Navigation Company undertook the task of improving the river, installing two sets of canals and locks, one around Little Falls and the other across the old portage from the Mohawk to Wood Creek, the beginning of waters flowing westward to Oneida Lake. Rapidly mounting tolls taken at Little Falls encouraged financial speculation in river improvements in general, and provided good arguments to be used later in furthering the great Erie Canal. Among the earlier advocates of a canal to connect the Hudson River with the Great Lakes was Judge William Cooper of Cooperstown, who warned in 1808: "The trade of this vast country must be divided between Montreal and New York, and the half of it be thus lost to the United States unless an inland connection can be formed. . . . This project, worthy of a nation's enterprise, has been for some time meditated by individuals. Of its practicability there can be no doubt." The natural break in the Appalachian highlands represented by the Mohawk River and the low country extending westward from Oneida Lake pointed out the feasibility of the scheme.

It remained for Pennsylvania to propose the first canal-building projects to link its eastern and western rivers on a grand scale. The projectors, however, had inadequately reckoned with topographic conditions. It was planned first to canalize the lower Schuylkill River from Norristown to Philadelphia, but the trench, penetrating hard rock, was very expensive to dig and slow in construction. The proposal to connect the Schuylkill with the Susquehanna from Reading to Middletown also met with discouragement when careful surveys showed that the summit level between these two streams was more than 300 feet above them. Little was actually accomplished on the Pennsylvania canals during this period, but a decade later the "canal fever" broke out in renewed form. This time it was directed toward the building of a Pennsylvania canal which would be a rival of the Erie. The Appalachian heights westward of present-day Altoona (known to travelers today through the "horseshoe" bend of the railroad tracks) prohibited the fulfillment of so ambitious a scheme.

Similarly, the face of Nature prevented the completion of an early-day plan to connect the waters of the Potomac River with the headwaters of the Monongahela River, which at Pittsburgh joins the Allegheny in forming the Ohio. This project began in a thoroughly practical manner with the construction of canals and locks around the two sets of falls, known as Great and Little Falls, near the city of Washington. Viewing these canals as successful ventures, proponents urged that connection be established with westward-flowing rivers, but more careful surveys were to show that such a plan was altogether visionary. This canal bears in its name, Chesapeake and Ohio, an ideal rather than an accomplishment.

Proposals of the Gallatin survey. The impracticability of canal navigation across the Appalachians was recognized in the Gallatin report of 1808. The best that could be done, it said, was to provide river navigation to the limit of portages, which would represent a carry of some 50 or 75 miles.

To provide for through western travel and mail delivery, it was recommended that a national road be constructed across the mountain country to connect the growing cities of the new West — Detroit, Cincinnati, Nashville, Vincennes, St. Louis. It was felt that settlement at the time was not sufficient to attract private capital; and this being the case, the project should be subsidized by the Federal Government. The road that eventuated from this and earlier planning has become known as the National Road, or sometimes as the Cumberland Road (from its origin at Cumberland, Maryland), although this name is likely to confuse it with the Cumberland Gap route farther south, made famous by Daniel Boone and the Kentucky pioneers. The intended western end of the National Road shifted from time to time; at first it was to be Cincinnati, later Vincennes, and then St. Louis. Through this road, it was foreseen according to Jefferson, "we may accomplish a continued and advantageous line of connection from the seat of General Government to St. Louis, passing through several very interesting points of the Western Country."

Gallatin also recommended "Communications between the Atlantic Waters and Those of the St. Lawrence, and with the River St. Lawrence." Under this heading it was suggested that: (1) a canal be completed across New York State to Lake Ontario or Erie, and (2) another canal be projected from Lake Champlain to Montreal by way of the Richelieu River.

Finally, the Gallatin report envisioned a series of canals along the seacoast, cutting across the necks of many peninsulas so as to provide an inland passage for seagoing vessels from Massachusetts southward through North Carolina. Among the peninsulas thus to be severed were Cape Cod, New Jersey from the Raritan to the Delaware, Maryland from the Delaware to Chesapeake Bay, and the lowlands between Chesapeake and Albemarle Sound. At the time of the report, only the last-named project had been attempted in a narrow ditch 3 feet deep known as the Dismal Swamp Canal, used for hauling logs from that desolate wilderness. In the course of time, canals were cut across each of the peninsulas mentioned, but at considerably more than the cost of $3,500,000 estimated in 1808.

NATURAL RESOURCES POORLY KNOWN

The underground resources of the Eastern states were but little known at this time. Gone and almost forgotten were earlier rumors of precious metals somewhere beyond the settlements — rumors such as are likely to circulate in any new country. The numberless "mines" described by the writers of colonial advertising pamphlets had generally failed to materialize. The word "mines" as used in early reports, it should be added, did not indicate a worked deposit, but rather the existence of minerals, certain or conjectured.

Iron and coal of some importance. Small supplies of lead and bog-iron ore were known and used in Massachusetts, and local sand was the basis of glassworks in that state as well as in New Jersey. However, most of the metallic minerals other than iron were imported from foreign countries.

It was known, from more or less accidental discoveries in excavations for cellars and wells, that Pennsylvania was underlaid with extensive deposits of coal. The first marketing attempts met with discouragement, for it was a product unfamiliar to the people, whose equipment was designed to burn wood or charcoal. Even in 1792 the Lehigh Coal Company was in financial difficulties because of the prejudices against their product and the high cost of transporting it from the upper Schuylkill to the Philadelphia market. Further, the use of coal as ballast in incoming vessels from Britain and Virginia placed such low prices on the product that often the Pennsylvania coal was at a disadvantage — another case, it would seem, of "carrying coals to Newcastle." Iron was also produced locally in many parts of central Pennsylvania, often in conjunction with farming; that is, the owner of a farm might have a small mine or a furnace for smelting the product, or both — a dual enterprise which became more important after 1810, receiving the curious name of "iron plantation."

Forests and their resources. The forests were of outstanding importance among the natural resources during this period. Wood provided the principal fuel, either burned directly for cooking and space heating, or as charcoal, the form preferred for glassmaking and smelting ores. The drains thus made upon the forests were rivaled in the manufacture of potash, one of the chief products of export trade, and by the cutting of structural timber for new housing or the replacement of burned or antiquated buildings, as well as for the special demands of shipbuilding. Over the years, forest fires of natural or incendiary origin had reduced merchantable timber to a large but unknown extent. The total forested area of the seaboard states still exceeded that of the cleared land, but the high cost of transportation and its virtual nonexistence in areas accessible today reduced greatly the extent of the effective forests. Arbitrarily assuming that road services were confined to 20-mile strips (Fig. 29), we see that many forested sections of southern New England, the region most amply supplied with roads, were practically unavailable at this time.

Newspapers and magazines occasionally carried editorials discussing the problems raised by the diminishing forests and offering suggestions for their conservation. Such an article could be inserted in a newspaper of today without the reader's being aware of the substitution. For example, an article entitled " On the Importance of Preserving Our Forests," appearing in an issue of the *Weekly Magazine* in 1798, forecast a dark future unless conservation measures be promptly taken. The setting of fires should be regulated by law, it urged, and forest preserves established by state, county, and township. Moreover, forests have aesthetic as well as practical values, the article continued; hence they should be cared for along the rights of way and in other sightly places. Mature or old trees in the public forests should be culled to encourage the growth of younger stock, with proceeds from the sale of timber to be used for the maintenance of poorhouses. We have here one of the first known pleas for silviculture; but, as we know, it fell on deaf ears. Shortage of timber near the seaport cities was reflected in the high cost of those special timbers demanded by shipbuilders. It was said to be " not uncommon for the builder to send at this day from thirty to forty miles for timber, and the stock fast diminishing."

The average New England home in the year 1800 probably burned up 15 cords of wood, although for real comfort as many as 20 cords were often stored. Conservatively, then, 2,000,000 cords of wood, mostly oak, ash, hickory, and hard maple, were consumed in Massachusetts alone for firewood. Estimating a cord of wood to three-fifths of an acre of woodland, some 2,000 square miles of woodland or woodlot were culled in a typical year. Regrowth could scarcely have equaled the cut of cordwood. No wonder that Bostonians who were getting firewood from New Hampshire and Maine were vitally interested in the completion of the Middlesex Canal, which tapped the supposedly inexhaustible forests bordering Lake Winnepesaukee.

The conversion of hardwood logs into charcoal was an important activity of this period. Charcoal was the main source of heat in the smelting of iron before coal came into use. The practice in Pennsylvania, where a great deal of charcoal was made for use in the iron industry, was to set fire to large piles of logs covered with a layer of soil through which a vent allowed the escape of gases.

In the modern view, the burning of high-grade logs of birch, oak, maple, and beech to secure potash for fertilizer and soaps seems a wasteful process. Nevertheless, potash and the more refined product known as pearlash were made in large quantities. The reduction of the wood to ashes was simplicity itself, but

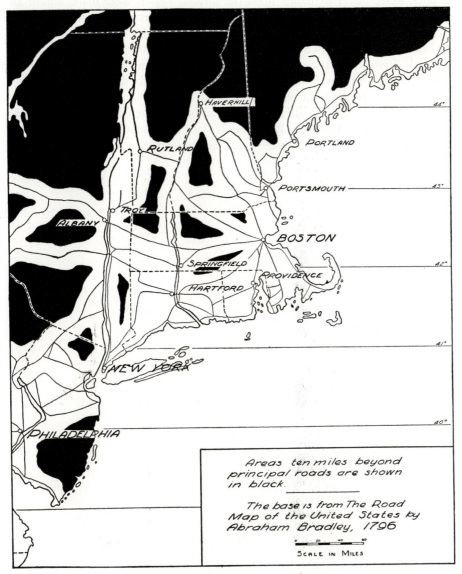

29 Accessibility in New England and adjacent areas as shown by 10-mile strips along the principal roads

different methods of leaching the ashes were devised; in fact, the first patent in this country was granted to Samuel Hopkins on July 31, 1790, for a method of leaching ashes and making pearlash. The product was sufficiently important as an export to require inspectors at some of the Northern ports, who passed upon the quality of the product.

Shipbuilding, which was largely concentrated in ports northward from Philadelphia, made heavy demands upon the forests. Vessels were made almost entirely of wood, and shipwrights, probably with good reason, demanded special types and grades of lumber. Fir was good enough for some purposes, especially for beams and braces, but deck and keel must be laid with sound oak, black birch, or beech. Resin and tar, called naval stores, came from the pine forests of the South. The life of a well-built vessel was perhaps a dozen years, for even if it did not succumb to one of many hazards, it was soon outmoded. The various fleets called for constant replacements and additions. The leading maritime position gained by the United States so soon after its formation as a country was owing in no small part to its varied and abundant forest reserves.

CHAPTER 7

The Sea: Its Industries and Commerce

IN THE year 1810 it seemed likely that the fishing industry would at last succumb to the economic ills to which it had long been subject. At best the hard-
won products of the sea — common whale oil and whalebone, spermaceti,
ambergris, fresh and salt cod, the very salt itself — made no great fortunes. Deli-
cately balanced between profit and loss, these American industries waged a re-
lentless battle on an economic front that included all countries of the North
Atlantic basin. That they did not always come out victorious is apparent from
the graph of ship tonnage registered in the fisheries from 1794 (Fig. 30), when
the data first became available. Disregarding the drop in tonnage from 1798 to
1800, possibly attributable to maritime difficulties with France, the fishing fleet
expanded encouragingly to 1807 only to collapse shortly thereafter. The graph
shows that nearly half the available tonnage was out of service at the close of
the decade, mainly because the owners of the vessels had found them unprofitable
for use.

Some authorities saw in the threatened collapse of the fishing industry a national calamity. Not only did the fisheries provide an outlet for other activities,
but the fleets were regarded as an insurance of maritime power. The fisheries as
a nursery for seamen was a favorite oratorical theme, but no one surpassed
Jefferson's seagoing version of the battle lost because of a horse improperly shod:
"The loss of seamen," he said sententiously in 1791, "would be followed by
other losses in a long train. If we have no seamen, our ships will be useless,
consequently our ship timber, iron, and hemp; our ship building will be at an
end, ship carpenters go over to other nations, our young men have no call to
the sea, our produce, carried in foreign bottoms, be saddled with war-freight and
insurance in time of war."

The fisheries, including whaling, were beset by numerous difficulties. The
marketing of fishery products had become a highly competitive business. Each
country was as determined as its neighbor to ensure maritime power through
encouragement of the fishing industry. All of them, with the possible exception
of France — Britain, Prussia, Holland, the Hanse towns — had surpluses
of fishery products. High tariff walls were erected to prevent importation
of their rivals' products. Some, in addition, paid bonuses to the fishermen, and
in this the United States followed suit. Great Britain, for example, paid bounties

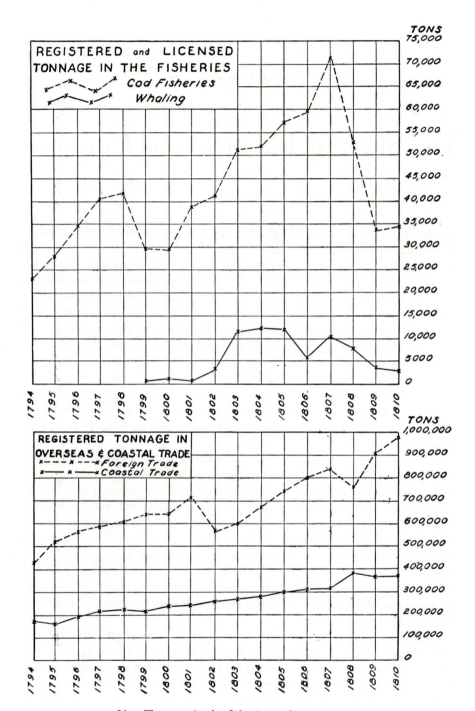

30   Tonnage in the fisheries and commerce

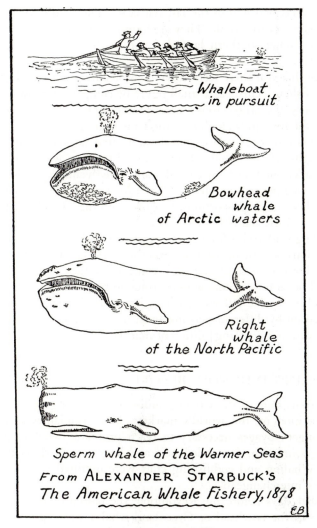

Whaleboat in pursuit

Bowhead whale of Arctic waters

Right whale of the North Pacific

Sperm whale of the Warmer Seas

From ALEXANDER STARBUCK'S
The American Whale Fishery, 1878

EB

31 Types of Whales

of from £18 to £50 on every fishing vessel complying with certain nominal requirements, and laid an import duty of £18 5s a ton on common whale oil. The higher grade spermaceti was not yet in such demand as to warrant large sales of it in Europe, tariffs being what they were.

The War of the Revolution was disastrous to many American industries. None suffered more than the fishing industry, for during the war the greater part of the fleet was destroyed or rendered unfit for further service. The work of rebuilding proceeded slowly, not reaching significant proportions until the turn of the century. In 1806 the Committee of Commerce and Manufactures took satisfaction in reporting to the Congress that the whale fishery of Nantucket

" has greatly increased within the last ten years. Their ships visit the most distant seas in search of the whale. They are found on the coast of Brazil, near Cape Horn, in the higher southern latitudes, and in the vicinity of Cape of Good Hope."

Actually in that year there were 10,685 tons of shipping licensed and employed in the whale fishery. This was a small figure by comparison with the 59,000 tons in the codfishery, the 341,000 tons employed in coastal trade, and the 808,000 tons registered in the foreign trade during the same year. The proportions devoted to these four major services varied sharply and often unpredictably from year to year, but roughly about two-thirds of the total tonnage was regularly engaged in foreign trade, one-fourth in coastal trade, one-twentieth in the codfisheries, and perhaps 1 or 2 per cent in whaling. It was not until the 1820's that the whaling industry reached major proportions, merging into the " Golden Age " with the second quarter of the century. (See Fig. 31.)

The whaling and cod-fishing fleets expanded and shrank in somewhat the same proportions because of conditions on the world's markets. Beyond this, and the fact that both were conducted in oceanic areas, they had little in common. Students and not a few writers who continue to fuse the two industries in their minds should memorize Jefferson's classic lines that the cod and whale fisheries were " carried on by different persons, from different ports, in different vessels, in different seas, and seek[ing] different markets."

THE WHALING INDUSTRY BEFORE ITS GOLDEN AGE

The precarious state of the whaling industry was owing only in part to economic competition on the world's markets. More fundamental were the increasingly longer voyages necessary to reach profitable whaling grounds; the longer voyages, in turn, demanded new and larger investments in vessels and equipment. Whaling and cod-fishing craft were outfitted very differently and thus were not interchangeable.

In the lusher days before the Revolution, the baleen or right whale (sometimes known as the bowhead or Greenland whale) was captured in relatively near-by waters of the North Atlantic, particularly along the edges of the Gulf Stream, where the huge animal found a variety of food. Though originally a closely guarded secret of the whaling industry, this eventually became well known, and through Benjamin Franklin's efforts in obtaining information from a Nantucket whaleman, a chart of that stream was published in a popular magazine (Fig. 32). The position of the Gulf Stream as shown thereon agrees with modern charts in that part of the western Atlantic where whaling had been carried on longest. East of the Newfoundland banks, whalemen and mariners " lost " the stream in a confused flow of surface water and countercurrents.

Whalers explore the South Pacific.   The depopulation of the more accessible whaling grounds led to longer cruises in vessels of larger capacity than had been necessary earlier. Voyages into the South Atlantic off Brazil were in due time

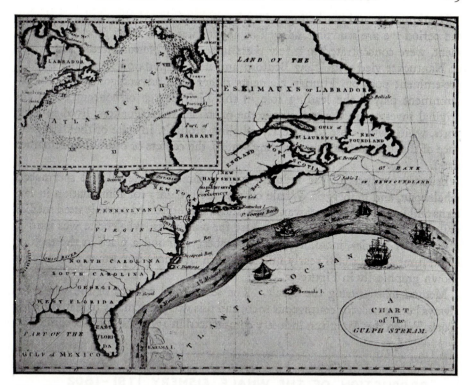

32   The Gulf Stream, from *The Complete Works of the Late Dr. Franklin,* Vol. 3,
     1806. The inset represents the presumed migration of herring.

followed by the rounding of Cape Horn and searches along the western coast
of South America. There the whalemen came upon the sperm whale, of a larger
species than the baleen. Two whaling fleets became recognized, the northern
and the southern, with the former's vessels averaging about 150 tons. Compared
with the monster vessels of today, such craft seem pitiably small for carrying out
so difficult an assignment.

The veil of professional secrecy was so well maintained that it is difficult to
learn all we would like to know about whaling operations in the pre-Golden
Age era. Perhaps one southern voyage, described in a letter written in 1792, was
typical of many: Leaving Nantucket in September, the whaler rounded Cape
Horn and sighted the first large school of whales off the desert coast of Chile.
After a voyage of fifteen months, the vessel returned with a cargo worth 6,000
pounds sterling, a figure possibly in exaggeration of the actual take. The captain
of this whaler reported that the weather of the desert coast of Chile offered
less difficulty in whaling operations than did the cold, stormy weather off Labrador and Greenland. It was said that " the ignorance of the Spaniards was such
that they could not understand what the North Americans came there to slay
whales for. Upon being made to understand that it was to make candles of
Spermaceti, they were very eager to get a few to show to their governor."

Headquarters and marketing. Headquarters of the whaling industry during the period we are studying, as well as at the later time of its greatest development, were concentrated in a few ports in southern Massachusetts. The island of Nantucket vied with New Bedford and near-by ports on Buzzards Bay for pre-eminent position. Human elements rather than advantages of natural environment played the leading role in this high degree of concentration; the original investors in the industry, some of whom were Quakers, lived in these ports, which were close to the early whaling grounds. In spite of the disappearance of the animal from surrounding waters, the centers of operations remained fixed.

Primary products of the industry were common whale oil and spermaceti, whalebone, and ambergris. Whale oil was used mainly for illumination in lanterns and lamps; spermaceti wax was made into candles and possibly used medicinally, as in more recent times, as a base for ointments; whalebone was used in a variety of articles, including corsets; ambergris found a place in the making of perfumes. The sharp yearly fluctuations in the more important products are shown graphically in Figure 33.

Method of capturing the whale. The search and capture of the whale has always been a task for courageous men, and this was particularly true in the early 1800's. When the American industry commenced in 1715, the animals came close

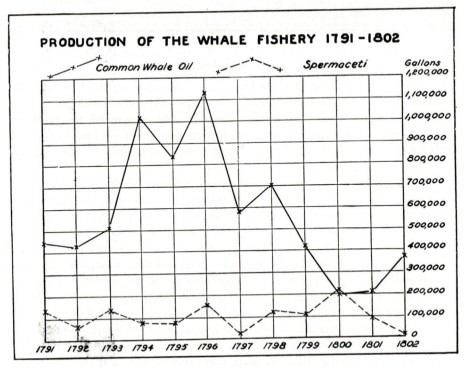

33   Production of the whale fishery, 1791–1802

enough to shore to permit approach to them in small boats; indeed, some whales were caught in shallow water into which they had unwisely swum at high tide. As the whale's habitat receded from the coast, larger vessels equipped for sustained voyages were necessary. Pursuit boats were carried on deck, each manned by a designated crew of three or four men. Upon the sighting of the whale one of the small boats was dispatched on its perilous mission, with the harpooner in the prow. A tempestuous ride was in store for the crew when the javelin, with rope attached, found its mark in the huge animal.

With the whale finally brought alongside the mother ship, there followed the difficult and unpleasant steps of cutting the carcass and rendering the products, especially the oil, which was then stored in barrels awaiting the end of the cruise. Because the men shared in the profits of the voyage there was an inducement to capture the maximum number of whales and also, upon returning to the home port, to keep silent as to the precise locations where they had met with their greatest successes; hence the secrecy mentioned above.

THE COD–FISHING INDUSTRY

Unlike whaling, the cod-fishing industry was conducted from a large number of New England ports, some of which were also busy with coastwise and foreign commerce. Among the leading cod-fishing centers were the Massachusetts ports of Gloucester and Marblehead, as well as Newburyport, Plymouth, Boston, and Provincetown; Waldoboro, Wiscasset, and Portland in Maine; Newport, Rhode Island, and New London, Connecticut. An occasional vessel was registered from Sag Harbor, New York, but rarely from any farther south. Cod-fishing was distinctly a Northern coast industry.

The nature of the fishing banks. Knowledge of the fishing banks was built up gradually from the experiences of men engaged in the industry. Of greatest concern were the locations and limits of the principal fishing grounds, as well as the depths of water in which fishing was most successful. This practical knowledge was supplemented by the more scientific information secured by such early-day hydrographers as Captain James Cook, Chabert, and Count de Fleurieu. The scientists were, of course, interested in the possible origins of the submarine platforms that were, in the popular language, the fishing banks.

It was found that the east coast of Newfoundland plunged beneath the sea to form a trough of deep water 60 miles wide, but beyond "The Ditch" (as this deep was suitably known), ocean depths became shallower. Within a vast triangular area of some 40,000 square miles, depths ranged from 50 to 100 fathoms, the depths preferred for fishing. This area became known as the Great Bank because it overshadowed in size all other submerged platforms in its vicinity. To the east of it was a small counterpart known as Outer or False Bank, in which Chabert had made soundings in 1750. Three banks — Jaquet, Whale, and Green — were separated from Great Bank by narrow troughs; they were essentially outliers, to the west of which were separate platforms named Porpoise, Banquereau, and Middle; and Sable Island. It may be presumed that the fishermen annually sought their favorite fishing areas within the limits of these various banks — the deep-sea equivalent of the " fishing holes " which are the subjects of so many campfire discussions by lake fishermen. (See Fig. 32, page 115.)

The original theory that these shallows in the otherwise deep sea were the tops of submerged mountains was losing favor by the early 1800's. More frequently it was being suggested that they were deposits of material washed from Newfoundland or the continent itself. Many believed that the Gulf Stream, and to a lesser degree other ocean currents, transported the waste material of the land areas and, with lessening current, deposited it in the North Atlantic. Observing that the Gulf Stream's course paralleled the Atlantic coast line to near Newfoundland and then turned southward (the contemporary, though mistaken, assumption), a French geographer announced that " the banks of Newfoundland merely constitute a bar at the mouth of the vast shoreless river." The modern theory which attributes much of the observed phenomena to deposits of glacial drift derived from the continent was not advanced until the latter part of the nineteenth century.

The contrasting temperatures of the ocean currents were assumed to play a part in the remarkable concentration of life forms on which the hungry cod depended, but to what extent was not known. Fishermen described the floors of the banks as being covered with vast quantities of shellfish of various kinds, but the handy collective word " plankton " had not yet been invented for them. There was a natural interest in the swarms of the small fish whose movements apparently regulated the presence of cod. Dependence of life forms one upon the other was not confined to the sea itself, but included the flocks of great auk and garefowl (at that time called penguins) which frequently hovered over those areas where surface-swimming fish could be snatched.

Fishing methods on the banks.   The operations of the banks fisheries were not materially different from those of the earlier Colonial period. Reliable accounts indicate that the banks were the common meeting place of 300 or 400 fishing vessels and a large flotilla of smaller craft, manned by seamen from all of the important countries, as in earlier days; but fishermen from Britain, especially Jersey and Guernsey, predominated. In official references Newfoundland was likened to a " great English ship, moored near the Banks during the fishing season for the convenience of English fishermen." This advantage came to Britain through the Treaty of Utrecht (1713). By its terms, subjects of France were given the right to dry fish on the shores of the great island from Cape Bonavista northward and on the west coast southward to Point Rich, so long as permanent structures were not erected. These coasts were the least accessible to the principal fishing grounds, a handicap partially offset by France's retention of the small islands of St. Pierre and Great and Little Miquelon.

Fishing was done by means of hand lines baited with pieces of cod or capelin, a small fish found near shore. A fisherman could handle one or more of these lines. After the fish were beheaded and partly cleaned, they were generally salted down in the hold. Relatively few New England fishermen dried their catches near the banks. They preferred either to make port and then complete the curing process, or to go directly to Mediterranean or African markets with the green cod. Visitors to the New England fishing towns report seeing — perhaps after first smelling — large areas whitened with the drying cod.

Offshore and inshore fishing. Scarcely less important were the various fishing operations conducted near enough to shore to require only short voyages from home ports. They were recommended particularly because such fishing could be carried on during the winter, while the banks fisheries were summertime operations only. It was said, too, that winter-caught fish were superior in flesh to those taken at other seasons.

Not far from Cape Cod and the coast of Maine were fishing grounds famous for their cod and haddock, caught with hook and line, and also pollock, mackerel, and herring, taken in seines. Seine or net fishing was frequently practiced in river fishing for salmon and shad, which in the spring swarmed up from the bays to spawn in fresh water. The salmon take in the Maine rivers was very large in these earlier days, and so many sturgeon were caught in the Hudson River that it could be bought very cheaply, sometimes under its nickname of " Albany beef." Oysters, crabs, sea bass, and a half-dozen other varieties of sea food were sought during the appropriate seasons, and many river fish were taken in summer by farmers and townspeople who salted them down for family use during the winter.

The manufacture of salt. Salt imported from Europe was a large element in the cost of preparing dried cod for market. One of the first legislative acts of Massachusetts provided for the repayment of import duties on salt to those who used it principally in the codfisheries. This procedure, known as a " drawback," was followed in many other industries which imported goods from abroad, and also, as we shall presently learn, in the re-export trade to the West Indies. Although the extraction of salt from sea water was a relatively simple process and was one of the first home industries, little was so derived commercially until the beginning of the nineteenth century.

The early method, as developed on Cape Cod, was to pump sea water into large, shallow tanks exposed to the sun, tanks which could be covered when rain threatened. Fires underneath the vats hastened the natural evaporation process. Shortly after this coastal development, additional supplies of salt were discovered in central New York near the present city of Syracuse, and this soon became the leading center of the salt industry. Before the year 1810 some 60,000 bushels of salt were annually produced from springs in that locality. It was some time, however, before the seaboard states were independent of other countries for this important and then costly product.

COMMERCE OF THE UNITED STATES

The remarkable growth of the seaborne commerce of the United States from the time of the origin of the nation to the difficulties which preceded the War of 1812 has been the subject of frequent comment.

Ship tonnage engaged in the foreign trade doubled in twenty years, climbing steadily, except for slight interruptions in 1801 and 1807, to nearly 1,000,000 tons in 1810. (See Fig. 30, page 112.) This was a tremendous figure for those days, when the largest vessels, from 200 to 300 tons capacity, appear Lilliputian in comparison with modern tonnage. During a few days of submarine warfare in 1944, a comparable tonnage was sunk in the North Atlantic trade lane alone. Tonnages employed in the coastwise trade — which theoretically was domestic commerce between the states, but often extended to Canada and Florida as well — also expanded during this period, but at a slower rate. Less affected by world-wide conditions than was overseas trade, and protected from the enemy seizures which marked the years before the War of 1812, coastwise tonnage grew slowly but steadily to about 400,000 tons in 1810. The total commercial tonnage in that year was nearly 14,000,000 tons. So far as individual vessels were concerned, overseas and coastwise trade were not mutually exclusive. That is, between major cruises vessels normally carrying on overseas trade were sometimes diverted to runs along the coast. It should also be observed that commerce was then, as now, a two-way affair. American vessels did not take care of all of this country's trade. It is estimated that some 4,000 vessels of foreign countries called at Atlantic coast ports in the year 1800.

Looked at from this distance in time, the commerce of the country during this period assumes a simplicity which actually it did not possess. Commerce was then a very complex business, involving as it did: (1) direct trade with western Europe and the Orient; (2) the " three-cornered " trade, of which the other two apexes of the assumed "triangle" were Europe-Africa and the West Indies; (3a) direct trade with the West Indies, and (3b) the so-called re-export trade with the same islands, which did not imply the sale of domestic products; and (4) coastwise trade, of which the most important phase was interstate commerce by sea, with extralegal extensions northward into Maritime Canada and southward into Florida and neighboring islands. Each of these aspects of commerce will be briefly investigated.

Direct trade with Europe. The declaration of political independence of the United States did not significantly alter the commercial relationships between England and this country. With the coming of peace following the Revolution, the North Atlantic trade lane resumed its earlier significance. The location of this trading route connecting Britain and continental Europe with American ports bore a more definite relation to the Gulf Stream than it does today. Sailing vessels then used in overseas commerce — mainly brigs and ships — were more dependent on prevailing winds and ocean-current flow than is the modern steamer. Due account was therefore taken of the rate of flow of the Gulf Stream.

It was computed that vessels attempting to stem the current on a westward voyage from Liverpool to New York were held back as much as 70 miles a day because of the current. The recommended practice, then, was to cross the stream as nearly at a right angle as conditions permitted and thereafter to keep between the current and the land in the western part of the ocean.

An alternative route, followed especially in the triangular trade, was to avoid the Gulf Stream by a westward crossing of the Atlantic in lower latitudes. Furthermore, the northeast trades were favorable to passages in that direction. Much remained to be known about the circulation of prevailing winds and currents, but experienced seamen were reasonably familiar with the clockwise circulation of both winds and currents about the dreaded Sargasso Sea. The northeast trades and the variable westerlies were well-known winds at this time. Crossing the Atlantic meant a voyage of approximately a month. The voyage of the schooner *Juno,* for example, from New Haven to Spain, consumed twenty-six days.

The greater part of our European trade was with England. Items imported from England included a variety of manufactured goods to be exchanged for the agricultural products and raw materials of this country — and for money, to the continued dismay of the country's leaders, who did not like to see money leaving this country. The cargo the *President Adams* of Boston unloaded on the wharves of Liverpool in June, 1809, is a good example of American exports. It included some 200 tons of cotton, potash and pearlash, flour, and tobacco. Cargo taken in return included window glass, lead, dry goods, and liquors. Some of this return cargo was destined eventually for West Indian markets, not for direct sale in the United States. The transaction of the *President Adams* is also historically significant, since it marked the reopening of trade with England following the lifting of the Non-Intercourse Act passed two years before. (See Fig. 34.)

Many other European ports also shared in our transatlantic commerce, notably Leghorn, Lisbon, Marseille, Copenhagen, and Hamburg. The vessels that cleared the customhouse at Charleston, South Carolina, in 1801 show that this famous Southern port was trading with half the world.

ORIGIN OF VESSELS ARRIVING AT CHARLESTON, S.C., IN 1801

Other ports of the United States	586
Great Britain	98
South America	36
Germany	35
Mediterranean countries	22
Spain	16
France	15
East Florida	23
Madeira Islands	12
Dutch Netherlands	11
Others: Russia, Prussia, Denmark, Portugal	5
TOTAL	859

New trade connections with the Orient. If Charleston's trade was semi-global, that of some Northern ports assumed truly global proportions. In addi-

34   The Port of Boston. From Charles W. Janson, *The Stranger in America,* London, 1807.

tion to the long-standing commerce with Europe and the African west coast, the Northern ports also traded with the Far East — India, the Spice Islands, China, and Japan. This Oriental trade is identified largely with Salem and Beverly, Massachusetts, now of little significance in this respect, and also with Boston, Providence, New York, Philadelphia, and Baltimore.

Within a dozen years after the first American vessels had ventured to the Orient, practical navigators were prepared to lay out " approved courses " for the young men to whose hands this trade was largely entrusted. Three courses were given varying degrees of approval.

1. Because it was known to be a dangerous passage, the route southward around Cape Horn, up the South American west coast and across the comparatively unknown Pacific, was least approved. A variation of this route included the Pacific coast of North America, where trade in sea-otter skins offered some attractions. As many as 29 American vessels traded on the northwest coast (present-day Oregon and Washington) in 1792. At least one company, says Howard Corning, used this route around Cape Horn in its trade with Canton. Sealskins were obtained at a small island of the Juan Fernandez group off the coast of Chile, where a few men were landed to capture the seals and to prepare the skins for market. Customarily, the detachment of men was left on this islet to be picked up with their peltry on the next year's voyage.

2. More acceptable was the route southward from Atlantic ports to the West Indies and coastal Brazil to the latitude of Montevideo, which, as a glance at a map will show, lies in the position of Cape of Good Hope. Thence, an eastward passage across the Atlantic in the prevailing westerlies of the Southern Hemi-

sphere brought the vessel into the Indian Ocean, where stops were commonly made at Mauritius (then called Isle de France) in preparation for the journey to an Oriental destination.

3. A third recommended route, proposed by Nathaniel Bowditch, the leading navigator of his time if not of all time (his book on the subject is still required reading for naval trainees), ran southeast across the Atlantic to the Ivory Coast of Africa, followed by a coastal voyage to Cape of Good Hope and then into the Indian Ocean.

Eastward from Mauritius and back to that small but important island, the master of a vessel was pretty much on his own. The timing of a voyage to India appears to have been adjusted to the monsoon winds; however, the probability of securing seasonal cargoes of pepper in the Spice Islands may have played an equally important role in determining the time of the voyage. Sailing under orders from Salem or Beverly to obtain cargoes at Calcutta or Java, the master of a ship might use his judgment as to changes of destination. Reports picked up on the way as to market conditions or changes of price, even " hunches " on the part of the commander, often abrogated original sailing orders.

A round-trip voyage to the Orient, even over one of the most approved courses, required several months. A few known examples of voyages from Salem, believed to be typical, are as follows: The *Union* made the round trip to Canton between March 23, 1802, and February 1, 1803; the *Astrea* was 129 days on her outward voyage to Manila and 153 days on her return: the *Putnam*, leaving Salem late in November, 1802, reached Sumatra at the end of the next April. Stopovers at ports partly accounted for the length of round-trip voyages. The *America*, for example, lay over for two months and three days in Calcutta Harbor for outfitting, repairing, and the buying and loading of return cargo.

We cannot be positive about the character of the trade with the Orient, because reliable records are extremely limited. The commodities brought to and from China, for example, were as varied as human ingenuity could devise. American shipowners guessed what the Chinese would take in exchange for their own goods, or acted on advice furnished by agents stationed at Canton, the leading foreign port of that country. The Canton trade was already highly competitive, with vessels and merchants from all the maritime countries of Europe on hand.

American trading ships at Canton necessarily submitted to local regulations and customs. Incoming vessels first stopped at Macao, a Portuguese settlement on the island of that name in the mouth of the Canton River. If inspectors found conditions satisfactory, a Chinese pilot brought the vessel to Whampoa, a dozen miles below the city, where all foreign trading ships anchored. Lighterage service was available to Canton itself, where trading was carried on by means of barter. It is because of this arrangement that extant logbooks of Cantonese traders refer constantly to Whampoa rather than to Canton as the commercial center.

Commodities taken on board at Whampoa included teas, chinaware, sugar, cassia, various types of cloth — especially nankeens and other cotton goods — art objects, and ginseng. The *Union*, for example, bought 139 bales of nankeens in her 1802 voyage. It is reported that ginseng, which enjoyed a reputation as a panacea for various ailments, was an especially valuable commodity. Ginseng of Tibetan origin was priced at $10,000 a pecul (133⅓ pounds). The *Empress of China,* out of New York in 1794, is accredited as the first American vessel to trade at Whampoa. Twenty-eight vessels from this country stopped there in the year 1805 — 12 from Philadelphia, 8 from Boston, 5 from New York, and 1 each from Salem, Providence, and New London.

Prominent among ports of call in the Orient trade were Aden in Arabia, Calcutta in India, various ports on Java, Sumatra, the Celebes (Spice Islands), and Manila in the Philippines. Occasional stops were also made at Yokahama. The pepper business was very important. The *Putnam* of Beverly in its 1803 voyage secured a cargo of pepper at Meulaboh and other north-coast ports of Sumatra, arriving there in April when the kernels were in their prime. In the year 1803, Sumatra alone exported 54,600 peculs of pepper, or roughly 7,000,000 pounds. Some vessels bound for the pepper market of Java stopped on the way for other products in India and Arabia. For example, the *America* of Salem secured supplies of gum arabic, senna, and goatskins at Aden on her way to the Spice Islands.

Some vessels traded at Japanese ports, long antedating the much-publicized opening of trade with the Japanese Empire. The records of the ship *Franklin* of Boston show that she went to Japan in 1798, receiving soybeans, dried apricots, rice, cinnamon, umbrellas, and fans as part of the return cargo.

Mentioned above as commodities in the return cargoes from the Orient are those commonly referred to in ships' logs still available — bulky commodities, usually perishable or consumable. In addition were a thousand and one articles of decorative or artistic character — carvings in ivory, inlays of rare woods, jewelry, and oddments of various sorts, picked up by crewmen on shore leave as souvenirs from a strange land. The display cases in the Marine Museum and Essex Institute of Salem, Massachusetts, are the best available evidence of the great trade which marked the first contacts of Americans with Oriental peoples.

The West Indian trade. Direct trade with the West Indies was a natural result of the climatic and cultural differences between the islands and the seaboard states, and of the relatively short and safe trade routes which connected them. A voyage down-coast from New York, even to the more remote islands, was a matter of a month's time; round trips might be made in fifty days, allowing for loading time at the port of destination. Never far from the mainland and often in the lee of islands, southward-bound vessels were aided by favoring trade winds south of Florida. Vessels not rugged or large enough for an Oriental voyage could be economically used on West Indian runs. Diversion from coastwise trade to the West Indian run was a frequent practice.

Political conditions, however, intervened to prevent a full realization of the natural advantages for commerce with the West Indies. The United States owned none of the islands. Simmering international rivalries between Great Britain and France frequently approached the boiling point in seizures or threats of such action, causing many of our ships to proceed in convoy. An apparently typical case was that of the *Commerce,* New London, which traded at Martinique in February and March 1799, leaving the French island on March 22 with about 50 other vessels, including the armed ship *George Washington* and the brig *Pinckney.* Trade with the French and Dutch islands was less subject to restrictions, hence most commercial contacts were maintained with Dutch-owned Curaçao and the French islands of Martinique, Guadeloupe, Saint-Barthélemy, and Hispaniola.

Direct West Indian trade may be illustrated by the movements of two vessels for which good records are available, the brig *Retrieve* of Newburyport, and the schooner *Hannah* of Boston. The *Retrieve* cleared Newburyport in May, 1796, with lumber, shingles, rum, fish, meats, and candles. A direct voyage brought her to Saint-Barthélemy in the Leewards on June 17. Here some of the candles were disposed of, whereupon she set sail for St. Christopher (St. Kitts), a British island. Sugar was taken on board there. The next stop was at Jacmel, on the south coast of Santo Domingo (Haiti), on July 10. Early in August, the *Retrieve* started her homeward voyage, touching first at Cayes on Santo Domingo, and disposing of some of the cargo at Charleston, South Carolina. " So ends " (to borrow an everyday logbook phrase) the record of this voyage.

The schooner *Hannah* cleared Boston Harbor on December 15, 1802, arriving at Martinique on January 10 with lumber, staves, shingles, cheese and butter, barreled pork and beef, and salt fish. Some of the cargo was disposed of at Martinique and some later at the island of St. Croix, where special market needs enforced a side trip to Savannah, Georgia. The schooner arrived at Savannah on February 16, loading more lumber and barrel staves, as well as rice, ham, and tobacco. The return voyage to St. Croix was made in twenty-seven days. The lumber and rice and possibly other stores were exchanged for sugar, molasses, and money. On May 27 the schooner took leave of St. Croix and on June 16 stood in at Boston, from which port she had been absent for 143 days.

Re-export trade also added to the commercial activities of the Atlantic coastal ports. The so-called West Indian re-export commerce was a partially successful means whereby countries of continental Europe maintained trade relations with their island possessions during this period of intense maritime rivalries. France was particularly concerned, because its merchant marine was at low ebb and there was always the danger of British seizures of vessels engaged in such trade. American shipowners were ready to sell cargo space to the French, and merchants in the seaboard ports were eager for the profits to be made from re-export trade, which was carried on in the following manner: Merchants in the seaboard ports, such as Philadelphia, would import goods from France and then advertise them for re-export to a French colony — to Martinique, for example. Typical of these advertisements is one appearing in a Philadelphia trade paper which announced the arrival from Bordeaux of dry goods, sweet oil, aniseed oil, and brandied fruit, " put up for the West Indies market." When the goods were re-exported, the merchant was entitled to a refund of the import duties he had originally paid. Repackaged or relabeled in Philadelphia, the goods were dispatched to their destination in an American-owned vessel. If they were seized on the way, it could be claimed that the cargo was of American origin. The procedure also worked in the reverse direction: West Indian produce destined for Europe was landed in American ports only to continue on its way in Europe-bound vessels.

The West Indies were linked commercially with Africa by the long-standing triangular trade, which continued, although on a reduced scale. One leg of the triangle connected West Africa with the Caribbean islands. In earlier days before the Revolution, slaves were purchased or otherwise secured in Africa, to which goods of various sorts were brought on the outward voyage. The slaves were sold on the markets of the West Indies or in the American colonies. West Indian products also came northward on the slave ships, many of which were registered in New England ports. The enactment of state laws prohibiting the traffic in human cargo greatly reduced triangular trade connections with the Old World.

Domestic coastwise trade of the United States. After these excursions far asea and the complexities surrounding the re-export trade, it may be somewhat of a relief to consider the relatively simple coastwise commerce. Although the colonies had exchanged products by sea, the growth of this form of communication began on a large scale with the formation of the United States. With the increasing economic differentiation of the various states and the growth in population, there was more and more opportunity in this branch of commerce. Climatic contrasts between the Northern and Southern states were sufficient to bring about the differences in surpluses and deficiencies of products which form the basis of trade. The development of manufacturing in the Northern cities was a particularly important factor in the growth of this commerce, cotton being one of the main raw materials demanded by the growing factories of New England. Freight haulage by land for any considerable distance was next to impossible, the roads being what they were. Rivers were of little service in this capacity, for their directions were roughly at right angles to the north-south trade.

No country in the world in 1810 could boast of so many natural harbors and man-made ports as the United States. " The vast extent of seacoast," said the geographer Morse, " the number of excellent harbors and sea-port towns, the numerous creeks and immense bays, which indent the coast; and the rivers, lakes, and canals which peninsulate the whole country; added to its agricultural advantages and improvements, give this part of the world superior advantages for trade."

Because of the shallow drafts of the carriers then in use, a great many harbors now of little commercial importance were linked to coastal services. From the standpoint of coastal commerce, the harbor of Machias, Maine, was not inferior to New York Harbor, although the latter had much more trade because of a heavily populated hinterland. Many of the coastal vessels in use were registered at less than 20 tons each, and the average was not greatly in excess of 100 tons.

The busiest section of the coast line was that between Boston and New York. Regular services were maintained on a weekly or biweekly basis between neighboring ports, such as Boston, New Haven, New London, Providence, and New Bedford. Scarcely less important was the trade of Chesapeake Bay, with numerous craft connecting Maryland's east and west shores, and Delaware with Maryland and Virginia. The people of Chesapeake Bay, it has frequently been said, lived amphibiously.

Statistical records of arrivals of coastwise vessels at specific harbors are limited, and probably not so complete as similar records relating to the foreign trade. It is known, however, that 800 coasters arrived at Philadelphia in 1797, and 1,600 at Boston in the year 1800. Of the 1,600 vessels just mentioned, about one-third came from other New England ports — Newburyport, Salem, Marblehead, Ipswich, Plymouth, Provincetown, New London, Portsmouth, Bath, Portland.

The rate of travel by sea was comparable to that on land between the same points. In general, there was less certainty in traveling by sea, for sailing times could not be definitely forecast and events on the way were unpredictable. Actual records of vessels show that two took fourteen days each to go from New York to Philadelphia in 1800, and one somehow consumed a whole month on a trip from Boston to Philadelphia. These were not typical cases, however. The usual sailing time from Boston to Philadelphia was five or six days, to Charleston, South Carolina, ten or twelve — about the same rate as overland. Coasting vessels sometimes carried passengers from one port to another, but their main business was hauling freight.

Coasters engaged in local trade carried the products of farm and forest to the cities and returned with part cargoes of manufactured goods or with more bulky produce which was in transit from some distant point. Thus much of the trade between the many ports on Long Island Sound was in perishable products — butter and cheese, meats, apples, potatoes, in addition to cider and hay. Tanbark, in transit from inland and Southern localities, was redistributed from the larger ports to tanyards in the smaller towns. Lumber, firewood, and livestock were characteristic items in the local trade of the Northern ports.

More significant were the commodities transported over longer distances. Generally speaking, southbound cargoes were more varied than those going in the opposite direction. Southward from New England and New York went manufactured goods — shoes, hats, vehicles, ironware, saddlery, dry goods, books, liquors. Flour was a leading export from the Chesapeake Bay ports, destined for points both north and south as well as overseas. Fish in various forms of preservation went in large quantities to Southern plantations; indeed, some of the fish from the North were even delivered alive in Charleston. This remarkable feat was accomplished by admitting sufficient water into the hold of the vessel, a " dogger," to keep the fish alive during their ten- or twelve-day voyage.

One of the more interesting products in the southbound trade was ice, cut in fresh-water ponds in the Boston region. The originator of this trade, Frederic Tudor, wrote that he commenced the transporting of ice with " a shipment of a single cargo of a hundred and thirty tons, in a brig belonging to myself, to the Island of Martinique." His contemporaries at first considered this " a mad project " and it " elicited the derision of the whole town," but it paid handsomely. Warehouses for ice were established in many Southern ports, including Charleston and New Orleans, whose warm winters prohibited local supplies.

Northbound coasting vessels carried domestic produce from the plantations or Southern forests, and also West Indian cargoes in transit to Northern ports for transshipment abroad. Tar, pitch, turpentine, rice, and cotton were domestically produced; items in transit included muscovado (unrefined) sugar, coffee, chocolate, and salt. Out of the port of Boston, an important transshipment port, went an amazing assortment of commodities brought there by coasters from the South. In the early 1800's, Boston regularly exported $1,000,000 worth of naval stores, rice, and cotton, produced far to the south.

The United States also conducted trade with Maritime Canada and Florida, British and Spanish possessions respectively. Actually this was foreign trade, but it is to be suspected that much was carried on extra-legally. Although few statistical records are available, the trade with Nova Scotia and New Brunswick was probably of major proportions.

Poverty-stricken Florida had no great trade with any part of the world, but it is of interest to note that much of what it had was with the United States. In the year 1800, for example, 20 vessels sailed from St. Augustine to the following destinations: 7 to Havana; 5 to Charleston; 3 to New York; 4 to Georgia — Savannah and St. Marys; 1 to other parts of Florida.

A committee of Barcelona merchants had earlier reported to the officials their view that " The region around St. Augustine is very poor, with a small population, and consequently with little commerce, and we have been told that Bostonians, flying the Spanish flag, are supplying the natives with flour, salt meat, and some common dry goods and that all the return or marketable products of that country consists of a small supply of peltry." This was one side of the picture of Florida trade and probably very nearly the correct one; the other side was supplied by Vincente de Céspedes, Governor of Florida in 1787, who understandably wished to make out a good case for his colony. He listed the Florida products " immediately available " as including timber, myrtle wax, beeswax, honey, herbs and medicinal plants, oranges, salt, fish, vegetables, and, above all, inexhaustible sources of pitch, tar, resin, and spirits of turpentine. The exports listed on January 15, 1789, were as follows:

FLORIDA EXPORTS LISTED IN 1789

Product	Pesos' Worth
Indigo	325,000
* Surplus tobacco	100,000
Peltry	115,000
Lumber	85,000
Rice	20,000
Salt meat	10,000
Pitch	5,000
TOTAL	660,000

* Produced in excess of the amount purchased by the King.

Comparison of the trade of Atlantic ports. A question that naturally arises is, What were the leading ports from 1800 to 1810? The answer is difficult, because official data are given by states rather than by ports. On the basis of total value of exports in foreign trade in 1810, the leading states, all with $1,000,000 or more of export value, ranked as follows:

RANK IN EXPORT VALUE, 1810

1. New York
2. Massachusetts
3. Pennsylvania
4. Maryland
5. South Carolina
6. Virginia
7. Georgia

On the basis of customs payments recorded in 1802, a not wholly satisfactory method of comparison, the leading ports in that year were:

RANK AS PORTS, 1802

1. New York
2. Philadelphia
3. Boston
4. Baltimore
5. Charleston
6. Norfolk
7. Savannah

It will be noted that the ranking of the leading ports agrees with the ranking of states, except for the interchanged position of Boston and Philadelphia. The combined commerce of the many ports of Massachusetts surpassed that of the single great port of Pennsylvania.

CHAPTER 8

Regional Studies: The South

COMMENT on the differences between the North and the South occupies many pages of the geographies published from the 1790's on. Said one:

The northern and southern states differ widely in their customs, climate, produce, and in the general face of the country. The fisheries and commerce are the sinews of the north, tobacco, rice, and indigo of the south; the northern states are commodiously situated for trade and manufactures, the southern to furnish provisions and raw materials.

At the turn of the nineteenth century the cultural differences between the two great groups of Eastern states were more sharply defined than at any previous time. Continuing at an advanced pace the trends of the Colonial period, plantation economy had invaded vast regions of the Piedmont or Upper Country from Maryland southward to Georgia. While expansion to the westward did result in a slight withdrawal from the impoverished soils of the tidewater country, this partial depopulation did not reduce the importance of plantation economy. At the same time that tobacco plantations pushed into the stronger soils of the Virginia Piedmont, cotton was asserting its dominance in the corresponding portions of the deeper South. Upland cotton, not yet " king " in the South Carolina Piedmont, was well on the way to its coronation, with indigo and rice surviving under increasing difficulties, the latter on reclaimed lands which paralleled the rivers and threaded the pine barrens of the low country. The people who formed the tide of western settlement in the South were in part drawn from the older-settled tidewater country whose rural districts thus became locally depopulated. Others came down from the North, notably from Pennsylvania, bringing with them the practices of that region. Hence islands of free-labor farms, such as those of the Germans and the Scotch-Irish in North Carolina, occurred within the vast expanse of the plantation country. Even east of the Appalachians the South was far from being exclusively a slave-plantation country.

Not only were there more plantations in the early 1800's than before, but there is some evidence to suggest that the average size of the tidewater plantation was greater by this time. The planters who had withstood the impacts of change in crop staples, and in some instances declining market prices, often acquired the abandoned lands of their less-successful neighbors. " The larger estates grew larger," says Professor Avery O. Craven, speaking particularly of Virginia, " and the great planter assumed an even more dominating position in agricultural production." This assertion could, however, be accepted with more complete confidence if more data were available on the actual property limits of a wide sampling of plantations.

It is to be feared that popular concepts of the Southern landed estate have been derived largely from a few examples romanticized in novels or filmed for the screen. Estates owned by famous persons were often not representative of the average plantation. For example, George Washington's Mount Vernon, with four " farms " aggregating 8,000 acres, of which about 25 per cent was plowable, was much more extensive than the ordinary plantation. It is well to remember that in its original usage the term " plantation " applied to the cleared and cultivated portion of a wooded area. Plantations were usually larger than the land-holdings called farms in the East, but this was only one of their features, perhaps not the most important one. Before the War between the States, the plantation was a way of life, often one of gentility and refinement, based upon an abundance of labor. To a degree self-contained, the plantation derived its main income from the sale of staple products.

The distribution of slavery in the early nineteenth century. The area of slavery extended far beyond the limits of plantation economy, but northward of the Chesapeake Bay country slaves constituted less than 10 per cent of the total population except in small districts. The four Northern states of New England had no slaves in 1810 and later (Fig. 35), though free Negroes resided there as well as in the slaveless counties of New York and Pennsylvania. Slaves were relatively most important in three great areas southward of the Potomac: eastern Virginia and adjacent North Carolina, coastal South Carolina and Georgia, and the lower Mississippi River in Louisiana. Within the regions of maximum slaveownership there were great contrasts in the proportion of slaves to the total population. In the Charleston district of South Carolina, for example, about 85 of 100 persons were slaves, while in near-by Orangeburg less than one-third of the population was held in bondage. Free Negroes also lived in the plantation country. A prominent Southerner pointed out in 1795 that " in a tract of country comprehending more than one-half of the population of Virginia, there are more blacks, and even more slaves, than free white persons." The same observer, who was writing to an acquaintance in New England, attributed the greater number of slaves in his state to " climate and a baneful policy," and doubted the possibility of the extermination of the practice. Many were the plans advanced by both Northerners and Southerners to cope with the increasing problem of slavery in America, but none, as we know, was successful. The vicious cycle of slavery was well phrased by a French visitor in 1799 who observed of South Carolina that since " Rice can only be cultivated by negroes . . . Slavery, therefore, confirms the planter in his prejudice for rice, and the cultivation of rice, on the other hand, attaches him to slavery."

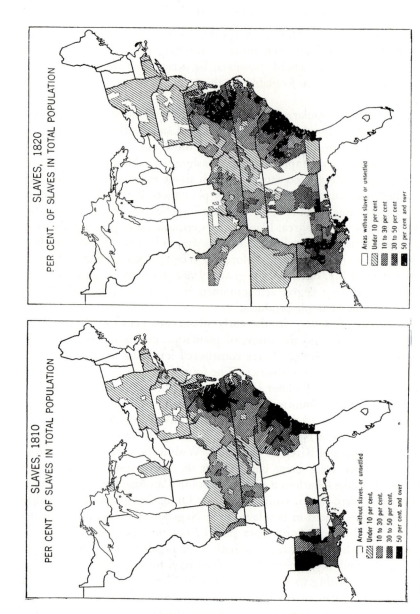

35 Proportion of slaves to total population, 1810 and 1820. From C. O. Paullin's *Atlas of the Historical Geography of the United States*. Courtesy of the Carnegie Institution and the American Geographical Society.

THE TOBACCO COUNTRY OF EASTERN VIRGINIA

The rise of tobacco as a staple commodity in colonial Virginia has already been discussed. In those earlier days the chief centers of production were in the tidewater regions around Chesapeake Bay, the largest inland waterway on the Atlantic coast. By the year 1800, however, most of the tobacco came from the Piedmont region above the Fall Line, and from the inner Coastal Plain. This shift of production is an essential part of the economic history of eastern Virginia.

Many circumstances favored the spread of tobacco culture in tidewater Virginia, notably the availability of water transport and an abundance of good soil needing only clearing to make it ready for use. Since tobacco culture was "hard on the soil," promoting erosion and drawing heavily on its nutrient elements, an essential and almost perennial task required of the slaves on a plantation was the clearing of land for new fields. After three or four seasons of tobacco cultivation, a field was either abandoned or relegated to crops that were commercially inferior, such as corn or wheat. An abandoned field, eventually overgrown with weeds, brush, or pine trees and perhaps riddled by gully erosion, would be recognizable for years to come as a former site of tobacco production. One of the most long-continued effects of the erosion of worn-out fields was the sedimentation of rivers and channels tributary to Chesapeake Bay. A recent investigator has stated that when Captain John Smith first saw the Patapsco River, whose main estuary forms Baltimore Harbor, "the limit of open tidewater was 7 miles farther inland than it is today." It is further stated that two early colonial ports in Maryland — Hartford-on-the-Bush and Joppa Town — are at the present time 2 or more miles from navigable water. Port Tobacco, Maryland, important in Colonial times and still in some use at the time of the War between the States, is now far above the navigation limit. (See Fig. 36.)

36
Diagrammatic view of (*above*) original and (*below*) present conditions at Port Tobacco, Maryland (*center of diagram*), which was at one time an actual port on the Potomac River but is now above the head of navigation through the filling-in of the channel. Reproduced by courtesy of L. C. Gottschalk and the *Geographical Review,* published by the American Geographical Society of New York.

Records left by travelers through tidewater Virginia in the early 1800's picture the region as one of partial abandonment, of formerly elegant mansions in a derelict condition, taken over for poor and mean uses — in short, having " seen better days." The traveler Weld, for example, crossing the Potomac at Port Tobacco by ferry, saw in the ferryhouse "one of those old dilapidated mansions that formerly was the residence perhaps of some wealthy planter," now descended to " the picture of wretchedness and poverty." The country roundabout " for miles together " was an expanse of abandoned fields worn out by tobacco, now overgrown with yellow sedge, with here and there " the remains of several good houses, which shew that the country was once very different to what it is now." In Weld's view the country appeared to be a " perfect wilderness."

Scenes of desolation such as the one pictured were not universal, not even in the older-settled districts where tobacco had been grown for a century or more. Along the James and the York and the Rappahannock there were, as there are today, many fine estates still producing tobacco and other crops. These were the landed estates of influential slaveowners, some of whose landholdings had gained by the departure of former neighbors. The newer country above the Fall Line offered a much more pleasing landscape, but in older and newer districts alike the steps in producing the leaf were essentially the same.

Labor requirements in tobacco production. A hogshead of tobacco leaf delivered at a Virginia inspection station in the early 1800's represented a large amount of tedious hand labor under constant, intelligent planning and management.

The preparation of " new ground " by clearing woodland and grubbing out the stumps was only one of the operations necessary in the average year. The logs thus produced were used for building purposes and for making hogsheads and constructing worm and panel fences. Seedbeds were started, often as early as the Christmas season, in outdoor " plant patches " when danger of frost had passed. An important seasonal task was the " pitching " or transplanting of the seedlings in the prepared fields, perhaps in late April or early May, to coincide with the rains of the so-called " long season." With plenty of labor on hand, hoes rather than plows prepared the fields to receive the crop. In pitching the small plants and for cultivation during the long growing season, different types of hoes known as the " sprouting " hoe and the " narrow " or " hilling " hoe were used, the last-named for setting the plants in hills about 3 or 4 feet apart. Periods of cultivation throughout the growing season alternated with other operations, such as " topping " and " suckering " — that is, the pinching off by hand of superfluous sprouts as a means of controlling the heading of the plant. Hand labor was also employed in " worming " the plant, or freeing it from the attacks of pests such as the green hornworm.

Harvest brought anxiety for the management and more hard labor for the workers. The ripened plants, cut with a hand knife, were " threaded " on pointed sticks punched through a split in the thick stalk; this was properly the first step in the curing process. Several " threads " of tobacco were hung on movable scaffolds and taken to barns or sheds adjacent to the fields or in near-by woods. Here the plants were hung in closely spaced rows to cure, with occasional "firing" to regulate temperature and moisture. When this process was complete, the cured leaves were stripped from the stalks and then "prized" or compressed into bundles so as to reduce shipping space. These operations are pictured in Figure 37, a contemporary print.

The finished product was transported by various means to the inspection station, where the planter was given a formal receipt or note for his crop. For short distances, canoes joined in parallel were sometimes used to float hogsheads of tobacco to the station; or single hogsheads were rolled to market behind horses or mules attached by shafts to the barrel, which was strengthened by extra hoops. Heavier loads, perhaps the combined product of several plantations, were

37

Steps in the production of tobacco as pictured in *An Historical and Practical Essay on the Culture and Commerce of Tobacco,* by William Tatham, London, 1800. a. Tobacco house. b. Threads of tobacco on scaffold. c. Prizing or compressing tobacco leaves. d. Inside view of tobacco house. e. Outside view of public warehouse. f. Inside view of public warehouse, with inspectors.

carried longer distances in wagons or by water in upland boats. (See Fig. 38.) Carrying distances had been decreased with the establishment by 1800 of inspection stations, usually privately operated but subject to regulation by state legislatures, in the newly developing tobacco country above the Fall Line and even in the Ohio River country.

Providence Forge, a Virginia plantation. The foregoing observations may be pointed up by reference to a Virginia plantation for which some specific records are available. (See Fig. 39.)

The area to be considered, about midway between Richmond and Williamsburg, is the site of a plantation which came into being before the Revolution and was known originally as Providence Forge, a name now attached to the

38

Transporting tobacco to market, according to Tatham's essay of 1800. a. Canoes joined for heavy loads. b. Upland boat. c. Wagon for longer journeys. d. Rolling hogsheads, protected by extra hoops, to market.

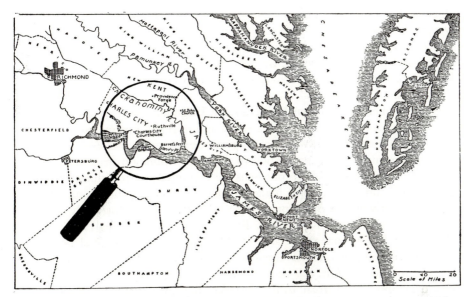

39   General map of the peninsulas of eastern Virginia, localizing the lower Chickahominy River, as discussed in the text

crossroads village of today. Navigation on the Chickahominy River was a factor
in the location of the original buildings, which included a forge and a gristmill,
but the stream has greatly diminished in depth since that time. The irregular
boundaries of the estate enclosed 3,200 acres of land in 1823, possibly less than
when first settled. The Forge estate in the same year reported 110 slaves, of
whom 43 were under fifteen years old. There is no record of the amount of cultivated land on the estate at that time, but among livestock and material items
inventoried were 15 mules and horses, 90 cows, 500 sheep, 200 hogs, 14 plows,
12 narrow hoes, and many wagons and carts.

Tobacco was the original staple of Providence Forge, but the scattered records
available indicate its dwindling production, probably because of soil exhaustion
and uncertain market values. Two hogsheads of tobacco totaling 3,026 pounds,
possibly representing the produce of 3 acres, were sold from the estate in the year
1810; if more was sold, there is no record of it.

From then on to the middle of the century the crops mentioned most frequently in the reports of the plantation manager are corn, broomcorn, wheat,
and vegetables. In 1830, for example, the plantation yielded 1,500 bushels of
wheat at a sale price of $1 a bushel. Cotton was also raised, but apparently not
on an extensive scale. Quantities of fish, mainly shad and herring, were seined
in the Chickahominy, and from it in the winter ice was cut and stored for later
use. Hogs, livestock, and poultry added to the variety of production.

In 1835 the estate was divided, and thereafter operated as two plantations,
the new one being named Mount Sterling. (See Fig. 40.) Two years after the division, Mount Sterling's slave population of 64 was valued at $21,375. The evidence

suggests that this plantation, like many others in the South at that time, was oversupplied with slaves. The staple crop, which had formerly required the services of many slaves — field workers, house servants, weavers, shopmen, and so on — had all but disappeared from the picture. Throughout the South during the first half of the nineteenth century there were many such "slave-poor" plantations.

Towns and cities of eastern Maryland and Virginia. Many of the plantations fronting on the almost innumerable rivers and inlets of Virginia and Maryland performed those functions which often give rise to towns; as a result, there were fewer towns and cities in proportion to the total population than in the Northern states. Although hundreds of towns were granted charters during the Colonial period, and efforts were made to establish communities in the English tradition, relatively few came into being, and of those established only a few survived the chaos of the Revolution. By 1800, places of original settlement on Chesapeake Bay — Jamestown and St. Marys, for example — had been ghost towns for several generations. Annapolis, originally called Severn from the river at whose mouth it stands, was chosen as the capital of Maryland when the village offered prospects of a great future. In 1800, the dwellings scattered along the streets of Annapolis, radiating from the state house in the center, numbered only 300, and its small commerce was a further disappointment. The great city of the Chesapeake Bay country was Baltimore, at the head of Patapsco Bay, popularly referred to at the opening of the nineteenth century as the fastest-growing town in the country. Baltimore was then third or fourth in population (26,000 in 1800) as well as in value of commerce. The city had outgrown its reputation for unhealthfulness sufficiently in 1800 to permit a geographer to say, somewhat guardedly, that certain improvements "have corrected the dampness of the air, and [the city] is now judged to be tolerably healthy."

That Williamsburg alone of Virginia's eastern cities was without water transport in 1800 was considered remarkable at the time. Once important as the colonial capital of Virginia, Williamsburg had suffered from the transfer of governmental activities to Richmond, and from the loss of surrounding population through the impoverishment of the soil. A visitor in 1799 saw the town with a somewhat jaundiced eye as a main street with the College of William and Mary at one ex-

40

Mount Sterling mansion as it appeared in 1937. The unshuttered windows represent rooms in the home occupied at the time.

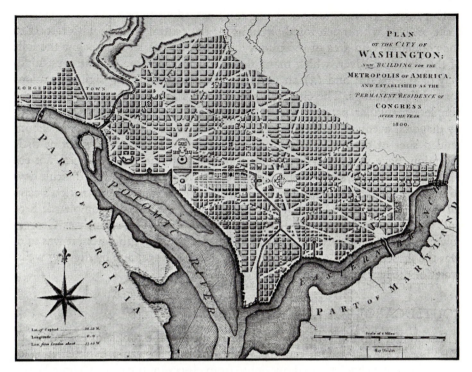

41   Proposed plan of Washington, D.C., at the time of its founding (1800) as the
      national capital, from an original copy in the Library of Congress

tremity and " at the other, the old capitol or statehouse, a capacious building
of brick, now crumbling to pieces from negligence. The houses around it are
mostly uninhabited and present a melancholy picture." These remarks would seem
to have done scant justice to Williamsburg, for the population of the town at
that time was nearly 1,500. The "crumbling" ruins of other days, as is well
known, have been restored to their original handsome state, and the college
which in 1796 had only a hundred students is now a leading educational center.

Richmond, at the Fall Line on the James River, in 1800 was nearly four times
the size of Williamsburg, deriving its importance from functioning as the state
capital. Further advantages were anticipated with the completion of a canal from
the head of large-boat navigation 20 miles distant, lighterage service being used
in the meantime. Petersburg, similarly situated near falls on the Appomattox, in
its range of industries and services came very close to being the typical Virginia
city. Several warehouses received annually some 20,000 hogsheads of tobacco,
and considerable manufactures of flour and other products were increasingly
important. Of little account in 1800 were Yorktown and Newport, but Yorktown " will ever be famous in American annals for the capture of Lord Corn-
wallis and his army by the combined forces of the United States and France,
which took place on the 19th of October, 1781."

The city of Washington was being built according to preconceived plans on a site selected with much forethought as to: (1) central position with respect to the population and area of the country at the time; (2) location below the falls of the Potomac River, which many thought would become the east-west highway of the nation; and (3) an undulating surface permitting sightly locations for public buildings. The city plan selected (Fig. 41) was an adaptation of the simple rectangular pattern of streets as typified by Philadelphia's, elaborated by diagonal avenues converging at circles or squares, or leading toward the intended sites of edifices. These basic arrangements, however excellent at their inception, have necessarily been altered by the introduction of features not envisioned at the time, such as railroads, not to mention airfields. It is difficult now to imagine the newborn city in 1800, just starting its career as the nation's capital—its streets unpaved, only a few public buildings partially completed; here and there groups of houses which were the original villages, such as Georgetown, of the Federal District. One of the attractions of Washington, it was said, was the presence of " a great number of excellent springs; and by digging wells, water of the best quality may readily be had."

SOUTH CAROLINA LOW COUNTRY

Essentially, two kinds of land were recognized by the people of coastal South Carolina in the eighteenth century: pine barrens and swamp. Neither kind of surface was of a character to draw praise from observant travelers. George Washington viewed the country, with some moderation of statement, as a land of " sand and pine barrens, with very few inhabitants " along the rights of way; a " perfect sameness seems to run through all the rest of the country." To others it was a somber country, with longleaf pines rising branchless to majestic heights, their crowns draped with the gray moss then descriptively called Spanish beard. The floor of the forest was surprisingly free from undergrowth, possibly due to burnings. Roads were often blocked by fallen trees. Understandably, the barrens had acquired a reputation for infertility, a view the more acceptable because of the task of clearing the land for cultivation. Since they served merely as a source of turpentine and timber, not until the opening of the nineteenth century with the new demands of commercial cotton production were the barrens seriously considered for agricultural purposes.

Swamps influential in locating plantations.   Swamps, it seemed, were everywhere. Strangest of all in their occurrence were the " inland swamps "—scattered small areas apparently unrelated to surface drainage lines or perceptible changes in slope. These inland swamps sometimes served as reservoirs of fresh water for the flooding of rice fields. No less important in rice economy were the " high-river swamps " occupying elevated portions of river plains above the ordinary limit of floods. Most widespread were the " tidal " swamps bordering the rivers — Pee Dee, Santee, Edisto, Coosahatchie, and Savannah — formed when the advancing tide turned back the river current and flooded the adjacent lowlands. In the lower river courses the salt in the overflowing water was detrimental to cultivation, but a few miles upstream the water in such swamps was fresh. Salt marsh bordering the river mouths, coasts, and off-lying islands was of little agricultural importance. The prevalent fear of harmful " effluvia " or gases rising from swampy areas at first discouraged settlement, but with the introduction of Oriental rice, in spite of the persistence of this view beyond the eighteenth century, rice plantations spread through the swamp country with its natural opportunities for raising this staple.

Characteristics of the average rice plantation. The average plantation with an area of less than 1,000 acres included perhaps 100 acres of diked land for rice and an equal acreage beyond the original limits of the swamps and suitable for the growth of cotton, indigo, and supply crops such as corn, peas, and sweet potatoes. In 1800 the chief staple was rice, although cotton was increasingly important. Indigo, extensively grown in Colonial times, had all but disappeared from the economic scene. The plantation " mansion " — no elaborate affair but rather like a hunting lodge, as indeed many of them have become in these days — was occupied by the well-to-do planter and his family for only a month or two in midwinter, when there was thought to be less danger from fevers. The remainder of the year was spent in residences in Charleston or on the low islands fringing the coast. With its cluster of outbuildings and slave quarters, the mansion was usually located beyond the river swamp on a clearing of higher ground, a tiny island in a sea of forest. The roads followed the higher ground, with the result that visitors unfamiliar with the country supposed it to be a thinly populated land. In contrast to the Virginia plantation, overlooking the river which served as its highway for travel and transportation, the rice estate was peculiarly isolated and difficult of access.

Rice culture in that environment required an enormous amount of labor under very difficult circumstances. It is superfluous to say that slavery was the answer, or seemed to be at the time. The work began with the reclamation of the swampland and continued through a nine-month season of care and harvesting. But when the last pound of rice was poured into the last keg, there was no three-month vacation for the laboring force.

Preparation of new rice ground was scarcely less taxing or unpleasant than the fabled cleansing of the Augean stables. The section of swamp to be reclaimed was first surrounded by a wide ditch, the excavated material being piled up to form the dike. The outer dike paralleling the river was built to exceed the height of the highest high tide — the spring tide. Openings or " trunks " through the dike permitted the flooding and drainage of the fields behind it. These preliminary tasks completed, the swamp was cleared of its heavy growth of tangled vegetation. Pioneer-fashion, stumps were often left in the miry ground and planting went on around them. Additional dikes, called " cross dams," were erected within the outer embankments, enclosing fields an acre or two in extent. These were also fitted with trunks and sluices in order to control water depth and to permit the drainage or the flooding of different fields. In general, the flooding operation occurred at high tide, when the gates in the trunks permitted the inrush of water, and drainage occurred at low tide. On many plantations the diked fields were linked to an inland swamp which served as a reservoir in seasons when the rivers were low.

The planting of the rice seed in hoe-dug pits was often done by women. About two bushels of seed were planted to the acre; if all went well, the yield might be 60 bushels at harvest. The early-April planting time was followed by the "sprout flow" or flooding to hasten the germination of the seed and to drown insects. Within a week or two the water was drained off and the slaves were set to work at weeding the grain, until the "long flow," a period of nearly a month during which the water overtopped the growing plants, now 5 or 6 inches tall. Again the fields were drained, permitting dry cultivation until the August "lay-by flow," the last of the flooding operations. During the lay-by, the Negroes were dispatched to the near-by woods to make ready kegs and barrels for the expected crop. The ripening of the shoulder-high grain in October was usually marked by the invasion of "ricebirds," and by the employment of children to stand on the dikes to frighten the birds away.

The grain was cut by hand and bundled much as wheat is handled on some farms today. In the early days rice was milled by hand in mortars excavated from tree trunks, but by the 1790's these were being displaced by mills operated by tidal power. These mills, often called pecker mills because of their manner of operation, also fanned out the winnowings and assorted the grain into sizes. (See Fig. 42.) After the rice was packed in barrels and inspected by officers appointed for the purpose, it was floated to market in plantation barges or in *perriaugers* made from cypress logs.

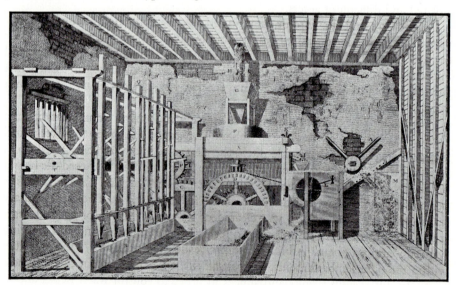

42   A rice mill in South Carolina, from Drayton's *View,* 1802

The foregoing description is taken from eyewitness accounts available about 1810. Rice-producing methods varied but little during the following decades. Thus according to the account of Frederick Law Olmsted, written on his journey in 1856:

An expanse of old rice ground, a nearly perfect plain surface with its waving, clean, bright verdure, stretching unbroken except by the straight and parallel lines of ditch and wall to the horizon's edge before you, bounded on one side by the silver thread of the river, on the other by the dark curtain of the pine forest, is said to be a beautiful sight. But the new plantation as I saw it in February, the ground covered thickly with small stumps and strewn with brands and cinders and half-burnt logs . . . with a company of clumsy and uncouth black women armed with axes, shovels and hoes, and directed by a stalwart black man armed with a whip, all slopping about in the black, unctuous mire at the bottom of the ditches, is a very dreary scene.

Factors in the decline of rice and indigo production. By the opening of the nineteenth century, rice acreage in South Carolina was reaching a period of stability. Thereafter, the reclamation of swampland became less common, and gradually old fields were diverted to other uses. By this time, thousands of acres of land had been diked and drained, upsetting the natural balance between runoff and deposit. Reading between the lines of eyewitness accounts written before the days of systematic physiography, we find evidence of increased filling of stream channels and greater variations of stream flow, both reasonable expectations under the circumstances. According to one reporter, the rivers carried more sediment than in earlier times and " while the stream is encreased, the bed of the river is narrowed." Overflowing, therefore, was more common. To straighten the channels, " cutting off their numerous windings by small canals " was suggested as a remedy, but the more practical-minded viewed this as an impossible undertaking.

A few scattered records lead to the inference that floods were more frequent in the later stages of rice cultivation than they had been at earlier times. Floods which overtopped the dikes or crevassed their sides, spreading debris in the rice plots, were disastrous in their results. In other years the opposite catastrophe occurred: Low water levels resulted from droughts. In 1752, for example, there was a report of

. . . the greatest drought here ever known, which still continues, whereby the crops of rice, corn, and indigo have suffered extremely. It is so great that the beasts of the field are almost starved in the pastures, and travellers call in at houses to draw water out of the wells for their horses, wherefore tomorrow [July 24, 1752] is by proclamation, appointed for a solemn fast on this occasion throughout the province.

During another brief period thirty years later, the sale of rice was prohibited because of the shortages resulting from a long drought. Uncertain market values and increased competition from other producing regions were added factors in the diminishing popularity of rice.

Indigo culture in 1800 may properly be viewed as a survival in a labor-rich region where its original culture was encouraged by the payment of bounties. For indigo, like rice, demanded a large amount of labor under extremely unpleasant conditions. It was intensively cultivated as an annual plant in relatively small patches of the better soils. The seeds were sown in April in rows sufficiently wide to permit repeated cultivations and weedings. During a favorable year there were two or three cuttings of leaves, the first one when the plant was 2½ feet tall. The leaves were put into shallow vats to ferment for a day, after which the liquor was drawn off and churned, with the addition of lime to cause the indigo to settle to the bottom. The sediment was partly dried, spread out on cloths, and then placed in boxes or bags for pressing. The final step in manufacture was the cutting of the blue paste into small squares, which were packed in casks for shipment. (See Fig. 43.) Planters figured on a yield of 50 pounds an acre, perhaps the season's work of one slave.

When competition from other parts of the world, especially the Orient, threatened the industry, the newly formed United States Government considered various measures for preserving the industry. It was thought, for example, that the adoption of a blue color for military uniforms would create a market sufficient to encourage the continued growing of indigo. Nevertheless, competition proved too strong, and eventually spelled the disappearance of this crop from plantation economy in the United States.

Cotton supplanted indigo as a staple, becoming in a short time far more important than its predecessor had ever been. The soil requirements were much the

43

Steps in the manufacture of indigo in the South. One of the few known pictures showing the preparation of this commodity, this derives from the elaborate title of a *Map of South Carolina and a Part of Georgia,* sometimes known as the Stuart Map and published in London in 1780. From an original copy in the John Carter Brown Library.

same. According to a writer in 1803, " by an easy transition, and without much
expence, the indigo planters driven, by necessity, to search out other sources of
industry, have directed their attention to the planting of cotton." Some rice
fields were also converted to the new and more profitable use.

THE UPPER COUNTRY OF SOUTH CAROLINA

The rice country extended about 90 miles inland to a belt of higher land known
as the High Hills of Santee. These sandy hills would have been insignificant
in a rugged region, but rising here to heights of from 50 to 200 feet above
the uniform Coastal Plain level, they gave an impressive appearance of altitude. Covered with stunted pine and scrub oak, which connoted an infertile
soil, the High Hills were of little agricultural significance. They enjoyed a reputation for healthfulness, in contrast to the swampy rice country from which
financially able planters emigrated seasonally to escape the fevers; the Hills thus
shared favor with the coastal islands as places of hot-weather residence.

The belt of country between the High Hills and the Fall Line, a space of
some 50 miles, was termed the Middle Country by informed writers of the time.
It was and is the transition area from the Coastal Plain to the rolling Piedmont.
Soils recognized as being stronger and richer than those of the Coastal Plain
made this a region of rapid agricultural settlement during the first half of the

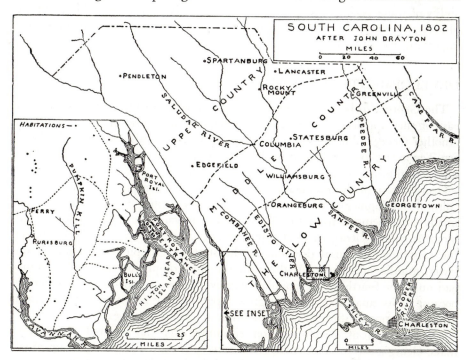

44   The regions of South Carolina as outlined by John Drayton in 1802

nineteenth century,—the region into which upland cotton first extended in its westward march beyond the Coastal Plain. Rice was never important here, not only because of an unsuitable environment but because its decline as a plantation product had already begun when the Middle Country was opening up. Settled mainly by South Carolinians and adapted to cotton and tobacco culture, the Middle Country developed into a plantation area in which the slave population equaled that of the earlier-settled areas of the state. (See Fig. 44.)

The heart of the Upper Country, lying between the Fall Line and the Appalachian Mountains, was the region of distinctively new settlement in the early 1800's. Settlers came not only from other parts of South Carolina and Georgia but also from states farther north. Tobacco and cotton were the leading crops and slave population was high, but there was much wheat raised on slaveless farms and stock-raising was more important than elsewhere. Many of the larger cities of interior South Carolina originated at this time, and giving promise of future growth were towns at the Fall Line: Columbia, situated on the east side of the Congaree just below the confluence of the Saluda and Broad rivers, as can be seen from a modern map, had been selected as the new capital of the state. Slightly larger than Columbia was Camden on the east bank of the Wateree, a strategic place because of navigation on the lower river. Like other Fall Line cities, Camden's location and early growth was owing to its position at the head of navigation; its later and more rapid expansion was stimulated by the availability of water power for the manufacturing of tobacco products, flour, and textiles. Among the other inland villages, small in 1800 but destined to become more important, were Orangeburg on the Edisto, Statesburg, and Granby.

DEVELOPMENTS IN GEORGIA

The Georgia to be considered here is that portion of the present state lying east of the Appalachians, with natural regions like those of South Carolina. Another Georgia, known at the opening of the nineteenth century as the Western Territories and extending to the Mississippi River, will be considered in a more appropriate place.

Georgia east of the mountains was extensive, and surprisingly varied in its cultural development. As in South Carolina, the center of population was annually on the move from the Coastal Plain toward the more inviting Piedmont. In giving Georgia a total population of 82,848, the 1790 census recognized the existence of natural divisions in the state by grouping the counties into lower, middle, and upper. At this time the area comprising the lower counties had only one-fourth of the population; nevertheless it had the greater density because of its small size. Georgia grew rapidly in the next two decades, reaching a population in 1810 of 252,433, of whom 105,218 were slaves.

The triumph of slave-plantation economy over the original attempts to make Georgia a free-labor, small-farm country is shown in the make-up of the population as well as in the major uses of the land. The Coastal Plain region with its predominant staple-crop economy had the largest slave population, roughly 60 per cent of all inhabitants. A third of the people in the lower Piedmont (Middle Country) were held in bondage, and even in the upper Piedmont and mountains 23 per cent of the total population was slave.

The plantation economy of Georgia.   Rice dominated the plantation system of the Coastal Plain region, but as in South Carolina, cotton was assuming greater importance. The rice plantations clung to the low swamplands along the Savannah, Ogeechee, and Altamaha rivers and to the salt-free soils near the coast contemporarily called hammock lands. The majority of the plantations raised other crops, for sale and for local use, in the drier soils cleared from oak-hickory and pine forests. Records of the Hopeton Plantation are perhaps representative of the more extensive Georgia estates — and there were many of them. Hopeton was established in 1805 on the south bank of the Altamaha River a few miles above Darien. Its area included 4,500 acres, more than half of which remained in woodland. Sea-island cotton was the earliest crop, followed later by sugar cane; but ultimately rice became the chief dependence. It is reported that the plantation " was worked by six hundred slaves or more," which must be regarded as an unusually large labor force even for so extensive a unit.

A traveler descending the lower Savannah River in July, 1792, reported " a continued Succession of beauteous Farms and elegant Buildings " and " on both Sides of the River very extensive Fields of Corn, Rice and Indigo, convenient to which are Mills, Vats, etc., to manufacture the Produce." Georgia's chief export in 1810 was cotton, from the immediate coastal districts and the interior, totaling 11,000,000 pounds and worth $1,500,000. This was ten times the value of rice exported during the same year.

Decadent and growing towns in eastern Georgia.   Gone from the economy of the lower Georgia country were most of the experimental crops and industries envisioned by the founders of the colony. Silk, for example, was no longer produced. According to Marguerite B. Hamer, " Planters found it more profitable to employ their slaves in making rice and indigo," and " after 1771 even the people of Ebenezer, the most devoted to the silk project, took up the culture of maize, rice, indigo, hemp, and tobacco."

The trend toward plantation economy and local shifts in population distribution had resulted, on the one hand, in the decadence of several early-day towns in the lower country and, on the other, in the increasing importance of Savannah. The " dead towns " of Georgia, such as Purisburg, Sunbury, Frederica, and Old Ebenezer, have been the subjects of lengthy and interesting studies. Old Ebenezer, originally laid out by a group of German immigrants known as Salzburgers, was abandoned, and by the middle of the eighteenth century had been replaced by Ebenezer New Town, the one generally located on maps. A visitor described Purisburg in the 1790's as an " almost depopulated town on the north side of the River which was once to Savannah what Georgetown is [1792] to Philadelphia." Sunbury, another thriving community of pre-Revolutionary times, was mostly in ruins in 1790, its docks in dilapidated condition and the former farm land overgrown with myrtle bush and Bermuda grass. And Frederica on St. Simons Island, once a thriving frontier post, was at the same period almost a ghost town, its broad but silent streets shaded with uncared-for orange trees.

In contrast to these decadent communities, Savannah had grown rapidly, rising with little apparent effect from the ashes of a great fire in 1796. Located some 20 miles from the ocean, it was already the principal town of the state. George Washington saw the city in the summer of 1791, as recorded in his diary, standing

. . . upon what may be called high ground for this Country. . . . The town on 3 sides is surrounded with cultivated Rice fields which have a rich and luxuriant appearance. On the 4th or back side it is a fine sand. Rice and tobacco (the last of which is greatly increasing) are the principal exports — Lumber and Indigo are also Exported, but the latter is on the decline [supplanted] it is supposed by Hemp & Cotton. Ship timber, viz: live oak and Cedar is (and may be more so) valuable in the exp[ortation].

Washington as well as other visitors questioned the healthfulness of Savannah, but conceded that the bluff (if it could be so called) saved the city from the " dangerous miasmata " of the surrounding swamps. Fears of insalubrity to the contrary, the city had grown from 2,300 in 1787 to 5,146 in 1800, and to 5,215 in 1810. In the latter year, the Negro population of Savannah was 2,725, of whom only 530 were free.

Piedmont Georgia.   Geographical writers in the early 1800's, with no promotional axes to grind, considered the Piedmont to be a " more desirable country," not only because of its presumed healthfulness but because of the stronger and richer soils. Piedmont soils above flood plains were referred to descriptively as " mulatto " and " gray " lands, anticipating by over a century the modern terminology of soil classification. New settlers taking up land in the rapidly developing Piedmont paid close attention to the soil types, rating oak-hickory or mulatto land better than the gray lands associated with mixed growths of hardwood and pine. Note was taken of the reddish or yellowish subsoil with its clay admixture — good because it formed a firm base for the topsoil. Cotton and tobacco were the principal products of early Piedmont agriculture, along with corn, flax, beans, root vegetables, and hemp. There was much stock-raising in the new country, one beneficial result of which was an annual supply of manure. " Cow-penning " was a practice of the time, inherited from earlier days; that is, forming temporary enclosures for cattle whose accumulated droppings were plowed in when the field was thought ready for cultivation.

The new towns of Georgia in the early 1800's were in the Middle and Upper countries. Augusta, laid out in 1735 at the head of navigation for 50-ton boats on the Savannah, had grown by 1810 to a city of 2,500. Augusta's trade was largely in tobacco and cotton, boated to Savannah 125 miles downstream. Similarly situated on the Oconee was Milledgeville (population in 1810, 1,250), but the river was not navigable by large boats. Athens on the same river could already boast that it was a university town, even though smaller than other places, such as

Louisville on the Ogeechee. There was no village by the name of Atlanta at this stage of development.

FLORIDA SERVES ANOTHER TERM UNDER SPAIN

What little is definitely known about Florida at a comparable period can be briefly summarized. There were two Floridas, East and West, administrative units established by the British during their rule from 1763 to 1783 and retained by the Spanish at the resumption of their control.

The new Spanish control, it must be said, was not very effective. Still concerned with the Indian problem, but interested no longer in supporting missions, Spain regarrisoned the existing forts, particularly San Marcos. Apparently realizing that so vast a frontier could not be held against the advancing wave of American settlement in Georgia, even if the Indians were checked, the Spanish Government offered greater inducements to settlers and traders: "What missionary and soldier could not do," suggests Professor Whitaker, "might be accomplished by trade and toleration." But results were unfavorable; few Spaniards came to take up the land. Moreover, the principal trading company, operating with official permission, was of English origin. Known as Panton, Leslie & Company, the firm traded mainly with the Creek Nations from Pensacola and other Gulf ports in West Florida. Fort St. Marks on Apalachee Bay was reestablished in 1787 to protect Panton's trade and to prevent freebooting.

The few settlers who came from Spain apparently remained in St. Augustine or its vicinity. The plantations and towns developed by the British during their twenty-year period of stewardship became decadent — or rather, more decadent than before. Most interesting of these was New Smyrna, 60 miles south of St. Augustine on a small and shallow bay called Mosquito Inlet. To this place in 1767 came about 1,500 people in one group, perhaps the largest single importation of foreign peoples into the New World in all its settlement period. And many of the New Smyrna immigrants were alien indeed, such as those from Greece and the Minorcan Islands among others from the British Isles. A more strange assemblage of people could scarcely be imagined, but the project takes on some sense when viewed in the light of its background.

The originator of the colony, Dr. Andrew Turnbull, who had a wealthy Greek wife, envisioned a Utopia in the New World, its people living the good life and supplying England with rare commodities. Recruits in silk culture and weaving, vineyard cultivation and wine-making, were brought from various Mediterranean areas. Never prospering, because the plans behind the scheme were no more solid than the sands on which the town was built, the New Smyrna colony survived for only a few years. Loss of life, probably through malaria and poor sanitation, was tremendous. The dissatisfied if not desperate survivors revolted in 1773, scattering to Georgia and South Carolina or taking refuge in St. Augustine, and by 1800 there was only a remnant of the colony.

Gone even more completely were other British-sponsored ventures in land settlement on the St. Johns River west of St. Augustine. One such place was Rollestown, named for Denys Rolle, in whose visionary mind a colony somewhere in Florida had taken form before he secured a grant of land and set out with a few followers. Short-lived indeed, Rollestown was in ruins at the time of William Bartram's visit near the end of the period of British occupancy, when he beheld structures " mouldering to earth, except the mansion house [which was] yet in tolerable repair, and inhabited by an overseer and his family. There is also a blacksmith with his shop and family at a small distance from it."

Florida trade dwindled to negligible proportions, only 20 vessels clearing St. Augustine Harbor in the year 1800. The Spanish King frequently received advice from authorities to give up the peninsula. José Salcedo pointed out that Florida " has no port, only what is called one," and little prospect of furnishing important trade in the future. The Americans, perhaps not with entire sincerity, assured the King that Florida was " little better than a wilderness," the maintenance of which could not possibly " compensate for the expense . . . in supporting the government of St. Augustine." By 1819 the United States was ready to take over, but many long years were to elapse before Florida's period of modern development began.

CHAPTER 9

Regional Studies: The North

ALMOST obscured in the great main stream of Western settlement were innumerable countercurrents such as appear in a river when viewed from a bridge. Hence in studying the Northern states not only must the general westward sweep of the frontier be considered, — the main current — but also the redistribution of inhabitants within the settled area — the countercurrents. Increasing numbers of immigrants from Europe contributed to the power of these currents during the opening years of the nineteenth century.

INDUSTRIES AND CITIES OF NEW ENGLAND

This was a period of unprecedented city growth, mainly under the impetus of industrialization. The factory system brought new communities into being and gave a new stimulus to the growth of existent cities formerly dependent upon commerce or the fisheries. In Massachusetts, for example, the center of population advanced westward from 1765 to 1800, not very far, but nevertheless in that direction. Then between 1800 and 1840 the center retreated eastward, nearly to the point where it had been seventy-five years before. This shows that despite the ever advancing frontier, population growth following 1800 was greater in and near Boston than elsewhere in the state. In fact, Boston and its contiguous towns now forming the metropolitan district grew at a rate nearly four times that of inland cities and towns. Few if any places were spared the effects of this phase of the Industrial Revolution. Upland rural villages occupying hilltop sites above the streams often ceased growing or actually lost in population to the river towns which mushroomed about factories near water power. Settlement progressively moved downslope during this period of readjustment to new conditions.

Development of manufacturing. The availability of many widely scattered water-power sites in New England was of course a prime factor in the localization of milling industries. Hardly a stream was without one or more waterfalls capable of being harnessed for power with the means then available. The Merrimack, Taunton, Blackstone, Willimantic, Connecticut, and Housatonic rivers were only the larger streams of southern New England to present numerous falls. The majority of these rivers were the more useful in the beginning stages of industrialization because they presented no serious obstacles to development. But something more than convenient waterfalls — namely, capital — was required to start New England upon its manufacturing career. Other regions had water power. In the South, " white coal " was available along the Fall Line and within the Piedmont, but capital in that region was largely invested in the land or in new slaves for further agricultural enterprise. It is reported, for example, that between 1804 and 1808, 200 slave ships entered the port of Charleston, South Carolina, and that 30,000 slaves were sold there. The expenditure for slaves of possibly $300,000 would have been enough to have financed many small mills of the type being erected near New England waterfalls and millponds during the same period.

The Northern states were ripe for the manufacturing period. A long background in home industries had developed a potential supply of skilled labor. Also, the already existent compact villages and numerous small cities invited new industries. Investors who had accumulated capital in other enterprises, notably those connected with foreign and domestic commerce, were seeking new outlets for investment as a remedy for the uncertainties brought on by the Embargo and Non-Intercourse acts, climaxed by the War of 1812. Moreover, the commercial dominance of the Northern states brought to their ports large quantities of raw materials — cotton from the South, minerals from Europe, and hides from Spanish America. Why not use them for manufacturing? Human ingenuity also played a leading role in the beginnings of manufacturing as well as later. The power machinery in the famous Slater textile mill, erected in 1791 near Providence, Rhode Island, was built in imitation of British inventions which Samuel Slater saw during a stay in England. There were at least 25 similar mills in the same city by 1809.

Products of New England manufacture. When the president of Yale College set out on a tour of New England at the turn of the nineteenth century, he intended to make a complete record of his observations, following the example of many travelers. He had not gone very far, however, before deciding to omit further mention of sawmills and gristmills because " There is scarcely a township . . . which does not have a complete set." The grinding of corn and small grains was one of the first manufactural uses of water power, although some early-day flour mills were driven by draught animals or by wind. Small in capacity because they drew upon only local supplies of grain, gristmills often occupied choice water-power sites later acquired by other manufacturers.

Very common too in the beginning stages of manufacturing were carding and fulling mills, the former for preparing wool, flax, or cotton fiber for spinning, and the latter for compacting or shrinking woolen cloth. These processes were elaborations of similar ones conducted in the home, representing a transitional stage between pure home industries and the factory system. Family-woven woolens and worsteds were often taken to the fuller for more expert attention. By the year 1810 there were more than 400 carding and fulling machines in New England, perhaps twice as many as in the region south of the Potomac. A related manufacturing industry was the making of carding machines. The processing of farm products locally derived thus constituted the most widespread manufacturing industries of early New England. Less important, but based on agriculture, were the refining of West Indian and Louisiana sugar and the making of rum, distilled liquors, and malt.

The spinning of cotton into yarn by means of spinning jennies was largely confined to the Northern states and to New England in particular. (See Fig. 45.) Another distinctive industry of the new factory era was the weaving of cloth. Power looms turned out various kinds of goods, basically cotton but often mixed with wool or linen: according to weave and pattern, kerseymeres, fustians, cords, diaper (a material of varied uses with a small woven pattern such as diamond), bedticking, osnaberg, sailcloth, shirtings, coach lace, and ginghams.

Although the mineral resources of New England were limited in kind and amount, metal industries developed at a surprisingly early time. A few cities in Massachusetts and Connecticut turned out iron, copper, and brass products which derived their value more from the skilled labor they represented than from their material content.

Encouraging though it was, the manufacturing output fell short of domestic needs, and large importations of manufactured goods from foreign countries continued. With a view to encouraging " infant industries " the United States placed high tariffs on competing goods imported from abroad and sought by other means to encourage entrepreneurs. These procedures met with some disfavor, especially in the agricultural regions of the South and the West.

The spread of manufacturing. New England enterprises, as distinct from home industries, first sprang up in several coastal towns and cities which presented one or more advantages, such as water power, supplies of raw material or labor, and markets for the sale of finished products or means of transportation to such centers. It is also reasonable to suppose that not a few industries developed in a particular site because of some whim or fancy of the promoter. The enterprises were characteristically varied during the earlier years, but within a decade or two certain limited areas or river valleys became identified with one or two major industries, such as cotton spinning or weaving, and boot and shoe manufacture. Imitation of existing industries, even if they had been only mildly successful, was a potent factor in the localization of similar industries in close proximity.

By the middle of the nineteenth century, manufacturing plants had invaded all of New England save the interior of Maine and the more remote and mountainous parts of Vermont and New Hampshire. To trace this evolution would go far beyond the limits of this study. One authority points out that, fortunately for New England, " its factories became firmly rooted before coal was used for power purposes." Had coal preceded water power in this use, he continues, " many inland towns and cities of Massachusetts would never have been much more than summer resorts." In this view, the small water-power sites effected an early start in manufacturing and encouraged the dispersal of industry from

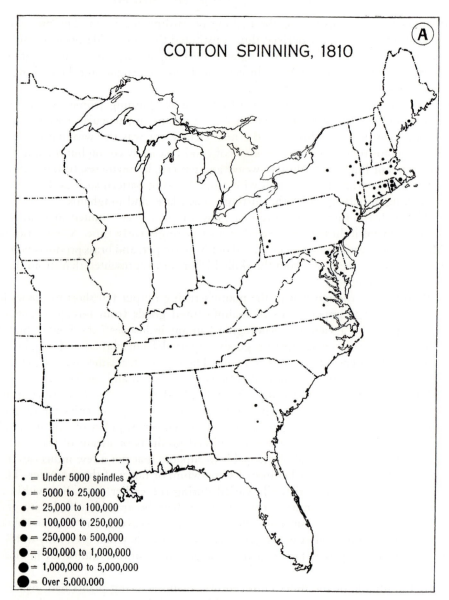

45 Cotton-spinning works in the United States in 1810. Reproduced by permission from C. O. Paullin's *Atlas of the Historical Geography of the United States*, published jointly by the Carnegie Institution of Washington and the American Geographical Society of New York.

originating centers, but they were not large enough to sustain the factories during their period of growth. The manufacturing plants usually outran the available water power and were forced to draw upon additional energy from coal. A mill once established would in all likelihood remain fixed in site even after the disappearance of the natural advantage which originally located it.

Early manufacturing centers.   In the larger cities and town-clusters of coastal New England, manufacturing industries of the new era competed for a brief period with other occupations surviving from earlier days. A catalogue of industries in the leading manufacturing centers of the early 1800's offers convincing proof of their varied character, together with plenty of evidence of the trend toward textiles even as early as this. Outstanding industrial centers or regions at the time were New Haven, the Narragansett Bay country, the Boston district, and the lower Merrimack Valley.

New Haven was a city of some 4,000, too small to permit its consideration as one of the great cities of the country. Among its older industries were flour-milling and distilling, and possibly also the making of buttons. Signs of the new day were clearly evident in cotton and linen mills, as well as factories for the manufacture of carding machinery, and paper mills using rag stock for raw material. New Haven was not a one-industry town then or later, although the textile business was beginning to take a firm hold.

Several of the cities around Narragansett Bay in Rhode Island and in Massachusetts showed similar trends toward textile manufacture. Here also were many occupations inherited from an earlier day: candles were made of spermaceti, and in other " works " sugar was refined or grains were distilled or malted. The manufacture of felt and the related hat industry was also of early origin and long remained a stand-by. Cotton spinning was comparatively new, although it was eventually to dominate the economic scene. Including near-by Pawtucket, where Samuel Slater's mill stood, the Providence region in 1810 had 150,000 spindles which transformed 320 tons of cotton into 250 tons of cotton yarn. Nails and other iron products, including anchors, came from the Providence region during that early period. The situation of Fall River in Massachusetts, with deep-water transportation almost reaching the falls for which the place was named, was particularly well suited to cotton-textile industries based on raw materials from the Southern states.

Boston ranked among the great cities of the country in 1810, with 33,000 inhabitants within the city limits; to this number 10,000 more can be added for Charlestown, Cambridge, and Roxbury, which were then, as now, integral parts of the urban area. A complete list of Boston's industries would run to great length, commencing with over two dozen distilleries and breweries, followed by a half-dozen sugar refineries and several ropewalks. Among industries requiring heat rather than power, glassmaking was most important, although other factories made stoneware and bricks and there were several foundries and casting plants.

Northward of Boston, more detached physically from it than now, was the

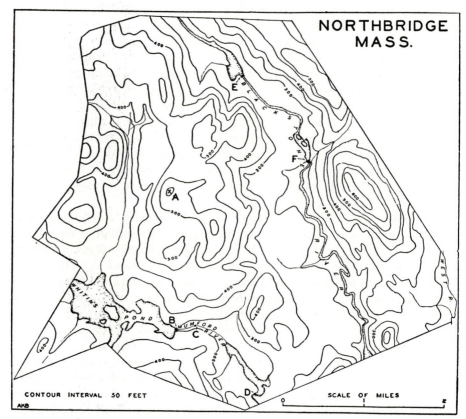

46a Topographic map of Northbridge, Mass. A. Site chosen for village. B, C, D. Falls and dam sites on Mumford River. E, F. Dam sites on Blackstone River. Note that ponds are artificial and were not available at time of settlement. Reproduced by courtesy of Adelbert K. Botts.

town of Lynn, already the great shoemaking center of the country. This, perhaps the first concentrated industry in the United States, naturally drew the interested attention of travelers. As early as 1788 Brissot de Warville, on his trip from Boston to Portsmouth, made note of the making of women's shoes at Lynn and of men's at Reading. As many as 100,000 pairs of women's shoes were turned out of Lynn shops in the year 1800. It appears that the tanning of leather was an early industry in the locality and that women there, as elsewhere, had developed skill in making shoes as a home industry.

Perhaps no one would have predicted in the year 1810 that the lower Merrimack Valley would become a leading textile center within the next quarter-century. The river-mouth town of Newburyport was an old-time shipbuilding center whose inhabitants, a charitable writer said, were " characterized by their hospitality and amiable manners." Upstream was Haverhill, where sailcloth had been made since 1789, possibly the beginning stage of textile manufacture in

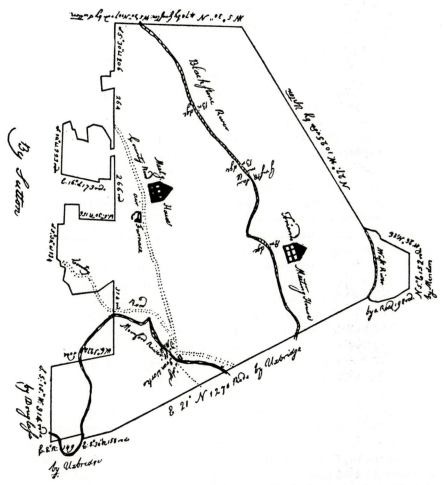

46b Map of Northbridge, 1795, when the township had a population of less than 600 persons. Among the representations are ironworks, gristmills, and a sawmill. Typical of the manuscript maps of early townships and villages in New England. Reproduced by courtesy of Adelbert K. Botts.

that area. Lowell and Lawrence with their great woolen mills came into being at a later period.

Water power and local population changes. The next stage of New England's industrialization was marked by the inland spread of factories. The rough upland country into which industry spread, mainly by way of the river valleys, had had little manufactural experience beyond that provided by home industries. It was a rural land, not far in miles from the sea but deriving little benefit from approximate coastal position. The population of the inland towns was adjusted to a self-sufficing agricultural economy. Many of the villages occupied hillsides or hilltops, so selected at an earlier time because of presumed soil superiority, or for the view, or to enjoy greater security from surprise Indian attacks. But such villages were poorly placed for a factory economy in which water power was a controlling element, and the result can easily be surmised, especially now that we know what *did* happen: New villages developed near the water-power sites, draining population from the older communities and acting as magnets for immigrants newly arrived from Europe. Also influential in the downslope trend of population was the new alignment of highways (still later accentuated by railroads), which in traversing the upland country between main points naturally followed the lines of least resistance. Cut off from these routes and too high above water level to gain advantages from water power, the older villages often lost population or remained essentially stabilized.

Northbridge, Massachusetts, provides an instructive case study in understanding these historical changes. The Northbridge story may be said to start in 1772, when the northern part of the still older township of Uxbridge was separated to form a new governmental unit. In the view of the Town Fathers, it was important that the town hall and the church be located in a sightly spot; therefore a hilltop was selected, rising 300 feet above the Blackstone and Mumford rivers, the main streams of this locality. (See Figs. 46a and 46b.) Despite relatively poor soil, agriculture became the chief industry of the people of Northbridge. It scarcely need be said that the farming was of the subsistence type, including the crops and the livestock usual to post-Revolutionary New England.

Between 1807 and 1814, into this more or less static scene came the first factories of the new era, acquiring sites formerly occupied by lumber mills and gristmills. The Blackstone and the Mumford presented the essential requirements of water-power sites — a small but dependable " head " of water, and level land near by for factories. Natural facilities were enhanced by impounding water in millponds. Labor supply for the factories was at first recruited from near-by farms, but as the industries grew, greater numbers of the hands were immigrants. During the first half of the century four new villages developed: Whitinsville (named for its promoter), Rockdale, Riverdale, and Linwood. Their combined populations soon outstripped that of the older village of Northbridge, which remained static in size and essentially unchanged in make-up as to nationality.

Population movements in New Hampshire. Conclusions of similar import have been reached by Professor J. W. Goldthwait in a study growing out of the preparation of a topographic map of Lyme Township in northwestern New Hampshire. The survey brought to light numerous abandoned roads, vacant cellar holes, and large areas of former fields (as shown by remnants of stone walls) reverted to woodland, relic features which could be understood only in terms of past periods of occupancy. This led to the preparation of similar maps of the same area at earlier stages, reconstructed from town records and other reliable evidence. For such a study the Lyme area is most instructive because the town's western portion borders the Connecticut Valley, with its flood plain and alluvial terraces, while the eastern limits lie in the rough, hilly upland typical of interior New England. Culminating points, locally called mountains (such as Hardscrabble Mountain), are 2,000 feet above the flood plain. (See Fig. 47.)

This region of varied surface came within the frontier of settlement soon after the Revolution, developing a self-sufficing rural economy. From the beginning of settlement to about 1830 the population steadily advanced and farms over-spread lowland and highland in almost equal proportions. In fact, the evidence suggests that hillsides were preferred to the low country because the sloping land afforded better drainage and the soils were thought to be more durable than

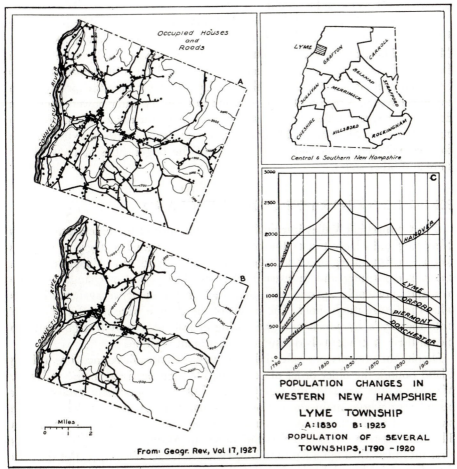

47   The township of Lyme, New Hampshire, at two different periods in its devel-ment, and a graph of population growth and decline in Lyme and neighboring towns from 1790 to 1925. Adapted from illustrative material in the paper by J. W. Goldthwait, "A Town That Has Gone Downhill," *Geographical Re-view*, Vol. 17 (1927), pp. 527–57, with permission of Mr. Goldthwait and the American Geographical Society of New York, publisher of the *Geographical Review*.

those of the bottom lands. During this period of advancing settlement large areas were cleared, first of woods and then of boulders, the latter proving useful in home-building and for erecting stone walls to enclose small, irregularly shaped fields. Reaching the peak of population in 1830, Lyme Township thereafter declined, and at the present time is little if any larger than it was in the 1790's. Furthermore, the passing years have witnessed a greater concentration of people in the village clusters of Lyme Center and Lyme Plain. The process is well summed up in the title chosen by the author for his study of the area: " A Town That Has Gone Downhill."

Chief among the causes of the general abandonment of the higher and rougher lands was the opening up of superior farming country in New York and the Midwest. Many of the Western settlers came from towns like Lyme. Soon their farm products were flooding Eastern markets, and the hill country could no longer compete in agriculture. Neither did Lyme benefit from the factory epoch; though it was in a region of rapid streams, none of its water powers invited industrial enterprise. Other areas near by were more fortunate; Manchester, for example, on the Merrimack. Many of Lyme's residents, particularly the younger folk, contributed to the industrial growth of the larger cities of New Hampshire and other states.

REGIONAL CONTRASTS IN NEW ENGLAND

The Connecticut Valley in transition.   At the turn of the nineteenth century, New England's largest river lowland was in the beginning stages of its transformation from a region of subsistence agriculture and rural villages to one of specialized farming and industrialized cities. The period of change was slow to arrive, nor could anyone have predicted on the evidence available in 1800 what the future might hold. The effects of the change were not clearly evident until the 1850's, by which time the raising of leaf tobacco by foreign-born peoples or their descendants had assumed a dominant position.

Despite the presence of a splendid waterway with oceanic connections in Long Island Sound, the older order of economic life long persisted in the valley. As Martha Genthe has said, the valley lowland of the Connecticut evolved as an inland area whose main connections were overland to the east. This appears paradoxical unless the peculiar character of the Connecticut lowland is known. Through western Massachusetts and down to Middletown, Connecticut, the river meanders through a flat-to-rolling valley some 20 miles wide. But the river then leaves its broad lowland and follows a comparatively narrow river-cut valley through the hard-rock upland country. The lowland itself, a slice of rich soils dropped down, as it were, between the rugged upland country on either hand, continues on southward to Long Island Sound at New Haven, whereas the mouth of the river is at Saybrook, some 30 miles to the east.

The advantage of north-south transportation on the river, improved by a half-dozen canals by 1825, was perhaps more than offset by the breaking of travel in the other direction. The wide river delayed the erection of bridges, enforcing dependence on costly and time-consuming ferries. Costly too was the maintenance of deep-water navigation from Saybrook to Hartford, a stretch of 50 miles into which ocean-going vessels often ventured. In all probability, Hartford profited more from its position at a river crossing and from its productive hinterland than it did from maritime trade.

Descriptions of the Connecticut Valley in the early 1800's emphasize its fertility and its wide variety of products. "The chief agricultural wealth consists in the pastures and mowing lands," said traveler Edward A. Kendall in 1809 — just as it did nearly a half-century before when Robert Rogers of Rangers fame wrote of the large quantities of black cattle, horses, and swine to be seen in the intervale lands. But we may infer that the raising of sheep was new and that authorities considered it worthy of further encouragement as a basis for woolen and worsted manufacturing. At any rate, an act was passed granting "a deduction from the amount of ratable property, of seventy-five cents for shorn sheep ten months old, and sheared in the season preceding the making out of the list."

In descriptions of the use of cultivated lands on the higher terraces we find more positive evidence of change. Since wheat was cheaper to import from regions more suited to its growth, it was passing out of the picture. Increasing difficulties with the Hessian fly and the more or less mysterious "blasting" of wheat also led to the more extensive raising of the hardier rye and meslin, a mixture of rye and wheat which was still used for bread grain in the early 1800's. The first intensively tilled crop of the upper valley was broomcorn. According to the historian Sylvester Judd, broomcorn was introduced from India as early as 1785, but its growth did not become general for a dozen years or more. It is said that "strangers who were passing after the tall broom corn had put forth its panicles considered what it was and stopped to make inquiries." The manufacture of whisk brooms from the dried panicles was one of the first industries of many towns, such as Hadley and Easthampton.

The cultivation of onions was becoming increasingly important at this time, spreading northward from Wethersfield, Connecticut, where it was introduced at least by the year 1765. Travelers going up and down the valley through the one-street village of Wethersfield made reference to its surrounding fields of onions. According to Brissot de Warville's description in 1788, "Wethersfield is remarkable for its vast fields uniformly covered with onions; of which vast quantities are exported to the West Indies." It should be noted that Brissot, an emigré from the French Revolution, saw America as a great, bright land for which the most complimentary adjectives were inadequate; his "vast fields" were actually a few acres, and the onion exportation quite limited. But we do know from corroborative accounts that Wethersfield was the center from which the lowly onion spread through the valley lands. Its presence in valley economy facilitated later settlement by north-European immigrants, because it was an intensively tilled and profitable crop and capable of being grown in small patches.

The plots were at first rented from resident owners; later the frugal immigrants purchased the land and themselves became landlords.

The changes in population in the Connecticut lowland during this period of readjustment were of a more complex character than those seen in less attractive agricultural areas of New England. Here as elsewhere the opening up of the Midwest in the 1830's and later, and the greater attraction of cities, led to the abandonment of farms and the general loss of rural population; but here the decline was only temporary, because the land was promptly taken over by incoming immigrants, particularly those from Poland and Lithuania. Coming from a region not unlike the Connecticut Valley, these people could engage in familiar occupations. In their case, too, the accompanying growth of industrial cities was important, because members of the family could find productive employment in textile mills, if not the year round, at least during the winter season. Relative proximity to ports of entry was also a factor in the increasing foreign populations of the valley farms and cities.

Manufacturing in Connecticut Valley cities in the early 1800's was characteristically varied, but with emphasis on textiles and papermaking. Northampton was the largest city in the Massachusetts portion of the valley, with Springfield forming a poor second. Both were river-crossing points of long standing. Just starting were the paper mills of South Hadley Falls and Holyoke, now great industries. Greenfield was a place of less than 1,500 people, contemporarily described in a gazetteer as a "handsome, flourishing town." The manufacture of machine tools and armaments, in modern times typical of Greenfield, Millers Falls, and Springfield, was not among the original industries of the valley towns. The chief Connecticut city was Hartford, already the state capital. Laid out as early as 1636, the town had grown to nearly 5,000 by the year 1810, and was important for manufacturing.

Cape Cod, Martha's Vineyard, and Nantucket. Cape Cod and Cape Ann, the two projecting points of Massachusetts, are identified historically with maritime affairs. Only to name the Cape Ann ports of Gloucester and Marblehead is to suggest their long, almost uninterrupted connection with the fishing industry. Cape Cod's coastal towns of Provincetown, Chatham, Falmouth, Sandwich, and others are also old-time fishing ports, which in modern times have acquired additional characteristics as haunts of artists and antique-lovers. The greater extent of Cape Cod, which is properly speaking a peninsula, endows it with a variety of surface features and economic activities not possessed by the more limited Cape Ann north of Boston.

Strictly speaking, Cape Cod extends from the isthmus between Cape Cod Bay and Buzzards Bay, now cut by a ship canal, to Provincetown at the outer hook, a distance of 50 miles by road. By extension, the Cape country includes adjacent portions of Plymouth and Bristol counties and the larger islands off the south shore, notably Martha's Vineyard and Nantucket. The Cape and the islands belong physically to the Coastal Plain — in the more descriptive terminology of an earlier day, the Region of Sea Sand. The major characteristics of the Cape environment resemble those of the Coastal Plain elsewhere along the Atlantic. The use of the term " desert " was not uncommon on early-day coastal maps.

Cape Cod is a region naturally subject to changes in shore line and surface detail, the more so because the peninsula lacks a solid rock foundation. This has been no academic matter with generations of resourceful people. Severely practical problems were the making of substantial cellar holes in the unsubstantial earth and the protection of planting-fields from blowing sand. Cellars were sometimes made in circular form to secure greater strength, and trees were planted and cared for where they might serve as windbreaks.

Such planting of trees as occurred in the late eighteenth century, however, can be considered only a partial restoration of areas cleared by previous generations. The constant need of firewood in the homes was met in part by cuttings in patches of jack pine and post oak, never at any time abundant on the Cape. There is record of a near-by island, extinct by 1800, from whose originally wooded surface of 20 acres the people of Nantucket secured fuel. It would seem probable that the removal of the protective covering from the area, named on early maps as Webb Island, hastened its disappearance under the combined onslaught of wind and wave. Beginning in the late 1790's, saltmakers added to the demand for fuel, although most of the wood they consumed in evaporating sea water came across Cape Cod Bay from Boston and Portsmouth.

As the people became less dependent upon the fisheries and more upon agriculture, wooded swamps were cleared and partly drained to provide pastures for cattle. Chatham town records indicate that many swamps had been cleared by the year 1800, when only one-tenth of a square mile of woodland remained in its 12 square miles of area. Still other records indicate that the Cape had lost much of its original woodland during a century and a half of settlement. It was noted, for example, that the stumps of large trees were exposed at low tide near Provincetown. The Cape environment, naturally a poor one, appears to have depreciated during the first century or more of occupancy. Some visitors, if not residents, viewed the outer cape as " the most ungrateful soil in the world." Paul B. Sears's *Deserts on the March* (Simon and Schuster, 1937) might well have begun on Cape Cod, a bridgehead of original settlement.

Each of the twenty Cape towns relied on the fisheries, but none so much as the Truros and Provincetown at Land's End, which could boast of little except landing places and fairly good harbors. Timothy Dwight viewed Provincetown as a " mere residence " for its thousand inhabitants, and considered the three villages of Truro (Center, North, and South) as " Bleak, barren, and desolate, as if never designed to be the home of man." Provincetown's stake in the banks fishery was at that time represented by about 40 sailing vessels which regularly visited the Grand Banks, or more exactly the Strait of Belleisle. Three voyages each season were made to the distant straits between Newfoundland and Labrador.

During the interval between the outward voyage and return, relative quiet prevailed, but when the sails stood in with the new catch, usually in May, July, and October, the village came to life. In readiness on the beaches were the fish flakes or frames, a dozen yards long and raised 2 feet above the ground. Almost everyone found employment in transferring the catch from the bankers and preparing the already partly cleaned cod for the drying process.

More in the daily routine was the catching of fish in the bay and digging for clams, periwinkles, and mussels in the shallower water near shore. The occasional sighting of whales doubtless reminded the older residents of the days when the so-called common whale was really common. It is reported that in the early years of the nineteenth century, swarms of blackfish sometimes arrived near shore, whereupon the people of Truro and other Cape towns " put off in boats, get without them, and drive them like so many cattle on to the shore and flats, where they are left by the tide and fall an easy prey." The carcasses of the blackfish, a source of liver oil, littered the beaches for many days after one of these visitations.

Southward of the Truros, agriculture played an increasing role in economic life. The people of the towns of Brewster, Falmouth, Dennis, Orleans, and Sandwich combined fishing and farming. Perhaps it would be truer to say that there was a division according to age, for an observer said that the land of Orleans was cultivated by old men and boys, while " the flower of the people, between the ages of 12 and 45 are engaged in the cod-fishing." Seafaring men turning, reluctantly it must be assumed, from the seine to the plow, found that the apparently stubborn soil was moderately productive under proper management and crop selection.

Sandy-loam soils fertilized with seaweed were found to yield good crops of the common grains, and experiments with fruit-raising proved successful. More surprisingly, marsh hay was found to offer a good substitute for superior grasses, and many people felt that manure from it was superior to other types. A resident of Sandwich speaks of the " great extent and excellence of the marshes and meadows of this place," enabling the maintenance of large stocks of cattle in the winter and providing food for their subsistence through the remainder of the year, if necessary. Sandwich looked more hopefully to the future than did contiguous towns, because it lay astride the peninsula where surveys had been taken for the ship canal.

The extraction of salt from sea water in the manner described earlier was the only manufacturing industry of the Cape proper in the early 1800's. Within its immediate vicinity, however, were several busy manufacturing centers, including Taunton, Raynham, and Plymouth, which together formed probably the first iron-and-steel center of the country. Local supplies of bog-iron ore, considered at the time to be inexhaustible, had led to the early establishment of forges and bloomeries in Plymouth and Bristol counties. Indeed, Raynham claimed the first forge in America, established in 1652. Other related industries requiring skilled labor developed in the course of time — wiredrawing, nail manufacturing, firearms and armaments, farm tools, and bells. Perhaps the largest smelting plant in the country in 1810 was the Federal Furnace at Plymouth.

The general principle that islands tend to preserve older features of cultural life longer than do their near-by mainlands is partly borne out in the 1800 geography of Martha's Vineyard and Nantucket.

Martha's Vineyard was one of the few remaining areas of southern New England to have an Indian population at this time. Its 300 Indians lived mainly at Gay Head, a western cape now locally known for the bright colors of exposed shale beds which in early times furnished a small exportation of pipe clay from Edgartown, the principal port. Agriculture and home industries rather than fishing were the leading occupations of the Vineyard, even though some two-thirds of its surface was then, as now, an unproductive scrub-oak plain. Nantucket's separation from the mainland was doubtless responsible for the preservation there longer than elsewhere of " common-land " practices typical of the colonial New England towns but which disappeared during the eighteenth century.

Down in Maine. One of the earliest historians of northern New England, dutifully listing major events and accomplishments year by year, came to 1800 and remarked: " Settlements are now distributed & established upon the margin of all the tide-waters of Maine." This was the Maine of the early nineteenth century — nearly 250 miles of rugged coastland on whose almost innumerable

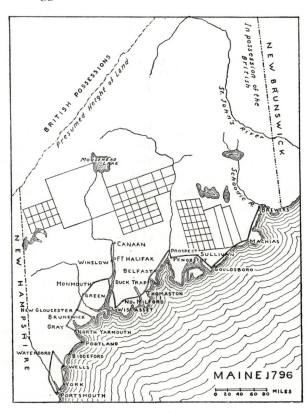

48

A map of Maine in 1796, derived from the Bradley map of post roads issued in that year and revised at later times. The map emphasizes the restriction of settlement to the coastal areas. Augusta, for example, does not appear on the 1796 map.

bays and terrace-bordered estuaries lived the quarter-million persons who formed this jurisdiction of Massachusetts. The interior of Maine, beyond a few miles of the head of tidewater, was of little consequence. (See Fig. 48.)

The now familiar expression " down in Maine," which in all probability was in good use at the time, referred to this bold coastland, more varied in topographic detail than any other section of the Atlantic seaboard of the United States. Because it bore little resemblance to Massachusetts and, in terms of travel of that day, was remote from Boston, Maine's separation from the parent state was urged at an early time. A Maine orator remarked in 1791 that " our detached and already dismembered situation from the other parts of the Commonwealth " made advisable a new government which " might be constructed in such a manner as to apply directly to the local situation, climate, habits and business of every part of the territory." Despite numerous proposals of similar emphasis, the District, as it was called, remained under the wing of Massachusetts until 1821.

Noting that the coast of Maine runs more east-west than north-south, early geographical writers divided the area for discussion into three principal sections: (1) western coast from the New Hampshire line to Casco Bay and Portland, (2) middle coast from Kennebec River to the Penobscot River, and (3) eastern coast from the Penobscot to Passamaquoddy Bay.

The western coast, with Casco Bay, was the most completely settled area by the year 1810. Here were the growing towns, named from south to north, of Kittery, York, Berwick, Wells, Biddeford, and Portland. All seaport towns, each combined the maritime activities of fishing and boatbuilding with some agriculture and forest industries. A description of York in 1794 has this to say:

The soil is rocky and very hard of cultivation, especially on the sea-coast and the northerly parts of the town. Indeed a large proportion of it, perhaps two-thirds, is incapable of any other cultivation than what spontaneously arises. The principal settlements and improvements are within a mile and a quarter of the largest inlet and upon each side thereof. . . . The principal employment of the inhabitants is agriculture, many of whom must be frugal and industrious to obtain a subsistence [from corn, barley, wheat, rye, potatoes].

Already the largest town of the western coast was Portland (nearly 8,000 inhabitants in 1810), on a peninsula of Casco Bay. Its deep, safe, and ample harbor, which was seldom closed in winter, was busy with shipbuilding and coastal trade. Large quantities of lumber and cordwood went out of Portland and Casco Bay to southern New England. Augusta, the future capital of Maine, was a small town of about 2,000 in 1810.

Maine's middle coast contains the largest indentation — the estuary of the Penobscot — and the greatest array of off-lying islands. This area was settled later than was the Kennebec estuary; hence there were no communities comparable in size to Portland. The historical development of Ellsworth at the head of Union River estuary, seemingly typical of early Maine settlements, has been

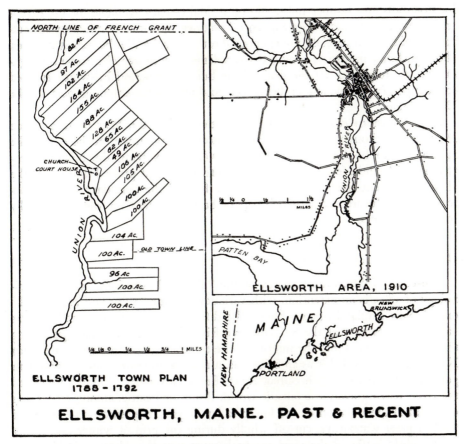

ELLSWORTH, MAINE. PAST & RECENT

49 Ellsworth, Maine, showing the original town plat of 1790 and the present-day situation of the village. For details on the area consult Derwent Whittlesey, " Coastland and Interior Mountain Valley: A Geographical Study of Two Typical Localities in Northern New England," in *New England's Prospect,* American Geographical Society, Special Publication 16, 1933.

touched upon in several places. The town of Ellsworth was carved out of an earlier French grant by order of the General Court in 1787, its original settlers coming from Biddeford and Scarboro and selecting lots which were surveyed between 1788 and 1793. Incorporated under the name of Sumner by court order in 1800, the town was renamed Ellsworth at a later time. (See Fig. 49.)

According to Professor Derwent Whittlesey, the narrow coastal lowlands which form the town site were essentially in their naturally wooded condition at the time of settlement. The nonagricultural Indian population was presumably small; in any case, " Indians when near the coast were fully occupied in catching and curing fish and game." Ellsworth was situated at an early crossing place on the Union River, at the lower end of a series of rapids which provided power for gristmills and lumber mills, and on a tidal estuary available for use except from December to May. (See Fig. 49.) The town remained dominantly agricultural until the commercial-lumber epoch shortly after the War between the States, although forest industries provided a supplementary source of income throughout the entire period. At the peak of the lumbering period Ellsworth enjoyed the temporary distinction of being the leading lumber-shipping port in the United States.

Maine's eastern coast was but little settled before the War of 1812, when Machias was thought of as the "farthest-north" large town on the coast. The future was to hold some international troubles involving the boundary between Maine and New Brunswick, but until settlement pressed northward the simple statement that the St. Croix River formed the boundary was satisfactory. Let the future decide which part or branch of the river was intended by the treaty-makers.

UP THE ST. LAWRENCE

The coast of Maritime Canada, or the "British Possessions," in the terminology of 1800, is an extension, with variations, of the "stern and rockbound" one of New England's poetic fame. The difference of greatest magnitude was (and is) the estuary of the St. Lawrence River, which permits passage during the summer months into the interior of the continent. No other river of eastern North America rivaled it as an open-season route to interior points; it was with good reason often called the Great River. From November to March ice closed the river, barring away the outside world. Professor Peattie, among others, has emphasized the isolation of the lower valley despite its position on one of the world's great waterways, cut off wholly during the grip of winter and faring only slightly better in the open season because vessels trading to Quebec had little occasion, other than the delivery of mail, to stop on the way. Wintertime mail and small-package freight went in and out of Quebec and other river points by an overland route opened in 1783 from the Rivière du Loup to St. John in New Brunswick. This road, more than 600 miles long, was sometimes known as the Temiscouata Portage route, a section of which is shown in Figure 50.

Summer-season navigation of the St. Lawrence has been greatly altered by river improvements. In its original and natural state, ocean-going vessels proceeded without interruption to Quebec, which was considered the head of deep-water navigation. Some large vessels ventured into the swifter water and dangerous channels between Quebec and Montreal, but smaller boats generally handled the traffic in this section. Ten miles above the island of Montreal, navigation was again interrupted by the Lachine (China) Rapids, so named in the earliest days when the discovery of a Northwest Passage to the Orient was confidently expected, and the size of North America was grossly underestimated.

The 200 miles of river above the rapids to Kingston on Lake Ontario were negotiated by other boats called batteaux by their French oarsmen, of whom

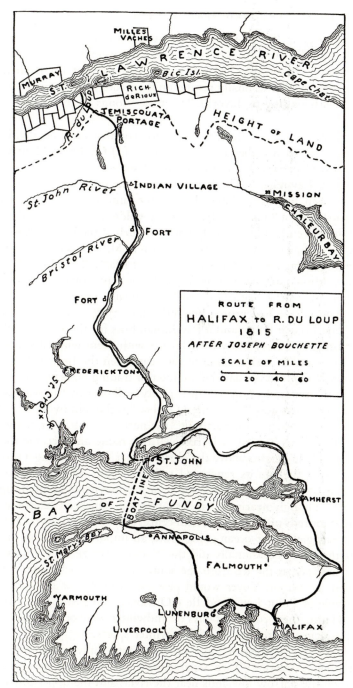

50 A section of the large map showing the Temiscouata Portage route from the St. Lawrence River to New Brunswick and Nova Scotia. From Joseph Bouchette, *Topographical Description*, 1815, opposite p. 536.

four made up a crew. To go up-river against the strong and variable currents encountered from Montreal to Kingston required a week's time; the return was an easy journey of three days in craft laden with bales of fur from the back country, the crewmen occasionally resting on their oars while the current carried them along, perhaps singing favorite " Canuck " songs in their joy at heading homeward.

For descriptive purposes the St. Lawrence country may be divided into: (1) the lower river, (2) Quebec and the Narrows, (3) Quebec to Montreal — the heart of French Canada, and (4) the Montreal section.

The lower St. Lawrence.   The lower river, at the opening of the nineteenth century, had been but little changed since the time of Cartier. Said traveler Patrick Campbell of it in 1793, " The gloomy wilderness in which the traveler is often lost has no end and is inhabited only by such of the savage tribe as prefer shade to light." A few extensive seigniories, such as Milles Vaches and Rimouski, and the trading village of Tadoussac, comprised nearly the sum total of settlement on this portion of the river. The frequent representation on maps of Tadoussac, at the mouth of the Saguenay, gave it a greater importance than its size warranted. The village had grown but little since 1746, when it was described as having " one French house and a few Indian huts for the savages, who come here at fair time, and carry away their booths with them when it is over." The " fair time " referred to is the season of the year when the Indians brought furs to the river settlements in the days before interior trading posts became common; that phase of the fur trade, however, was pretty well over by the year 1800.

Quebec at the Narrows.   The name " Quebec " is thought by some authorities to derive from an Indian word meaning " the narrows "; at any rate the French town established here in 1608 early received this name and became the capital of New France. The heights above the older quarter, commanding a broad view of the river, gave the site its renowned military value. The location of a city at the first narrows going upstream was as nearly inevitable as anything can be in geography. Though nearly 400 miles upstream, Quebec's harbor could accommodate hundreds of early-nineteenth-century vessels; and it was at this time the head of navigation for ocean-going craft, an important position during the winter months. Only occasionally did the Narrows freeze over solidly enough to permit travel across the ice from the south shore. At such times a local authority called the Grand Voyer would pass on its safety for transportation; if safe, the people of Point Levis and Ile d'Orléans could easily cross over to the larger city. Hence, these cold *pont* days of midwinter were occasions of rejoicing and of horse-racing on the ice and other winter sports.

In 1810 Quebec was a city of some 12,000 persons, fully two-thirds of whom were of French extraction. Two separate town nuclei were recognized: the lower town on the narrow lowlands near the river, and the upper town situated on the heights which rise abruptly, almost perpendicularly. In the words of Isaac Weld, who visited Quebec in 1800, " there is a communication between the two towns, by means of streets winding up the side of [the bluff], though even here the ascent is so great that there are long flights of stairs at one side of the street, for the accommodation of foot passengers."

The St. Lawrence Valley from Quebec to Montreal.   The heart of Lower or French Canada lay between Quebec and Montreal, a stretch of about 200 miles. Here lived by far the greater proportion of the estimated 200,000 people of Lower Canada. They occupied the lowlands and terraces on both sides of the St. Lawrence River as well as its numerous tributaries. Visitors were uniformly impressed with the " street-village " type of occupancy to which reference has already been made. Continued subdivisions of the seigniories had resulted in close spacing of houses. The average of 10 houses to the mile was occasionally interrupted by large towns such as Trois Rivières (Three Rivers). The report of one traveler, typical of many, states that the road from Quebec to Montreal

. . . differs from all others I have seen, in this, that it may be said to be almost a continued street; one house succeeds another so quickly that I believe I may safely say there is not a mile without one. Except for the town of Trois rivières, you have scarcely any place that deserves the name of a town: but every parish church has a village in its neighborhood and of these there are between Quebec and Montreal, upwards of twenty.

The seigniories of Lower Canada (see Fig. 11, page 47) were grouped by the British into three administrative areas known as District of Quebec, with 87 seigniories, District of Trois Rivières with 40, and District of Montreal, with 55. Together they included about 2,750,000 acres of improved land, most of which was in the lower lands and terraces near the river. Extending well inland, the holdings included higher and rougher pasture land and woodland, with varied soils which contributed to the self-sufficing economy of the people. Many who have condemned the method of land subdivision which developed here have failed to appreciate the fact that each unit included a variety of soils and resources that another system might not have provided.

French-Canadian agriculture was emphatically self-sufficing, with arable land used for crops such as potatoes, onions, corn, and some small cereals. Sheep, horses, and cattle were grazed in meadows and upland pastures and in the wooded tracts. The family produced its own dairy products and meat, and clothing was made from wool woven in the household. Woodland areas furnished raw materials for building and cordwood for fuel, as well as maple sap for syrup and sugar, a substitute for cane sugar. Apples were abundantly produced, and from them cider was pressed. In addition each habitant maintained a garden and kept poultry, and there was always the river from which fish could be secured. It will be seen that commercial towns found little place in this type of economy.

The notable exception was the town of Trois Rivières, so named from the apparent confluence of three rivers midway between Quebec and Montreal on the north shore where the St. Maurice River breaks into a number of separate channels. Founded as early as 1610, the community grew with the fur trade, especially in the earlier period when Indians brought their peltry to the annual fair. Some of its original advantages were lost, however, with the increasing importance of Montreal, which was nearer the source of furs and the newly established posts in the interior. Compensating for these trade losses was the large extent of productive land within the District of Trois Rivières.

The island city of Montreal.   In 1800, Montreal was a picturesque place about the size of Quebec, with an interesting past but no bright prospects for the future. Its site was a small portion of one of the islands formed by the splitting of the St. Lawrence River into three branches. In aboriginal days there had been a village here (Hochelaga), and still later a town named Ville Marie, from which Montreal grew, but of the ancient walls which had enclosed the town only the gates remained. In the parlance of the time, the built-up areas beyond the walls or their crumbled remains were known as the suburbs. Even the traveler Weld, who was more enthusiastic about Canada than about the United States, found the homes of the old city of " very gloomy appearance, and look like so many prisons, being all furnished at the outside with sheet iron shutters to the doors and windows, which are regularly closed towards evening, in order to guard against fire." The walls were serviceable in early days " when the large fairs used to be held in Montreal, to which the Indians from all parts of the country resorted with their furs . . . as the inhabitants were thereby enabled to shut out the Indians at night."

From the eminence of Mount Royal an attractive and extensive countryside was seen, and another visitor " beheld many lively landscapes. The city and the islands in the river, or rather lake which surrounds the island and mountain of Montreal, and Isle Jésu, unite in entertaining the sight in endless variety. This is the magazine for fruit, in particular for apples for the province."

Montreal looked more to the west than to the east before the days of river improvement. By interior lake and river the city was connected with a tenuous string of forts and posts where the fur trade in the manner of the nineteenth century was being conducted. Gone were the days when the Indians docilely came to the settlements with their peltry, perhaps to be tricked by sharp merchants; now the trading companies were dispatching their employees to the Indian country. No doubt the Indian was still the loser, but the change in procedure, to be discussed in the next section, reacted to the benefit of Montreal.

Frontiers of the Seaboard States and the St. Lawrence Valley

Penetration of the "back country," first by trader and then by settler, was a continuous process during the eighteenth century, with the greatest gains in the Southern states. It is notable, for example, that the original Western states were Kentucky and Tennessee, the former reaching statehood in 1792 and the latter four years later. In contrast, the larger part of the Territory Northwest of the Ohio River was still essentially Indian country to 1810, with only Ohio as a full-fledged state (1803).

The greater encroachments on the erstwhile Indian country in the South were first emphasized by Frederick Jackson Turner, whose teachings and writings in the field of frontier history have become classic. Turner early pointed out that "the leaders of this southern element came in considerable measure from the well-to-do classes, who migrated to improve their conditions in the freer opportunity of a new country." The main body of pioneer settlers in Kentucky and Tennessee was represented by the poorer classes, not slaveholders — a democratic society augmented by Germans and Scotch-Irish. Not only did the Southern settlers move into the valleys of the Appalachians and beyond them through natural openings into Tennessee and Kentucky, but according to Turner they also "furnished the great bulk of settlers north of the Ohio" at a later time.

The frontier zone of 1810 straddled the Appalachian highlands and extended as bulges of "white man's country" into the already famed Nashville Basin and the Kentucky Bluegrass region. Extending northward, the zone of new settlement swung eastward through Pennsylvania and upstate New York, regions which had been only recently wrested from aboriginal hands. Canada's frontier pressed closely on the very borders of the St. Lawrence lowland, from which the Laurentian uplands rose in forbidding fashion — forbidding, that is, to the farmer, yet attractive to the fur trader. As Arthur R. M. Lower has said, the Laurentian uplands "interpose the most formidable of obstacles between the usable regions of the East and the fertile ones of the West." Because the uplands north of the Great Lakes have changed less than have the other areas which were called " Western " in the early years of the past century, this reconstruction of our early American frontier commences with that region and proceeds south-ward.

THE FUR TRADE COUNTRY NORTH OF THE GREAT LAKES

The vast extent of the fur-trade country is suggested in Figure 51. During this period and for some time thereafter Montreal was the Eastern entrepôt, although some cities in the United States, earlier rivaling Montreal (for example, Albany), still profited from the trade. With big and powerful companies in control, the day of the small-time trader was pretty well over. Naturally enough, as Sir Alexander Mackenzie said in 1801, " the animals whose skins were precious " had become extinct near the settlements, so that longer and longer journeys must be made to reach profitable territory. Long trips required more adequate financing than could be accomplished by a free-lance trader; financing was also necessary in the purchasing of trading goods and the maintenance of posts in the distant interior. The leading company, with headquarters in Montreal, was the North West Company, which, says Professor Innis, " had its origin in the demand for increasing capital following the extension of trade into the Athabaska country." The North West Company, organized in 1783–84, was largely directed by Englishmen and Scots and within a short time developed systematic procedures.

Routes from Montreal to interior establishments.   Montreal with its outpost

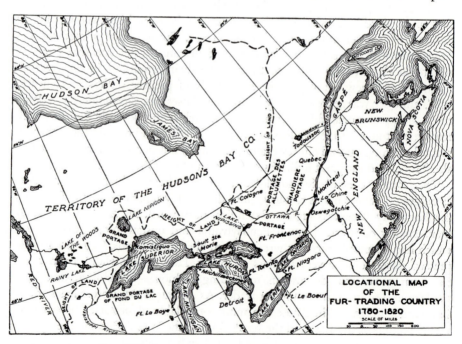

51   The fur-trading country tributary to Montreal

of Lachine at the head of the rapids was a natural focus of water routes over which the trade circulated. The city is at the node of a Y of which the two limbs are represented by the rivers Ottawa and upper St. Lawrence. Both were important in the fur trade, but especially so was the Ottawa, which cut westward into the wilderness and offered a fairly direct route to Georgian Bay of Lake Huron, through Lake Nipissing and French (or Frenchman's) River. By this route Michilimackinac and Sault Ste. Marie were some 700 miles away — a journey of a month or six weeks for experienced voyageurs.

The Island of Michilimackinac, or Mackinac as it is known today (pronounced măk'ĭ·naw), was the most important post within the fur country. From this strategic place, goods and supplies brought up from Montreal were distributed to inland posts or " wintering stations," some of which had only temporary existence, and the furs and peltry secured during the winter season were assembled and baled for transportation to Montreal. On the island and at near-by St. Ignace on the northern mainland of the straits were Indian missions. A visitor to Michilimackinac in 1820 described the town, harbor, and Forts Mackinac and Holmes built upon it as

. . . picturesque and sublime. The Town contains 100 buildings, including a Court-house and jail; the houses are generally constructed of bark. The population is chiefly French who are mostly very poor. At this place is stationed the Head Quarters of the American Fur Company; this company is very extensive and their establishments are spread over all the country between the Mississippi & the great lakes. They have about 300 men in their employment who come to Mackinac in the spring with the fur collected during the winter, where they stay from one to three months, when they receive another assortment of [trading] goods and proceed to their wintering grounds.

Patterned after Mackinac, but on a smaller scale, were many other posts or " establishments " as they were then called, such as Sault Ste. Marie, La Pointe (near present-day Ashland, Wisconsin), and Sandy Lake, one of the headwaters of the Mississippi River in Minnesota.

The operations of the North West Company were regulated to a great extent by the seasons. During the winter in Montreal, preparations were made for the departure of the trading canoes when the rivers and lakes should open in the spring. The canoes were about 35 feet long, 4½ feet wide, and 30 inches deep, so constructed as to float over 4 tons of burden, and light enough for portaging. Trading goods and provisions were packaged into 80-pound bundles for convenience in handling and portaging, the load of a voyageur being two such packages. According to Mackenzie, a trading canoe setting out from Lachine would have a crew of eight or ten men

. . . and their baggage; and sixty-five packages of goods, six hundred weight of biscuit, two hundred weight of pork, three bushels of pease, for the men's provisions; two oil cloths to cover the goods, a sail, etc., an axe, a towing line, a kettle, and a sponge for bailing out the water, with a quantity of gum, bark, and watape [pliant spruce roots] to repair the vessle.

It is not surprising that the so-called canoes were loaded to the gunwales upon departure from Lachine. They were dispatched in " brigades " of 50 or more, early in May. George Heriot, an eyewitness, reported seeing the departure of one such brigade with a human cargo of 373 men of whom " three hundred and fifty are navigators, eighteen are guides, and five are clerks."

The journey up the Ottawa and across to Lake Nipissing and Frenchman's River was interrupted by frequent portages and half-portages; here was a nice distinction defined by Mackenzie thus: " The place where the goods alone are carried, is called a Décharge [half-portage], and that where the goods and canoes are both transported, is denominated a Portage." Another definition, that " a portage is the longest distance between two points," takes on meaning when it is realized that the portage paths around falls or between rivers were likely to become gutters of mud in rainy weather and that the voyageur's load was two packs of goods, weighing together 160 pounds, carried on the back with straps around the forehead. There were 10 portages and décharges on the Ottawa, followed by a portage to Lake Nipissing, and others down Frenchman's River to Georgian Bay. Mackenzie realistically describes some of those encountered on the Ottawa: At Chaudière portage (see Fig. 51, page 174),

. . . the rock is so steep and difficult of access that it requires twelve men to take the canoe out of the water: it is then carried by six men. . . . From hence to the next is but a short distance, in which they make two trips to the second Portage de Chaudière, which is seven hundred paces, to the carrying place alone. From hence to the next and last Chaudière, or Portage des Chênes, is about six miles, with a very strong current, where the goods are carried seven hundred and forty paces; the canoe being towed up by the line, when the water is not very high.

Other Ottawa portages were Des Allumettes, Des Sables, Grand Calumet, and Roche Capitaine, with décharges at Derige and Trou. There were 36 carrying places on the Ottawa-Nipissing route, according to the traveler Joseph Hadfield.

From the mouth of Frenchman's River the voyage was by lake shore to Mackinac, where the goods were distributed to other posts. These included stations on Lake Superior and Rainy River by way of Kamistigua, where Fort William is now located, and over the Grand Portage of Pigeon River. Care should be taken to distinguish the two Grand Portages of the Lake Superior country, the better known of which is on the Pigeon River-Rainy River route. Somewhat less important was the Grand Portage of Fond du Lac, from above present Duluth to the Mississippi headwaters at Sandy Lake. The men who transferred the goods to the lesser interior stations were referred to, apparently with some disdain, as Goers and Comers or Pork-eaters.

Trader Long relates the activities of a typical wintering station north of Lake Nipigon. In April, he says, a large band of Indians came to the post with the winter's catch, and " having disposed of all my merchandise except a few articles, and a small quantity of rum . . . we baled up our peltry, and on the 23rd of May left Lac la Mort, with four small birch canoes richly laden with the skins

of beavers, otters, martens, minx, loup seviers, beaver eaters, foxes, bears, etc."
Accompanying the party of sixteen Canadian traders were about twenty Indians
who assisted at carrying places. He delivered his cargo of 140 packs of furs on
August 10 and "loaded the canoes with fresh goods; then taking leave of my
companions, prepared for my departure for the Inlands, to winter another year
among the Nipegon Savages." Long felt that his salary of £150 for the year
was no more than enough.

Fur types from the interior. The Laurentian uplands and the prairie plains
to the west were the natural habitat of many types of animals supplying either
"fancy fur" for coats and neckpieces, or skins and felting hair. Most in demand
at this time was the beaver, the rapid extermination of which in older hunting
grounds led to swift advances into virgin territory. The beavers' habits of life,
which confined them to local habitats largely of their own making, made them
an easy prey to experienced hunters, who opened the water-margin dens with
trenching tools through the winter ice. In this manner entire families were
secured, effectively limiting the reproduction rate, which even under natural
conditions was relatively low.

Other important skins were those of fox, deer, wolf, wolverine, fisher, raccoon,
and bear. Bison still ranged as far east as the Mississippi River in the United States
and northward to Great Slave Lake; hence buffalo robes were shipped from
Mackinac. "The . . . furs and skins which are collected annually at Mackinac
and the north west country are supposed to be 5 or 6,000 packs valued at £15 stg.
per pack," said Hadfield, a close observer of the fur trade, in 1785. In that year
Detroit exported about half that amount. The North West Company produced
the following numbers of fur pelts and skins in 1798, according to Mackenzie:

PELTS TAKEN IN 1798

(North West Company)

Beaver	106,000
Marten	32,000
Muskrat	17,000
Lynx	6,000
Fox	5,500
Otter	4,600
Wolf	3,800
Bear	2,100
Deer	1,950
Mink	1,800
Fisher	1,650
Elk	700
Wolverine	600
Buffalo robes	500
Raccoon	100
TOTAL	184,300

BOOM SETTLEMENT IN UPSTATE NEW YORK

While French voyageurs were toiling through the Laurentian wilderness, the advance guard of pioneers was transforming the lands of the Onondaga and the Mohawk into white man's country. The invasion was little short of epic. Until the 1780's, the frontier line in New York remained stationary at Rome, or the site of Fort Stanwix. Beyond were the villages and hunting grounds of the strong Six Nations, occasionally visited by adventurous missionaries and traders but seldom by anyone intending to remain permanently. Reports filtering back to the old towns in the lower Mohawk Valley encouraged land-seekers to believe that it was a fine country, as indeed it later proved to be.

The evacuation of the Indian peoples began with the military raids of Generals John Sullivan and James Clinton in 1779 and concluded with a series of treaties, of which the most notable was the Treaty of Canandaigua in 1794. By this time most of the few Indians remaining in western New York were on reservations. Portion by portion, vast areas passed from the former claimants to the ownership of the state, of great land companies, and of individuals. In no other Eastern state was so large an area of potentially valuable country made available for white settlement in so short a time. That is why New York State experienced a boom unmatched by the other seaboard states. As many as 60,000 people streamed into the country beyond Rome within the two decades following 1790. Because many of the processes were later repeated on an even grander scale in the Ohio River country, a study of this movement, involving as it did promotion activities by land companies, is of special interest.

As early as 1791 it was reported of upstate New York that "immigrants are swarming into this fertile region in shoals like the ancient Israelites seeking the land of promise." In the majority opinion, the bounty lands of the Military Tract and the newly opened Genesee Country offered great opportunities. Beyond the possibilities of farming, there were known resources of water power and lumber, and the presence of minerals was strongly suspected. Moreover, the natural groove through the Appalachian Highlands, known as the Mohawk Lowland, provided an easy route to the lower Great Lakes. The heights to the south of the lowland received special approval, for here were excellent soils at various levels of the plateau surface. Rivers flowing northward across the plateau presented two or more series of falls as they plunged down the eroded faces of escarpments, or "steeps" as they were then called. The Genesee Falls, upper and lower, for example, were 60 and 90 feet respectively, and it was freely predicted that they would become centers of manufacturing.

Most famous of New York's waterfalls was Niagara. Although not yet significant for water power, Niagara attracted many travelers, whose descriptions of the cataract and the country on the way are of great interest. On approaching the falls of Niagara, said Volney, "attention is at first awakened by a dull and rumbling sound like the roar of a remote sea"; the portion of the falls beyond Goat Island "moulds itself into the form of a horseshoe. . . . For more than eighteen hundred feet round the spray fills the air, and descending in columns, wets the spectator to the skin."

The chasm below the falls was interpreted as the result of the retreat of the falls in past ages, but the time that this would have required conflicted seriously with Biblical interpretations. A Mr. Robert M'Causlin, who had observed the falls for nine years by 1793, reflected: " If we adopt the opinion of the Falls having retreated six miles, and if we suppose the world to be 5700 years old, this will give above 56 inches and a half a year, or sixteen yards and two thirds for nine years, which I can venture to say has not been the case since 1774." Andrew Ellicott prophesied that the retreat of the falls would some day provide a time scale for the age of the earth.

The great extent of treeless country was an impressive feature to travelers through western New York. On such a journey Timothy Bigelow noted in the vicinity of present-day Batavia " hundreds of acres of open country with but a few log huts upon it. . . . Glancing the eye over these open grounds, they look like a settled and cultivated country; but the want of houses and fences and more especially the solemn stillness that prevails over them, admonish you that you are in a wilderness." Bigelow and others inferred that many of the openings were caused by Indian fires that were set " so that the tender grass, afterwards springing up, might entice the deer and other game out into a situation where they would be exposed to the hunter." There were also countless Indian old fields near the sites of former Indian villages, for the members of the Six Nations in their unmolested state were sedentary and agricultural. Aboriginal farming was so advanced that orchards were found by the first settlers near Geneva.

Of the extensive tracts of land into which upstate New York was divided in the boom settlement period, three will be discussed in some detail: the New Military Tract, the Genesee Country, and the Macomb Tract. (See Fig. 52.)

The New Military Tract. Western settlement was off to a good start with the designation of a part of the newly acquired territory as a reserve within which veterans of the Revolution could take up their bounty lands. Actually, a Military Tract had been in existence since 1781, but its location in the then remote north-eastern part of the state rendered it unattractive to settlers. Veterans who had been reluctant to seek bounty lands near Lake Champlain might be expected to show interest in the *New* Military Tract — often appearing on maps and in writings without the first adjective.

The New Military Tract of the 1790's included 1,500,000 acres of land in east-central New York, corresponding roughly to the present-day counties of Onondaga, Cayuga, Tompkins, and Cortland. The region may also be identified as the eastern portion of the Finger Lake country, in the early 1800's, as now, unsurpassed in natural charm and variety of resources. We may be sure that even if there had been no deliberate stimulation, this area would have been rapidly settled. Nature had endowed it with qualities sufficient to satisfy a land-hungry people — good soil, timber, water power, proved mineral resources in the form of salt, location on the way to the Far West through the Mohawk

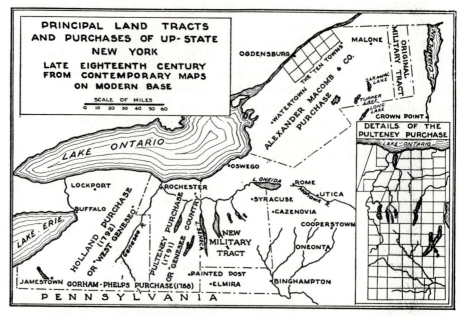

52 The land settlement tracts of New York State in the late eighteenth century. This illustration is based upon many contemporary maps, particularly one published by the promoters of the Genesee Tract in *Observations on the Proposed State Road,* New York, 1811.

Lowland, and approaches from the south by way of the upper Susquehanna River.

The Military Tract was probably superior to the regions east of it where boom settlements had already occurred, such as the one reported by Judge William Cooper of Cooperstown. In 1785 Judge Cooper visited " the hilly country of Otsego, where there existed not an inhabitant, nor any trace of a road "; but in May, 1786, " I opened the sales of 40,000 acres which, in sixteen days, were all taken up by the poorest order of man."

The Military Tract was surveyed into square-mile sections and made available for patenting by veterans, only a few of whom when put to the test proved to be genuine settlers. Instead, the " scrip " which entitled each veteran to a section of land soon acquired a market value, and most of it was bought up by real-estate agents. A historian's comment that " the lots became a rich mine for active and often unscrupulous speculators " is confirmed by several contemporary visitors who on their way to Niagara Falls paused in the Tract to witness American settlement in practice. Said John Maude in the year 1800, " These patents were soon bought up by the speculators, who very rarely gave more than eight dollars, or half a joe, for each patent of six hundred acres, now selling from three to six dollars per acre."

Many land-buyers arrived only to find their lots occupied by squatters who were fully prepared to assert their claims to priority. Disputes to titles notwith-standing, there were at least 30,000 people in the Tract in 1804 and others were on the way. The great majority were native-born families from near-by states. An eyewitness found that most of the settlers between Seneca and Cayuga lakes were from Pennsylvania, having come up the Susquehanna River route, with New Englanders predominating elsewhere. Probably typical of the Military Tract settler was Jedediah Barber, who as a young man set out from Woodstock, Connecticut, for Onondaga, where older members of his family were already in residence. Barber became a pioneer citizen of Homer, developing a general store under the momentous title of " The Great Western Store." Homer is one of many cities and towns of the Military Tract bearing classical names, in har-mony with the " classical revival " of this period, revealed in architecture and other forms of art. Syracuse, Marathon, Manlius, Camillus, Marcellus, Tully, Pompey, and Cincinnatus are interesting ingredients of the potpourri of Ameri-can place names.

The principal early industry of the Military Tract was agriculture, with wheat as the main crop. The making of salt near Syracuse was also of significance. Springs emptying into Salt Lake provided some of the many early saltworks at the village appropriately called Salina. The annual product of 60,000 bushels was considered remarkable in the early 1800's.

Genesee country.   To the emigrant of the 1790's, " Genesee country " meant almost all of western New York just as, at a later time, " Pike's Peak country " embraced the Colorado Rockies. To be specific, the Genesee country was a rec-tangular tract extending west of the military lands to the Genesee River and from Lake Ontario to the Pennsylvania line — 2,250,000 acres of opportunity. The east and west limits of Steuben County, if extended to Lake Ontario, give an approximation of the extent of this tract within which the first large-scale scheme of land settlement was worked out. Plans for its settlement were of British origin, modified to suit American conditions as then understood. In 1791 the tract was purchased from its American owners by Sir William Pulteney, a wealthy Scot-tish landowner who during the next few years exerted remote control over its destinies through agents, of whom the first and most influential was a Captain Charles Williamson.

A profusion of advertising literature in the form of anonymous pamphlets and maps attributed to Williamson or his coworkers brought the story of the tract to the attention of readers in this country, in Britain, and in France. These promotional writings, as may be suspected, placed regional opportunities in a favorable light and sought to break down the prevalent idea that the Genesee country was " unhealthy." Emphasis was laid on the excellent farming land, the extensive forests and mineral resources, the favorable climate (because of prox-imity to Lake Ontario, it was said), and the probability of canal communica-tions with the Hudson River and the lower Great Lakes. Moreover, it was urged, the Genesee country possessed a secondary outlet to world markets through the Susquehanna River route to Baltimore and Chesapeake Bay. Appealing to the good sense of emigrants, the pamphleteers reasoned against going far out into the Ohio country for good land when there was plenty of it " close in " along the Genesee.

Promotional advertising of the Genesee area had a large element of painting the lily, and it is to the credit of the management that their descriptions and maps were of a comparatively high order. In an attempt to avoid the evils of land speculation, the management limited the amount purchasable by an individual; residence and early improvement of the property were also required — provisions not unlike those of the national Homestead Acts of a later time. Plans also included the predetermination of the sites of towns and villages. A dozen or more community sites were selected and named before the tide of settlement broke on the Genesee. Gifted with no more than the usual foresight, the managers were not wholly successful in planning towns before the need arose; some towns failed to live beyond the blueprint stage, others actually came into existence but did not progress as was anticipated.

Bath, now the county seat of Steuben County, was selected as the future metropolis of the interior, while Rochester was not included in the original plans. A visitor to Bath in 1795 remarked that so rapidly was the country being occupied and so evident " the busy hum of men, that instead of being indebted for their support, they will henceforth annually supply the low country, Baltimore especially, with many hundred barrels of flour and head of cattle." The development of the Genesee Tract and all of New York to the west of it (originally known as " West Genesao ") into one of the most densely populated parts of the country justifies the faith that the promoters and the settlers had in it.

The Macomb Tract and the Ten Towns. While emigrants were pouring into the Genesee country, the State of New York continued to look with anxiety upon its still-empty northern frontier. Actual fortification of the " danger zone " along the Canadian border was not seriously considered, but people in high places nevertheless thought it desirable to have a solid line of settlements in the north country. The old military bounty-land provisions in the counties of Franklin, Essex, and Clinton had failed to accomplish their purpose, but something might yet be done. Between 1782 and 1795 this huge area northward of the Adirondacks had been purchased from the Indians, who, while having few villages there, had regarded it as their hunting grounds for deer and beaver.

Unfortunately for state policies, the citizens of New York viewed the area in somewhat similar terms, questioning the possibilities of actual land settlement. Washington Irving visited the Black River country in 1803 and returned with a discouraging account of its bad roads and extensive forests. " When we were out of the woods," said Irving, " we had nothing to entertain the sight but fields . . . disfigured with burnt roots & stumps & fallen bodies of trees. Now and then in the course of a few miles you may pass by a log house round which the land is partially cleared, a dreary scene."

Legislative plans to settle the north country took shape in an act empowering the Board of Land Commissioners to lay out ten townships along the St. Lawrence and to dispose of the nearly 4,000,000 acres of back country. Out of this plan came the so-called Ten Towns of the St. Lawrence, or Canadian Ten Towns. The townships, of 100 square miles each, were surveyed in two tiers of five, with one tier stretching 50 miles along the river. The intention of the state as shown by the original act (abrogated in 1830) was to sell the land in moderate-sized plots to a large number of purchasers; but like many another plan, this one did not work out as anticipated. When put up at public auction in New York City, the towns and back country, all except 2 square miles in each township, were sold to wealthy Alexander Macomb — the first in a series of land deals which finally reached down to individual buyers and genuine settlers. There was no great rush to the Ten Towns, and gaps in frontier settlement long remained more prominent than solid fronts. Deliberate efforts to stimulate border settlement gradually disappeared with the coming of more peaceful relations between the United States and Britain.

THE APPALACHIAN COUNTRY AND BEYOND

When Volney, the sensitive French geographer, reached the trans-Appalachian country in 1796, he observed "a singular, though natural circumstance, that I had scarcely crossed the Alleganies before I heard the borderers of the great Kanhaway and the Ohio give in their turn the name of Back Country to the Atlantic coast, which shows that their geographical situation has given their views and interests a new direction, conformable to that of the waters which afford them means of conveyance towards the Gulf of Mexico." It is never safe, as we all know, for a much-used pot to call a kettle black, but city dwellers along the seaboard would doubtless have been astonished to hear themselves called back-country people.

The Appalachian Highlands, scored though they were with many fertile valleys and cut by numerous passageways east and west, served to separate the people of the new West from the older Atlantic seaboard. It was a different country, in which settlement was keynoted by spontaneity. There were no great companies with ready-made schemes for land disposal, no agents with contracts awaiting signatures. Land jobbers, like "revenooers," remained obscurely in the background. Individuals, families, and groups of families, with their household effects and livestock, took to the trails and roads "on their own."

Some of the states had issued military scrip to veterans, but the several governments made little attempt to direct land settlement. Perhaps this was just as well, because the people early showed a great disdain for established authority. The movement toward formation of an independent state of Franklin, in what is now East Tennessee, reflected the prevalent attitude. As Frederick Turner has said, the objective of the frontiersmen was to better their circumstances — just how, perhaps few of them could have clearly said. At any rate they were ready to take the chance, in a mountain empire that offered so much variety and had been, by 1800, freed from Indian troubles.

In taking up new land in the Appalachian country, the qualities of the soil for agriculture played a dominant role; settlers also looked to the possibilities of grazing, the wealth of near-by forests, and the availability of a good supply of water. If, in addition, there were salt licks and opportunities for getting fish and game, the site was considered ideal. Coal was discovered in various Appalachian regions by 1750 at least, and it was soon put to various uses, but that mineral seems to have had little effect in localizing original settlement. The early development of Pennsylvania's iron resources was not as an independent industry but was allied to agriculture; moreover, the fuel first used on the so-called iron plantations was charcoal made from hickory and other hardwoods. These various factors will be considered, after a survey of routes into and across the highland area.

Appalachian routes.   In all the years since 1803, no one has improved on the simple statement of the Reverend Thaddeus Mason Harris: " It is only in particular places that the ridges can be crossed. Generally the road leads through gaps, and winds around the sides of mountains; and even at these places is steep and difficult." Long before the arrival of white men, migratory deer and buffalo in their searches for feeding grounds, water, and salt had learned that movement in the highland country was confined to " particular places." A traveler of 1797 pointed out that licks were

. . . nothing but salt springs and the ground in their neighborhood is *licked* up for a considerable distance by the deer, buffalo, and other wild animals, who frequent them at certain seasons of the year, and in such astonishing quantities, that a lick is easily found out by the road which is made by the frequent passing and repassing of these animals.

Many of the animal traces became well-worn Indian paths linking hunting grounds and villages, and these in turn often evolved into the trails and early roads of the frontiersman. Studies are sufficient to show that few pioneer trails were strictly original; rather, pre-existent paths were here and there straightened and united by new links to form long-distance routes toward well-defined objectives.

These objectives were clear enough by the 1790's and remained but little changed until the railroad era. There were essentially three focusing points for the transmontane routes: the Forks of the Ohio, Cumberland Gap, and the Valley of East Tennessee. Each was a *point de réunion* analogous to a knot binding several strands of rope, whose separate lengths flare outward in various directions.

Converging at the Forks of the Ohio (Pittsburgh and vicinity) were several major and minor routes with originating points in eastern Pennsylvania and Maryland. Most direct, because it did not conform to the irregularities of a drainage system, was the southern Pennsylvania route, sometimes called the Forbes Road. From Harrisburg to Carlisle, the Forbes Road followed the Great Valley and then crossed successive ridges, passing through Shippensburg and Bedford (in early days a fort) to the Loyalhanna sources of the Ohio. Easiest to follow on a map is the Juniata Route, also beginning at Harrisburg, and snaking its way through the parallel-ridge-and-valley country to the massive Allegheny Front west of present-day Altoona, surmounting the Front with difficulty to reach the headwaters of the Allegheny.

Movement over the Pennsylvania routes to the west had reached flood tide early in the nineteenth century, when traveler Harris found:

The settlements on both sides of the Monongahela river are fine and extensive, and the land is good and well cultivated. Numerous trading and family boats pass continually. In the spring and fall the river seems covered with them. The former, laden with flour, whiskey, peach-brandy, cider, bacon, iron, potter's ware, cabinet work, etc., all the produce of the country, and destined for Kentucky and New Orleans or the towns on the Spanish side of the Mississippi. The latter convey the families of emigrants, with their furniture, farming utensils, etc., to the new settlements they have in view.

Also leading to the Forks of the Ohio was the route up the Potomac and across the narrow divide to the Youghiogheny. By the year 1800, this old-time way of travel had become the beginning of the National Road, sometimes called the Cumberland Road — to the confusion of generations of students who assume incorrectly that it must run through the famous Cumberland Gap. The National Road is entitled to alternate reference as Cumberland Road because of the early importance of a fort of that name in western Maryland, within whose protection the present city of Cumberland grew. The advantage of the Potomac route was heightened not only by the improvement of the road for heavy traffic but by the canalization of the river. It was freely predicted at the time that the Potomac route would become the master artery of east-west travel in the United States. (See Fig. 53.)

Rivaling the Forks of the Ohio in importance as a route focus of the mountain country was Cumberland Gap, a 1600-foot-deep notch through Cumberland Mountain near the southern end of the Virginia-Kentucky boundary. It was through this gap, and the related Pine Mountain Gap, that the Wilderness Road struck the headwaters of the Kentucky River, ultimately to branch by alternative routes either to the Bluegrass country or to the Nashville Basin. Speaking in strict terms, the Wilderness Road began at Fort Chiswell in the Shenandoah Valley, but it should be noted that tributary routes from many Eastern cities, such as Richmond and Fredericksburg, were essentially continuous with it. It would be analogous to say that the Ohio River begins at Pittsburgh, forgetting the tributary sources of the Allegheny and the Monongahela. The main stem, up the Shenandoah Valley from Harpers Ferry, was the easiest and most heavily traveled approach to the Wilderness Road. The Shenandoah, or Valley of Virginia, was well settled even by the time of the Revolution, hence the contrast with the "wilderness" borders on the west. The most difficult section of the Wilderness Road was the crossing of the upper Holston and Powell rivers and their intervening ridges before reaching Cumberland Gap. Emigrants from the North as well as from Virginia and North Carolina sought the new West

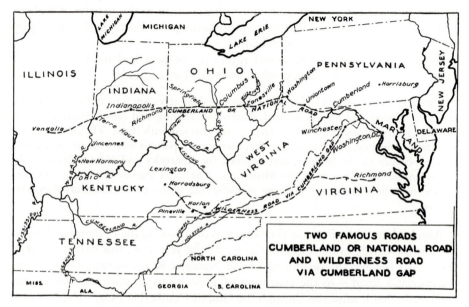

53   Two main routes across the Appalachians

through Cumberland Gap, especially in the earlier days when hostile Indians held the Ohio River portal. (See Fig. 54.)

The third plexus of trans-Appalachian routes was the Valley of East Tennessee just southward from Cumberland Gap. An extension of the Shenandoah Valley and, like it, a part of the great trough which strikes through the highlands from Pennsylvania to Georgia, the Valley of East Tennessee was " good country " to the frontiersman. Sections of it soon became identified with the river sources of the Tennessee; thus one spoke of the settlements of Watauga, Nolichucky, French Broad, Holston, and Clinch. The " valley," if so diverse an area may be so called, was approached with relative ease not only from the Shenandoah but from the east by way of gaps in the bordering mountain ramparts. In perhaps no other Appalachian section was the pioneer character more strongly developed.

Settlement in the mountains.   Not all emigrants who set out to make new homes west of the mountains actually reached their destination. There were too many attractions on the way. The Juniata route, for example, intersected a half-dozen valleys in the parallel-ridge-and-valley country, and occasionally followed one of them for several miles, giving emigrants a chance to assess their possibilities. The typical Pennsylvania " canoe-shaped " valley, perhaps five miles wide and ten times as long, its axis floored with limestone, and lines of springs along the margins where shale underlay the limestone, was attractive indeed. Just such a valley is the Kishacoquillas in central Pennsylvania, over the mountain from Nittany Valley, in which Penn State College is located.

The first settlers in the Kishacoquillas (a name of Indian origin) being Scotch-

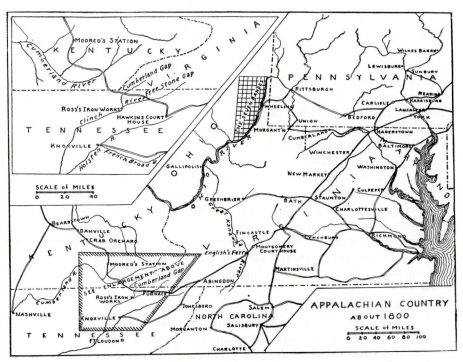

54   This map of the Appalachian area derives basically from the Bradley road map
      of 1796, with a few additions from other maps of comparable date.

Irish of the pioneer type, it was not long before they were eager to move on
again, and many of their farms were bought by the advance guard of Amish
people, representing a branch of the Mennonite Church. These industrious folk
still further improved the land of their less-patient predecessors and proceeded
to reduce the entire floor of the valley to the purposes of agriculture. Lovers of
the soil, the Amish made no attempt to continue the early manufactuiing ventures of the Scotch-Irish; that they were and are a farming people is apparent
to anyone visiting the Kishacoquillas today.

It is not to be inferred that each valley of the ridge country had the same order
of settlement or developed in the same manner as the one just described, but in
many known cases the original settlers did eventually " sell out to the Dutch,"
who proved to be the more permanent occupants. Many western Pennsylvania
valleys, following a preliminary agricultural development, became iron-and-
steel centers later in the nineteenth century. The story of Johnstown in Cone-
maugh Valley has been detailed by Professor Raymond E. Murphy, who points
out that the original village, named after its founder Mr. John, depended largely
on farm and forest industries until its selection as the site for a steel plant.
Thereafter, Johnstown grew rapidly, and the whole basis of life changed.

The first settlers of the Cumberland Mountains of Kentucky came there by
way of the Cumberland Gap, their eyes set on distant horizons but ready to

stop where conditions met their fancy. "Many of the frontiersmen were so attracted by the opportunities of the mountains that they abandoned the idea of pushing on to the west," says Professor Darrell H. Davis. Though in today's view this area seems to hold little promise, it was well suited to pioneering. The hillsides were forested with excellent timber, there was game in the woods and fish in the streams, and sufficient level land for a modest agriculture. In the drier seasons the creeks, too shallow for navigation, often served as roadbeds.

Accretions to the original population came from its own prolific ranks, and from other emigrants who settled down instead of going on " somewheres else." As the population increased, original farms were subdivided among the children, and often a creek valley became a neighborhood of relatives. Few Negroes mingled with this otherwise varied ethnic group which, assembled in a new and for many generations an isolated environment, acquired traits of speech that stamped its members as " mountain folk." For at least a century a self-sufficient agriculture was topped off by home manufacture of clothing and equipment. Even today there are occasional areas in this maze of V-shaped valleys and towering slopes where the way of life has changed but little from that of the earliest days.

Bluegrass and barrens.   The end of the Kentucky rainbow rested, for the time being at least, on the Bluegrass country. Even the " knobs " and " barrens," margins of the Bluegrass, were not unattractive once it became known that " barren " did not mean inherent sterility. How unfortunate that the term " Kentucky meadows " was restricted to scientific literature! A newcomer like the botanist André Michaux in 1802 " expected to cross over a naked space " in the 60-mile stretch beyond Little Barren River, but " Instead of finding a country as it had been depicted to me, I was agreeably surprised to see a beautiful meadow, where the grass was from two to three feet tall." Land-seekers preferred the inner Bluegrass to the barrens, which when seen by Michaux were thinly populated, " for on the road where the plantations are closest together we counted but eighteen in a space of sixty or eighty miles."

The Bluegrass proper was a land of undulating surface where groves of deciduous trees alternated with grassy savannas in parklike fashion. The region was approached not only through Cumberland Gap but also by way of the Ohio River, the favored stopping-point being Limestone, now called Maysville, on the left bank. Michaux said of Limestone in 1802: " This little town, built upwards of fifteen years, one could imagine to be more extensive. It has been the place where all the emigrants landed who came from the northern states by the way of Pittsburg, and it is still the staple for all sorts of merchandise sent from Philadelphia and Baltimore to Kentucky." The early village of Boonesborough, a terminus of the pioneering trail of Daniel Boone, was soon outstripped by other communities of the inner Bluegrass: Lexington, Harrodsburg, Danville.

Watauga settlements and the Nashville area.   The first settlements in Tennessee were made in 1768 on Watauga Old Fields, presumably a former Indian clearing. Others quickly followed, reaching in 1800 an estimated population in the East Tennessee Valley of 70,000, of whom 3,000 were slaves. (See Fig. 35, page 132.) It seemed probable to the traveler-botanist André Michaux that the earlier idea of a " State of Franklin " would be revived, because a " division into East and West Tennessee is commanded on the one hand by the boundaries that Nature herself has prescribed between the two countries . . . and on the other by their commerce, which is wholly different, since the Cumberland carries on its trade by the Ohio and Mississippi." The people who first came to " West Tennessee " or the middle Cumberland Valley (now called Middle Tennessee) were of a different background from that of the hardy settlers of the Watauga. Favorable if not glowing accounts of the Cumberland attracted wealthy men and a few land speculators, who soon acquired the more desirable areas. Land values rose sharply and there was soon a renting class, unusual in the border country. In many respects the society that developed was not unlike that of eastern Virginia. Favored by good soils and accessibility by river and roads, Nashville — at first called French Lick and later Nashborough — grew rapidly.

Georgia Western Territories. The vast country south of Tennessee out of which Alabama and Mississippi were later carved was "beyond the frontier" in 1800. Nevertheless it was an area much in the public mind because of the circulation in 1795 and 1796 of advertising matter by land companies operating under the supposition that they owned much of the territory. By legislative act on January 7, 1795, the State of Georgia sold nearly all of the land west of the Alabama River to the Mississippi, and northward of the old Spanish boundary, to four companies whose ambitious schemes are reflected in the princely domains involved. The Tennessee Company bought a generous strip along the Tennessee River in what is now Alabama; the Upper Mississippi Company was content with the present northwestern Mississippi; the Georgia Company secured the territory west of the Tombigbee River and north of the Yazoo mouth; and the remainder went to the Georgia Mississippi Company. At least 22,000,000 acres of land, at a cost of $500,000, were included in the four " deals." (See Fig. 55.)

But this was only the first step in transactions involving high finance and big territories. The original companies promptly sold their holdings to various individuals in the Northern and Eastern states who had visions of promoting large-scale colonization. Within the next few months, however, certain Georgia leaders declared the sales were " opposed to the good of the State, and obtained by fraud, atrocious speculation, corruption, and collusion." The result of this agitation was another legislative act of February 13, 1796, nullifying the original transactions and ruling that " said property was the property of the State." This was not the last of the legal complications arising from the so-called Natchez land frauds, for the United States in turn contested the claim of Georgia to the territory, the litigation extending over thirty years; but enough has been said to show why this flurry of colonization was short-lived.

By the year 1800, the public had returned to the earlier view that the Georgia Western Territories were Indian country, and remained unexcited by encouraging reports of soil fertility and wealth of resources. What mattered it if the country's

55   The southern interior. This map is a simplified redrawing of a folded map prepared by Abraham Bradley for inclusion in the most widely read geography of
the early 1800's, *American Universal Geography* by Jedidiah Morse.

official geographer had reported that "the climate is healthy and temperate,
the country delightful and well watered, and the prospect is beautiful and extensive; variegated by innumerable copses, the trees of which are of different
kinds but mostly of walnut and oak"? It was known that the Territories were
inhabited by several Indian nations mustering some 20,000 warriors or " gunmen."

Beyond the Tombigbee River were the compact villages of Cherokee, Chickasaw, and Choctaw Indians, with perhaps 6,000 warriors rather determined to hold
their fine country against the whites. Along the upper Alabama River, especially
near the junction of the Coosa and the Tallapoosa, were the lands of the Upper
Creek people. Allied with them were the Lower Creeks on the Chattahoochee
River; together these were known as the Nations, for they had succeeded in
forming out of many remnant tribes a confederacy rivaled in strength only by
the Six Nations. It is significant that in its various land deals the State of Georgia
made no attempt to " sell " the homeland of the Creeks, and it was not until
1814 that military raids upon them were successful. The following table from
Jervis Cutler's *Topographic Description of Ohio* (1812) presents a conservative
estimate of the numbers of Indian peoples south of the Ohio River at this period.

INDIANS SOUTH OF THE OHIO, 1812

Nation	Number of Warriors	Total Population
Catawba	150	450
Cherokee	1,500	4,000
Chickasaw	575	1,725
Choctaw	4,041	12,128
Creek	6,000	26,000
TOTAL	12,266	44,303

The people of the Nations had developed an orderly existence based essentially on farming and stock-raising, combined with some trade in deerskins with white traders resident in their villages or at near-by posts curiously named, such as " New York " and " Vanstown." According to the traders and Indian agents from the United States, the Upper Creeks followed the usual Indian practice of " settling out in villages " — that is, forming new communities when the original village had outgrown its local resources or had become unhealthful through poor sanitation. In many cases the village name or a variation of it was transferred along with the village itself, leading to much confusion in contemporary reports and maps. There were Great Koussadee and Koussadee, for example, and when Tukubachee split in 1797, according to the Indian agent Benjamin Hawkins, who was on the scene at the time, one of the villages became " Tukubacheelellawhassee."

Only a few white people ventured to settle within this Indian country, the last extensive area held by the aborigines in the East. There were perhaps 2,000 people on the United States bank of the Mississippi River at Natchez and along the lower Yazoo River. There was also a small settlement on the lower Tombigbee River at " Walker Shoals " at the head of tidewater, near present-day Jackson, Alabama. Safe beyond the Indian country was New Orleans and its tributary area. Bordering the river for nearly 100 miles were settlements of French Acadians who originally came in 1763, and German immigrants of a later date. By the turn of the century there were as many as 7,000 slaves in the lower Mississippi River settlements at work on plantations yielding cotton, rice, sugar, tobacco, and supply products.

Part Three

THE OHIO RIVER
AND LOWER GREAT LAKES REGIONS,
TO 1830

CHAPTER II

A General View of the Land

A STRANGER stopping at a tavern on the Illinois frontier in 1819 drew many questioning glances when he declined the host's request to sign the register. A breach of etiquette which at a later time and farther west might have led to gunfire ended here to the amusement of all present; for after quenching his thirst, the aloof visitor announced to the barkeeper in a voice loud enough for all to hear: "My name is Robinson. I objected to mentioning it, fearing you would name a town after me."

Thus with sly humor did the author of this anecdote, the traveler Richard Lee Mason, call attention to the wave of town-building and farm extension which by 1819 had reached the triangle formed by the Illinois and Mississippi rivers. Northward from Alton, Illinois, near which other towns had mushroomed (some to live for only a brief period), lay 3,500,000 acres of bounty land. This was Big Prairie country, with grass so thick and tall that government surveyors were experiencing difficulty in marking out quarter-sections. Prairies were no new thing to settlers by this stage of Ohio Valley settlement, but those back in Ohio and Indiana were small affairs, better called "openings" in forested country. To the botanical-minded, the small prairies were "savannas." The Big Prairie was something different, for out on its broad expanse farmers would be separated from useful timber and firewood and perhaps also from good water. Would the multiplication of towns continue in the Illinois Bounty Lands? "Mr. Robinson" had no doubt that it would, and history has confirmed his opinion. (See Fig. 56.)

OHIO RIVER COUNTRY, THE NEW PROMISED LAND

By 1820, the southern portion of the Territory Northwest of the Ohio River had won a favorable reputation among people in the source regions of settlement. Attention has already been called to the then prevalent belief that its climate was superior to that of the older states in the same latitudinal position. Settlers had learned by experience that the climate did not permit the wide range of products that advance report had suggested, but there was little ground for serious dissatisfaction on that score. In amount and distribution of rainfall Ohio River lands were "well watered," and in length of growing season the whole drain-

56   The United States in 1820. Note that the Military Bounty Lands of Illinois are prominently identified. Original map, in greater detail, was drawn by John Melish.

age basin was clearly the equal of the central Atlantic states and far better than New England.

Traveler Bradbury's description with its strange mixture of fact and fancy is typical of the accounts before many data had been accumulated. Writing in 1811, he pointed out: "The seasons and general state of weather are comparable with similar latitudes in upper Louisiana: — in spring heavy rains; in summer an almost cloudless sky, with heavy dews at night; in autumn some rain followed by the Indian summer; and the winter from ten weeks to three months long, which is dry, sharp, and pleasant." There were the usual questions about the "salubrity" of the climate and, as usual, the doubts he expressed did not check settlement. As an Irish observer of the American scene had pointed out in 1799, "If the lands in one part of the country are superior to those of another in fertility, if they are in the neighborhood of a navigable river, or situated conveniently to a good market; if they are cheap and rising in value, thither the American will gladly emigrate let the climate be ever so unfriendly to the human system."

The state of medical knowledge in the early nineteenth century was such as to allow various interpretations of the causes of malaria, "intermittent fevers," "milksick," ague, and cholera, and many were inclined to charge them up to "insalubrity," which was vague enough to include any of them. The high death rate of the members of the Harmony Society from 1814 to 1824 apparently did not discourage Robert Owen and his associates from engrafting upon the original Rappite community his New Harmony venture (pages 246–50). Besides, newcomers were inclined to think that stories of epidemics and plagues were overdone in newspaper accounts. Thus in October, 1832, a citizen of Cincinnati wrote to a friend: "You have doubtless heard by this time, probably in exaggerated terms, of the dreadful visitation of cholera which has burst upon us since you left here and has plunged the whole city into mourning."

The Ohio River a natural highway. For the first time in the settlement of the country, a great natural highway extended in the general direction of movement. For over 1,000 miles, the Ohio River presented no serious interruptions for navigation by ordinary boats. By 1820 its surface was alive with steamboats (60 by that year), barges, schooner boats, keelboats, flatboats, Kentucky and New Orleans boats, skiffs, rowboats, and ordinary rafts. Said a contemporary riverman: "No form of water craft so whimsical, no shape so outlandish can well be imagined but what, in descending from Pittsburg to New Orleans, it may somewhere be seen lying at the shore or floating on the river." (See Fig. 57.)

Should you want to go down-river, you had merely to construct your own craft or, better still, join forces with another traveler bound in the same direction. For those with cash, passage could readily be purchased at numerous points, but possibly at the cost of some discomfort also. Perhaps many were as discontented as Amos Wheeler, who went by keelboat from Beaver, western Pennsylvania, to St. Louis in the early summer of 1816. "The longer I am on board the less I like my situation," complained Wheeler. "Sleep is now my only recourse to wear away the time. I have not accommodations for comfortable sitting." But even Mr. Wheeler found occasional interest in watching the panorama of "improving farms" and forested solitudes, not to mention an accident to a steamboat near Marietta, Ohio. The steamer "started from here to go down the River, but was not yet a mile before the boiler burst. Killed 6, drowned 1, & wounded 11, most of whom were badly burnt & scalded, but are on their [way to] recovery."

A full discussion of Ohio River navigation is reserved for a later chapter, but here it may be pointed out that the portion most used by travelers was that from Pittsburgh to Cincinnati, for reasons inferable from the map. Below Cincinnati, the river bears sharply to the south, a favorable direction for trade by way of the Mississippi River, but an unfavorable direction for emigrants who were bound for the interior of Indiana and Illinois. Many of the emigrants, in fact, came

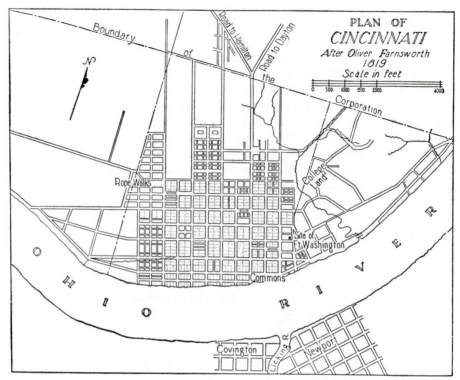

57   Plan of the city of Cincinnati, about 1820. Courtesy of the Library of Cincinnati.

from the Southern states and were heading for the newly opened Northwest territories, partly in an effort to escape the growing slavery problems south of the Ohio. As a consequence, the Big Bend below Cincinnati became an accustomed place at which to leave the river and set out overland, by wagon or perhaps on foot. Undoubtedly, Cincinnati derived much of its early importance from its position near the point where the Ohio River changes its direction. (See Fig. 59, page 214.)

Although the river was a highway available to all, experience in its use was desirable. Among the hazards were occasional rapids such as the Falls of Louisville, and dangers to boats from concealed snags, "sawyers," and "planters" (submerged logs). Furthermore, navigation on the river had its seasonal highs and lows, influenced by changes of depth during the open season and by winter ice floes. The wise traveler timed his departures to take advantage of the more favorable seasons.

Tributaries to the Ohio River.   The natural means of communication offered by the main stream were greatly extended, north and south, by the larger tributaries. The Muskingum, the Scioto, and the Wabash aided in the opening up of the Northwest Territory, while southern tributaries such as the Licking and Kentucky rivers were vital to the commercial agriculture of Kentucky. The ancient town of Vincennes on the Big Wabash, for example, was favored with 200 miles of navigable water to the Ohio River. Topographical surveys before 1790 had pointed to the possibility of connecting the Ohio tributaries with rivers flowing northward into Lake Erie, because the divide in northern Ohio and Indiana was comparatively low and the headwaters came close together. When the success of the Erie Canal was assured, ambitious river-improvement projects were carried through in the Northwest Territory.

Northern Ohio easily reached. Northern Ohio, especially the large section of it which was included in the Connecticut Western Reserve, was also easily reached from eastern points, and some of the early settlers arrived at southern Lake Erie ports on sailing vessels from Buffalo and Erie, Pennsylvania. Even after regular steamboat navigation appeared on the lower Great Lakes in the early 1820's, however, by far the greater number of emigrants reached the Reserve by overland routes. The most common overland approach to Cleveland was by way of the Great Ridge Road from Erie, following one of the shore lines formed during the glacial period when Lake Erie occupied a much more extensive basin than it does today. Many also came to northern Ohio from across the state, having left the Ohio River at Steubenville, Wheeling, or Marietta. For many years travel by land westward of the Connecticut Reserve territory was virtually prohibited by the notorious Black Swamp, which overspread much of what now constitutes the counties of Sandusky, Ottawa, and Wood. This "fearsome" swamp effectually isolated Detroit from the growing towns of northern Ohio. A pioneer of Cleveland recalled that the delivery of mail to Detroit required a journey of six days, and that the water of the swamp was likely to be from 2 to 6 inches in depth. The completion of a military road across the swamp in the 1830's and its final drainage a quarter-century later were both hailed as major improvements.

INDUSTRIES ATTRACTED BY REPORTS OF MINERAL RESOURCES

Enough was known about mineral resources by 1830 to lead to confidence in the future development of many industries in the Ohio country. A few coal beds in northern Ohio were already in production, iron ores were known to exist and others were suspected in various localities, and several saline deposits were annually yielding thousands of bushels of salt.

Saltmaking was, in fact, the first mineral industry along the now highly industrialized Ohio River. The principal springs and salt wells of the 1820's were near the junction of the Ohio with two major tributaries: the Great Kanawha and the Wabash. Already abandoned by that time were the salines near Zanesville, which preceded the Kanawha supplies in use. First developed in a primitive fashion as early as 1797, the Kanawha springs (also known as Great Buffalo Lick) had been visited in succession by buffalo, Indian, and pioneer to obtain salt. Large-scale operations on the Kanawha commenced in 1808, and the "establishments " there were soon supplying the major salt needs of the West. The springs of the lower Wabash, known as the Ohio Saline, came into production in 1815, when a well was sunk 420 feet — an " astonishing depth " in the opinion of *Niles' Weekly Register.*

To secure salt water, wells were bored or dug to various depths, from which the water was dipped or pumped to the surface, unless it issued forth of its own pressure. If the well were to be a shallow one, the opening was protected from slumping and infiltration of fresh water by a hollowed tree trunk. According to John A. Bradbury, the wooden well casing, some 3 or 4 feet in diameter, was called a " gum, for although many species of trees are liable to become hollow, yet none are so perfectly hollowed as the gum tree (*Liquidamber strycafolia*). These trees, as I am informed, are often found so completely hollowed to leave the sound part not more than an inch in thickness, and the inside surface perfectly smooth." For greater depths, metal casings were employed for the same purpose. Cased borings of from 60 to 80 feet were not uncommon.

The salt water was pumped into large kettles, each holding a dozen gallons. Heat for the evaporation process was derived from wood in the earlier years but mainly from coal after 1817. For this reason a salt " establishment " was often called a furnace, of which there were some 30 in the Kanawha area during the 1820's. One saltmaker announced with some pride that he had invented a way of raising salt water " with buckets which empty themselves when drawn up by a machine worked by a horse, without the help of a hand." The annual production of the fine-grained Kanawha salt, which had a reputation for excellence in pickling, was about 700,000 bushels, reaching its peak in the 1850's, when the output was over 3,000,000 bushels. Salt was one of the chief freighting products on the Ohio River during the early part of the past century, but the industry declined with the exhaustion of supplies and the opening up of greater deposits in Kansas and elsewhere. Nevertheless, the present-day chemical industries of the Kanawha River near Charleston, West Virginia, may have derived in part from this earlier activity.

The great coal supplies of eastern Ohio could only be guessed at, and nothing appears to have been known of the petroleum of the Lima region. One of the early coal-mining centers was in the vicinity of Tallmadge and Guildford, a locality now familiar as the better-known city of Akron. In 1822 this coal deposit was referred to as " the only one on waters emptying into Lake Erie, and this being within 3 miles of the boatable waters of the Cuyahoga must be of importance as soon as the canal is opened."

The year 1808 appears to have marked the beginning of the now great Youngstown steel industry, for then a furnace was built in the vicinity. No great iron-ore deposits had been found, but the presence of iron was indicated in various places. Hematite, or " flag ore," to use its earlier name, was known to occur in the eastern coal fields, but at such depths as to discourage its mining. The Yellow Springs from which the present city derives its name were presumed to indicate underlying iron ores. Already well known, Yellow Springs were described in

1805 as having " a beautiful, cold and limpid water, issuing out of nearly the top of a hill, about eighty or ninety feet high." The springs enjoyed a reputation as a health resort.

LAND SURFACE FAVORABLE TO SETTLEMENT

Prospective settlers found assurance in numerous reports that the Ohio country was, to say the least, agriculturally promising. As gathered from printed " travels " and guidebooks available by 1825, the general picture was that of an area as extensive as some European countries, with bottom lands and lowland plains swelling here and there into low hills that were themselves arable — an attractive picture, modified but not greatly altered by increasing knowledge over the years. Probably many who came to take up the land had received advance report in letters written back East to relatives or friends. A typical folksy account was the message of Ephraim Brown from central Ohio in the fall of 1816. He said in part:

You will perhaps wish to know something about the Soil, Climate, etc. of this country. So much has already been said that I cannot add to it unless I say that it has been over rated by some and under rated by others. For a general observation, it is a level country tho' there are many exceptions — there are many hills but no mountains. The Rivers and Creeks mostly are sluggish & form extensive bottoms (or as it is termed in New England, meadows); these bottoms . . . are often found without timber on them & sometimes covered with Elm, Walnut, Butternut, Basswood & Sycamore. The Uplands are generally covered with Oak, Chestnut, Poplar, Hic'ry, Basswood, Cucumber, etc. etc. and what is very remarkable you will find these sorts all mixed together. In many places where the land is covered it is wet, but I have observed that when cleared and opened to the sun it becomes dry enough to plough. Grassland can not be purchased here short of from three to five and ½ dollars an acre in small quantities — say 100-acre lots.

The new West also had its detractors, no doubt inspired by the overdrawn accounts circulated in the interests of land companies operating in Ohio. The " antis," many of whom were New Englanders, probably had little effect in checking the emigration they so greatly deplored. One literary curiosity from this source was a pamphlet printed in Providence with the title *Western Emigration: Journal of Doctor Jeremiah Simpleton's Tour to Ohio* (1826). Henry Trumbull, the author, assures his readers that " the substance of the following pages is founded on fact, and nothing but a ludicrous coloring constitutes the *Fable* of the writer." In an imaginary dialogue it appears that Doctor Jeremiah Simpleton has visited Ohio and, returning, reports to " Mr. Scruple," in part as follows:

Dr. Jerry. Yes, fags, I've been to the Ohio! And if the *crows* do not deprive me of all that remains of poor old Dobbin, ere I can reach once more the neighborhood of the comfortable dwelling which, like a Tom fool, I was persuaded to barter away for Ohio lands, I will sit myself down contented to remain all the days of my life an inhabitant of old Massachusetts — and thankful even for a scanty meal of codfish and potatoes!

Mr. Scruple. With the *most* flattering expectations of exchanging my situation for the better, I have too, sir, just been persuaded by a land jobber to exchange my snug little farm in *Main,* for four times the number of acres in Ohio — represented to me to be equal to the Garden of Eden — producing almost everything spontaneously — indeed where a plentiful crop may be *reaped* without *sowing!*

Jerry. Ha! Ha! — another Tom Fool (saving your presence, friend Scruple) caught by these pesket [*sic*] land jobbers, as well as myself!

On the more serious side, we learn from topographical accounts of the first quarter of the nineteenth century that attention was directed to four contrasted areas: (1) the river hills and bottom lands of the Ohio River and its northern tributaries, (2) the hill country of eastern Ohio, (3) Lake Erie watershed and bordering plain, and (4) the Pickaway Plains of the Scioto.

River hills and bottoms of the Ohio. Edwin James, the topographer of the Long expedition of 1820, was perhaps the first to place on record the two grand divisions of the land along the Ohio — the upper hill country and the lower alluvial plain. The point of separation was said to be Rockport, in southwestern Indiana. Above that place the Ohio flows through steep, conical hills, products of its own downcutting; the lower river, in contrast, is bordered by alluvial banks in a broad flood plain which in the far distance terminates in low bluffs.

The hazard of floods was increased in this low country by the gradual slope of the plain away from the river, said topographer James; " Hence, when the waters are sufficiently swollen to flow over the banks, they inundate extensive tracts, from which they cannot return to the channel of the river and are left stagnant during the summer months." The dikes and levees which are now designed to hold the lower Ohio in check had not been constructed at the time we are considering, but the need of them was recognized, if man hoped ever to use the fertile soils. The alleged monotony of the lower Ohio country before the days of modern improvements was depressing to visitors, one of whom expressed " a degree of impatience at finding all our prospects limited by an inconsiderable extent of low muddy bottom lands, and the unrelieved gloom of the forest."

The more varied landscape in the long stretch from Pittsburgh to Rockport naturally drew the greatest amount of attention, and occasional bursts of eloquence. Daniel Drake, pioneer scientist of Cincinnati, wrote:

The Ohio River is generally serpentine, and presents to the eye of the voyager an uniform succession of hills and declivities which display, in spring, the blooming elegance of a luxurious garden; in summer, the rich verdure of a lofty and boundless forest; and in autumn, a splendid tissue of green, gold, and crimson foliage. In winter, an occasional precipice with a brow overhung by red cedars, exhibits considerable grandeur — but variety and sublimity are not predominant features of this scenery, and the pleasure it affords is chiefly referable to its beauty, freshness, and tranquility.

The bordering hills of the Ohio presented all kinds of slopes and exposures, but almost everyone agreed that their fertile soils could be put to productive uses, perhaps for orchards and grazing. The structure of the hills, said topographer James in 1820, " does not so much differ from the Alleghany Mountains as their form and position," for they represent remnants of a continuous and nearly horizontal structure " which the flowing of water, during the lapse of ages, has channelled and excavated to its present form." Important to settlers too were occasional " bottoms " which rose like steps from the water's edge. To the observant Jervis Cutler in 1812, the bottoms appeared as " a sort of glacis," suggesting to this army officer a defensive slope in front of a fortification. The Cutler description, appearing as a roughhewn gem in a matrix of mediocre reports, deserves a fuller quotation:

> The base of some of the hills extends to the banks of the river, others recede leaving wide bottoms of a very rich and deep soil. When the hills approach the river on one side, they usually recede from it, on the other, so that there are wide bottoms, alternately, on both sides of the river. Much of the soil of these bottoms, especially the first (for there are two or three bottoms, rising one above the other, forming a sort of glacis), has been found as deep as the river. The hills are clothed with a thick forest of trees, consisting of white, red and black oak, hickory, ash, chestnut, poplar, sassafras, dogwood and grapevine. The bottoms are covered with a heavy growth. . . . The passenger, gliding down the river in the summer, is amused and delighted with the appearance of . . . vines on the upper branches and tops of the trees, forming large canopies, festoons, arbours, and grottoes, with numerous other fantastic figures. Some of the trunks of these trees are of a size which will admit them to be split into four rails for fence.

The hill country of eastern Ohio. In early descriptions, the dissected plateau region of eastern Ohio was most frequently referred to as the Seven Ranges, a usage that grew out of the rectangular survey system adopted by the Ordinance of 1785 and first applied here. North-south lines, 6 miles apart and parallel to the western boundary of Pennsylvania (Ellicott's Line), were surveyed to form seven ranges of townships, under the personal direction of Thomas Hutchins, official geographer of the country. It was from the field reports of the corps of surveyors that the first specific knowledge of the area was derived. The reports were far from encouraging to settlers, in anticipation of whose presumed needs the survey was made.

Throughout the field operations, protection from roving Indian bands was provided by troops sent out from Fort Harmar, but perhaps more serious than this hazard were the delays caused by the rugged wilderness and the cold winters of 1786 and 1787. Hutchins wrote to one of the military aides in August, 1786: " I might enumerate many difficulties occasioned by mirey swamps and the ruggedness of several parts of the Country; but as both my duty and intentions lead me rather to surmount them, than to complain of difficulties, I will dwell no longer on this disagreeable subject."

By the time the Seven Ranges were thrown open to settlement the Indian menace was well in hand, but the area within them, physically a portion of the dissected Allegheny plateau, still remained less attractive than the lowland plains of central Ohio. The river valleys of the Beaver and the Mahoning, providing the most practicable routes northwestward to the Connecticut Reserve, were the principal areas of settlement other than those along the Ohio River itself. The coal measures which underlie this area did not become an effective environmental feature until the middle of the century.

Lake Erie watershed.   The "ridge of hills" separating the headwaters of rivers flowing into Lake Erie from those tributary to the Ohio was considered a significant landmark in a region generally devoid of prominent surface features. Early reports pointed out that the divide did not everywhere appear as an easily recognizable ridge; it was rather a "height of land" spreading out into extensive tablelands. Water power was said to be available in the upper courses of the Lake Erie rivers, such as the Cuyahoga, but far downstream they flowed sluggishly across the ancient lake plain. With the eye of a physiographer, traveler William Darby observed that the lake-border plain "has all the features of recent alluvion: the streams are sluggish in their motions, their beds having but little elevation, the land along the banks is the highest part of the ground; the interstream spaces are low and mostly swampy."

The most extensive of the swamps, as already mentioned, was the now extinct Black Swamp, extending from Sandusky to the Maumee River. Much literature was circulated in the Eastern states assuring prospective settlers that northern Ohio, despite an admittedly large extent of marshland, was mainly a "healthy" region with fertile soils. Although the period we are considering long antedated modern theories of continental glaciation, the more competent observers recognized the lowlands as an ancient lake bed. Former shore lines 2 miles inland from the present beaches were familiarly known, and the Ridge Road followed one of them for long distances.

The Pickaway Plains of the Scioto.   The most enthusiastic accounts of Ohio came from settlers in and visitors to central Ohio, particularly the Scioto basin from Chillicothe to Columbus. Passing from the hilly and forested belt bordering the Ohio River, settlers were here greeted with their first large sample of open prairie, with which they inevitably became more familiar as the frontier line spread westward. Search of the original records has failed to bring to light any suggestion on the part of the settlers that they believed the soils were infertile because they were treeless. The open country was not called "barrens," for example, but prairie or "praira" from the very first, and all descriptions emphasize the fertility and productivity of the land.

The Pickaway Plains, in the strict sense, lay to the west of the Scioto River in present-day Pickaway County, an area now much altered from its original state. Twenty miles long and 4 broad, with a surface slightly higher than the bordering forests, these plains were originally covered with a thick carpet of grass. Settlement within them was so prompt that even in 1805 the greater portion was in agricultural use. When seen in September 1807 by R. Ricks, an emigrant from Virginia in search of a new home, Pickaway was " a beautiful plain containing eight or nine thousand acres of land clear of timber except a very few Copses; lies high and well for Cultivation and is exceedingly fertile Soil said to be from two to two & one half feet deep, produceth either Corn or Wheat to admiration." At the time of Ricks's visit, Chillicothe was a bustling town of 2,000 inhabitants, in a part of the country

held by me in a very favorable view. I traveled in getting here 603 miles. — Being now satisfied with Exploring the Country & thinking it advisable, if ever I should think proper to remain in the state, to proceed to Chillacotha & there take a temporary residence in order to acquire a more perfect knowledge of the Soil, Neighborhoods, Conveniences, & Inconveniences of particular places, than can possibly be acquired by a trancient excursion over the Country. . . .

" Trancients over the Country " were different from Mr. Ricks in this: They were more likely to leave a permanent record of their impressions and observations, for that was their avocation; the " Mr. Rickses " were more notable for practical deeds than for literary works. And so we have a surplus of travelers' thoughts on the Pickaway Plains and a shortage of those coming from settlers on the land. In the view of Jervis Cutler, the plains were " not entirely level, but interspersed with gentle swells, which render the prospect the more agreeable. This tract is destitute of trees and shrubs, excepting a few compact clusters of trees surrounded with thick bushes, appearing like scattered islands in a bay. The soil is good, and a fine stream of water passes on the south side." Traveler Josiah Espy was impressed by the " sublimity of the scene," while Thomas Ashe (whose testimony cannot always be relied upon) could " not conceive that the world entire could furnish so grand, so great, or so sublime a position for a capital or great flourishing town."

Clearly evident at the time of settlement were earthworks and mounds which have been the subject of much intensive archaeological study in more recent years. Of most interest to the newcomers were the large rectangular and circular earthworks in Circleville. As reported by *Niles' Weekly Register* in 1816:

In the centre of the town, is a small vacant circle. Emanating from this focuss, the streams diverge in regular radii, intersecting the walls at equal distances. The town is mostly built in the circle and hence derives its name. The variety of this amphitheatre is not ascribed to the builders of the town, but to the plan which an unknown cause has designated. The [town] square is in the east of the circle. On it a few buildings are erected.

Observers in the 1820's generally agreed that the mounds were erected for ceremonial or defensive purposes by an extinct Indian race, but none cared to say how long an interval separated the mound-builders from the Miamis and Wyandots known to them. They rather thought there was no connection. Trees growing in the mounds had every appearance of being as old as those in the woods roundabout. A Mr. N. Little in 1802 made note near Chillicothe of a

" circular fortification " 30 feet in height " on which is now growing 5 sugar maples of a good size. Some old stumps yet remain on the Mound, one of which I observed must have been a very large tree of white oak or Black walnut. At present the owner of the lot has an ice house on the side of it. By what information I could obtain there had never been any particular examination of this mound."

Doubtless Mr. Ricks reported the average settler's view of the Circleville mounds that " this plain is surrounded by several old fortifications, one of which is said to contain, by a late survey, 40 acres of ground & altho' no traditional acc[ount] is to be obtained respecting the people who formerly occupied those forts, yet it is believed the plain has been cultivated in former days." So thinking, the new settlers proceeded at once to level with their plows the earthly monuments of their prehistoric forerunners, thus creating new problems to puzzle the archaeologists of a later day.

THE PRAIRIE ENVIRONMENT OF THE WESTERN OHIO COUNTRY

Contemporary descriptions of Ohio west of the Miami rivers and of Indiana and Illinois give most attention to the prairie environment, and properly so. The grassy expanses presented a natural combination new to the great majority of the people who came upon them.

Almost invariably the many prairie types aroused the wonder of visitors who beheld them for the first time. There was the strange silence of the big prairie — " Not a living thing could I see or hear, except a large hawk or eagle wheeling about over my head " — and there was the apparent artificiality of the small prairie, reminding Englishman Morris Birkbeck of " some well-cultivated vale in Europe surrounded by wooded uplands; and forgetting that we were in fact on the very frontiers, beyond which few had penetrated, we were transported in idea to the fully peopled regions we had left so far behind us."

Government surveyors usually made note of the surface cover in their plat books, but there seems to be no comprehensive map of the original distribution of the arable prairies at the time of settlement. The earliest official map, issued in 1858, distinguishes between dry (short-grass) and arable (tall-grass) prairie, and agrees very closely with modern maps on the same scale. The map (Fig. 58) fails to show relatively small, but nevertheless important, prairie areas within the forested regions of central Ohio and Indiana. These smaller prairies, first encountered by the westward-moving frontier, offered no serious obstacles to settlement. In fact, as Shaler pointed out, " It was holiday work to subdue the prairie to men who for generations had been engaged in a battle with the primitive forests of the Atlantic coast." The sod could be cut and turned with plows then in use, and wood was easily accessible. In occupying them, settlers gained experience which was greatly to their advantage when they came to the extensive, tough-sodded grasslands farther west.

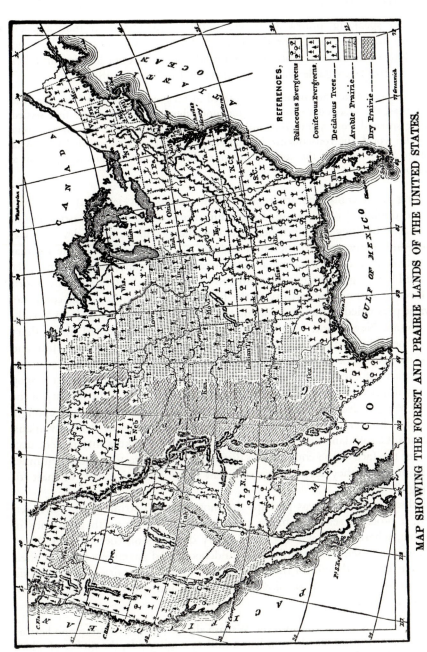

MAP SHOWING THE FOREST AND PRAIRIE LANDS OF THE UNITED STATES.

REFERENCES:

Foliaceous Evergreens ————
Coniferous Evergreens ————
Deciduous Trees ————
Arable Prairie ————
Dry Prairie ————

58   Distribution of forest and prairie lands of the United States. From *Report of the Commissioner of Patents, 1857.*
       Frontispiece.

Generally speaking, prairie areas were settled somewhat later than adjacent wooded or forested tracts. For this relative delay many causes have been advanced. One of the main reasons is to be found in their interior location and their remoteness from navigable water. Said traveler Bradbury in 1810:

Had this portion of the country been placed at no greater distance from the Alleghanies than the wooded region, it would undoubtedly have been the first settled; but being situated from 500 to 1000 miles from them by one of the most fertile countries in the world, the consequence is, that emigrants are so well satisfied with what advantage a first view of the country presents, that they are anxious to sit down as soon as possible.

Judging from contemporary reports of numerous travelers and a few residents, no doubts were entertained regarding the fertility of the prairies, big or little. Naturally they distinguished between the productivity of dry and wet prairies, and many avoided the latter because of the association in the popular mind between swampy " miasmata " and disease — especially, in Illinois, malaria. Even the Doubting Thomases who came to Illinois prejudiced against the prairie were forced to admit the fertility of the black soil; nevertheless, they could not always be persuaded to stay and take up the land. Such a visitor was John Wright from upstate New York, who in entering Illinois in 1819, noted in his diary that he " beheld a vast and almost boundless body of land, stretching before and around me; equal, or nearly so, in point of fertility, to the boasted swales of the western parts of New York; every thing seemed to invite me to select a spot, begin my improvements, and enjoy my happy fate." In spite of the fertility of the soil, Mr. Wright decided to return to his home state because, curiously enough, the people who were already there were " a motly assemblage of Pennsylvanians, Virginians, Carolinians and Kentuckians with a few Yankees intermixed, scattered over the face of the country at a distance of from two to eight or ten miles apart in order, as they say, to have sufficient range for their cattle, or mast for their hogs."

The absence of wood was perhaps the most serious detriment to prairie settlement, a problem reaching major proportions in the far-north grasslands of Minnesota, where frigid winters made heavy demands on fuel supplies. Newcomers were advised by the authors of guidebooks and gazetteers to locate their farms so as to include within them forest land as well as prairie — not too difficult to arrange in regions of alternating woods and grass. Said the *Western Gazetteer* in 1817:

. . . the streams which run into the Wabash divide one prairie from another; on the streams are strips of woods from half a mile to a mile wide, the timber of which is excellent; the soil of the prairies is a black vegetable mould intermixed with fine sand and sometimes gravel. In choosing a situation for a farm it is important so to locate a tract as to have half prairie and half wood land, by which means you have a plantation cleared to your hand.

This nice arrangement was quite impossible to achieve in the Big Prairie country of the Illinois, the sequence of settlement in which has been carefully traced by Professor Harlan H. Barrows.

The original farm homes, says Barrows, were located on prairie margins near springs; "in consequence the small prairies were presently encircled with a belt of farms. Later, another ring was established . . . farther out on the prairies, and by a continuation of the process the entire prairie was finally occupied." In his study of Princeton in Bureau County, Illinois, Professor Stanley D. Dodge was able to generalize from the reminiscences of early pioneers: "In the beginning of settlement, the settlers erected cabins in the margin of the woods with small fields for the growth of crops and larger prairie pastures for the grazing of cattle, and here they lived until more substantial dwellings could be built." It was not until 1854, however, that the Bureau County prairies as well as the woodland had been entered for settlement and "houses were scattered over most of the prairie shortly thereafter."

This was the prairie. Original descriptions of the unmodified prairie rank high among efforts in American geography. In their realism they give one the feel of the land, the more remarkable because their nonprofessional authors elsewhere rarely rose above literary mediocrity. One can only surmise that before alteration by succeeding generations the prairie setting was quietly but grandly impressive, forcing the committing of thoughts to paper. A few selections follow:

General Josiah Harmar to Secretary of War Henry Knox, on November 24, 1787:

These prairies are very extensive natural meadows, covered with long grass. One in particular which we crossed was 8 leagues in breadth. They run in general from north to south, and like the Ocean, as far as the eye can see, the view is terminated by the horizon. Here & there a copse of woods is interspersed. They are free from brush & undergrowth, and not the least vestige of their ever having been cultivated. The country is excellent for grazing, and abounds in Buffalo, Deer, Bears etc. It is a matter of speculation to account for the formation of the Prairies.

Henry Newberry on Sandusky prairies, 1822:

This part of the prairies struck me as being very uncommon in its appearance; generally speaking there is no wood nor shrubbery growing in them, but there are ranges of timber running in various directions not generally more than 2 or 4 rods wide which appear as if planted by art to determine the boundaries of fields; in other places it is in clumps as if planted for ornament. Its appearance is highly beautiful. Beyond this are occasional pieces of timbered land and prairies of thousands of acres without a single tree — and when they approach the woodland the termination is as sudden as from any improvement in a heavily timbered country to the surrounding primitive forest. These large prairies are covered mostly with tall grass and flowering and other plants but in no instance did I find them wet or mirey — indeed they are the *highest land* in the vicinity — and when cultivated produce abundant crops and fruit trees flourish wherever they have been planted. These prairies extend for about

12 miles south of Portland to the vicinity of Milan, or Indian village as it is called, altho there is now no appearance of the aborigines there.

William Newnham Blane, on the prairies west of Vincennes, 1824:

I am at a loss to account for the formation of these extraordinary meadows, and all the theories I have read upon the subject appear to me to be very unsatisfactory. The wood, wherever it intersects them, or runs in at points, does not gradually decrease in size, but remains as lofty as elsewhere, and gives the ground the appearance of having once been cleared. The fertility of the soil renders it still more astonishing that the wood should terminate so abruptly as sometimes even to resemble a wall. Those who are of opinion that the Prairies are artificial maintain that they were caused by the fires which the Indians make in the autumn and winter. But these plains increase in magnitude as one advances west, and after crossing the Mississippi between that river and Mexico, is, with very little exception, one immense Prairie.

I do not know anything that struck me more forcibly than the sensation of solitude I experienced in crossing this, and some of the other large Prairies. I was perfectly alone, and could see nothing in any direction but sky and grass. Leaving the wood appeared like embarking alone upon the ocean; and, upon again approaching the wood, I felt as if returning to land. Sometimes again, when I perceived a small stunted solitary tree that had been planted by some fortuitous circumstances, I could hardly help supposing it to be the mast of a vessel. No doubt the great stillness added very much to this strange illusion. Not a living thing could I see or hear, except the occasional rising of some prairie fowl, or perhaps a large hawk or eagle wheeling about over my head. In the woods I have often experienced this silence and solitude, but it struck me more forcibly in these boundless meadows.

William Blane on a prairie fire between Kaskaskia and St. Louis, 1824:

How shall I describe the sublime spectacle that then presented itself? I have seen the old Atlantic in his fury, a thunder storm in the Alps, and the cataracts of Niagara; but nothing could be compared to what I saw at this moment. The line of flame rushed through the long grass with tremendous violence, and a noise like thunder. With such vehemence did the wind drive along the flames, that large masses of them appeared actually to leap forward and dart into the grass several yards in advance of the line. It passed me like a whirlwind, and with a fury I shall never forget. As far as the eye could reach, nothing was to be seen but one uniform black surface, looking like a vast plain of charcoal.

Theories of prairie origin. Of theories regarding the origin of the prairies there were many by 1830, all having a modern flavor. Perhaps the majority of observers felt that the grass on the plains was culturally induced or, to use the contemporary expression, " artificial." The aftereffects of prairie fires were familiar to resident and traveler alike; they reasoned that the original burning of the trees was followed by the destruction of seeds, hence the grasses assumed dominance. The abrupt wall of the forest on prairie margins often coincided with a stream or slough whose moisture would conceivably protect the woodland from successive fires. This theory satisfied the observed conditions of many large prairies, but was applied with increasing difficulty to regions of alternating tongues of grass and woods. Others believed that the prairie environment was due, at least in part, to browsing animals, especially the buffalo in earlier days; trees and shrubs, they argued, could not long endure the shearing off of their growing stems and shoots. Some support for this theory came from the observed effects of cattle-grazing in forest areas; the native covering of trees often was gradually displaced by white clover and bluegrass, " as frequent pasturing seems to give those plants ascendancy over the others." The treelessness of the wet prairies was most often ascribed to the height of the water table, which was unfavorable to arborescent growth except for a few water-loving trees, many of which (for example, tamarack, spruce) were not native to the area. A people who had learned much about the habitats of broad-leaved trees did not expect to find them growing in land constantly moist.

Perhaps the most advanced theory of this period conceived " predisposing causes " — that is, causes more remote than the effects of fire or grazing or inundations. This was well expressed by David Thomas, who in 1816 attributed treeless ground covers to underlying hardpan or

. . . level rock [which] I have noticed in the wet prairies. The same rock extending under the drier parts, confines the roots, and intercepts the supply of moisture that sub-soils generally contribute. The trees, thus stunted, admit amongst them a luxuriant herbage; in autumn it is speedily dried by the sun and wind, and the underbrush perishes in the annual conflagration. Near the borders sufficient evidence of this was often before us in the stools of oaks, with shoots from one to six feet in height, which were blasted by recent fires.

Similar theories of prairie origin in the humid Midwest, where acclimated trees were found to grow well if planted, have prevailed to the present time.

CHAPTER 12

People in the Land:
The State of Ohio

IN EARLY May of 1789 General Josiah Harmar, commandant of the fort bearing his name opposite the then year-old village of Marietta at the mouth of the Muskingum, reported: "The emigration continues if possible more rapid than ever; within these 20 days not less than one hundred souls have passed daily." The destination of these 2,000 persons was the guess of all the soldiery; in General Harmar's opinion they were headed for the lower river country, perhaps beyond the United States. In fact he allowed himself some heavy humor in adding that "the people are all taken up with Col. Morgan's New Madrid; they are in my opinion *mad rid* indeed. The Generality of the Inhabitants of Kaskaskia and a number of those at Post Vincennes, I am informed, have quit those villages & gone over to the Spanish side."

Each day's quota of emigrants, spreading into so vast a country populated mainly by unfriendly Indians, added to the responsibilities of the military, requiring three additional regiments of infantry, for "beyond a doubt a lesser number is insufficient to guard & protect this Western World." Fearing that the "old states must certainly be drained of their inhabitants" should the emigration maintain its pace, the General had ordered an accurate count of the people migrating down-river at two different periods, with results as follows:

EMIGRATION DOWN THE OHIO

	From June 1 to Dec. 9, 1787	From Dec. 4, 1788 to May 8, 1789
Boats	146	185
Persons	3,196	3,151
Horses	1,381	1,294
Cattle	171	453
Sheep	245	581
Wagons	165	58

Within all the Territory Northwest of the Ohio River (to give the new country its official title) there were, at the beginning of white settlement, probably about 8,000 warriors, representing four times that number of Indians. Some of the nations were presumably too remote from the Ohio River to cause much concern to the new settlements: The Ojibway and the Potawatomi, for example, lived in the remote upper Great Lakes country. Nearer at hand were the Shawnee, the Delaware, the Miami, and the Wyandot, together with remnants of the Six Nations evacuated from New York. The following data from Jervis Cutler give a fair appproximation.

INDIANS IN THE OHIO COUNTRY

	Warriors	Total Number
Six Nations	1,400	4,500
Wyandot tribes	550	1,800
Delaware	600	2,000
Shawnee	300	900
Ottawa	900	3,000
Miami	300	1,000
Chippewa	1,550	4,000
Potawatomi	500	2,000
Others	3,810	13,700
TOTALS	9,910	32,900

Scattered as they were over a large territory and uprooted from earlier residences and hunting grounds, the resentful Indians created a military problem difficult to handle in the traditional manner. Unexpected raids, their damage done before troops could reach the spot, would occasionally interrupt an interval of apparent peace. A typical report was one of Harmar's on May 8, 1789:

The Indians according to custom take the Liberty of Killing & Scalping defenseless people now and then. Five persons have been murdered on Dunkard's Creek in Washington County; two in Judge Symme's Settlement [near Cincinnati], and what is the worst of all, Captain [Zebulon] King of our Neighbors, a few days ago, was killed in the new settlement which the New England Gentlemen are about making down below [Ohio Company of Associates, pages 215–18].

Occasionally, as in October, 1790, trained troops and Indians met in more formal combat, and not always to the glory of the white forces.

Indian territory and white man's country. The military strength of the United States in the upper Ohio country before 1800 was represented by some twoscore forts and posts distributed in an arclike arrangement along the Ohio River and northward to the present-day Toledo region or, as then known, the "Miami of the Lakes." At strategic points to the west of Fort Harmar, and garrisoned by less than 600 militia, were a dozen forts or cantonments, of which the most influential was Fort Washington, forerunner of present-day Cincinnati. The western line of forts included, named from south to north, St. Clair (1791), Jefferson (1793), Greenville (1793), Recovery (1793), Wayne (1795) — this, of course, in present-day northeastern Indiana — and Deposit (1794). Still others, such as McArthur, Meigs, and Seneca, came into existence during the troubled year of 1812. (See Fig. 59.)

Beyond this crescent line of frontier forts and supply stations lay Indian country, officially recognized by the Treaty of Greenville of 1795. This important treaty was concluded on August 3 of that year between General Anthony Wayne and chiefs representing the Delaware, Shawnee, Wyandot, and Miami confederacies. The resulting boundary line in north-central Ohio and extending into adjacent Indiana is sometimes known as Wayne's Treaty Line. (See Fig. 59.) It established a definite line of separation within the Northwest Territory between Indian lands and those open to white settlement. Lands westward and northward of the Treaty Line were reserved to the Indians, except Detroit and other specified French settlements. Affirmed by the same treaty was a United States claim to a tract of land at Sault Ste. Marie, earlier granted to this country by France.

The Indians perhaps regarded the treaty line as a permanent one, but within the ensuing quarter-century they gave up their claims to much of the territory set off by it in a series of sales and treaties involving tracts of land whose boundaries were often found to overlap in a most confusing manner. (See Fig. 65, page 237.) Although the Greenville Treaty Line proved not to be so permanent as the Indian chiefs had assumed, it gives us a good approximation of Indian territory and white man's country in Ohio during the early years of the nineteenth century.

With the opening up of Ohio south and east of the treaty line, and north of it in the Connecticut Reserve, a great wave of settlement began. Large sections were soon purchased by land companies, of which the more important are outlined in Figure 59. Discussion will first be directed to the tracts acquired by the Ohio Company of Associates and the Scioto Company. This will be followed

59

Graphical summary of the land purchases, survey tracts, and land grants in Ohio by a study of the special conditions obtaining in the huge Connecticut Reserve Fire Lands area. Attention will then be turned to the small-scale or individual settlement in the areas identified as Congressional or military lands, wedged between the holdings of the company projects. Finally, another large company project outlined on the map, the Symmes Purchase, including the city of Cincinnati, will be considered.

THE OHIO COMPANY OF ASSOCIATES

Settlement of that part of Ohio west of the Seven Ranges was promoted by a New England group which had purchased directly from the Federal Government 1,500,000 acres of land for a few cents an acre. Among the officials of the new company were several who had served in the Revolutionary War and were well known to George Washington. Personal friendship may have played some part in his public approval of the company, which was given in the following words: " No colony in America was ever settled under such favorable auspices as that which has just begun on the banks of the Muskingum. Information, property, and strength will be its characteristics." The motives of the company were, indeed, of a high order. As expressed by a ranking official, the Reverend Manasseh Cutler, the Ohio Associates wished their settlement to serve as a model for similar attempts that were sure to follow. Furthermore, the lands they had chosen for the great experiment lay just beyond the already settled area (the Seven Ranges) and thus, it was said, represented a desirable progression of occupied territory. High motives were equally evident in the reservations of land set aside for the support of churches and schools. They possibly served as precedents for school reservations in townships surveyed at a later time in other Western states.

Each shareholder of the purchase received a final apportionment of 1,173.33 acres, made up of a full section of land (640 acres), in addition to fractions of other sections, and ⅓ acre for a house lot. There was here little of the speculation in real estate that distinguished the Military Tract of New York, partly, no doubt, because of the wealth of land available in other parts of Ohio.

Factors influencing selection. Several factors were considered by the Ohio Associates in the location of their purchase. One factor was the protection, or sense of protection, afforded by Fort Harmar. The country adjacent to the Muskingum was at a respectful distance from the Indian settlements, and derived presumed advantages from a frontage of over 100 miles on the Ohio River. As Major Ebenezer Denny wrote in his military journal in 1788, " A number of the proprietors and directors had come on and fixed upon the ground at the confluence of the Muskingum and Ohio rivers, as a central situation from which they could extend their operations, and at the same time to be protected by the garrison at Fort Harmar." (See Fig. 60.)

The proximity to areas already settled in the Seven Ranges and across the river in Virginia also influenced the selection. Furthermore, that part of Ohio west

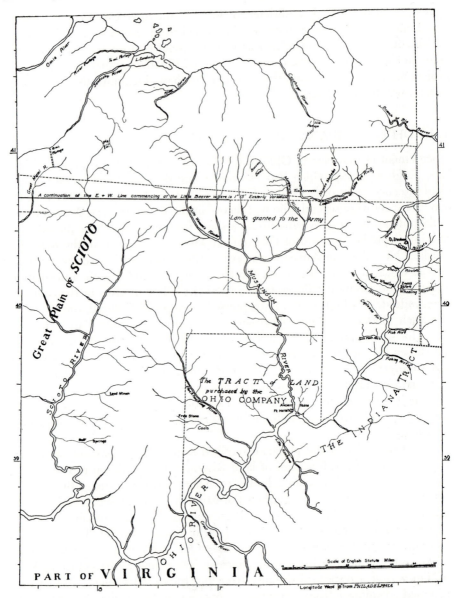

60   Copy of one of the first maps of the Ohio country, following the Ordinance of
1787 and showing the purchase of the Ohio Company of Associates

of the Seven Ranges was one of the few large units of Ohio — and the company
thought in large terms — to which clear title could be given. Prior claims to
the lands west of the Scioto and along Lake Erie had been entered by Virginia
and Connecticut, respectively.

The Ohio Associates' faith in the future of their purchase was genuine. In pointing out the agricultural possibilities of the tract, promotional literature was not overly extravagant when considered in the light of knowledge available at the time. Manasseh Cutler's writings include lengthy endorsements of the area by Thomas Hutchins, whose position as Congressional Geographer added weight to whatever he said in such matters. And there was plenty of other contemporary support for favorable comment on this part of the Ohio country. Even before the settlement of the tract, General Harmar stated:

> . . . the million of acres which is to be bounded South by the Ohio company purchase, I believe will be found to be excellent Land, especially if it should take in the Lands of the Muskingum & its branches. . . . From all accounts the Muskingum River inclines more to the eastward than is laid down in Captain Hutchins' maps & if so the Tract reserved for the late Army will be very valuable.

Prospectuses available to the average emigrant encouraged a more favorable impression of the " lay " of the land bordering this section of the Ohio River than was justified by the facts. This disparity resulted, however, more from the difficulties inherent in preparing realistic descriptions of topographical details than from deliberate attempts to mislead prospective buyers. Many who came were disappointed with the land and pushed on to the broader expanses of the Scioto.

Marietta, official town of the Ohio Associates. Marietta was the first and principal settlement of the Ohio Associates, and as such drew an extraordinary amount of attention; first from Fort Harmar's soldiers, who saw it take form, and later from travelers up and down the river, who considered their duty unfulfilled without some reference to it. Rightly or wrongly, Marietta was considered as a barometer of the company's success in its colonizing venture. When the town approached its twentieth year of life, the *Western Gazetteer* passed judgment in the remark that it " has not kept pace with public expectations," others adding that town growth was at least consistent with settlement of the tributary area, which was slow but sure. Much of the company's tract, said traveler Fortescue Cuming, was " broken and hilly, and the hills mostly poor compared with those farther to the westward on both sides of the river," hence a town larger than Marietta could not reasonably be expected.

Although drawn to a pattern too large for immediate attainment, Marietta was carefully planned. Within its expansive site, streets 90 feet wide were marked out on the land, and ample areas were reserved for public purposes. As Major Denny pointed out, Marietta took form " upon the site of a very ancient and very extraordinary fortification," where was erected " a place of arms and security called Campus Martius." Within the Campus (still so named) stood a large two-story building of hewn timber, " with strong block-houses at each angle, leaving a considerable area; here their stores, etc., were lodged and some families, perhaps more timid than others, reside."

By the year 1810 Marietta had grown to nearly 200 houses and had spread to the opposite banks and the site of Fort Harmar, which was at this time no longer in existence. A " handsomely situated town " in the opinion of early visitors, but exposed to floods rising above the ordinary level. From among the many accounts of early-day floods at Marietta we select one contained in a letter written from Point Harmar in the winter of 1813: "The Ohio has been 4½ feet higher the week past than it has been known since the settlement of the town. It has thrown such immense quantities of ice on the banks and bottoms as to render the River roads entirely impassable. It will be 2 or 3 months before it will be thawed. The damage has been very great, probably within this Town & neighbourhood ten thousand dollars." The chief early industries of the town were shipbuilding and the manufacture of rope, but other cities up and down the river surpassed Marietta in both activities. A comparatively unknown traveler, Christian Schultz, anticipated innumerable writers since his time in viewing Marietta, which was named after Queen Marie Antoinette, as "New England in miniature."

THE SCIOTO COMPANY, GALLIPOLIS, AND
THE FRENCH GRANT

The origin of the Ohio Associates and of other companies yet to be considered can be understood only by reference to time and place or, more exactly, to time and *space*. The vastness of the public domain northwest of the Ohio was matched by grandiose schemes of settlement under conditions that were never again to be duplicated. It was a time when, for example, it seemed reasonable for a citizen named Nathaniel Sackett, representing an associated group, to memorialize the Congress for a grant of about one-third of the State of Ohio; specifically, all the country between the Muskingum and the Scioto and from the Ohio River to Lake Erie. More remarkable still, Sackett and his associates proposed that "no consideration be paid the United States therefor except an ear of Indian corn annually, if demanded, as an acknowledgment of their sovereignty." On their part, the Sackett associates would see to it that the Indian frontier was properly settled, which, they thought, was the urgent need of the moment.

Sackett and his associates were not granted the kingdom they asked for, but another company contemporary with them and with the Ohio Associates negotiated a purchase of some 3,000,000 acres of the Scioto Basin— or thought they did. This has become known as the Scioto Company, whose dealings led to as strange a sequel as could well be imagined. That the make-up of the Scioto Company remains obscure is more important to history than to geography, but it is necessary to realize that the company was unable to meet its heavy financial obligations, and further, that errors were made in the limits of the property they had "purchased." Neither of these uncertainties appeared in the company's operations, which centered in Paris under the direction of Joel Barlow.

The advertising literature circulated in France, translated of course into French, approached a kind of fantasy worthy perhaps of a poet of Barlow's talents, but bearing little resemblance to the geography of the Scioto. The French readers were urged to consider a land of beautiful rivers and rich soils, productive of all kinds of foods — even, amazingly, sugar from native trees — with plenty of fish and wild game; and over all this bright land was a healthy and delightful climate of frostless winters. As the French geographer Volney said a dozen years later when he visited the Scioto:

> The offerers of so many benefits did not say that these fine forests were a preliminary obstacle to every sort of cultivation, that all provisions must be secured from a distance for at least a year, that these excellent lands were in the neighbourhood of a species of ferocious animal worse than wolves and tigers, the man called savage, then at war with the United States.

In the throes of their political revolution, the French people were in a mood to believe that the world contained so idyllic a spot somewhere beyond France. A further inducement was the low price of the land, possibly as little as $1 an acre. " A kind of contagious enthusiasm and credulity had seized men's minds," said Volney; " the picture was too brilliant, and the inconveniences too remote for the bait not to take effect. . . . Nothing was talked of in Parisian circles but the free and rural life to be led on the banks of the Scioto." This was doubtless an exaggeration, but much land was indeed sold to individuals of many professions and occupations, the latter including a few practical farmers.

Gallipolis in Gallia County.   As many as 500 French persons — some reports place the figure higher — set out from Le Havre, Bordeaux, and Nantes, arriving at Alexandria, Virginia, in the fall of 1790. There they learned that the lands they had supposedly bought lay within the limits of the Ohio Associates' purchase. In these straits, the immigrants won the assistance of the Government to the extent of free transportation to their lands, which lay opposite the mouth of the Great Kanawha. In the meantime, by arrangement with the Ohio Associates, a partly fortified village of two double rows of cabins or barracks had been constructed. This was Gallipolis, the City of Gauls, in present-day Gallia County.

The French immigrants were now confronted with the necessity of buying their lands once again at a cost of $1.25 an acre, and some 20 families so complied. Others returned to their home country or sought refuge in the French region of Louisiana. In March, 1795, the sympathetic Federal Government, with plenty of land available, granted 24,000 acres as a recompense for the invalid titles. By this time, however, many of the people had gone elsewhere. John Kilbourn's *Ohio Gazetteer* reported in 1816 that " there are not more than eight or ten French families who now reside upon it [French Grant], the other portion of the population being composed of emigrants from Vermont and other states." The substitute grant, where each settler of eighteen years or older was entitled to a share of the land, was located near modern Portsmouth in Scioto County. (See Fig. 59, page 214.)

When Volney reached Gallipolis in July, 1796, he was struck by the primitive surroundings of his unfortunate countrymen. They then lived in " whitewashed log cabins . . . built contiguous, no doubt that they might all be burnt up at once. . . . I could have wished to leave this colony with a persuasion that it may grow stronger and prosper," he added; but here, as elsewhere, he took the pessimistic view, concluding that " the French are not so well adapted for establishing farming settlements as emigrants from England, Ireland, or Germany." Another traveling Frenchman, André Michaux, was more positive, asserting that his countrymen were unsuccessful because they were less persevering than others and because " not a tenth part were fit for the toils they were destined to endure."

Gallipolis did grow and prosper, so much so that in 1807 it consisted of more than 50 houses built around the original spacious square on which, said Cuming, who stopped there on his tour, " they are now making brick to build a court-house for Gallia County." The people of the town long remained sensitive to the difficulties attending its origin, and felt that their community was unfairly pictured by many visitors. Christian Schultz was among those to remark that Gallipolis showed signs of decadence, whereupon in 1817 the home-town paper retorted with spirit: " In the first instance, the town at the time you *pretended* to have visited it, contained as many houses as at any previous date, and owing to the remarkable healthiness of the place, and other very flattering natural advantages, has ever since been rapidly growing." With true loyalty, the *Evening Standard* pointed out that the town was more than 14 feet above high-water mark and " at this time consists of one hundred houses, built on a solid foundation, which has certainly never been reached by any flood since the days of Noah, and will remain till ages after the Travels of Christian Schultz, Jr., Esq., are forgotten."

THE CONNECTICUT RESERVE

Among company-organized settlement projects of eastern Ohio, none is of greater interest or more worthy of study than the area blocked out as the Connecticut Western Reserve (or the Connecticut Reserve), and the Fire Lands. The extent and variety of eyewitness records, for the most part kept at the Western Reserve Historical Society in Cleveland, suggest that interest in the region began with the very origin of the Connecticut Land Company and continued through the period of its operations. From these records we are enabled to trace the " opening-up " of the tract, which commenced with the original survey of the Reserve and the contiguous Fire Lands, and was promptly followed by permanent settlement by farmers and town dwellers. It appears that the methodical procedures of the Connecticut Land Company are reflected in the relative completeness of the available record.

The origin of the Connecticut Reserve and the Connecticut Land Company, which promoted the settlement of the greater part of it, must first of all be briefly traced. In the year 1786, the State of Connecticut joined other Eastern states in ceding to the newly formed Federal Government its claims to Western territories, but differed from its neighbors in retaining possession of some 5,000 square miles in the northeastern corner of the present State of Ohio. This area immediately became known as the Connecticut Western Reserve, or, less properly, as " New Connecticut." In area, it was almost equal to the parent state, although, as will appear, there were some misconceptions regarding the actual acreage within it.

The deed of cession of September 13, 1786, established the reservation as the territory included between the 41st parallel and Lake Erie, and westward 120 miles from the western boundary of Pennsylvania. On the modern map, the 41st parallel corresponds to the southern boundaries of the counties of Portage, Medina, and Huron; the western limit of the Reserve is shown by the eastern boundaries of the counties of Seneca and Sandusky.

Shortly after the reservation was made, the residents of several Connecticut towns and cities, including Danbury, Ridgefield, Greenwich, New Haven, East Haven, Fairchild, Norwalk, New London, and Groton, petitioned the state government for compensation for losses by fire during the Revolution. In recognition of this petition, in 1791 the Connecticut Legislature designated the western part of the Reserve, consisting of some 500,000 acres, as the Fire Sufferers' Lands or Fire Lands. The eventual sale of these lands contributed to the support of the named communities, just as the sum derived from the disposal of the remainder of the Reserve went toward the support of Connecticut's schools.

Plans for the sale of Reserve land. Preliminary plans were early made for the sale of Reserve land, though final negotiations were not completed until 1795. According to legislative resolutions, that portion of the Reserve east of the Cuyahoga River was first to be marketed at not less than 3 shillings (about 50 cents) an acre. It was also decided that the Reserve should be surveyed into rectangular townships after the manner of the Seven Ranges, but with townships of 25 square miles each instead of the standard 36. Reservations were also made in each township — 500 acres for the support of schools and an equal amount for religious aid, with an additional 240 acres for the first minister who should settle in each town.

The first purchase within the Reserve was known as the Salt Spring Tract of 25,250 acres near the Mahoning River in the northeastern corner. The property was later subdivided by General Parsons, its original owner. In the fall of 1795, Oliver Phelps and a group of associates made a contract with the State of Connecticut for the purchase of the entire remaining tract of the Reserve, exclusive of the Fire Lands, for the sum of $1,200,000. The purchasers immediately organized the Connecticut Land Company, among whose members lots were to be distributed according to their respective investments. Prior to the allotment, twelve of the members, representing the counties of New London and Windham, considering it advantageous to draw their shares in one large tract, formed the Erie Company, of which Moses Cleaveland, for whom the city of Cleveland was named, was a trustee. This subsidiary company functioned until March, 1808, a year before the dissolution of the Connecticut Land Company.

In computing the acreage within the Reserve, the latter company was of course guided by available maps, which showed the southern shore of Lake Erie trending more directly east and west than is actually the case. Three million acres, it was calculated, were included in the company's purchase, but others guessed that the figure was higher. Out of this confusion developed what has become known as the Excess Company, which proposed to buy at a pro-rata price all the land over the 3,000,000 figure that more accurate surveys might bring to light. The survey, as a matter of fact, showed an area somewhat less than was anticipated, whereupon the Excess Company passed out of existence.

A possibility of confusion arises here in the frequent reference to the " surplus lands " of the Connecticut Reserve. The " surplus lands " resulted from an error in the running of the boundary between the Fire Lands and the property of the Connecticut Land Company. A corrected north-south line showed that about 5,300 acres of land had not been properly accounted for by the company, and the area within the " gore " thus formed was declared to be " surplus land " and was divided into 200-acre plots to be sold at an average price of $1 an acre. A summary of the acreages within the various tracts of the Connecticut Reserve follows.

QUANTITY OF LAND IN THE CONNECTICUT RESERVE

(From the draft book of General Simon Perkins)

Area	Acres
Salt Spring Tract	25,450
Connecticut Land Company	
East of the Cuyahoga River	2,002,970
West of the Cuyahoga River exclusive of the surplus lands and islands	827,291
Surplus lands	5,286
Islands	5,924
Fire Lands	500,000
TOTAL	3,366,921

Steps in settlement: surveying the land.   The advance guard of settlement in the Reserve was the surveying party consisting of about 50 persons who collected at Buffalo in June, 1796, and arrived at the mouth of Conneaut Creek on July 4. Until their surveying work was done, no settlement could properly take place. Theirs was the job of laying out township and range lines, plotting river courses and existent Indian paths, applying names to natural features and the squared spaces that were to become townships. The majority of the surveyors were experienced in the new kind of rectangular survey. The principal surveyor of this, the first of several parties, was Augustus Porter, who had served his apprenticeship in " gridding " the Holland Purchase of western New York; one of his aides was Seth Pease, a mathematician of ability, who was named chief surveyor in the following year. In the words of one of the party, " a large portion were young enterprising men whose greatest object was to see the country. Many had studied the superficial parts of the surveyor's art and were looking for employment in that business."

The success of the first surveying party may be attributed as much to the relatively subdued topography of the area and to freedom from Indian troubles, as to the experience of the men. The part of the Reserve east of the Cuyahoga River, surveyed during the first two years, seems to have been an essentially empty land just prior to colonization. Hunting ground it was, according to the word of the surveyors and confirmed by their maps, which show occasional Indian paths; but it was probably not permanently occupied by the aborigines. Even in the region west of the Cuyahoga, title to which was not cleared by treaty until 1805, and in the Fire Lands, only a few Indians lived. Amizi Atwater, of the first surveying party, reported upon arrival at Conneaut Creek the presence of 15 Indian families, but they had disappeared by the next year. A few Seneca lived near Grand River, and Indians from " Huron and Sandusky continued to resort there until nearly the commencement of the late War [1812]." In Atwater's view, supported by actual developments, the remaining Indians aided rather than interfered with white settlement.

From headquarters in a building called the Stone Castle, hastily erected on the east side of Conneaut Creek, the men of the transit and theodolite began their work at the Ellicott Line of western Pennsylvania, which they found regrown with brush since its first survey. Hacking a new swath 2 rods wide, the party finally established a post at the 41st parallel, from which the rectangular grid, eventually to cover the entire area, was extended. There were some disappointments, says Atwater, partly from the difficulty of securing supplies, and " others occasioned by our ignorance of the Geogrify of the Country, but not as many as might be expected." The progress of the work at the end of the second year is shown in the manuscript map of Seth Pease (Fig. 61). The map contains evidence of the care with which the work was done. The township acreages were precisely measured and topographical features were accurately represented. The map compares favorably with modern maps of the same area. As has been noted, each township approximates 25 square miles rather than the 36 square miles established by the Hutchins survey in the Seven Ranges.

All parts of the Reserve, as already implied, were not surveyed at the same time, a fact of some importance in understanding the settlement of northern Ohio. Settlers continued to refer to the three survey units of the Reserve as the eastern, central, and western sections, and reached them by different routes from Ohio River points. After the 1796-97 survey east of the Cuyahoga River there was a break of eight years before the survey of the land west of the river to the border of the Fire Lands was completed. The survey of the second unit could not be undertaken until the Indian title to that part of the Reserve was extinguished, which event occurred in 1805. Similarly, the preliminary survey of the Fire Lands, arranged by the company of that name, had to wait until an agreement was reached with the Indians in 1806.

Not the least significant contribution of the surveyors and company agents was the nomenclature which they applied to the Reserve. Basically, the still-existent names they bestowed were of three sources: (1) Indian names, (2) other names

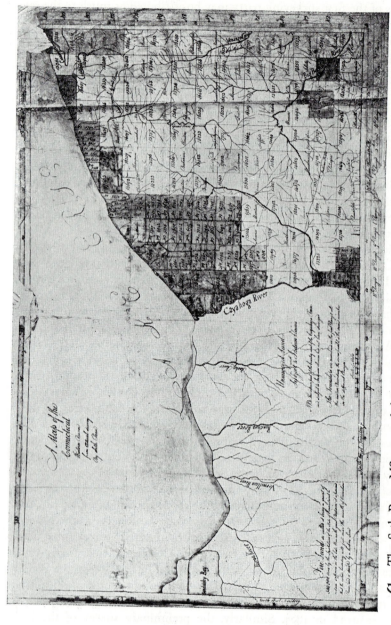

61 The Seth Pease MS. map of the eastern Connecticut Reserve to the Cuyahoga River. Figures within townships show acreage of land. Darkened portions were lands sold at time of survey. Inscription in lower left-hand corner begins: "Fire Land so called it being a grant . . . to certain sufferers in the late War with great Britain . . ." Original map in Western Reserve Historical Society; reproduced by permission.

transferred from cities or features in the East, especially Connecticut names, and (3) still others commemorating individuals prominent either in the nation or in the affairs of the Connecticut Land Company. Some of the surveyors even " amused themselves," as they said, by decorating the new maps with their own names.

Among aboriginal names are Chippewa Lake, Geauga, and Cuyahoga (spelled Cayahoga by Pease). Names of townships apparently borrowed from Eastern states are Hudson, Suffield, Milford, Windsor, and New London. Among those places named for individuals are Cleveland, Trumbull (a governor of Connecticut), and Atwater (one of the surveyors). Many original names have been changed. There are, as usual, some imaginative names, and others whose origins are subject to different interpretations. Mesopotamia Township was evidently so named because of its position between two branches of Grand River; but what is the origin of the name River Chagrin? According to Atwater:

It is believed by some that the Chagrin River was named on account of a disappointment of surveying parties mistaking it for the Cayahoga River through bad information. . . . It might probably have been named so at the time if it had not been so named before. It had long before been known by that name . . . in consequence of a French crew being cast away and suffered there. The particulars I do not know. We were very ready to confirm the name.

The coming of settlers: routes from the East and the South: The first permanent settlers in the Reserve included some of the surveyors, at least seven of whom decided to remain. It appears that the field men were allowed to select any township they fancied, to be divided into 320-acre plots and paid for at a minimum price on long credit. According to Augustus Porter, writing from memory in 1843, the granting of this privilege did not reflect altruistic motives on the part of the company but was a device of Moses Cleaveland's to quell a " disposition in camp to mutiny, or what would now be called a strike for higher wages." At all events, the surveyors chose the township adjoining Cleveland on the east, naming it Euclid in honor of the great " patron saint " of their profession; hence also Euclid Avenue, one of the principal thoroughfares of Cleveland.

The settlement of the Reserve by emigrants from the Eastern states was marked by solidity and strength rather than by speculative booms. There appears to have been no extravagant advertising, the promoters perhaps having the view that the region could speak for itself. Efforts to stimulate or aid new settlement were often of a constructive nature. For instance, the company voted to grant " a sum not exceeding $200 or loan not exceeding $500 without interest until April, 1802, to any person or persons who shall build a good grist mill in Ts. 9 in the 9th Range " — that is, the township of Willoughby. It would appear that similar provisions were applied elsewhere in the eastern part of the Reserve. Also the company appointed a committee in 1798 to survey the possibilities of road-building from eastern points. Upon the recommendation of the committee, the famous " Girdled Road " from the Pennsylvania line to Cleveland was soon constructed. Twenty-five feet wide, the road was cut through underbrush and among girdled trees along the old beach ridge from Conneaut, connecting the present towns of Austinburg and Concord with Cleveland via Euclid Avenue.

Among frontier regions, the Reserve was exceptional in its accessibility from the source regions of settlement. Its long frontage on Lake Erie ensured communication by lake-sailing vessels at first, and later by steamers when they began to ply the lakes in the early 1820's. Overland routes were also facilitated by numerous river valleys and by the low divides separating Lake Erie drainage from Ohio River tributaries. Indian trails showed the incoming people the shortest and best land routes to new objectives.

The most important route into the Reserve utilized Lake Erie for at least part of the distance from Buffalo. First used by the surveyors, this entrance increased in significance after 1818, when Buffalo and Cleveland were connected by steamboat line. Typical of many was the journey of settler Darius Lyman. Setting out from Northampton, Massachusetts, on June 21, 1816, he arrived at Buffalo on June 26, took a boat to Erie and then another to Grand River, reaching his destination, Ravenna, on July 8.

Settlers from Pennsylvania bound for the eastern section of the Reserve often followed the Beaver River to its junction with the Mahoning, then continued up its branches to the height of land. According to early accounts and maps, a main Indian path led from here to the Cuyahoga at Kent — Standing Rock, as it was then called, doubtless in apt description of a local landmark. A case in point is the journey of William Eldredge of New London, Connecticut, who came to Windsor to inspect his land. Starting from New London on May 14, 1806, he reached Cleveland on June 12 by way of Pittsburgh, Youngstown, and Warren. Mr. Eldredge found his land " very good, far surpassing our expectations (as well as the Town in general) both in point of Soils & Situation."

An alternative route from the east and south branched off from the Ohio River at Yellow Creek, in southern Columbiana County, thence led up the Tuscarawas (originally called Little Muskingum) and into the Reserve by White Woman's River. In the course of time, and with the opening-up of the western sections of the Reserve, other routes and roads came into being. The Conestoga wagon, sometimes called the Dutch wagon, was the favorite vehicle for transporting household goods and farm equipment into the new Promised Land.

The spread of settlement. Broadly considered, Western Reserve settlement advanced from east to west and not, as might be supposed, from the lake front inland. Occupation of the land followed closely upon the surveyors' operations and they, in turn, upon the extinction of Indian claims. Generally, too, the advance was from heavily timbered country into mixed forest and prairie and finally into the open prairie of the Sandusky plains. Beyond the latter, settlement was halted by the notorious Black Swamp and by Indian-held country.

Many of the communities of the Reserve not only bore the names of older villages in the East, but came to resemble them also in appearance. Familiar

features were village greens bordered by town halls and churches, the architec-
tural styles of which were reminiscent of New England. Outlying farms were not
greatly different from Eastern farms, and were productive of similar crops.
Nevertheless, there was much of the rawness of the frontier during the early
years of development. A Bloomfield pioneer, in picturing his new surroundings
for a friend " back East," said that he was writing from

. . . the Portico of a log house fronting the south. The Portico is supported by six columns. I am not a conoisseur [sic] in architecture, and cannot tell you what order they
are, but I can tell you they have rec'd no polish or ornament from art other than being
divested of their bark. This mansion house on your canvas must be placed nearly in the
center of a small opening or clearing like an island in the midst of a vast ocean of a dark
green forest. Your imagination must supply the rest as I am but poor in description.

It was perhaps inevitable that town clusters should develop at river-mouth
locations on Lake Erie and that some of these should grow into large cities —
Cleveland, for instance. Even before the forming of the Connecticut Land Company, the mouth of the Cuyahoga was a port of entry for vessels from Detroit;
furs were sometimes unloaded here and sent overland to the Ohio River. Further,
the Reverend John G. E. Heckewelder had pointed out, in advance of planning,
that there were many fine places for settlement along Lake Erie, and " particular
Spots far preferable to others; one of the best places is Cyjahoga ": It provided
a good harbor, it was navigable for small boats to the falls 60 miles inland,
and " there is the best prospect of water communication from Lake Erie to the
Ohio by way of the Cyjahoga and Muskingum Rivers." Moreover, near-by
waters provided a fishery and there was good drinking water in the vicinity.
Perhaps the most important of all, the surrounding land was of first quality and
there was prospect of easy road-building along the lake shore.

These advantages played a part in the selection of the Cleveland site and
the early growth of the city, which, however, until the railroad era and the improvement of the lower river, was by no means remarkable. By 1820 Cleveland
consisted of less than 100 houses on the right bank of the Cuyahoga a half-mile
from the lake. Said Daniel Blowe's *Geographical View*:

Its site is dry, sandy, and elevated 200 feet above the level of the river and lake;
nevertheless billious fevers and agues have frequently affected the inhabitants. The
cause is to be ascribed to the surf of the lake, choking up the river, and causing a
stagnation of its waters for three miles upward.

Sandusky, which came into being as Portland, was described in 1822 by traveler
Henry Newberry as a " little, dusty village " of a few homes and stores " doing
very little business, and one or two shut up: two poor taverns and quite as good
as the circumstances of the place will warrant." Nevertheless, Sandusky's natural
advantages were evident, with a harbor at that time admitting vessels of 8-foot
draft. " Sandusky will eventually become a great city," said William Woodbridge of Detroit in a letter in 1815.

SETTLEMENT OF CONGRESS AND MILITARY LANDS

Among the lands not acquired by large companies were some of the most attractive regions of eastern Ohio. These became known as Congress Lands and when surveyed into townships and minor divisions, were available for individual purchase at sums per acre which now seem ridiculously small. The systematic procedure provided by the rectangular network in the disposal of government land to settlers was further advanced by the division of the state into districts. (See Fig. 62.) Land offices within the districts became very busy places indeed as intending settlers came to inspect the plat books and selected the farms of their choice. The original Seven Ranges became the Steubenville and Marietta districts. The Canton District, sometimes called the " New Purchase " because the area was acquired after the Treaty of Greenville, lay between the Connecticut Reserve and the Zanesville District. Farther west were the districts of Chillicothe and Cincinnati.

62   The public-land districts of Ohio about 1825. Zane's Trace and other trails are shown.

In the view of the majority of prospective settlers, the Congress Lands were inferior to others in only one major particular: Their inland position reduced accessibility. Isolated from both the Ohio River and Lake Erie (the building of canals was still a subject for the vaguest speculation), the only solution was the building of roads. The extent to which the road network was advanced in the 1820's is illustrated in Figure 63, which is a simplified copy of a contemporary map. Each of the roads shown upon it has its own history, but one of them, Zane's Trace, deserves a special note.

The town and trace of Ebenezer Zane.   Interesting as an example of personal vision and energy is the story of the present city of Zanesville, which originated in the year 1800 and within a few years became one of the leading communities of Ohio. To understand the beginnings of Zanesville one must first consider Zane's Trace or Road, which for a generation was a chief route of land travel through southeastern Ohio. According to Clement L. Martzolff, Colonel Eben-

63   Simplified copy of a map of Ohio of the 1820's

ezer Zane was a practical road-maker who first opened a trail from Pittsburgh to Wheeling.

This route proved to be of such value to settlers that Zane became " more sanguine regarding a road connecting the Ohio with the Ohio and running through what was the garden spot of the state." A petition to Congress in 1796 for land patents was finally approved, and Zane laid out his trace, first as a bridle path and later improved as to surface and width. The route of the completed road, portions of which followed pre-existent Indian paths, is shown in Figure 63, extending from Wheeling through Zanesville, Lancaster, and Chillicothe to a point opposite Limestone in Kentucky. From all accounts, the road paid little respect to topographic features, aiming straight at its objectives, running over difficult hills east of the Muskingum, and elsewhere foundering in wet ground over insecure corduroy. Nevertheless, Zane's Trace was the only inland highway for many years, and it contributed greatly to the development of the state. The depth of its ruts was a measure of its great use.

The town that Zane founded received the approval of all travelers who placed their observations on record. Located on the then navigable Muskingum and also near falls of the tributary Licking River, with good land in the vicinity, Zanesville seemed on its way to becoming a leading city in the new state. Said Espy in 1805:

This place is not only handsomely situated, but possesses many and peculiar advantages which promise to make it a flourishing town. The falls afford seats for all kinds of valuable water works and two or three excellent mills are already erected. The navigation of the river all the way to its mouth is nearly equal to the Ohio, and the country above is said to be fertile and healthy.

By the year of Mr. Zane's death (1823) his town had about 3,000 population, a dam had been constructed to increase the natural endowment of water power, and there were many substantial manufacturing industries. Strolling through town in 1823, the English visitor William Faux saw a glass factory and several other mills. In the same year Professor William H. Keating made note of the manufacture of nails and hollow ware, and of china from local supplies of high-grade clay. As observed elsewhere, the early saltworks of Zanesville had been abandoned since the discovery of more concentrated supplies farther downstream.

Early developments in the central Scioto Basin. In many respects the development of the central basin of the Scioto was an epitome of the state as a whole. Here were group settlements by people linguistically allied, and land-company projects were here drawn to a more modest scale than elsewhere in Ohio. In addition, there was the usual farm settlement by individuals, and cities and towns more than kept pace in their growth with others of the surrounding country.

In the summer of 1801 two men from a Welsh community in Cambria County, Pennsylvania, reached the Scioto to select a tract of land suitable for settlement by their people. After some careful inspection of the land and plat books, they chose 1,800 acres in the northwest corner of Granville Township in Licking County. Soon thereafter a modest immigration set in, requiring the purchase of still more land for the incoming Welsh people. The area they selected, notable for its hilly and varied surface, is still called the Welsh Hills. This was not the only Ohio area to which Welsh people came in groups; other settlements developed in Gallia County and near Cincinnati.

Licking County was also of interest to a group of citizens of East Granville in southwestern Massachusetts. The example set by the emigration of many of their neighbors led to a meeting on April 23, 1804, to consider the purchase of lands somewhere in Ohio. They, like many others at the time, believed it advisable to settle in a group rather than singly, and as a first step commissioned a locating party to find a suitable site. While the locating party was on its tour of inspection the associates formally organized, at first calling themselves the Scioto Land Company. This title, however, had unpleasant connections by that time; their final selection of the title Licking Land Company was more appropriate in another way as well, for the chosen area was not directly on the Scioto River. Four townships were selected by the agents in the Military Tract of Licking County. In the traditional manner, the settlers arrived by ox team and successfully established themselves, after which the company was dissolved (1808).

The designation of Columbus as the capital city of the state was guided in part by its central position relative to the area of the state; the site had advantages also because of the growing productivity of its surrounding area, and its location on the Scioto River. The town was laid out in 1812, and lots with standing timber still on them were immediately placed on the market. Town growth was very rapid, leading to a population of some 3,000 within the next seven years. Said Timothy Flint's *A Condensed Geography*: " It is a memorable example of a town that has grown up from the woods, like a prophet's gourd, in a night." Foreign visitors, accustomed to a slower tempo, were more amazed than were native citizens at developments of this sort. Duke Karl Bernhard was astonished at what he saw in 1825 and joined with others in freely predicting that the capital city would soon " rival the first cities in the western country."

THE SYMMES PATENT AND CINCINNATI

Contemporary with the operations of the Ohio Associates and the Scioto Company was the personal venture in Ohio colonization of John Cleves Symmes of New Jersey. An officer of the Revolutionary army, Symmes had acquired a large fortune, but also a temporary and less enviable reputation in America and abroad for his eccentric views concerning the nature of the globe. According to Professor Keating of the Long expedition, " he appears conversant with every work of travels from Hearne's to Humboldt's, and there is not a fact to be found in these works which he does not manage, with considerable ingenuity, to bring to the support of his favourite doctrine " — namely, that the earth's surface is concave. Nevertheless, Symmes talked rationally on all other subjects, and he certainly showed good judgment in the purchase of the tract between the Little and Big Miami rivers. At first presumed to include a million acres, the area was shown by more accurate surveys to total less than 600,000 acres, about 10 per cent of which was reserved for public purposes.

Early referred to as a " little Mesopotamia " because of its position between two rivers, the Symmes Patent then lay next door to the Indian country. Military aid was promptly sought from General Harmar, who informed Secretary Knox on September 7, 1788:

. . . the honorable John Cleves Symmes, Esqr. . . . has purchased of the United States a tract of land between the Miami Rivers, where he means to establish a Settlement. He has made Application for a party of men to be stationed at the Old Fort for his Protection. I should cheerfully comply with his Request, but at present the situation of Affairs would by no means admit of it. I have given him every Reason to hope that as soon as it is provident & practicable, a Party of troops shall be stationed near the mouth of the Miami for the Protection of his settlement.

By August of 1789 the time was evidently propitious, for Harmar ordered one of his officers, Major John Doughty, to select a fort site near the mouth of the Great Miami or between the two Miamis. Since the selection led to Cincinnati's location, it may be well to quote Harmar's directions in full: " I would have you carefully to Reconnoitre for a high, healthy Spot, with Springs at hand on the margins of the River Ohio, never subject to inundations, and there to erect our works. A good & safe harbour for our boats is also an object of very great importance and Strictly to be attended to." The place selected, it should be observed, lay between the mouths of the Miami and Little Miami rivers, opposite the Licking River of Kentucky, a southern tributary of the Ohio.

Origin and early growth of Cincinnati. The result of these orders, or directives as they would now be called, was Fort Washington — located, in reference to the present city of Cincinnati, at Third Street between Ludlow and Broadway. It was in the shelter of the fort that settlement first began, spreading upstream and downstream and, more cautiously, into the interior. The civil community that developed near Fort Washington (nonexistent by 1810) was first named Columbia; when it grew larger, Dr. John Filson, famous Kentucky scholar, proposed that the name be changed to Losantiville (a Latinized abbreviation of " the city opposite the mouth of the Licking River "). This suggestion, however, was successfully resisted in favor of the name Cincinnati, in honor of the society of former officers in the Revolutionary Army.

Even in 1815 the city was being referred to as the metropolis or capital of the Western country, not altogether to the approval of Louisville, and before 1830 it was predicted that the city would " with great ease increase in population to about 50,000 inhabitants. Its increase beyond that number depends on so many causes, not yet fully developed, that human foresight cannot scan them." With greater emotion, a citizen pontificated that the city "will hold the same rank among the cities of the Union that the great State, of which she is the ornament, now possesses in the American Confederacy."

As to the "ornamental" qualities of Cincinnati during its early years of growth there was the usual difference of opinion. To an Englishman traveling down the river in 1822, Cincinnati appeared as a great slash in the wilderness, the inhabitants of which were apparently guiltless of any taste for the picturesque. "All the land in the immediate neighbourhood," said Blane, "is without a tree upon it. This is the case with all American towns, which consequently have an appearance of nakedness and coldness that forcibly strikes an Englishman, particularly as before arriving at them he must have passed through immense forests." A resident of Cincinnati from 1817 to 1821 recalled a quarter-century later:

. . . its appearance . . . struck me at first rather unfavorably. Its size and population was less than I had supposed, nor did it in other respects equal the picture my imagination had drawn of it. There was an air of life, a bustle and activity about it, and yet, taken together, it had a raw, unfinished and slovenly aspect. The bank of the river in front of the town was not only unsightly, but calculated to make an unfavorable impression upon the mind of a stranger. It was, in short, ragged, broken, and verdureless — without tree or shrub, without wall or railing, protection, or ornament.

The absence of docks and piers was a striking feature to many visitors; instead of the usual landing places, chains were used to make boats fast to the paved bank.

It was not until 1810 that Cincinnati advanced from the status of an ordinary river village to the rank of a major town. With the coming of steamboat transportation and the further development of the tributary region, Cincinnati grew rapidly as is shown in the following table.

POPULATION OF CINCINNATI

1795 . . . 500	1813 . . . 4,000	1826 . . . 16,250
1800 . . . 750	1815 . . . 6,000	1829 . . . 25,000
1805 . . . 950	1818 . . . 9,000	1830 . . . 27,000
1810 . . . 2,320	1820 . . . 12,016	1831 . . . 30,000

The commerce of the city was almost as extensive as the river system on which it was an important entrepôt, and inevitably the flow of commerce led to the development of manufacturing. Early industries included cotton spinning, hollow ware and pottery, saddlery, glassmaking, the production of white and red lead, and the making of liquors. Shipbuilding was also important, with as many as 5 boats in the process of construction when traveler Wright visited the city in 1819. It is recorded that 60 steamboats representing 11,225 tons were built at Cincinnati by the year 1828. The leading exports and imports in 1826 according to Drake and Mansfield were as follows:

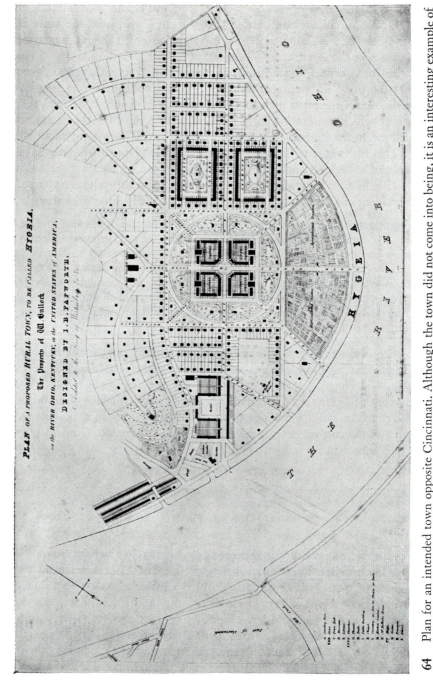

PLAN OF A PROPOSED RURAL TOWN, TO BE CALLED *HYGEIA*.

The Property of *Wⁱˡˡ Bullock*

on the RIVER OHIO, KENTUCKY, in the UNITED STATES of AMERICA.

DESIGNED BY J. B. PAPWORTH.

64   Plan for an intended town opposite Cincinnati. Although the town did not come into being, it is an interesting example of similar projects in the Ohio country at the time.

CINCINNATI EXPORTS AND IMPORTS, 1826

Exports		Imports	
Flour	$165,000	Iron (bar, cast, pig)	$225,290
Pork, lard, ham, bacon	223,000	Dry goods	1,100,000
Whisky	101,500	Tea and coffee	406,000
Feathers	78,520	Liquors	200,000
Hats	75,000	TOTAL	$1,931,290
Clothing	50,000		
Cabinet furniture	47,000		
TOTAL	$740,020		

The exceptional growth of Cincinnati was of interest not only to inhabitants of this country but also to those overseas, where favorable accounts of the city and of Ohio in general were widely circulated. It seems probable that, for example, the flattering description written by Duke Karl Bernhard in 1825 played some part in encouraging the large German emigration to this area in the ensuing years. Karl Bernhard told his countrymen:

We found the shores of the Ohio well cultivated, with orchards and Indian corn; we observed several very pretty country-seats. These shores are mostly elevated, and at a distance of about a mile we could perceive a chain of hills covered with woods, which made a fine prospect. Cincinnati is situated on the right shore of the Ohio, and built at the foot of a hill, which is surrounded by a half circle of higher hills covered with forests. The city presents a very fine aspect. The hills on the opposite side likewise form a half circle, and in this manner the hill on which Cincinnati is built, lies as it were in a basin. . . . The shores near Cincinnati are rather steep, and to render the loading and unloading of boats more convenient, they are paved and provided with rings and chains of iron.

An Englishman by the name of W. Bullock, foreseeing that Cincinnati would some day become a great city, made plans to develop a suburb across the river in Kentucky where Covington is now located. In a " Notice to the Public," published in London in 1827, Mr. Bullock stated that he had purchased " an extentive estate with a handsome home there "; and on returning to England he engaged an architect to lay out a town plan for the development of a beautiful community. The plan (Fig. 64) is perhaps the most elaborate ever fashioned for an American city, but the town, provisionally named Hygeia, never came into existence. The reduction of the original map necessary to fit it to page size makes it impossible to identify details, but the general pattern of this idealistic community is clearly apparent.

CHAPTER 13

People in the Land:
Down-river Country

THE importance of the Ohio River in Western settlement can scarcely be over-estimated. Its broad surface was common property, opening an easy way to the west or, as below the Big Bend, to the southwest.

The pronounced change in direction below Cincinnati was at first advantageous because in following it emigrants skirted the edge of the Indian country. The map showing the extinction of Indian claims, as illustrated by Indiana (Fig. 65), is a valuable reminder that during the beginning stages of the great westward push, much of the inland territory was unavailable for white settlement. It will be noted that the treaties of Vincennes and Grouseland of 1804 and 1805, which eased the way for occupation of southern Indiana, were not immediately followed by the extinction of Indian claims farther from the river. Not until 1818 was central Indiana opened up by the Treaty of St. Marys, sometimes called the New Purchase. Out of this cession, accomplished at the expense of a lump sum of $13,000 and small annuities, 37 counties have since been carved. Not only a new purchase, one would say, but a shrewd one as well.

Avoiding Indian-held country, the Western frontier extended rapidly downstream, leaving in its wake a string of hamlets and villages which have since grown into towns and cities. Within a dozen years this migration wave of Eastern origin extended the entire length of the Indiana shore and over a hundred miles up the Wabash, reaching Vincennes and other French settlements firmly rooted there after three-quarters of a century of growth. The advance across Illinois toward St. Louis was the work of another decade. It is estimated that the frontier advanced along the Ohio ten times more rapidly than elsewhere in the territory northwest of the river.

These swift, almost overnight changes in the human geography of the lower Ohio country find easy illustration in the migration of the capital city of Indiana. At first, and naturally enough, the capital was Vincennes, which remained for many years the largest town in the Territory. "A handsome, thriving place," said a visitor in 1812, although, he added, "the inhabitants still are largely French." To accept a French town as the capital of an American Territory did

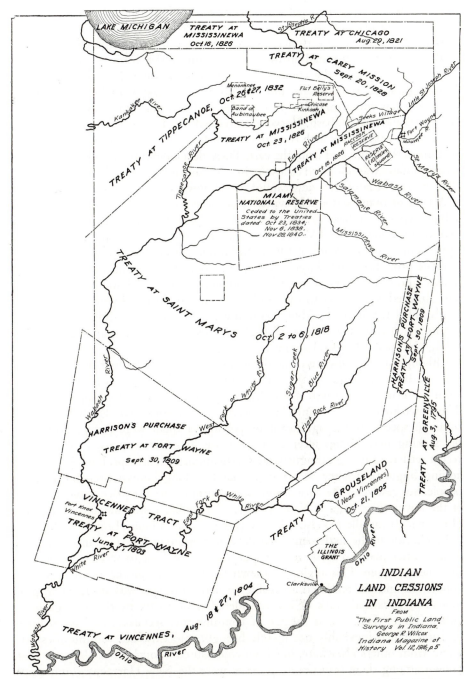

65 Indian land cessions in Indiana. Adapted from *Indiana Magazine of History* with permission of its editor.

not meet with the approval of the more recent settlers, especially because many other bustling places were nearer the new center of Indiana population. A bill to remove the seat of government from Vincennes, introduced in the legislature in December, 1811, touched off many rival claims to the distinction of becoming its successor. Among the competitors were Charlestown, Madison, and New Washington, all river towns, but the final choice was Corydon in Harrison County, a few miles inland from the river and at a point midway between the Big Bend and the Wabash. Corydon remained the Territorial and State capital from 1813 to 1824, by which time settlement had advanced into interior Indiana both from the south and from the east. These developments had been anticipated when Indiana was admitted as a state in 1816, for the Congress had then granted four sections of land for a new capital to be known as Indianapolis.

A land of many settlement types.   For variety of human population and resultant types of settlement, no region of comparable size in the United States exceeded the lower Ohio Valley. It was more truly a melting pot than was the upper valley, in the State of Ohio. No ambitious land companies, tending to regulate procedures over large tracts of land, operated here, as they did in Ohio. Those who came to the lower valley did so of their own initiative and choice, and attached themselves to the land according to their individual wishes and needs. This freedom of activity naturally led to variety, as did two other determining factors: (1) the varied backgrounds of the settlers, and (2) the differing objectives of several community projects.

Although, in the absence of land-company projects, there had been a notable lack of advance advertising, the majority of lower-valley settlers came down-river from Eastern and Southern states, drawn by the prospect of fresh opportunities. The newcomers were mainly Americans, in the sense that English was the common speech, but a significant proportion of them were foreign-born people seeking new homes after trial residence in other sections. Chief among recent settlers of foreign tongue were Germans and French-speaking Swiss, each adding linguistic variety to a region that had long known French-Canadian people. Suggestive of the varied human background are the place names of some of the lower river cities — New Albany, Clarksville; Louisville and Vincennes (French), Evansville (Welsh), Vevay (Swiss), and Albion (English).

In addition to the settlements that developed more or less spontaneously were communities planned to serve new purposes, or at least to serve old purposes in a new region. This region, somewhat removed from the main center of population and yet rendered accessible by natural routes, was attractive to promoters of advanced ways of life considered unorthodox by the average individual. Here, then, was a theater of communistic, sectarian, or " better-life " ventures which inevitably not merely brought into existence communities different from others elsewhere, but even contributed a touch of the bizarre. Best known among these community projects were the New Harmony community on the Big Wabash in southwestern Indiana, and the English Settlement on the Little Wabash in Illinois.

To illustrate the varied human geography of the lower Ohio country during the first quarter of the past century, selected districts will be studied in the order met with on a downstream journey, as follows: (1) Vevay in Switzerland County, southeastern Indiana; (2) the cluster of cities and towns around the Falls of the Ohio; (3) colonies on the lower Wabash — the New Harmony community, and the English Settlement in Illinois; and (4) Vincennes, as the chief center of the French settlements.

A SWISS SETTLEMENT: VEVAY, INDIANA

The southeastern corner of Indiana comprises Switzerland County, bounded on two sides by the Ohio River. Though it is a remarkably hilly region, its name derives from original settlement by Swiss vintners, not from a fancied resemblance to its European namesake. The first Swiss families of wine-makers came to the Indiana side of the Ohio in 1804 after an earlier residence on the Kentucky River, where they had developed what was known among them as the First Vineyard. It was in 1796 that a representative of the District of Vevay in Switzerland came to America to prospect for vineyard sites as an outlet for a population outgrowing restricted quarters at home. The preliminary selection in Kentucky failing to measure up to expectations, further searches were made in the same general territory. The area that is now Switzerland County seems to have been selected because it offered the combined advantages of easy access, good water supply, and a variety of sun-exposed slopes suited, or so it was thought, to the cultivation of the delicate wine-grape vine.

The Swiss people were well received, not only because of their favorable reputation as settlers, but also because the authorities saw advantages in experimentation with the vineyard industry by a people acquainted with its many details. As early as 1810 the Swiss had developed, on the steep slopes rising above the " second bottom " of the river, 8 acres of vineyard, from which 2,400 gallons of wine were made in that year, in great wooden vats. Ten years later, according to *Niles' Weekly Register:* " About 24 acres are occupied by vineyards at Vevay, in Indiana, and in very prosperous cultivation by the industrious Swiss settlers. It is supposed that the present year's produce will exceed 5,000 gallons, though great quantities of grapes are disposed of for other purposes."

The wine yield to an acre, however, fell disappointingly short of the average in their home canton. Difficulties with drought and frost, and perhaps other factors not then fully understood, tended to discourage a continuation of the vintner's art in this part of Indiana. Among the species tried out, it was reported in 1819, " Madeira and the Cape of Good Hope have flourished better than any others. . . . The vines of each grow well, but the Cape being much less liable to injury by early frost is the least precarious and the most productive."

The eventual decline of the Vevay wine industry can be attributed not only to local difficulties in vineyard control, but to the product itself, which, according to the testimony of many travelers, was of poorer quality than other wines available on the market. " The wine is wholesome and not unpalatable," was the half-hearted verdict of E. Dana. " I drank of the wine," wrote Amos Wheeler in his travel diary on July 4, 1816; apparently, however, it was not a day of rejoicing, for the wine " was something like Fayal & poor. I was told that it was some damaged wine, that had been rectified, but that they made as good as Madeira."

Straw hats made in Switzerland County homes by women seem to have met with more general approval than did the wine. " They are made quite different from the common straw bonnets," said the *Western Gazetteer,* " by tying the straws together instead of plaiting and sewing the plaits. They are sold in great numbers in the neighboring settlements."

The town of Vevay, whose site was carefully selected so as to escape floods, was platted in the year 1813, when the total population of Switzerland County was about 1,000. Vevay doubled in size during the first year or two, but soon thereafter settled down to a less spectacular growth. With its assortment of brick and frame buildings, Vevay looked much like any other river village of comparable size to travelers passing by, but those who stopped were impressed by the presence of such refinements as a library and a seminary. It was said to be a " delightful village " in the 1820's, a phrase equally applicable today as well as a generation or two ago, when Vevay became known in the literary world as the locale of Edward Eggleston's *Hoosier Schoolmaster.*

LOUISVILLE AND NEIGHBORING TOWNS AT THE OHIO FALLS

A winding voyage of 70 miles downstream from Vevay brought the traveler to the Falls of the Ohio, the most serious obstacle to navigation in the entire thousand miles of the great river's course. An ominous acceleration of current was the first visible evidence of approach to the falls, although their dull roar during seasons of low water could be heard a quarter of a mile above. These forewarnings of danger came too late for inexperienced crews to save their raftlike boats from a headlong plunge into the twisting channels which then threaded the falls. Untold numbers of boats of all kinds were smashed in the churning water or were hung up on one of the many islands to await extrication by fellow boatmen. Other boats equally out of hand successfully raced through one of the " chutes," as they were called, much in the manner of a bobbing cork in a turbulent brook, emerging on the quiet water below apparently none the worse for wear. For a mismanaged boat to reach the lower end of the rapids successfully, the chances increased with the depth of the water.

Early characteristics of the Falls of the Ohio. The descent of the stream in this stretch of two miles was only a few feet, 25 at most, but there was plenty of action packed into that short distance. To rivermen these were falls, and so they should be known to us. No term of modification, such as " rapids," could do them justice; perhaps this violent stretch of water would have become known as " cascades " if it had been named by a less practical people. When seen in their natural state, unchanged by controls of river depth of the modern period, the falls were impressive — a mile wide and over two miles long. Near their foot the water, breaking on the rocks, made waves ten feet high, and a passage through the two-mile stretch required only fifteen minutes. Favorite descriptive phrases of the 1820's were " formidably grand " or " grand and remarkable," and the river above and below was often called " majestic."

The cause of the falls was only too apparent: a broad ledge of tough limestone between the Indiana "knobs" and the Silver Creek hills which outline the plain on which Louisville is located. The limestone ledge was broadly exposed in low water, showing up as pitted mounds of such a shape that they were popularly called " petrified wasps' nests." At high water the ledge appeared as islands of various sizes, likely places for boats to run aground and for driftwood to collect. Viewing the river from Louisville in 1822, an English visitor saw in midstream

. . . a large black line of drift-wood formed by quantities of fallen trees, logs, stumps, and branches; for, after a great fall of rain, the small streams and creeks overflow part of the neighbouring lands and float all the timber that has fallen, or that has been cut down. This drift-wood coming into the Ohio, forms itself into a line in the most rapid of the stream; and whenever a steam-boat has to cross from one side of the river to another, generally breaks one or two of the paddles.

The falls would have been quite impassable, even for boats going with the current, except for three channels or " chutes " whose characteristics were familiar to experienced rivermen. The three passageways were known as the Town Chute on the Kentucky side, the Middle Chute, and the Indiana Chute on the north side. It was not advisable for boats to attempt to pass through these channels except during stages of high water, and even then, preferably in charge of local pilots. The chutes were most dangerous in seasons of shallow water, at which time, especially in pre-canal days, the falls interposed a virtual break in transportation.

The varying functions of the towns at the falls. The section of the river at the Falls of the Ohio was one where communities were sure to develop and, once started, to grow with the increasing importance of navigation. By the 1820's there were six towns at the falls, or rather, five towns and one fair-sized city — Louisville, already the principal center, with a population of nearly 5,000 and most favorably located of all, at the junction of Beargrass Creek with the main stream, just at the beginning of the falls, where commercial boats were almost certain to stop. Besides Louisville on the Kentucky side were Shippingport and Portland, originally separate villages, which in due time were included within the limits of the principal city. On the Indiana side were three towns — Jeffersonville at the head of the falls, Clarksville at the foot of the Indiana Chute, and New Albany a mile below this point. (Fig. 66.)

It is not to be inferred that these communities originated at precisely the same time, nor that they duplicated one another in function. Louisville, the oldest

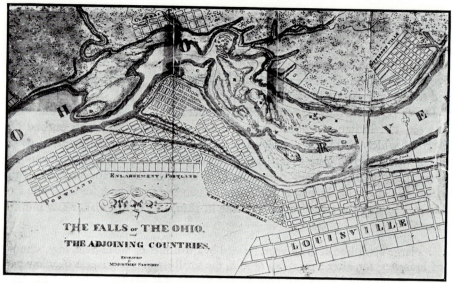

66   The towns at the Falls of the Ohio, from *Sketches of Louisville and Its Environs* by Henry McMurtrie, 1819

town on the Kentucky shore, is one of those rare communities for which the date of origin may be narrowed down to a particular day. A University of Chicago document headed " Falls of the Ohio " shows that " the intended Citizens of the Town of Louisville " met on April 24, 1779, to draw lots for half-acre plots in the townsite. It was stipulated that each person was to " clear the under-growth and to cultivate part thereof by the 10th of June and build thereon a good covered house 16 feet by 20 by the 25th of December."

Shippingport, at the foot of the Town Chute, was platted in 1803, but experienced little growth until 1806, when it became the favored stopping point for boats coming upstream from the lower Ohio and Mississippi rivers. The functions of Shippingport and Louisville were thus similar, the former profiting from boats bound upstream and the latter depending mainly on downstream traffic. Because of its somewhat rougher society, Shippingport was referred to by an early writer as the " Bois de Boulogne " of Louisville.

Portland originated in 1814, largely in anticipation of the building of a canal around the falls, a project which was completed in 1830. The weighty question as to the side of the river on which this canal was to be built was the subject of long and heated controversy between the people of Indiana and those of Kentucky. They seem to have agreed on only one point: that a canal around the falls was not only desirable but essential. Many were the petitions to the Congress seeking encouragement and support for the project, and several canal companies had a temporary existence.

An example is provided by a petition drawn up by three Hoosiers in January 1805, saying that they had " formed an association for considering, &, so far as in their power, for completing a work of no less magnitude than the opening of a passage for vessels of burthen from the head to the foot of the rapids of the Ohio River, by a canal and locks on the west side thereof." (Reference to the Indiana shore as the " west side " was sarcastically called a " trifling error " by rival interests in Kentucky.) The promoters of the Indiana canal merely asked that the Congress extend aid and encouragement " commensurate to the undertaking, either by a donation of twenty-five thousand acres of land or the privilege of a right of pre-emption of one hundred thousand acres in Indiana Territory."

Kentuckians countered with other proposals, especially after the advent of steam navigation in 1811. It was pointed out correctly that the hills bordering Indiana's shore would add greatly to the cost of canal construction, and also that such a canal would have to be more than three miles long. The natural " lay of the land," lower on the Kentucky shore, and the shorter length of canal required there, led to the construction of the Kentucky-Ohio Canal, and Portland, according to preconceived plans, became the downstream terminus.

Oldest town at the falls on the Indiana side was Clarksville, which originated in 1783 in what was known as the Illinois Grant. (Fig. 65, page 237.) It profited but little from the early river trade, which, as we shall see, was largely monopolized by the Kentucky cities. Jeffersonville, opposite Louisville, was laid out as a town in 1802, but showed no signs of profiting from its position at the head of the falls. New Albany below the falls was platted in 1814, the year of Portland's origin, and grew rapidly as the entrepôt of its expanding hinterland.

Louisville and Shippingport: river terminals. Louisville with its functional suburb of Shippingport was more truly a river city than was Cincinnati. Nearly every boat that moved on the lower Ohio paid tribute to one or the other of these terminals, more often to both. Their hold on river commerce began early, before the days of steam-powered craft, and continued late, becoming even stronger with the advent of steam and the completion of the canal. As to the canal, some interested observers had expressed fear that Louisville would lose its commercial importance when it was in operation. To this, Henry McMurtrie replied in 1819 by way of a question: " Do the gentlemen really believe that Louisville draws her importance solely from the obstruction to the navigation of the river, or do they pretend to assert . . . that a canal . . . has ever deducted from the population, wealth, or business of a town through which it has passed? "

Boats ordinarily stopped at Louisville or Shippingport for one or more of several reasons: 1. Much freight was discharged at one port or the other to be consumed locally or redistributed to the back country. 2. Cargo bound upstream or downstream was also unloaded, to be carried through the city and transferred to another vessel. In other words, for many boats the falls were the end of the voyage; having unloaded goods here from ports above or below, they reloaded with return cargo. 3. Furthermore, cargo was sometimes discharged to lighten a vessel preparatory to its passage through the chute, and having successfully negotiated this difficult part of the voyage, the boat would reload its freight at the other end of the falls. 4. Again, boats stopped at one port or the other to take on a pilot, and once safely through the channel, stopped again to discharge him. Pilotage of boats through the rapids, at one time for a fee of $2 a boat, was a regular and thriving business, having been authorized by the Kentucky Legislature in 1797.

Not only were the falls a break in freight traffic, but travel-weary passengers frequently interrupted their journey here. A large proportion of the people who thronged the streets of Louisville or sought recreation in Shippingport were strangers on their way to more distant places. Business houses in Louisville presumably profited by this early form of tourism. An interesting sidelight on comparative living costs between now and 1819 is contained in the comment of a transient who complained: " The tavern charges are the most extravagant I ever paid. Fifty cents for a common meal, 25 for a lodging, 25 for a gill of spirits, 75 for horse-keeping." A somewhat Pepysian visitor to the river city in 1829 wrote to a friend:

This evening I have been strolling up and down the streets, contemplating the artificial curiosities of the place, some of which are perfect anomalies, and again viewing the Majestick appearance of the Ohio whose surface is literally covered with steam-boats, skiffs, boats, and other mechanical constructions the names of which I have not learned. The city is in a perfect garboil and commotion from the innumerable drays, waggons, carriages, which are incessantly traversing the streets. I will drink a glass of lemonade and ice cream, believing you would willingly participate with me were you here.

Louisville had need of the stout limestone blocks with which its streets, like those of Cincinnati and Maysville, were then paved. Through-city traffic was very heavy before the completion of the canal. As Louisville grew and manufacturing developed, a greater proportion of the river-borne freight remained in the city instead of passing through. Most of all, though, Louisville was a commercial city, deriving its substance from a great traffic on a great river.

COLONIES ON THE LOWER WABASH

As we advance with these studies into Western frontiers we shall find that settlement by colonies was increasingly important. A colony in this sense implies a group of individuals allied by some bond of comradeship, and recognizing a centralized authority or leadership, who settled together in a site previously chosen for community development. Doubtless the best-known example is the Mormon colony which, after earlier trials in Nauvoo, Illinois, and other Eastern and Midwestern localities, occupied and developed under ecclesiastical authority the region about Great Salt Lake. But there were earlier instances of colony ventures, varying among themselves with regard to bases of unification and degree of centralized leadership. As instances of the loosely organized colony with nationality as the chief bond of comradeship, recall Vevay and the Welsh community studied in the preceding chapter. Allegiance to a faith, devotion to

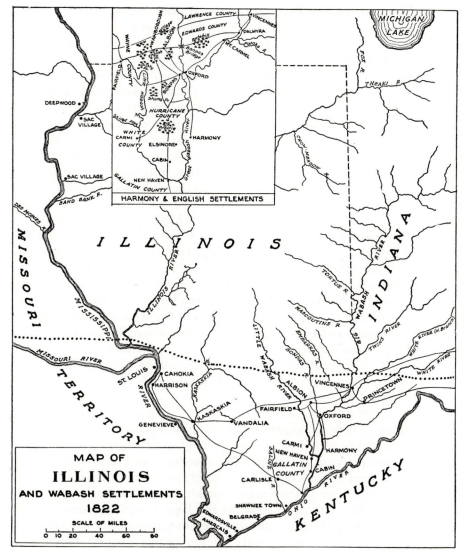

67   The Wabash settlements in Indiana and the State of Illinois in the 1820's. The
      inset represents the English Settlement between the Little Wabash and the
      Bonpas, on an enlarged scale.

a cause, a sense of fellowship provided by a foreign tongue, were common bases
for American frontier colonies. It is significant that the lower Wabash region
in the early 1800's provides a number of examples.

     Only two of the centers of colony development will be considered in detail:
(1) New Harmony, Indiana, on the Wabash River, and (2) the English Settlement, as it was called in the 1820's, on the Little Wabash in Illinois. (See Fig. 67.)

From Harmony to New Harmony on the Wabash.   The adjective " new " in New Harmony is itself significant, for here developed what has been called a "double-jointed communistic movement." At first, from 1814 to 1824, the town bore the name of Harmony, or more accurately, the German *Harmonie,* for it was developed by several hundred German sectarians representing a branch of the Lutheran Church. In 1824 the town was purchased lock, stock, and barrel (except for the residents) by a group of English and Scotch under the leadership of Robert Owen of Lanark, Scotland. It was at this time that the name New Harmony came into use; it is still retained by the present-day town, although the colony itself dissolved within a short time. The story of the transformation of the colony from one unusual type to another is remarkable; no less so is the record of the original community developed by the industrious German settlers. Visitors to Harmony just before its sale to Robert Owen for about $200,000 referred to it as " that wonder of the West," the achievement, said the *New Harmony Gazette* in 1825, of a " people who penetrated the wilderness and . . . redeemed [from it] in ten years . . . a village possessing advantages and comforts equal to any other within the United States."

The Rappites Begin the Colony.   The first colony site of the Harmony Society in America was on the Beaver River in western Butler County, Pennsylvania. It was established in 1803–04 by a large number of Germans who had emigrated from Württemberg under the leadership of Johann Georg Rapp, usually called George Rapp. A ten-year residence in western Pennsylvania resulted in the development of a thriving and prosperous community (reportedly sold for $100,000); nevertheless, the decision was reached to relocate themselves in the newly developing West.

The selection of a new site was entrusted to a locating party, which spent some six months on its difficult assignment. Needed was a place combining elements of environment that were basic not only to a self-sustaining community, but to one which also expected to market surplus products. In Pennsylvania, for example, the Harmonites (or Rappites, as they were more familiarly known) maintained a large warehouse in Pittsburgh from which they distributed agricultural and manufactured products. Location in the West would necessarily remove them from near-by markets, but this could be offset somewhat if natural waterways were available. The locating party also searched for a region offering good soil and water power. These various requirements were reasonably well supplied by the place chosen on the Wabash, some 40 miles above its junction with the Ohio.

A Decade of Growth.   As to the number of " Dutch " to arrive on the Wabash with the first contingent, there are many conflicting estimates. It seems safe to say that there were at least 300, for their numbers had increased through acquisition of new converts during their tenure of the Pennsylvania site. It should be remarked that the society was dependent for growth on recruits from among incoming German immigrants, because other nationalities were not welcome; further, and more important, regulations governing marriage prohibited natural increase. Marriage was not expressly forbidden, but it was discountenanced to such an extent as to be virtually prohibited. Children were sometimes adopted, but few were born in the colony, the men and women occupying separate quarters, perhaps in the same building. This being the case, said *Niles' Weekly Register* of August 21, 1819, " It is greatly to the credit of these people that only one or two children have been born in their settlement in the last five years." By other means must their numbers be increased, or even maintained.

Despite this attitude toward marriage and despite also a high death rate during the ten years on the Wabash, Harmony was larger in population in 1824 than it was in the beginning. Visitors were likely to overestimate the population, mainly because the amount of work accomplished by the colonists as evidenced in physical equipment and farm land, compared to that of the average frontier town of equal age, might well have been taken to indicate a much larger population than there actually was. A traveler passing through Harmony to the English Settlement in 1822 guessed that the population was " upwards of 800 members," while another in the same year put the number near 700. A visitor in 1817 mentions a church meeting where " three or four hundred of the Harmonites assembled." Since they often went to religious services and out to the fields in a military manner, men and women in separate groups, the total effect was startling to strangers.

Economic Aspects of the Community. The combined and supervised efforts of the colonists resulted in a community like no other in existence, certainly unlike any that would have been developed by people of a different origin and purpose in the same area. " They have indeed proceeded in everything with the greatest order and regularity," said traveler Blane in 1824. At that time the village consisted of some 200 buildings (some of which are still standing), including large community halls, a large granary, and of course a meetinghouse. The original log cabins, which in the beginning had been erected toward the back of the town lots to serve as temporary quarters, had been replaced by solid frame structures, many of them covered with stucco.

The village streets were planted with Lombardy poplars and mulberry trees; it was much later that the " golden-rain " trees which now give an exceptional beauty to the town were introduced from the Orient. In the village also were manufactories for making flour, hats, shoes, linen, and flannel, as well as distilleries, breweries, fulling mills, and a dye house. Surrounding the village were pastures and tilled land, orchards of apple, peach, and plum, and vineyards.

" The vineyards," it was said, " are on a steep hill, and planted around the hill so as to have several different aspects. Trees are laid to keep the earth from washing down. The paths between are sown with bluegrass." Another English traveler reported: " They have a fine vineyard in the vale and on the hills around, which are as beautiful as if formed by art to adorn the town. Not a spot but bears the most luxuriant vines, from which they make excellent wine. Their orchards, too, are of enormous size and fertility." As many as 2,000 sheep were grazed in the pastures in 1824, their wool supplying raw material for the manufacture of clothing which was designed for service rather than for style — a kind of uniform, " uncommonly plain," or so it appeared to visitors.

The Harmonites bought nothing they could possibly raise or make and they made much more than they actually needed. Although some of their products were sold in Shawneetown and other places on the Ohio River, the colonists mainly waited for the trade to come to them. People going through to take up claims of their own came to depend upon the Harmonites for essential goods, and neighboring towns survived their difficult beginning years with the aid of Harmony products. Among these were the English Settlement villages only 25 miles distant. A promoter of this settlement, George Flower, stated that some materials essential to the beginning of it came from Shawneetown, " But the chief supply of flour, meal, whiskey, woollen and cotton clothes, all the manufacture of the Harmonites, came from Harmony. My first bill with the Harmonites amounted to eleven thousand dollars, and I afterward paid them many large sums." His estimate was that between 1818 and 1828 " the Harmonites received from our Settlement, one hundred thousand dollars in hard cash."

Contemporary Appraisals of the Rappite Colony. The foregoing description of the Harmony Colony is derived primarily from eyewitness accounts, some of which were probably written from biased viewpoints. Promoters of colonies, and particularly those who were predisposed toward a planned economy, if not toward communism, naturally delighted in seeing so successful an example in operation. More grudging praise was given by other visitors who, on general principles, entertained opposite opinions about communistic life. Americans, it is said, regarded the Rappites jealously " for engrossing most of the business in this part of the country." Travelers often found the town of Harmony dull, its people phlegmatic or saturnine. One said of the women that " they are the least handsome I ever beheld." But they could not hide their admiration for this beehive of industry where so much was accomplished in so short a time.

Mainly, the efforts of the colonists were directed toward practical purposes, but there was one exception — the labyrinth, of which a modern replica is maintained in the town of New Harmony. Because it was so unexpected in a community inhabited by a people with such practical ideas of the meaning of life, nearly every visitor who wrote about Harmony told of the labyrinth in the public garden. The garden was of 5 acres, said Flower, " the outside square planted with fruit trees and vegetables, the inside with herbs, medicinal and botanical. In the centre is a rotunda of the rustic kind, standing in the midst of a labyrinth which exhibits more taste than I supposed to be found amongst the Harmonites." Another English visitor, who appears to have tried unsuccessfully to solve the mysteries of the maze, remarked: " None but those who formed it, or are acquainted with it, can find their way."

The New Harmony Colony Assumes Control. In 1824 the German community-builders disposed of their village and its 30,000 acres of land to Robert Owen, a Scottish reformer and philanthropist. Probably no greater change has occurred in any other American town within so short a time than that which resulted from this shift in ownership. The visionary plans of the newcomers were outlined in a speech by Mr. Owen in October, 1825, recorded as follows in the *New Harmony Gazette:*

I came to this country to introduce an entire new state of society; to change it from the ignorant, selfish system, to an enlightened, social system, which shall gradually unite all interests into one, and remove all cause of contest between individuals. I have bought this property, and have now come here to introduce this practice, and to render it familiar to all the inhabitants of this country. [Apparently this was not to be the final center of the movement, for] New-Harmony, the future name of this place, is the best halfway house I could procure for those who are going to travel this extraordinary journey with me; and although it is not intended to be our permanent residence, I hope it will be found an agreeable traveller's tavern, or temporary visiting place.

From the physical standpoint, the village was well equipped to support the "extraordinary journey" of the Owenites, but their unsympathetic critics, and even the new tenants themselves, soon realized that the plant was inadequately staffed. There was an oversupply of professional people and a shortage of artisans and skilled laborers, and even of plain workers.

Weak links in the chain of community maintenance are exposed by an inventory of the occupations and professions represented in 1825, appearing in the *New Harmony Gazette* in that year. Here are a few examples: The dye house, probably the equal of any then in existence in the United States, was idle because of "the want of a skilful person to undertake the direction of it." Not only was there no competent dyer, but should the great copper tanks need repair, there was no coppersmith to attend to them. The cotton-spinning factory, capable of turning out 400 pounds of yarn a week, "is under very good direction, but skilful and steady hands are much wanting." Four coopers were listed among the residents, but, so far as can be learned, there was no flour to place in their barrels; at least no mention is made of the operation of the flour mill with a capacity of 60 barrels a day. For working the 3,600 acres of improved land left by the Rappites, the new colony could supply but 36 hands. It would seem unlikely that one farmer could adequately care for 100 acres of improved land.

Or we may take one particular case, that of David Dale Owen (son of the founder), who later distinguished himself in geology. According to his father's plan, David Dale was to become a cotton-spinner, but the young man, who had been trained as a chemist in Scotland and Switzerland, felt that he could be of more service by continuing his studies. In later years his interests turned to geology, in the course of which time he transformed the four-storied Rappite granary into his first museum and lecture hall. There was no need for a granary in a community that had ceased to become economically productive; hence to the new residents this building was "the laboratory," one of the show places of

New Harmony. No change could better symbolize the transformation of the town.

In short, most of the basic industries developed by the Rappites were soon abandoned, and the colony as such rapidly disintegrated. The town indeed proved to be the " temporary visiting place " envisioned by the social reformer who had financed it, although it should be emphasized that New Harmony continued as the dwelling place of many people and the headquarters of a number of distinguished scientists.

The English Settlement in southeastern Illinois.   A study of the lower Ohio country as a frontier would be incomplete without reference to the so-called English Settlement at Albion, Illinois.

" Colony " would be a more appropriate term, because this was an organized development, beginning with the deliberate selection of the site for community purposes, and continuing with its later occupation by Englishmen arriving in a body in 1818. The English Settlement or colony, however, was not communistic, and in its separate villages authority was less centralized than that which marked near-by Harmony. The two promoters who activated the colony, Morris Birkbeck and George Flower, worked co-operatively for a few years, but later parted company. " Success was attained," said one of the promoters, " but harmony was not."

Both Birkbeck and Flower were well-to-do farmers of the English middle class who had become dissatisfied with economic and political conditions in England. They looked hopefully to the American Midwest for a solution to their problems. Flower arrived in this country in April, 1816, and visited various sections of the interior before settling down for the winter in Virginia. While there he approached Thomas Jefferson, then in retirement at Monticello, regarding the probability of securing a congressional grant of land for a " contemplated settlement." Jefferson pointed out that this would require an act of Congress unlikely to be passed unless some special national advantage, such as was anticipated from the Swiss settlement at Vevay, should clearly outweigh adherence to the general rule.

Flower finally decided to follow the general practice in buying land, but before doing so he had joined forces with Morris Birkbeck in Virginia. Birkbeck entertained definite ideas about colony development, believing that a site which combined prairie and woodland, and one outside the slaveholding part of the country, would be most likely to satisfy English people who were also discontented with conditions in the home country. Birkbeck became a persistent advocate of prairie settlement, issuing many publications, such as his *Letters from Illinois* (London, 1818), exhorting his countrymen to start life anew in the Midwest.

Promotion of Wanborough and Albion.   The search for a site led the English promoters to the southern Illinois frontier, where they found the kind of prairie-woodland country that measured up to their wishes. "For once the reality came up to the picture of imagination," thought Flower when crossing the Wabash River west of Harmony. "The whole presented a magnificence of park-scenery, complete from the hand of nature, and unrivalled by the same sort of scenery by European art." The first purchase of 3,000 acres was transacted at the land office in Shawneetown; in the next few months other purchases from the Government and from individuals brought the total to some 20,000 acres.

The contiguous holdings of Birkbeck and Flower were located on the higher land between the Bonpas and Little Wabash rivers in present-day Edwards County, Illinois. Although the promoters themselves called the holding Bolten-house Prairie, it became generally known as the English Prairie. Besides the English Prairie, which included about 16 square miles, were other similar park-like areas, such as Birkes, Bonpas, Burnt, Bushy, Long, and French Creek, which were settled in part by English families. This was the region on which some 200 English settlers were colonized before the close of the year 1818 — the same year that Illinois became a state.

These villages, it should be understood, were strictly on the frontier. The State of Illinois to the northward was virtually unsettled; at Peoria were the decaying ruins of a French fort, while at the site of Chicago there was a two-year-old fort named Dearborn, which provided headquarters for a few score of soldiers and an Indian agency. Settled Illinois consisted of two clusters of villages, one of them on the lower Wabash and Ohio, including the English Settlement, which was farthest on the frontier; and the other in the southwest near century-old Kaskaskia.

Each of the English promoters laid out a townsite within his property. Birkbeck's village of Wanborough consisted in 1822 of 25 cabins, a tavern, and a store or two. Flower's village of Albion, 2 miles east of it, answered a similar description in the same year. The colonists residing in these villages and on the near-by farms experienced hard times during the opening years; it is quite possible that they would not have survived except for the funds of the promoters and proximity to well-stocked Harmony. Not for six years did the efforts of the colonists yield a surplus permitting them to market their products. "The way they effected this," said Blane, who was in Albion in 1824, "was by loading several flat boats with corn, flour, pork, beef, sausages, etc., and floating them down the Wabash into the Ohio and thence down the Mississippi to New Orleans, a distance of 1,140 miles."

Growth and Importance of the English Colony. The contradictory accounts of Wanborough and Albion which were circulated in the home country led many English travelers to the Wabash to see for themselves the truth of the matter. Depending upon their preconceived ideas, they found the English villages either disappointing or gratifying. Perhaps the usual impression was best conveyed epigrammatically by Adlard Welby in 1820 thus: "If I picture to myself a giant and find a man of but ordinary proportions, is he to blame for this?" The settlement, that is to say, was much less imposing than he and others had anticipated; nevertheless the villages were all that could reasonably have been expected in view of all the conditions.

Welby felt that although Birkbeck had a right to live anywhere he desired, " when he publishes plausible representations to induce others to seek fortunes and independence in such situations, he is then doing that which he has no right to do and has much to account for." In preparation for his visit to Albion, traveler Blane had studied all the books and reviews " that have been written for and against this settlement," some of them picturing it as an earthly paradise and others as a miserable unhealthy swamp. "The truth," Blane found on reaching his destination, " is about midway between those extremes."

Albion and Wanborough competed for a time for leadership as the center of the English colony, a contest finally won by Albion. Birkbeck's Wanborough soon dwindled, and within a quarter-century ceased to exist even as a name. The prediction made by Elias Fordham in 1818 that Albion would become the county town came true a few years later. The original plan of the village, with its central public square, is still discernible in the present city of Albion. Many of the people in this part of Illinois are descendants of the English families who settled there over a century ago.

Historians have pointed out that although no great numbers of English people settled on the prairies that bore their name, the wide publicity which accompanied the early growth of the colony was influential in encouraging emigration to America. According to Frederic A. Ogg, the optimistic reports brought back to England provided a new stimulus to emigration, " though many of the persons thus attracted found land that suited them without going so far west as the English Prairies." Settlement by English people in Indiana cities, notably Vincennes, during the second quarter of the last century has also been attributed to the general publicity arising from the English colony on the Little Wabash.

VINCENNES

Differing from the varied assortment of towns round about, Vincennes has encompassed in its lifetime the entire period of white settlement in the lower Ohio country. The date of origin of Vincennes as a trading post and fort can be placed somewhere between 1717 and 1735, perhaps nearer the latter date. It was thus almost a century old by the time of the era of colony-planting on the lower Wabash. (See Fig. 68.)

The town was first known as Post Saint-Vincennes, or simply Post Vincennes, having been established by a French nobleman of that name at this Wabash River crossing about 120 miles above its mouth. Position at a strategic crossing ensured the continued importance of Vincennes; perhaps no less significant was the extensive prairie within which the town was situated. One approached the ancient town through a rolling country, said Welby in 1822,

. . . belted in with trees so fancifully disposed that one is apt to imagine the hand of art to have been employed: the land is not considered in general as of even second-rate quality, but it is dry and healthy, and when cultivated brings good corn if the summer is at all favourable; indeed, under the present drought I saw some fair crops at a few spots where squatters had fixed themselves. These barrens increase in size and number as we proceed westward until they end in the so much talked of prairie, or wild meadows: in the midst of one of which, and upon the Great Wabash river, stands the pleasant town of Vincennes upon a sandy gravel sub-soil, with excellent springs of water.

The sandy gravel subsoil which was so influential in determining the site of Vincennes is recognized by modern geographers, in the words of Dr. Alden Cutshall, as "a Maumee gravel terrace of about a mile in width, extending as an irregular tongue-like projection between the river and the eastern sand hills and bluffs. This terrace rises a few feet above the flood plain, but its lower portions have been subject to overflow in cases of unusually high water." The prairie areas inland from the gravel terrace were in early times divided into the narrow strip-farms characteristic of the French wherever they settled in the vicinity of a navigable waterway, each farmer securing in this way desired frontage upon the stream.

At the end of its first half-century of growth Vincennes was a straggling com-

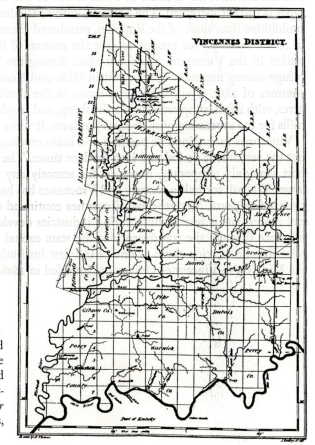

68

Harrison's Purchase and the Vincennes District. The original map illustrated *Travels through the Western Country in the Summer of 1816* by David Thomas, Auburn, N.Y., 1819.

munity, spreading in fact across the river, where several French farmers had taken up land. Because the town covered so much territory, travelers reached varying estimates of its population. In 1787, according to Major Denny, Post Vincennes was " the most capital village in the western country. There are about five hundred souls, French, and about half as many Americans." Denny's commanding officers, however, reached a higher figure at the same time: 900 French and 400 Americans. During the War of 1812 the population was judged to be about 2,000; by the 1820's it had increased by some 500 more.

Throughout this long period the physical appearance of Vincennes slowly changed. Although, as Welby said, " it has not yet by any means lost its cabin appearance," there were many new brick and frame structures " behind which its log huts are hiding their diminished heads." The population of the town had also changed in character, having attained a somewhat cosmopolitan quality in the 1820's. The larger number of people were still French Canadians, but there were also settlers from the Eastern states, recent immigrants from England, and a few Negroes and Indians. If one takes a larger view of Vincennes to include Shakertown, located 18 miles north of the city, the variety of human types is further increased. The Shakers, with restrictions on marriage even more prohibitive than those of the Rappites, numbered about 200 members. They lived in four " families " or groups, as was the custom of this religious sect. Having settled in the Vincennes site about 1800, during the War of 1812 they sought refuge among members of their sect in Ohio and Kentucky, but returned in the summer of 1815. The Shakertown estate in the 1820's consisted of about 1,500 acres, with a full complement of cattle, sheep, and cropland, together with various mills for the processing of their farm products. It was a self-sufficient community.

Vincennes maintained its position as a main crossing of the Wabash throughout the settlement period and into modern times. The town's position as a river port was only temporary, however, for scarcely any traffic has moved on the lower Wabash for half a century and Vincennes has had no river-borne trade for twenty-five years. Nevertheless, Vincennes continued to function as a commercial center, and a few manufacturing industries developed there. Its loss of importance through the transference of the state capital to Corydon was partially offset by the location there of one of the first institutions of higher learning in the Midwest — Vincennes University, founded in 1806.

CHAPTER 14

Travel and Trade on the Ohio River and Canals to the Great Lakes

I N THE long history of Ohio River navigation, no period was more productive of change than the one beginning with the Ordinance of 1787, which provided for the organization of the Northwest Territory, and ending with the completion of the Louisville-Portland Canal around the Falls of the Ohio in 1830. A first step in the organization of the Northwest Territory was the establishment of forts, whose garrisons and supplies were moved on the river and its tributaries. Once established, the forts were an invitation to emigrants to use the easily traveled river in their search for new homes in the West. Since most of the emigrants had no intention of retracing their journey, the great difficulty of going upstream was of no concern to them. This " flatboat era," as it has been called, predominated until about 1820, when the mastery of steam-propelled craft over the current was finally gained after a decade of trial.

The application of steam power did not immediately alter the nature or the direction of travel and trade on the river; we shall find that the eras of the flatboat and the steamboat overlapped by a quarter-century or more. The coming of mechanical power in 1811 was, however, a major event. Another date to remember in this survey is the year 1830, when the canal around the falls at Louisville was completed. The falls canal permitted new freedom of passage upstream and down and was the first in a long series of improvements that have continued into the present. It may be noted in passing that the first locks and dams were provided by the Congress in 1879 and that other controls were introduced at later times. Improvement for modern traffic began in the present century.

The combined effects of the improvements have, as intended, greatly altered the Ohio River, which now carries fully one-third of all river-borne traffic in the United States. To understand the Ohio River travel and trade as it was before extensive improvements were made, it is necessary to reconstruct from early-day accounts the natural characteristics of the stream and the various kinds of boats which floated upon it.

OHIO RIVER USE BEFORE IMPROVEMENT

In the early 1800's, the Ohio's annual range between high and low water was greater and more pronounced than it is now. The extreme range recorded by 1820 was 60 feet, but seasonal differences of 50 feet were common. At its lowest stage, usually from August to October, it was sometimes possible to ford the river at several places above Louisville, and in very dry years the chutes at the falls contracted to small proportions. One of the lowest river stages ever recorded at the Falls of the Ohio was in the autumn of 1819, when surveyors for the projected canal found the water " passing through a channel in the bed of the rock, not more than twenty-four feet wide; which was divided in the centre by a ledge of rock about a foot wide, extending the whole length of the channel, having much the appearance of masonry; so that with a couple of twelve-foot planks the river could have been crossed dry-shod." The momentum of the water was said to be astonishing, however, for " several attempts were made to ascertain its depth with a hickory handpike, but there was not a person in the company who could force it into the water more than one foot."

These seasonal changes in the depth of the Ohio were reflected in variations of current velocity. In periods of low water, the average velocity in navigable channels was about 2 miles an hour; at mean height the speed increased one-half, making it comparable to a walking pace. Converted into miles gained on a down-river voyage, this was a difference of perhaps 20 miles a day — something to consider on a trip made in the cramped quarters of a homemade craft cluttered with as great a medley of provisions, furniture, and animals as ever Noah could have stored in his miraculous vessel. The increased current at high stages was, however, not a clear gain, because at such times the surface of the river was strewn with logs and trees forming a minor hazard to navigation.

The Ohio may well have seemed longer in 1800 than it actually was and is today, the means of locomotion being what they were. Guidebooks calculated the distance from Pittsburgh to the falls at 560 miles, and to the mouth of the Ohio, at 1,280. Many emigrants began their journey at " embarkation points " above Pittsburgh on the Monongahela and Allegheny Rivers. On the latter stream, Olean in New York became a favorite starting point, for here were boat yards and stores catering to the needs of emigrants who were about to change their mode of transportation. A traveler in 1820 described Olean as " a point of embarkation where great numbers of families migrating from the northern and eastern states, have exchanged their various methods of slow and laborious progression by land, for the more convenient one of navigation of the Ohio." Below Olean, fleets of arks carried the necessities of settlement.

McKeesport on the Monongahela was also an important outfitting center, although there was less certainty of adequate water depth on this tributary than on the Allegheny. Families willing to endure the hardships and the cost of a somewhat longer land journey to gain surety of water depth made Pittsburgh or Wheeling their embarkation point.

Hazards to navigation in the days before river improvements varied with the depth of channels. Likely to be encountered anywhere were floating objects, snags, and sunken logs or " planters." A known hazard at any time of year was the tortuous raceway through the falls at Louisville. There were two other comparable difficulties, now of no importance because of river improvements. One was known as Le Tart's Rapids, 230 miles below Pittsburgh. Here was an acceleration of current rather dangerous in low water — dangerous, that is, for awkward and rudderless flat-bottomed boats — but obliterated in flood stages. The other was a limestone ledge known as the Grand Chain, near Shawneetown. Impassable by large boats in the lowest stage of water, the Grand Chain made a minor break in transportation. A similar obstruction in the Mississippi below Cape Girardeau was known as the Little Chain.

High water and downstream travel. From the foregoing discussion it will be seen why emigrants were well advised to time their departure from embarkation points at seasons of high water. Not only would they be likely to reach their destination in a shorter time because of the increased velocity of the current, but also the various obstructions would be passed with less difficulty and the increased current would tend to hold boats in midstream, away from the shore and the hundred or more river islands. " Land as seldom as possible " was one of the hard-and-fast rules laid down in the guidebooks that were issued for the benefit of the inexperienced river traveler.

There were two periods of normally high water, the spring flood from April to June, and a secondary rise in midwinter.

The time of the spring flood could be predicted with no more accuracy in early days than in recent times. Much depended on the amount of moisture locked in the snow of the preceding winter in the upper basin, on the relative speed of its release in the early part of the warmer season, and on the amount and character of the spring rains. Again, flash floods (or " freshes," as they were then known) in one or more of the Ohio tributaries influenced the height of water in the main stream. It was noted that floods in the Mississippi River also affected the height of water in the lower Ohio. In the words of Edwin W. James: " Floods in the Mississippi, happening when the Ohio is low, occasion a reflux of water in the latter, perceptible at Fort Massac, more than thirty miles above . . . [and] floods in the Ohio occasion a retardation of the Mississippi as far up as the Little Chain, ten miles below Cape Girardeau."

The secondary flood stage in winter was of course not recommended for emigrant travel. Not only would the traveler reach his destination at a poor time for setting up a new home, but there was danger from ice coming down from the upper basin. Generally speaking, navigation above Louisville was suspended for eight or ten weeks in midwinter. A letter from Fort Harmar on December 21, 1786, expressed fear of a flood and said: " You would have been surprized to see the Ohio when the Alleghany & Monongahela Ice came rushing down, sweeping all before it; Kentucky boats, canoes drifted by in great quantities, but it was impossible to take them up." Failure to follow the rule to suspend navigation in the winter occasioned the loss of at least one steamboat in the upper Ohio, and many unrecorded wrecks of ordinary boats.

Family boats and downstream passages. "Family boat" is a term under which may be grouped a variety of craft used for the down-river travel of emigrants. Some specific names for them were flatboats, sleds, ferry flats, and broadhorns, but in general a family boat was anything that would float and protect its human and physical contents. Such a boat differed from a raft in having high sides, and possibly such refinements as a partly covered deck. Blunt at both ends, the family boat differed from a raft, too, in being oblong rather than square. In the vernacular, such a boat was a broadhorn, although many so described were used to carry freight rather than families and their equipment. With some truth a family boat has been described as a house temporarily afloat. A typical boat of this kind was from 30 to 40 feet long, and cost about $1.25 a foot to construct.

The family boat was no easily managed craft. In setting out, its occupants quite literally committed themselves to the mercy of the current, with the fervent hope that all would go well. To be sure, there were steering devices at bow and stern — long sweep oars which, under normal conditions, would give some direction to the boat — but the boat lay flat and dead in the water, with a form and weight difficult to direct by the "gouger" in front or by any other kind of oar. Once out of control, as at the rapids, the occupants were in the hands of fate until quieter water was reached.

The time consumed in a passage from Pittsburgh to a given destination far down the Ohio depended not merely on conditions of depth and current but also upon individual decisions as to the advisability of night sailing, or floating. According to Zadok Cramer's *The Navigator* in 1814, a ten-day trip from Pittsburgh to the Louisville falls was "a quick passage, but sometimes a small boat will be 2 weeks in going to Limestone [Maysville], and in a very low state of water, 20 days."

Having reached its destination, the family boat was often hauled out of the water and its lumber converted into shanty, shed, or schoolhouse. Some boats, however, were sold, and some were even set adrift. According to a report by General Harmar in 1789, boats arriving at Maysville "are of scarcely any Value to the Owners. They are frequently set adrift in order to make room for the arrival of others."

The large number of flatboats on the river just before the steamboat period is shown in counts made at the Falls of the Ohio. From November 24, 1810, to January 24, 1811, the yearly low period in navigation, nearly 200 flatboats descended the falls at Louisville. From among the many descriptions of family and other flatboats, two contrasting ones may serve to point up the variety of accommodations they offered. Timothy Flint wrote in 1828:

We have seen boats of this description fitted up for the descent of families to the lower country, with a stove, comfortable apartments, beds, and arrangements for commodious habitancy. We see in them ladies, servants, cattle, horses, sheep, dogs, and poultry;

all floating on the same bottom, and on the roof the looms, ploughs, spinning wheels, and domestic equipment of the family.

Another traveler who took passage on a flat from Marietta to Cincinnati in January, 1811, declared to a friend that " on the whole . . . I do think this said passage . . . one of the most unpleasant, tedious, and disgusting scenes of human life that I ever witnessed." The trip was delayed because the captain dared not navigate at night; moreover,

. . . an apartment of twenty-two feet by twelve held twenty-one souls, among whom were eight children. After stowing ourselves away like slaves in a slave-ship, the little room that remained was about completely filled with the etceteras of household furniture. Heavy rains, too, for the great part of the time rendered escape from this dungeon to the roof entirely impracticable.

Kentucky and New Orleans boats. Similar in general appearance to the family boat were the larger and more rugged Kentucky boats and New Orleans boats, intended mainly for the downstream passage of freight. Each was an oblong ark provided with a sloping roof. Such a boat sometimes carried a mast for sails, although the very nature of travel on a winding river prevented any real reliance on the wind. Oars were used for giving the craft direction; and recommended equipment also included a steel cable which, when attached to a tree or other solid object on shore, could be used to hold the boat against a difficult stretch of water. Although these boats were sometimes equipped for short journeys against the current, they were usually sold at the downstream destination; on rare occasions, however, a boat was transported overland to the original point of departure.

The Kentucky boat and its more substantial cousin, the New Orleans boat, varied in length from 50 to 100 feet and were usually 20 feet wide. Because of their shallow draft, it has been said that they floated on the water rather than in it. They could carry from 300 to 400 barrels of flour or an equal weight in other products. Seeing a row of Kentucky boats at Pittsburgh, a curious visitor " concluded they were detached pieces of some ropewalk which had been carried off by the freshes from above." The warning signal heralding the boat's approach was a bugle, blown frequently when the boat glided with the current near shore. On such occasions, said a riverman: " Greetings, or rude defiances, or trials of wit, or proffers of love to the girls on the shore, or saucy messages, are scattered between them and the spectators on the banks."

The keelboat: " express " of the river country. Imagine a decked rowboat enlarged three or four times and the result is the Ohio-Mississippi keelboat. It was long (40 to 80 feet), slender (7 to 9 feet), narrow in the prow, comparatively light, and provided with a keel for greater manageability. As carriers for downstream navigation, keelboats were less efficient than flatboats, but — with much expenditure of labor — they could be pushed and pulled against the current. From six to eight hands were required for rowing upstream, fewer going down. Progress was occasionally aided by sails, or by setting-poles. When near the shore, the keelboat could be " cordelled " — that is, moved ahead by pulling on a cable attached to a tree. " Bushwhacking " was also resorted to in difficult stretches of water if the boat could be run close enough to shore to be pulled along by means of overhanging bushes.

Even after the introduction of steamboat navigation, the keelboat was much used in low stages of water and on the tributaries where the larger steamers could not go. An upstream journey in the " speedy " keelboat was very slow by modern standards. A trip from New Orleans to Louisville required from two to three months and to Pittsburgh at least five months. Ten miles a day was an average rate of travel against the current.

The keelboat was designed mainly to carry freight, but passengers were some-times taken aboard — and often put to work along with the hired hands. The following excerpts are taken from a diary kept on a keelboat journey from Pittsburgh to Portsmouth in 1816:

I have no accommodation for comfortable sitting. Although there are frequent bends and turns in the River, yet such is the form of the current that the boat will float down and seldom touch the shore, and, but for the logs, etc. in some places, no watch would be necessary. . . . In starting again [after stopping at Le Tart's Rapids] our boat got on to a stump and with difficulty we got off after two hours hard work. . . . Robin-son took no hands to work his Boat from Pittsburgh but depended on his passengers. Passed many keel boats with Salt from Kanawha bound to Pittsburgh. It is $6.00 per Bbl. (5 bushels).

STEAMBOATS ASSUME CONTROL OF NAVIGATION

The steamboat era of the inland waters was initiated in the winter of 1810 with the building at Pittsburgh of Fulton and Livingston's *New Orleans*. This first Ohio River steamboat, patterned after the original *Clermont* and launched in advance of the high-water season of 1811, was found to be ill-adapted to serv-ice in inland waterways. The engines and boilers of the *New Orleans* were not powerful enough to contend with the steady current of the Ohio. Moreover, the designers of the hull had followed too closely the lines of the *Clermont*, which had been intended for a different purpose. The *New Orleans* went downstream easily in the high-water season, more rapidly than any other craft had done up to that time, but upstream travel was difficult. Although she never returned to the upper basin, this boat saw many years of service in the quiet waters near the city whose name she bore.

A generation of boatbuilding on the Ohio before the arrival of the steam-boat had proved the serviceability of the flat-bottomed type of craft with its shallow draft and ferrylike capacity. The most essential need was an economical motive power capable of carrying freight and passengers upstream as well as down. Ship designers were not long in accepting the challenge, for soon they were turning out boats which, so the facetious ones said, could sail on a heavy dew. Strong engines and boilers, several boilers if necessary, were also added to the Ohio River steamboat. (See Fig. 69.)

69 The Cincinnati water front in the 1820's, showing typical steamboats in use at the time. From the original in the Public Library of Cincinnati.

It was in 1815 that two-way commerce on the Ohio-Mississippi River passed from the realm of probability to actuality. The *Aetna*, with 200 tons of freight and a few passengers, left New Orleans for Louisville, making the trip in sixty days. In the following year she went down in fifteen days and made the return trip in thirty. By 1816, therefore, the *Ohio Gazetteer* could truthfully say that "Steam boats have been found by actual experiment to be particularly well adapted for [river] navigation."

Steamboating on the Ohio and the lower Mississippi became a subject of country-wide interest, with news accounts and editorials appearing in many city newspapers. The *Detroit Gazette*, for instance, in March, 1819, considered it astonishing that

. . . there are now in full tide of success, on the Mississippi and its tributary streams, thirty-one steamboats, and thirty more are building, and nearly completed, for the same navigation. Allowing each boat to make three voyages in a year to New Orleans, at the present rates of freight and passage, the income of sixty-one boats is estimated at the enormous sum of $2,556,000 per annum. What a world of industry, enterprise, activity, and productiveness.

As Professor Almon E. Parkins has said: "The steamboat hastened the settlement of the [Ohio] basin. It carried settlers westward and afterward kept them in touch with the friends, relatives, and markets they had left behind. The increasing population, in turn, called for more steamboats."

Steamboat-building becomes a major industry. Within the decade following 1811, nearly 100 steamboats were built in Ohio River shipyards. One of the chief shipbuilding centers was Pittsburgh, sometimes called even at this early date the Birmingham of America. Observing its water front alive with boats of all kinds, a visitor in 1817 thought it not unusual to see 3 ships in the course of construction. The city's later reputation was foreshadowed in this early account: "Coal is used for domestic purposes as well as in their factories, and the city being hemmed in by the surrounding mountains, the air is always smoky." Other important shipyards on the Ohio were maintained at Wheeling, Marietta, Cincinnati, Louisville, and New Albany.

By 1827, according to an early tabulation, 233 steamboats had been built on the inland waters, and of this number 143 were in operation. Many of the boats had sunk when "stove in" by snags or by ice; a half-dozen others were burned when boilers became overheated — a common cause of disaster among steamers on the Ohio and other inland waters; and a great many had simply worn out or had become obsolete through improvements in design, power plants, and capacity. More detailed data are presented below.

NUMBER OF STEAMBOATS BUILT ON THE OHIO RIVER, 1811 TO 1826

Year	Number of Boats	Year	Number of Boats	Year	Number of Boats
1811	1	1818	25	1823	15
1814	1	1819	34	1824	16
1815	2	1820	10	1825	27
1816	3	1821	5	1826	56
1817	7	1822	13		

The average Ohio River steamer of a century and a quarter ago was the natural predecessor of passenger or excursion boats which are now seen on inland waters. It was perhaps 100 feet long, with two or three decks, and a tall smokestack near the bow. The river steamboat was usually a "side-wheeler," although this was not an invariable rule. Equipped to carry passengers as well as freight, the steamers were sometimes of a palatial character, much appreciated by travelers who in earlier days had complained bitterly of the hardships of river passage.

The largest steamer during this period was the *United States*, with the following specifications: length of keel, 165 feet 8 inches; length of deck, 176 feet 8 inches; depth of hold, 11 feet 3 inches; beam, 56 feet. This boat, considered "mammoth" at the time, was equipped with eight boilers and had "elegant accommodations for a large number of passengers." Perhaps the strangest-looking steamer ever built on the Ohio was the *Western Engineer*, launched at Pittsburgh in the spring of 1819. This ship was constructed specifically for the use of the Long expedition, a surveying party bound for the Missouri country and to which various references have already been made. According to the *New-York Commercial Advertiser*, the *Western Engineer*

. . . is well armed, and carries an elegant flag painted by Mr. Peale, representing a white man and an Indian shaking hands, the Calumet of peace and a sword. The boat is seventy-five feet long, thirteen feet beam, draws nineteen inches of water with her engine which, together with all the machinery, is placed below deck entirely out of sight. The steam passes off through the mouth of the figure-head, a large serpent. The wheels are placed in the stern, to avoid the snags and sawyers which are so common in those waters. She has a mast to ship or not as may be necessary.

This remarkable boat, decorated in a manner calculated to overawe the Indians, passed triumphantly down the Ohio and up the Mississippi to St. Louis and, what is still more remarkable, mastered the treacherous current and the mud of the Missouri for a distance of about 500 miles.

Passenger travel and freight traffic. For commercial data on Ohio River boats we must depend largely on a few records made at the Falls of the Ohio. With the coming of steamboats, the falls became increasingly important as a break in transportation. Louisville and Shippingport were stopping points for steamers, as well as for other boats, some remaining at one terminal or the other for weeks on end. The lower the water, the greater was the collection of boats at the head or foot of the falls. In the drought year of 1819, for instance, a traveler saw a dozen steamboats aground at Shippingport. The larger steamers moving on the lower Mississippi and Ohio usually ascended no farther than Shippingport, where cargo and passengers were discharged and received. The delay was often put to good advantage in replanking bottoms or otherwise refitting the vessels for further service.

No estimates can be made of the number of passengers carried on the Ohio in any year. Steamboats carried from 50 to 200 passengers, but many took passage on other boats even after the use of steam power became common. The annual total of passengers must have run into the thousands.

In the year 1822, nearly 78,000 tons of agricultural produce, valued at some $3,000,000, passed the Falls of the Ohio. The figures of the table below come from *Niles' Weekly Register* for 1823.

AGRICULTURAL PRODUCE PASSING FALLS OF THE OHIO, 1822

Number		Produce	Tons	Value
15,000	hogsheads	Tobacco	11,200	$ 600,000
10,000	hogsheads	Hams and shoulders	5,000	200,000
15,000	hogsheads	Hams and bacon	5,000	300,000
5,000	hogsheads	Corn meal	2,000	15,000
50,000	bbls.	Pork	7,500	250,000
5,000	bbls.	Beef	750	15,000
75,000	bbls.	Whisky	11,250	450,000
300,000	bbls.	Flour	30,000	900,000
5,000	bbls.	Beans	500	10,000
4,000	bbls.	Cider	600	800
8,000	bbls.	Apples	200	6,000
100,000	kegs	Lard	2,500	300,000
30,000	kegs	Butter	800	150,000
3,000	bales	Hay	450	2,000
		TOTALS	77,750	$3,198,800

It should be realized that Ohio River boats carried many other kinds of commodities, including lead from the Missouri mines; sugar, molasses, and cotton from the South; cabinetwork, wagons and other vehicles, tinware, copperware, and ironware, grindstones, and furs and peltry. Some vessels built on the Ohio were sent down to New Orleans in full cargo and sold for coastwise service.

One known example is that of the *Maria,* launched at Marietta in the spring of 1816. Loaded with pork, lard, and flour to the amount of 50 tons, the *Maria* passed Cincinnati en route, via New Orleans, to Boston where, judging from the lack of any other record, the boat and her cargo were disposed of. In the same year, the ship *Triton* of New Orleans passed the falls bound upriver for Cincinnati with the following cargo:

TRITON CARGO, 1816

Product	Amount
Louisiana sugar	75,000 lbs.
Molasses	1,000 gals.
Copperas	40 bbls.
Shad	10 bbls.
Mackerel	10 bbls.
Codfish	40 boxes
Queensware	66 crates
Logwood and Swedish iron	?

The *Triton's* freight, including many Eastern products such as codfish and mackerel, exemplifies the changing trend of Mississippi-Ohio commerce. Through the power of steam, passengers and produce could reach the growing cities of the interior by an all-water route.

CANALS

The Erie Canal speeds projects in the new West.   During the 1820's, the eyes of the nation were turned on the Erie Canal as it progressed across New York State. Even after three years' work upon it there were still some persons who doubted that the waters of Lake Erie and those of the Hudson River could be united. To them this was only " Clinton's Ditch," the fantastic promotional scheme of New York's Governor, De Witt Clinton. More than 360 miles separated the Hudson from Lake Erie. There were some difficult elevations to overcome on the way. Would not losses of water by leakage and evaporation prohibit a channel deep enough for barges laden with freight? And would rates on the canal, assuming it could be completed, greatly reduce transportation costs, after all?

Some of these doubts were removed in the summer of 1821 by the successful operation of the middle section of the canal. Newspaper readers were then informed that " elegant boats for the accommodation of passengers " were already plying between Utica and Lake Cayuga, passing horse-drawn barges carrying hundreds of tons of flour, salt, lumber, whisky, gypsum, and merchandise. Later in the same year the *Detroit Gazette* announced that " the operations of the eastern section of the Grand Canal have advanced to Schenectady Flats, within two miles of the city. The work is progressing with remarkable spirit, and promises completion much sooner than its warmest friends originally expected." The success of the New York canal was assured even before its completion.

No longer was it good form to speak of it scornfully as a ditch. It must now be called the Grand Canal, the New York Canal, or the Erie. To people beyond the Appalachians, where equally ambitious plans for other canals were already in the making, it was the Western Canal. Through it they hoped to find access to new markets by a route which would permit the transportation of their bulky and relatively low-priced farm produce. Midwestern farmers were confronted with the problem created by great surpluses from their large and fertile farms. The sale price of corn varied from 12½ to 25 cents a bushel; short of being converted into more valuable whisky or pork, it could not be sold on Eastern markets. Wheat in Ohio yielded 30 bushels to the acre; at a sale price of from 50 to 75 cents, the grain could not profitably reach distant markets except in the form of flour. At the same time people in Ohio and Indiana were paying high prices for commodities purchased in New England and Pennsylvania and brought in by combined land and water routes.

Popular demands for canals. A Bloomfield, Ohio, farmer expressed the general opinion in 1817 — the year of the commencement of the Erie Canal — in a letter to an Eastern friend, saying:

The season has been very fine. Indian corn looks well. English grain has done well. New England must send out a great many immigrants next year to take off our surplus produce or it will bear a low price. I hope it will be low. That will convince the people of the importance of canals. New York, I think, will succeed in accomplishing their great design. Ohio will I hope do her part in continuing the Great Canal by opening others from Lake Erie to the Ohio River. A Project for that purpose is now on foot. It is to connect the waters of Grand River which run northwardly into Lake Erie with those of the Mahoning or Big Beaver which runs southerly into the Ohio. The distance which must be excavated is not more than ten or a dozen miles and the summit level of such a canal for a guess will not exceed 30 feet. It may be less, but it will be soon known. A committee is to explore the route & make a report this month.

Illinoisans were no less interested in the Erie Canal than people in the states farther east, for projects were in hand to connect Lake Michigan with the Illinois River. Said a citizen of Vandalia in February, 1821:

The benefits we shall derive from it are incalculable. . . . To say nothing of the increase in population it will produce, by opening a water communication with North and Eastern States, it will afford to our citizens, upon the completion of the New York Canal, a sure and steady market for their produce. . . . It is said by some that nature designed the Mississippi as an outlet for our produce, and that New Orleans is our natural market! Be it so. To have a choice is at all times desirable, and we lose none of the advantages held out by New Orleans by connecting the Illinois with the Hudson.

The Erie Canal was officially opened on October 26, 1825, when a fleet of boats left Buffalo carrying, among other things, kegs of Lake Erie water to be poured into the Hudson upon arrival at Albany. The advance of the canal fleet was marked by the booming of cannon at frequent intervals. Had there been radio to carry a mile-by-mile account of this canal passage, no group of people would have been more interested listeners than Midwesterners. To them, this was the beginning of a new era.

Favorable reports of the Erie Canal even before it was in full operation furnished new grist for the mills of canal-promoters in the Ohio country. Heretofore the boosters of internal improvements had spoken in general terms. They had said, in effect, that canals could easily be constructed at a number of " levels " or old-time portages across the low divide separating the rivers tributary to the Great Lakes, and those flowing southward into the Ohio and Mississippi. As to just what rivers could thus be connected into through waterways there was considerable doubt and therefore much room for the pressing of particular schemes. Lacking was information concerning the: (1) exact altitudes of the summit levels, (2) length of portages, for example between the Maumee and the Wabash, and (3) dependability of " feeders " for supplying projected canals with the necessary depth of water.

Doubts concerning these matters were brushed aside in the clamor for canals which, promoters now said with confidence, would form extensions of the Erie Canal into the Mississippi Basin. A typical promoter was Benjamin Stickney, Indian agent stationed at Fort Wayne on the old-time portage from the Maumee to the Wabash. He wrote of his plans to no less a canal authority than De Witt Clinton, who replied somewhat pompously: " I have found the way to get into Lake Erie and you have shown me how to get out of it. . . . You have extended my project six hundred miles." Individual blessings such as this hastened canal-building schemes beyond the Appalachians.

Canal schemes.   Canal promotion in Ohio was publicly recognized in 1819 when the governor of the state, following legislative acts, appointed a Board of Commissioners. Their surveys were concentrated on the three main portage routes across the Lake Erie-Ohio River watershed.

Farthest east was the Mahoning Level, between the headwaters of the Cuyahoga and those of the Beaver and Muskingum, where the present-day city of Akron is located. The altitude of the Cuyahoga-Muskingum divide was found to be 377 feet above Lake Erie and 361 feet above Marietta; hence if a canal were to be dug, 700 feet of lockage would be necessary. The Sandusky-Scioto divide, known as the Tyamochte Level, would require 810 feet of lockage on a route connecting Sandusky on Lake Erie with Portsmouth on the Ohio. In western Ohio was the Maumee-Miami divide with a still greater lockage demand, since it was 389 feet above Lake Erie and 540 feet above the Ohio River at Cincinnati.

The surveys showed, in fact, that the extension of canals across Ohio would be far less simple than the armchair promoters had imagined. Besides the large lockage requirement there was the matter of water supply for long canals. On this point the commissioners agreed that the supply of water on the proposed Sandusky-Scioto route " would probably be insufficient to overcome the losses by leakage, evaporation, etc., and that it would have no supply of water for the passage of boats through the locks." Such questions as these, however, could not be decided solely by the totting up of engineering data. Each growing city in Ohio, and others that had hopes of growing, wanted to be on one of the canals. Interested persons in Columbus, for instance, felt that the capital city should be on any canal network which might be devised, even though the engineers had recommended avoidance of the Tyamochte Level. And Cincinnatians were equally insistent on recognition even though the city was not at a major stream junction.

The commissioners at first considered the possibility of one great project that would, at one fell swoop, satisfy the interests of Cleveland, Columbus, and Cincinnati. Their original plan, according to Professor Keating, was " to construct a canal which would unite the lake as near the north-east corner of the state as nature will permit, and passing through the great valley of the Muskingum, the Scioto, and the Miami, in a south-westwardly direction, and enter the Ohio near the south-west corner of the state." But this idea was soon admitted to be an idle dream. Two main canals instead of one resulted from the interplay of basic geographic factors and the promotional interests of the leading cities at a time when canals were thought to be the last word in speedy, efficient, and economical transportation. (See Fig. 70.)

Work on the Ohio and Erie Canal began on an auspicious date — July 4, 1825 — shortly before the Erie Canal was opened to through navigation. Following the Cuyahoga River to the Akron summit, the canal utilized the upper Mus-

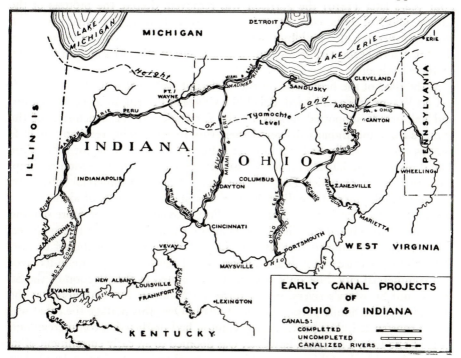

70 Canal projects of Ohio and Indiana

kingum and then swung across to the Scioto, thus satisfying the interests of Columbus. In its dimensions the new canal was a counterpart of the Erie; it was 307 miles long (320 with feeders), 40 feet wide at the top, and 20 feet wide at the bottom, and had a navigable depth of 4 feet. Of the 49 locks with which the canal was provided, 17 were in the short distance from Cleveland to the Akron level. The first canalboat passed from Akron to Cleveland on July 1, 1827, and a few years later barges were passing through the canal length at the rate of a brisk walk.

The growth of cities on the route, notably Cleveland, can be attributed in part to the services provided by the canal. When it was completed in 1832, Cleveland became the second most important port of Lake Erie, outranked only by Buffalo. Freight rates dropped to about one-tenth of their earlier figure, and there was some passenger travel. This canal and the 240-mile Miami and Erie Canal in western Ohio remained in use for about a quarter-century, waging for a few years a losing battle with the advancing railroads. Sections of Ohio's canals, though long out of use, can still be seen here and there.

Fort Wayne and the Wabash-Erie Canal. Of all the forts in the Ohio country, none was more strategically located than Fort Wayne. It was selected as a military site by General Anthony Wayne because of its command of the channel of communication between Lake Erie and the Wabash River. The fort built by Wayne was torn down and rebuilt in 1804, and again rebuilt in 1814 or 1815. Four years later (1819) the garrison was removed, despite the protests of the settlers who had gathered in its neighborhood. Following the usual history of frontier fortresses, the buildings which had formerly housed the troops were converted into headquarters for Indian agents and missionaries and, in this case, an Indian school.

At the time of the first plans for the Wabash-Erie Canal — in the early 1820's — Fort Wayne was a palisaded, Babel-like village of French, Indians, Americans, and half-breeds supported largely by the fur trade. At the conclusion of the winter's hunt the Indians delivered their furs in loose rolls, receiving as little as $1.25 for a deerskin, $1 for a raccoon skin, and from $3 to $5 for a bearskin. The skins were packaged and compressed at the village in preparation for shipment to Detroit, of which Fort Wayne was a kind of commercial subsidiary. The annual shipment from Fort Wayne was about 200 packs of skins valued at some $10,000. The frontier character of Fort Wayne appears the more striking when it is remembered that in 1820 Cincinnati was a city of some 12,000 people.

It was freely predicted that the site factors which had contributed to Fort Wayne's long service as a military outpost would continue to operate in its favor as a commercial city. Not only was the town located at the junction of the St. Joseph and St. Mary's rivers, which form the Maumee, but here also was the beginning of the 8-mile portage to the Wabash. Over this portage the canal was finally constructed, thus providing, as Clinton had predicted, a commercial outlet for Lake Erie. The canal, however, was doomed to an early curtailment of its service. As with the Ohio canals, this one was abandoned when railroads had

proved their greater serviceability. The canal was only an incident in the growth
of Fort Wayne, which, according to the predictions of more than a century ago,
has now become an important trade and manufacturing center.

The Chicago Portage. Chicago, like Fort Wayne, owed its original importance to command over a passageway from the Great Lakes to the Ohio-Mississippi Basin. In the 1820's there was a village of Chicago with a population of
less than 100, and there was also a garrison on the south shore of the Chicago
River, near its mouth. When Henry R. Schoolcraft visited the fort in 1820 it
appeared " like the majority of frontier posts, comprising a square stockade,
enclosing barracks, quarters for officers, a magazine, provision store, etc.,
and defended by bastions at the northwest and southeast angles. It is at present
occupied by a hundred and sixty men." Not long thereafter, Fort Dearborn was
abandoned as a military post.

The remarkable feature of the Chicago Portage was the slight difference of
altitude between the Chicago River and the upper branches of the Des Plaines,
headwater stream of the Illinois. Travelers estimated a difference of level of
less than a dozen feet and guessed, correctly, that the lake had overflowed into
the Illinois during earlier geological times. They could not, of course, forecast
that the Chicago River would again discharge in that direction when, in later
times, its flow was to be reversed through the will of man.

The length of the portage shrank and expanded according to the season, but
was generally from 4 to 9 miles. During very dry years the portage was nearly
20 miles, for boats could ascend the Illinois no farther than Joliet — Mount
Joliet, as it was earlier called. The portage route was not canalized until many
years after the period of this study. Unlike the other canals heretofore studied,
the Illinois and Michigan remains in use at the present time and is an essential
link in the Lakes-to-Gulf waterway.

Even though Chicago was a small village in 1820 and was not much larger
for another quarter-century, Schoolcraft predicted a great future for it. He found
the country roundabout to be one of the " finest lowland prairies " in the most
favored part of the Mississippi Valley. " To the ordinary advantages of an agricultural market town," he continued, " it must hereafter add that of a depot
for the inland commerce between the northern and southern sections of the
nation, and a great thoroughfare for strangers, merchants, and travellers."

CHAPTER 15

Detroit and Southeastern Michigan

A SLOW START

A STUDY of the modern map is poor preparation for understanding why south-eastern Michigan failed to share in the settlement wave that swept across adjacent Ohio in the early 1800's. Conditions have so greatly changed that there seems no possibility that the Detroit region was ever isolated from sources of emigration. Gone now is the Black Swamp of the Maumee, which in the early 1800's was an effectual land barrier. The approach from the east provided by Lake Erie and the Detroit River failed to offset the difficulties of travel to southeastern Michigan by land from Ohio. Until the advent of steam-powered craft in 1818, there was little passenger travel on the Great Lakes, even in summer, and many years passed before American-built shipping eclipsed that of the British. Furthermore, navigation on Lake Erie was completely closed in the winter season. Before 1800 little had been done to improve natural waterways. The River Rouge, now dredged to permit access of the largest freighters to the great Ford plant, was navigable for only 3 miles by sailing vessels of 150 tons and for 3 miles more by the small boats of French rural residents.

Isolation. Detroit and its contiguous settlements were cut off also from interior approaches. "For miles in every direction," said an early Detroiter, "lies a heavily timbered, level, muddy plain, where the soil is alluvial on the surface and a cold, squeezy, heavy clay beneath, through and over which even now transit is almost impossible." Modern hard-surfaced boulevards and arterial highways make it difficult for us to imagine the slow, costly, and seasonally impossible travel conditions of that time.

Political as well as physical conditions contributed to Detroit's early-day isolation. Across the narrow stretch of the Detroit River lay the British Possessions, controlled by a foreign power that was hostile to the United States. War clouds had been piling up for some time before the outbreak of hostilities known as the War of 1812, and did not disperse for many years after the end of the war.

One would surely not be expected to understand from modern information that Michigan Territory, beyond a dozen miles west of Detroit, was virtually unknown and, what is worse, was the subject of unfavorable report. In the fall of 1818 three Detroit citizens (Major Oliver Williams, Calvin Baker, and Jacob

Eilett) " resolved to penetrate into the interior and ascertain whether the country was or was not inhabitable." They followed the military road, which was an extension of Detroit's now famous Woodward Avenue, for a distance of 4 miles (not 40, which might appear more reasonable), and then were led by guides along an Indian trail to the plains beyond Royal Oak. Quite an adventure to take place within a half-dozen miles of Fort Shelby in Detroit, a town that had been founded over a century before! What the " explorers " found will be a matter for later discussion. The event is cited at this point as evidence of the nearness of the wall separating the known from the unknown in Michigan a dozen years after its organization as a Territory.

The growth of Michigan's population. Many thought that Michigan had been started too early upon the road to statehood. Territorial authority was granted on July 1, 1805, when its population was a scant 4,000. Included in this number were about 200 soldiers who could not properly be considered as settlers. Four-fifths of Michigan's population was of French extraction at the time the Territory was formed, the first trickle of American settlement having begun in 1796. Michigan's elevation to the status of Territory did not activate a new movement of emigration in that direction, as similar events had done and were to do elsewhere. The Territorial Act ostensibly gave intending settlers a vast theater of operations — all of the Southern Peninsula and the eastern part of the Northern as well. Nevertheless, there were few newcomers and the people already within the Territory clung closely to the lands bordering the two straits: the *détroit* between Lakes Erie and St. Clair, and the Straits of Mackinac far to the north.

The year 1805 was momentous in the river settlements for another reason — the conflagration which, according to an observer, left not a single house standing in Detroit. Since the destruction of the city, whose population was at that time about 750, made possible the replanning of its streets to accommodate an expected growth, many historians have maintained that the burning of old Detroit was a blessing in disguise. Victims of the fire's ravages doubtless felt differently.

Between 1810 and 1820 Michigan's population doubled in size, but was still less than that of the city of Cincinnati alone during the same period. Detroit could claim only 1,422 citizens in 1820, with settlements extending compactly up and down the river, but still confined to the very borders of the main stream and but a short distance up its principal tributaries — Raisin, Ecorse, Rouge, and Clinton (then called the Huron of St. Clair in distinction from the Huron of Lake Erie). The people were still dominantly French. A census-taker for the 1810 enumeration complained that the compensation of $1 for listing 100 persons was inadequate in a territory where the mass of the population used the French language and was acquainted with no other.

The slow growth of Michigan Territory and its principal city was by now a subject of much concern to prominent citizens, and especially to the *Detroit Gazette*. Said that newspaper in the winter of 1819, " The unfavorable reports of many interested individuals have, heretofore, so far succeeded in depreciating the character of our country in the public esteem, that the principal current from the usual source of emigration has been turned in other directions." This was an oblique reference to Ohio, whose more rapid growth and greater popularity were thought to reflect unfavorably on Michigan.

Perhaps, said some of Michigan's detractors, James Monroe was not far wrong in reporting to Thomas Jefferson: "A great part of the Territory is miserably poor, especially that near the Lake Michigan and Erie. . . . The districts, therefore, within which these fall will never contain a sufficient number of inhabitants to entitle them to membership in the confederacy." Pessimism was evident even in Detroit, in no less a person than William B. Woodbridge, one of the city's most prominent early citizens. Writing to John Quincy Adams in 1820, Woodbridge remarked: "Great as may be considered the commercial and natural advantages of this Territory, the number of emigrants is perhaps comparatively small who may find in so high latitudes inducements to settle among us."

But it is always darkest before the dawn, according to an old proverb. In the 1820's Michigan's population began to swing sharply upward, reaching 31,639 in 1830 and an amazing 212,267 ten years later. With its growth in numbers and a more accurate knowledge of the geography of the Southern Peninsula, the population was sprung loose from its river-border sites and distributed across the state toward Lake Michigan. In 1837, after the longest Territorial period of any state east of the Mississippi River, Michigan reached statehood and looked confidently to the future.

Michigan's shifting boundaries. Among Michigan's Territorial uncertainties, none were more important than those relating to areal limits. One quandary arose from provisions in the Ordinance of 1787 which stated that Congress should organize not less than three nor more than five states in the Northwest Territory. If five states were to be formed, the additional states were to be carved out of the territory which lay north of an " east and west line drawn through the southerly bend or extreme of Lake Michigan." (See Fig. 71.)

This apparently simple proviso, which had been disregarded in the addition of both Indiana and Illinois — notice that their limits extend northward of the tip of Lake Michigan — eventually led to a prolonged dispute between Ohio and Michigan. Ohio authorities had foreseen that the state might lose valuable frontage on Lake Erie if later surveys confirmed fears that a line projected eastward from the southern end of Lake Michigan would pass to the south of Maumee Bay. The following clause was therefore included in the Ohio constitution: " That if the southerly bend of Lake Michigan should extend so far south that a line drawn due east from it should not intersect Lake Erie, or if it should intersect the said Lake Erie east of the mouth of the Miami River of the Lake [Maumee River] then . . . the northern boundary of this State shall be established by . . . a direct line running from the southern extremity of Lake Michigan to the most northerly cape of the Miami [Maumee] Bay." Ohio's admission to the Union in 1803 involved an acceptance of this proviso in the state consti-

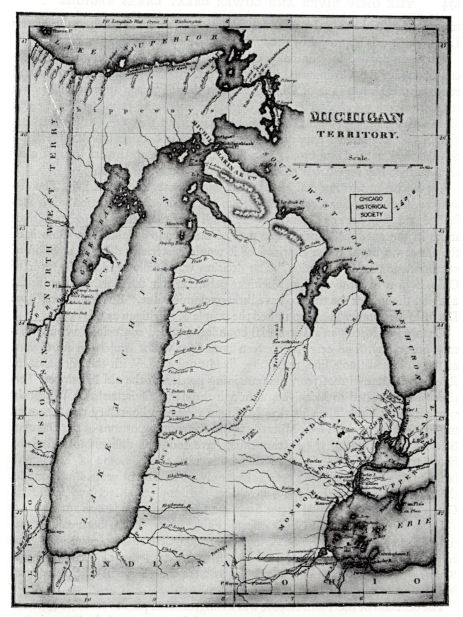

71 Michigan Territory in the early 1820's. Note that the Michigan-Ohio boundary assigns the Maumee Bay region to Michigan, although later interpretations gave this area to Ohio. The map shows how little was known about Michigan at the time. From the collection of the Chicago Historical Society.

tution, a foothold made the more secure by a later survey, known as the Harris Line, which was approved by the Ohio Legislature in 1818.

Michigan applied for admission as a Territory taking as its presumed southern boundary the Ordinance Line, which unfortunately was found to extend south of the Harris Line of Ohio. Although the difference appears slight on a map, involving an area of less than 500 square miles, the resulting dispute was long and heated. Spokesmen for Michigan claimed that the Ordinance Line should take precedence over any other, the more so because the Black Swamp formed the " natural and proper " limits of Ohio in the northwest. In their view the Maumee Bay region was allied to Michigan rather than to Ohio.

But Michigan was not concerned alone with frontage on Lake Erie. The disputed area, though small, was presumed to be valuable for its location; as Woodbridge said, " an acre of Country to the south is of more importance to us than miles in the north. A considerable part of the Country claimed by Ohio is of the finest we have; to be deprived of it would materially delay the period of our admission into the Union." The decision was finally rendered in favor of Ohio. By way of compensation, Michigan gained area in the Northern Peninsula, a region thought at the time to have little economic value. " But few issues," says Dr. Milo M. Quaife, " have so united the people of Michigan as this one."

Changes in Michigan's Territorial boundaries added confusion to contemporary geography. The original western boundary was a projection northward of the Indiana-Illinois line, remaining fixed until 1818. With the admission of Illinois as a state in that year, the remaining portion of the old Northwest Territory was attached to Michigan, although the name Ouisconsin or Wisconsin was currently used. Then in 1834 Michigan's western boundary was extended to include present-day Iowa, Minnesota, and the eastern portions of the Dakotas. Schoolchildren during these years must have found it difficult to " give the boundaries of Michigan " when called upon to do so. Some of Michigan's boundary-line problems have been solved only within recent years. For example, the Michigan-Wisconsin dispute involving the Montreal River and islands in Green Bay required United States Supreme Court action as late as 1926.

Unfavorable reports and their effect. Faulty maps, it has been said, sometimes cause a lot of history. So do hasty or incomplete reports, especially when issued as official documents. With such a report, sometimes called the Tiffin Report, we shall now be concerned just as were the people of Michigan upon its issuance in 1815.

The occasion of the Tiffin Report was a congressional plan to set aside 2,000,000 acres of the Southern Peninsula as bounty land for veterans of the War of 1812, or the War of 1812 to 1815, as early Michigan historians prefer to call it. A survey of the region was ordered and carried out by a field party, under the direction of the Surveyor General of Ohio, Edward Tiffin. The methods of the surveyors are not a matter of record, but it seems fair to infer from the rapidity with which 30,000 square miles of land were inspected that their observations were of a reconnaissance nature. The field observations were delivered to Tiffin, who wrote to Josiah Meigs, Commissioner of the General Land Office, on November 30, 1815: "The surveyors, who went to survey the military land in Michigan Territory, have been obliged to suspend operations until the country shall have been frozen over so as to bear man and beast."

This was an excellent topic sentence for a brief regional description which went from swamp to marsh and back again to swamp, pausing briefly to comment on thick underbrush and heavy timber interspersed with occasional patches of barren land. Tiffin's regional description of the Southern Peninsula was written with the finality of a report based upon exhaustive, firsthand inquiry. Notably absent were such phrases as "it is believed" or "until further information is secured we are forced to the conclusion that . . ." Observations so dogmatically made were accepted by other writers, except, of course, proponents of settlement in Michigan; and as the statements passed from one written page to another, distortions naturally entered the record. It will therefore be necessary to consult the original, in *American State Papers,* and abstract typical portions of the document.

Quotations from the Tiffin Report on Military Lands in Michigan Territory, 1815

The country on the Indian boundary line from the mouth of the great Auglaize river, and running thence for about fifty miles is (with some few exceptions) low wet land, with a thick growth of underbrush, intermixed with very bad marshes, but generally very heavy timbered . . . from thence continuing north and extending from the Indian boundary line eastward, the number and extent of the swamps increases with the addition of numbers of lakes. . . . Many of the lakes have extensive marshes adjoining their margins, sometimes thickly covered with a species of pine called tamirack, and other places covered with coarse high grass. . . . The intermediate space between the swamps and lakes, which is probably near one half the country is, with a very [few] exceptions, a poor barren, sandy land, on which scarcely any vegetation grows, except very small scrubby oaks. [Some of the dry land is sand hill country.

Streams are generally very narrow and deep,] the shores and bottoms of which are swampy beyond description. [Many of the marshes are thickly covered with a sward of grass, which is deceptive to one crossing such areas on foot.] The margins of many of the lakes and streams are in a similar situation, and in many places are literally afloat. [On the margin near the private claims the country is less swampy,] but the extreme sterility and barrenness of the soil continues the same.

Taking the country altogether, so far as has been explored, and to all appearances, together with the information received concerning, the balance is as bad, there could not be more than one acre out of a hundred, if there would be one out of a thousand, that would in any case admit of cultivation.

This description of southern Michigan as a morass scarcely worth the expense of surveying seemed credible to authorities in Washington. In his special message to the Congress on February 6, 1816, President Monroe recommended that Michigan's portion of the bounty lands, 1,000,000 acres for 6,800 men, be located in Illinois. It is to be presumed that the attitude of the Congress became widely known through newspaper comment and private communications. Influential also in spreading unfavorable ideas about Michigan were geographies and guide-books containing descriptions taken from the Tiffin Report or a derivative of it. If an emigrant going West failed to encounter one of the many descriptions available, he would likely meet with someone who had, and thereupon decide to take up land in a more promising locality.

Much effort and many years were required to break down the prejudices created by the accounts of this period. Spontaneous exploring parties such as the one referred to earlier set out from Detroit to determine the true prospects of land settlement. The patriotic *Detroit Gazette,* beginning in the winter of 1819, carried long and favorable descriptions of the region. Local residents attempted to dispel the libelous statements of the official surveyors, who they said must have been acting with ulterior motive. It was more than once suggested that interests seeking to preserve Michigan as a source of game and furs had arranged for a report that would keep settlers out.

Gradually a more nearly correct view of Michigan geography crept into the literature. Books written by travelers who could assure their readers of personal acquaintance with the region were especially influential. Such a visitor was Estwick Evans, author of the curiously titled *A Pedestrious Tour of Four Thousand Miles* (1818). He said:

I deem it my duty to express my high opinion of the Michigan Territory, because facts warrant such a course, and it is important that my fellow citizens . . . should possess every information on the subject. In travelling more than four thousand miles in the western parts of the United States, I met no tract of country which, on the whole, impressed my mind so favorably as the Michigan Territory. Erroneous ideas have heretofore been entertained respecting this territory. Indeed it has, until lately, been viewed as scarcely within the jurisdiction of the United States. Even some late geographers seem to have collected no other information respecting it, than what had been written by their predecessors. Some of this information, especially as it respects Detroit, does not apply to the present time.

SOUTHEASTERN MICHIGAN IN 1820

By 1820, the deservedly unpopular Tiffin Report had given way to others from which readers could obtain a fairly accurate picture of the Southern Peninsula as a field for possible settlement. Even at that time inhabited Michigan was unbelievably small. Within a short distance of the Detroit River lived most of the Territory's 9,000 people. Farthest inland, but only 40 miles from Detroit, was the new town of Pontiac, seat of the equally new Oakland County. Settlements extended along the river from Lake St. Clair southward to Monroe near the mouth of the River Raisin on Lake Erie.

The land surface.   The developed area was a flat plain rising gradually from the Detroit River to the rough hilly belt of Oakland County. Even the most enthusiastic descriptions of the 1820's frankly admitted that this was not the most favorable of environments for pioneering. Much of the surface of the plain was heavily timbered, large areas were poorly drained, and the heavy " squeezy " clay seemed to be almost everywhere.

Although the correct interpretation awaited scientific developments in glaciology, the dominant topographic features of the Detroit plain were the result of continental glaciation. In a hasty view this plain was devoid of all features, but close observers made note of the numerous beach ridges with a northeast-southwest trend within the limits of the Detroit area and farther inland. The gravelly surface of the beaches provided convenient lines for roads across the otherwise hard-to-travel plain, and furnished good building sites as well. As early as 1793 these minor but critical features were recognized as beach ridges by Jacob Lindley, who recorded that while in Detroit he

. . . walked out into the woods a mile and a half, when my further excursion was prevented by swamps, bogs, and marshes. In my route I found stones in divers places, such as are observed on the margin of a lake. The land in general is almost sunk under water. My mind was strongly impressed with the belief that lakes Huron, St. Clair, Erie, and Michigan were once united, and that tens of thousands of acres of low adjacent land were all overflowed. By the breaking and wearing away of the great falls mentioned before [Niagara], the water was lowered to the present surface.

The inner edge of the lake plain was observed to be bordered by a prominent ridge or belt of hilly country rising 100 feet or more above the general level, known in modern times as the Defiance Moraine. The Williams-Baker-Eilett exploring party earlier mentioned (page 270) had no knowledge of the glacial origin of this feature, but their descriptions of it and of the till plain that lay beyond proved the erroneous character of the Tiffin Report. An observer wrote:

The report that this party made of the beauty and fertility of the country they had seen after passing the belt of wet timbered lands, and the evidences they adduced, electrified the hearts of the Americans in Detroit, and utterly astounded the Frenchmen whose homes were near the riverside and whose aspirations seldom extended beyond the possession of a canoe, a spear, a few dozen hooks for fishing, with a wife and a half dozen dogs.

Agriculture in the Detroit area. By 1820, little change had occurred in the century-old agriculture of the French people along the strait between Lakes St. Clair and Erie.

The map of property divisions (Fig. 72) shows the characteristics made familiar by studies of other French-occupied districts in North America. The farms were parallelograms in shape, with water frontages of 3 or 4 French arpents or about one-tenth of a mile, and extending inland for variable distances. In this area of difficult land travel, access to water deep enough to float canoes and small boats was especially important. Frontage on the river also ensured advantages in fishing, and furnished supplies of water in an area notably lacking in good

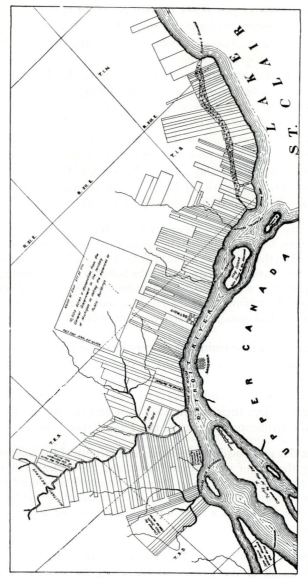

72 A section of a large map showing the property divisions near Detroit during the early days of the American occupation. From the Burton Historical Collections.

springs. From the River Rouge to Lake St. Clair, a distance of 12 miles, the river front resembled the suburbs of a large town, the houses being no more than 20 rods apart. Intervals of wooded country separated the River Rouge settlements from those of the Ecorse and more southern tributaries.

Observers found little to praise in the agricultural practices of the French inhabitants. Even the *Detroit Gazette,* which lost no opportunity to present attractive pictures of Michigan, was forced to conclude (January 22, 1819) that the lands were " owned by families who will not or who know not how to cultivate them; who only increase the demand for the necessities of life by their numbers and their negligence or ignorance of agricultural pursuits." This severe judgment finds support in the agricultural survey of the Indian agent Jouett, who found the soil inherently productive, although poorly managed. Of the Ecorse River settlements, 10 miles south of Detroit, Jouett said that the soil was rich " and sufficiently dry for any cultivation, yet the people are poor beyond conception, and no description can give an adequate idea of their servile and degraded situation." This comment or indictment perhaps shared with others the intolerance with which American-made descriptions of French settlements were flavored.

The French settlers were at their best, apparently, in gardening and raising fruits — apples, peaches, cherries, and pears. " Most of the farmers have been assiduously careful in the rearing of fruit trees," Jouett reported to authorities in Washington. " Their apple orchards are generally well enclosed with pickets, and produce fruit and cider in sufficient abundance for the consumption of the country and even for the supply of many of the Canadian settlements to which they are exported." But even here there should have been better management, said critics. Pruning was neglected and the replacement of aging trees by young orchards had not been properly seen to. Of the various kinds of fruit adaptable to this area, the pear was most widely raised, nearly every French family having a few trees.

Local agricultural production was inadequate to regional needs. The garrison and residents of Detroit were dependent on Ohio and western New York for a large share of their supplies.

The city of Detroit. Judged by ordinary standards, Detroit was of little importance in 1820. Its civil population of 1,450 occupied a diminutive checkerboard of eighteen streets on a slight rise above the river. Three hundred and fifty dwellings, some of brick, some of hewn logs, the majority of frame construction, nearly hid from view the picketed gardens of their occupants, about half of whom were French.

This was the civil town. A few rods to the west of the main street was the military post, Fort Shelby (so named upon reoccupation of the post by Americans following a British defeat in 1813). There had been a fort at Detroit, but not on this particular site, since the beginning of white settlement in 1701. Indeed, the old town of Detroit was itself the fort. (See Fig. 73.) Fort Shelby did not command the river as had its predecessor, but it was neat and impressive, one

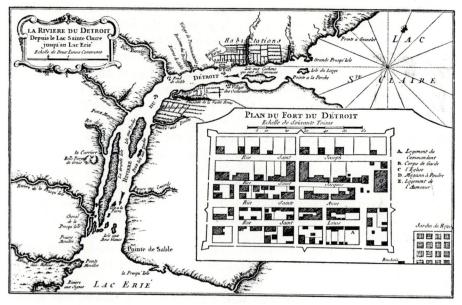

73   A composite plan of Detroit and the fort published in 1764. From the collection
of the William L. Clements Library.

of the major posts in the West. Those who remembered the old fort-town destroyed by the fire of 1805 agreed that the committee responsible for planning the
new town had acted with admirable vision. The planners were free to work
out their ideas with little opposition from surface features, but at the same
time with little hope of taking advantage of sightly elevations. In natural surface, present downtown Detroit differs but little from the original except that
a swampy watercourse known as Savoyard Creek is no longer in existence. In
outlining the new street pattern the planners assumed that the fort would soon
be abandoned by the Government, a forecast that came true in 1827. From the
lower end of the city in the direction of the River Rouge, there was no perceptible break between town and country, so closely spaced were the farm homes.

Detroit as a Frontier Town.   The importance of Detroit in 1820 cannot be
fairly estimated by its physical equipment or the number of its permanent residents. A large floating population considered the town as a temporary or seasonal headquarters: emigrants, fur traders, and adventurers, as well as Indians
of various Northern tribes. The last-named were a constant reminder of proximity to the frontier, for Detroit, seen in the large, was a connecting link between
the primitive heartland and the civilized Eastern regions.

The streets of Detroit in daytime were often crowded with Indians who had
come to trade their furs and skins for other commodities. Here also were prominent governmental authorities, since Detroit was the Territorial capital; prosperous tradesmen, military personnel, and the usual sprinkling of scamps. There
were also visitors from Canada just across the river, for this was a political

frontier as well as a social and economic borderland. President Monroe took due note of Detroit's two-way frontier on his visit in 1818. Addressing the citizens he expressed his pleasure at seeing Detroit " so rapidly regaining its beauty and consequence " after the fire a dozen years before. He was touring the frontier and especially the Great Lakes frontier, he said. in order to be better able " to devise the most efficient methods of defending [it]."

Visitors to the town at the straits were reminded of other similarly placed communities, such as Vincennes and Fort Wayne. Traveler Darby noted the resemblance of Detroit to Natchitoches on the Red River of the South. He commented:

Each place occupies the point of contact between the aboriginal inhabitants of the wilderness, and the civilized people who are pushing those natives backwards by the double force of physical and moral weight. In each place you behold at one glance the extremes of human improvement, costume, and manners. You behold the inhabitants in habiliments that would suit the walks of New York, Philadelphia, London, or Paris, and you also see the bushy, bare-headed savage, almost in primeval nudity. In the same storehouse you will see on the same shelf objects to supply the first and last wants of human nature.

Commercial Terminus on the Great Lakes. It was at the water front that the functional character of Detroit was best observed. Throughout the years, the town had maintained its far-flung trade connections, eminently justifying Cadillac's original choice of the straits for a site. Detroit originated in the period of French-British rivalry for the control of the continental interior, especially of its trade. The *détroit* was viewed as a strategic section of the trade route — a narrows between two larger bodies of water, all connected with the East. Some other spot on the straits might have served equally well the purposes which Detroit was designed to serve; the straits were nearly 30 miles long, and obviously there were two sides to them, a primary fact which led eventually to the placing of Britain's rival Fort Malden on the Canadian shore.

The Detroit site was not a natural focus of routes. Two Indian trails, referred to in the early records, apparently met at the straits at River Rouge. One of these has been called the Saginaw Trail, connecting the bay of that name with the Rouge. The other was the St. Joseph Trail, extending westward from the Rouge and Huron rivers to the St. Joseph of Lake Michigan. These trails were in use at the time of the American occupation, and many years elapsed before any other routes were made available. Detroit became the center of routes and, in due time, of railroads, because of its growing importance; the routes, in turn, contributed to the further growth of the city. It was an " eligible site " for a post and a fort and for the Indian town, Teuchsagondie, which antedated the French fortress, but by no means was it the *only* suitable place in that vicinity.

Character of Detroit's Trade. But it may at least be said of the site of Detroit that the banks rise gently from the water to the slightly higher land formed by the broad Detroit Moraine. The low banks allowed easy access to wharves, of

which there were three when the first steamboat on the lakes, *Walk in the Water,*
out of Buffalo, arrived on the morning of August 27, 1818. (See Fig. 74.) The date
and hour are well recorded, because this event was hailed as the beginning of a
new era. Hundreds of Detroiters lined the bank as the steamer puffed up
river; farther down the straits, astonished Indians at Fort Malden had shouted
exclamations at the " big canoe of the Long Knives." In its way, the *Walk in the
Water* became as famous as the *Griffon* of the Sieur de la Salle, the first vessel
to navigate the upper Great Lakes, launched in 1679. On the Buffalo-Detroit
trip the new steamboat consumed over 30 cords of wood, sufficient to maintain
a speed averaging 8 miles an hour. The passenger fare for the journey, which
could be made in a day and a half but usually required longer because of ports
of call on the way, was about $15. The *Walk in the Water* was contemporarily
described as a ship of " elegant fittings " — 135 feet long, 32-foot beam, drawing
8½ feet of water. Small as she was, travelers saw in the first steamer a great advance over slow-going, unreliable, and uncomfortable schooners. In the year
after her maiden voyage the *Walk in the Water* was extending her itinerary to
Mackinac, the round trip from Buffalo averaging twelve days. Advertisements
declared that the voyage was " so near a resemblance to the famous expedition
in the Heroic Age of Greece that expectation is quite alive on the subject."
Other steamers soon followed: *Rodgers* (1820), *Superior* (1822), *Chippewa*
(1825), *Henry Clay,* and *Pioneer.* Growth of steam shipping was relatively slow,
however. Less than a dozen steamers had been launched by 1830, but in the next
decade the number increased to nearly 75.

During the 1820's the tonnage of shipping was largely made up of sailing vessels. Detroit's commercial activity is suggested in the following table of port
activities for a week in 1820.

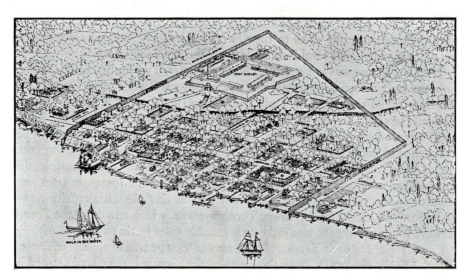

74   Detroit in 1818, from an original in the Burton Historical Collections

PORT OF DETROIT ARRIVALS AND CLEARANCES,
JUNE 29 TO JULY 7, 1820 *

Arrivals		From	Carrying
Steamboat	*Walk in the Water*	Buffalo	Passengers, freight
Schooners	*Hannah*	Buffalo	Merchandise
	Haskins	Ohio ports	Pork, cheese, bacon
	Night Hawk	Ohio ports	Stoves
	Happy Return	Ohio ports	Flour, whisky, pearlash
	Liberty	Cleveland	Country produce
	Erie	Buffalo	Merchandise
	General Johnson	Mackinac	Skins, furs, peltries, Indian sugar
Clearances		To	
Steamboat	*Rodgers*	Buffalo	Passengers
Schooners	*Merry Cabin*	Ohio ports	?
	Eliza Gallagher	Ohio ports	?
	Erie	Buffalo	Salt
	Liberty	Buffalo	Pork
	Belden	Mackinac	Flour, whisky, tobacco

* From the *Detroit Gazette*, July 7, 1820.

The annual value of Detroit's trade in the 1820's rarely exceeded $100,000. Detroit was a kind of halfway station for Great Lakes shipping. The furs, peltry, and salt of the Upper Lakes were often deposited at Detroit to be carried to Ohio, Pennsylvania, and New York ports by other vessels.

In turn, many products were redistributed from Detroit to the garrisons and posts of the upper Great Lakes — Mackinac, Green Bay, and Chicago. There was little penetration into Lake Superior because of the break in transportation caused by the rapids of the St. Mary's River, or Sault de Ste. Marie. Some of the exports to the Upper Lakes, such as merchandise and whisky (or at least some of the latter), were trading goods for the fur trade. Only a small proportion of the commodities entering into Detroit's commerce originated in the city; its exports regularly exceeded the imports, but many of the "exports" were goods or freight on the way to other destinations. The commodities in transit through the straits resembled those of the present time in only one particular: they were relatively cheap and bulky.

The activity of Detroit's water-borne trade, stimulated by the advent of steamboats, gave rise to many inspired and often overenthusiastic predictions as to the city's future grasp on Great Lakes commerce. It was a time of country-wide enthusiasms, particularly strong in Detroit, emerging as it was from dark clouds of unpopularity. With his customary pomposity, Schoolcraft said that even " a cursory view of the map of the United States will indicate [Detroit's] importance as a central military and commercial position. . . . It is destined to be to the regions of the north-west, what St. Louis is rapidly becoming to the south-west, the seat of its commerce, the repository of its wealth, and the grand focus of its moral, political, and physical energies." There was no basis then for knowing that iron ore, coal, and other bulky products would eventually constitute the chief cargoes of the lakes, and that many ports, not merely Detroit, would profit from this trade. But Schoolcraft was correct at least in assigning a great future to Detroit.

THE GROWTH OF DETROIT AND ITS HINTERLAND, 1820 TO 1830

" Every addition to the population of southern Michigan," says Professor Parkins, " had its effect in swelling the size and increasing the importance of the growing metropolis on the eastern border." The opening of the Erie Canal, the mounting numbers of steamboats on Lake Erie, the building of new roads, the opening of a land office in Detroit — all these were developments of the 1820's that contributed to the growth of Detroit and the Territory.

In 1825, *Niles' Weekly Register* reported: " Emigration is powerful to the west. The vessels are hardly able to carry the passengers and their goods, though the steamboats convey three hundred persons westward each week." It was estimated in July of that year that 4,000 persons had arrived at Detroit since the opening of warm-season navigation. The newer steamboats, fitted to transport household effects and livestock as well as the emigrants themselves, sometimes left Buffalo before the scheduled hour to avoid pressure of persons seeking passage.

Not all the incoming settlers were newly arrived from the Eastern states. Old-time residents of Michigan took special satisfaction in noticing that among the newcomers were many Ohioans, who would not have made this change, it was said, unless they believed that Michigan offered greater opportunities. Better means of communication by land as well as by water played a leading role in this interstate movement.

The conquest of the Black Swamp. The decade of the 1820's was a period of road-building *into* Detroit; the following ten years saw the opening of new land routes *out of* Detroit. Deserving of special mention is the road which after many years of planning and effort was completed across the Black Swamp in 1827.

The Black Swamp was recognized as a blemish on the fair land of Ohio in the Treaty of Brownstown (November 25, 1808). According to its Article 2, the Indians ceded " a tract of land for a road of one hundred and twenty feet in width . . . and all the land within one mile thereof " from the rapids of the Maumee to the western border of the Fire Lands.

The Black Swamp Road project was long delayed, however, unaccountably so in a country famed for prompt attention to major undertakings. Three years after the Treaty of Brownstown the President authorized a road survey through the swamp and appropriated $6,000 to see it through. But there was no time for carrying out the project then. The War of 1812 took Detroit into its zone of hostilities, virtually cutting it off from the United States. To reach the city, the little army of General William Hull hastily made a roadway by felling trees and building rude bridges across the bogs, but it scarcely served even military purposes. The want of a suitable road across the swamp, it was estimated, cost the Government $2,000,000 during the war.

Hull's makeshift road, little used thereafter, was soon overgrown with brush. Traces of it could be seen for some years, " principally indicated by the broken remnants of buggies, wagons, and gun carriages, scattered remains of flour barrels, and the moldering skeletons of horses and oxen, remaining as they were left just visible above the surface of the mud and water which destroyed them." The swamp was as much of a barrier as before the war.

After the border war the swamp-road project was dropped, much to the dissatisfaction of interests in Michigan and its principal city, Detroit. The able Territorial governor, Lewis Cass, kept hammering at military and governmental authorities concerning the need for a land connection with Ohio. He wrote General Duncan McArthur on January 30, 1818: " To reach the territory of Michigan from any part of Ohio by land, this swamp must be crossed. No description can convey to a person who is unacquainted with it an adequate idea of the difficulties to be encountered before a tolerable road can be formed through the country [which] in its present situation renders the territory of Michigan an insulated point upon the map of the nation." It was pointed out that the swamp-road project should logically be allied to the Cumberland, or National, Road scheme. (See Fig. 53, page 186.)

Not a little sectional feeling was developed by the apparent indifference of national authorities. Michigan people noted that public moneys were being expended for improvements in the Eastern part of the country. They asked: Was not a road to Michigan more important than the protection of " some insignificant island or headland along the Atlantic seaboard? " Besides, the Government should carry out its pledge in the Brownstown Treaty and provide for the delivery of mail to Detroit. By 1820 a road known as the River Road had been extended by Detroit soldiers to the edge of the swamp, but the morass still remained impassable.

Stirred to action in 1823, the Congress granted land and funds for the building of the road, the first subsidy made by the Federal Government with a view to promoting the settlement and defense of Michigan. The work of construction extended over four years, testimony to the difficulty of the undertaking. Road-builders regarded the swamp as 30 miles of bog, bayou, tangled brush, grassy quagmire, and small timber, with a slope so slight (4 feet to the mile) that streams could not drain it. Beneath the aquatic vegetation was a stratum of impervious clay which originated, according to modern physiographers, when all this part of Ohio was occupied by the glacial lakes Maumee, Whittlesey, and Warren. Some of the road at least was built by subcontractors who received land grants as compensation. One man, for example, agreed to " make the Twenty-third mile of the Road leading from Maumee to this place [Lower Sandusky] to the fire lands for one thousand four hundred and fifty dollars in land to be selected by me out of the land belonging to the road fund." Others were paid in cash at comparable rates.

The completion of the road to Detroit in 1827 was hailed as a major accomplishment, as indeed it was. The first stagecoach line from Ohio to Detroit was established in that year, contributing to the emigration to Michigan Territory and obviating further deliveries of mail by horseback travel. The final draining of the swamp, another major project, was accomplished in the early 1850's.

INTERIOR SETTLEMENT, 1830 TO 1840

At last connected with the East, Michigan entered with new energy upon a program to link the straits settlements with the interior. Route-planning involved a consideration of distant objectives (for example, Chicago), existent trails (St. Joseph Trail), the location of rivers tributary to Lakes Erie and Michigan (Huron and Grand rivers), and areas of new settlement such as Saginaw.

First authorized by Congress was the Chicago Road, completed in 1833. The course of this Territorial road, initiated with an appropriation of $3,000, may be followed on a modern map by way of the places which developed along it — Ypsilanti, Ann Arbor, Jackson, Marshall, Three Rivers. Next in order and with equal justification was a road from Detroit to Fort Gratiot near Port Huron, and another to Saginaw and Bay City, points of new settlement in the 1830's.

These roads and others soon to follow — to Lansing, Kalamazoo, and Grand Rapids — were narrow and poorly constructed, and in the Detroit region were further handicapped by the clayey soil. According to George B. Catlin, eastern Michigan had no good roads until the Plank Road Act was passed in 1848 authorizing the laying of wooden planks over the worst stretches of oozy clay. But the poor roads served their purposes; as Parkins has said: "Along them thousands of settlers passed from Detroit to the interior in search of fertile land. Back along them the farmer kept in touch with the outside world and sent his produce to the market at Detroit."

Most eagerly sought by settlers were the "oak openings" made accessible by the territorial roads. The environment of alternating oak groves and prairies was (and is) typical of much of central Michigan, pre-eminently so in the counties of Calhoun, Kalamazoo, and Cass in the southwest. The first settlers came here in the early 1830's, locating, as others had done in Indiana and Illinois, on the prairie margins. A typical and well-studied example is that of Prairie Ronde in southwestern Kalamazoo County. Here a New England emigrant filed on 720 acres which included mostly prairie land, margined with timber. Characteristically, the home was built in the shelter of a projecting tongue of woods. Other settlers soon followed, eventually establishing the village of Schoolcraft near the center of the "round" prairie.

From an exhaustive study of land entries of Prairie Ronde, George N. Fuller has found that " nearly all the prairie land, amounting to thirteen thousand acres, was taken up before the neighboring timber, except along the margin." A similar process occurred in other Kalamazoo County oak openings: Little Prairie Ronde (settled in 1833); Gourdneck, Goguec, and Dry Prairie (settled 1831–32). It is said that 1,440 acres of Dry Prairie were filed upon by actual settlers in one day, providing good evidence of the popularity of this kind of environment among pioneers.

During the 1830's the population of Michigan and of Detroit increased sevenfold and threefold respectively. In 1837, when Michigan was admitted as a state, internal improvements were proposed on a grand scale. State aid was given for improvements of the Grand and Kalamazoo rivers. Railroad lines were projected, this within ten years of the first important railroad operating in the United States. The " civilizing rails " pushed out from Detroit, often along the old stage lines, reaching Lake Michigan in 1849. With the completion of the Michigan Central to Chicago in 1852, Michigan's modern era may be said to have begun.

Part Four

THE NEW NORTHWEST,
1820–1870

CHAPTER 16

The Upper Lakes Country:
Fur Trade, Mining Industries, and
Forest Exploitation

Dᴇᴛʀᴏɪᴛ, Mackinac, Sault Ste. Marie: these were the places most commonly associated with Michigan during its early Territorial period. Each commanded a narrows in the Upper Lakes system, exercising influence as an emporium of the fur trade and a center of military authority. Detroit soon became something more, but Mackinac and Sault Ste. Marie long remained limited to the functions which had brought them into existence during the French and British regimes. They were old places by the time Easterners came to know much about them through the reports of travelers and explorers. (See Fig. 75.)

The forested empire to which Mackinac and Sault Ste. Marie were gateways was likewise old in terms of human occupancy, but its true character had not become part of American knowledge in 1820. For a century and a half, fur traders had skirted the shores of Lake Superior, stopping at widely spaced trading posts, heading into the many rivers tributary to the lake, and toiling over the portages into the basin of the Mississippi. They were searching not only for fur-bearing animals but also for the friendly Indians who made the pelts commercially valuable. The traders and the voyageurs, and probably also the Indians, knew the country well, but they were not the type who could systematize their knowledge or make it generally available. " No part of the United States is less well known," said the *Cleveland Herald* of March 21, 1820, expressing the general thought of the time. The only corrective for this state of affairs was exploration and map-making by trained individuals acting on their own initiative or under governmental authority.

Official knowledge of this north country, including Michigan's Upper Peninsula and the Lake Superior regions of present-day Wisconsin and Minnesota, was greatly to be desired. Precisely where was the boundary between the United States and the British Possessions? The treaty had referred to the headwaters of the Mississippi as a critical point on this boundary. Where did the " Father of Waters " rise? Fur traders possibly could have told, but it was not until 1832

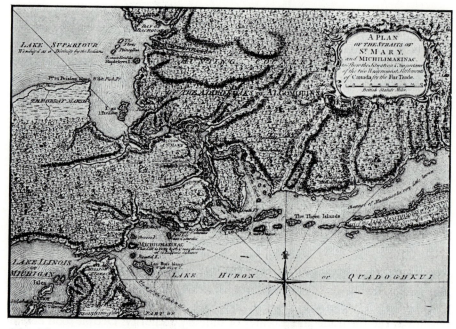

75   The Straits of Mackinac and Sault Ste. Marie as shown on a British map of the
late eighteenth century

that the source of the river was discovered, in the true meaning of this expression.
And, granted that the boundary could be determined, to what extent were British
traders poaching on the fur territory of the United States?

Again, copper was greatly needed for ship fittings by the United States merchant marine. Was there any basis for the vague rumors of the occurrence of the
valuable metal somewhere on the south shore of Lake Superior? This must be
determined forthwith. Also, the Indian nations were showing evidence of
becoming unruly; a display of power and the building of forts should put them
in their proper place. These were just a few of the questions which led to new
expeditions and surveys of the Upper Lakes country in the 1820's. The list of
questions did not contain the usual ones relating to agricultural opportunity.
Everyone agreed that this region lay too far north to permit serious thought
of farming.

Stages of occupancy.   This study begins with the burst of exploration into
the Upper Lakes country of the early 1820's, when fur-trading was still the
dominant activity. But this age-old occupation was soon on the wane, evidenced
by the abandonment of posts even far into the Minnesota area, and climaxed by
the decline of the American Fur Company, chief operator, in the 1840's. A study
of this twenty-year period of fur-trading, the first stage of occupancy, will necessarily involve a large areal coverage, because by its very nature this occupation
was a wide-spreading one. In an industry of many uncertainties this alone was

sure: It would withdraw from older centers into new country, a long jump ahead of permanent settlement.

By the time the Upper Lakes fur trade was in its waning stages Wisconsin and Minnesota had become official Territories, largely through the advance of the agricultural frontier into those portions contiguous to Illinois and Iowa. The boundaries of both Territories were extended northward to the lakes and the international boundary, against the advice of many legislators who held the upper country to be valueless, a burden to be carried by the productive areas.

Mining, the second stage of development, began toward the close of the fur-trade era, but this was largely coincidental. The experience of the fur traders did not contribute to the opening of the first Lake Superior mines, although the reports of individual traders served to keep alive rumors of the occurrence of metals recorded by missionaries before their time. In general, the official policy of fur-trading companies was antagonistic to the development of other occupations which might in the end destroy the industry on which they depended. A study of copper mining and iron mining from the 1840's to 1870 requires a restriction of view to limited areas in northern Michigan. Copper mining was largely confined to the Keweenaw Peninsula, where it began. Iron mining passed through several evolutionary stages during this quarter-century, but remained limited to the Marquette Range, inland from the port city of that name. It was not until the 1880's that the still greater supplies of Minnesota, especially those of the Mesabi Range, came into production.

The period of forest exploitation originated in part as a result of mining, for much lumber was consumed in the making of charcoal for local smelting processes. Later, as the mines went deeper into the earth, quantities of props and timbers were needed. The timber supply seemed endless, even when lumber companies, in Paul Bunyan fashion, were harvesting the crop of the centuries for shipment to distant markets. A study of this third stage of occupancy will require another broad view of the Upper Lakes region and the Northern forest belt. Lumbering advanced from the Atlantic seaboard westward across the Appalachians into northern Wisconsin and Minnesota, where its closing phases were reached toward the end of the century.

THE FUR TRADE

A familiar sign in the window of shop or store on Main Street reads: " Under New Management." Go inside and you will find new decorations and perhaps new equipment, almost certainly a different personnel, but the business carried on is essentially the same.

This analogy is not without merit by way of introduction to the fur trade of the interior Northwest south of the Canadian border from 1820 to the 1840's. Under new management it surely was, because now the American Fur Company of John Jacob Astor was largely in control. The old North West Company, of British origin, merging in 1820 with its former rival the Hudson's Bay

Company, transferred its activities to the northward regions. The North West Company's principal interior establishment, the Grand Portage of Pigeon River (see Chapter 10), was moved to the mouth of the Kamistigua River, where Fort William was built. Other posts not so well known were also abandoned, some of them to be reoccupied by agents of the new American Fur Company with headquarters at Mackinac and in New York City.

The American Fur Company.   The American Fur Company was "big business" in the best American tradition. Fur was its chief stock in trade, but the new management dealt also in minerals, "Indian sugar," products of the fisheries, and real estate; they also manufactured articles exchanged for the peltries, and furnished transportation facilities and mail service. With a regard for diversity of environment and of Indian nations within the interior Northwest, the company divided the whole area into departments. There was, for example, the Fond du Lac Department of the north, inhabited mostly by the Chippewa, and the Western or Sioux Department of Minnesota beyond the Mississippi River. Big and diverse as it was, the departmentalized Northwest was viewed as merely a part of the company's far-flung territory, which extended to the Oregon country. We should adopt a similar view here, realizing that attention is being focused on a small section of a very large picture.

It is also helpful to know that from 1795 to 1822 a chain of government-owned and government-operated stores was established, and included northwest branches at Fort Wayne, Mackinac, Green Bay, Prairie du Chien, and Chicago. The purposes of the "Indian factory system," according to Professor Edgar B. Wesley, were to: (1) strengthen military policy, (2) promote peace on the frontier, (3) offset the influence of British and Spanish traders, and (4) protect the Indians against exploitation by private traders. The last-named purpose was considered a threat by fur companies, which immediately arose to their own defense in a variety of ways. They said, more or less politely, that the Government was stepping out of its field; the fur trade could best be conducted by persons experienced in its many problems. No tears were shed at the American Fur Company's posts in 1822 when the government-store plan was declared to be a failure and was abandoned.

The Indians and the fur trade.   Under the threat of a possible governmental monopoly of the fur business and competition from private companies, such as the XY, and individuals operating on their own behalf, spokesmen for the American Fur Company made many pronouncements from Mackinac. The following (*Detroit Gazette,* December 5, 1820) was one of them: "When the persons engaged in this trade are assembled at Michilimackinac, men can be found acquainted with every foot of the country, and with every influential Indian on this side of the Mississippi, including the heads of that river, the river St. Peters [Minnesota], and the heads of the Wabash and Illinois." Possibly this was true, but Indian chieftains must be reckoned with, and they were sometimes men of temporary influence, their people unpredictable.

It was with families of Indians that the traders or company *engagées* dealt --

not at Mackinac headquarters, or even at Grand Portage of the Fond du Lac, but at remote wintering stations on Minnesota's Leech Lake or far up the Minnesota River at Lac Qui Parle, locked in ice and snow and accessible only by dog sledges or *traineaux de glace*. A wintering station was rarely established near a native village, nor was it expected that Indians would collect around it, except perhaps to deliver their promised furs at the end of the hunting season. Setting up a wintering station in an inhabited area would only result in early extinction of the game on which the trade depended. To understand this strange and primitive business, we must consider the Indian people during the quarter-century of their contact with the white man.

Two linguistic groups, the Chippewa and the Sioux, were the principal Indians with whom the traders dealt in the interior Northwest. Enmity which had originated at an earlier day prevailed between them. The Chippewa, because of their Eastern derivation, were the first to be equipped with firearms, steel hatchets, and other implements of the white man. With their superior weapons, they advanced into Sioux territory and gradually pushed the latter out of the northern forests toward the prairie plains beyond the Mississippi. By the 1820's the Sioux had not become wholly dwellers of the plains, an environment with which American readers now associate them, nor had the Chippewa won all of the northern forested country. A debatable land or buffer zone of varying width, subject to incursions by one or the other, lay between them.

This was the situation in the summer of 1820 when the officially sponsored Cass expedition arrived on the upper Mississippi, and when Fort Snelling or its predecessor was established at the junction of the Minnesota River with the Mississippi. One of the objectives, in fact, of the Cass expedition was to effectuate a peace between the warring tribes. After a brief lull filled with oratory and pledge-making, the Chippewa and the Sioux resumed their forays, even down to the period of pioneer settlement in southern Minnesota, when they found a common enemy among them.

These two tribes could not very well be hunting and trapping animals while engaged in their attempts to kill each other, and results were evident, especially on the border zone of conflict. Upon his return to Detroit, Governor Cass informed Secretary of War John C. Calhoun:

> In this debatable land the game is very abundant. Buffaloes, Elk, & deer range unharmed and unconscious of harm. The mutual hostilities of the Chippeways & Sioux render it dangerous for either, unless in strong parties, to visit this portion of the Country. The consequence of this has been a great increase of all the animals whose flesh is used for food or whose fur is valuable for market. We found herds of Buffalo quietly feeding on the plains. There is little difficulty in approaching sufficiently near to kill them.

The Chippewa of the North. In warrior strength the Chippewa numbered about 1,500, implying a total population of 4,000. Away from the zone of conflict they lived peaceably enough, settled in villages near good fishing on Lake

Superior or at river rapids here and there over the North country. Their principal food was fish, caught in scoop nets or speared at rudely improvised weirs. In 1820 some 50 families lived at the foot of the rapids of the St. Mary's, and there were 5 permanent lodges of 60 Chippewa at the mouth of the Ontonagon. Each group depended on sturgeon, whitefish, and tullibee (called by them *too-nee-bee*), supplemented by wild foods of various sorts. At the Ontonagon a weir was stretched entirely across the river:

> . . . in the lower side seats are constructed on which they [the Indians] may sit with perfect ease, holding in their hands a long pole to which is attached an iron hook, and with this when the fish are dropping against the weir, they make a dexterous and sudden pull which fastens it in the body of the finny prisoner. This manner of taking their food is peculiarly adapted to the indolent habits of an indian, and here they sometimes sit from morning till night, imagining themselves, if we may judge from appearances, the happiest mortals in existence.

Besides part of the fish catch dried for preservation, Indian fare included wild plants and the meat of animals and birds, although the price of powder at a beaver skin for a gill was too high to permit taking much game except in wooden traps. Wild rice was the most prized of the native plant foods. The harvesting of rice was the duty of squaws, two or more of whom would guide a canoe through the shallow margins of lakes where the reedlike plant grew in abundance. While one managed the canoe, the companion would bend the stalks over its side, beating out the grain with short paddles. Rice was prepared for eating either by parching it in a kettle or by drying on a platform built over a slow fire or, more simply, in the sun. Food was also obtained from the bulbous roots of the common arrowhead and from several other common plants of the northern forests. Only the rudest sort of agriculture was practiced by the Chippewa, who sometimes poached upon the gardens at the trading posts.

The Sioux of the South. The Dakota or Sisseton Sioux outnumbered the Chippewa; at least in 1834 there were over 7,000 Sioux within the area of Minnesota and in the part of South Dakota adjacent to Lakes Big Stone and Traverse. They lived very much as the Chippewa did, but with more dependence on agriculture and the products of the chase. Their more southern location permitted the growing of corn, frequently mentioned in exploratory journals of the early 1800's. The Cass expedition, for example, was regaled with home-grown products in a welcoming feast on August 2, 1820, at a Sioux village named Kaposia in what is now South St. Paul. The Sioux explained that they were a poor people, but nevertheless declared a feast day in the main hut, where there were

> . . . four or five fires, over each of which hung a large brass kettle filled with corn; around these fires they danced and sang until the corn was sufficiently boiled, when having made an offering of a small part of it to the Great Spirit, each one filled his wooden bowl, holding probably two gallons, and commenced eating.

The land. When the American Fur Company began its operations, the interior Northwest had been but little altered by the preceding century of fur-

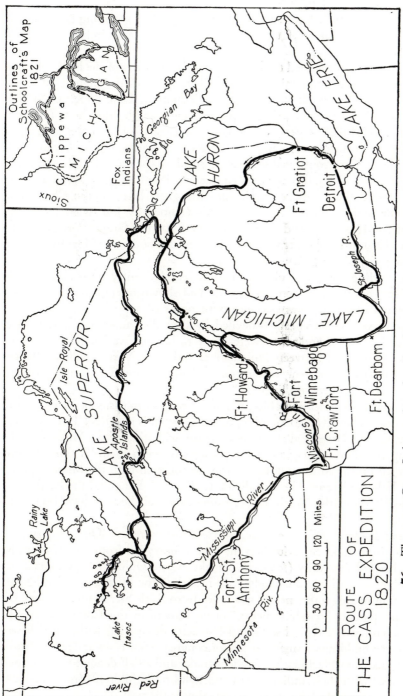

76 The upper Great Lakes region, showing the route of the Cass expedition of 1820.

trading. It was still a forested solitude, interrupted by gleaming lakes and rivers and the tiny clearings of trading posts, stockades, and Indian villages. (See Fig. 76.)

The sea of forest tended to obscure the rough features of the land, which, here and there, rose to mountainous proportions. Some of the highest altitudes lay along the main route of travel — the south shore of Lake Superior. "Cabotian Mountains" was the fantastic group name suggested by Bouchette for the lofty masses of solid rock which rim the Lake Superior basin; but this nomenclature was too artificial for acceptance by the severely practical people who sought a living there. They continued to speak, instead, of the Grand Sable and Pictured Rocks west of Whitefish Bay; of Keweenaw Point and the Porcupine Mountains beyond that long peninsula into the great lake; of the Chequamegon Peninsula and its related Apostle Islands (named by Jonathan Carver in the distant past); of the Fond du Lac of Lake Superior, Grand Portage, Thunder Bay, and hundreds of other features which needed or deserved identifying names. The majority of early names are still in use.

The trading routes. This was hard-to-travel country even along the lake-and-river routes, which long experience had shown offered the least resistance. Voyageurs, straining over portages with packs of supplies and trading goods strapped over the forehead, bedeviled by deer flies and gnats and with deep mud or hard rock underfoot, were likely to become well acquainted with the routes. "The road between Philadelphia and New York," said the American Fur Company, "is scarcely better known than are the different routes which are pursued in the course of this trade."

The general courses and objectives of the routes can easily be stated; to follow them closely, however, a map of topographic detail is required. Two main routes connected the Great Lakes drainage basin with the upper Mississippi River, seeking the shortest height-of-land portages between them. A third communication led up the Minnesota River from its junction with the Mississippi to Big Stone Lake and across the low divide to Traverse Lake and the headwaters of the Red River of the North. Lesser routes in use at the time have been omitted from this discussion.

Grand Portage of Fond du Lac, and Savanna Portage. The principal trading channel from Lake Superior into the back country led from the St. Louis River at the head or extremity (*fond*) of the lake, where Duluth is now located, across the height of land into the Sandy Lake branch of the Mississippi River. Near the beginning of this route, nearly 500 miles from Sault Ste. Marie, was one of the principal posts or "establishments" of the American Fur Company. The Fond du Lac post was a typical station: a few acres of clearing within which were a half-dozen buildings, a small garden for potatoes, a few cows and horses (brought by bateaux from Mackinac), a resident trader and a half-dozen French-Canadian employees with their Indian wives and half-breed children (*bois brulés*). Usually, a few dozen Indians were encamped near the post.

Grand Portage, strictly speaking, consisted of two river portages around diffi-

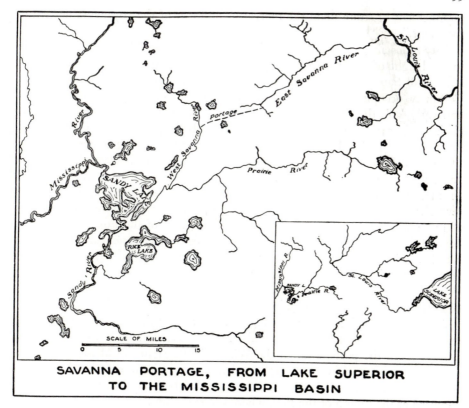

SAVANNA PORTAGE, FROM LAKE SUPERIOR
TO THE MISSISSIPPI BASIN

77 A typical portage of the Upper Lakes fur-trading country: the Savanna Portage
from the St. Louis River, flowing into Lake Superior at Duluth, to the Sandy
Lake source of the Mississippi. Adapted from Irving H. Hart, *Minnesota
History*, 1927.

cult stretches in the St. Louis River. The Grand Portage route, however, was
more than this, for its objective was the upper Mississippi River by way of the
Sandy Lake source, the West Savanna, which rises near a small affluent of the
St. Louis. Hence, the route involved the passage of two rapids on the St. Louis
in addition to the portage across the divide. (See Fig. 77.)

Going upstream from the Fond du Lac post, the first portage led around 8
miles of swift and shallow water through which laden canoes could not safely
pass. In the traders' measure of distance, the length of this portage was nineteen
" pauses " — that is, resting places spaced at quarter- or half-mile intervals. The
ancient practice was still followed in the 1820's: The voyageurs would deposit
their loads at the nearest pause, then return to the starting point for a new load,
and so on.

Four miles beyond the first stream interruption, traders came to another called
Knife Portage. Here was a ledge of slate lying in perpendicular strata resembling,
said one explorer, " the leaves of a book standing edgewise. The effect of this

arrangement of strata upon the moccasins and feet of the voyageurs has led to the name."

Sixty miles above Knife Portage the traders' route ascended the East Savanna to the height of land; then came 7 miles of portage to the West Savanna, an affluent of Sandy Lake. Here was another principal post of the American Fur Company, occupied still earlier by the North West Company. During the 1820's and early '30's the Sandy Lake post was serving mainly as a rendezvous for clerks and agents on the move between the Mississippi and the Great Lakes, having gradually lost its former significance as a fur-collecting center.

The Fox-Wisconsin Route. Early-day communications between Lake Michigan and the Mississippi were much easier, by comparison with the foregoing. From Green Bay the route led into the Fox River, whose various rapids required several portages or half-portages (see page 176) before reaching the broad surface of Lake Winnebago. The portage between the head of the Fox and the great bend of the Wisconsin River was little over a mile; in fact, canoes and small boats could occasionally, at times of high water, pass uninterruptedly from one drainage basin to the other. In the 1820's the site of the portage was occupied by a Winnebago Indian village, and soon thereafter by Fort Winnebago; now the city of Portage stands there. The map on page 317 shows most of the route.

A small connecting ditch was dug as early as 1766; the prediction of many explorers that a canal would eventually replace it came true in the 1850's. The passage from the portage down the Wisconsin River to the Mississippi, a distance of nearly 170 miles, met with moderate difficulties in occasional shallows, sandbars, and partly sunken logs. Forts guarded both ends of this route: Fort Howard at the mouth of the Fox, whose site is within the present city of Green Bay, and Fort Crawford at Prairie du Chien. The new and the old were combined at Prairie du Chien: the town itself, settled by French people, was a century old when Fort Crawford was erected in 1816. The fort, it was said, " is handsomely built, and is the only ornament to the place."

From the Minnesota to the Red River of the North. Traders and explorers were led to the West and the Northwest by way of the Minnesota River, which rises in Big Stone Lake very close to the Lake Traverse head of the Red River of the North. Because its native life had been but little disturbed by man, the region along this route was of particular interest to fur traders during this period. Here were the natural habitats of bison, deer, beaver, otter, and many other animals furnishing valuable pelts.

The Federal Government also was concerned with the upper Minnesota and Red River country. Available accounts and rumors were contradictory, some picturing it as a worthless desert and others as a wonderfully productive land. Furthermore, the position of the international boundary awaited solution. Here was a proper field of action for an official exploring party, mentioned in earlier chapters as the Stephen H. Long expedition of 1823. The party included a full complement of scientists, interpreters, and soldiers as well as an Italian adventurer, Giacomo Constantino Beltrami, whose somewhat theatrical activities have inspired many writings. Before the Long expedition had reached its objective, Beltrami detached himself from the party in a personal endeavor to find the source of the Mississippi River. In this he was unsuccessful, not particularly to his discredit considering the extremely involved drainage pattern of the upper basin. Beltrami's explorations are suitably commemorated in the name of a Minnesota county.

There were several establishments, or permanent trading posts, on the Minnesota-Red River route. At the mouth of the Minnesota River was Mendota, near Fort Snelling; farther upstream were Traverse des Sioux and Lac Qui Parle; near the international boundary was Pembina.

Operations of the fur trade. For a full view of the fur trade of the second quarter of the past century we must return in imagination from Pembina and other remote stations to Mackinac, headquarters and main distributing center of the American Fur Company.

The name Mackinac (shorn of its prefix "Michili," much to the satisfaction of map makers cramped for lettering space) applied specifically to the island located 4 miles from the mainland, but in a general sense identified also the straits and the settlements on both sides of them. Mackinac, the island, then contained a village at its principal harbor, and also two forts: Mackinac and Holmes, both built by the British, the former in 1780 and the latter in 1812. Further evidence of the strategic significance of the straits was to be seen in the ruins of a still earlier fort on the southern mainland, the defense work of Robert Rogers. This has been restored within recent years and is a point of interest to visitors to Mackinaw City, which is nearly opposite the island.

The village on the island of Mackinac was busiest in summer, when company employees assembled from the length and breadth of the fur country. At that time the traders secured goods of the kinds that would appeal to the Indians of their district — thread, needles, beads, firearms, canned meats, clothes, common tools — and in sufficient quantities to see them through the year. Goods destined for remote stations left Mackinac as early as June; other goods intended for the nearer stations were sent later. Large boats (bateaux) transported the packaged goods to stations on Lake Superior, but the trading canoe, capable of being portaged, was used on the river routes. Main establishments, such as Fond du Lac, Sandy Lake, and Mendota, served as supply depots for the less permanent interior or wintering stations.

As in earlier days, winter was the season for seeking the finer furs, and it was also a time of activity for the agent. "Runners" were periodically sent out from post and wintering station to collect the furs that had accumulated and to replenish the supplies of the Indians. The dog sledge saw good service during this period. Continuing contact between trader and hunter was highly recommended by headquarters; for, they said, "By these means the Indians are not obliged to assemble from great distances and to remain lounging about the posts, with the usual improvidence of savages and often with the necessity of losing their winter's hunt."

It was estimated that during the fall and winter a hunter would collect a pack of peltry worth from $80 to $100 at Mackinac prices. The traders, of course, sought to purchase the catch at the lowest possible price. According to a narrator of the Cass expedition:

> All the goods are sold and reckoned by skins; a [beaver?] skin is estimated at $2. A blanket is sold by 4 to 6 skins . . . a knife 1 skin, 1 fathom of Twist tobacco 2 skins . . . a hatchet 1 skin. . . . If an indian obtains credit for these articles, he expects to be furnished gratis with a flint, needle, aul, gun worm, rings, tobacco, and a little vermilion; and in a credit of 600 skins, the trader considers himself recompensed (because he is obliged to do so) if he receives 300 in return.

Many traders, as the above implies, sought to keep the Indian hunter in debt, with the expectation that furs would be delivered over a long period to satisfy the indebtedness.

The furs collected during the winter at interior stations were brought to the main posts, where they were prepared for transportation to Mackinac, generally reaching the island in June. The trader then settled his account with headquarters, and indulged in some recreation at this outpost of civilization. " New agreements are formed or the old one renewed," it was said, " and the importer of goods and the collector of furs part to pursue their respective vocations, and to meet upon the same spot during the ensuing year."

Decline of the fur trade. The fur trade declined gradually, but not at the same rate or time throughout the entire region. Generally speaking, the decline spread from east to west, the industry remaining active longer in western Minnesota than in Wisconsin. As late as 1835, according to Professor Theodore Blegen, the Mendota post handled the peltries of 391,500 muskrats and muskrat " kittens," 3,230 minks, 3,200 deer, 2,000 raccoons, more than 1,000 otters and buffaloes, and hundreds of bears, fishers, martens, and foxes.

The decline of the industry was inevitable. When the Indians ceded their lands to the United States, they usually received in return annuity payments; these payments, though not large by modern standards, were sufficient to encourage them to neglect work so difficult and regular as hunting and trapping. Other more fundamental factors are suggested by Henry H. Sibley, agent for the American Fur Company at Mendota. Writing in 1842 under the pseudonym "Hal — A Dacotah," he states: " A residence of twelve years on the west side of the Mississippi, during which time I have made many hunting excursions, has satisfied me that the larger animals are fast disappearing, and will soon be exterminated." A few years before, " Elk and Buffalo were to be found by hundreds and by thousands," but " the hunter may now roam for days together without encountering a single herd." The improvident killing of the young, the slaughter of many times the number of animals that were needed, the impairment of natural habitats — these were basic causes for the gradual disappearance of the fur trade from the Upper Lakes region.

THE MINING INDUSTRY

The occurrence of minerals in the Lake Superior region had been suspected long before mining began in the middle 1840's. Jesuit missionaries in the seventeenth century stated that the Indians used copper for ornamental purposes and that the metal was derived from local deposits somewhere in the North country. Various explorers in succession reported that they had found copper and knew the location of the "mines" — by which term, as has been noted, they meant mineral deposits rather than actual producing areas. A certain vagueness, perhaps not unintended, accompanied these early reports until the 1760's, when a mining company actually mined copper, though without commercial success.

Following this first, and historically unimportant, venture in Lake Superior mining, the region became more productive of rumors about minerals than of minerals themselves. This is not altogether surprising; for it was a likely rumor factory, with its great areas of solid rock outcroppings and exposed mineral veins of a sort commonly found in mountainous regions (of which this was one in past geological times). For eighty years these stories circulated, altering, as such reports are apt to do, as they passed from one person to another. Gold and silver became part of the legendary tales about Lake Superior wealth, but nothing so commonplace as iron seems to have stirred public interest.

Ontonagon copper: " A mineralogical curiosity." Interest of the Federal Government in finding domestic supplies of copper led to the first authentic account of this mineral near Lake Superior, but not directly to the commercial production of it.

The Cass expedition of 1820 was instructed, among other duties, to examine a copper deposit which was then reported to lie on the upper Ontonagon River. " I anticipate no difficulty in reaching this spot," said Cass, " and it may be highly important to the Government to divide this mass and to transport it to the sea board for naval purposes." Arriving at the mouth of the Ontonagon late in June, the scientific staff toiled upriver for 30 miles and found a rock mass of serpentine veined with pure, malleable copper — something of a disappointment, however, because advance information had pictured a pure metallic mass. A brief reconnaissance of the surrounding area revealed no deposits of similar character. " Thus ended all the marvellous stories we have heard about the copper mines of Lake Superior, which some had gone so far as to represent inexhaustible," wrote Charles C. Trowbridge, a diarist of the expedition.

But the " marvellous stories " were not entirely ended for those who were soon reading the narrative of Henry Schoolcraft, the party's mineralogist, whose enthusiasm surpassed his technical knowledge. The copper rock had been much diminished in size since its first discovery, he and others said, as evidenced in chippings and old chisels scattered about, but nevertheless " it may still be considered one of the largest and most remarkable bodies of native copper on the globe." On more sober thought, Governor Cass informed the Secretary of War that " common report has greatly magnified the quantity, although enough remains, even under rigid examination, to render it a mineralogical curiosity." The importance of this discovery, despite the initial disappointment that accompanied it, should not be overlooked. It was conclusive proof of the occurrence not merely of copper, but of copper in its native form, showing where Indians had secured some of their supplies.

Keweenaw copper: The beginning of mining.   Interestingly enough, the Cass party on its way to the Ontonagon had passed within a short distance of the now famous copper deposits of the Upper Peninsula.

Jutting out from the mainland is Keweenaw Point, about 100 miles long, an annoying detour in a shore passage from Sault Ste. Marie to western points on the lake. To go around it was not only time-consuming, but was definitely dangerous for small, heavily laden trading canoes and bateaux. The lake is not one to be trifled with at any time, with its choppy, cold waters easily whipped by sudden storms into waves much like those of the ocean. However, near the base of Keweenaw Point Nature had conveniently arranged a water route known as Portage Lake and Portage River, by which traders were able to cross the point and thus avoid the many miles of its rough shore line. The route is now an excavated channel, with Houghton, Hancock, and other centers of population clustered near it. This was the locality where copper mining developed when knowledge of the deposit became available. The first systematic study of this mineralized area was made by Dr. Douglass Houghton, who lost his life by drowning near the scene of his important scientific work, shortly after his principal report was issued.

The first actual mining of Keweenaw copper was in 1844, when a few tons of oxide ore (not native copper) were produced. For many years after the opening of the pioneer Cliff mine in 1845 the tonnage yield was very small; nevertheless it represented the greater part of the copper mined in the United States, as indicated in the following table.

ANNUAL PRODUCTION, LAKE SUPERIOR COPPER DISTRICT

(Compared with annual production of the United States, 1850–1870, and 1919 for comparison)

	U.S. Long Tons	Michigan Long Tons	Percentage of Total Production
1850	650	572	88
1855	3,000	2,593	86
1860	7,200	5,388	74
1865	8,500	6,410	75
1870	12,600	10,992	87
1919	493,705	99,545	20

The Michigan mines regularly occupied first position in American production until 1887, when they were surpassed by those of Butte, Montana. The annually increasing output was made possible by the opening of new mines and by extensions in depth. At the present time the mines of Michigan are among the deepest in the country.

The development of the Keweenaw mines led to renewed searches for minerals in other Lake Superior areas. On Isle Royale, for example, copper mining started soon after the opening of the Cliff mine, with increasing production up to 1855. The island's resident population was small and the activity drew but few newcomers, with the result that Isle Royale mining has since been of an intermittent character. In general, however, copper mining has attracted large numbers of people to the Upper Lakes country and has encouraged developments along other lines.

Iron mining in the Marquette Range. During the 1840's various exploring parties, some with official connections and others "on their own," were scouring the North country for hidden mineral wealth. A company of explorers from Jackson, Michigan, searching the Upper Peninsula for copper, gold, and silver, encountered an Indian half-breed at Sault Ste. Marie who volunteered to guide them to a deposit of iron ore. This search proved unfruitful, but soon thereafter an Indian chief directed the party to the actual site.

The outcropping of iron ore was on a wooded hill, apparently no different from many in its vicinity, where the mining town of Negaunee is now located. It was a claim and a hope in 1845, this slope named Jackson Hill, but no white people lived in the vicinity. There was no Ishpeming, now adjoining Negaunee, nor was there a Marquette on the lake shore, although explorers had predicted that a town would surely be located there at some future time. Like all the country roundabout, it was green in the brief, cool summer and white with snow in the frigid winter when Presque Isle Bay was locked in ice. Sleds drawn by horses provided the best means of transportation over the rough country and down the slope of the Lake Superior escarpment a dozen miles away. It is important to remember, too, that there was no Soo Canal providing access to the other lakes when Negaunee was laid out as a claim.

With these factors of site and situation in mind, and also knowing that the Marquette Range is still productive of iron ore, we may consider its first quarter-century of development. Professor J. R. Whitaker refers to this period as the beginning of the "open-pit sequence." That is, iron mining here began with the stripping of near-surface deposits, a kind of mining which dominated the area until 1885, when shaft mining at depth became more common. The "open-pit sequence" passed through three stages: (1) infancy, 1846–55; (2) youth, 1855–70; and (3) maturity, 1870–85.

Open-Pit Mining; from Infancy to 1855. The first mines in this area were scarcely more than shallow quarries opened in the ores, which were close to the surface. As a result of the ice scour from continental glaciation in past ages, there was little "overburden" or mantle rock in the Marquette Range. The ore was pried loose with hand implements and crushed with ordinary sledges, then shoveled into carts or sleds for shipment. Production from these open pits would doubtless have been greater than it was, even with such primitive methods, had there been an adequate market.

The principal market for the ore was, in fact, Negaunee itself and other centers which developed near by. Forges appeared, using charcoal prepared from the locally abundant hardwoods. But the experience of a few years showed that the product of the forges, called blooms, could not be profitably exported. " The movement of machinery, supplies, and men into the area, and the assembly of the ore and charcoal, and the export of the blooms — all met the handicaps of costly transportation," says Professor Whitaker.

Small quantities of ore were taken by slow-moving sleds to the lake shore, there to await the opening of summer navigation. Upon arrival of a boat headed for Sault Ste. Marie the ore was trundled into the hold with wheelbarrows. Reaching the Soo, the ore was unloaded, carted around the rapids, and then reloaded for passing down the lakes to Ohio ports. Only a few hundred tons of ore could be shipped out in this slow and costly manner during the season of navigation. Notwithstanding all these difficulties, the Marquette mines survived until developments brought them into closer contact with the outside world.

Open-Pit Mining; Youth, 1855–70. During the next fifteen years the Marquette mining district experienced its greatest period of expansion. Most important to the mines of the Upper Peninsula, and to others later to be developed in Wisconsin and Minnesota, was the opening of a safe channel of communication through the rapids of the St. Mary's River. This stream gains its rare natural beauty, along with a natural barrier to travel, from a descent of 25 feet in ½ mile over a ledge of red sandstone. For large boats in precanal days this was an unavoidable break in transportation, and even trading canoes had to be unloaded before proceeding in either direction. Although Michigan's early schemes for internal improvements (see Chapter 15) included a proposal for a Soo Canal, little was accomplished during the Territorial period beyond surveying and paper work. From the 1840's on there was much agitation for a canal, at first as an aid to the fisheries and then in the interests of the growing mineral industries of Marquette and Keweenaw Point. Congress granted the requested aid in 1852, and in the summer of 1855 the new channel and locks were in operation. Since that time they have been much changed, enlarged, and even multiplied.

The completion of the first Soo Canal was a great triumph that immediately found reflection in the mining industry. The beneficial effect of the canal was magnified by two other improvements in transportation closer to Marquette: a new plank-surfaced road from Ishpeming and Negaunee to the port, and soon thereafter the first railroad in the mining country. The plank road was intended to be nothing more than its name implied — a highway surfaced with planks; but it was completed as a tramway for the passage of mule-drawn ore cars from the mines to newly constructed docks at Marquette. Wooden rails, protected by strips of steel, permitted the passage of heavily laden ore cars at a rate that was then considered very rapid.

The tramway had hardly been given a fair trial before the first railroad reached the mines in 1857. This new conquest over distance immediately resulted in a great saving in the cost of transportation. After the railroad was in operation, ore could be shipped from Negaunee to Marquette at less than one-third of its former cost. A further improvement was registered in 1857 when the leading mining company provided a dock with ore pockets into which ore could be dumped to be held until ready for filling by gravity the holds of waiting vessels.

This period of youth in mining development also encompassed the period of the War between the States, with its new demands for steel and more steel at almost any cost. The Marquette mines were ready to supply some of the needs of the Northern states, just as in the recent world conflict the Lake Superior mines sent millions of tons of ore through the Soo canals for war industries.

The vigor of youth was evident in the Marquette mining district in various ways: in the growth of small villages to substantial cities of 3,000 or 4,000 persons; in the continual enlargement and deepening of existing pits and the opening of new ones; and in the development of industries related to mining. It was no doubt evident, if less tangibly so, in the spirit and outlook of the people. Open-pit methods remained dominant, although in some cases as many as 40 feet of overburden and an equal thickness of rock were removed to get at the ore. This suggests that the people were delaying the inevitable underground methods of mining as long as possible in order to reap the advantages of open-pit mining.

Two main advantages pertained to open-pit methods: (1) a saving in skilled labor, because much of the work could be done by contractors with ordinary excavating equipment, and (2) the avoidance of large investments in shafts, timbering, and ventilation. Nevertheless there were some difficulties. Occasionally, piles of waste rock which had been stripped from an ore body had to be moved, perhaps more than once, to uncover underlying ore. In winter the falling and drifting snow, caught in the open pits, tended to slow up mining operations. But this was not too serious, because rail service to Marquette was sometimes interrupted by the same conditions. As late as 1864 the line ceased operations at the first snowfall, and the lake route to distant markets was closed.

Not all the ore was sent down the lakes to Eastern steel centers. It was found that blast furnaces using local charcoal were profitable now that cheaper transportation was available. In 1860 there were 10 furnaces in Marquette County, one of which, in a typical year, consumed the timber from at least 1,500 acres of land. The clearing of land to feed the furnaces near town sometimes resulted in the discovery of new ore bodies and provided clearings for farming, but furnaces remote from settlement " simply converted virgin forest into cut-over."

Later Stages in the Marquette Mining Industry. After the climax of the youthful period of open-pit mining about 1870, the output from new mines " did little more than offset the decline of production from the older ones." This was a period of stability, when the mining cities grew but little and output remained on a level. The miners had to go deeper into the earth by means of shafts. At first, the attack on the new supplies led to increased output; then, following 1910, evidences of decline appeared. Shaft mining required the services of skillful and willing underground workers, some of whom were immigrants from Cornwall, England, where mining was an old and declining industry. The new kind of mining also brought increased demands upon the forest.

EXPLOITATION OF THE FORESTS

The industries of the Upper Lakes region were all dependent on the forest cover, but in opposite ways. To the fur trader, the preservation of natural habitats was vital; even an apparently slight alteration of ground cover might upset the delicate balance of nature and lead to the extinction of game. To the miner, the forest cover was at first an encumbrance on the land, hiding mineral vein and surface deposit, or at least making them difficult to retrieve. When mining passed its experimental period, however, the forests served as a source of logs for buildings and for charcoal; with the development of shaft mining, timber was required in great quantities for mine props.

With the extension of surface mining and the penetration of mines in depth, and with increasing demands for charcoal, the clearings advanced into the forest around the mining towns. Some of this land was useful for farming; most of it was not, being stony, sandy, or poorly drained. In any case, the short summer of the Northland made difficult a well-rounded farm economy. Thus there developed a widening zone of cutover land between the mining towns and the untouched forest a few miles beyond.

Demands for lumber in the mining industry were slight compared to the increasing markets in the agricultural regions, both of the continental interior and of the Eastern states. By 1860, the commercial lumber industry was rapidly advancing westward from its original base in Maine and Maritime Canada. Many of the lumberjacks, swampers, camp crews, and overseers also drifted westward with the lumber camps. The 1870's were the heyday of lumbering in northern Wisconsin, while in Minnesota that period came a decade or two later. By the turn of the century, forest resources were fairly well exhausted.

The extent of the Northern forests. The interior advance of the lumber industry becomes more understandable when the continuity of the Northern forests is appreciated. Figure 78 shows the vegetation areas of North America according to the best information available in 1860. The map, one of the first issued by the United States Department of Agriculture, compares favorably with modern maps of similar content and scale. A different nomenclature is used, but the regions are easily identifiable.

Chiefly to be noted here is the Northern forested belt, extending inland from the Eastern seaboard and narrowing to a point at the Red River of the North. This is the " Canadian " section of the Lacustrian (lake) Province; the unforested region to the west and south was then known as the Campestrian (plains) Province.

The " Canadian " forest of mixed hardwoods and conifers was rich in valuable timber. Generally speaking, the white pine, most prized of all its species, was

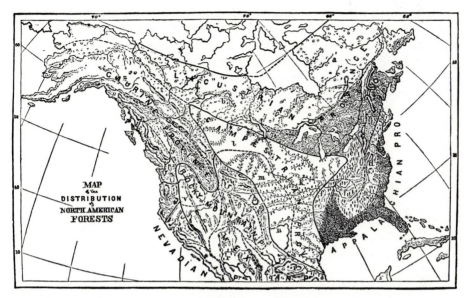

78 Vegetation regions of North America as mapped in 1860. *From Report of the Commissioner of Patents* (Executive Doc. 48, 36th Congress, 2d Session).

associated with the less well-drained but not swampy areas; the red pine of Wisconsin and Minnesota was found in higher and stonier land. Red pine became popularly known as Norway pine, one explanation being that many of the first lumberjacks came from Norway, Maine. Hardwoods mixed with conifers occupied the well-drained soils. These mixed stands included sugar maple, yellow birch, and basswood, to name the more valuable species. Aspens and oaks were also typical, the former especially advancing quickly into the cutover areas left in the wake of the sawmills. "For almost half a century," says Professor Guy-Harold Smith, "the pioneer woodsmen extended their salients up the rivers and later along the railroads until the primeval forest was separated into isolated areas of unconquered pine."

The methods of the Upper Lakes lumber industry need no lengthy discussion. Very little of the timber was finished in the area of production, the trimmed logs being sent down the streams, when streams were available, to sawmills nearer the markets. It has been said that the rivers not only drained the land, but also drained the forests into the growing population centers to the south. The St. Croix River, for example, served as a main channel for log transportation from the forests of northwestern Wisconsin and a part of adjacent Minnesota. St. Croix Falls, Wisconsin, and Stillwater, Minnesota, were early lumber towns. On the Mississippi, the Twin Cities with water power available at the Falls of St. Anthony became lumber-manufacturing centers.

The story of the wasteful methods used by the lumber industry in that period is too well known to require repetition. A cutover tract was a sorry sight, particularly so after a destructive fire, often the concluding stage of its ruin. A famous example is the Peshtigo, Wisconsin, forest fire in the fall of 1871, a dry season, when 1,280,000 acres were burned and about 1,500 human lives were lost. The deforested areas were less valuable for farm land than were the cutover lands in the southern hardwood regions. The northern cutover was a frontier of agricultural settlement that has persisted into modern times.

CHAPTER 17

From Mining to Farming in Southern Wisconsin

"THE Bright Land" it was called, by a novelist who told of the coming of people to the lead-mining region centering upon Galena, Illinois, and spreading into the adjacent corners of Iowa and Wisconsin. In the 1820's, this was a new land to the westward-moving settlers, attracted here by plentiful deposits of lead ore. After a quarter-century or more of mining, the more easily won ore was exhausted, but not before settlement had become firmly established. Many of the people then departed for more promising mining districts, but a greater number remained, and still others came from the East. Their main activity turned from mining to agriculture; instead of "raising lead," it has been said, they raised wheat and other crops, for this mining area, unlike many others, was potential farming country.

Thus settlement spread from original centers such as Galena, and Dubuque, Iowa, northward into the Wisconsin area, where scattered deposits of lead ore formed the original attraction. This was before the name Wisconsin had political identity, for the Territory was not organized until 1836; twelve years later the state was formed, the seventeenth to be admitted into the Union. In southwest Wisconsin, as in near-by Illinois, the lead veins played out and their richer veins were early mined out, but this too was good farming land. Still better for farming, after the Indians were eliminated in the early 1830's, was that part of Wisconsin east of the lead region. Into this rolling prairie-woodland region came the advancing wave of emigration pushing up from Illinois — not a mining people, but land-seekers, many of them recent arrivals from western Europe. By the time Wisconsin reached statehood in 1848 a "thin film of population" had spread over all of Wisconsin from Lake Michigan westward to the Fox-Wisconsin portage route. This was the beginning of the "New Northwest" of the 1840's; later, in the popular mind, this regional term included all of Minnesota.

Such, in brief, is the story of Wisconsin's early years of development — not a particularly dramatic story, but one needing careful attention. First to be considered is the lead-mining region, sometimes called the Tristate Mining District, for Illinois, Iowa, and Wisconsin share in it. Remember, however, that during the beginning phases of active mining Illinois alone of the three was a state. To the west was "unorganized territory," a part of the Louisiana Purchase, and to the north was a portion of Michigan Territory from which Wisconsin was to be carved.

LEAD MINING

Early lead mining. References to the lead region of the upper Mississippi Basin appear at a remarkably early time. By 1690 at least, French fur traders brought lead to various interior posts, some of it from eastern Iowa and some from Missouri. The metal was probably secured from the Indians, who had learned the relatively simple method of separating the lead from its ore by heating the ore under fires of brush and timber. Throughout the eighteenth century small amounts of lead came out of this region, the traders competing among themselves for the Indian-made product.

By 1800 the chief figure in the lead business of the upper Mississippi Basin was a Frenchman, one Julien Dubuque, for whom the present city is named. Dubuque had acquired a proprietary estate on the western bank of the Mississippi River, a type of holding unusual in Midwestern history, by purchasing from the Fox Indians a large block of land which enclosed some of the richer ores. The estate extended for over 20 miles north and south between the mouths of the Little Maquoketa and Têtes des Morts rivers, with an inland depth of about 10 miles. On the estate were numerous "Indian diggings," perhaps as many as 50 of which were deep enough to be called pits. Most of the diggings were near the mouth of the Têtes des Morts, convenient to transportation on the Mississippi River.

The death of Julien Dubuque marked the end of this phase of lead mining. Resentment among the Indians, built up during the despotic regime of their former master, found immediate release in home-burning and general destruction. But the hostility of the Indians was not wholly centered upon Dubuque, nor was it expended in one outburst. By various acts they let it be known that white settlement in their land was unwelcome. When Schoolcraft visited the Dubuque-Galena mines in 1820 he commented upon the sullen attitude of the Foxes who were disposing of their lead to agents of the American Fur Company or to other traders. Their economic position was little advanced by exchanging lead in baskets holding 120 pounds for $2 worth of trading goods.

The surface occurrence of the lead ore and its wide scattering over the country were well suited to the improvident habits of the Indians. "Few persons are so industrious as to dig deep into the earth," said a visitor in 1820, "rather choosing to abandon the digging when it becomes laborious, thereby losing perhaps the richest fruits of their perseverance." The Indians were in constant search of new and easy diggings, and also obtained lead in the ash heaps of earlier smelting pits.

The Fever River mines at Galena. Active mining of lead ore by American settlers began in the 1820's, not on the Iowa side of the river but on the Fever

River of northwestern Illinois. Here Galena came into being, a name significant in itself, being a technical word for the lead-sulphide ore typical of this region. The ore occurred within 50 feet of the surface, some of it literally on the surface, in vertical crevices well above the water table. The rock formation of greatest occurrence in this locality has become known to geologists as the Galena dolomite. Characteristically, the veins were in groups, not difficult to find by the incoming mining people. Rule-of-thumb methods, such as distinguishing rock colors, were followed by miners in their prospecting for new ore. The sites of earlier Indian diggings, and loose pieces or " float " strewn on the surface, also served as clues to deposits.

Galena soon became the principal trading town in the upper Mississippi Basin. It served as the main gateway to the mining region and, when mining activity had passed its peak, to the farming country farther upstream. Galena was also a supply center and the main shipping point for lead. To understand Galena's hold upon navigation it must be realized that the Fever River, a tributary of the Mississippi, was navigable for commercial boats a century ago; today it is a shallow, insignificant stream scarcely 100 feet wide. Deposits in the stream channel resulting from abnormal erosion in the rough, hilly country of its basin have been the principal cause of this change.

The first river steamer arrived at Galena in 1822, and five years later a regular line was in operation to St. Louis. In 1829, when the Fever River population had shot up to nearly 10,000, there were close to 100 steamboat arrivals at Galena, some boats, of course, making three or four calls during the open season. River navigation was not without its difficulties, however. The annual peak of lead production was reached in late summer, when the river was at its lowest stage and the rapids above Rock Island, Illinois, were difficult to pass except by small boats. Nevertheless, as many as 5,000 tons of lead were annually shipped downstream from Galena during the 1830's.

Mining and smelting methods. The mines at Galena and in the surrounding territory were of the vertical-shaft type, rarely more than 40 feet deep. Early mining processes thus were exceedingly simple in comparison with those of other regions. As the test pits deepened into mines, the ore could be pried from the enclosing rock with ordinary tools and raised to the surface by hand-operated windlasses. The openings seldom extended beneath the water table in the early days, because the galena was largely confined to the water-free zone. It was not until the 1860's that the zinc blende or " jack " beneath the water table was mined to satisfy new market demands.

As the Indians had shown, recovery of the lead from the ore involved no great difficulty. In fact, the first furnaces were patterned after the aboriginal methods. The ore was simply piled on a log fire, and the melted lead filtered to the bottom, where it was collected the next day. An improved method introduced about 1820 made use of a hopperlike pit, in the bottom of which flat stones served as a grate. Leading from the bottom of the pit to the side hill was a small trench which directed the flow of molten lead into bowl-shaped excavations, where the metal solidified into 70-pound pigs or "plats." Wood or logs, easily secured locally, were used for fuel. In the 1860's a still more efficient blast furnace, adapted from similar types in England, came into use. This, the Scotch hearth furnace, consisted of a tall chimney with an oven beneath, into which a blast was directed by mechanically operated bellows. These more elaborate furnaces were usually located near streams, which furnished the power to operate the bellows, as well as the means of transporting the heavy pigs.

Extension of lead mining into Wisconsin. It was in 1823 that the first lead mines were opened in the Wisconsin area, a natural extension of the same activity in Illinois. The wide diffusion of the surface deposits invited prospecting by those who had become familiar with this industry either in the Galena district or in the more distant Missouri mines. The early miners, therefore, were a rather homogeneous group, deriving from southern localities of the region. As the mining fever spread, however, adventurers arrived from distant places, adding variety to the population. Irish and Welsh immigrants predominated in the late 1820's, and the next decade saw an influx of Cornishmen. The gradual exhaustion of the mines in Cornwall was thus reflected in the lead diggings of southwest Wisconsin. Mining towns quickly took form, some of them to last only a few years.

Among the more important places originating in this period were Mineral Point (for many years the largest Wisconsin city), Dodgeville, and Platteville (Fig. 79). Others, such as Old Helena and Paris, disappeared within a few years. So rapidly did the lead country fill up that influential political leaders considered it the most suitable region for the capital when Wisconsin should achieve statehood. The village of Belmont, now Leslie, was in fact chosen as the capital, and a building was constructed for legislative purposes. Only one session was

79

Location map of southern Wisconsin and the lead region

held in it, however; settlement had already spread so far into southeastern Wisconsin that centrally located Madison was the ultimate choice for the seat of government.

Decline of Wisconsin lead mining.   Scarcely a quarter-century intervened between the opening of the first lead mines in Wisconsin and the peak year of production, 1845. In that year, lead metal to the amount of some 25,000 tons was made in the upper Mississippi Basin. It may be observed for comparison that in the same year the iron deposits of upper Michigan had only recently been opened up.

Evidences of decline in lead mining were apparent by 1847, with dwindling output of the mines and a general drift of miners to other localities. It is estimated that nearly one-half of the mining population of this area joined the trek to the California gold mines in 1848; other mining districts also lured people away. Some miners found they could make a better living by farming, or by combining part-time work in the mines with agriculture. The railroads were pushing out into the Midwest, offering comparatively high wages for labor in laying the tracks. It was at this time, also, that tariffs on lead imports were reduced, lowering the market value of the product at a time when costs of production were mounting.

The fundamental reason for the decline in lead mining was, of course, the exhaustion of the richer and more accessible ore. Shallow deposits, even though widely distributed, could not last very long. With depth, two difficulties were encountered: (1) infiltration of water when the mines reached the water table, and (2) an increased mixture of zinc in the ore. Expensive pumping equipment was necessary to counteract water seepages, and new methods were required to separate the zinc blende from the galena. Until the 1860's there was little market for zinc, but with the exhaustion of the richer lead ores, zinc became the chief product. Zinc smelters began operations at this time, the first one being erected at La Salle, Illinois, soon followed by another at Mineral Point, Wisconsin. Most of the zinc mines, according to Professor William O. Blanchard, were further developments in depth of old lead-mine shafts.

THE DEVELOPMENT OF AGRICULTURE

To understand the slow development of agriculture in the lead region we must return in thought to the earlier years of mining settlement. It was then that the profits from mining were most certain, for the deposits of ore were widespread, and its recovery involved no great expenditure of capital. The possibility of finding an unusually productive vein was a temptation to scour the country for its hidden wealth. Regional opportunities were thought to begin and end with mining, thus attracting a people with little experience or interest in other occupations.

The United States Government, adopting here an unusual policy, ruled that the mineral deposits were Federal property subject to a leasing system. Lands were not sold directly to individuals, hence the frequent references to the " public mines " in early reports. The leasing system, possibly good in theory, led to much confusion and uncertainty because of incomplete knowledge of the location and the extent of ore bodies. The system also encouraged a somewhat aimless drifting of miners from one prospect or partially worked " diggings " to others. " They are constantly changing from one place to another," complained an official report to the Congress in 1826, twenty years after the leasing system was put into effect.

The government leasing system virtually prohibited agriculture in the lead region. The standard claim for an individual was a mere strip 300 yards in width, although leases of a half-section (320 acres) were made to public smelters. Along with each claim the miner was allowed a plot for his own use, garden-sized and altogether too small for genuine farming. This restriction was no doubt often evaded in order to avoid the high prices for food products prevailing in local markets, but it was clearly discouraging to immigrants who wished to develop the land. The leasing system, with its good and bad results, finally gave way to the more usual procedure of selling land to individuals, but it was not until 1846 that public-land sales were common in the Wisconsin area.

Other factors which tended to delay agricultural colonization are the location of the leases in sites unsuitable for farming, and the lack of trustworthy geographical descriptions for this part of the Midwest.

The great majority of the mining leases were on the steep, river-cut slopes which distinguish this region — now widely known as the Driftless Area — from the surrounding country. Preferred locations also included timber useful not only for fuel in smelting but also for building purposes. The mines were therefore located in sites ill-adapted to farming. Few claims extended up-slope to include the broad, rolling summits between the river valleys. Prairies and oak openings predominated in the interstream areas, but these were of little significance in regional economy until the mining industry began to wane in the 1840's. (See Fig. 80.)

Early reports of the lead region were naturally of a specialized character. They stressed the minerals and mining possibilities, with slight or incidental reference to those features which would be informative to agricultural pioneers. Nor was it made clear in early accounts that the striking features of the mining region extended northward beyond the mineralized zone into Wisconsin and Minnesota, to include an area as large as all of southern New England. In the absence of comprehensive reports people in the Eastern and Southern states assumed that this part of Wisconsin resembled other sections of Michigan Territory, of which it was a part. It will be recalled that in the 1820's unfavorable accounts of Michigan were widely circulated. Thus southwestern Wisconsin was pictured as a land of lakes and swamps and unproductive soil, which was true only in part. Furthermore, many prospective settlers questioned the possibility of raising such common crops as corn and wheat in a region that lay north of proved

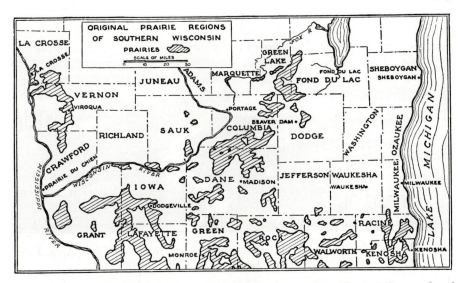

80   The prairies of southern Wisconsin. Adapted from *The Physical Geography of Wisconsin* by Lawrence Martin, Figs. 38 and 115.

farming country. They had no means of knowing that tobacco would in time become one of the chief cash crops of the Driftless Area. The cold of the winters and the shortness of the summers were exaggerated in the popular mind.

Transition to farming industries.   These fears and doubts were not dispelled for many years. Perhaps the first scientist to visit the Driftless Area and to describe its contrasts with the glaciated country round about was Professor W. H. Keating of Long's second expedition in 1823. He was impressed, as others have since been, by the sharp relief features, the relative shallowness of the soil, and the absence of erratic (or transported) boulders. Crossing the Driftless Area in a northwesterly direction for nearly 100 miles, Keating noted the resumption of the subdued topography and boulder-strewn drift in the vicinity of Lake Pepin, a widening in the Mississippi River above the mouth of the Chippewa. " A very great change in the country above Lake Pepin was visible," wrote Keating. " The bluffs are not so high, they are more frequently interrupted, and give a new character to the scenery of the [Mississippi] river."

Other travelers and geologists in later years emphasized the natural beauties and attractions of the Driftless Area. David Dale Owen in 1848 commented that the " features are less grand and bold than those of a mountainous region, but are yet impressive and strongly marked. From the hill-tops the intervening valleys wear the aspects of cultivated meadows. The whole combination suggests the idea, not of an aboriginal wilderness . . . but of a country lately under a high state of cultivation and suddenly deserted by its inhabitants." (See Fig. 81.) The absence of boulders, deep drift, and lakes and swamps, features so prevalent in adjacent parts of Wisconsin and Minnesota, continued to impress

81   View of the Turkey Hills, northeastern Iowa, in the Driftless Area. From David Dale Owen, *Report on the Chippewa Land District,* 1848.

thoughtful travelers long before an acceptable explanation was proposed. In his description of the lead region in 1854 Edward Daniels, the first state geologist of Wisconsin, observed:

A remarkable fact in the superficial deposits of this region is the entire absence of the drift so abundantly represented over the north-west generally, by boulders, gravels, sands, and clay. So far as my observation extends, not a single boulder or gravel stone can be found over the whole district. Widely removed as this circumstance may seem from practical matters, it has nevertheless a most important bearing upon the economic value of the district. For had it been otherwise the whole surface would have been covered with loose deposits often of great thickness, burying all indications of the presence of lead veins, rendering discovery exceedingly doubtful, and profitable mining a practical impossibility.

The beauties of the Driftless Area were not lost upon scientists such as Daniels, whose reports did much to make the region known to intending settlers:

About one-third of the surface is prairie, dotted and belted with beautiful groves and oak-openings. The scenery combines every element of beauty and grandeur — giving us the sunlit prairie, with its soft swell, waving grass and thousands of flowers, the sombre depths of primeval forests; the castellated cliffs, rising hundreds of feet, with beetling crags which a Titan might have piled for his fortress.

Until the 1860's, physiographers assumed that the driftless character of the area was owing to protection from the floods which had inundated surrounding regions and deposited in them a deep mantle of alluvium and detritus. Later they developed the theory, now unquestioned, that lobes of the advancing ice-sheets of the Glacial Period failed to penetrate this part of the Midwest. As Colonel Lawrence Martin has said: "Much of the United States is also driftless, as in the southern states and a large part of the West. . . . These regions are not spoken of as driftless areas or thought of as exceptional in any essential respect. The Driftless Area in Wisconsin, however, is famous the world over because it is completely surrounded by glaciated territory."

Agricultural settlement: New Glarus and other examples. By the 1840's farming opportunities had largely replaced mining as the principal attraction to new settlement in the Driftless Area. Settlement spread into the numerous river valleys between and beyond the mining towns, and advanced into the prairie land of the rolling uplands. It is estimated that nearly 40 per cent of the upland country was relatively free of timber at this time, but most farms were large enough to include slopes clothed with timber. This combination of prairie and woodland was much sought for by settlers here, as it was in other Midwestern regions.

The opening up of the Driftless Area to agriculture counteracted the loss of population through the decline of mining, and added variety as well. Immigrants fresh from Europe contributed significantly to the tide of northwestward settlement during the third quarter of the past century. Coming from regions in central or northern Europe not dissimilar from southwestern Wisconsin, they found it much to their liking. A case in point is that of the German-Swiss colony of New Glarus in Green County, near the eastern edge of the Driftless Area.

New Glarus, Wisconsin, like Vevay in southern Indiana, had its origin in the overpopulation of a Swiss mountain valley — in this case Canton Glarus. About 1840 it was apparent that emigration was necessary, and with characteristic forethought a locating party was sent to the United States to find a suitable place. Since dairying was the principal industry of the people, the searching party looked for pastures, fertile soils, and good water supply. No doubt, too, they were influenced in their final choice by aesthetic properties of the landscape. A lowland plain would scarcely be acceptable even if other conditions satisfied the practical needs of the dairymen.

The Driftless Area, though not at all a counterpart of Switzerland, seemed a reasonable fulfillment of their wishes. In the year 1845 the Swiss filed upon about 1,000 acres of woodland-prairie in northwestern Green County for division among the 108 colonists, who arrived shortly thereafter and named their community New Glarus. These thrifty people at once set about subduing the " bright land " to their special needs, many of the men seeking temporary or seasonal employment in mining and other industries during the first years of colonization. Their principal product was cheese, well suited to the relatively slow transportation methods of the time. Swiss cheese-making here was a domestic task until about 1870, when the first factory was started.

The growth of New Glarus and its cheese industry was comparatively slow at first, but reports of the success of the new colony brought many more Swiss to this area. The unfamiliar brown cattle of the German-Swiss drew frequent comment from travelers. The present-day visitor will still see the Swiss-bred cattle in Green County and other parts of the Driftless Area, and he may stop long enough at the New Glarus town square to read the dedication on the monument erected to the community founders, who were among the pioneers to build the Midwest of today.

Beginning with the 1860's, Scandinavians also colonized portions of the Driftless Area. In the valley of the Kickapoo River, a northern tributary of the Wisconsin, and throughout the counties of La Crosse, Vernon, and Crawford, numerous Norwegian, Swedish, and Danish communities took root. Examples may be cited, though not a complete list: Westby, Onalaska, and Viroqua. The coming here of Scandinavian and other foreign-born settlers during the 1860's and later is in part related to efforts by the State of Wisconsin to attract immigrants to its own area in competition with other Midwestern states. These measures will be outlined after a brief consideration of the settlement of southeastern Wisconsin.

THE SETTLEMENT OF SOUTHEASTERN WISCONSIN

No natural boundaries separate the region of southeastern Wisconsin from bordering territory in the same state or in Illinois. Lacking them, we should have in mind in this discussion that great area, roughly triangular in shape, which extends from the corner of Illinois at Lake Michigan to the Fox-Wisconsin portage route. In surface it is typically drift-covered, but no sharply defined line separates the glaciated from the driftless area. One type of surface merges into the other, requiring a sharp and practiced eye to distinguish the common border of the two. Roughly, the edge of the drift country passes north and south about 20 miles west of Madison. Generally speaking, the surface of southeastern Wisconsin becomes more hilly and diversified as one advances from northern Illinois and the shore of Lake Michigan toward the Fox-Wisconsin portage route. It is a region of pleasing variety but with few prominent features, and has been much altered by occupancy and development since the 1830's. According to early accounts, it was a beautiful country before the beginning of white settlement, and few doubted that it would eventually become a region of dense population.

That some 8,500 square miles of this region are within the State of Illinois rather than Wisconsin can be viewed with less emotion now than a century ago. Until the 1840's the political division of this area was a hotly contested issue, growing out of the Ordinance of 1787. As previously mentioned, the Ordinance provided that an east-west line touching the southern end of Lake Michigan should serve as the boundary of states eventually to be formed. This provision had been avoided in describing the northern boundaries of Ohio and Indiana and, to an even greater degree, that of Illinois. The enabling act which provided for the entrance of Illinois into the Union established the north line as the parallel of 42° 50', thus ensuring a lake frontage of about 60 miles.

Possession being nine points of the law, Illinois maintained an attitude of indifference when Wisconsin Territory petitioned the Congress for a restoration of the boundary according to the Ordinance. Residents on both sides of the Illinois line were naturally concerned with the outcome of the dispute, sometimes with loyalties that might not have been predicted. For example, delegates from northern Illinois met in Rockford in 1840 and resolved that northern Illinois rightfully belonged to Wisconsin. The issue was settled in 1846, when the Congress admitted Wisconsin into the Union with the parallel of 42° 30' as its southern boundary. Hence one addresses a letter to Chicago, Illinois, not to Chicago, Wisconsin.

Until 1832, southeastern Wisconsin was unavailable to white settlement. It was strongly held Indian country, ringed by a few frontier fortresses, such as Fort Howard at the site of present-day Green Bay, and Fort Winnebago at Portage. The famous Black Hawk War of 1832 ended in the submission or dispersal of the various Indian tribes, and was a curtain raiser for the immigration period. At this time, it should be recalled, southwestern Wisconsin and adjacent Illinois were well along in the process of settlement. This historical fact is well brought out in the great seal of Wisconsin, which, using the symbols of pick and shovel, a pyramid of pig lead, and the figure of a miner, clearly identifies that part of the state. According to some interpretations, the badger on the state seal also symbolizes the mining industry — a burrowing animal signifying an activity carried on partly underground.

By 1850, the frontier line in Wisconsin extended diagonally across the state, roughly following the Fox-Wisconsin route. A decade later, population had greatly increased within the settled area and had advanced toward the St. Croix River in the northwest. (See Fig. 82.) The process of land occupancy involved few features not covered in this study in connection with the growth of other regions. Selection of the land was largely an individual matter, since no great land companies operated here as did those in Ohio. Road extension followed closely upon settlement, providing easy access to markets. Development was essentially on a rural basis, for minerals played no part in this southeastern region. The alternation of prairie and wooded country was well suited to pioneering needs.

Contrasts of settlement in prairie and forest. From the standpoint of natural cover, southeastern Wisconsin represents the transition from the open prairies of the south to the forested land of the north. Reference to Figure 80 (page 317) will show that the two counties of Kenosha and Racine, in the southeastern corner of the state, originally contained large prairies. These two counties also presented to the pioneer extensive oak openings — not shown on the map. In contrast to the varied cover of Kenosha and Racine were the heavily forested counties of Milwaukee and Ozaukee just to the northward and also fronting on Lake Michigan. These two pairs of counties, essentially alike in climate and accessibility but differing in surface cover, were selected by the late Joseph Schafer for an intensive study of settlement history. Three main points stand out in his long and careful inquiry.

First, the oak openings were preferred by settlers to either open prairie or heavily wooded land. The timber of the openings was not an obstacle to cultivation, and it served for fencing, building material, and fuel. " Unless supplies

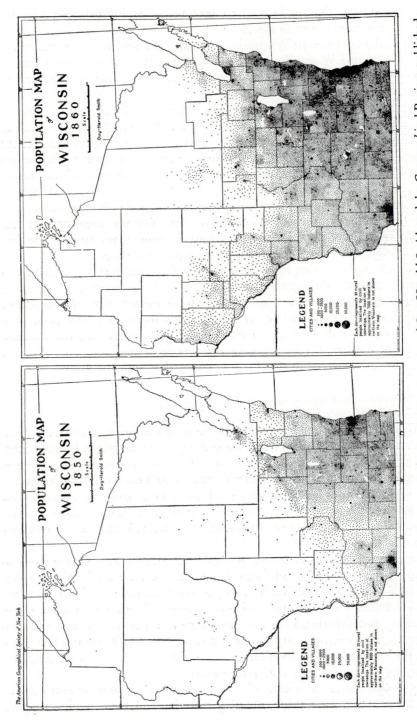

82   Population distribution in Wisconsin, 1850 and 1860. Courtesy of Guy-Harold Smith and the *Geographical Review*, published by the American Geographical Society of New York.

of timber were easily accessible," Schafer concluded, " settlers preferred the openings as farm land to the treeless prairies."

Second among the major conclusions of Schafer's study was the evident preference of settlers who arrived in Wisconsin with more than the average capital for the prairie lands in Kenosha and Racine counties. It was not a region for the empty-handed pioneer, because the expenditures for building, fencing, and well-digging were higher than in the similarly situated but wooded counties of Milwaukee and Ozaukee. According to Schafer: " The prairie . . . was indeed to many the most beautiful aspect of such a land as Wisconsin. But to the prospective farmer, life on the open prairie had its draw-backs as well as advantages." The frigid winters of Wisconsin, compared with those of Ohio, made heavier demands upon fuel wood, and upon timber for the construction of substantial dwellings. Even though the prairie could be put to cultivation more easily than the heavily forested land, it was found that the larger prairies near the lake shore remained in the public domain " some years after all the timbered lands, with prairies adjoining them, had been taken up."

Third, it was found that the timbered land of the two northern counties was the place for the poor man to begin farming. Here were the subsistence farmers, many of them foreign-born immigrants, who possessed little cash or lacked sufficient credit for making improvements in the more productive open land. They gradually made clearings in the forest, and in many instances disposed of their land and improvements preparatory to moving on to more promising farming areas.

THE IMMIGRATION POLICY OF WISCONSIN

Wisconsin was the first of the Northwestern states to set up an Office of Emigration. This step was taken in 1852 when the flood of emigrants from the Eastern and Southern states was being augmented by people from northern Europe. Because Wisconsin lay to the north of the main direction of movement, it was felt that the state would not receive its rightful share of settlers unless deliberate measures were taken toward attracting them. Illinois and Iowa, perhaps even Minnesota, might be considered more desirable for settlement of new homes.

The time had come, therefore, to speak forthrightly on the advantages to be found in Wisconsin. People were needed to make a state, " men and ever more men of capacity, endurance, strength and adaptability [to] break up the prairie sod, clear the brush from the slopes, drain the marshes, build the railroads, and do the thousand and one jobs incident to pioneer life, and then turn to the building of factories and towns and cities." In 1852 Wisconsin had much land and relatively few people; population growth had been encouraging, but authorities felt that it was less than was needed.

The great reservoir of immigrants was seen to be the ports of entry on the Atlantic coast, especially the port of New York. It was quite in order, therefore, for the first Commissioner of Emigration to reside in New York City, where he could keep in close touch with other agencies concerned with the incoming aliens and where he could personally meet the arrivals. As assistants he employed persons familiar with the Scandinavian and German languages who could interview immigrants as they arrived and put in a good word for Wisconsin.

Printed matter to supplement the oral communications was promptly made available. Pamphlets describing the state were at first circulated in New York and other cities in this country, and later distributed in European cities. During the first year of operation, according to Professor Theodore C. Blegen, an authority in this field, "Twenty thousand of these pamphlets were printed in the German, five thousand in the Norwegian, and four thousand in the Dutch language."

When immigrants arrived at the ports, various agents seem to have descended, vulturelike, upon them. Railroad agents were looking for laborers to build their lines, and business enterprises in New York City and leading industrial centers were on the watch for cheap labor. The Wisconsin Commissioner of Emigration, therefore, was not without competition even when he began his activities. Soon thereafter other Midwestern states followed Wisconsin's example by establishing boards of immigration with similar functions. In his report of 1853 the Wisconsin commissioner said: " For years past, emigrants, especially those landing in New York, have been systematically plundered, for which shameless wrong not only the hireling sub-agents, runners, etc., are responsible, but especially those who retain these unprincipled subjects in their employ." The immigration authorities did not devote full time to aliens, but turned their attention also to prospective settlers throughout the country. It is said that an agent for the Wisconsin office traveled 42,000 miles in the United States in 1853 and inserted descriptions of his state in over 900 newspapers.

Wisconsin discontinued its emigration office from 1855 to 1867, partly because of political opposition but also as a result of the sharp drop in immigrants arriving from Europe, and domestic problems caused by the War between the States. The work was resumed in 1867 by a Board of Immigration consisting of the governor, the secretary of state, and six others. From this office there flowed a stream of guidebooks for emigrants containing directions for reaching Wisconsin, comment on the variety of occupations and current wages, data as to land and its cost, as well as notes on climate, resources, and postal facilities. Pocket maps with data printed in gazetteer-like manner were an especially effective type of advertising. In the year 1880 the Wisconsin board issued 10,000 maps of the state printed in English, German, and Norwegian.

It is difficult if not impossible to measure the effectiveness of state-supported efforts to attract immigrants. The Wisconsin board was just one of many influences, tangible and intangible, which drew people to the state. Its literature had the advantage of official origin and thus might have been considered more reliable than promotional writings issued by private agencies. The board's promotional literature, in the opinion of Professor Blegen, maintained a high standard. As one of the commissioners said in 1871: "One principle I have laid down for my guidance, viz., to give the facts just as they exist, unvarnished and uncolored."

Wisconsin received thousands of foreign-born immigrants during the period of operation of the immigrant board. In 1853, for example, it was estimated that immigration to the state was as follows:

IMMIGRATION TO WISCONSIN, 1853

From	Numbers
Germany	16,000–18,000
Ireland	4,000– 5,000
Norway	3,000– 4,000
Other countries	2,000– 3,000
TOTAL	25,000–30,000

It is safe to presume that many of these newcomers would have settled in Wisconsin even if no efforts had been made to attract them there. Probably a letter written back home by an immigrant who had already settled in this country had more effect than a packet of attractively printed descriptions and maps. In any event, it can be said that official inducements to immigration, and the interstate competition in the Northwest, contributed in no small measure to the great influx of Scandinavian and German peoples into Wisconsin, Iowa, and Minnesota.

CHAPTER 18

Minnesota: Territory and State

WHEN Minnesota was granted Territorial status in 1849, few cared to predict that it would soon become a full-fledged state. With a population no greater than that of an average township in the East, Minnesota seemed likely to be destined for a Territorial period fully as long as Michigan's had been. Some 6,000 Minnesotans in 1850 were huddled in a few villages not far from Fort Snelling at the junction of the Mississippi and Minnesota rivers. Even the most enthusiastic citizens could detect no sure signs of an influx of settlers sufficient to justify application for statehood within a reasonable time. According to the accepted formula, 60,000 inhabitants made a state, ten times the number then living in " Minnesota East " — that is, the portion east of the Mississippi River. " Minnesota West " was largely Indian country, extending far beyond the present state boundaries to the Missouri and White rivers of the Dakotas.

Compared with Iowa, which had been a state since 1846, Minnesota seemed to have little to offer. The new Territory lay to one side of the main route of migration, northward of proved farm country. Iowa contained an abundance of land — good land, in the judgment of experienced farming people — and Wisconsin was capable of absorbing many of the settlers who might otherwise have pushed on to the upper Mississippi. There was plenty of opportunity in other regions of the Northwest, not to mention attractions in the Far West, especially the gold fields of California.

Grave doubts were expressed regarding the desirability of settling in Minnesota. Stories of Sioux Indian raids, losing nothing in the retelling, were sufficient to cause many people to seek homes elsewhere. Bulking large in popular thought were the frigid winters of this remote region. One of the Territorial governors said that " during the past year I have received almost innumerable letters from the middle states propounding a variety of questions about our territory, desiring to know if our winters are not very long and so exceedingly cold that stock freezes to death and man hardly dare venture out of his domicile." Even Minnesota's first Congressman could paint no favorable picture of his Territory. " These people have emigrated to the remote region they now inhabit under many disadvantages," he said. "They have not been attracted thither by the glitter of inexhaustible gold mines, but with the same spirit which has actuated all other pioneers of civilization. They have gone there to labor with the axe, the anvil, and the plough."

Despite these forebodings, more than 150,000 persons came to the new Territory within the next ten years, clearly beyond the number of the minimum requirement for admission to the Union. Minnesota became a state in 1858, with boundaries essentially those of the present. Nearly all of Minnesota West had been acquired by purchase or by cession from the Indians, and thus a great area was opened up for new settlement. Between 1860 and 1870 the population of the state increased from about 172,000 to over 439,000, a rate of increase not equaled in later years. This was the beginning of the great period of foreign-born immigration — a period which will require careful study at the proper place. Settlement spread northwestward across the state, and in the early 1870's was much influenced by railroad lines which were heading for the Pacific coast. The quarter-century following 1850, which encompasses the main features of the growth of Minnesota, will provide the time limits for this study of the interior Northwest.

MINNESOTA GEOGRAPHY: PRE-SETTLEMENT PERIOD

Minnesota was a well-explored area by the time the Territorial government was organized. Official explorations commenced in 1805, when Zebulon Pike charted the course of the upper Mississippi and recommended sites for military bases, and ended with the more extensive and general survey of Joseph Nicollet from 1836 to 1843. Between these surveys were several others. Stephen H. Long led two expeditions into the Minnesota country, the first in 1817 with objectives similar to those of Pike, and the more wide-ranging tour of 1823, which went from the Minnesota River to the Red River and finally to Lake Winnipeg, with Professor W. H. Keating as the geologist-geographer. Mention has been made earlier of the Cass expedition of 1820, which entered Minnesota over the Fond du Lac and Sandy Lake portages and followed down the Mississippi River to Prairie du Chien. A member of the Cass party, Henry Schoolcraft, returned to Minnesota in 1832 heading his own expedition, with the main purpose of discovering the source of the Mississippi River. The objective was successfully attained, and resulted in several papers and books — for Schoolcraft was a busy writer — which told of his exploits and, incidentally, described the region covered by his journey.

Many of the observations and maps made by Pike, Long, and Cass were obsolete by the time the gifted French geographer Joseph Nicollet commenced his work for the War Department in 1836. Contemporary with the studies of Nicollet, but operating independently, were the topographic surveys of southern Minnesota of George W. Featherstonhaugh and Lieutenant Albert M. Lea. Many Minnesotans know that the city of Albert Lea in Freeborn County com-

83   The Coteau des Prairies as represented in the Hayden Survey, 1871

memorates in its name the able topographer who did much to give an unbiased view of the southeastern prairie country in 1836.

The Nicollet report, with its map, was the most influential of all the documents which, in one way or another, threw new light on the geography of Minnesota. Not that the Nicollet description was widely read; like all official documents of the time, its circulation was limited. Nevertheless, it was occasionally used by the authors of articles, geographies, and emigrant guidebooks which were made available to the general public when Minnesota was reaching out, far and wide, for new settlers. In this way the scholarly observations of Nicollet, who was aided for part of the time by the more famous John C. Frémont, reached down to the rank and file, where they were effective in directing general opinion. The secondhand versions were rarely masterpieces of reproduction. It may well be imagined that the writer of a guidebook seeking to promote settlement in Minnesota, as well as the sale of his book, colored the original to suit his own purposes. Only brief portions of the promotional writings derived from the Nicollet and other documents, and even these passages were sometimes altered beyond recognition.

The prairies in southern and western Minnesota. The Nicollet report of Iowa Territory, which then included most of what came to be Minnesota, paid much attention to the southern prairie region. This is an important consideration, because the southern region, adjacent to Iowa and Wisconsin and rendered accessible by river routes, was bound to become the first area of settlement.

Nicollet's account of the prairie country veered toward the favorable view, although the author presumably had no ulterior motive in giving this impression. He told of the gently rolling prairies, interspersed with oak openings and threaded by many rivers and creeks. He bestowed the fanciful name "Undine Region" upon that part of the southern plains centering upon the elbow of the Minnesota River near Mankato. Because "Undine" identifies a fabled water sprite, we may infer that Nicollet was impressed by the well-watered character of this area. The writers of many popular books adopted this regional name for that general part of the state, retaining elsewhere such practical expressions as Minnesota Valley, Red River Slope, and Lake Superior Slope. Regional names sometimes have strange bedfellows.

The culminating physical feature of the prairie country was observed to be in the southwest, in the form of the Coteau (edge) des Prairies (Fig. 83). This was and is the height of land dividing the waters of the Minnesota River from those of the Des Moines and some Missouri River tributaries. Rising nearly 500 feet above the general level, this upland prairie, decorated with groves of broad-leaved trees, added variety and beauty to the sea of waving grass. Nicollet ventured the prediction that " in future time this region will be the summer resort of the wealthy of the land." How eagerly this chance observation was pounced upon by promoters, especially by railroad-builders of a later day, can readily be imagined.

The prairies of Minnesota were not carefully mapped in the presettlement period. About fifty years later, however, the distribution of forest and prairie was represented as shown in Figure 84. It will be seen that the prairies formed an L-shaped belt, with the hollow of the L occupied by the forest-covered lands of the north and east. The settlement of Minnesota cannot very well be understood without constant reference to this map of surface cover.

The Big Woods north of the prairie. A region of great importance in the settlement period was known as the Big Woods. This was a term in common usage by the people who settled the country, not one handed down by scientists or explorers, and thus deserves special attention. It referred to the belt of deciduous hardwoods extending along the Minnesota River from the elbow

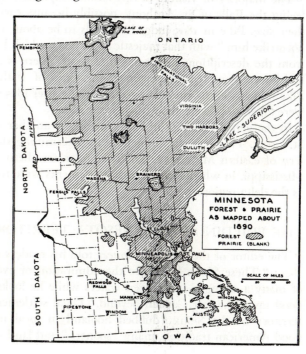

84

The distribution of forest and prairie in Minnesota. From a manuscript map prepared for the Minnesota Geological Survey about 1890.

northward to the Mississippi, but not, as one might at first suppose, to the extensive pine forests of the north. In short, the Big Woods lay between the southern prairie and the northern pineries, close to the main routes of travel from the East. The woods were good hunting grounds before white settlement, and as the pioneer homeseekers came in they furnished fuel and building material in a land where both were greatly needed. When the land had been cleared and the stumps removed, it was found to be comparable in productivity with the prairies. For all of these reasons, the Big Woods became a favorite region for homesteading. So little of the original Big Woods now remains that efforts are being directed to preserve a few acres which escaped the ax and plow of the pioneers.

Early importance of the Minnesota-Mississippi junction. In this immensity of space, white man had made but few changes before Minnesota Territory was created. The principal settlements were near the junction of the Minnesota and Mississippi rivers, an area then known as St. Peter's, the original name of the Minnesota River. Here were (and are) the village of Mendota and Fort Snelling, the latter influential in attracting further settlement in its vicinity. Fort Snelling was a unit in frontier defenses, built on a high bluff after a year's trial at another site nearer water level, and named in 1820 for its commandant. The first name of the fort was St. Anthony, a name also applicable to the falls in the Mississippi River just above the confluence site, a natural factor which led to the location of Minneapolis.

The majority of visitors to this locality expressed their disappointment upon seeing the Falls of St. Anthony, possibly because earlier stories had magnified their size. Pike in 1805 judged the falls to be about 15 feet high, and they did not strike him " with that majestic appearance which I had been taught to expect from the descriptions of former travelers." There is a possibility that the falls had lowered appreciably between the time of Father Hennepin's visit and Pike's. In any event, they changed so rapidly after 1805 that engineering measures were taken to prevent their further recession.

In the general vicinity of Fort Snelling is another river junction, that of the St. Croix. This also was influential in determining the original settlement pattern of eastern Minnesota. The triangular area between the St. Croix and the Mississippi, in which several early settlements were made, is sometimes known as the delta region.

THE BUILDING OF MINNESOTA TERRITORY

The editor of the *St. Paul Pioneer* told his readers in the issue of August 16, 1849: " These Sioux lands are the admiration of every body, and the mouth of many a stranger and citizen waters while he looks beyond the Mississippi's flood upon the fair Canaan beyond." Legal settlement could not occur in the territory of the Sioux (dubbed Sooland in local newspapers), although, in good American tradition, many " sooners " and land speculators had gone there in advance of survey and treaty. For the first two years of its existence as a Territory, Minnesota was confined to the small area east of the Mississippi River, to which immigrants were coming, clamoring for land. The Treaties of Traverse des Sioux and Mendota made Sooland available in 1851, an event followed by a great rush to the west. As one historian has said, " These were stirring years, filled with vigorous planning and building, with big enterprises and ideas." Special factors that need consideration are: (1) the development of river transportation, (2) the building of military and other roads into the interior, and (3) the location of new forts and towns in the erstwhile Sooland.

Navigation on the Mississippi and the Minnesota. The Mississippi River provided the chief means of entrance to Minnesota Territory, and St. Paul, so to speak, was the port of entry. An upriver journey by steamer from Galena or Dubuque required four or five days, with many stops on the way to permit passengers to leave at places of their choice, such as Winona and Red Wing. Arriving at St. Paul in October of 1850, a passenger graphically stated that " every boat spills out from 40 to 75 passengers " on the wharves.

A measure of the number of emigrants coming to Minnesota during the Territorial period and early years of statehood is gained from the following official table of steamboat arrivals at St. Paul. It should be realized that one boat was capable of making several round trips between Dubuque and St. Paul during the open season. After 1862, the number of steamboat arrivals steadily declined, amounting to only 218 in 1874, when railroads had become a competitive factor. Assuming an average of 50 passengers to a boat, it appears that 50,000 people came to St. Paul in the year 1862. On some days, 8 or 10 boats arrived at the head of navigation.

STEAMBOAT ARRIVALS AT ST. PAUL, 1849–1862

1849	. . .	95	1854	. . .	256	1859	. . .	808
1850	. . .	104	1855	. . .	560	1860	. . .	775
1851	. . .	119	1856	. . .	857	1861	. . .	937
1852	. . .	171	1857	. . .	1,025	1862	. . .	1,015
1853	. . .	200	1858	. . .	1,068			

St. Paul, as seen by traveler J. C. Laird in 1850, was " the great depot of Minnesota," containing " 6 churches, about 25 stores, 6 taverns, groceries and gambling houses too numerous to mention, about 50 Lawyers and Land Agents, 250 gamblers, and about 15 or 1800 inhabitants." Political leaders in St. Paul were already making it known that this was the logical center for the state capital when the permanent government should be formed. Many rival claims were soon put forward, and not everyone agreed that the port city was the best choice. Mr. Laird felt that " it will not always remain the seat of government as it is too much to one side of the territory, but it is a great place now."

The Minnesota River was also navigable during the early days, but it has seen little commercial use since 1871. With its narrow channel, small volume of water in midsummer, and limited season of navigation, the Minnesota was by no means an ideal river for transportation. Nevertheless it was preferable to the only other means of freight haulage then available — by ox team over poor roads. The following table shows the rise of navigation on the Minnesota and then its rapid decline, brought about by the combined effects of sedimentation in the channel and the competition of railroads.

MINNESOTA RIVER NAVIGATION, 1850–1872

(Steamboat trips below Mankato)

Year	Trips	Year	Trips	Year	Trips
1850	4	1858	394	1866	100
1851	3	1859	300	1867	100
1852	13	1860	250	1868	80
1853	49	1861	318	1869	50
1854	30	1862	413	1870	50
1855	109	1863	177	1871	50
1856	207	1864	166	1872	1
1857	292	1865	195		

Roads to the interior. It was only natural that St. Paul and its near-by rival village of St. Anthony (now Minneapolis) should become the center of roads leading into the newly opened country. Because of the expense of building roads and their usefulness in Indian defense, the Territory called upon the Congress for aid. In response, the War Department undertook the construction of four roads leading from St. Paul into southeastern Minnesota. These routes came to be known as military roads, although they were not intended for purely military purposes.

Named from east to west, the military roads were as follows: 1. The west bank of the Mississippi River to Lake Pepin. As its special function, this route was to connect with river transportation below Lake Pepin, which because of its quiet water remained locked in ice longer than the river below and thus isolated, for a time, the upper river section. 2. The Faribault Road, essentially U. S. Highway 65 of today, heading southward from St. Paul to points in northern Iowa. 3. The Big Sioux or Dodd Road, which cut through the Big Woods to St. Peter and Mankato on the Minnesota River. 4. The St. Anthony-Fort Ridgely Road, which went through Shakopee and across country to Fort Ridgely, near the present city of Redwood Falls.

These primary roads were greatly extended during the ten years of the Territorial period. They were used not only by the typical prairie schooners of the emigrant, but also by stagecoach companies who contracted to carry passengers and deliver mail. It was often to the advantage of the stage companies to aid in the improvement of the roads over which they operated. The new roads contributed to the extension of farms and the growth of the towns through which the stages went. They also led to the development of new towns, for it was characteristic of this booming region that roads were pushed out far in advance of actual settlement.

New forts and towns. Although the Sioux had signed away their long-held hunting lands, the Indians themselves remained in considerable numbers on near-by reservations. This led to a demand for new military posts beyond the range of Fort Snelling. In 1853, out of this demand came Fort Ridgely and the Redwood Indian Agency. The wisdom of this move became apparent when the Sioux attacked the agency in 1862 and raided much of the surrounding country.

The rapidity with which the prairie country of southeastern Minnesota filled up during the ten years of Territorial growth can scarcely be appreciated. As examples note the growth of two cities, St. Peter and Faribault, both resulting mainly from the needs of the farming country roundabout.

Writing from St. Peter on January 9, 1858, Congressman William Hines remarked that although it was in the depth of winter:

The carpenters are still doing out-door work in the way of building. Indeed our town has now so extended its limits that it needs no puffing up to be called quite a city. That you may know of the importance of the place which has grown upon our beautiful prairie in one year and a half, I send you a partial directory of our business houses as taken from the *St. Peter Courier.*

The list, which will be omitted here, contains the names of various kinds of mills, as well as wagon factories and stores. The appearance of a newspaper within a year after the founding of the village is also typical of booming times.

In the summer of 1857, the new town of Faribault was said to be so full of strangers that

. . . it was almost impossible to get a place to sleep at any price. Real estate dealers, lawyers, and business men in general are here by hundreds. The opening up of the land office has drawn them. It is estimated that over 1,000 men have arrived within the last two days. Board at the best houses ranges at from 3 to 6 dollars a day. No one grumbles, for a good many are making thousands daily.

Almost forgotten were the days, only a dozen years before, when serious doubts were expressed that Minnesota would prove to be a favorable place of residence.

AGRICULTURAL EXPANSION IN THE NEW STATE

" The sudden transition of Indian hunting ground . . . to the first rank of northwestern states," said the Commissioner of Agriculture in his report of 1863, " directed much attention to Minnesota." The naming of the new state on May 11, 1858, was publicized throughout the country. Its thousands of square miles of public lands had not been " picked over " by land-seekers as had the farming regions of the older states near by. Besides, the old question of public-land policy, which had been a political issue ever since the acquisition of the Northwest Territory, now assumed a new meaning. A growing popular demand for free land was finally answered in 1862 by the Homestead Act permitting selections of quarter-sections of surveyed areas. The Homestead Act greatly stimulated Western settlement, and was particularly important to Minnesota because of its admission into the Union on the eve of the passage of the act.

Even if no deliberate effort had been made to attract people to Minnesota, there seems little doubt that the new state would have received a large share of the westward-moving immigration. Because of the filling-up of Wisconsin and the improvement of means of transportation, Minnesota seemed less remote. Furthermore, actual experience had swept aside some of the doubts regarding agricultural possibilities. The southern tiers of counties became known, geographically, as an extension of Iowa and Wisconsin. There remained many doubts concerning the suitability of the central and northern parts of the state, and some of these have not been removed even at the present time.

Minnesotans were not quite sure that it had been wise to give prominence to the expression "North Star State," appearing on the great seal as "L'Etoile du Nord." The frigid winters that this phrase suggested probably discouraged immigration from the south. On the other hand, the high latitude position of the state was a point in its favor among people arriving from northern Europe. "What a glorious new Scandinavia might not Minnesota become," said Frederika Bremer several years before Minnesota became a state and when less than a dozen Norwegians and Swedes lived west of the Mississippi River. By 1890 there were over 200,000 Scandinavians within the state of Minnesota.

Invitations to settle in Minnesota. People learned about Minnesota during its early years of statehood through letters written "back East," newspaper editorials, printed pamphlets, maps, emigrant guidebooks, and descriptive works which might well be called amateur geographies. An example of the latter, with a title suggesting the nature of its appeal, was *Rural Sketches of Minnesota: The El Dorado of the Northwest* by H. W. Hamilton.

We cannot pretend to summarize the extended and scattered writings of a quarter-century, nor is it possible to evaluate in certain terms their influence on public thought. It can be said that they played a vital role in the continued growth of population, for, by and large, they painted a glowing picture of opportunity. In the manner characteristic of promotional literature, the printed material minimized unfavorable features and magnified the favorable ones. To the average reader of the 1860's, the one who made the decisions, "Minnesota" came to be known as the southern part of the state, not all of the area within its boundaries. The less said about the far north of Minnesota, perhaps the better — at least when appeals went out to people looking for farm land.

The climate of Minnesota received much attention in both the letters of emigrants and the published descriptions. This would not be unexpected, because it was assumed, probably correctly, that popular impressions trended toward the unfavorable. Furthermore, it was a relatively intangible aspect of the total environment, one that permitted much ingenuity in the manipulation of data. It was admitted that the winters were cold, but it was a "dry cold," more endurable than similar temperatures in the humid East. This was stated a thousand and one times, and was powerfully supplemented by the testimony of pioneers who spoke with the authority of the man who has been there. It was also pointed out, correctly, that snowfall was far less in southern Minnesota than in the

Northeastern states. Among a number of examples, there are the letters of
L. W. Dibble, who emigrated to Minnesota in 1865 and wrote frequently to his
relatives in Connecticut. "It is not so cold here as I expected," said Dibble on
one occasion when there was scarcely enough snow to permit sleighing. Two
years later, Dibble wrote from Le Sueur saying:

The winter here is the finest I ever saw. There has been but very little wind and
more sunshine than I ever saw in the east. Indeed a cloudy day here is a rare thing
unless it is snowy. This is my third winter here. The air is still dry cold, and one
is rarely seen with his teeth chattering. The difference is so great it would seem
proper if possible to have some variation in the thermometer, like an almanac calculated for different latitudes. It is impossible for you to understand the difference
without experiencing it.

Mr. Dibble's letters by themselves probably had limited influence in allaying
doubts about Minnesota's climate, but there were thousands of Dibbles, writing
in various languages, who conveyed similar information to relatives in this
country and in Europe.

With one eye to malaria-ridden parts of the South and the other to the preva-
lence of tuberculosis (then called "consumptive diseases") in the East and
elsewhere, the State Board of Health and many private physicians lent their
authority to proclamations of the salubrity and health-restoring qualities of the
Minnesota climate. Broad claims were made, with a forcefulness which was
scarcely justified by available knowledge of either climate or disease. Said one
pamphlet: "The whole world cannot produce a climate more salubrious than
that of Minnesota."

In an essay awarded a prize by the State Board of Immigration, when in 1865
it conducted a state-wide competition on the topic "Minnesota as a Home for
Immigrants," a Mary J. Colburn went far beyond her depth in recommending
the state for invalids and those who wished to preserve their health. Miss Colburn observed that many people had left the "comparatively healthy climates of
New England to find untimely graves in the rich soil of Indiana, Illinois, Missouri, and Iowa." But this fate would surely not overtake those who went to
Minnesota, where there are "no stagnant pools to send forth poisonous exhala-
tions." Stirred by such advice, bearing the approval of medical authorities of the
time, a large but unknown number of people came to the state. Not immigrants
in the usual sense, they often sought occupations in the growing communities
and lived long and useful lives. Some health-seekers, such as Henry David
Thoreau, were disappointed in their quest and remained only a short time.

Other points that were suggested in favor of Minnesota's climate may be listed
briefly: 1. The high latitude position of the state made for longer daylight hours
in summer, thus increasing the productivity of the land. 2. Crops were known
to yield more abundantly toward the limit of their range, not within the area
where conditions were best for growth. 3. The rainfall, though admittedly bordering upon the minimum for successful farming, was favorably distributed

during the year; the amount falling during the growing season was " fully equal to that of noted agricultural districts." 4. Appeal was made to the glories of the seasons, especially the long autumn with its weeks of " Indian summer " and the rich colorings of leafy vegetation.

It should be re-emphasized that favorable advertising was only one of the many factors which contributed to the rapid increase of Minnesota's population during its first quarter-century of statehood. This was a period of ever increasing expansion to the West, and many states shared in its benefits. The provisions of the Homestead Act of 1862 deserve special mention here, because Minnesota presented such vast areas of public land. The original act provided that the head of a family could receive a quarter-section (160 acres) by the simple procedure of filing upon it with the payment of a small fee, usually not exceeding $15. After a residence of five years the homesteader received title to the property. The original act was modified in several particulars during the succeeding decades, usually in the direction of liberality.

Some idea of the great area thus opened to new settlement is gained by the following calculation. Of the 23,040 acres in the standard government township, 8 quarter-sections or 1,280 acres were reserved for school purposes. There remained 21,760 acres of land which could be divided into 136 farms, each with the 160 acres provided by the Homestead Act. A county of average size, such as Mower on the Iowa line, contains 20 townships, therefore providing for well over 2,500 farms. There are 32 counties in Minnesota between the Iowa line and the Minnesota River.

GROWTH TO A WHEAT EMPIRE

The Homestead Act, long in the making, went into effect in a nation torn by civil strife. Its benefits were therefore counterbalanced by several years of disastrous war and painful reconstruction. Human energy and natural resources were diverted into new directions, noticeably slowing up the westward drift of population. For a time, the American people were less mobile than was their habit. The population of Minnesota and other states on the frontier continued to increase, but at a slower rate than might otherwise have been expected.

Two additional factors tended to delay the effect of the free-land law in Minnesota: (1) the Sioux uprising of 1862, and (2) the searing drought of the same year.

The Sioux outbreak has been adequately discussed by historians and thus will be referred to here only briefly. The uprising was a series of frontier raids and counterraids of exceptional violence, well up to the moving-picture version of clashes between the white man and the Indian. Stories of the raids filtering back into the Eastern states caused many people to reconsider plans they might have had for going to Minnesota. According to the Commissioner of Agriculture, the Sioux outbreak checked new settlement to such an extent that "its effect was still visible in March, 1863."

The drought of 1862 and 1863 also retarded settlement in Minnesota, not so much during the dry period as somewhat later when the event became known in the Eastern states. The practically snowless winter of 1862 caused no great concern among the pioneers, for the " rainy season " of early summer was confidently expected. But instead of the usual rains, the skies remained clear, and hot winds from the southwest swept over the land. Rains finally came in August, 1863, too late to be of benefit to the crops. This was not a protracted drought, as others were to be, nor was it accompanied by locust invasions; nevertheless it caused local distress and confirmed doubts as to the dependability of climatic conditions on the Western frontier.

At the time of the drought of 1862 and other coinciding events, Minnesota agriculture was in rapid transition from the subsistence or self-sustaining type to commercial grain farming. In taking up a new farmstead, preferably a quarter-section containing a wood lot, the settler was advised to break some of the prairie immediately. Experience had shown that newly plowed prairie sod did not yield well until the following year. Prairie grass should also be harvested, and shelter provided for animals as well as for the family. The first habitations were rudely constructed sod houses or log cabins, the latter more common in the Big Woods region than farther to the west. It was a common practice for the homesteader to plant trees for windbreaks around his home. Beginning agriculture consisted of raising a variety of crops, such as potatoes, corn, oats, and wheat, with supplemental stock-raising.

A New Yorker who traveled by railroad across southern Minnesota from Winona to Mankato in 1867, looking over " the vast expanse in right good earnest," has left a vivid picture of a landscape that was undergoing change. Much of the prairie was still in its natural state, looking like " nothing else but a vast ocean of long rolling swells, with an occasional great wave which overtops the rest, and as the cars pass they seem to be rolling away to the eastward and are lost to my view; but others are following them in quick succession as we go rolling on." The beginnings of settlement were also impressive, the traveler being " lost in wonder and admiration of the sight presented to my view. I see the smoke ascending from the settlers' cabins in every direction. The numerous little groves which dot the prairie on every hand, indicating the settler's domicile, tell the story of his industry in a commendable effort to supply by the cunning of his hands that which nature has failed to furnish."

He estimated that not one-fourth of the homesteaded land had yet been fenced, because of the limited supplies of posts and rails — barbed wire not having been invented as yet. He wondered if the settlers did not need more fuel than they possessed, " especially because of being in the open land receiving the full effect of the wind." Little was being done, apparently, to refertilize the land that had been used for cultivation; he saw great piles of manure but " sometimes thought (judging from appearances) that perhaps they made it a practice of moving their barns at certain periods, to avoid handling the article." Southern Minnesota was a typical frontier country in 1867.

85   Wheat production in Minnesota, 1870 and 1890. One dot represents 2,000 bushels. From " Some Notes on the Growth of Population in Minnesota " by Leonard S. Wilson, *Geographical Review,* Vol. 30 (1940), pp. 660–64. Courtesy of the author and the *Geographical Review,* published by the American Geographical Society.

The trials of the pioneer stage gradually passed away. Hovels became homes; from tracks across the prairie, acknowledged highways evolved. Crossroads hamlets grew into substantial towns and cities, and commercial agriculture, dominated by wheat, replaced the subsistence type.

The wheat-production maps for 1870 and 1890 give testimony to the rapid rise of commercial farming. From them also the distribution of population may be inferred. By comparing the wheat-production maps with the map of forest and prairie, it will be seen that settlement and wheat farming spread from the tree-bordered rivers of the southeast and the fringes of the Big Woods into the long-grass prairie of the west (Fig. 85, and Fig. 84, page 329). Then settlement moved northward into the shorter-grass country of the Red River of the North and into the subhumid climatic area. Thus the state of Minnesota occupies a critical place in the study of historical geography, because it bridges a main climatic belt of the country — from humid to semiarid.

It will not be surprising to learn that the growth of the wheat empire from 1870 to 1890 affected the development of industries and city growth on the eastern border. The flour-milling industry centered at Minneapolis, where the Falls of St. Anthony furnished the water power. Minneapolis became known as the Flour City and by 1890 was the leading milling center of the country. Three-fourths of the annual product was shipped to the East, much of it by way of Duluth through the Great Lakes.

FOREIGN-BORN IMMIGRATION INTO MINNESOTA

The bulk of the settlers who came to Minnesota during the Territorial days were of native stock or, if foreign-born, had lived for a time in some other state. Very few immigrants came directly from a foreign country to the Territory. This was partly because much land remained to be taken up in more accessible Midwestern regions. In the 1850 census, for instance, the Territory of Minnesota listed only 12 Scandinavians; Wisconsin had 8,885, of whom 86 per cent were Norwegians. People of German origin or parentage far exceeded other foreign peoples in both Wisconsin and Minnesota Territory, for immigration from the Scandinavian countries did not set in until a later time. Irish people also outnumbered Scandinavians in the early years of Minnesota immigration. It may come as a surprise to many who associate Scandinavians with Minnesota to learn that people of other nationalities were more numerous in the beginning years of its settlement.

During the 1860's there was a marked increase in the percentage of first- and second-generation north-Europeans among immigrants to Minnesota. From 1860 to 1870, for example, the number of German-born inhabitants in the state rose from 18,400 to 48,457. The Scandinavian element in Wisconsin and Minnesota offers interesting comparisons if viewed over a period of time.

SCANDINAVIAN ELEMENT IN WISCONSIN AND MINNESOTA, 1870 AND 1890

	Wisconsin		*Minnesota*	
	1870	*1890*	*1870*	*1890*
Norwegians	40,046	65,696	35,940	101,169
Swedes	2,799	20,157	20,987	99,913
Danes	5,212	13,885	1,910	14,133
TOTALS	48,057	99,738	58,837	215,215

The data indicate that by 1890 Minnesota had taken first place as a choice of residence by people of Scandinavian origin.

German immigration. We have seen that during earlier decades German immigration into Minnesota was far more significant than that of the Scandinavian countries. In fact, it has been found that " the number of German-born inhabitants in Minnesota was larger than that of any other single non-American nationality group until 1910," when for the first time they were outnumbered by Swedes.

The spread of German stock in Minnesota did not differ markedly from that of peoples of other national origins. In 1870, German people lived in some numbers throughout all settled parts of Minnesota. Some 23 per cent of these Germans lived in cities and towns, only one of which, New Ulm, can be considered of German origin. For the most part they took up residence in cities that were in existence at the time of their arrival: the Twin Cities, Duluth, Rochester, and many others. In them they followed trades or professions with which they were familiar. Probably they had been city dwellers in the country of their origin.

The two main concentrations of rural German population can be easily identified on the map, which is based on township data (Fig. 86). Standing out clearly is the German-settled belt extending northeast-southwest along the lower Minnesota River Valley. When this section was taken up by the original German pioneers in the 1850's, it lay west of the main occupied area of Minnesota, and twenty years later it was still beyond the center of population. This German area was in the Big Woods region, with timber conveniently at hand; perhaps earlier experience led the settlers to associate superior soils with a forest cover of this type. The open prairies seem to have been avoided. The lower Minnesota River, which was navigable at the time, may have provided an additional incentive to fix upon this part of the state.

Until original records are made available one can only speculate upon the factors which drew Germans to this section rather than to some other equally accessible at the time. The German element continued to predominate along the lower Minnesota, not moving northwestward with the rapidly advancing frontier. Germans preferred to settle among Germans, says a leading authority in this field. National cohesion was very strong, and " was exclusively responsible for Germans settling in townships where the soils, the timber supply, and transportation facilities were no better than those of neighboring townships where they did not settle."

Loyalties within loyalties seem to have been largely responsible for the second main center of German settlement — northward of the Twin Cities in

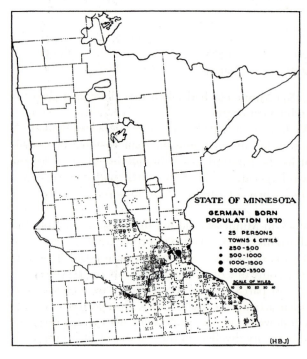

86

German-born population in Minnesota in 1870. This map is reproduced through the courtesy of Hildegard Binder Johnson, who supplied all the data for it and personally supervised its construction. In her paper " The Distribution of the German Pioneer in Minnesota " (*Rural Sociology,* March 1941), Mrs. Johnson presents a similarly detailed map based on percentages of German stock to the total population of Minnesota in 1870.

present-day Stearns County, of which St. Cloud is the principal city. The central figure in the origin of this German-held area was a dynamic priest, Father Franz Pierz, whose name is preserved in one of the local towns. Father Pierz came to Minnesota as a missionary to the Chippewa Indians, and after some investigation decided to center his activities near St. Cloud. Without any question, this was beyond the frontier, showing once again that when occasion demanded, German-Americans struck out far from the settlements, even into Indian country. Wooded country, like the lands along the Minnesota River, was chosen for this northern settlement, near the limit of the Big Woods and in the vicinity of a navigable stream.

Father Pierz drew about him German followers of the Roman Catholic Church. He told them, perhaps in a moment of pleasant imagination, that Minnesota " has a mild climate, like that of Germany." With more truth, he informed his compatriots that they would find here good soil, meadows, woods and wild game, adequate water supply, and transportation facilities. He urged that they make haste " to join the stream of immigration, for the sooner you come the better will be your opportunity to choose a good place to settle."

A new Scandinavia. Probably no profound knowledge lay behind Frederika Bremer's oft-quoted prophecy concerning Minnesota's future as a new Scandinavia. " The climate, the situation, the character of the scenery," she said, " agrees with our people better than that of any other of the American states, and none of them appear to me to have a greater or more beautiful future than Minnesota." With more moderation it might have been said that Minnesota shares with Scandinavia certain broad resemblances of climate and landscape, as do also other states and regions in the North and Canada. As the state having the largest remaining area of good farm land at the time of the principal Scandinavian immigration to America, Minnesota was in a position to receive a large portion of it.

Some of the lands settled solidly by Norwegians and Swedes bore little resemblance to the country of their origin. Houston County in southeastern Minnesota, originally called Norwegian Ridge, and a point of dispersal for incoming immigrants from Scandinavia, was typical prairie-woodland country; the woodland, at least, gave some suggestion of Norway. Spreading rapidly with the frontier or, more truly, carrying the frontier with them, the people from rugged Norway took up the level prairie land and fashioned for themselves a new way of life. The newcomers showed great adaptability in extending their settlements into nearly all parts of the state, not only on farms but in towns and cities.

Deliberate efforts were made to attract Scandinavians to Minnesota. The State Board of Immigration took a leading hand in this, thus coming into competition with similar agencies in Wisconsin. Favored by a liberal appropriation, Minnesota sent agents to Eastern ports to meet the immigrants and, to make sure that they were not diverted on the way, accompany them on the westward trip. Temporary homes sometimes awaited the newcomers when they reached the state, and aid was extended them in filing upon land. Especially influential was a Swedish-American agent who it is reported made trips to Sweden, and on one occasion led to America a party of 800 Swedish immigrants. Descriptive literature was printed and circulated by various state bureaus.

In their aggressive campaign for Scandinavian immigrants, the state agencies were aided by railroad companies and commercial firms of various types. Railroads were extending into the state in the eventful year of 1862, introducing a new factor into Minnesota settlement. It was to the advantage of the railroads to have people along their rights of way, not only assuring them of freight revenue but enabling them to dispose of the " railroad land " that had been granted by the Government as an inducement to extend their lines. The railroads did not direct their appeals exclusively to Swedish or Norwegian immigrants, but accepted all comers, in a procedure which became common at later times in the parts of the United States farther west.

RAILROADS AS FACTORS IN NEW SETTLEMENT

The first Minnesota railroads, advancing westward from Wisconsin and northward from Iowa, entered areas already occupied and, for a brief period, ended at existent towns and cities. Soon, however, the steel rails were extending beyond the developed regions, heading for distant objectives. Anticipating the routes the railroads would take became a favorite topic of discussion at general stores and neighborhood gatherings. A stranger appearing in such a community, especially one bearing equipment that might be identified as a tripod or a theodolite, was immediately suspect as a railroad surveyor, and was the central point of rumors that spread like wildfire throughout the countryside. To locate along a railroad, especially in advance of its arrival, was an achievement often rewarded by increased land values.

The tracing of a developing railroad pattern is a special kind of history, necessarily long and involved, and will not be attempted here. The accomplishments of ten years in Minnesota are shown in the map of railroad lines for 1869 and 1879, a critical period in the development of the state (Fig. 87). It is especially important to know that these new lines of travel led to developments which were far less spontaneous than those which accompanied the military and stage roads of the earlier day. Between their main points of origin and destination, the railroad companies played a leading part in deciding where towns were to be located. Taken into consideration were such items as the spacing of stations to accommodate expected settlement, and convenient locations for division points and freight yards.

Many of the railroad companies platted towns along the rights of way and thus determined the town plan for years to come. They also bestowed names on the towns when they existed merely as checkerboard lines on blueprints. Most commonly selected were names that could be easily enunciated, and not likely to be confused with some other name on the same railroad. Descriptive names

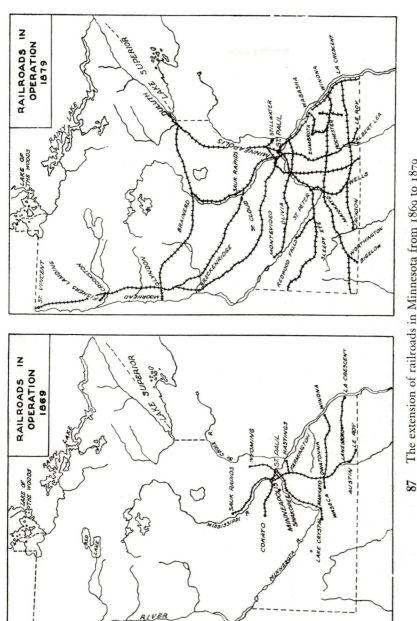

87   The extension of railroads in Minnesota from 1869 to 1879

and names of Indian origin, unless satisfying the test of pronounceability, were largely discarded. Thus on the Northern Pacific line between Brainerd and Moorhead, one encounters such names as Aldrich, Verndale, New York Mills, Frazee, and Detroit Lakes.

Great areas of public land were granted to the railroad companies building across Minnesota. Two such railroads, eventually to become transcontinental ones, were the Northern Pacific and the Chicago, Milwaukee, St. Paul & Pacific. As a means of getting their lands into the hands of settlers, real-estate companies of a special variety were organized. The ambitious nature of one of them is suggested by its title: Lake Superior and Puget Sound Company. The activities of the land companies were varied and far-reaching: they platted towns, advertised opportunities for settlement, organized colonies, and aided colonists in getting a start in their new venture. They accepted part payment for railroad land and, on occasion, built houses to be paid for in installments. The companies adopted aggressive methods, because the more land they sold, the greater was the reward.

Many of the towns and cities along the Brainerd-to-Moorhead stretch of the Northern Pacific came into being in this manner. Two of them, Detroit Lakes and Hawley, will serve as examples of the new kind of human geography introduced by the railroad.

Detroit Lakes, now one of the larger cities of western Minnesota, originated in 1871 as a colony. Its site was selected as a suitable place for a town. Soon after it was platted, the railroad constructed a number of houses to be paid for by those who were to come. Advertising matter of the promoters pointed out that the region was blessed with an excellent climate, the soils were deep and fertile, the surrounding forests were a source of future wealth, and the country was "well watered." Many of the first colonists were disappointed upon their arrival, remembering something of the advance advertising. They agreed that the land was indeed well watered, with its extensive lakes and swamps, but felt that the promoters had overestimated the depth of the soil and other advantages. The initial disappointment was finally overcome and Detroit Lakes grew substantially, as its present population of about 5,000 will indicate.

The town of Hawley, farther west on the same railroad, originated as an English colony. The Reverend George Rodgers of Stalbridge, England, on salary from the Northern Pacific, came to this country in 1872 to select a suitable place for a group of his countrymen to settle in. After some inspection of various possibilities he pronounced Minnesota to be a favorable place for colonization and, not unexpectedly in view of his sponsorship, placed his stamp of approval on the Hawley site. The people came to take up the land in 1873. Other English colonies, such as Furness, developed on the railroad lands of northwestern Minnesota. Still others took root in the southern part of the state, including the city of Fairmont in Martin County, near the Iowa line.

CHAPTER 19

The United States in 1870

REGION by region, state by state, we have advanced with the crest of settle-ment to the Far West of the 1870's. From this vantage point, bordering the lands of uncertain rainfall, it will be desirable to obtain an over-all picture of the Republic that now extended from coast to coast. A back-tracking journey to the East will permit attention to major developments in various regions since the period of their discussion in foregoing pages. Atlantic seaboard geography, for example, contained in 1870 elements not present fifty years before, and the South had also changed in many particulars. A forward look toward the Pacific will serve as preparation for chapters to follow on various parts of the West — the Great Plains, the Rocky Mountains, the Southwest, and the Pacific Coast. The signpost for this chapter, then, points in two directions — forward and back.

The United States in 1870 was continental, with an area computed by the geographer of the United States census at 3,025,600 square miles. The Census Bureau, not so sure of the size of recently-acquired Alaska, usually excluded that detached territory from its computations of area, population, and resources, for its character was poorly understood. Purchased from Russia through the influence of William H. Seward, Secretary of State, it was popularly known as Seward's Folly or Seward's Icebox.

The handiwork of the empire-builders, of whom Seward was then the most recent example, was apparent in the map of the West. Through conquest and annexation, purchase and international agreement, the boundaries of the nation had been thrown around 2,000,000 square miles of Western land. All this had been accomplished within less than half a century, under the observation of thousands of persons then living. To learn these acquisitions was a part of the geography lesson of those days: the Louisiana Purchase, Texas (which actually included eastern New Mexico and southern Colorado), the First Mexican Cession (California, Nevada, Utah), and the Second Cession, otherwise known as the Gadsden Purchase. The accessions of territory in continental United States, with dates and cumulative areas, are shown in the following table.

UNITED STATES TERRITORIAL ACCESSIONS

Accession	Area of Accession (in square miles)	Total Area (in square miles)
Original territory	827,844	827,844
Louisiana, 1803, Oregon, 1846	1,171,931	1,999,775
Florida, 1821	59,268	2,059,043
Texas, 1845	376,163	2,435,206
First Mexican Cession, 1848	545,753	2,980,959
Gadsden Purchase, 1853	44,641	3,025,600

The people of the United States at first viewed these territorial gains with a divided national mind. To many they were a fulfillment of the country's destiny, foreseen when the Mississippi River formed the western boundary. The new possessions, poorly known as they were, furnished themes for orations and books on " manifest destiny " and the " march of empire " to the westward. Others considered the Far West to be beyond the reach of the Eastern settlements, not likely ever to serve useful purposes. They were perhaps familiar with existing maps on which " Great American Desert " was boldly printed across the interior, or were moved by the words of William Cullen Bryant, who spoke of

> The continuous woods where rolls the Oregon
> And knows no sound save its own dashings.

Gradually the public was educated to think in continental terms. Within a year after the First Mexican Cession came reports of precious metals in California and the beginning of the gold rush to the " diggings " on Sutter's Creek. Many people had never heard the name " California " until this event, but soon thereafter the world was talking about it, even in remote China. Following in chronological sequence was the Gadsden Purchase of southern Arizona from Mexico in 1853, involving an area perhaps not intrinsically valuable but vital to the control of southern routes to the new El Dorado.

To link the new settlements on the Pacific with the settled East became the great project of the day. Written communication across the intervening space was more quickly accomplished, however, than was mass transportation of people and supplies. The swift pony-express rider bridged the gap until he was displaced by the even faster telegraph and railroad. The announcement in 1848 of a proposed Atlantic and Pacific telegraph appeared utterly visionary to most people, including government officials. At that time the First Telegraph Range linked the Atlantic States with St. Louis, Keokuk, Davenport, and Dubuque; to extend it farther seemed chimerical indeed. The very title adopted by the telegraph company enforced continental thinking.

Iron rails extending westward from Omaha and eastward from Sacramento met near Ogden, Utah, in 1869, only twenty years after the discovery of California gold. On this occasion the *" Life "* magazine of its time, Frank Leslie's *Illustrated Newspaper,* exclaimed:

See now the changes produced in the brief space of twenty years! Notwithstanding the drawbacks connected with such a civil war as the world has never seen before . . . the vast region between the Mississippi River and the Pacific Ocean has been divided into organized States and Territories, and our boundaries pushed twelve hundred miles out into the Pacific Ocean, and up into the Arctic regions, by the acquisition of Alaska — with railroad facilities transporting passengers in palace-cars within a week between New York and San Francisco, and with telegraphs that furnish news of the business-day of London and New York in time for the California merchants to operate . . . several hours before the apparent time at which they started, beating the sun itself in their transit across the continent.

While the nation was adding vast Western territories, the population was constantly increasing. Year by year from 1790 to 1860, the statisticians had announced percentage increases varying from 3.2 to 3.6. This record was shattered during the war-torn years of the 1860's, years also of diminished immigration, when the annual increase was only 2 per cent. But by 1870 the rate of population increase approached its earlier figure, a temporary recovery followed by an increment during the decade 1880–90 of 24.86 per cent. The center of population advanced to the west at about 4 miles a year, from Baltimore in 1790 to Cincinnati in 1880 (Fig. 88). The precise center of population during the century was affected mainly by Western settlement and by annexations, the War between the States, and the great increase in Southern population following the war and reconstruction.

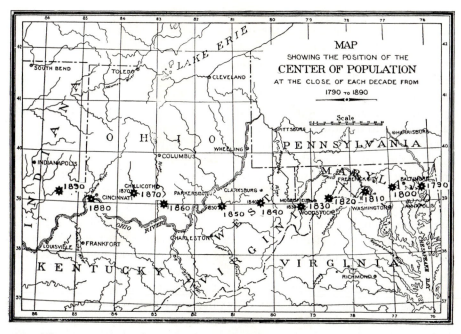

88   The center of population by decades, from 1790 to 1890. From Henry Gannett, *Statistical Atlas of the United States*, 1898.

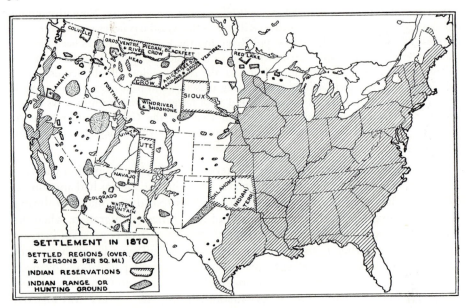

89   Settlement of the United States in 1870. Simplified from a map in Henry Gannett, *Statistical Atlas of the United States,* 1898.

Accessions of Western territories necessarily caused variations in the density of population as calculated from the decennial censuses. The number of people to a square mile was 6.41 in 1800, but with the Louisiana Purchase added, the figure dropped to 3.62 in 1810. For the next two decades population density increased gradually to 8.29. The Western acquisitions of the 1850's again reduced the population density, this time to 7.78, but subsequent decades have shown a continual upward trend. In 1870 the United States was a land-rich nation, counting only 12.74 persons to the square mile.

The geography student of today should have no difficulty in recognizing the states of the East, the South, and the Midwest as they were in 1870. In number and outline they were the same as now; no territories remained for further division east of the Mississippi River. The Eastern states contained 90 per cent of the country's population, which in 1870 had increased to 38,558,371 — an impressive figure, though it fell far short of the optimistic predictions of the 1790's.

A generalized view of inhabited United States emphasizes the continuity of the settled area from the Atlantic coast to eastern Nebraska and Kansas (Fig. 89). The north-south line marking the limit of interior settlement may be easily kept in mind as the 97th meridian, which it closely approximated. The map does not bring out variations in density of population, which was heaviest in southern New England, the central seaboard states, and westward through the Ohio Valley and bordering the lower Great Lakes. New York, Pennsylvania, Illinois, and Ohio were then, as now, the four ranking states in numbers of inhabitants. Rhode Island, with over 300 persons to the square mile, was the most densely populated state, followed closely by Massachusetts. Unsettled areas, with less than 2 persons to the square mile, were where they would be expected — southern Florida, northwestern Maine, the Adirondacks of New York, and portions of upper Michigan, Wisconsin, and Minnesota.

THE MAGIC OF THE RAILROADS

Undoubtedly, the most effective agent of change had been the railroad. The expanding network of iron rails (not steel until the 1870's) was in part the effect and in part the cause of industrial changes of the time. It contributed to the transformation of small towns to commercial and industrial cities, and opened up resources which had theretofore been of little significance. Changes wrought by the railroads included also the development of great inland cities such as Chicago, the extension of agriculture into vast areas of land inaccessible by water, and an enormous increase in movement of persons and freight from place to place. Railroad depot or junction competed with ocean port and river landing as nuclei of settlement.

The year of birth of the American railroad system was 1830 and the place was Maryland, where fifteen miles of track were laid for the Baltimore & Ohio. Within ten years there were about 20 disconnected lines scattered over the Eastern states. Boston, Philadelphia, and Baltimore, the first ocean-port terminals of rail lines, were soon rivaled by New York and Washington. Inland cities such as Cincinnati, Cleveland, and Detroit, formerly linked to trade by road and waterway, were quickly transformed into rail centers. Indianapolis, originally located without reference to water transport, became the hub of a rail center with lines running in all directions. Most surprising was Chicago, a small town in 1840, which burgeoned to a city of 300,000 in 1871, the year of its great fire. As seen by a British visitor, Chicago was a city of crowded, bustling, and busy thoroughfares, " abounding in signs of life and energy " — the same impression that is received by a visitor of today.

All through the first half-century of railroad building in the Eastern states there were never enough lines to take care of freight and passenger demands. With 50,000 miles of track in operation in 1870, enough to girdle the earth twice, plans for the extension of other lines were announced almost daily (Fig. 90). A new route connecting the Atlantic seaboard with the Ohio Valley was " imperatively needed " to accommodate existing traffic. It was estimated that each year 50,000,000 tons of Midwestern and Southern produce — grain, flour, cattle, tobacco, cotton — must be moved to Eastern cities and Atlantic ports.

The Chesapeake & Ohio was projected at this time, not only for the purpose of moving existing traffic, but to enable the opening-up of coal mines in West Virginia, whose resources were known to be huge but, so far, impractical of development. Observers in 1870 considered it fortunate that " another trunk line to the West is nearly completed, which will connect the unfailing naviga-

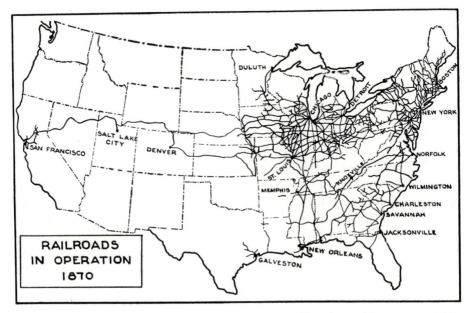

90   Railroads in operation, 1870. Reproduced by permission from C. O. Paullin's *Atlas of the Historical Geography of the United States,* published jointly by the Carnegie Institution of Washington and the American Geographical Society of New York, 1932.

tion of the great Chesapeake Bay with the chief railroad and river cities of the West by a route shorter and of easier grades than the older lines." Plans of still other railroad companies were hailed with equal optimism, apparently by everyone except proponents of river navigation.

Declining canal traffic. Before the coming of the railroad, the Erie Canal was the greatest achievement in internal communication, forerunner of other canals of nearly equal dimensions. Although the Erie was ready for operation only five years before tracks were first laid in Maryland, two decades elapsed before the railroads were sufficiently unified and extensive to be viewed as a serious threat to slow-moving, if cheaper, canal traffic. Many people spoke of the puffing locomotive with scorn, just as at a later day the " horseless buggy " was for a time an object of derision.

During this period of grace, Midwestern canals were being rushed to completion, and bulk traffic moved by water across New York State with no sure signs of decline. But the decline was inevitable. Tracks were laid alongside the canals and navigable rivers, or wherever they were thought to be necessary or profitable. Shipping costs by rail were gradually lowered to be within hailing distance of canal rates. Cheapening of rail movement was accomplished by the consolidation of formerly separate lines, and by technical improvements of equipment and roadbeds. It was soon found that solid roadbeds with fewer curves could accommodate larger rolling stock and faster-moving locomotives. Road-beds were widened to permit double tracks, in answer to ever increasing demands for speedy service. Of all technical changes, perhaps the most far-reaching and least conspicuous was the substitution of steel rails for those made of wrought iron.

In their eagerness to serve the public better than their waterway competitors had done, railroad companies contracted to handle freight that was at first un-profitable, only to find that shipments were so greatly increased that even at the lowered rates the business yielded a profit. More than this, railroad com-panies competed with each other, leading to a " railroad war " which lowered freight rates to 3 cents a ton mile in 1860, higher than rates for canal-borne traffic, but offset by speed of delivery. Cheap and bulky commodities not requiring quick passage to market were still transported by canals and rivers in those regions so provided, but railroads absorbed ever increasing amounts of the more valuable freight and passenger traffic. Elimination of canal tolls, a final desperate effort to keep canal traffic alive, was unavailing. By the 1860's water-way transportation was distinctly subordinate to railway traffic — and the canal period was over.

OVERSEAS COMMERCE, COASTWISE TRADE, GREAT LAKES SHIPPING

When we last considered maritime industries, the United States was a small, newly formed nation facing on the Atlantic Ocean. Until enterprising merchant-men entered the field, the Atlantic trade had been all but entirely divided be-tween the British, the Dutch, and the Hanse Towns. Formidable competition though this was, United States commerce rapidly increased, reaching a cul-minating point in 1810, when nearly 90 per cent of our commerce was being carried in American vessels. Then came the restrictive measures preceding the War of 1812, followed by the war itself and that, in turn, by a five-year depres-sion. So much has been related more fully in earlier pages.

A condensed survey of American commerce from 1820 to 1870 first takes note of the rapid recovery of maritime activities following the stagnation of the period of the War of 1812. From 1820 to 1830, American shipyards were again busy turning out vessels with all kinds of rigging, and in short order these boats were carrying nine-tenths of the country's foreign commerce. " In every respect," according to one authority, " we may say that this period represents the most flourishing condition of shipping in American history." There were few dis-turbing circumstances at home or abroad, tonnage engaged in shipping con-stantly mounted, and it appeared likely that the chief commercial rival, Great Britain, would soon be forced into second place.

But again the carrying trade declined, and for reasons not fully understood at the time. The 1830's were the beginning of a period of major change in types of ocean carriers, with steam-powered craft displacing wooden sailing vessels.

For the time being the United States was at a disadvantage, because England, more advanced in industrialization, was in a better position to supply modernized equipment. The famed clipper ship, respected in all parts of the world, was about to meet her master, just as in earlier days American sailing vessels had shown their superiority to foreign-built ships. Steam-powered, screw-propelled craft, built mainly in Britain, captured the more profitable trade. The new ships held closely to the major trade lanes of short hauls and valuable cargo, leaving to sailing vessels the long voyages for bulk products — somewhat paralleling the canal-railroad situation.

The building of wooden ships powered by steam or sail continued in American shipyards, for there was a great domestic business to be carried on. Consider a single aspect of it: the movement of people and supplies to the gold fields of California. Thousands of gold-seekers were determined to go there; any kind of route, by land or water, would do. A route favored by many " rushers " was by water, down-coast to the Gulf of Mexico and the Caribbean, then by land across the Isthmus of Panama to await passage by another boat to San Francisco. Others rounded Cape Horn, going " all the way by sea to California." All this stimulated a demand for American ships — an artificial demand, it has been called — that tended to make the country more dependent upon foreign vessels in its overseas commerce.

Following this period of renewed activity came the paralyzing effects of the War between the States. By the end of the war, less than one-third of our imports and exports was carried in American bottoms. Not all of this reduction can be attributed to wartime conditions. It must be borne in mind that the country's interests had turned landward. Internal improvements, such as roads and railroads, became paramount; agriculture and manufacturing absorbed the energy of the people. In short, the United States had become a continental rather than a maritime country. Through its expansion, the nation now faced on two oceans three thousand miles apart. Disparities being what they were, it is not surprising that Bostonians were amazed to read news accounts of a new kind of immigration to America — that of Chinese to California. Steerage passage from Hong Kong to San Francisco cost about $50, and entitled the immigrant to his subsistence from port to port. " The Chinese have crowded out an army of white laborers," the press complained, at the same time granting that the Chinese " are quiet and inoffensive, doing their work conscientiously, and retiring peacefully at night to their own quarters."

Unhampered by international difficulties, the domestic coastwise trade continued its upward trend throughout the first half of the nineteenth century, reaching its culminating point in 1860. Tonnage enrolled in the coastal trade in that year was 2,764,589, greater by 300,000 tons than the shipping licensed for foreign trade.

Shipping on the Great Lakes also increased in importance throughout the century. Mounting demands for iron, copper, and lumber, as well as the extension of wheat cultivation in Minnesota, naturally resulted in greatly increased tonnages passing from the upper lakes to the East. During the seven months of navigation in 1870, for example, 690,000 tons of cargo were locked through the Soo Canal. Parenthetically, it may be pointed out that the Soo Canal was not at that time a close rival of the Suez Canal, with which it is now often compared. It was in 1889, when over 7,000,000 tons passed through the Soo locks, that the American canal first surpassed the Suez in tonnage.

Not only were there more Great Lakes vessels built each year, but the average size constantly increased, embodying new developments in design and power. Great Lakes navigation became integrated with rail transportation, in marked contrast to the competitive spirit which prevailed between railroads and inland canals. The advantage of a combined lake-and-rail haul was more positive than it is today. In 1870 it cost 33.3 cents to haul a bushel of wheat from Chicago to New York by rail, while a combined lake-and-rail haul cost 17.1 cents.

THE FISHING INDUSTRIES

Deep-sea fishing industries, it may be recalled, barely survived the difficulties of the early years of the nineteenth century. Hardest hit was whaling. With the virtual extermination of whales in near-by waters, American whalers were forced to journey halfway around the world to reach profitable ground. This could not be done with outmoded equipment, hence the industry was faced with a severe test of readjustment. The whaling fleets all but disappeared, only a few shipowners holding on in the old ports.

These ports—New Bedford, Nantucket, and Barnstable—were again to know the activity of earlier times. The industry revived in the 1830's and continued on the upgrade until 1862, the period known as the Golden Age of the whale fishery. Newly outfitted boats sought the whale in the North and the South Pacific, and the products of bone and oil were sold on a world-wide market. A few additional whaling bases developed in New England, and the appearance of San Francisco on the list of whaling ports pointed up a shift of operations to the Pacific. But before the Pacific-based whaling fleets reached significant size, the industry was heading toward its final decline. Depredations upon whaling boats by Confederate cruisers were not so important in bringing the Golden Age to an end as the appearance on the markets of products competing with those of whaling. Coal oil was found superior to whale oil, and steel made better corset stays than did whalebone.

The codfishery also reached its culminating point in 1862, when 230,000 tons were enrolled. Cod-fishing, like whaling, remained largely a New England industry, although a few vessels were registered from Virginia, Florida, and California. Old fishing grounds were annually visited, with new equipment and more modern methods. Seining and netting, replacing hand methods of catching fish, greatly increased the take on fishing voyages. Inshore and river fishing were also modernized throughout the nineteenth century, but the overfishing and the increasing pollution of rivers, into which drained the waste of cities and factories, gradually reduced the size of the salmon and shad runs. Each spring season, great nets were taken out of storage in fishing shacks and spread in Northern rivers at the height of the shad run. A favored netting spot on the Delaware was Gloucester Point, a short distance below Philadelphia.

Fishing both in the deep sea and near shore fared poorly in a country constantly expanding inland, and in which all manner of new industries were daily appearing.

INDUSTRIAL DEVELOPMENTS

Labor was cheap and raw materials were plentiful in the United States a century ago. In 1850, adult hands in Rhode Island woolen mills worked fourteen hours a day at 4½ cents an hour. During the next ten years, such workers were paid 5 cents an hour; by 1867, 7½ cents. In 1870, textile weavers in the same state worked only a twelve-hour day at 8 cents an hour, thus earning a daily wage of about $1. Workers in Philadelphia in a locomotive works received a weekly wage of $12, firemen in gasworks $3 a day, common laborers about $1.50 a day. Passenger-car conductors were plutocratic, receiving a daily wage of $3.85. It is estimated that the average daily earnings of all gainfully employed persons in Illinois in 1870 were about $2. These wages, however, bought far more in necessities than a similar amount does today. The foregoing statistics help one to understand why investment in manufacturing enterprises was attractive to men with accumulated capital. In 1870, a moderate-sized factory cost about $8,000, an amount within the reach of many persons.

Besides these labor conditions, there was an abundance of raw materials and of partly fabricated products adaptable to new uses or needing change to a new form. The annual cotton yield after 1865 approached 2,500,000 bales, the growing of which gave employment to the largest number of persons engaged in any agricultural industry. Cotton by itself, however, was of little value; it must be spun into yarn and woven into fabrics. Of cereal grains, mostly wheat, there were 1,500,000,000 bushels a year; various food-processing industries derived from this rich annual harvest. A million tons of pig iron were drawn from blast furnaces each year in the 1860's. Some of it went into open-hearth and crucible steel, and this in turn was made into a variety of products. The growing railroad system placed increasing demands on iron and coal mines, not only for rails, but for equipment that moved over them. In 1870, the Baldwin Locomotive Works were producing a standard engine for $12,000, and were exporting many of these to Europe. There was demand for plows, wagons, tools of all kinds, clothing, household equipment, machines to make machines — a thousand and one types of consumer goods.

In 1876 the Centennial Exposition in Philadelphia gave visitors a concentrated view of the country's industrial development up to that time. The Main Building, sprawling over 21 acres, housed the departments of mining and manufactures; another structure, covering 14 acres, was devoted to machinery. Standing before the 700-ton Corliss steam engine in the Machine Building, President Grant chose appropriate words to open the exposition:

One hundred years ago our country was new and but partially settled. Our necessities have compelled us to chiefly expend our means and time in felling forests, subduing prairies, building dwellings, factories, ships, docks, warehouses, roads, canals, and machinery. Burdened by these great primal works of necessity, which could not be delayed, we have yet done what this Exposition will show in the direction of rivaling older and more advanced nations in law, medicine, and theology, in science, literature, philosophy, and the fine arts. While we are proud of what we have done, we regret that we have not done more. Our achievements have been great enough, however, to make it easy for our people to acknowledge merit wherever found.

In the opinion of the President, ours was a materialistic nation.

American-made products alone did not fill these acres of buildings, for there were exhibits from a score of other countries. Some foreign products on display were viewed as novelties, their potential development in American manufacture undreamed-of. The India Rubber Exhibit, for example, was assembled by New York and Boston firms because of the " great ignorance regarding this important article of commerce," first imported into the United States in 1830. But rubber consumption had increased to 7,000 tons in 1876, years before its suitability for tires had been considered.

In a tour through the Centennial Exposition the visitor could see such products of American manufacture as the new wallpaper-printing press; tools and cutlery from Connecticut; sewing machines from New Jersey; Waltham watches from New York and Elgins from Chicago; Joseph Gillott's steel pens; Prince's Improved Fountain Pen, " guaranteed to write ten hours "; the typewriter, " a machine to supersede the pen for all kinds of writing except book-keeping "; glove-fitting corsets with steel braces from New York; Knabe pianos from Baltimore; organs and melodeons from Buffalo; Reliance Clothes Wringers from Providence; Tiffany's jewelry; ornamental-iron and bronzed-iron bedsteads; shoe machinery from Lynn, Massachusetts, where most of the country's shoes were made; baseballs from Nassau Street; Powell guns from Cincinnati; furnaces, steam engines, carriages, and wagons from various cities of the East and the Midwest; and, for the children, magic lanterns and " sciopticans " from Philadelphia.

In short, American manufactures were highly varied, reflecting inventiveness, enterprise, capital funds, cheap labor, abundance of raw materials, an insatiable public demand, and ease of transportation. The following statistics indicate in round numbers the general rise of the manufacturing industries over a thirty-year period.

AMERICAN MANUFACTURING, 1850–1880

Capital Invested		Value of Product	
1850	$500,000,000	1850	$500,000,000
1860	1,000,000,000	1860	750,000,000
1870	1,750,000,000	1870	1,230,000,000
1880	2,750,000,000	1880	2,000,000,000

Average Capital per Establishment		Number of Persons Employed	
1850	$4,000	1850	900,000
1860	7,000	1860	1,130,000
1870	6,800	1870	2,000,000
1880	11,000	1880	2,700,000

Average Yearly Wages per Employee	
1850	$250
1860	290
1870	310
1880	340

CITIES AND MANUFACTURING

In 1870, within the limits of a dozen major cities was concentrated the greater part of the country's billion-dollar manufacturing industry. Perhaps 90 per cent of these industries were within the northeastern " rectangle," with its four " corners " at Boston, Baltimore, St. Louis, and Chicago. We can further localize the manufacturing area by considering Pittsburgh to be its center of gravity. Pittsburgh itself was not one of the great cities of 1870, if we consider the minimum of greatness to be represented by the population figure of 100,000. In round numbers, the larger cities ranked as follows:

COMPARATIVE CITY POPULATIONS, 1870
(in thousands)

New York	942	Cincinnati	216
Philadelphia	674	New Orleans	192
Brooklyn	396	San Francisco	150
St. Louis	311	Buffalo	117
Chicago	300	Washington	110
Baltimore	267	Newark	105
Boston	250	Louisville	100

Location on navigable water was perhaps the only common characteristic of the major cities in 1870. In other respects they were noticeably diverse, especially in their degree of industrialization. Washington, San Francisco, and New Orleans, mainly political or commercial centers, showed no indications of great manufacturing enterprise. On the other hand, Philadelphia had shown industrial trends almost from the outset. The combined populations of New York, Brooklyn, and Newark gave to that limited area the leading position both in commerce and in manufacturing. New York, already metropolitan, was experiencing problems of congestion in its downtown section, and this led to various projects for harbor improvement and more rapid transportation within the city. A survey conducted under the direction of General George B. McClellan of war fame showed to the satisfaction of New Yorkers that " our metropolis is unrivalled in its position as a great maritime and commercial mart," yet it was capable of improvement. The construction of a river wall some 200 feet into the East River and the Hudson, and filling in behind, was seen as the best means of creating a new shore line from which docks could project into deep water along 25 miles of harbor. Residents of the city were also asked to consider at this time the possibility of an elevated railroad system to relieve traffic on the crowded streets of Manhattan.

Types of manufacturing dependent more on skilled labor than on large amounts of raw material were localized in southern New England, eastern New York and Pennsylvania, and adjacent portions of New Jersey and Maryland. Here were industries such as the making of watches and clocks, high-grade textiles, and machine and hand tools, the value of all these being derived mainly from skilled labor. The heavy industries of iron and steel, milling, and food processing were more widely distributed, gravitating toward the supplies of raw material and coal. Hence the iron and steel industries centered about western Pennsylvania near the ore and the developing coal mines (in which there were already serious labor troubles). A general ranking of the major industries in 1870 is offered below.

MAJOR AMERICAN INDUSTRIES, 1870

1. Lumber and woodworking industries
2. Flour-mill and gristmill products
3. Clothing
4. Iron and steel
5. Foundry and machine-shop products
6. Printing and publishing
7. Cotton goods
8. Boots and shoes
9. Woolen and worsted goods
10. Railroad cars
11. Tobacco products
12. Leather
13. Bakery products
14. Sugar and molasses refining
15. Carriages and wagons

AGRICULTURE, ESPECIALLY IN THE SOUTH

The foregoing discussion of manufacturing may have given the impression that the United States had become mainly a manufacturing country in the 1870's. So to think would be erroneous. Agriculture and stock-raising were still the predominant occupations, and lumbering was high on the list. These facts are suggested in the inventory of manufactures, which emphasizes farm and raw-material products. It has been said that manufacturing was a billion-dollar industry in 1870. Using this as a rough basis for comparisons, it appears that at the same time the combined value of farm machinery and implements was $8,000,000,000, and that the wheat crop of Minnesota alone far exceeded the value of all manufactured goods. Mining, though increasingly important, employed relatively few persons, with an annual value of product worth less than $500,000,000. Furthermore, the rural or small-town population far exceeded the city population. The geographer of the census considered as an urban element " that portion of the population which lived in cities of 8,000 inhabitants or more." The ratio had increased through the years at an accelerating rate, but in 1870 city dwellers represented only one-fifth of the total population. It may not be surprising to learn that the states with the largest total populations were also the states having the highest ratio of city dwellers.

RATIO OF URBAN TO TOTAL POPULATION, 1790–1870

1790	3.35	1820	4.93	1850	12.49
1800	3.97	1830	6.72	1860	16.13
1810	4.93	1840	8.52	1870	20.93

The South was the most truly rural section of the United States. Industries other than agriculture had made little headway before the onset of the civil conflict, from which a rapid recovery could not have been expected. Cotton manufacturing was fairly widespread in the antebellum period, with the largest concentration of mills along the Fall Line of the Piedmont, particularly in Georgia. Many of the mills were patterned after those of the Northern states. The iron industries were of little significance during this period, but the outbreak of hostilities led to the hasty erection of forges and bloomeries near sources of iron ore. Manufacturing developments were so limited that new ventures were given more publicity than similar events received in the industrialized North. Thus the announcement of a new rolling mill in Atlanta in 1858 led to widespread comment. Relatively, however, Southern manufacturing declined as cotton-growing expanded into new areas. Of the destruction caused by the war it need only be remarked that nearly all Southern industrial plants and great mileages of railroad within the zone of conflict were destroyed or put out of commission.

The period of the War between the States and recovery has long been accepted as a dividing point in Southern development. In 1850, the South had 39 per cent of the country's population, which was less proportionally than in earlier times. A few examples may suffice for illustrative purposes. Charleston, fourth in size among American cities in 1790, was twenty-sixth in position in 1870. Virginia, first state in population until 1810, dropped to fifth place in the same period, and North Carolina plunged from third to twelfth place. Many factors were accountable for this change, but writers are agreed that the institution of slavery was chiefly responsible. European immigrants tended to avoid the South as a place of settlement; furthermore, the Cotton Belt lost a large percentage of its natural population increase through emigration to the North and the West. Small-scale farmers or nonslaveowners or renters whose ties to the land were insecure added to the tide of Western emigration. Many persons were out of sympathy with prevailing institutions, or had suffered economic loss from the one-crop cotton economy which led to soil impoverishment and erosion.

The reader should remember that only one-half of the landowners in the Southern states held slaves, and that not more than one-third of the white population was slaveowning.

Following the war and reconstruction, population increased and spread into new areas to which cotton and other Southern staples were adapted. With the annexation of Texas a new frontier opened up, and the Cotton Belt bulged into the humid eastern portion of the new state. Population growth in the South following the war, as well as a trend toward manufacturing, is well shown in the rise of Southern cities. A striking example is Atlanta, which grew from a hilltop railroad station in the 1830's to a city of nearly 22,000 in 1870. Atlanta's location in the Piedmont region, at the southern end of the rugged Appalachians, endowed it with advantages which became apparent as the railroad system expanded in the new era. Atlanta was the first of the major Southern cities to develop without facilities for water transport. Other Southern cities which showed evidence of renewed growth in the 1870's were Mobile, Montgomery, Vicksburg, and Nashville.

BEYOND THE NINETY–SEVENTH MERIDIAN

One-half the nation's area, but in 1870 only one-tenth of its population, lay westward of the 97th meridian. It was called " Our New West " by Editor Samuel Bowles, one of the first of a number of distinguished observers to travel over the Union Pacific to California after completion of the road in 1869. The land *was* new to the great majority of American citizens, but it was old in written annals. For well over a century, explorers and surveyors had traveled over the great spaces and mountain ranges. Sixty-five years before Bowles set out westward in the luxury of a railroad car, Lewis and Clark began their epochal journey up the Missouri to the then unknown Oregon country.

The Lewis and Clark expedition was only the first of many exploring parties to be dispatched across the West. During the 1840's and 1850's the number of surveyors became so great as to defy an orderly listing of their movements. The objectives of the explorers became increasingly comprehensive as great areas fell within the domain of the United States. One objective, however, provided a common thread for a half-century of exploratory effort and report: the finding of routes across the Great Plains, over or through the Rocky Mountains and the interior plateaus, to the Pacific coast. Routes, therefore, will concern us very largely in the chapters to follow, just as they were emphasized on the map that Bowles ordered to be printed in 1869 (Fig. 91).

To the average traveler in 1870, Western routes were reduced to a simplicity unknown to his predecessors. There was one completed railroad, the Union Pacific, following for the most part the old-time central or overland trail to Salt Lake City and California. But its beginning was different, for the railroad took off — the expression is thoughtfully chosen — from Omaha, while Independence or Kansas City, Missouri, was the earlier beginning of the trail. On the

MAP TO ACCOMPANY "OUR NEW WEST" BY SAMUEL BOWLES.

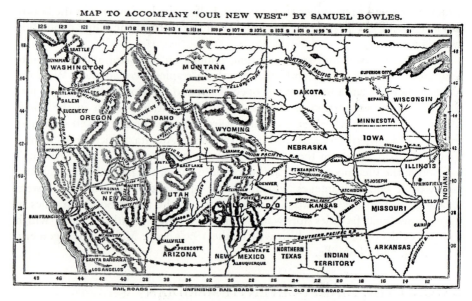

91   A generalized view of western United States in 1869. From *Our New West,* by
Samuel Bowles, Hartford, 1869.

maps of the 1870's the trail appears as the Old Stage Road, for that had been
its principal use just prior to the railroad era. One other rail line stretched across
the plains, from Kansas City to Denver. This was the Kansas Pacific, not yet
completed beyond Denver but projected, and soon completed, to Cheyenne. To
preserve a sense of proportion in a chapter that has discussed the great cities
of the Eastern states, it should be pointed out that in 1870 Denver was a town
of 5,000 inhabitants in the Territory of Colorado. Denver was the largest center
in all the space between Kansas City and the Rocky Mountains, then as now,
and more closely identified with the mountains than with the Great Plains.

In addition to the operating Western railroads there were a number of projected lines, more or less approximating the original trails of explorers and emigrants. Some of these had been given names which, when completed, they
actually assumed, examples being the Northern Pacific and the Southern Pacific.
Other rail lines appearing on the maps reflected the hope and faith of a country
aiming at great conquests, boldly assuming the future settlement of areas im-
perfectly known. It should be emphasized that the Bowles map is a simplified
view of the West and its routes, suitable for introductory purposes.

Regions of settlement. In studying the settlement map of the West (Fig. 89,
page 348), it is well to recall the discussion in Part One of colonial settlement in
the Southwest and California. In those earlier years, colonization had extended
into portions of present-day Texas and New Mexico and the coastal valleys of
the Pacific coast. The years intervening between the Colonial period and 1875
had witnessed an expansion within these earlier centers, particularly in Cali-

fornia following the gold rush of 1849. Within a year after that event, California was admitted as a state, having, unlike all other Western political areas, by-passed a Territorial period. California's population in 1870 was nearly 600,000, and the original small village of San Francisco was a big city of 150,000, typically American in character (Fig. 92).

With but slight interruptions, West-coast settlement extended into the Willamette Valley of Oregon, across the lower Columbia River, and into the Cowlitz Valley of Washington. A measure of Oregon's early development was its admission as a Territory in 1848.

The Rio Grande settlements of the Colonial period had enlarged, and by 1870

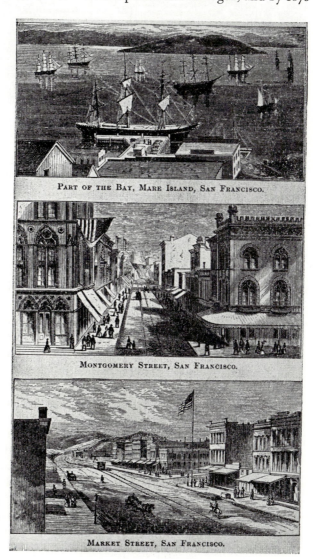

PART OF THE BAY, MARE ISLAND, SAN FRANCISCO.

MONTGOMERY STREET, SAN FRANCISCO.

MARKET STREET, SAN FRANCISCO.

92
Views of San Francisco in 1869. From Samuel Bowles, *Our New West,* Hartford 1869.

93   Austin, Nevada, in 1869. From Samuel Bowles, *Our New West,* Hartford, 1869.

joined the more recently developed mining and irrigation area of the Colorado mountain front and piedmont. Chiefly responsible for the beginning of Colorado settlement was the discovery of gold near Denver in 1858, and similar discoveries at other places in its mineralized zone. Colorado's population had reached less than 100,000 when its Territorial government was transformed into that of a state in 1876, from which date Colorado is sometimes known as the Centennial State.

A third main area of permanent settlement lay about midway between Colorado and California — in Utah. This appears on the map as a narrow north-south belt extending from southern Idaho through Logan and Salt Lake City into the Sevier River Valley of southern Utah. Selected in 1846 by the Mormons, this region has become a classic example of group settlement in the West.

Beyond these major belts of the inhabited West, white settlements appear as small, scattered islands. This impression is, in part, a fault of the map, which excludes from consideration those areas with less than 2 persons to a square mile. The extensive blank areas on the map were not so devoid of population as these suggest. Cattle ranches had by this time developed in the Great Plains region south of the Platte River. Their extensive areas contained many cattle, but few people. The Iliff Ranch in northern Colorado, for example, counted its cattle in such numbers that to lose 2,000 in one blizzard was not considered a great calamity. Iliff followed the practice of his contemporaries in ranging his stock over the public lands, operating from a " home ranch " near water supply. This was the " day of the cattleman," of which it has been said that Uncle Sam provided the land, Westerners contributed the experience in cattle-raising, and Easterners furnished the capital.

Some of the small dots of settlement scattered over the West were villages or forts, on trail or river; others were farming centers based on irrigation; and a great many were mining towns. Austin, Nevada, contained many of the features typical of early-day mining communities in the Rocky Mountain and Great Basin areas (Fig. 93). The main street of Cheyenne, Wyoming, in the same year suggests the village type developing on the main routes of travel on the western edge of the Great Plains. (See Fig. 94.) The use of the name Pike's Peak (always so spelled then) for business houses — the one in the photograph a jewelry " manufactory " — was a favorite practice.

INDIAN RESERVATIONS AND HUNTING GROUNDS

Not since early Colonial times had the American people been brought into such close contact with the Indians as in the quarter-century following the War between the States. The problem, as it indeed became, had been in the making for a long time, ever since the first removal of Eastern tribes and nations to trans-Mississippi reservations. The advancing frontier had now caught up with the reserved areas and was sending out lines of communication that could scarcely avoid skirting, or indeed penetrating, Indian-held territory. As one writer has said, " a barrier of Indians had been banked up against the western expansion of settlements."

The stronghold of the stolid and now determined Indian was the trans-Missouri country in present-day South Dakota and Montana. Here two incompatible races fought out the concluding phases of two centuries of conflict. The attitude of the Northern nations was well phrased by Chief Bear Rib of the Unkpapa Sioux at the discussion of the Harney Treaty at Fort Pierre (near present Pierre, South Dakota) in 1866. He asked with primitive eloquence:

94
Main Street of Cheyenne, Wyoming, 1869. Photograph by W. H. Jackson, courtesy of the U.S. Geological Survey.

To whom does this land belong? I believe it belongs to me. If you ask me for a piece of land I would not give it. I cannot spare it, and I like it very much. All this country on each side of this river belongs to me. I know that from the Mississippi to this river the country all belongs to us, and that we have travelled from the Yellowstone to the Platte. All this country, as I have said, is ours, and if you, my brother, should ask me for it, I would not give it to you, for I like it and I hope you will listen to me.

Indian spokesmen found many listeners, but were to experience a pardonable bewilderment when decisions were finally rendered. A changing and frequently conflicting policy was a major factor in misunderstandings that soon arose. During the 1860's, the trend was toward treating the Indian tribes as independent nations, with relations established by formal treaties to be ratified by the Indians and the United States Senate. Many of these treaties sought to cancel the Indian titles to their ceded lands, in return for which reserved lands or amnesty goods were given. As the supply of lands suitable for reservations approached exhaustion, amnesty payments became greater. Possibly the Indians viewed the payments as bribes to keep the peace; thus the more trouble they caused, the bigger would the payments become. At least this was the contention of the War Department, which was called upon with increasing frequency to quell disturbances. The War Department and the Indian Bureau were at odds in their attitudes and policies. Said General John Pope:

Both in an economic and humane view, the present Indian policy has been a woeful failure. Instead of preventing, it has been, beyond doubt, the source of all the Indian wars which have occurred of late years. So long as present Indian policy prevails, the money and goods furnished to the Indians will be a constant and sufficient temptation to unscrupulous white men, and so long may we expect outrages and Indian outbreaks on the frontier.

Good or bad, the Indian policy from 1820 to 1870 had resulted in enormous tracts of land reserved to the native people. The reservations reached their maximum size in 1870, comprehending a combined area larger than the states of California and Oregon together.

Indian Territory and Oklahoma. First in order of development was the officially named Indian Territory, since 1907 a part of the State of Oklahoma. Within Indian Territory was to be found the most varied assortment of Indian tribes and nations in America. Eastern and Western tribes occupied different sections. The Choctaw was the first nation to be transferred here, in 1820; then came other Muskogee peoples from the Southeast: Chickasaw, Creek, and Seminole. Remnants of tribes native to the lands north of the Ohio, such as the Seneca, the Shawnee, and the Wyandot, were grouped in the northeast corner. Potawatomi and Sac and Fox from Wisconsin found themselves neighbors again in their enforced new home.

Some order of geography was observed in assigning the western part of the Indian Territory to Western tribes, for here, toward the Texas border, were Kiowa and Comanche, Cheyenne and Arapaho — the latter from the mountains of Colorado. However, the Western tribes were cut off from the Osage, also a Western Indian, by the famous Cherokee Outlet (or Strip), extending toward the panhandle of Oklahoma. When Indian Territory was originally selected, it was considered remote enough to answer all purposes, but by 1870 the reservation was practically engulfed by the advancing tide of settlement.

Reservations of the Northern plains and mountains. Rivaling Indian Territory in size, but not in variety of inhabitants, were the trans-Missouri reservations north of Nebraska. All of South Dakota beyond the Missouri was the Big Sioux Reservation. Gold was already known to lie in the Black Hills, within the reservation, from which fact troubles were soon to come. Farther up the Missouri, in present-day North Dakota, was the reservation of Arikarees, Mandans, and Gros Ventres. South of the Yellowstone in Montana, shortly to be made famous by Custer's indiscretions, was the Crow Reservation, established in 1868. Nearly all of Montana north of the Missouri was set aside for other Crow Indians, as well as Blackfoot, Gros Ventre, and Piegan. Note should be made of the Wind River reserve in west-central Wyoming, still in existence in smaller size, and the enormous Ute reserve occupying much of western Colorado.

To name all of the reservations and hunting grounds throughout the West would require more space than is available in this volume. Many of the reservation boundaries were drawn to enclose Indians within their habitual place of residence, so that no transference was required. This was notably true of the more restricted areas occupied by the Pueblo Indians of the Southwest. In general it may be said that the Western tribes were in happier relation to their lands than were those who were removed from Eastern and Southern localities. The Sioux and the Blackfoot and the Crow knew this kind of country, they " liked it very much," as Bear Rib had said. Within or near their reservations were the greatest numbers of bison (buffalo) then remaining within the United States, and on this hulking, untamable beast the Northern tribes greatly depended. Here also were other animals useful for food or raw material, as well as native plant foods. The Indian way of life was based on an abundance of living space.

Indian strength and opposing military forces. Estimates of the numbers of Indians in the West in 1870 vary from 175,000 to 190,000. Official reports to the Congress assign 80,000 Indians to California, 15,000 to New Mexico, and about 55,000 to the Northern Plains. Estimates for other Western regions seem to be less reliable. For comparison, it may be pointed out that in 1942, there were 368,920 Indians on reservations or under the jurisdiction of the Office of Indian Affairs.

Since the Indians of the Plains region were perhaps most significant in the advance of the frontier, it seems desirable to indicate their strength in some detail. There were " fifty thousand hostile Indians " between the Missouri and the Rockies, said the Commissioner of Agriculture in 1869, exhibiting " a stolidity of character and an inaccessibility to civilizing influences which are remarkable even in this strange race of men."

The Sioux, most numerous and most powerful, were all but successful in combining their various tribes into a formidable organization. Against this Indian population of the West there were over 100 forts, manned by about 25,000 troops. The tables below present details.

UPPER MISSOURI INDIANS ABOUT 1860

	Lodges	Souls
Sioux	3,000	30,000
Blackfoot	1,200	9,600
Assiniboin	1,500	4,800
Crow	400	4,800
Cheyenne	300	3,000
Arikaree	200	1,500
Gros Ventre	85	700
Mandan	50	150
TOTALS	6,735	54,550

U.S. MILITARY STRENGTH, UPPER MISSOURI COUNTRY

	Number of Posts	Garrison	Average
1860	73	13,069	180
1864	101	21,291	210
1867	116	24,598	212
1870	111	22,789	205

It was into this land, varied in geography and native life, that settlement was advancing during the nineteenth century. As in the foregoing chapters, emphasis will be laid on the changing geography of the West and, no less important, the changing ideas about Western geography.

Part Five

THE GREAT PLAINS
AND BORDERING REGIONS,
TO 1870

CHAPTER 20

The Great Plains Region:
What It Was, and What It Was
Thought to Be

I N HIS book *The Great Plains* (Ginn, 1931), Walter Prescott Webb has shown how poorly the American people were prepared for occupying the semiarid West. Their equipment and institutions were adapted to life in the forests and humid prairies of the eastern third of the United States; and to fit this new and very different environment, the equipment, the tools, the whole way of life, had to be altered and bolstered by new devices.

The explorers and surveyors who were commissioned to report on the trans-Mississippi country also came from the East — Zebulon Pike, John C. Frémont, Stephen H. Long, Meriwether Lewis, William Clark, and a score of able army officers. We are reminded that Pike and Frémont served their apprenticeships as explorers in Minnesota, and the surveys of Long have likewise been touched upon in previous chapters.

These many explorers brought with them into the Western plains and mountains their compasses and surveying instruments and, no less important, a humid-land terminology. The surveying tools worked as well in the sand hills of Nebraska as they had in the upper Mississippi region. Proof of this lies in the maps that were produced, surprisingly accurate in the position and courses of rivers, topographic features, Indian villages, forts, and routes of travel. However, that most sensitive of instruments, the language, did not fit the new land so well. That this was so justifies a chapter title which distinguishes between what the region of the Great Plains really was and what people thought it was.

Few of the explorers were learned men. They seem not to have read widely in the literature of the Old World, where semiarid lands had been well described. They were as unaccustomed to the Great Plains region as were those they now sought to inform. There was a natural tendency to apply familiar expressions to unfamiliar objects. If familiar terms were not available, new ones were created which might have little meaning to a reader in the Eastern states. An example of the innovated term was " prairie dog," referring to the small burrowing marmot that is neither dog nor a prairie dweller. Within the memory of men then living, no bison had existed east of the Mississippi River except perhaps in captivity, but out on the Plains, where there were millions, they became known as the buffalo. Were the reports correct in describing as treeless a land wherein a place called Council Grove was already famous? How could one make clear to people familiar with New England brooks or Kentucky creeks the true nature of the Cimarron River, the Canadian, or the Platte? What was a coulee, a butte, a bench? The term *" mauvaises terres,"* used for a kind of land, baffled untold thousands of Eastern readers. The fierce, horse-riding Indians of the Plains, armed with revolvers instead of bows and arrows, were also a mystery to people who had never seen an Indian and perhaps had no wish to see one. They could better understand such a one as Queue de Bœuf, a Sioux chief who in his attire and bearing showed the dubious effects of civilizing influences. Queue de Bœuf is described as wandering into the camp of Major Osborne Cross near the Forks of the Platte dressed in a bottle-green frock coat reaching to his ankles and decorated with well-worn epaulets, and wearing a grizzly-bear cap to which was fastened a long red feather; suspended from his neck was a medallion made in 1809, bearing the likeness of President Madison.

THE HIGH PLAINS BECOME A DESERT — ON THE MAPS

For half a century the idea of a Great American Desert extending eastward of the Rocky Mountains existed in the official records, and for a longer time in the unofficial, but equally influential, popular writings.

The seeds of the idea of the High Plains desert were sown by Pike in his report on explorations in 1806. His observations on the " internal deserts " might, however, have remained locked in the pages of his journal had they not been supported by similar views deriving from the Long expedition of 1819–20. The conclusions of both Pike and Long were expressed in quotable phrases that were popularized in magazines and newspapers with various colorings. A popular idea so firmly grounded was bound to survive beyond the time of the original pronouncement. Geography textbooks took up the refrain, adding apparent authenticity with their maps, which carried the words " Unexplored Deserts " or " Great American Desert " over the western portions of present-day Nebraska and Kansas.

The majority of military reports to the Congress in the 1840's and 1850's confirmed the idea of a High Plains desert, especially if the reader did not inspect the document closely. Travelers and amateur geographers were also effective agents in nurturing the idea of the desert character of the Plains. When they returned home and wrote their books, their words carried weight because each could say, " I have been there."

Signs of the breakdown of the desert idea first appeared officially with the railroad surveys of 1855, when at last the High Plains were compared to the steppes of Russia. Authors were even venturing such expressions as " subhumid "

and " semiarid " — common enough with us but new to that time. Soon thereafter the travelers began to revise the estimates of those who had preceded them.
Said Editor Bowles when he was leaving Fort Kearny, Nebraska Territory, on
his first westward journey in 1865: " This is called The Great Central Desert
of the continent and uninhabitable space, yet [it is] not a desert such as is commonly interpreted — not worthless by any means. The soil is fat indeed compared to your New England pine plains." In 1870, Ferdinand V. Hayden of the
Geological Survey pointed out that " every year as we know more and more
about the country this [desert] belt becomes narrower and narrower, and as a
continuous area has already ceased to exist even in the imagination."

The descriptions of Pike and Long. The instructions given to Pike on June 24,
1806, were both specific and general. He was to conciliate Indian tribes; to conduct certain Osage Indians, who had been on visits to the East, to their homes
in western Missouri; to make " careful geographical observations upon the
region traversed "; and, so far as possible, to " ascertain the direction, extent,
and navigation of the Arkansas and Red rivers." He therefore crossed the southern Plains, usually not far from river courses; but his was not a river journey,
as was that of Lewis and Clark. For the first 300 miles of his journey — namely,
across the present State of Missouri — Pike saw no particular change; indeed
" the country will admit of a numerous, extensive, and compact population," he
thought. But beyond this limit the land became less attractive, apparently limited
to stock-raising — if, indeed, it were ever inhabited. The future residents could
raise cattle, horses, sheep, and goats, " the earth producing spontaneously sufficient for their support." Nearer the Rocky Mountains, desert characteristics
became more prevalent, with vast plains which " may become in time as celebrated as the sandy wastes of Africa." On this route were " tracts of many leagues
where the wind had thrown up the sand in all the fanciful forms of the ocean's
rolling wave, and on which not a speck of vegetable matter existed."

There is no doubt that Pike encountered sand-hill and sand-dune areas, for
some of these still exist on his line of march; and if his journey coincided with a
drought period, his impression of the region as an arid desert is the more understandable. At the same time it is probable that Pike used the word " desert " for
want of a more suitable expression. He was, indeed, not too careful with his
terms, with which he was inadequately equipped for the kind of country
he was traversing, and in which he met several disasters. His conclusions, when
they finally took form, may have been colored by his misfortunes: the hardships
of a frigid winter in the Rockies; his failure to find the sources of the Red River;
his capture by Mexican troops in present-day Colorado and imprisonment in
Chihuahua.

Carrying his Eastern terminology into the western Plains, Pike told of the
" immense prairies " which would at least serve to restrict " our population to certain limits." The American people were altogether too prone to rambling, he
thought, taking some satisfaction in believing that these " prairies " which were
incapable of cultivation would be left to " the wandering and uncivilized abo-

rigines of the country." Pike's early promise as an explorer in Minnesota was somewhat dimmed by his later experience in the Great Plains, which he failed fully to understand.

Edwin James, geographer of the Long expedition, who has been made known in earlier pages for his helpful observations on the Ohio River, identified the High Plains as that part of the continental interior extending 500 or 600 miles eastward of the base of the Rocky Mountains, formerly called the Mexican Desert. James did not hesitate to say of this region that " it is almost wholly unfit for cultivation, and of course uninhabitable by a people depending upon agriculture for their subsistence." This could easily be interpreted by Eastern readers to mean that the country was a desert, although other occupations were said to be possible. James viewed the scarcity of wood and water as an obstacle to future settlement. The Plains represented a frontier of infinite importance to the United States " inasmuch as it is calculated to serve as a barrier to prevent too great an expansion of our population westward."

The journals of the Pike and Long expeditions greatly influenced contemporary thought. They were favorite sources of journalists, book-writers, and stay-at-home geographers, many of whom copied freely from others. The view of the High Plains as a barrier to expansion was reasserted over a great many years, and often quite independently; so also the word " desert " was applied in such a way as to suggest that the author did not mean desert in the strict sense. Thus in 1858, G. K. Warren remarked:

> The people on the extreme frontiers of Nebraska are near the western limit of the fertile portions of the prairie lands, and a *desert space* separates them from the fertile and desirable region in the western mountains. They are, as it were, on the shore of a sea, up to which population and agriculture may advance and no further.

A "desert space" would not necessarily imply an arid land, but in the next sentence Warren raises the old question of aridity by predicting that " as soon as the wave of emigration [attracted by gold in the Rockies] has passed over the desert portion of the plains," then " the present frontier will become the starting point of all products from the Mississippi Valley."

DEFINING THE LIMITS OF THE HIGH PLAINS

The early explorers experienced many difficulties in conveying their information to others. Not only was the region different from any in the East, but they could find no satisfactory method of showing on a map where the Great Plains were. The particular problem was on the east, where the High Plains and the Prairie Plains merged imperceptibly into each other. Here and there were conspicuous elevations, such as the Coteau du Missouri of the Dakotas, or the Flint Hills of Kansas, but they were discontinuous features, not useful as regional boundaries. It thus became common practice, in this region of few identifying features or names, to indicate the beginning of the High Plains by reference to a certain

95   The plains of southwest Kansas, showing a " buffalo wallow." View in Haskell
      County, taken in 1899 by Willard Johnson, used by courtesy of the U.S. Geo-
      logical Survey.

meridian, such as the 96th or the 98th. Present-day authors have also used this
device — not meaning thereby that geographical conditions abruptly change at
the chosen line.

There was general agreement among observers that the High Plains region
began somewhere near the 96th meridian and was bounded on the west by the
Rocky Mountains. One of the first attempts to delimit the Plains was that of
Adolph Wislizenus, scientist for a military survey in 1846. It was suggested that
Council Grove, on the Neosho in eastern Kansas, was

. . . a dividing point in the character of the country. The country east of it is formed
of prairie, with slight ascents and descents — constant undulations, as I might call
them, sometimes shorter and more rapid; sometimes larger and fuller, resembling the
waves of the ocean. . . . This eastern portion is well watered, and along the water
courses sufficiently timbered to sustain settlements. . . . A short distance west, the
country rises to the elevation of 1,500 feet, and ascends gradually towards the Arkansas to 2,000 and more feet above the sea. The intermediate country yet exhibits sometimes the short, wavelike form of the eastern portion, but oftener it resembles . . . the
plateaux or high plains between the Arkansas and Cimarron, those representatives
of the calm, immense, high seas, where the horizon extends further, the soil becomes
drier and more sandy, the vegetation scantier and water more rare.

Few descriptions of the transition country from the humid to the semiarid
written in the last century have surpassed the foregoing one of the foreign nat-
uralist-geographer.

The term " Great Plains " for the region thus defined is of relatively modern
origin, having gained currency among geographers since the Fenneman study
of physiographic regions a quarter of a century ago. Before this, the region was
almost invariably called the High Plains in distinction from the lower Prairie

Plains of the Midwestern States. In some respects it has been unfortunate that the accepted descriptive term of earlier days was discarded. At least it should be known that the classic study of the region is Willard Johnson's "The High Plains" in the *Twenty-first Annual Report of the U.S. Geological Survey, 1899–1900*. (See Fig. 95.)

LEARNING THE CLIMATE OF THE PLAINS

Until the 1850's, conclusions regarding the climate of the Plains, especially the rainfall, were based on impressions gained from the appearance of the vegetation — not until then were instrumental records available. Readings of temperature and precipitation were made at a few widely spaced forts, some of which were actual military posts while others were trading stations, without garrisons, but built in fortlike manner.

The first records, necessarily limited to only a year or two, confirmed the general opinion that the rainfall diminished from east to west, with the most noticeable change beyond the 103rd meridian. By the time of the railroad-route surveys, it was also clear that rainfall was variable from year to year, but no definite trends could be detected from so limited a series of observations. With Hays, in western Kansas, receiving as much as 20 inches in some years, the Plains were decidedly not the "rainless region" which had been pictured by many persons.

Advancing knowledge of the Plains climate was indicated in 1855 when this region was compared with the steppes of Russia. With some inaccuracy, the Congress was informed that descriptions of the Russian steppes "might be applied almost verbatim to Nebraska." Similarities of vegetation were related to resemblances in rainfall, most of which in both regions was concentrated in the warmer season. The coincidence of maximum rainfall with the growing season was shown to offset the small amount of moisture the region received. It was reported in 1870 that at Fort Riley 69 per cent of the annual moisture occurred during the growing season, at Fort Kearny 81 per cent, and at Fort Laramie 72 per cent. These percentages imply an accuracy which the limited observations did not justify, but they represented the information on which action was taken at the time.

The known extent in latitude of the Great Plains, from the Gulf to the Canada line, made it reasonable to suppose that the region was not a climatic unit. As in Territorial Minnesota, there was a natural tendency to overemphasize the severity of the winters in the Plains north of the Missouri, and on the part of promoters there was also a similar effort to break down preconceived ideas. Initiators of the Western railroads asserted that the Plains winters were by no means so unendurable as was popularly supposed, and further pointed out that great railroads operated in other countries that were just as cold. Admittedly, the climate of the "Nebraska Region" — that is, the Plains northward from the Missouri — was "the most unfavorable on the proposed route," but to regard the winters as Arctic was erroneous. Records taken in 1858–59 at Fort Benton, head of navigation on the Missouri, indicated temperatures several degrees warmer than those of Montreal in about the same latitude.

Of winter snow, little was actually known at this time, but there were the usual beliefs and suppositions. Snow was believed to accumulate to greater depths than was actually the case. This belief delayed the extension of cattle-grazing into the Northern Plains, for many cattle-owners felt that it would be impossible to winter-graze their stock in the far North. Observations in the Black Hills indicated that even in that area of increased precipitation, snowfall was not very heavy. The streams issuing from these hills gave no evidence of spring freshets caused by melting snow, nor were small trees bent over by drifts. On the other hand, the snow of the Black Hills must be deep enough to hide trails and landmarks, because surveyors found that the " main Indian trails were marked by stones placed in the forks of trees or by one or more sets of blazes, the oldest almost overgrown by the bark."

TREELESS PLAINS, WOODED WATERCOURSES, AND FORESTED MOUNTAINS

Everyone agreed that the most striking feature of the Plains was the absence of trees. The " great open spaces " emphasized the extent of the Plains, which seemed endless to travelers plodding on foot or drawn in a slow-moving wagon train to reach the reputedly better country beyond them. It was quite natural that the western Plains grassland would popularly be called " prairie," although the better-informed soon pointed out that this was not good usage. Many new grass species were identified: the tall bluestem in the area of more ample rainfall, the little bluestem and needle grass farther west, and the still shorter buffalo grass and grama of the western High Plains. Broadly considered, the Plains grassland was a transition belt between the humid prairies of the Midwest and the true desert grasslands of the Southwest.

Deficiency of rainfall was at first generally assumed to be the cause for the absence of trees, although some considered it possible for trees to grow if planted, cared for, and protected from fire. " If this country is ever densely populated by agriculturists," said Randolph B. Marcy in 1854, " a new era of husbandry must be instituted. Nature seems to demand this. Instead of clearing up the timbered lands for the plough, as in the eastern states, it will be necessary to cultivate timber; indeed this has already been commenced in some western prairies with successful results." As the Plains gradually lost their reputation as a desert, opinion swung to the other extreme: Trees could be grown and, in growing, would become a factor in causing the rainfall to increase.

No less an early authority than F. V. Hayden of the Geological Survey changed his views regarding the suitability of the Plains for tree growth. Hayden wrote in 1869 that " until two years ago I believed with other easterners that trees cannot be grown due to unfavorable climate and soils." But now he thought otherwise; indigenous trees, such as cottonwood, soft maple, elm, basswood, black walnut, honey locust, and various willows, could be planted and cultivated. Not only would the trees increase in value, but the tree growth would improve the climate, which " has already changed for the better along the Missouri in Nebraska." Views such as this were influential in the passage by the Congress of the Timber Culture Act of 1873, one of whose objectives was the encouragement of tree growth in the West.

Grazing possibilities early recognized.   The presence of numerous herds of buffalo on the Plains and of elk nearer the mountains in the early days was sufficient to show that the grasses were good for grazing. Equally convincing evidence came from the trans-Mississippi wagon trains hauled by oxen, cattle, or mules, which depended on native pastures for weeks at a time. When it was learned that cattle could forage for themselves even during the northern winter, the economic future of the region seemed assured. Doubtless there were many people who learned, by accident or through necessity, that the short-grass country was suitable for year-round grazing.

During the great emigration to California in 1849, animals were pastured at all seasons without imported hay or grain, and frontier armies depended on the grasses for the support of their trains. " In the 1859 emigration," said the Commissioner of Agriculture, " winter grazing was put to the test and found successful." The favorite wintering ground of one of the great trading companies, Russell, Majors & Waddell, was the area between the present cities of Greeley, Colorado, and Buffalo, Wyoming, where, said Russell, " I have never had less than 500 head of work cattle, and for two winters, those of 1857 and 1858, I wintered 15,000 head of heavy work-oxen on the plains each winter." In the best opinion of the time,

. . . the bunch and buffalo grasses are highly nutritious. They are of quick growth, ripen rapidly, and by early summer are as perfectly cured as possible. Standing in this condition throughout the winter, animals find excellent grazing during the entire year without human aid. It is a great grazing country and can support in the aggregate great herds of cattle.

Woods along the streams.   Nearly all the rivers were bordered by strips of woodland extending from ¼ mile to ½ mile from the water's edge. The most widespread species, especially in the north, was the Western cottonwood. Although making an inferior lumber, the cottonwood was very important in a region otherwise lacking timber. It was one of the main sources of fuel in the homes and was used by steamboats on the upper Missouri during the river's brief period of navigation in the 1860's. Steamboats made frequent stops along the banks, picking up cordwood to feed the hungry boilers, for they could not possibly store enough to last the long miles to Fort Benton.

Cottonwood was also sawed into lumber and made into siding and shingles, substituting for better woods that were not available. The shingles warped and split when they became dry, and the sidings resisted coats of paint; nevertheless, the cottonwood contributed to the development of the region. The groves were also sought by emigrants as stopping places on the long trek across the Plains. They furnished shade and shelter, and were likely to indicate the presence of water.

The Cross Timbers. Of particular significance in the southern Plains were the Cross Timbers of Texas and Indian Territory (Oklahoma). Early governmental reports refer to these strips of woods cutting across the edge of the Great Plains as the " celebrated Cross Timbers." The belt achieved much notoriety of a favorable sort, not only because it appeared in an area otherwise treeless, but because it contained woods useful to man.

The Cross Timbers was (and is) a belt of small hardwood trees, from 5 to 30 miles in width, extending from the Arkansas River southwestward to the Brazos River, a distance of about 400 miles. Routes to the Southwest originating at Fort Smith, Arkansas, or Fort Gibson and the near-by Choteau Trading House on the Canadian River, intersected this belt of timber. According to Marcy, who crossed the belt many times in his various surveying tours, this woodland consisted principally of post oak and black jack, standing at such intervals that " wagons can without difficulty pass between them in any direction. The soil is thin, sandy, and poorly watered." Trees other than post oak to be found here in the early days were black walnut, hackberry, chinquapin (dwarf chestnut), and elm.

Wagon trains headed for the long journey to El Paso and beyond reaped advantages from the brief trip through the Cross Timbers. Here new axletrees were cut and attached, and broken spokes replaced. Authors of emigrant guidebooks did not fail to advise the traveler to " provide himself with such extra material as, in his providence, he may think necessary."

The mesquite of the Southwest. Farther to the west in Texas and New Mexico, but not confined to the strict limits of a belt, was the mesquite, another small but useful tree of the semiarid country. Growing widely spaced in its natural state, the mesquite reminded approaching travelers of an orchard, but closer examination showed small trees whose thick, stocky trunks bore crooked and thorny limbs. The trunk and long roots of the mesquite made an excellent, long-lasting fire, and its beanlike fruit has also proved useful to generations of mankind. It was an essential part of the diet of the Apache, the Pima, and many other tribes of New Mexico and Arizona. Travelers, both white and Indian, chewed the pods while on the march, finding them useful not only as a food but as a preventive of thirst.

The Indians prepared many dishes from mesquite pods. There was the hot or cold porridge or mush made from the fresh fruit, eaten by all in camp grouped around a common bowl. The dry pods were also gathered for winter use. For this purpose the beans were reduced to flour, in which the larvae of insects would develop, forming a homogeneous mass of animal and vegetable substance. The aboriginal uses of the mesquite did not end here: it found service as the basis of a fermented drink, as feed for horses and cattle, and as a hairdressing; and fibers from the tree bark were made into twine and woven into skirts and baskets.

The forested Black Hills of South Dakota.   There were two Black Hills regions in early descriptions of the West; though they are widely separated in space, the repetition of the name nevertheless has caused some confusion among writers. An arm of the Rockies projecting into the Plains in Wyoming, afterward called the Laramie Mountains, became known among early travelers and settlers as the Black Hills; but this name has been obsolete for many years.

The Black Hills of South Dakota, still so known today, were viewed in early times, as now, as " an oasis of verdure among the open and level plains." When seen from a distance the forested slopes of the mountains appeared dark or black, hence the descriptive name.

The Black Hills of South Dakota were at first regarded as a storehouse of forest wealth, with a variety of trees useful to settlers and railroad builders. A new interest was stirred by reports of gold in the late 1860's, but soon thereafter the region was set aside as part of the Big Sioux Reservation. According to the terms, white men were not permitted to enter the mountains except by special permission. People waiting impatiently for the opening up of the Black Hills were assured by government surveyors: " There is gold from the grass roots down, but there is *more gold* from the grass roots up. No matter how rich the gold-placers may prove to be, the great business of this region in the future will be stock-raising, dairying, and farming." In addition to the useful mountain forests, the hills contained extensive areas of grassy glade and meadow, which it was thought would make the mountains a chief center of the grazing industry. The gold rush of 1878 set the stage for the occupation of the Black Hills and stimulated development in the trans-Missouri country.

THE BISON OF THE PLAINS AND MOUNTAINS

The usual association of the bison or American buffalo with the Western Plains and mountains has resulted from the distribution of that animal at the time the West became generally known.

Before 1800 the bison ranged over two-thirds of the North American continent, from the Appalachians to the Great Basin of Nevada, and from the Gulf of Mexico to Great Slave Lake (Fig. 96). Within a quarter-century the eastern limit of the range had withdrawn before the advancing frontier of settlement, beyond the Mississippi River. Little change in the extent of the range occurred during the next twenty-five years, but the bison rapidly diminished in numbers as new weapons for their slaughter came into use. It was during this period, from 1825 to 1850, that Frémont said: " A traveler may start from any given point south or north of the Rocky Mountain range, and during the whole distance, his road would always be among large herds of buffalo, which would never be out of his view until he arrived within sight of the abodes of civiliza-

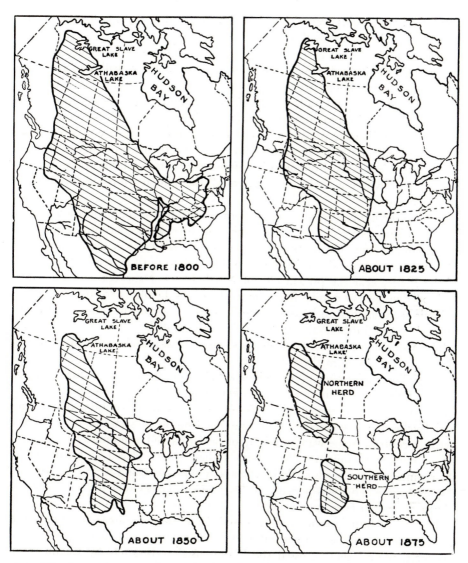

96   The diminishing range of the bison. Simplified from a map in " The American Bison, Living and Extinct " by J. A. Allen, *Memoirs, Museum of Comparative Zoology,* Vol. 4, No. 10, Harvard University Press, 1876.

tion." Emigrant trains were delayed for hours at a time waiting for the passage of straggling herds across their route.

Where the buffalo was not actually to be seen, there were evidences of his existence in the form of skulls, skeletons, and trails. The " wallows," popularly attributed to the bison, were presumably caused by natural agencies. (See Fig. 95, page 373.) The trails were said to be innumerable, leading from rivers and salt supplies into ravines or over bluffs where grass could be found. Some of the wide trails were pressed a foot or more into the soil; easy to follow, they were especially useful to surveyors and explorers. In his trail-finding through the Rocky Mountains, Frémont often followed existent buffalo trails, and discovered that where a choice was presented, the animal paths led to the more accessible passes.

By 1850 the herds were dispersing from the vicinity of the main routes to the West, and survivors of the accelerating slaughter were concentrating toward the mountain front. On his westward journey to Salt Lake in 1851, the explorer Howard Stansbury did not encounter a live buffalo until he reached the Forks of the Platte, near the present city of North Platte, Nebraska, and even then had to " diverge 4 or 5 miles from the road back of the bluffs, for these sagacious animals have learned to become shy of approaching wagon trains." Herds remained longest in the Plains north of the 36th parallel.

The Montana mountain front was a stronghold of buffalo herds in the 1860's, as one can gather from the reports of General W. F. Raynolds. In his Yellowstone Valley exploration of 1858–60, Raynolds found the area " literally black with buffalo, grazing in an enormous herd whose numbers defy computation." In this mountain setting, particularly in the Wind River country, the Indians had developed a new practice of hunting, favoring the preservation of remaining herds in contrast to the wanton killing of earlier days. The animals were penned up in narrow mountain valleys, with Indian lodges placed at points where the remnants of the herds could be effectively controlled, and were killed only as the need arose. This was perhaps as close to herding as either the buffalo or the Northern Indian ever approached.

By 1875 the buffalo range had been split into two main areas — the northern and southern herds, never to be reunited. Significantly, the break occurred where the main central route crossed the Plains, used successively by wagon train, stage, pony express, and railroad. Thereafter the slaughter continued so rapidly that field parties of the Smithsonian Institution experienced difficulty in obtaining specimens. A herd of about 50 head was found in 1886 about 75 miles northwest of Miles City, Montana, and a few scattered herds were known to be in existence in Yellowstone Park and the panhandle of Texas.

There were few people who looked upon the near-extinction of the buffalo as a tragedy. Granted that buffalo meat and skins had served useful purposes, it seemed to the majority of observers that these advantages were outweighed by various drawbacks. The animal apparently was incapable of domestication and of interbreeding with a more tractable beast; calves could be raised in captivity,

97   Part of the herd of 700 buffaloes on the Phillips estate near Fort Pierre, South
Dakota, about 1890. Photo by E. T. Hancock, used by courtesy of the U.S.
Geological Survey.

but on reaching maturity they became unruly and difficult, if not impossible, to
confine. Efforts at domestication led to unsatisfactory results, although much was
written in advocacy of more determined experiments. (See Fig. 97.)

Products of the buffalo hunt. " It is vain to remonstrate against this whole-
sale destruction," said Stansbury in 1851, upon seeing the slaughter at its height.
The supply of buffalo seemed unlimited and the needs were great. Furthermore,
the beast was fairly easy prey, having taken a last stand in a region well suited
to his ultimate destruction. Indian methods of hunting, adapted to open country
and made more effective by the use of firearms, included both stalking or still-
hunting animals straggling from the main herd and larger-scale operations depending on the stampede. Large herds, frenzied by horse-riding Indians, were
driven over the edge of an abrupt terrace slope or " bench," at the bottom of which,
with maimed bodies and broken bones, they were subject to easy killing by
other Indians who were stationed there. Such slopes were called " buffalo kills,"
and old-time residents of the Plains will still point out where they are.

The buffalo was not a ferocious animal, except in protection of the young or
in advanced age, and only a few firsthand observers regarded him as sagacious.
Seen in retrospect, the slow-moving, poor-sighted buffalo was not the kind of
animal fitted to survive in the open Plains country.

The choicer parts of the buffalo were used for food by Indian, emigrant, and
frontier army on the march. Held in highest regard was the meat of the shoulder
and ribs, the latter called fleece and belly fleece in the special terminology of the
Plains. The broad, fat part extending from shoulder to tail, known as the *depuis,*
was also prepared for eating. The greater part of the carcass, stripped of its better
portions, was usually left to the coyotes and buzzards unless the party was under
privation.

Bleached buffalo bones, strewn along the trails and around former camp sites, added a touch of desolation to the Plains journey. The remains were most abundant in Indian-held country or its vicinity. In such areas, fear of building fires, the smoke of which might attract the enemy, prevented the full use of the buffalo for food.

Liver, blood, lungs, portions of the intestines, ribs, bone marrow, and brains could be eaten raw. Among the Indians the buffalo brain was a special delicacy. The brain was sometimes obtained by shattering the forehead with tomahawk or ax, and many emigrants were mystified at seeing along their line of travel numerous punctured buffalo skulls. It was estimated that a party of six men could feast on a freshly killed buffalo without starting a fire. This was a real advantage to emigrants short of food or fearing they soon would be, traveling across a country filled with big bison but offering almost no other fuel for cooking and campfires than the dried dung or " chips " of the buffalo itself.

The skins of buffalo cows and calves were also valuable, at first to the Indian, who used them for lodge coverings, robes, rugs, and blankets, and then to the white man for various purposes. The more favorable season for dressing the skins was from November to March, which was not the time of the great buffalo hunts. Even when the skin was prime for robes, no more than one-third of the animals killed were stripped for making them. According to Frémont in 1843, " the skins of bulls are never taken off or dressed as robes at any season," only the skins of females being considered valuable by traders. Bulls greatly outnumbered cows in the average herd, and if over three years of age, their skins were rarely used except for lodge coverings, nor was their meat eaten if better food was available.

A little-known type of river craft, the bullboat, deserves a place in this discussion. A full account of travel across the Plains is reserved for the next chapter, but here it is well to point out that it was often necessary for a wagon train to cross the main rivers, such as the Platte, and the many tributaries that intersected the route westward. In high water this operation was full of difficulties. Often the contents of the wagons were unloaded to be floated across the river in bullboats made of buffalo skins stretched over wooden ribs; thus emptied, the wagons could be hauled through at a shallower point.

On one recorded occasion in 1846, the party of Overton Johnson and William H. Winter, not having previously provided themselves with bullboats, resorted to an ingenious method of getting across the river. The swollen Platte was reached 85 miles above the Forks, where it was decided that a sort of boat would have to be constructed. Green buffalo hides were first sewed together; these the men " stretched over the wagon beds as tight as we could, with the flesh side out, and then turned them up in the sun to dry; and when they became thoroughly dry, we covered them with tallow and ashes, in order to render them more impervious to the water." Thus put together, the boat successfully negotiated the mile-wide Platte with a crew of six men. Bullboats were also used on the Missouri River.

In view of the wanton killing described above, statistics of buffalo hides and robes sold on markets are a poor index of the importance of the buffalo or of the number of animals killed. In the 1840's, some 90,000 buffalo robes, exclusive of skins, were marketed each year, with St. Louis as the chief distributing center in the United States. The American Fur Company and the Hudson's Bay Company were the principal marketing agencies.

OTHER ANIMALS OF THE PLAINS

Other grass-eating animals, better adapted to the semiarid Plains environment than the massive buffalo, were the pronghorn or American antelope, prairie dogs, squirrels of various types, and jack rabbits.

The pronghorn, capable of subsisting on grass and little water, " is the purest type of Plains animal, and seems to have developed only in the Great Plains of North America," according to Professor Webb. Wary, fleet of foot, and sharp-eyed, the antelope usually maintained a safe distance from known enemies, but his timidity was sometimes overcome by an almost equal curiosity, which impelled him to approach unknown objects too closely for his own safety. Marcy was perhaps the first to record the strange mixture of fear and inquisitiveness of the antelope, noted many times since by close observers. When the long-range rifle came into use, methods of hunting this shy animal depended much on its mental quirks. The method followed by the Gilfillan family, pioneers of North Dakota in the 1860's, illustrates the point. It is reported that Mr. Gilfillan, " riding in front, would see one, immediately would lie down in the grass and flag them, waving the flag to and fro. In this way, their curiosity being excited, [the antelopes] would come nearer and nearer to see what it was till at last they got within range, when a shot would ring out, and we would see the others scampering away."

A protective device of the antelope, the expansible white patch on his rump, has been referred to by Ernest Thompson Seton as saving many flocks. When danger is apprehended, the patch enlarges, at the same time exuding an odor, warning other animals to be on the alert. Through the use of firearms, pronghorn meat became a common and welcome dish to travelers and settlers alike.

Prairie dogs and jack rabbits, also capable of getting along with little or no water, and referred to by early travelers as curiosities, have been of significance in the later settlement of the Plains. Prairie-dog towns, intricate systems of underground channels, have often been the beginning points of serious soil erosion, and jack rabbits are notoriously destructive of farm produce. Many of the counties and towns of the Great Plains conduct widespread rabbit hunts each year as a means of protection from the damage done by these animals.

Meat-eating animals have also played roles in Great Plains development. Despised by early explorer and more recent settler alike are the destructive, if cowardly, coyote and wolf. One of the suggested reasons for the rapid extinction of the buffalo near the mountain border before the great hunts reached so far was the increased number of wolves which destroyed buffalo calves. Raynolds arrived at that conclusion in his Yellowstone exploration, suggesting a bounty on the wolf, and it seems to find support in Hayden's later comment on the Laramie Plains west of the mountains of that name. There were large flocks of antelope, Hayden noted, " but the buffalo has disappeared forever." The Laramie Plains, it may be mentioned, are surrounded by mountain country, a favorite habitat of the timber wolf.

FLIGHTS OF MELANOPLUS SPRETUS, THE LOCUST

Locust invasions of Western settlements were first brought to public attention, if not to understanding, through reports of the hordes of grasshoppers which descended upon the fields of the Mormons in Utah only to be dispersed by sea gulls. Similar flights, which fell upon the land like a plague or blight, are recorded in the descriptions of the Great Plains and adjacent areas. Naturally enough, little was heard about these invasions until settlement advanced to the border-lands of the Great Plains. In 1864 and 1866, and at too-frequent intervals during the succeeding quarter-century, the skies were darkened by immense numbers of the insects which, though insignificant individually, were mighty collectively.

Eyewitness accounts of locust flights are among the more awesome features of Western literature, passing credulity in many instances. First seen on the western horizon, the flight appeared like a black cloud or a dust storm, but on nearer approach the ominous noise, suggesting a distant railroad train, warned people that this was another plague. Said a pioneer of North Dakota: " Grasshoppers came that first year, 1871. They darkened the sky which, when looked up at, shone like silver with their flashing wings. They ate the sides out of our tents, the linen coat off my father's back while he was mowing." A Coloradan told of the flight across the Snowy Range " filling the air as much higher as they could be distinguished with a good field-glass." And at Colorado Springs in August 1875 the insects came with the wind and alighted in the rain, covering the ground to a depth of about 2 inches, sometimes halting railroad trains on the upgrade because of the oil crushed from their bodies.

The sudden appearance and disappearance of locusts were often attributed to supernatural powers, even after the first official study conducted by the Department of Agriculture in 1877. This analysis cleared up many of the mysteries: how the grasshoppers moved so rapidly, how they accomplished such swift destruction, why they were present in some years all the time and only occasionally in others.

Source regions and temporary areas of locusts. In the first place, it was discovered that the Rocky Mountain locust, naturally strong of wing, was assisted in its flight by numerous air sacs that gave it buoyancy. In still air, the insects whirled about like swarming bees, but with a wind they were buoyed along in its direction. With a favorable wind they were capable of advancing at least 20 miles a day, sometimes a much greater distance. The more extensive the uninhabited area, the longer were the flights, for the insect seemed to sense an ap-

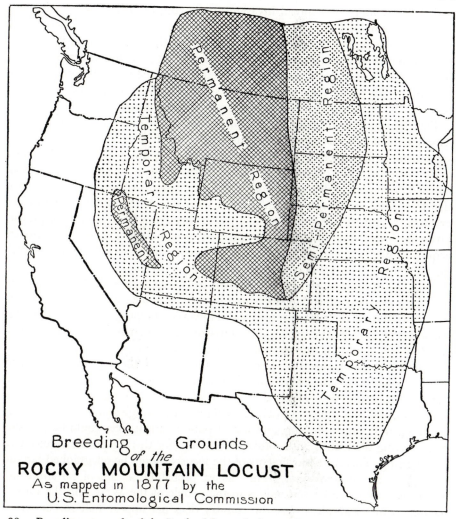

98   Breeding grounds of the Rocky Mountain locust. From *Report of the Commissioner of Agriculture*, 1877.

proach to cultivated fields. The entomologists of that time concluded that local
flights for food were possible at all times, but "the general movement east of
the mountains is conspicuously toward the south and southeast," possibly in
obedience to other laws.

Apparent oddities, such as the alternating periods of locust invasions, were
expressed in terms of types of breeding grounds: (1) the permanent, (2) the
subpermanent, and (3) the temporary (Fig. 98).

In the permanent region, or native breeding grounds (crosshatched on the
map), the species was reported to be present all the time. This was the source

region of the more widespread invasions, occupying the Rocky Mountains and the drier plains of Colorado, Wyoming, Montana, and adjacent Alberta. The subpermanent region, a narrow belt to the east of this, was the area frequently invaded by *spretus,* and in which " it can perpetuate itself for several years, but from which in time it disappears." Finally there was the vast temporary region, covering nearly all the arid, semiarid, and subhumid West, which the pest visited periodically, but from which it disappeared within a year.

The destructiveness of the Rocky Mountain locust, once settled in an area, temporarily or otherwise, was owing to its powerful jaws, an efficient digestive system, and phenomenal reproductive powers. The full-grown insect's ability to eat great quantities of food was equaled by that of its wingless progeny, which hatched preferably in dry, sandy soil. The Commissioner of Agriculture reported that the " little creatures are often so thick soon after hatching that they blacken everything, and their hopping, as one passes through a field or piece of prairie, gives the impression, at a short distance, of heat flickering in the air." Insects acquiring wings in the temporary region were capable of leaving for new conquests before additional hordes appeared from the permanent breeding grounds.

These were the essential facts as known to entomologists by 1877. It scarcely need be added that much has since been learned, in some cases contradicting the understanding of the earlier generation. However, the purpose of this brief discussion is to consider this aspect of the environment in terms of the period when the Rocky Mountain locust was most destructive.

Protection against locusts. For protection against these pests, whose permanent breeding grounds were not to be disturbed or destroyed for years to come, the experts recommended: (1) destruction of the eggs by plowing, harrowing, irrigation, and tramping; and (2) destruction of the wingless insects by burning, crushing, trapping, collecting, and use of poisons. Fruit trees could be guarded by encircling the trunks with cotton batting, but for this the people would need forewarning. Therefore movements of the locusts should be telegraphed far and wide. Said an entomologist: " The ' locust probabilities ' are of far more importance than weather probabilities to the people of the West, and the idea of having them telegraphed over the country does not appear half so chimerical to us now as that of having weather foreshadowed a few years ago."

TOPOGRAPHIC VARIETY IN THE PLAINS

There is some danger that Figure 95 (page 373), a scene in southwest Kansas, will be taken as representing the entire Plains region. The picture is truly typical of extensive areas in earlier days; it would fit conditions as they were in portions of Montana, South Dakota, eastern Wyoming, and Colorado. The picture could almost be labeled " The Llano Estacado " or Staked Plains of northwest Texas and eastern New Mexico. This area was so flat and featureless that stakes or buffalo bones had to be set out to mark the routes of travel. Of the Llano a military officer said in 1849, " Whilst upon the staked plains [the traveler] sees

99   Scott's Bluff on the North Platte, an early-day landmark and fort site, and present-day city. From the *Hayden Preliminary Report* of 1870.

what he has not before seen during his whole route — an uninterrupted expanse of dead-level prairie, with not a tree anywhere upon it to vary the scene."

But there were many other surface types. There were the sharp terraces along the Missouri River, providing sites for cities-to-be, terraces which were correctly interpreted as resulting from "oscillations of level, and in the past each formed the bed of the river." There were the Big Bad Lands or Mauvaises Terres of western South Dakota, and other badlands in Nebraska and Montana. (See Fig. 99.) They were called badlands because of the difficulties of travel, and were already famous among geologists for the remains of extinct animals to be found among the cream-colored, stratified beds. Hayden came upon the Big Bad Lands in 1866, first seeing a long range of peaks and domes, even though this was not an elevated region. Instead, here was "a simple washing out of the country into innumerable gullies or canyons . . . leaving only isolated pyramids, peaks, and columns as witnesses." The Big Bad Lands are near the Black Hills, already mentioned as adding variety to the Great Plains.

Most familiar to travelers, of course, was the country on the main routes. It was a region in which landmarks assumed great significance, where various rocks, groves, and river bends were specifically identified.

CHAPTER 21

Passage across the Plains: Routes
of Trade and Migration

I T WAS trade that first caused movement across the Plains. In the earlier days,
furs lured trappers and traders to the Rocky Mountains and the Pacific Northwest; following the 1820's, commodity markets attracted traders to the Southwest. Soon after the Mexican commerce with Santa Fe and Chihuahua was established, the first trickle of migration commenced, swelling to major proportions
with the opening of the Oregon country in the 1840's. While the trade to Mexico
was continuing in the Southwest, new migrations broke across the Central and
Northern Plains: the Mormons pushed to Utah and beyond, gold-seekers went
to California in 1849, and both gold-seekers and health-seekers settled in Colorado within the next decade.

Traders and travelers alike needed protection during the long trek across
the open Plains, which were still regarded by some Indians as their land. Forts
were therefore established at strategic points along the traveled ways; these in
turn created new traffic demands. Troops were shuttled from fort to fort or
dispatched on surveying missions. Each detachment required the transportation
of supplies from Eastern depots. The United States Army contracted with private
companies to haul food and other necessities to the forts. This traffic brought
into being caravans so great as to cause Horace Greeley to exclaim on arrival at
Leavenworth in 1859: "Such acres of wagons! such pyramids of axletrees! such
hordes of oxen! such regiments of drivers and other employees!"

The majority of traders and emigrants viewed the Plains only as an area to
be crossed in order to reach more attractive goals. On the central route, for
example, more than 500 dreary and dangerous miles must be covered. At the
eastern approach to this route was Independence, Missouri, which became a
major outfitting point for travel across the Plains. Five hundred miles to the
west was Independence Rock in Wyoming, a landmark at the entrance to South
Pass in the Rocky Mountains. In good American fashion, many a traveler memo-
rialized his arrival here by scratching or painting his name on the rock, perhaps
looking back upon the Plains journey with few regrets at leaving it behind. The

routes across the Plains were aimed straight at distant objectives — or as straight as land surface, river courses, and water and grass supply permitted. The last two were the primary needs of travelers on the march, at least until the coming of the stage lines in the 1850's, when such problems were left to the managers.

These distant objectives were trading centers such as Santa Fe, mining camps in the Rockies, and passes in the mountains, of which South Pass, through its central position and ease of crossing, became the most important. It should be realized that the majority of those who crossed the Plains heading for Santa Fe, Denver, Great Salt Lake, California, or Oregon did not return, nor did they intend to do so. It was a one-way passage, to be completed as rapidly as possible.

THE SANTA FE TRADE AND TRAIL

The western objective of the " commerce of the prairies," as the trade to the Southwest was called, was a definite place — Santa Fe. The means of getting there varied from time to time. When the first caravan drove into the public square of Sante Fe in 1822, this northern outpost of Mexico was a city of some 3,000 inhabitants. Although it was the administrative center of the upper river country (Rio Arriba), Santa Fe was scarcely better suited for assuming the functions of a trading center than was St. Augustine, a city of comparable age in another part of Spanish America. Situated a few miles east of the Rio Grande, which was the main focus of routes, Santa Fe was reached with difficulty from the east by passage through the rough Sangre de Cristo-Culebra range.

Allied commercially to Santa Fe were the three towns of Taos — San Fernandez, Ranchos de Taos, and Pueblo de Taos, altogether representing a population of about 1,000 Indians and Mexicans. The towns of Taos, a half-dozen miles from the base of the mountains, were even more difficult to reach than Santa Fe. Lured by profitable trade, wagon trains nevertheless reached the Taos villages, either from Santa Fe or by secondary routes from Wagon Mound.

The New Mexican towns at the western end of the trail seem to have profited from the trade; at least Santa Fe had grown to a city of some 5,000 in 1848, when it became a United States city (Fig. 100). Chief center of interest to the traders was the plaza or public square of some 3 acres, upon the corners of which the main streets converged. Here was (and is) the Governor's Palace, a one-story building occupying the entire north side of the square; the courthouse, the old Mexican Military Palace (then used as a church); and about 25 stores. Scattered about were the adobe dwellings of the villagers. Fort Marcy, erected during the Mexican War and now falling into ruins, was part of the scene.

Santa Fe was not a particularly impressive place in the eyes of Wislizenus, who saw it in 1847. He relates that his expectations of seeing a fine city had already been cooled down by previous accounts; " however, when I perceived before me that irregular cluster of low, flat-roofed, mud-built, dirty houses, called Santa Fe, and resembling in the distance more a prairie-dog village than a capital, I had to lower them yet by some degrees."

100   Santa Fe, New Mexico, in 1848. From J. J. Abert, *A Report and Map of the Expedition to New Mexico,* Exec. Document 23, 30th Congress, 1st Session, 1847–48.

The beginning of the Santa Fe Trail. Like a river that originates in several tributaries, all of apparently equal size, the Santa Fe Trail had several upper sources. Franklin in Missouri, the original starting point, was soon to be replaced by Independence, already a thriving town in 1822 and situated only a dozen miles from the "Indian Border," as the Kansas line was then known. Independence maintained a share of the trade even when the "starting point" advanced to the west, first to Westport (founded in 1833), then to Kansas City and other places beyond. It was not until the 1850's that Independence lost its position of supremacy to other outfitting points. In 1846, for example, caravans aggregating 363 wagons, 50 carriages, and 750 men, transporting nearly 10,000 bales of merchandise valued at $1,000,000, left Independence on the 780-mile trip to New Mexico.

A visitor to Independence in that year was struck by " its varied crowd of strangers, composed of the most different materials, all united in one object — that is, to launch themselves upon the waste ocean of the prairies, and to steer through it in some western direction." The town swarmed not only with traders but with hordes of emigrants, who upon their departure would come to a fork in the road a few miles out and a sign saying " To Oregon."

Council Grove, Kansas, came to be considered by many people as the beginning of the Sante Fe Trail. This famous spot, 150 miles from Independence, was on the edge of the High Plains. Here in 1825 representatives of the United States had held a conference with Osage Indians, but no real village took root until the 1840's. The site was a woodland strip along the Neosho River, a southward-flowing tributary of the Arkansas. A focus of routes, one of which came from

Forts Riley and Leavenworth, contributed to the importance of **Council Grove** as an outfitting and trading center, with supply stores and shops for repairing and blacksmithing.

It was customary for traders to organize at Council Grove, the caravans proceeding from there in military fashion. The necessity of close organization becomes apparent from a picture of a single caravan consisting of 25 or more heavy wagons (some of them made by Studebaker), 200 mules, and 20 oxen, with a crew of 40 men. If escorted by troops, as was sometimes the case from 1829 to the 1840's, additional teams made up this land-going fleet. The wagons, loaded with 2 tons of cargo each, were hauled by 6, 8, or 10 mules or oxen.

Around many a campfire discussions were held as to the merits of the mule versus the ox as a beast of burden on the Sante Fe Trail. Josiah Gregg, a principal trader, held that the mule was superior in this job; oxen developed foot trouble, and their strength waned when they reached the drier, shorter grass of the western Plains. Few knew the art of shoeing oxen, said Gregg, with the result that the impoverished, footsore beasts arrived at Sante Fe worth no more than $10 a yoke. However, they could pull more weight and were preferred by some traders, especially if their feet were protected with buffalo-skin moccasins and grain was taken on board for feed.

The course of the Santa Fe Trail. The eastern stretch of the Santa Fe Trail, from Council Grove to the Great Bend of the Arkansas, remained practically unchanged from the beginning of trade over it in 1822 to the arrival of the railroad lines which rendered its use obsolete. (See Fig. 101.) From Council Grove, the trail headed straight for the Great Bend, meeting the river at Pawnee Rock (also known as Painted Rock or Rock Point), a famous landmark. Leaving the Great Bend, the trail clung to the left bank of the Arkansas, as far as a point near the site of present-day Dodge City.

Beyond Dodge City, two sections of the trail must be distinguished: one was

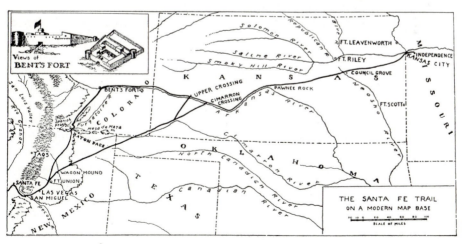

101   The Santa Fe Trail, on a modern map base

known as the Mountain Division and the other as the Cimarron Division or Cutoff. The Mountain Division, used during the earlier years and later by occasional traders and military detachments as well as by the United States mail, followed the Arkansas into Colorado. Here was Bent's Fort, a privately owned trading post, not a military establishment. From this point the trail struck southward up the Purgatoire and Timpas rivers to Raton Mesa near the southern boundary of Colorado. This was the most difficult part of the route, especially the steep grade over Raton Pass between Trinidad, Colorado, and Raton, New Mexico. As the map suggests, this route was an indirect approach to the objective, besides requiring a great expenditure of mule power.

The more direct route across the Plains from the Arkansas to the Cimarron and Wagon Mound, while avoiding the difficulties of the Mountain Division, was for the most part a waterless route, thus involving some hazards. For part of the distance, known as Cimarron Crossing, the trail followed the upper part of the river of that name, but for nearly 70 miles beyond no water was to be had and the grass was poor. Even the buffalo had disappeared from the desolate Cimarron plains by 1846 when an explorer failed to find evidences of his former existence, and antelope were rare.

Conduct and cargoes of the trade.   Early summer was the usual time of embarkation from Independence or Council Grove, with expected arrival at Santa Fe within forty or sixty days. Some of the teams and wagons were disposed of at the end of the trail, just as today automobiles are driven across country and sold at the journey's end. The fall-season return parties usually left Santa Fe after four or five weeks' stay, with lighter loads than they had brought in. There were several reasons for the reduced cargoes going east from Santa Fe: 1. The grass was poorer in the fall, thus putting limits on the number of draft animals. 2. Traveling must be faster to avoid a possible early winter. 3. Remittances were chiefly in money, bullion, and compact goods such as rugs and blankets, occupying less space than the cargoes brought to New Mexico.

The high rates charged for freighting, approaching 10 cents a pound, were a measure of several risks, physical and political, to be met with on the way. There was some danger of plundering by Apaches on the approach to the mountain country, and thus a need for military protection, which was sometimes afforded. During the War between the States there were additional risks which are apparent if one remembers the " Bloody Kansas " of that period. At that time new forts came into being: Forts Zarah and Larned near the Great Bend, Fort Dodge, Fort Lyons near present-day Las Animas, Colorado, and Fort Union in New Mexico. By the time of the war, the heavily subsidized Santa Fe Mail Line was in operation over the Mountain Division. The time from Kansas City to Santa Fe in light wagons or " celerity coaches " was cut down to two weeks — no doubt at the cost of great discomfort to passengers. (See Fig. 102.)

Political difficulties before 1848 arose from the international character of the trade. Mexican officials issued edicts and orders covering the kinds of goods that could be imported and exported, as well as the amount of duties. Increasing

102 The Overland Mail, changing from stagecoach to light wagon. From *Leslie's Weekly,* October 1858.

restrictions hampered traffic, such as the tariff of April 30, 1842, prohibiting the importation of many classes of goods and forbidding exportation of silver. Later in the same year, Mexico decreed the closing of customhouses in Taos, El Paso, and Presidio del Norte in Chihuahua. Under these restrictions the commerce might not have survived but for the enterprise of the traders and the high returns in favorable years. It was estimated that in 1857 the value of goods brought to New Mexico, including freight paid, approached $1,000,000, with net profits ranging from 10 to 40 per cent.

The bulk of the cargo trundled westward over the route consisted of goods put up expressly for the Santa Fe market, such as trinkets, shirtings, calicoes, hose, woolens, pelisse cloths, cutlery, silk shawls, and looking-glasses. Arriving at Sante Fe, part of the goods was redistributed to other towns in New Mexico as well as to Chihuahua in Old Mexico. The value of the trade varied much from year to year, another indication of the risks involved. No accurate records seem to have been kept after 1843, when the restrictive measures of Mexico first took effect. The table on the next page is taken from the well-known *Commerce of the Prairies* by Josiah Gregg, the only trader to have left a chronicle of the commerce to the Southwest.

SANTA FE TRADE

(Value of merchandise at probable cost in Eastern cities)

Year	Value	Transferred to Chihuahua
1822	$ 15,000	
1824	35,000	$ 3,000
1826	90,000	7,000
1828	150,000	20,000
1830	120,000	20,000
1832	140,000	50,000
1834	150,000	70,000
1836	130,000	60,000
1838	90,000	40,000
1840	50,000	10,000
1842	160,000	90,000
1843	450,000	300,000

THE CENTRAL ROUTE OF MIGRATION AND FREIGHTING

The valley of the Platte River was the great channel of communication across the Plains. It offered a fairly direct connection between points of emigrant concentration on the frontier and the main opening through the Rockies in west-central Wyoming, known as South Pass. Furthermore, the valley afforded water, grass, and wood for fuel in greater abundance than elsewhere, and comparative freedom from Indian troubles.

The Platte Route may be pictured as a trunk line consisting of two strands, one on each side of the river. The road on the north side, known as the Mormon Trail after the 1840's, originated near Council Bluffs and Omaha (then called " Winter Quarters "), and thus reached the Platte near its mouth. The south-bank route, in contrast, first met the river about 200 miles upstream at Fort Kearny, opposite the present-day city of Kearney, Nebraska. This was a point of convergence for emigrant and freighting trains that had commenced the westward journey at Independence, Westport, Kansas City, Atchison, and a number of other places. According to some historians, the Oregon Trail began at Fort Kearny; others would place its origin much farther west, perhaps at South Pass, where travelers crossed into the region of Pacific-flowing rivers. Fort Kearny was to the Central Route what Council Grove was to the Santa Fe Trail — the gathering point of several roads connecting with towns on the frontier.

The unnavigable Platte. Travel along the Platte Valley was entirely by land, for the river was then as unnavigable as it is today. " It is but a drain for the melting snows from the mountains," said Major Cross disdainfully in 1850, " and can only be [considered] remarkable for forming more sand bars, and having less depth of water and more islands half covered with useless timber, than any other stream of its size in the country." In high water the Platte rarely exceeded 5 feet in depth, and ordinarily it was divided into numerous channels winding about over its sandy flood plain. The term " braided stream " for such a river had not been invented at the time of the great emigration, but in their descriptions observers left no doubt as to the twisted character of the Platte's current. The maximum degree of channel division or braiding was reached at Grand Island below Fort Kearny. Here were innumerable winding channels, varying in width from 30 to 300 yards, forming numerous islands, collectively called Grand Island. Average depth of water at this island was 2 feet, with sand and water scarcely distinguishable because both were in a state of motion.

Useless as a means of navigation upstream and downstream, the Platte also formed a virtual barrier to travel across it. Thus the two main roads paralleling its course were essentially independent of one another. The astonishing width of the river (fully a mile wide above Grand Island), coupled with its sandy bed and many channels, prohibited cross movements except at a few fords and ferrying points. The stream was sometimes forded at Fort Kearny and below Grand Island, but owing to shifting sands little reliance could be placed on either of these fording places.

Obstructions to road travel were also presented by the tributaries, of which by far the largest was the Loup River, entering from the north. The Loup was another Platte, except that its lower section, where necessarily it must be crossed by the Mormon Trail, was deeper than the main stream and had a more rapid current. There was "no permanency about its banks," said the railroad surveyors of the Loup, nor was the ford near its mouth dependable. One surveying party ferried across the Platte near the Loup entrance only to find on returning a month later that sand bars had formed, and the "train was gotten over by the men wading by the side of the boat, winding about among its bars hunting out the deepest water."

The Platte Route from Fort Kearny to Fort Laramie. When wagon trains first rolled over it in the 1840's, the Platte River Route was a swath cut in the approximate center of a wide expanse of grazing land. For purposes of travel the grass was as important as the track, because the animals which hauled the wagons had to subsist on the land as they went. The route was therefore very wide, and it was long too, with 500 miles lying between Fort Kearny and the outposts of civilization on the Rocky Mountain front.

Fort Kearny, in the opinion of an officer, had "nothing to recommend it in the way of beauty," located as it was between unprepossessing sand dunes and the muddy river, here destitute of tree growth. The buildings were constructed of sward cut in the form of adobe bricks. These sod houses were typical of frontier dwellings on the treeless plains. Fort Kearny offered the usual layout of quarters for troops, a shop or two, and a building that passed for a hospital. Perhaps uninviting in appearance, the fort was nevertheless well located to check Pawnee and Sioux raids on emigrant trains.

Five hundred miles to the west in the upper Platte Valley were the "Laramie Forts" or trading stations, the most important of which was Fort Laramie, established in 1834. Fort Laramie was strategically located at the junction of Laramie Creek and the North Platte, about 100 miles from the present Wyoming city of Laramie. The fort graduated to the position of an actual military base

103   Fort Laramie in 1868, important station on the central route. This is not the site of the present-day city of Laramie. Photo by W. H. Jackson, courtesy of the U.S. Geological Survey.

in 1849, with thick walls 12 feet high, topped by pickets or spikes, and enclosing an open square in which the barracks, storerooms, and blacksmith shops were located. A few acres of gardens were also attached to the fort.

Other trading stations near by were Fort William, Fort Platte, and Fort John, the last-named located a mile below Fort Laramie. These forts were of a temporary character; Fort John, for example, was acquired and demolished by the American Fur Company in the early 1850's. Fort Laramie, functioning as a military base until its abandonment in 1890, was therefore an important way station for a generation of trail-users — emigrants in wagon trains or on foot, freighters, stagecoach and mail-coach drivers, pony-express riders, explorers, surveyors, and soldiers (Fig. 103).

The first great emigration over the Platte Route, a wagon train three miles long, was conducted by Colonel Stephen W. Kearny in 1845. Three years later as many as 6,000 emigrants passed over the roads on either side of the Platte, on their way to Great Salt Lake and the Oregon country. As a result of these great migrations, said Major Cross, the trail soon became a road

. . . as large as any public highway in the United States. Large trains were coming [to Fort Kearny] from all points of the Missouri River, on trails intersecting this great highway. . . . All these trails followed ridges, which placed the wagons frequently in such positions that they seemed to be crossing the prairie in every direction, and, as their white covers were well trimmed, they looked at a distance not unlike vessels on the wide ocean, steering for different parts of the globe.

The route was most serviceable as a highway during the first few years of its use. Signs of deterioration soon appeared in the deepening of the ruts and impoverishment of the grazing lands within easy reach. As early as 1850 one traveler said that the road was " so cut up by successive emigrations that we found much trouble in travelling." The summer period of maximum traffic was also the time of heaviest rainfall, favorable for the maintenance of grass cover but unfavorable for freighting with heavy wagons.

Soon emigrants calculated their chances of a successful passage to Fort Laramie on the basis of the number of trains that had preceded them. Counts of trains at Fort Kearny in June, 1850, indicated that more than 4,000 wagons had passed, not including those that had followed the Mormon Trail, which could not be seen from the fort. A seasonal aggregate of 10,000 wagons and 50,000 oxen or steers was therefore not unusual. " Trains could be seen as far as the eye extended. To look at them, it would seem impossible that grazing could be found for such immense numbers of cattle that must be thrown together when it becomes necessary to stop for water."

The covered wagons of emigrants were not the only vehicles to pass over the trunk highway to Fort Laramie. Commercial freighting companies ran fleets of wagons over it, the army quartermaster paying as much as $1.50 for hauling 100 pounds of produce each 100 miles for the 645-mile journey from Leavenworth to Laramie. A line of the Overland Mail also followed the Platte on its route to Salt Lake. Government ox trains were occasionally to be seen on the Platte Route, like the one pictured by the explorer Howard Stansbury, who passed an outfit on its way to provision a fort beyond South Pass. This train " consisted of thirty-one heavy wagons, four hundred oxen, and about forty men. At night the wagons are drawn into a circle, in the open plain, away from any covert, and chained together," leaving a small space into which the cattle were driven. This was the usual method adopted by wagon trains for protection against surprise Indian forays.

Not to be wholly forgotten in an account of movement across the Plains are the pedestrians who pushed handcarts containing a minimum of equipment. This has been called " handcart migration " by the historian Le Roy R. Hafen, who has made a special study of it. Leaders of the Mormon Church encouraged this method of travel between 1856 and 1860, providing carts similar to those used by porters and street-cleaners. The advantage of the handcart was its mobility — it was capable of twice the daily speed of an ox train — but the human endurance that it required limited the method to a comparatively few persons for a short period. Dr. Hafen states that during the handcart migration period 662 carts were employed in the transportation of 2,969 persons.

When Editor Bowles traveled by stage over the Platte Route in 1865, the railroad not having reached so far, the scene was very different from its appearance twenty years before. In 1865 the road was lined with telegraph poles and wires, and

. . . every ten or fifteen miles is a stable of the stage proprietors, and every other ten or fifteen miles an eating-house; perhaps as often a petty ranch or farm-house, whose owner lives by selling hay to the trains of emigrants or freighters; every fifty to one hundred miles you will find a small grocery and blacksmith shop, and about as frequently is a military station with a company or two of United States troops for protection against the Indians. This makes up all the civilization of the Plains.

From Fort Laramie to South Pass.   One of the most difficult sections of the Central Route was the 250-mile stretch across Wyoming from Fort Laramie to the Sweetwater, headstream of the North Platte rising near South Pass. Much of it was rough terrain with short grass indicative of the diminishing rainfall. It was in this section that travelers became accustomed to evidences of discouragement and disaster: discarded equipment that the emigrants had jettisoned as wagons gave out or oxen died.

On his trip west from Fort Laramie in 1850, Stansbury soon came upon " melancholy evidences of the difficulties encountered by those who are ahead of us. Before halting at noon we found eleven wagons that had been broken up, the spokes of the wheels taken to make pack-saddles, and the rest burned or otherwise destroyed. The road has been literally strewn with articles that have been thrown away " — bar iron, steel chains, anvils, bellows, crowbars, plows, grindstones, harness, ovens, and even clothing. The trunks and other baggage of passengers with whom Stansbury had traveled to St. Louis were recognizable along the roadside. Occasional crosses or markers commemorating travelers who had died on the way added final touches of desolation to the scene.

Many of the animals died on the way or were slaughtered for food; others escaped or were traded for fresh stock to settlers who had shrewdly established themselves at strategic points along the trails. Under the circumstances, trading was usually to the advantage of the settler. One known character, with an eye to emigrant business, settled near South Pass about 1840; having begun with little more than a keen business sense, he had acquired in twenty years " fifty horses, three or four hundred cattle, three squaws, and any number of half-breed children." These roadside settlers traded livestock one for two (or more, on occasion); that is, giving one fresh cow for two beasts worn out by a 500-mile trip on poor grass. Thus did the herds multiply.

Roads were free, but bridges and ferries across rivers in the line of march were not. Ferry charges, not regulated as they are today by public authority, were changed from time to time. For example, charges for crossing the Laramie and the North Platte varied from $3 to $6 a wagon, depending on the depth of water. With payments of $2 here and $5 there at different places on the South Pass route, an emigrant could be $25 poorer within a few miles. Loose stock were charged for separately, at one time as much as 25 cents a head — another reason for the disposal of animals before reaching Fort Laramie. An army officer estimated that tolls paid by overland emigrants aggregated some $50,000 a year. Thus many emigrants reached South Pass considerably reduced in equipment, livestock, and money with which they had hopefully set out from Fort Kearny.

South Pass, principal route-focus of the Rockies.   There are literally hundreds of passes across the Continental Divide formed by the Rocky Mountains, and many of them were known a century ago, but none attained the significance

of South Pass in west-central Wyoming. For that matter, no pass is like South
Pass, for it is a wide break in the otherwise continuous mountain system which
runs athwart east-west lines of travel. South Pass is no narrow defile through
winding mountain gorges, but a major break in the Rocky Mountain system,
and it was so recognized at an early time. Efforts have been made to name the dis-
coverer of South Pass, with little success; it was made generally known, at least,
by fur traders in the early 1820's. Factors contributing to its great use as a way
through the mountains include: (1) comparatively low altitude, hence longer
snow-free season than in many other passes; (2) ease of approach, especially from
the east; and (3) advantageous position with respect to major routes of east-west
travel.

This pass possibly attained the adjective " South " as a means of distinguishing
it from the Montana passes made known by Lewis and Clark. It would be more
correctly called now the Central Pass, or, as some observant travelers have put
it, the Great Gap. Actually, South Pass is about 20 miles wide, approached from
the east by the Sweetwater River and from the west by Sandy Creek, an affluent
of Green River (Fig. 104). The approaches were easy of ascent, the road hard
and compact by comparison with the rough going across Wyoming from Fort
Laramie. So gradual was the ascent that many travelers could not recognize the
actual divide between Atlantic and Pacific drainage.

The width of the pass permitted the building of a number of roads in it; moreover, the varied destinations beyond called for more than one highway. The two
main objectives immediately beyond were Fort Hall to the northwest, and Salt

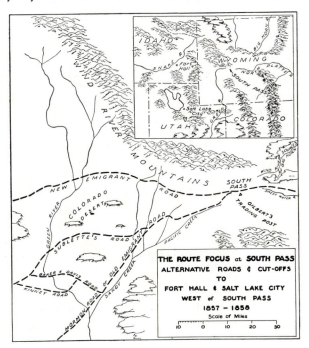

104

South Pass and the various
roads leading to the West,
1858

105   South Pass City, near the eastern approach to the pass, in 1868. Photo by W. H.
Jackson, courtesy of the U.S. Geological Survey.

Lake toward the southwest. To reach these places, several roads or " cutoffs "
were constructed by the late 1850's, and all had their advocates. Each one required the use of a ferry, and it was from his ferry that the road-builder received
his recompense. Of the several shown on the map, Figure 104, the Mormon and
Kinney roads were operated by the Mormons, while Sublette's Road was the
" cutoff " of William Sublette, an early-day trader of the mountain country. The
emigrant was advised in guidebooks to be wary of the claims made by the
projectors of the South Pass roads, because they were in competition with each
other for the emigrant trade. He was also advised to inquire at Gilbert's trading
post at the pass itself, or at South Pass City near it, as to the condition of the
roads. (See Fig. 105.)

No systematic counts were made of emigrant trains going through South Pass.
Traffic in the fall of 1858, not the time of heaviest travel (since 6 inches of snow
lay in the pass by November 30 of that year), is shown in the following table.

WAGON TRAINS AT SOUTH PASS, OCTOBER–NOVEMBER,1858

	October	November
Outfits	59	36
Men	838	528
Women and children	9	
Horses	91	100
Mules	369	207
Oxen	4,851	932
Wagons	490	107

ADVICE TO WESTERN TRAVELERS, 1859

Drawing upon his experience of many years of successful exploration in the Plains, Randolph B. Marcy turned from his writing of narratives to the preparation of a little book for the use of emigrants. He called it *The Prairie Traveler*. It is full of advice to emigrants unfamiliar with the trans-Mississippi country, and makes good reading now. The major points of Marcy's advice are as follows:

I. In selecting the route, emigrants should always remember that " there are several different routes which may be taken with wagons, each having its advocates in persons directly or indirectly interested in attracting the tide of emigration to travel over them." Chief consideration should be given to place of departure and destination, seasons of year of commencing journey, and character of means of transportation.

II. Start as early in the season as possible. Cropping of the grass by previous parties reduces the amount available by late summer. In August 1858, " I seldom found myself out of sight of dead cattle for 500 miles along the road, and this was an unusually favorable year for grass, and before the main body of animals had passed for that season."

III. Organize into companies before venturing on the Plains, preferably with 50 or 70 armed men under an elected captain. Pay attention to such details as the wood used in the spokes of wheels: bois d'arc (Osage orange) is recommended because it shrinks but little. Never load a 6-mule wagon with more than a ton. *The success of the journey depends on the care of animals.* Mules are to be preferred in settled country where grain can be procured and for a journey of up to 1,000 miles if grass is abundant. Oxen are preferable elsewhere: they are cheaper, less likely to be stampeded, can be overtaken by horsemen if they stray, and can be used for beef if supplies run short. Cows are not to be despised as draft animals.

IV. On the march, post both advance and rear guard and establish pickets at night. Select camping grounds with reference to water, fuel, and defense. Water supplies can be foretold by converging animal trails or flights of birds. Concave bends of rivers are desirable for camps; away from rivers select a point near the crest of a hill or bluff, not at the base. Start the march early in the morning, planning on a daily journey of from 16 to 18 miles. Avoid danger of overdoing because, to repeat, *the care of the animals will determine success or failure.*

MISSOURI RIVER ROUTE TO THE NORTHERN PLAINS
AND MOUNTAINS

The Missouri River was but little used as a through route from the eastern frontier to the Pacific coast. The great majority of settlers of the Oregon country reached there by way of the Central Route, over South Pass to Fort Hall and down the Snake-Columbia River, rather than by the route made forever famous by Lewis and Clark. For all that it seemed to lead in the right direction, the general course of the Missouri River route penetrated country long held by the Indian, as can be seen from the map showing reservations (Fig. 89, page 348). Nor did the river route become important even with the dissolution of the reservations, for by that time roads and railroads were pushing across the Plains from Minnesota and the eastern Dakotas.

Nevertheless, the Missouri provided a means of transportation within its drainage basin, promoting movement between the Plains and the mountains to the west of them. Official use of the Missouri was for transporting troops and supplies among the many forts of the interior Northwest. Furthermore, the supplying of Indians, who had become abject wards of the Indian Bureau, was often accomplished by means of river boats. Unofficially, the river was used for transportation by the American Fur Company and by miners or would-be miners in the various gold rushes to the Montana mountains. A high proportion of the mineral yield of Montana during the 1860's sought Eastern markets by the long, winding route of the Missouri, which, said the historian Hiram M. Crittenden with poetic license, "is like a great spiral stairway leading from the ocean to the mountains."

Natural impediments to river travel. The Missouri had little to recommend it as a navigable stream even when there were few other means of getting about. Its great length, 2,000 miles from Omaha to Fort Benton, early-day head of navigation, was almost its only asset. As a Sioux City newspaper remarked in 1868, in a manner suggesting that the writer knew whereof he spoke: "Of all variable things in creation, the most uncertain are the action of a jury, the state of a woman's mind, and the condition of the Missouri River."

From the middle of May to the first of July there was a period of comparatively high water, long enough, perhaps, for a steamer to puff its way from Omaha to the Yellowstone, but with little time to spare. During the remainder of the year navigation proceeded with increasing difficulties, the shallowing water forcing larger vessels off the river at different points throughout its great length. Winter closed navigation at varying dates: about November 10 at Sioux City and December 1 at Leavenworth. The early arrival of winter in Montana also imposed limitations; the advantages of going high up on the Missouri were counterbalanced by the possibility of an early freeze. Other difficulties were the many sand bars, snags, and logs partly obscured by water that was usually muddy, thus prohibiting clear vision of these hazards.

River boats on the Missouri. Commercial boats on the Missouri from the 1840's to about 1870 included the Mackinaw boat, the keelboat, and the steamboat, each adapted in size and draft to Missouri River conditions.

The Mackinaw boat, 50 feet long, was built at upstream points where suitable lumber could be found. Filled with cargoes of furs or mineral products, the boat was navigated downstream, preferably at high water, and sold along with the products it carried at St. Louis or some other city. A return journey of 2,000 miles against the current, which would have to be made the following year, was obviously not economical; better to sell the boat for $10 at St. Louis. Mackinaw boats were also used in the upper tributaries, where the water was too shallow for larger craft. On the Yellowstone, for example, Mackinaw boats made the 225 miles between Fort Union on the North Dakota-Montana border and Fort Alexander Sarpy on the Yellowstone in fifteen or twenty days in country where no roads were available.

The keelboat was a standard carrier on the Missouri. Sixty or 70 feet long, with a cargo box rising 5 feet above the deck, the keelboat was powered by various kinds of equipment — oars, poles, sails, and the cordelle (long rope for pulling). The main reliance was the cordelle, sometimes 1,000 feet long; fastened to the top of the mast, it was pulled by a crew walking alongshore. The absence of established towpaths increased the difficulties of this method, the more so because the boat was constantly in danger of being hung by snags or made fast to a sunken island of sand. The propelling of a keelboat upstream was an all-summer job.

Steamboats appeared on the Missouri as an extension of Mississippi traffic, and became quite common in the 1860's. The first steamer reached Fort Benton, earliest upper-river town and head of navigation, in 1859. The typical steamer was a three-decker with a cupolalike "texas" (pilot house) rising above the main structure.

Steamers proceeded slowly up and down the Missouri, especially up. Much time, perhaps as much again as their total running time, was lost by lying up at night, to avoid running aground or being "stove" by snags. But even the best-managed boat would meet with difficulties in broad daylight. A passenger in 1853 thus describes the "ordinary events that transpire" in running into a sand bar: "the grating sound, the trembling motion of the boat as it comes to rest, inclination from stem to stern, ringing of bells to stop the engines"; but this "failing to relieve the boat from its awkward position, the resort is to the double set of spars, pulleys, and tackling with which every Missouri River steamboat is furnished."

It was estimated that on an average in each running season six or eight weeks were lost in various delays. Two hours of each day were consumed in securing wood to feed the boilers. In the lower river, fuel wood could be bought at from $2 to $2.50 a cord at woodyards. The owner of the yard would indicate his ability to supply fuel by raising a conspicuous signal, and an approaching steamer would signify its needs by tooting the whistle on drawing near. In the upper river, however, the crew often had to rustle its own wood, preferably dead trees or windfalls that could be burned immediately. The consuming capacity of a steamboat, 2 cords of wood an hour, imposed a very real burden on steam navigation. On the other hand, the banks of the Missouri were the most heavily timbered of any of the Great Plains rivers, a factor which contributed to the use of the stream for steamboats.

Steamers on the Missouri, as well as those on the Ohio, occasionally met with total disaster, possibly from the muddy water, which clogged boilers and machinery. On one known occasion in 1861, on the way to Fort Benton a steamer's cargo of smuggled alcohol and whisky caught fire, causing the vessel to blow up.

Movement of cargo and passengers on the Missouri. Government freight represented perhaps two-fifths of the cargo moved on the Missouri during its most active period of navigation, from 1860 to 1870. The large number of river forts in the Dakotas and Montana made this use logical enough. In the Dakotas were such forts as Randall, Sully, Berthold, and Union, while upstream was Fort Alexander Sarpy. Flour, meat, forage, ammunition, and other military supplies were moved by water before other means of travel were available. Indians received their annuity goods, and troops were often transferred, by water. Non-government cargo consisted mainly of furs and minerals.

The year 1867 was the time of greatest steamboat activity on the upper Missouri, as shown by the following table:

STEAMBOAT ARRIVALS AT FORT BENTON, 1859–1874 *

1859	1	1865	8	1871	6
1860	2	1866	31	1872	12
1861	0	1867	39	1873	7
1862	4	1868	35	1874	6
1863	2	1869	24		
1864	4	1870	8		

* *Montana Historical Collections*, Vol. I, 1876.

THE SOUTHERN TRANSCONTINENTAL ROUTE

Mention has been made of the numerous railroad surveys of the early 1850's. These were organized to determine the more suitable routes for rail lines from the eastern frontier of the Plains to the Pacific. Most of the reports were ready for publication in 1855, when the director stated that " if results of the explorations did not furnish data to solve every problem, they at least give a large amount of reliable information and place the question in a tolerably clear light." Anyone who has dipped into the massive volumes of the Pacific Railroad surveys is quite sure that the information is large in quantity; it is also, for the most part, high in quality. In their reports the various surveyors took account of topographic features, heights of mountain passes and gradient of ascents to them, timber available for construction of rail lines, fuel and water supplies, actual and prospective settlement, and existent routes which might be converted into rail routes. For all of these matters the railroad surveys are a mine of information.

The surveys for future rail routes were conducted systematically. The West was divided into five east-west strips, identified by parallels of latitude, and with specific assignment of responsibility. The plan and personnel appear below in condensed form.

I. Near the 47th parallel — North Dakota to Washington; under direction of Governor I. I. Stevens of Washington Territory.

II. Near the 41st and 42nd parallels — Nebraska, Wyoming, to California. From the Missouri River to Fort Bridger, Wyoming, not surveyed with special reference to a rail line, the report depending on previous surveys of Colonel John C. Frémont and Captain Howard Stansbury.

III. Near the 38th and 39th parallels — Colorado and Utah; under the direction of Captain Gunnison, who while in this work was killed by Indians on the Sevier River in Utah.

IV. Near the 35th parallel — northern Texas, New Mexico, and Arizona; under the direction of Lieutenant A. W. Whipple.

V. Near the 32nd parallel — southern Texas, New Mexico, and Arizona; under the direction of Captain John Pope from the Red River to the Rio Grande, and Lieutenant J. G. Parke from the Rio Grande to the Gila. Surveys still farther west were conducted by W. H. Emory and Lieutenant R. S. Williamson.

The southern route from Fort Smith to El Paso and beyond. It is the southern route, Number V above, with which we are now concerned. Various parts of this route had been in use for travel before the grand project of a railroad was considered.

For purposes of a rail line from Fort Smith, Arkansas, to the Pacific coast, a route near the 32nd parallel was seen to have some advantages and some disadvantages. (See Fig. 107.) Among the former were: (1) relatively short distance to the Pacific coast — 1,618 miles — costing perhaps $20,000,000 less than the least expensive of the other proposed transcontinental routes; (2) open passes with low summits; (3) mild winters and temperate summers, thus no apparent difficulty with snow and ice; (4) coal fields near the Brazos in Texas and possibly elsewhere; (5) population already in residence. Chief among the foreseen disadvantages were: (1) high construction costs between the Pecos and the Rio Grande; (2) high sums of ascents and descents over the rough terrain, even though individual passes were not high in altitude; (3) scanty water supplies in the desert country west of the Pecos; (4) the circuitous route to San Francisco from Los Angeles, requiring a secondary crossing of mountain ranges.

The popular press made much of the circuitous nature of any route that would approach San Francisco by way of the 32nd parallel. The projected line, indif-

106   Fort Smith, Arkansas. From *Leslie's Weekly*, October, 1858.

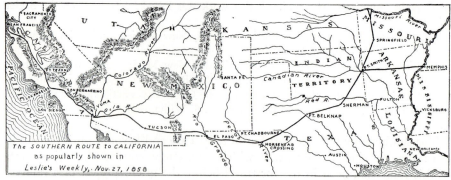

The SOUTHERN ROUTE to CALIFORNIA
as popularly shown in
Leslie's Weekly, Nov. 27, 1858

107   Popular interest in Western routes during and after the gold rush led to the publication of maps in many magazines and newspapers. This is a facsimile of a map extending across the top half of two pages of *Leslie's Weekly* for November 27, 1858.

ferently spoken of as the Fort Smith Route, was also labeled as a side line, or the " Horseshoe " or " Oxbow " Route. Since to the majority of Easterners at that time " San Francisco " and " California " were synonymous, there was some justification for reference to the route as a side line. This characteristic is well brought out on a popular map of 1858 showing the line of the United States Mail from Fort Smith to El Paso, Yuma, Los Angeles, and San Francisco (Fig. 107). The route was one of the many to be brought within the ever widening territory served by the Overland Mail Company. To supply water for men and animals in this Southwestern country of desert rainfall conditions, the company organized mule-drawn water trains of wagons fitted with metal tanks. Beyond El Paso the route followed closely the track known as the Cooke Trail, the control of which was obtained with the Gadsden Purchase.

The southern route to the West was not greatly used by emigrants who were bound for San Francisco or the gold fields, which were far to the north of the point where the road first met the Pacific. In the settlement of Texas, however, this route and others paralleling it became of much importance. But for the inopportune occurrence of the War between the States, the southern route to the West might have rivaled other routes. It has been pointed out that the civil conflict " finally decided the contest between sections over the continental mail in favor of the North."

CHAPTER 22

Settlement in the Central
and Northern Plains

THE first settlements in the Central and Northern Plains resulted from the
needs of travelers and freighters on the trails. Considering the means of locomotion in use, the most essential needs were water and feed for the draft animals
as well as for the " loose stock " (cows, hogs, horses) which usually accompanied
the trains. As a matter of course people depended on the natural grass for the
support of their grazing animals and, staying close to the rivers, found water
also along the routes.

Enough has been said to suggest the gradual depletion of the grass accessible
to the main routes, especially in the later weeks of each emigration season.
Recognizing this situation, enterprising persons established themselves here and
there along the roads, prepared to furnish native hay and cared-for pasture to
passing trains. The operators of these roadside ranches, early-day counterpart
of the modern filling station, were not averse to making a profit in other ways,
such as trading livestock and repairing wagons. This was the beginning of the
grazing industry of the Plains, which has ever since been the dominant regional
occupation.

Other needs of travelers contributed to the bases for settlement. Eating-houses
or taverns appeared at frequent intervals, especially with the advent of the stagecoach as the chief means of passenger travel. Villages tended to grow at customary stopping points, as well as at ferry crossings. Throughout the period of
wagon travel the matter of defense against Indian attack was a prime consideration, reflected in the forts, which multiplied with the years. Within the neighborhood of the forts other villages were almost certain to develop, as at Fort
Dodge, Kansas, and near Fort Pierre (pronounced " peer "), South Dakota.

A special type of pastoral activity developed along the Rocky Mountain front
incident to the gold rushes into Colorado and Montana. Incoming gold-seekers,
finding it impractical to drive their livestock into the mining area, especially in
the face of prevailing fears of terrible winters in the mountain country, often
left the cattle in the care of ranchers along the mountain border. When, as sometimes occurred, the owner failed to return to claim his stock, possibly because his

interests were diverted in other directions, the rancher enjoyed a profitable increase in his herds.

Naturally enough, the people who collected at these various locations turned their attention to the grazing industry rather than to agriculture. Beginning as a subsistence activity, restricted to the vicinity of the highways and the mountain border, the industry rapidly assumed commercial characteristics. Millions of acres of grazing land became available with the reduction of the " Indian barrier " of the Dakotas and Montana in the 1870's, at which time, too, railroads were advancing from the east. Indeed, the available area expanded more rapidly than did the cattle population. The stocking of the Northern Plains with Texas cattle driven over the trails furnishes one of the more dramatic episodes of settlement in the Plains, a favorite theme of story and moving picture.

This was the " day of the cattleman," when the ranges northward of Texas were being stocked, when the grass was not yet overgrazed and prices were high on accessible markets, and before many sheepmen or farmers had arrived. The " open-range " period of the Plains cattle industry ended with the advance of the agricultural frontier. When barbed-wire fences appeared in the range land, and plows bit into the topsoil, the cattle industry had to readjust itself to a new set of conditions.

SUBSISTENCE STOCK-RAISING IN THE PLAINS

The beginning period of stock-raising in the High Plains has often been disregarded, perhaps because it is more interesting to talk about roundups and cattle drives and cowboys with six-shooters than about plodding oxen and unspectacular drivers. The first stock-herding on the Plains, more properly called livestock *care* than " raising," is drab by comparison with the cattleman's heyday; but nevertheless it is of importance in understanding the more interesting variety.

It should be known, first of all, that the freighting companies had to acquire experience in handling big herds of livestock in the open Plains northward from Texas. Until the land had been tried out by the hard test of experience, there was no means of knowing the capacity of the range grass to support browsing animals. The extent of the buffalo herds argued in favor of a high carrying capacity, but what was good for a native beast might not be favorable for a tame one. Particularly, there was doubt concerning winter grazing. Before it was found that the natural range was available for grazing in winter as well as in summer, the traders' livestock was commonly driven to winter quarters to be maintained on stored feed.

Authorities agree that the first demonstrations of the fitness of the northern range for winter feeding were made by freighting companies which employed herds of oxen as beasts of burden. There is a healthy disagreement as to where, when, and by whom the first test was made, the probability being that this was an original discovery of many individuals in different places and at different times. The most commonly repeated story is that of a trader, E. S.

Newman by name, who was snowed up in the Laramie Plains in the winter of 1864–65 with a large bunch of oxen that were not in the best condition. Turning them loose with no expectation of seeing his herd again, he was surprised next spring to find the animals not merely alive, but fat and sleek, as they certainly had not been in the fall.

The story had a precedent, but Mr. Newman may never have swapped experiences with General Raynolds of the Yellowstone expedition of several years before (1859), on which the latter found after a bitter winter that his cattle were in excellent condition. It is certain that by the 1860's experienced cattlemen knew that the capacity of the northern range could be estimated in terms of winter as well as summer grazing, granting that the winter meant some hazards in the rearing of livestock.

Consider the practical problems in animal husbandry that were faced by one trading company mentioned in an earlier chapter — Russell, Majors & Waddell. Originally connected with the Sante Fe trade, this company in 1854 undertook to deliver government stores to the various army posts and Indian agencies of Nebraska and Wyoming territories and elsewhere. During the disturbances of 1857 and 1858, for example, the army required the use of nearly 47,000 oxen and 6,000 mules, hauling a flotilla of some 5,000 wagons. An authority on the cattle industry, Louis Pelzer, states that the Russell firm at the peak of its growth controlled more than 75,000 oxen, and that over 18,000 tons of stores were delivered " to 21 army posts and Indian agencies during the year ending June, 1865." The point intended to be brought out here is not so much the magnitude of the trade as the experience gained in the handling of livestock on natural range land. Later stock-raisers profited much from these experiences.

The trading companies did not, however, contribute appreciably to the permanent stocking of the available range land. Oxen and mules are incapable of reproducing their kind; moreover, after 1868 the ox was a less vital factor in transportation, being considered more important for meat than for power.

Stock-building commenced in a small way when emigrants in their passage to distant goals abandoned cows and bulls on the Plains. Coming as they did from the East, the emigrants brought with them the breeds of cattle typical of that region. Not well adapted to life on the open Plains, these animals were referred to disdainfully as " barn cattle," or " pilgrims," and more expertly, as native cattle. Nevertheless they were self-perpetuating livestock, and they soon became mixed with more hardy varieties. Cattle came in from Oregon, over the passes into Montana and Wyoming, and in increasing numbers were driven northward from Texas, which was the reservoir of the longhorn, a typical range animal. Hence in a relatively few years the term " range cattle " as used in the Northern Plains referred generically to a mixture of Eastern-derived stock with the Texas longhorn of Spanish-Mexican origin.

DEVELOPING PRACTICES IN CATTLE–HERDING

Although the herding of cattle and other livestock had been characteristic of the frontier as it advanced westward from the Atlantic seaboard, there was little precedent for the management of herds on the High Plains. Livestock-raising on the frontier fringe of Kentucky, Ohio, and other Eastern areas was a more or less temporary undertaking in humid forest or forest-and-prairie country, land soon to be pre-empted by farmers. The agricultural frontier thus quickly overran the cattle frontier, with the result that the raising, tending, and fattening of animals for market was soon identified with general farm practices. In the High Plains, by contrast, the livestock industry advanced into an environment so different that new institutions had to be developed.

Perhaps the most far-reaching among the new practices of cattle-raising in the semiarid Plains was the acquisition of " range rights " in public land. To understand this we may seek an analogy in the better-known staking of mining claims in the gold regions of Colorado and California. A miner was considered to have a valid claim to the development of the ore in vein or creek bed in a prospect once it had been staked out and advertised according to local procedures. Furthermore, if the miner used water from a stream to wash out his gold, as he did in placer mining, he became invested with the right to use the same amount of water so long as it was put to beneficial purposes.

This right in water use took precedence over the claims of later arrivals and could be transmitted to heirs or assigned to others. This has become known as the doctrine of prior appropriation, a feature of the common law that was elevated to actual statute law and thus made defensible in courts of the Western states. The analogy with range rights is pertinent to this point and no further, for, as we shall see, the range rights of a cattleman were not backed by legal rulings.

The acquisition of range rights by a stock-raiser also resulted from the appropriation of water and, in this case, the public land contiguous to it. The semiarid grasslands of the Plains beyond reach of water supplies, which the animals needed as much as they did grass, were of little value for cattle-raising. The effective range of a cattle herd, especially of the earlier " pilgrims," was thus confined to a day's roving distance, possibly a dozen miles. More self-reliant and faster-of-foot cattle, such as the longhorn, could range farther, but even for them water supply set the main limits.

Water, therefore, controlled the range; and water, in the High Plains, meant rivers of various sizes, not " water holes " as it did in the desert country of Utah and Arizona. The habitual range of a cattle herd established the " range rights " of its owner — in the common understanding of the early-day cattlemen of a neighborhood. This ordinarily implied a generous strip of land stretching along a river, sometimes on both sides of the stream, possibly extending to the next stream divide.

Inasmuch as water partings seldom are plainly marked topographical features in the Plains, there was a strong tendency for the herds of different owners to mingle during the grazing season. Even more likely was the intermingling of herds upstream and downstream, for here natural boundaries were still less clearly marked. Had there been water holes to determine the effective range in all directions, the problems of management would have been much simplified, and herding on the Plains would have assumed different aspects.

This common practice of establishing rights to segments of range land worked rather well in the beginning stages of cattle-raising. Of range land owned by the Government there was enough and to spare, especially with the elimination of the Indian menace and the extension of new lines of transportation. In the cattle kingdom fashioned by the men first on the ground, a kind of good-neighbor policy prevailed — so long as the neighbor was not too close. What was "too close" is hard to define. Another cattleman with range rights 10 or 15 miles away was near enough — perhaps too near, depending on the livestock actually owned or hoped for at some future time.

If cattle of Owner A were found grazing in the accustomed range of Owner B, the cow hands were instructed to "drift" them back to their proper sphere. Identification marks of ownership existed on the animals in the form of brands, which, through publication, were known to all who had any occasion to be concerned. If Owner C decided to sell a bunch of cattle — "bunch," not "herd," in this Western country — to Owner D, it was generally understood that their habitual range was a part of the deal.

This was an extralegal or nonlegal transaction, but understandable in terms of the evolution of the Plains cattle industry. Courts of law could not raise this practice to statutory level as other courts had upheld the common law in the gold-mining districts. The practice violated the very traditions of the American people, because some of the range rights involved thousands of acres of land, not, as in the case of mining communities, a few square yards at the apex of a mineral vein or a strip of creek bottom from one mountain wall to the other.

The whole matter was admirably phrased by a cattleman who at the height of the cattle boom in 1879 gave testimony before the Public Land Commission. Said he:

Wherever there is water there is a ranch. On my own ranch [320 acres] I have two miles of running water; that accounts for my ranch being where it is. The next water from me in one direction is twenty-three miles; now no man can have a ranch between these two places. *I have control of the grass, the same as though I owned it.* . . . Six miles east of me, there is another ranch, for there is water at that place. . . . Water accounts for nine-tenths of the population in the West on ranches.

EXTENSION OF RANGE LAND AND CATTLE DRIVES TO THE NORTH

From these considerations one can appreciate why a new arrival within the range was, to put it mildly, unwelcome. The stranger might not recognize range rights in an unfenced country known to be a part of the public domain. The

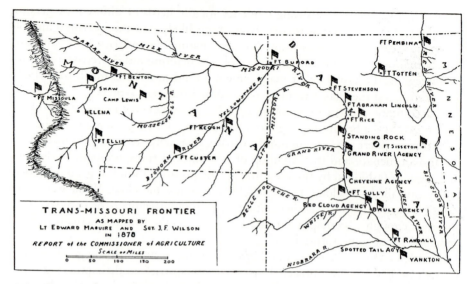

108   Forts, Indian agencies, and settlements in the Northern Plains, 1878. This is a
facsimile redrawing of a folded map attached to an article on " Forestry of the
Western States and Territories " published in the *Report of the Commissioner
of Agriculture* for 1878.

day of ultimate conflict between the old-timers and the newcomers was appreciably delayed, however, by the expanding field of operations.

The vast plains of the north in Colorado, Wyoming, and Montana lay awaiting the arrival of the cattleman — and the departure of the hostile Indian. No
great expansion occurred until well into the seventies, because of the existence
of so many Indian reservations and outlying hunting grounds. Early residents
of the Territories petitioned Congress for more determined action against Indian
hostilities, pointing out the inferior strength of all the army detachments that
had been sent into the field, and the wide spacing of the forts. The defeat of the
1876 offensive, of which Custer's annihilation was a part, served to confirm these
memorials to the Congress; but for many years large sections remained unavailable for occupation. The reservations were viewed as extensive fortresses into which
the hostile Sioux could withdraw after devastating forays upon isolated fort,
lonely freighter, or adventurous settler far beyond the limits of the reserved
territory. Even as late as 1880 all of the trans-Missouri country of South Dakota
to the Nebraska line (with the exception of the Black Hills area) was Indian
land or was considered unsafe for settlement. (See map, page 348.)

With the gold rushes into the Black Hills and the mountains of Montana,
interest was aroused in the grazing possibilities of the Northern Plains. Successes
in the Indian wars also spelled the coming of a new day. With the opening up
of the Northern Plains, the greatest need of the cattlemen was cattle. The great
reservoir of cattle for stocking purposes was Texas, whose markets had been

cut off or severely reduced during the War between the States. The herds had so multiplied that — so it was said — the measure of a man's poverty was the number of Texas steers in his possession.

From the Texas cattle reservoir, herds began to move northward over the trails crossing the Red River. These "drives" to the north had several objectives, the best-known among them being the heads of railroad lines as they advanced across Missouri and Kansas. Cattle were driven to the "cow towns" at the temporary ends of the rail lines, where they were bought for shipment to Eastern slaughterhouses. These were important drives, to be discussed in the next chapter. We are concerned here, however, with two other northward drives, somewhat less publicized: (1) to the Northern Plains for breeding and stocking purposes, and (2) to the Indian agencies of the Dakotas and Montana for beef supply. (See Fig. 108.)

As early as 1859, longhorns were driven from Texas and Indian Territory into eastern Colorado to stock the then empty ranges of that area. The year is significant, for it was near the beginning of the gold rush into the Denver region, with high prices for beef prevailing locally. The first big drive of Texas stock into Wyoming, according to Professor Osgood, was in 1867. This venture resulted from an arrangement made by two cattle kings, Iliff of northern Colorado and Goodnight of Texas, buyer and seller respectively. The longhorns were drifted up from Texas through the Pecos Valley and across the Arkansas, reaching Cheyenne in February, 1868. "In May of that year he [Iliff] was selling a thousand head to the local meat dealers at five cents a pound gross," says Professor Osgood. This success, and others like it, did much to encourage the spread of grazing in the empty Plains of the north.

The advantages of Montana and elsewhere were extolled by railroad companies, which envisioned new sources of revenue. A surgeon for the Northern Pacific, Dr. Henry Latham, wrote many promotional pamphlets depicting the wonderfully nutritious grasses not yet damaged by years of grazing. Less-prejudiced observers pointed out that, while the grasses of the north were virgin, nevertheless the winters were boisterous and cattlemen must be prepared to stand occasional huge losses. The winter of 1871–72, which came in with a November blizzard and remained cold and snowy through March, was often mentioned as disastrous. A writer for *Harpers' Weekly* pointed out that during that "old-fashioned" winter: "In all the Texas herds held in Kansas, the losses were heavy. Hardly a herd lost less than 50 per cent, and 60, 70, and 80 per cent losses were common. The creeks were dammed with the decaying carcasses of cattle."

Expected profits, however, outweighed reported difficulties, with the result that Texas cattle continued to come up from the south. These drives were usually organized by professional drovers, not by cattle-owners. The drover contracted with a Northern buyer to deliver to him cattle with certain specifications as to age, sex, and condition. The drover then went to the locality where he expected to find stock meeting the specifications of the contract. A dozen cowboys were employed for each drove, and horses to the number of 40 to 2,500 cattle were provided for their use on the journey. The drive, when organized, was directed by a captain or boss driver, upon whom fell the chief responsibilities of controlling the cattle on the trail.

Tallies of cattle driven northward across Indian Territory were made in 1880, when there were 103 drives. From the table below it will be noted that by far the greater number of cattle were intended as stock for the northern ranges or as supply for Indian agencies; a relatively small proportion were driven to Kansas City for market.

DESTINATION AND CHARACTER OF CATTLE DROVES ACROSS INDIAN
TERRITORY, 1880 *

	To Nebraska, Wyoming, Dakota, Montana	To Upper Missouri Indian agencies for Beef	Direct to Indian Territory for Breeding Purposes	To Colorado for Stocking	Sold in Kansas City
Yearlings	49,777		11,652	2,050	
2-year-olds	52,879		13,092	1,250	
3-year-olds	18,080	13,508	879	1,075	26,990
4-year-olds	10,470	7,821	748	200	21,007
Dry cows	11,606	8,671	811	535	
Cows and calves	518		31	400	
TOTAL CATTLE	143,330	30,000	27,213	5,510	47,997

* From the *Tenth Census*, 1880, Vol. 3.

In addition to the tallied drives as shown above, there were 164 other contract droves, aggregating 384,147 head of cattle. It is estimated that 75 per cent of the animals driven northward, originating mainly in the Nueces River region of southeast Texas, were intended for stock purposes or for grazing, and the remainder for slaughter, either at once or according to the demands for beef at the Indian agencies of the upper Missouri region and Indian Territory. Time allowances for the drives northward from originating centers in 1880 were ninety days to Ogallala, Nebraska, thirty-five days to Fort Dodge, Kansas, and seventy-five days to Pueblo, Colorado.

As a result of this invasion of Texas cattle, the longhorn strain became evident in range cattle, the proportion of Texas blood becoming progressively less toward the north. Thus, according to the *Tenth Census* (1880):

Texas characteristics in Montana stock are scarcely observable. In 1865 the bringing in of stock became a regular business, the stock coming from various states to the east, from Oregon and the northwest, and a few cattle were brought in from Texas in 1866, 1867, 1868; and also in 1879 and 1880.

Montanans spoke with some pride of the purity of their stock, holding that a Montana steer was superior to one from Texas and brought a higher market price.

END OF THE OPEN-RANGE INDUSTRY

The early 1880's mark the closing phases of the raising of cattle on the open range in the Central and Northern Plains. It was not, of course, the demise of the cattle industry, but a change of land control to a ranch basis. The distinction between range and ranch was well brought out by Joseph Nimmo in 1885, thus: Range cattle are those which are fattened on public lands, or on unfenced lands generally, where herds of different proprietors freely range and intermingle; ranch cattle, in contrast, are raised within enclosures, on lands belonging to cattlemen, on which their own cattle graze. The change from the range industry to the ranch business was a gradual process, not occurring at the same time throughout the Plains region.

The end of the open-range industry cannot be attributed to any one cause, but rather to the coincidence of a number of factors. The leading causes suggested by authorities are these:

1. Economic collapse, following an unhealthy boom, resulting from overspeculation by capitalists who had invested large sums in ambitious cattle companies. For example, the biggest Montana outfit, the Swan Land and Cattle Company, went into receivership in 1887 after several years of heavy losses.

2. Lowering or unstable prices of meat on Eastern markets.

3. A series of disastrous winters, such as that of 1887, causing widespread losses. When, in the spring of 1888, says Professor Osgood, cattlemen saw the emaciated remnants of their herds, " men revolted against the whole range system."

4. Overcrowding of the ranges, which only a few years before were virtually empty. Cattlemen had loaded the range too heavily and newcomers had " nested " within the accustomed ranges of the original appropriators. Attempts to protect their ranges from invasion by others had proved unavailing. Lacking the support of public law, the cattlemen tried boycotts through local associations, which boldly proclaimed specified areas of public land to be reserved for their use and " positively decline allowing any outside party, or any party's herds upon the range, the use of our corrals, nor will they be permitted to join in any roundup on said range from and after this date." Such statements were as ineffectual against the powerful forces at work as barriers of sand against a river flood.

5. The extension of sheepherding, leading to the deterioration of the grass, because sheep clipped the grass shorter than did cattle.

6. The advance of the agricultural frontier onto the semiarid Plains. This involved the fencing of land taken up legally by farmers under the Homestead Act and various modifications of it. Professor Webb has placed great emphasis upon the effect of barbed wire as fencing material in the treeless plains. He points out that the first piece of barbed wire was marketed in this country in 1874, and thereafter the wire was strung over large sections of the former open range. Such fences were especially effective in cutting up the ranges, prohibiting movement of animals within their habitual range and on drives across country. " This cheap and easy fencing," says Professor Osgood, " spread so rapidly that the whole range industry was in danger of being strangled to death in a web of its own making."

Since this chapter is primarily concerned with settlement in the Plains, of which the cattle industry was the first stage, item 6 above will be singled out for further consideration.

CONDITIONS FAVORING AGRICULTURAL SETTLEMENT

The original idea that the High Plains formed a region uninhabitable by a farming population had all but disappeared by the 1870's. Settlement based on the grazing industry was taken as concrete evidence of error in the original view. Man had now conquered the Plains, it was asserted, not only by means of his settlements, but also by extending railroads across them. Original conditions no longer obtained, or were set aside by other things. Furthermore, crops were being raised in various sections, first in the vicinities of the forts and Indian agencies, and then by ranchers as an adjunct to the grazing industry. Small-scale irrigation had developed here and there and was declared to be successful. Not a few influential individuals stated that crops could be raised in the Plains better than in the humid Eastern states. (See Fig. 109.)

The general land policy of the United States was a powerful influence in encouraging agricultural settlement in the Plains region. The public domain was regarded as valuable only if it became available in relatively small units to individual landowners. As the National Resources Board said in 1934:

Throughout the period of westward expansion the public policy was one of getting the land settled and improved as rapidly as possible. Certain features of this policy, as exemplified by the homestead laws, established a size of farm and a type of farming pattern poorly adapted to many areas, especially in the drier, more inaccessible or otherwise poorer lands of the semi-arid West. Under the assumption that the process of carving out farms could continue successfully in the semiarid regions if the

109   Omaha in 1858. From *Leslie's Weekly*, November 6, 1858.

160-acre homestead were increased, the Enlarged Homestead Act of 1911 and the Stock-raising Homestead Act of 1916 were passed, permitting entry of 320- and 640-acre homesteads respectively.

By the 1870's the better and more accessible lands of the states east of the Mississippi River were fairly well taken up. Land-seekers therefore were prepared to consider acquiring homesteads in the very area which only a few years before had been publicly condemned for agricultural settlement. Private interests joined with the public-land policy in offering inducements to Western settlers, as is shown by the following advertisement that ran in the summer issues of *Leslie's Weekly* in 1871.

1,700,000 ACRES IN IOWA!
180,000 ACRES IN NEBRASKA!

The

R. R. Land Companies

of Iowa and Nebraska

offer

the above land to settlers

at

$3 to $10 per acre, on time,

at 6%, or for cash.

Best Lands in the Best States!

Land exploring tickets

at Cedar Rapids and Chicago.

The Government, for its part, encouraged Western settlement by continuing its policy of granting land for internal improvements, and by offering modifications of the Homestead Act designed to fit the environment of the treeless and more arid lands. The extent of land grants for internal improvements throughout the country by 1880 is shown in Figure 110. Note should be taken of the broad strips across the West within which major transcontinental railroads were constructed. The general policy was to grant to the railroads alternate sections within these strips, leaving the other sections available for individual entry.

That the attempts to adapt land policy to suit the new conditions in the West were short of perfect will become apparent from a consideration of legislation through the 1870's. Chief among the pieces of legislation were the Timber Culture Act and the Desert Land Act.

The Timber Culture Act of 1873. This legislation, entitled " An act to en-

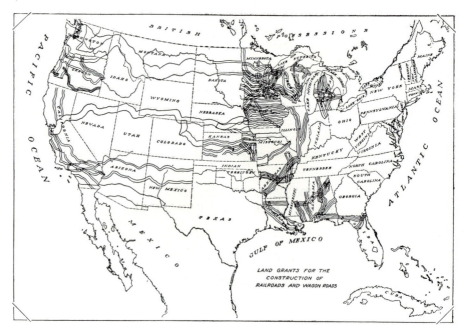

110   Land grants for internal improvements up to 1878. From the J. W. Powell *Report on the Lands of the Arid Region of the United States, 1879.*

courage the growth of timber on western prairies," did not, as is commonly stated, grow "out of the recognition of the desirability of having timber and forests on the Great Plains." It was framed more particularly for the possible benefit of homesteaders in the *humid* prairies, where experience had demonstrated that trees could grow, and grow well, if planted and cared for during the earlier years of their growth. As the provisions of the act became popularly known, "tree claims" were taken up in the prairie regions, with many social benefits accruing to later generations. Many a farmer's wood lot in the prairie regions of Iowa and Minnesota derives from a tree claim taken up by a homesteader a half-century ago, probably in addition to the quarter-section allowed him under the basic Homestead Act. These wood lots have furnished fuel, fencing material, and pasture for cattle and hogs for later residents in the farming country who may be unaware how the wood lot came into being.

However, the Timber Culture Act was not restricted to the prairie region. Under it, tree claims could be taken out in the public domain, which then overspread a vast region of varied topography, climate, and soils. By 1873 the largest remaining areas of the domain lay to the west of the Mississippi River, with the natural result that tree claims were taken up in the semiarid and even the arid regions.

The original act stated that any person who should plant, protect, and keep in a healthy growing condition for ten years 40 acres of timber, with trees not more than 12 feet apart, would receive title to the quarter-section of which the 40 acres was a part. Homeseekers in the humid prairies naturally found this a wise and beneficial act; they also viewed it as a means of acquiring an additional 160 acres of land. Settlers out on the semiarid Plains were even more desperately in need of timber than was the prairie farmer. If government authorities thought he could grow trees in an area called a desert only a quarter-century before, there was no reason why he shouldn't try. As to the depth of his faith in eventual success there is little evidence, for homesteaders who took out tree claims seldom left records revealing their views on this matter.

The tree-claimers did register disapproval of specific provisions of the act. It was said that to plant and care for 40 acres of trees was ridiculously impossible, for the farmer must devote most of his time to income-producing activities. In response, the Government reduced the requirement to 10 acres, but it took four years to bring about this change of law. Fraudulent practices were easily devised. Actual settlement on the tree claim was not required; one need not even be a resident of the same state in which the claim was taken up. Consequently there was many a nonresident tree-claimer who after making slight improvements quietly withdrew to await the time when he would own the quarter-section.

Many claims were taken up in blocks by employees of cattle companies that hoped, by this and other legal means, to acquire the size of landholdings which they thought necessary and which the law, as strictly interpreted, denied them. In a well-known case in South Dakota, a cattle company thus acquired 26¼ sections of land along streams. Other cattle companies sought to " fence off " large areas of range land by having employees file on tree claims so placed as to encompass the desired area. Speaking of western Nebraska, the Commissioner of the Land Office said:

My experience leads me to the conclusion that the majority of entries are made for speculative purposes, and not for the cultivation of timber. My information is that no trees are to be seen over vast regions of country where timber-culture entries have been numerous. Probably one in a hundred entries are made in good faith.

These malpractices, however, should not condemn the act itself, which was repealed in 1891. It worked many benefits, not only in the true prairie country, but in the transition belt of subhumid climate farther to the west. It was also beneficial in those parts of the semiarid Plains where water was available to tree roots most of the year.

The Desert Land Act of 1877. The Desert Land Act originated in a genuine desire to encourage Western settlement, but contained impractical provisions which reveal a lack of understanding of irrigation farming.

Briefly stated, the act provided for the sale of a section of land in specific Western states, at the rate of $1.25 an acre, to each settler who would irrigate it within a three-year period. Under this act, " desert land " could be bought in the Rocky Mountain states, as well as in Dakota Territory, Arizona, Nevada, and southern California. This vast area included much land in which agriculture of any sort was impossible, and other areas potentially suitable for farming without resort to irrigation. Excluded were western Nebraska and Kansas and Texas, where irrigation would be as advantageous as in other Western areas.

Not all the weaknesses of the act were immediately apparent, nor was it foreseen that fraud could easily be practiced. One of the first questions to be asked was, Why put a price on desert land when good farm land elsewhere was subject to homesteading? More important, What was meant by the irrigation of a section of land? Did this mean the entire square mile, or such portions of it as could be supplied with water by gravity flow? Who was responsible for the idea that an irrigated farm should be four times the size of an ordinary farm — that is, a whole section, compared to the usual 160-acre homestead? Although little was known about irrigation, it was generally assumed to be an intensive type of farming suitable for small holdings.

Since the provisions of the act were impossible of fulfillment, settlers in desert land felt that they could be forgiven for evasions of the letter of the law. The act was used to build up landholdings, just as was the Timber Culture Act. " By living a little and lying a little," says Professor Webb humorously, " it was possible for one man to bring together a considerable body of land which could be used for a stock ranch." By means of all kinds of devices known to man, the " irrigators " of desert land sought to satisfy the inspectors. Concerning these fraudulent schemes it would be hard to improve upon Professor Benjamin H. Hibbard's observation that in Wyoming " a great deal of so-called ditching was done by plowing a few furrows. Moreover, these ditches failed to follow the contour of the land with reference to the habits of water, and often they began where there was no water to be conducted and ended where there was no field to receive it."

Nevertheless, some semiarid and desert land was developed by settlers into small irrigation projects. Such land was often used for raising hay and fodder, or for irrigated pastures in connection with the livestock industry.

THE POWELL REPORT ON THE ARID LANDS

The most enlightened program for disposal of lands in the states and Territories west of the 100th meridian was prepared by Major John W. Powell, government geologist, and published in 1878. The Powell *Report on the Lands of the Arid Region of the United States* came out of a careful survey of the natural environment of the West and its social problems, which by then had reached a critical stage. It remains as a classic in its field. Reference to Powell's work as a " report " is likely to convey the wrong impression; it was no routine office job, but a thorough, hard-hitting analysis, accompanied by recommendations for legislation.

Powell's " Arid Region " included the true desert west of the Rocky Mountains and the semiarid belt to the east of them; in his view, the same problems related to both areas. This embraced four-tenths of continental United States where " the mean annual rainfall is insufficient for agriculture, but in certain seasons some localities, now here, now there, receive more than their average supply."

Excluding the forested mountains, there were said to be two main classes of land: irrigable and pasturage, with the latter predominating. Only a small proportion of the Arid Region could ever be irrigated, because of limited water supply. A land unit in the irrigable area should not exceed 80 acres. The farm unit in the pasturage districts, in contrast, should be four full sections of land (2,560 acres) and each unit should have some irrigable land attached to it.

It was further recommended that the rectangular survey system be abandoned in favor of divisional surveys conforming to topographic features. " Many a brook which runs but a short distance will afford sufficient water for a number of pasturage farms," said Powell, " but if the lands are surveyed in rectangular tracts as square miles or townships, all the water sufficient for a number of pasturage farms may fall entirely within one division." Emphasis was placed on the desirability of the colony plan of settlement in arid lands, which will always " maintain but a scanty population." Reference was made to the success of colony settlements in agricultural and mining districts in which

. . . local rules and regulations . . . are managed better than they could possibly be under specific statutes of the United States. Customs are forming and regulations are being made by common consent among the people in some districts already; but these provide no means for acquirement of titles to land, no motive is given to the improvement of the country, and no legal security to pasturage rights.

Powell's factual report and its recommendations were followed by two bills introduced in the Congress, one to authorize the organization of irrigation districts and the other to enable the formation of pasturage districts. The bills did not meet with congressional approval, apparently because of the many innovations contained in them. A point of particular attack was the provision for a homestead of 2,560 acres of land, which seemed to legislators from Eastern states out of all reason. As a matter of fact, Powell's figure of four sections of land was the absolute minimum which he had found necessary. In a footnote he recorded his " fears that this estimate will seem insufficient to many of his western friends who will think he has placed the minimum too low."

Broadly speaking, Powell sought to legalize practices which the people already living in the region had developed. He felt it desirable to relieve them from the necessity of resorting to subterfuge and extralegal land entries in acquiring the extent of acreage which a stock farm must have for successful operation. But the American people were not ready to accept the farsighted recommendations of the one-armed geologist in charge of the United States Geographical and Geological Survey of the Rocky Mountain Region.

RAINFALL AND SETTLEMENT

We now know that the rainfall of the Great Plains is distributed over the years in cyclical fashion — that is, a few consecutive years of above-average rainfall are likely to be followed by another period of years when the rainfall is far below the average. For example, western Nebraska sometimes receives as much rainfall as Ohio, and again as little as does the Arizona desert. No definite periodicity in these cycles is as yet clear, at least not sufficiently so for purposes of prediction. It is known, however, that few areas in the Great Plains receive above-average rainfall in as many years as below-average rainfall is experienced. Dr. J. B. Kincer has pointed out that in more than half the years, the Great Plains receive less than the average rainfall.

These facts were of course not known in the 1870's, when agricultural settlement in the Plains was receiving much encouragement from various sources. Few rainfall records were available even to the better-informed, and no weather station had been maintained long enough to show trends over a considerable period of time.

Particular attention was drawn to the periods of more ample rainfall, one of which lasted from about 1875 to 1880 in the Central Plains. Many interpreted this as a change for the better in the climate, a good omen for the future. This supposed change of climate seemed natural enough to those who believed that rainfall " follows the plow " — that is, that settlement somehow induces greater precipitation. In later years of similar upward trends in rainfall, attention was called to the probable effects of irrigation, which was supposed to contribute more moisture to the air and thus to increase the probabilities of rainfall. Fantastic as these views appear to be today, they were nevertheless widely held in earlier times.

The years of increased rainfall, along with other factors, encouraged greater settlement in the Plains region. During the brief periods of above-average moisture, when, in fact, the rainfall equaled that of states farther east, wheat yields were satisfactory. The Wheat Belt, which had for a century been advancing across the country from the Atlantic seaboard, edged onto the drier lands and, as Figure 111 suggests, by 1880 " islands " of wheat cultivation appeared in the more favorable areas. Reports of good wheat crops in the Dakotas and Montana reached the source regions of emigration, perhaps in exaggerated form, and stimulated further development. Often the emigrants acted upon information that was already obsolete, for by the time they reached their newly selected homesteads the drought years had set in.

To many, a year or two of drought was no cause for great alarm; in the long run, it was confidently believed, the climate was changing for the better. Advocates of " dry farming " were prompt to point out that with careful tillage of the soil to retain moisture by retarding evaporation, farmers could do with less than the amount of rainfall that was supposed to be necessary. During long-continued droughts, many settlers were forced to give up their homesteaded land

and return to the Midwest or the East. Dry-land farmers they had become with a vengeance, as may be recalled from the most recent drought of the middle 1930's when the term "Dust Bowl" was popularly applied to this region or to parts of it.

Although there were alternating periods of agricultural advance into the Plains and withdrawal therefrom, a gain in population was usually registered over a long period of time. The effect of rainfall on settlement can easily be overstressed; commonly it was a contributing factor rather than a wholly independent cause. Many other factors played their parts in determining the ebb and flow of High Plains settlement. Country-wide conditions of depression and prosperity were registered in advances and retreats of the "frontier line." Elements operating to induce continued settlement in the High Plains included: (1) the continued immigration from foreign countries and the "filling-up" of the potential farming lands in states farther east; (2) the extension of railroads and the efforts made by their subsidiary land companies to dispose of lands along the rights of way; and (3) the gradual removal of the Indian barrier. Thus was settlement encouraged in a great area which Isaiah Bowman has aptly called a land of risk.

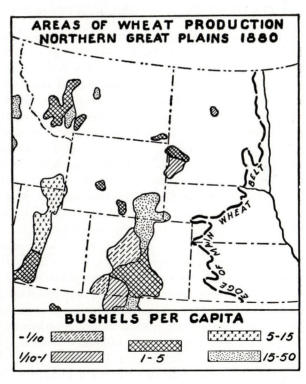

111

The limited extent of agriculture in the Northern Plains in 1880 is suggested by this sketch taken from the *Census of the United States* for that year.

112   Fort Randall, on the Missouri River, Gregory County, South Dakota, in 1858. The arrangement of the barracks, storehouses, and other buildings is typical of frontier forts of that period. From *Leslie's Weekly,* July 3, 1858.

SETTLEMENT IN A PLAINS STATE: SOUTH DAKOTA

The many factors which operated in the agricultural settlement of the Great Plains are well illustrated by a brief review of the historical geography of South Dakota. The greater part of this state lies in the Great Plains, although it should be realized that the eastern portion is more truly subhumid, and in the southwestern corner further variety is offered in the Black Hills.

Lying off the main routes of Western migration, and long held by hostile Indians, South Dakota was scantily populated until after the War between the States. In fact, the Territorial government was not formed until 1861, when its small population was confined to the Sioux Valley in the southeastern corner. At that time, Yankton was the Territorial capital. Even this small area was almost depopulated after the Sioux raids of 1862. Fort Randall on the Missouri River in present-day Gregory County was considered far out on the frontier during this period. (See Fig. 112, also Fig. 108, page 412.)

The first Dakota boom, according to the study made by Professor Stephen S. Visher, extended from 1868 to 1873. It was initiated by a period of goodcrop years and further extended by the approach or arrival of railroads. Furthermore, nearly all the better lands of Iowa had been taken up, and emigrants accordingly turned northward into the adjacent territory. Organized efforts to attract people to the state were also effective in inducing settlement.

The next stimulus to South Dakota settlement resulted from the discovery of gold in the Black Hills in 1874. The reports had their usual effect in attracting people to the state. Although the Black Hills were Indian country, the lure of precious metal was so powerful that prospecting parties set out for the mountains in spite of military opposition. The actual gold rush occurred in 1878 in

Deadwood Gulch. The booming mining camps provided a new market for agricultural products; hence, and with government encouragement, farmers were also attracted to the region. Many who originally came to mine gold remained as farmers or ranchers in the mountains or near them.

The so-called Great Dakota Boom occurred during the period from 1879 to 1886 when, says Professor Visher, "What a few years before had been an almost uninhabited expanse of prairie, became a fairly populous farming region, soon to be admitted as a state."

Several consecutive years of above-normal precipitation greatly contributed to this boom period. The winter of 1880–81 was a hard one, setting in with an October blizzard, with deep accumulations of snow during the season. While this unusually severe winter contributed to the bad reputation of the area, it did yield some unexpected benefits, for the melting snow saturated the soil (which had not frozen under its blanket) and filled many a shallow depression with water. "Certain it is," says Professor Visher, "that this snow, by creating thousands of lakes, suggested a humid climate, a condition highly attractive to prospective settlers." By no means unimportant as a factor in the Great Dakota Boom was the further extension of rail lines, which linked the farming areas with profitable markets.

The boom times were brought to an end in 1886 by a drought and consequent crop failures. The drought continued for two or three years, which saw the departure of many settlers and most of the land speculators. Many persons had come to South Dakota, as to other Western states, chiefly to secure title to homestead land; not being genuine settlers, they could quite easily be induced to leave. The drought considerably delayed the admission of South Dakota as a state, an event which occurred in 1889.

CHAPTER 23

Texas: Farming Frontier and Cattle Kingdom

Texas within its present boundaries first appeared on maps in the year 1850. Before then, the name was applied to a still larger area which included the present state of New Mexico east of the Rio Grande and, for good measure, a strip extending into Colorado. Even in its reduced form, Texas was still (as now) the giant of American states in area — but small in population.

The Texans of the 1850's, numbering about 250,000, were thinly scattered over the eastern third of the state. Here and there were a few villages and towns, some newly founded, others reaching back to the early Spanish period of colonization. San Antonio, with about 3,000 inhabitants, was the largest town in 1850 and remained in first position until the modern period. On the fringe of settlement were a number of forts, many of them established during the war with Mexico or as a consequence of it. San Antonio, dominantly Mexican in population, was on the frontier, as were also Austin, Waco, and Fort Worth to the north. A line joining these places with Laredo on the Rio Grande represents the approximate frontier when the boundaries of Texas were stabilized nearly a century ago.

It is with the eastern third of Texas, mainly a humid land but including also drier grasslands and creosote-bush country south of the Nueces Valley, that this chapter is largely concerned. A relatively small part of East Texas is included in the Great Plains region, but a true understanding of the Western cattle industry requires attention to this Southern land of varied natural landscape. It was here that the range cattle industry first developed, and after the War between the States it reached gigantic proportions. East Texas was more than a reservoir of cattle for Northern ranches and markets; here also was vigorous agricultural settlement by people of many conditions and many national backgrounds. Climatically allied to the Cotton Belt, this became a region of staple-crop production, with large landholdings and slavery as characteristic features. Do not be misled into thinking of humid East Texas as a small region because it is only a third of the whole state. The area between the Gulf Coast and the frontier line above suggested is as large as Indiana, with room and to spare for industries based on the soil, even though one of them — cattle-grazing — required extensive acreages.

THE REGION OF EAST TEXAS IN THE 1850's

East Texas was viewed by visitors a century ago as a region of unusual charm and promise for the future. Descriptions emphasize the mildness of the seasons and the dependability of the rainfall, the evident fertility of the soil, the luxuriance and variety of the vegetation, the favorable conditions for the grazing industry, and the apparent success of settlements which had sprung up after Texas became a state in 1845.

Approached from the Gulf of Mexico, Texas was described as a low shore line of elongated islands forming lagoons, with occasional " passes " giving entrance to deeper bays. Thus Laguna de Madre, extending for over 100 miles from the mouth of the Rio Grande northward to San Antonio Bay, was separated from the Gulf by a nearly continuous line of barrier-beach islands, such as Padre, Mustang, St. Joseph, and Matagorda. Mustang Island, off Corpus Christi Bay, was aptly named for the wild horses which lived there as well as on the adjacent mainland. Also prevalent here were herds of deer and beef cattle, subsisting on the rich natural grasses.

When John R. Bartlett, government surveyor, entered Corpus Christi Bay in 1854, he found the lagoon " covered with myriads of water fowl, including cranes, swans, herons, ibises, geese, ducks, curlews, and sand pipers. The large cranes and swans stood in lines extending for miles, appearing like a sandy beach or white cliff." Coming upon the birds unexpectedly, he observed that " they would rise in one continuous flock and make a noise like thunder as they flapped their wings on emerging from the water." A few villages situated toward the heads of the larger bays were beginning to feel the effect of new settlement, but commerce had not grown to large proportions. Among the more important ports of this period was Corpus Christi, which was expanding from its original site on the low beach to the higher bluffs.

Even more attractive than the immediate shore was the wide-sweeping coastal plain which, as W. H. Emory pointed out, comprised " alternating beds of alluvial and oceanic deposits, showing how gradual and well contested have been the encroachments of the land upon the sea." Traversing these alternating deposits were the great, almost equidistant rivers of East Texas, — Sabine, Trinity, Brazos, Colorado, San Antonio, and Nueces, named from north to south (Fig. 113). Unnavigable except in their lower portions, the rivers rendered service by furnishing water for the stock-raising industry and occasionally for irrigation, as at San Antonio.

The more striking features of the inner coastal plain of Texas were related to vegetation types rather than to topographic features. In the unanimous opinion of observers, East Texas was a beautiful country in the 1850's, diversified by belts of forest and no less luxuriant prairie, kept green most of the year by the abundant rainfall and the mild winters. The terms "black prairie" and "black waxy prairie" are of more modern invention, but the grassy regions were recognized, as were also the Upper and Lower Cross Timbers.

Early residents of Texas referred to the prairie-woodland country as "mottes," a term comparable to "oak openings" as used by Northerners. Thus Emory refers to the "clumps of post-oak called *mots*" which his party encountered after crossing the black-prairie belt and a "ridge of low sand hills which seem to mark the former limits of the coast." Many visitors were impressed with the parklike nature of the landscape, as though the hand of man had been concerned in the creation of it. The surveyor for the western railroad said of the upper Trinity Valley near present-day Dallas that the land

. . . presents the most charming views, as of a country in the highest state of cultivation, and you are startled at the summit of each swell of the prairie with a prospect of groves, parks, and forests, with intervening plains of luxuriant grass, over which the eye in vain wanders in search of the white village or the stately house which seem alone wanting in the scene.

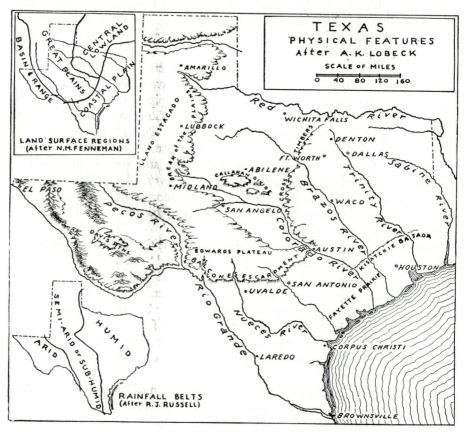

113   Physical map of Texas

During his surveys of the Red and other rivers of North Texas from 1852 to 1854, the explorer Randolph B. Marcy also found natural beauty in an area not yet settled by white men, and described it in the extravagant language of that period. Reaching the summit level between the Trinity, Brazos, and Little Wichita rivers north of Fort Belknap, Marcy and his party found that

. . . a most beautiful panorama was opened to our view. On our left, in the distance, could be seen the lofty cliffs bordering the Brazos, while in front of us, towards the sources of the Little Wichita, were numerous conical mounds, whose regular and symmetrical outlines were exhibited with remarkable truth and distinctiveness upon a ground of transparent blue sky. On our right several tributaries of the Little Wichita embellished with light fringes of trees, flowed in graceful sinuosities among green flowering meadows, through a basin of surpassing beauty and loveliness as far to the east as the eye could reach; all contributing enticing features to the romantic scenery, and producing the most pleasing appearance upon the senses.

Similarly, a view across the fertile San Antonio Valley from Goliad comprehended a surface of

. . . gentle undulations, not densely wooded enough to form a wilderness, but bearing here and there clumps of trees, disposed so regularly as to give the landscape a rural aspect. So closely do the clusters of live-oaks resemble orchards, and the recently burnt prairies, with the newly-springing grass [resemble] meadows, that one finds it difficult to convince himself that he is not passing through a highly cultivated district.

Such a rare combination of luxuriant grasses, belts of timber, ample water supplies, mild winters, and coastal position made this one of the finest grazing regions in all of North America. "The country between the Nueces and the Brazos is fine for grazing," said Emory. "Formerly there were incredible numbers of horses and cattle, and to this day [1857] the remnants of this immense stock are running wild on the prairies between the two rivers." Professor Webb has concluded that this southern Texas region was the cradle of the North American cattle industry. He pictures the diamond-shaped region below the Nueces as offering "almost perfect conditions for raising cattle" — grass and timber, mild climate, adequate or plentiful water supplies, and protection from Indian attack.

SETTLEMENTS, OLD AND YOUNG, IN EAST TEXAS

The belted coastal plain of East Texas was not entirely a magnificent solitude of luxuriant grasses and half-wild cattle, although this was its dominant aspect. There were many settlement clusters, some of them deeply rooted in the past and still growing, others existent only in ruins — monuments of the early Spanish period or the wreckage of warfare for Texas independence — and still others of more recent origin. The important settlements are shown on the general map of 1858 (Fig. 114). Note the ring of forts which marked the frontier, and the

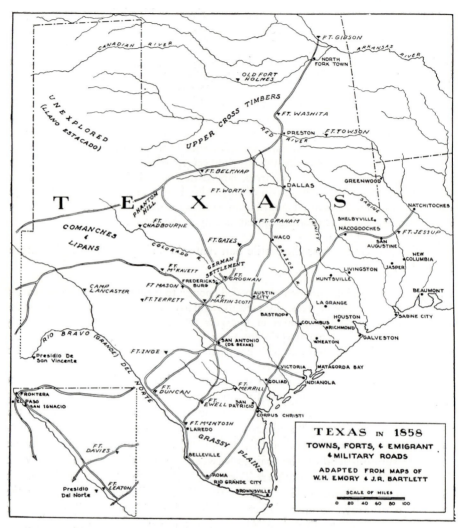

114   General map of towns, forts, and roads of Texas in 1858. Adapted from con-temporary maps.

main emigrant roads roughly paralleling the coast or extending from coastal localities across the then uninhabited wastes of West Texas, to reach El Paso. It appears that all the important towns were situated on rivers, particularly at points where they were crossed by the main roads. Many other factors were involved, however, as can be seen from brief studies of such typical places as Goliad, San Antonio, Austin, and Fredericksburg.

Old and new Goliad on the lower San Antonio River.   Some appreciation of the long period of white settlement in East Texas is gained by a consideration of Goliad in the present-day county of that name on the lower San Antonio

River. In the 1850's there were two Goliads, the old and the new, about 2 miles apart. New Goliad had developed with the wave of immigration which followed upon the admission of Texas as a state and the peace ensuing after the war with Mexico. Old Goliad, on the west bank of the river at its highest navigable point, was the principal settlement in the area from the time of its founding in the Spanish Colonial period through the struggle for Texan independence — that is, until 1836.

From the partially occupied ruins of old Goliad in 1850, visitors could reconstruct its original appearance as a Spanish mission. Grouped in one enclosure were a church, a fort, and some 20 structures built for residential purposes. Only the church was in tolerable repair in 1854, when it was in use as a dwelling. The walls, made of a locally derived soft limestone (which apparently hardened somewhat on exposure), were prostrate, as were also most of the other buildings. The ruins of old Goliad recorded not merely the effects of time and neglect on weak building material, but also the troubled state of affairs in Texas prior to its arrival at statehood. With each successive capture of Goliad during the war for independence, the buildings were impaired, and after the decisive battle of San Jacinto the work of destruction was completed by the retreating Mexicans.

The original importance of old Goliad was enhanced by its position near the head of navigation on the San Antonio River; though 40 miles inland, it was the collecting point for revenue taken at the small ports on the bay. New Goliad never achieved this degree of regional importance, but remained a small town far surpassed by other centers of southeast Texas.

San Antonio. Main center of Spanish colonization in the previous century, San Antonio remained the metropolis of Texas after its American accession. Situated in the center of a productive agricultural and grazing region, San Antonio would inevitably grow in importance. Signs of growth were already apparent, for its population of 2,000 at the close of the war with Mexico more than doubled within the next decade. San Antonio's importance derived in part from the productivity of its hinterland and in part from control over southern-Texan trade. It was a focus of routes. Ox trains connected the inland town with coastal ports, making the 130 miles in five or six days; reaching the town, the freight was redistributed to distant localities. In competition with the Santa Fe trade, long trains frequently set out for El Paso, Eagle Pass, and other border towns.

Visitors found San Antonio a century ago a strange mixture of sleepy old Spanish buildings and more alert-looking American structures, inhabited by Mexicans, French, Germans, and recent immigrants from the United States. The plaza itself was set off by an assortment of buildings, dominated by the old church, which seemed more like a citadel than a place of worship (Fig. 115). The church, in fact, had been occupied for military purposes during the war of independence, and the famous Alamo was used in 1854 as a depot for the Quartermaster Corps.

The Alamo had suffered much from the ravages of war, only its Moorish door-

115   Military Plaza, San Antonio, Texas. From William H. Emory, *Report on the United States and Mexican Boundary Survey*, 1857.

way remaining essentially intact. In a sorrier state were the outlying missions: San José, San Juan Espada, and Concepción, monastic fortresses whose stately ruins told of their former grandeur. San José with its near-by convent, 5 miles from the Alamo, had suffered from military occupancy and was used as a farmer's dwelling. Concepción was not only desolated but desecrated; the church enclosure was used as a cattle corral, and bats flitted about in the neglected dome and towers.

Farming in the San Antonio region depended on irrigation from the San Pedro, a tributary of the San Antonio; but a century of irrigation with improper tillage and poor drainage had resulted in alkali accumulations sufficient to reduce crop yields. Some persons felt, indeed, that irrigation was doing more harm than good. For miles around the city, however, grazing conditions were excellent for the self-reliant longhorn cattle of the period.

The colony of Stephen Austin.   The earliest American colonization scheme in Texas was promoted by Stephen F. Austin, sometimes referred to therefor as the "father of Texas." Austin brought his plans to completion in 1821, the year of Mexico's emancipation from Spain, choosing for his colony a site on the accessible Gulf coast, an initial venture in Anglo-American settlement. The selection was an excellent one in terms of environment, for here were combined vegetation and soil types described as typical of the more favored sections of the coastal plain. Although descriptions of the colony naturally made the most of the advantages, advertising literature held to a rather high level. The colony drew much attention to this part of Mexico, and a few other settlements were established near by. However, no great influx of immigrants occurred, possibly because of uncertain political conditions.

German settlements on the frontier.   Germans were among the first European immigrants to come to Texas during its decade as a republic, from 1836 to 1845. The Texas Republic, recognized as a sovereign state by the United States and some European countries, adopted a liberal policy toward foreign immigration, well shown in 1843, when the legislature ordered the publication of the laws of Texas in the German language.

The German settlements to be considered here, however, came into being in 1847 as a result of a mass migration encouraged by a group of German colonizers who formed the Adelsverein " for the protection of German immigrants in Texas." Under this plan, from 1847 to 1850 some 17,000 Germans took passage from Bremen and Antwerp and settled in previously selected sites within a limited area beyond Austin.

One of the leaders of this venture in frontier settlement was Karl, Prince Solms-Braunfels, who (according to his own account) arrived in Texas in 1844 to establish a colony of the Adelsverein. Possibly the promotional writings of the Austin colony led him to the Colorado River; at all events he found here an area to his liking — a healthful climate on the higher lands of the plain at a considerable distance from the coast.

Looking about him, Solms-Braunfels saw little to commend in the American settlements already established in Texas. American backwoodsmen, he observed, used little forethought in moving into a new area. He concluded that while " such people are used to sacrifices and hardships of this sort," a different procedure was necessary for German colonists. Their equipment must be such as to carry them successfully through the difficult first year or two. Furthermore, they should not settle the land individually; in numbers there was strength. The German colonization of the Adelsverein was to be different from the haphazard ways of the " ever-moving American squatter family." The aristocrat laid down two rules for his people: 1. Never establish a settlement farther than 40 miles from an old colony. 2. Never allow a mixture of Germans and Americans as long as the colony is in its infancy.

Solms-Braunfels returned to Germany in 1845, leaving his work to be carried further by others. It is reported that Adelsverein officials spent more than a year visiting different parts of Texas, including Galveston, Houston, and San Felipe. They deliberated on the advantages and disadvantages of this and that area, finally choosing the inland frontier site which had received the favor of Solms-Braunfels.

Permanent settlements were formed in Fredericksburg (Gillespie County), New Braunfels (Comal County), and Castell (Llano County), all on the frontier at the time. Of these, the one considered most likely to develop into a large city was Fredericksburg. When Bartlett visited there in 1854 he classed it as a " flourishing German settlement " of about 500 persons. The surrounding fields were well cultivated, there was evidence of prosperity and well-being, and Bartlett was particularly surprised to find an excellent library in this new town. " The stores were filled with goods adapted to the Indian trade, as the place is on the very border of civilization, resorted to by numbers of Indian tribes contiguous." Not far from Fredericksburg was the Mormon colony of Zodiac. Here also the land had been improved with remarkable rapidity, the fields were well cultivated and fenced, and the homes cozily built.

If the promoters of the Adelsverein had in mind the creation of a New Germany in America, as has been suggested, their plans did not carry through. Nevertheless, the percentage of German-born people in Texas exceeded that of other states at the time, including Wisconsin. The interest which the colonies generated induced many Germans to settle in other parts of Texas, notably in San Antonio, where in the troublous days before 1861 some ill feeling developed between them and native-born inhabitants. As Dr. J. A. Hawgood has said in his recent book: " The German in Texas became a German-American and remained so for half a century. Time and the passing of the original settlers began to dissolve the hyphen, and the breakdown . . . of German Texas was beginning to be evident at about the turn of the century."

THE COTTON BELT EXPANDS INTO TEXAS

It was learned by experience that the climate of East Texas differed in no essential respect from that of the older cotton region. The process of learning began in 1821 when, under powerful forces of expansion, cotton culture pushed into Mexican territory, carrying with it the institution of slavery, in defiance of the Mexican constitution. Southern planters, continually seeking new frontiers as older producing areas became impoverished, found in East Texas an attractive new field. Thus American settlers in the Texas area brought cotton with them, setting the stage for later developments on a larger scale.

The expansion of the Cotton Belt throughout the years is shown in Figure 116. With the northward spread of cotton culture restricted by the long growing sea-

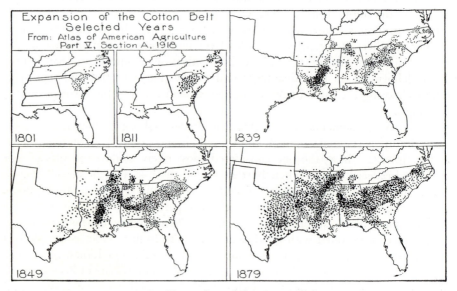

116   Expansion of the Cotton Belt.

son of some seven months, expansion following the 1820's was mainly to the west. By 1821 the Mississippi River had been crossed, and soon East Texas was invaded. Decade by decade, cotton culture pushed westward with the frontier until by the 1890's it had reached the arid border.

The Texas area offered not merely a favorable climate, but also extensive areas of fertile soil in prairie regions where the work of preparing the land for cultivation was at a minimum. Texas climbed rapidly in the list of cotton-producing states, ranking fifth in the prewar year 1859.

COTTON PRODUCTION IN THE UNITED STATES, 1859

(Total U.S. production, 4,369,000 bales)

	Bales
Mississippi	992,000
Alabama	791,000
Louisiana	622,000
Georgia	561,000
Texas	346,000

The westward expansion of the Cotton Belt to include part of Texas is likewise reflected in the proportion of slaves in the population. The following census figures show that, between 1850 and 1860, the slave population perceptibly increased.

TEXAS POPULATION, 1850 AND 1860

(in thousands)

	White	Slave	Total
1850	154	58	212
1860	422	180	602

THE TEXAS CATTLE INDUSTRY

Like a slow-growing plant which gathers strength for a brief blossoming period and then quickly fades, the Texas cattle industry was nurtured by favoring circumstances for many years before it burst forth as a phenomenon of the period after the War between the States, and then, within a quarter-century, declined to unspectacular proportions.

No one seems to know just when Andalusian cattle, foundation of Mexican breeds, were driven across the Rio Grande into the Nueces Valley of southern Texas. Perhaps the exact decade doesn't matter if it is known that the event was contemporary with the American Revolution. In 1775, possibly earlier, ranches extended into the green country of the Nueces, and by the early 1800's extensive herds of cattle, horses, and sheep grazed over the land. Records show that during the Mexican Revolution (1830–36) cattle were running wild in southeastern Texas, multiplying prodigiously in this favoring environment. At this time, cattle of other breeds were driven in, " pilgrims " with the settlers of Austin's colony, and French stock from Louisiana. By 1830 there must have been 100,000 cattle in Texas, with Spanish-bred types predominating five to one. Intermingling occurred, slowly at first, to form a common stock differing from the original Mexican variety. (See Fig. 117.)

Texas cattle, as they became known in the 1840's, were well adapted to range life; the steers later proved their capacity for long drives from range to market, although the cows were often considered poor walkers. Varied in coloration, Texas steers were nervous in manner, small in intestinal organization, and tough in meat; they were distinguished by their lightness of body, their long legs and narrow head and muzzle, and by the overly developed horns which gave them their common name. Half-wild or partly tame, longhorns showed self-reliant traits, such as an instinct for seeking food and water and for self-preservation during inclement weather. They were " good rustlers " and they needed to be so, even in humid-temperate southern Texas. Before the days of the long drives they were rounded up by cowboys to be slaughtered for hides and tallow, or driven to interior markets.

Texas cattle on the hoof became known east of the Sabine as early as 1842, when some of them were driven to market in New Orleans. Shipment by steamer occurred soon thereafter. The first authenticated long drive was to Ohio in 1846. Four years later, cattle were driven to California, and an event of 1856 was the delivery of Texas stock in Chicago.

Cattle drives to the North from 1846 to 1861 were irregular, and the War between the States virtually put a stop to them. Some cattle were delivered to Confederate forces until the Old South was severed from the New South by Union control of the Mississippi River. Then many herds remained untended while owners served with the Confederate army. During this period, says Professor Webb, " cattle accumulated; the calves remained unbranded, mingling

117   Longhorn cattle of Texas, as pictured in *Report of the Commissioner of Agriculture for the Year 1870*, Washington, 1871

with the old stock hardened and toughened by age and the experiences of precarious survival." On the eve of the war Texas had become "the cattle hive of North America," with an estimated 4,785,400 head in 1860. This was not the sum total of livestock in Texas at that time, for records indicate 1,187,000 sheep, 2,509,000 hogs, and uncounted numbers of horses.

The home ranches of southern Texas. After the War between the States, Texas cattle were held in herds varying in size from a few hundred to well over 70,000. Favored locations for ranches were the Nueces Valley and other river valleys near, or directly on, the Gulf coast; also important was the mesquite-grass and creosote-bush country of the immediate interior and the lower Rio Grande Valley. This was the original core area of the range cattle industry. With the extension of agriculture, a higher economic use of the well-watered coastlands, there soon came a general shift of ranching toward the higher prairies of central and northern Texas, and finally into the great expanse of semiarid West Texas. The "day of the cattleman" in East Texas was relatively short-lived, as it proved to be also in the north.

A few examples of the large-scale holdings or "outfits" may contribute to this picture of the geography of southeastern Texas. In 1870, the Robideaux Ranch spread over nearly 143,000 acres of a peninsula jutting out into the Gulf of Mexico south of the Nueces River. The Gulf provided natural limits on three sides, while 30 miles of plank fencing across the isthmus, derived from local timber, completed the enclosure for 30,000 head of beef cattle and other stock. There was also the O'Connor Ranch below Goliad on the San Antonio, with 40,000 cattle in 1862, grown from only 1,500 ten years before. Famous among early-day ranches was the Santa Gertrudis of Colonel Richard King, comprising 84,000 acres on which grazed 65,000 cattle, 10,000 horses, 7,000 sheep, and 8,000 goats, requiring the services of 300 herdsmen. Some 12,000 calves were branded each year in Santa Cabrutas corrals, and perhaps as many as 10,000 head were sold for marketing or stocking purposes.

A shifting toward the interior, where there was less competition with agricultural land uses, was evident in 1870. Exemplifying this trend was the ranch of John Hittson, who emigrated in 1852 from Rhea County, Tennessee, to Palo Pinto County on the Brazos. Starting "on a shoestring," eighteen years later Hittson was the owner of a ranch of 50,000 acres and as many cattle, employing 50 herders. He also acquired a ranch on the South Platte near Fort Morgan, Colorado, where he wintered some of his stock.

Cattle trails and drives from Texas. As pointed out earlier, this cattle reservoir was connected with Northern markets by various trails. The delivery point shifted with the westward advance of settlement and active railroad-building across the Plains from Kansas City and other centers. One of the first objectives was Sedalia, Missouri, on the Missouri Pacific Railroad, which was then pushing southwest. But to reach Sedalia the trails must necessarily cross settled country. Fear of the spread of "Texas fever," and of other damages resulting from large herds moving over trails and roads, provoked antagonism and brought about the eventual abandonment of the more eastern trails. Sedalia had, as a consequence, a short-lived career as a marketing point for Texas steers.

The construction of the Kansas Pacific, now the Union Pacific, soon made it possible to deliver cattle over routes beyond the settled frontier during that brief interval before settlement overtook the trails. Thus Abilene in Kansas became a " cow town " where Southern drovers and Northern buyers met at the rail line. Cattle were first driven to Abilene in 1867; a few years later, stock was being delivered at railheads or depots at Ellsworth, Ellis, and Colby in northern Kansas, as well as at Caldwell, Hunnewell, and Dodge City in the southern part of the state. Other herds moved beyond the rail depots, destined for stocking the ranges, or for slaughter at Indian agencies. Among examples of the latter use was a herd of 25,000 steers purchased by buyers holding contracts with the Department of the Interior to supply beef to the agencies, and driven from the Nueces to South Dakota in 1867.

The trails were permanent enough to be identified by various names, such as Chisholm's Trail, laid out by Jesse Chisholm, a half-breed Indian trader;

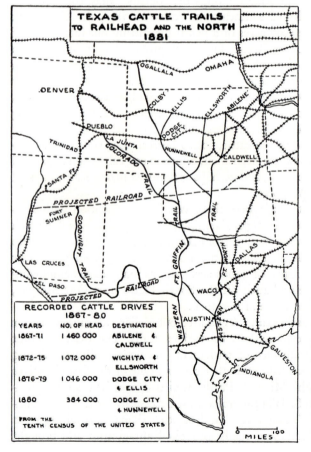

118

Texas cattle trails in 1881. The Texas portion of this map is taken from a " Map of Texas, Showing Routes of Transportation of Cattle," United States Department of the Interior. Original copy in Division of Maps, Library of Congress.

Old Shawnee Trail to Baxter Springs; Middle Trail, West Shawnee, and so on. The main routes in 1881, when railroads in Texas had displaced the more eastern trails, are shown in Figure 118. At this time the two trunk lines, so to speak, were the Eastern or Fort Worth and the Western or Fort Griffin trails. More than 1,000,000 cattle were driven annually over these trails from 1867 to 1881.

The map of cattle trails in 1881, taken from official sources, also shows the

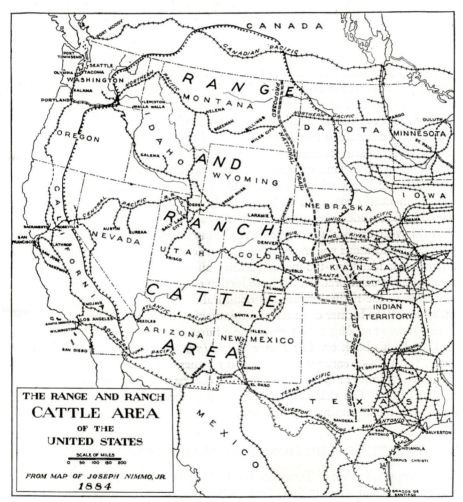

119 The range and ranch cattle area of the West, as shown by Joseph Nimmo, Jr., Chief of the Bureau of Statistics, in 1884. This is a simplified redrawing of a large and detailed map published in 1885 and found in two sources, both entitled " Report on the Internal Commerce of the United States," Government Printing Office, Washington: *Treasury Department Report*, Vol. 1; and House Exec. Doc. 7, Part 3, 48th Congress, 1st Session.

westward shift of stock-raising into the semiarid Great Plains region of Texas. West from San Angelo the Goodnight-Loving trail led to New Mexico and El Paso, where great ranches were at this time developing, and where they remained intact for the longest period. Droves on the western trails and into Colorado met with opposition from Indians; on the eastern, they met more effective resistance from land settlers. The native attitude was illustrated by Colorow, a Ute Indian, who spoke thus: " Colorow owns this country. Buffalo are Indian cattle. White man's cattle eat all grass, buffalo die, no feed. No hunting, no meat, no robes. White man must go damn quick. Colorow no big fool. No more talk."

The rapid extinction of the cattle trails is emphasized by an official map prepared under the direction of the Chief of the Bureau of Statistics in 1884 (Fig. 119). By that year, the Fort Worth Trail had been eliminated as a result of the westward extension of the farming frontier and north-south railroad lines. The Western or Fort Griffin Trail was still functioning, particularly as a route for the delivery of cattle to Northern ranges and military posts. The 1884 map also shows the proposed " National Cattle Trail " offered as a solution to the problem of driving cattle beyond quarantine lines proclaimed by Kansas and Colorado. The National Trail, which never advanced beyond the planning stage, would have been nearly 700 miles in length and, with an average width of 3 miles, would have included over 2,000 square miles of land.

In this year of 1884, the range cattle industry was reaching its peak of prosperity. An enormous volume of capital, some of it foreign, had been poured into an overexpanded and too-well-advertised business; overloading of the range resulted in its deterioration; the introduction of sheep further limited the browsing value of the natural grasses; agricultural settlers in ever increasing volume pressed into the former open range land, making it less suitable for the original uses. " It was not long until there came a bursting of the bubble," says Edward E. Dale in his book on *The Range Cattle Industry* (University of Oklahoma Press, 1930) " — a collapse of prices and a general decline of the whole movement, which brought to the ranchmen dire distress and, in many cases, complete financial ruin." The 1884 map of Nimmo, therefore, coincided with the end of an era and the beginning of a new one.

TEXAS BEYOND THE HUNDREDTH MERIDIAN

The natural division of Texas into humid East Texas and dry-land West Texas was recognized at an early time. Perhaps the first to give the appproximate position of the dividing zone was Marcy in his explorations of the Red River from 1852 to 1854. Where the Upper Cross Timbers meet the Great Plains, it seemed to the explorer, " the entire face of the country, as if by the wand of a magician, suddenly changes its character."

By contrast with the pleasant landscape farther east, this was a desolate and inhospitable land devoid of wood and lacking in water. It seemed probable that

" this section was not designed by the Creator for occupation, and I question if the next century will see it populated by civilized man." In declaring that the western country " is subject to periodical droughts," Marcy went beyond known facts, for there were no climatic data available; but a multitude of data collected since that time, as well as the tragic experiences of many homesteaders, have amply demonstrated the truth of the observation. The most recent drought occurred only a decade ago, when " dust-bowl " conditions prevailed in West Texas. A recent study by Professor Richard J. Russell, based on more than a hundred rainfall records, supports the earlier views. The simplified map derived from Russell (lower inset, Fig. 113, page 428) shows the humid-semiarid boundary roughly following the 100th meridian (which coincides with the eastern boundary of the Panhandle) and swinging sharply toward the coast in central Texas.

Attempts at desert conquest. The meeting of the frontier and the arid lands of Texas led to new experiments in methods of conquest, which now appear fantastic. One of these ventures was the importation of Saharan camels, intended for use in transportation across the wastelands. A congressional appropriation of $30,000 in 1855 culminated in the arrival of two boatloads of these " ships of the desert " at Indianola, whence they were sent to interior points. They were used for short journeys in Texas, and comprised one caravan to California, from which many did not return. This novel experiment ended in failure, as did also an attempt to create rainfall in West Texas. The publication in 1871 of a book on the presumed effects of battles on rainfall captured the attention of a Senator who petitioned the Congress for a grant to put the theory to practical test. The plea was further strengthened by the issuance in 1880 of a patent covering rain-making apparatus. Congress responded at different times to the total of $14,000 in an attempt to legislate rain.

The work was put in charge of Major R. G. Dyrenforth, who assembled his equipment in the summer of 1891 at Midland, Texas. The apparatus was awe-inspiring, including explosives, chemicals for generating oxygen and hydrogen, balloons, and kites. For several years this army officer was a man of importance, to be interviewed whenever he appeared in town. However, the experiments gathered more publicity than clouds, and the Major — sometimes known as Dryhenceforth — was the butt of a good deal of ribaldry.

The Llano Estacado — America's " Zahara." West Texas remained terra incognita until after the close of the Mexican War. Before that time, explorers had avoided this area, as well as other parts of Texas, perhaps because it was Mexican territory until 1836 and for the next few years a region of uncertain political status — at least it was not part of the United States. During the war with Mexico, the principal military forces dispatched to objectives south of the Rio Grande reached there by sea, or over the familiar Santa Fe Trail and southward through El Paso; hence very little was learned about West Texas at this time.

The Staked Plains (Llano Estacado) of northwest Texas, when seen by Marcy in 1849, appeared to him even more forbidding than advance report had pictured them. Reached by easy ascent from the headwaters of the Canadian and the Brazos and the tributaries of the Red, the high plain appeared as boundless as the ocean. Marcy wrote of it, with more than his customary emotion:

Not a tree, shrub, or any other object, either animate or inanimate, relieved the dreary monotony of the prospect. It is a vast, illimitable expanse of desert prairie — the dreaded Llano Estacado, the great Zahara of North America. It is a region almost as vast and trailless as the ocean — a land where no man, either savage or civilized, permanently abides; it spreads forth into a treeless, desolate waste of uninhabited solitude, which always has been and must continue uninhabited forever; even the savage does not venture to cross it except at two or three places where they know water can be found.

Later surveys of the Llano served to correct some of Marcy's hasty conclusions. The surveyor for the western railroad in 1853 admitted that the " scarcity of water will limit agriculture," but contended that the land was good for sheep-grazing and possibly for cattle if artesian water could be found. Furthermore, the land was not wholly treeless, for in protected places, such as the northern and eastern bluffs, stunted growths of piñon pine and cedars were found. The conclusion was drawn that the " treelessness " of the Llano was as much the result of strong winds as of aridity. Although bison did not permanently inhabit the Staked Plains, they did nevertheless include them in their migrations, and this region came in time to be one of their last strongholds. Comanche tribes, some of whom were known as " buffalo-eaters," followed the migrations of the bison across the high plains of West Texas.

Early attempts to obtain artesian water from borings met with discouragement. Further search was finally rewarded, but without mechanical aid water could not be lifted from deep wells economically, and it was not until 1873 that wind-mills were manufactured on a large scale in this country. Under these circumstances, the Staked Plains remained essentially uninhabited until 1910, when new forces and attractions, such as oil near Amarillo, came into operation.

EL PASO ON THE RIO GRANDE

Letters addressed to El Paso in the 1850's were delivered not to a United States El Paso, but to the city on the Mexican side of the Rio Grande. El Paso del Norte, as the Mexican place was officially called, was then a city of some 5,000 persons. There was only a suggestion of an American city of El Paso in a collection of buildings known as Magoffinsville.

El Paso in Chihuahua was less a town than a succession of plantations extending 10 or 12 miles along the valley. A cluster of structures around a plaza, after the usual pattern of the Mexican village, indicated the center of activity. Here were the cathedral and the customhouse, flanked by stores, public buildings, and dwellings. On every hand there were vineyards, as well as " flower gardens, orchards, and shrubbery, loaded with foliage and fruits, and little canals conveyed water along nearly all the streets, and through the gardens and yards, adding to the pleasantness of the scene," said W. W. H. Davis in 1857. Crude adobe buildings amidst these surroundings " appeared much more pleasant than mud houses ever did before."

Water supply for irrigation was derived from a dam a mile above the town, from which an acequia (canal) extended the length of the inhabited area. Several miles above the dam, where two gristmills were operated by water power, the river broke through the mountains in a narrow " pass "; it is from this the name El Paso is thought to have derived. The land was more truly inundated than irrigated, the soil being well saturated with water in advance of the planting season. A great variety of products was raised — vegetables, fruits (peaches, pears, quinces, figs), wheat, oats (the latter introduced in 1851) — but most of the irrigated land was used for raising grapes, a culture of long standing. The vines were carefully pruned and tended, and bedded down with straw during the brief winter. Grapes were made into wine by reducing them to a mulch which was later compressed in bags of oxhide. Brandy, also made from grapes and known as Pass whisky, was an article of trade even in distant localities. The annual output in 1847 was about 200,000 gallons, according to *De Bow's Review* of that year.

The many villages on both sides of the river, and on islands within it, reflected the strategic importance of the El Paso region. On the American side, besides Magoffinsville there were (and are) Ysleta, Socorro, and San Elizario. El Paso, Texas, is largely a product of the railroad era, during which period the city has gradually assumed command of the trade, national and international, that is focused upon this site.

CHAPTER 24

Gold in the Hills and Water on the Plains: Colorado

Geographical accounts of the West a century ago permitted but few rays of light to play upon a canvas done in the monotones of real or imaginary deserts. One of the few bright spots on the Western picture of that day was the Rocky Mountain front or, more precisely, the plains rising to the foothills and the ranges just beyond them. Since little was known of the vast field of mountains which actually form the Rockies, a certain indefiniteness as to the extent of the region is to be expected. Precious metals and water were viewed as the magical elements which would retrieve the mountain belt from the inferior position of a grazing land.

Reports of minerals, already in circulation, became more common and credible with the discovery of gold in California in 1848. If the Sierras contained gold, why should not the Colorado (then Kansas) Rockies? And no one could reasonably doubt the availability of water. Any number of streams, forming the headwaters of the Missouri, the Platte, and the Arkansas, poured out from mountain gulches, promising the basis of irrigation. The enthusiasm with which this region was greeted by writers on Western geography is reflected in their exaggerated estimates of potential wealth in minerals and water. As the authors of an 1846 guidebook for emigrants remarked, " Men are apt to expect too much — to draw their pictures too fair; they look to those wild and distant regions for something surpassing nature, and they are disappointed."

The actual discovery of gold in Colorado in the summer of 1858 seemed a fulfillment of existent beliefs. This was the curtain raiser to a drama whose major scenes have been made familiar by constant repetition. The site of the original discovery was on Cherry Creek near its junction with the Platte — in a word, present-day Denver, a dozen miles east of the mountains. To this site, within four months enough people had come to make necessary the organization of two towns, Auraria and Denver City. Rivals for nearly two years, the twin villages on Cherry Creek united to form Denver, " a curious ensemble of wretched architecture," as it was described at the time.

Denver was soon to learn the uncertainties which beset a mining camp, for

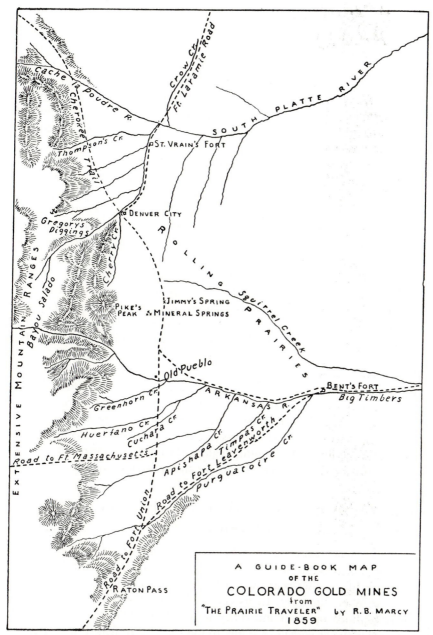

A GUIDE-BOOK MAP
OF THE
COLORADO GOLD MINES
from
"THE PRAIRIE TRAVELER" by R.B. MARCY
1859

120   "Sketch of the Country in the Vicinity of the Gold Region near Pike's
       Peak and Cherry Creek" — facsimile redrawing of a map prepared by a vet-
       eran explorer and cartographer, Randolph B. Marcy, for the use of emigrants
       and gold-seekers. With his clientele in mind, Marcy did not strive for the carto-
       graphic fineries which distinguished his official reports. Instead, this specimen
       is notable for boldness and simplicity.

within a year half of its houses were deserted. Many people had turned back east, toiling over trails where, full of hope but otherwise poorly equipped, they had traveled west a few months before. The greater number, however, were off to a new " strike " in the near-by foothills. The new discovery was in a tributary of Clear Creek, a spot at first called Gregory Diggings and later, when several hundred tents and shacks had been set up, Mountain City. (See Fig. 120.) More permanent towns which grew here became known as Blackhawk, Central City, Nevadaville, among other lesser places.

Shortly there were several thousand people within a dozen miles of the original Gregory Diggings, and those that had been there a month were thought of as old settlers. Denver itself was recovering from the shock of its partial desertion. Elsewhere in Colorado other discoveries gave new impetus to the gold rush, so many within a few years as to prevent a full record in limited space. Participants in the rushes to gold and silver camps were not the type to leave records of their activities, or to describe in broad terms the regions in which mining developed. Many of the eyewitness accounts prepared by visitors uninformed in the mining industry are so obviously in error as to make them unsafe for use. We shall therefore depend upon descriptions and surveys prepared after 1865, when mining was more firmly established and when competent witnesses were on hand. Other mining centers in the Rockies will also be briefly considered.

Mining, however, was only one phase of regional development in the Rockies. Less well known, but more important in the long run, was the establishment of several irrigation colonies in Colorado within that belt for which promising forecasts had been made earlier. They were near enough to the mining camps to supply them with some of their necessities, thus pointing to the complementary nature of the mining and farming regions. From these centers of settlement have grown many of the present-day towns and cities of Colorado.

COLORADO MINING DEVELOPMENTS: THE CLEAR CREEK OR CENTRAL CITY DISTRICT

The Clear Creek district, toward the northern limits of Colorado's mineralized belt, provides a good case study of the mining industry. Clear Creek, a tributary of the South Platte, rises near the Continental Divide and drains a typical portion of the mountain front. In its course through the foothills, the stream is narrowly confined by steep and rocky walls which, at varying altitudes above stream level, slope at widening angles to the rounded or flattish interstream uplands. As a downcutting stream Clear Creek had deposited but little sedimentary material in its bed; the aggrading tributary creeks or gulches, in contrast, were floored with somewhat more extensive deposits of sand and gravel. So much, at least, may be told of original conditions in an area which has been greatly changed by mining activities.

The rapid extension of mining into the mountains west of Denver is graphi-

121   Central City, Colorado, as it appeared in 1928. Photograph by Charles F. Snow, Boulder, Colorado.

cally told by eyewitnesses in 1865. Although only six years had elapsed since the original strike in Gregory Gulch, fully 7,000 persons had gathered here, some to mine and many others to live off the miners. Central City, well named for its situation relative to the developing mines, was already the principal town. No longer strictly a camp, Central City was acquiring the solid brick and stone buildings for which it is still distinguished among Colorado mining towns of similar size (Fig. 121). The bustling town appeared to one visitor as " most uncomfortably squeezed into narrow ravines, and stuck into the hillsides, on streets the narrowest and most tortuous I ever saw in America." The author of this statement, Samuel Bowles, was not the last to comment on the apparent insecurity with which the residences of Central City clung to the steep hillsides.

The hands of many men had transformed the original, and no doubt lovely, landscape into a series of ugly gashes. The pinewoods which must have clothed the ravines, especially on shaded slopes where snow remained the longest, had all but vanished. Tree stumps had been pulled out in the search for fuel, leaving unsightly scars of soil erosion. Yellowing piles of waste from mining and milling operations spotted the encircling mountainsides. In local terminology the mountains were hills (except to the most recent arrivals), and were named, clockwise around Central City, Nigger's, Winnebago, Mammoth, Quartz, and Nevada.

Clear Creek no longer deserved its name, for its waters had been clouded by mine refuse draining into it by way of the gulches — Gregory, Eureka, Chase,

Spring, Nevada, and several others. Their narrow beds contained the wreckage of equipment which had served briefly in placer mining — that is, the separation of gold flakes or nuggets from the gravels by washing. The silence was rent by many noises — occasional blasts in underground workings, the endless crushing of hard quartz in stamp mills, and the clattering of wagons hauling the quartz from mine openings to mills. Central City was not to hear the sound of a locomotive whistle for another half-dozen years. The isolation of the mines from the outside world is told in part by the high prices paid for food and other necessities, secured mainly from Denver, which was now less a mining town than a distributing center.

Stages of mining. I: From placering to surface quartz mining. The usually short-lived placering, to use a textbook name for an operation known in Colorado as gulch mining, ran a particularly rapid course in this district. The limited amount of stream gravels within the 100-foot claims was soon exhausted. Elaborate machinery in such an area was scarcely justified; the simplest equipment was commonly employed. The more efficient processes depended here, as elsewhere, on sluice boxes or troughs designed to lead water over gravels shoveled into them. By 1865, most of the stream beds had been dug up and worked over, sometimes more than once, leaving pits and piles of sand which added to the general disorder. Gulch mining was still being carried on in 1865 toward the less accessible upper portions of the tributary gulches, where deposits were more extensive.

Mining in the lodes had largely replaced gulch mining by 1865, but this transition caused far less difficulty than later changes were to bring forth. The weathered ore near the surface, " rotten quartz " in the common language, demanded little skill and machinery to give satisfactory results. The digging of the quartz veins was at first a pick-and-shovel operation, and the crushing of it could be accomplished on a small scale by homemade devices. For pulverizing the gold-bearing quartz, arrastras were sometimes used. A device long associated with mining in Mexico, the arrastra consisted of a circular stone bed in which quartz fragments were mechanically pulverized. Heavy rocks, drawn by mules or horses plodding around the shallow basin, often supplied the grinders for this primitive mill. It is estimated that some 40 or 50 arrastras were in use in the Clear Creek mines until they were rendered obsolete by more efficient methods.

Milling machinery known as stamp mills, adapted from types successfully used in California, was introduced into the Central City area and soon provided the principal means of milling. A stamp mill consisted essentially of a battery of miniature pile-drivers of sufficient weight to crush the quartz. Falling vertically in trip-hammer blows, the heavy stamps reduced the ore to a pulp, which was then washed and coated with quicksilver. The union of gold with quicksilver formed an amalgam which was later separated, under high temperatures, into the same two elements.

The stamping-quicksilver process of gold recovery was highly variable in its returns and never very effective; some authorities estimate that no more than one-half of the precious metal was saved. Much of the gold in the pulp thus went into the tailings, possibly to be recovered at a later time when more efficient methods were known. Nothing was more common in the later phases of mining than the reworking of tailings, the waste thrown aside when ore was rich and plentiful.

The free-milling ore held in veins above the water table sustained mining at a high pitch for several years. New strikes were daily recorded in local papers, and stories swept like wildfire through the saloons and business houses of Central City. Should a glum-faced prospector return to town with a hard-luck tale, fellow miners were as likely as not to assume that he was trying to keep secret a profitable " lead," and they would speculate on its probable location. No lodes were discovered here that were to become world-famous, such as the Comstock Ledge of Nevada, but there were several dependable producers. Average yields allowed a profit from much hard work. It was estimated at the time that average ore yielded about $100 a cord (8 tons) under the stamp-mill process, with mining costs at $40, hauling at $5, and crushing and extraction at $20.

It was found that, contrary to earlier beliefs, mining could be carried on throughout the year. Back in '59, September was assumed to be the end of the mining season, and a large percentage of the gold-seekers withdrew then from the mountain country. Winters proved to be less severe than was anticipated; snow occasionally suspended the hauling of ore, but work in the mines continued with little interruption. It was during the colder season that much " dead work " was put through — enlarging mine entrances and tunnels, and making other improvements.

Mines went down into proved veins, and buildings went up on the hillsides and gulch bottoms. Thick as anthills were diggings or test pits into pre-empted claims on the slopes of Quartz Hill. Central City and Blackhawk expanded down and up the narrow gulch until they became indistinguishable as separate towns. Central City-Blackhawk grew in population because more people came in than departed for other localities. Attractions near by were represented by the booming camps of Idaho Springs, Georgetown, Empire, and Russell Gulch, all within the drainage area of Clear Creek. Northward across the ridge, another cluster of mining towns was forming on Boulder Creek, at whose point of exit to the Plains Boulder City had formed. Far to the south was the " Pike's Peak country " as strictly interpreted, although in the popular mind this phrase covered much of Colorado's mountain area. Many gold-seekers who had originally set out for Cripple Creek near Pikes Peak were diverted, by stories picked up on the way, to one or the other of the camps mentioned above. The mining population was a highly migratory one. (See maps, Figs. 120 and 124.)

Stages of mining. II: Mining in deeper ores. As the mines struck deeper into the veins, costs of mining necessarily increased but also, and more important, the ore was chemically different. At depth, very little of the gold was found free in the quartz, but was rather closely associated with silver and pyrites. As Samuel Bowles remarked in 1865, " The plague and the mystery are the sulphurates that

122   Site of the first gold lode mine in Colorado, near Blackhawk. Picture by Charles
       F. Snow, Boulder, 1928. The placard, erected by the State Historical and Nat-
       ural History Society of Colorado, reads as follows: " On this ground, later
       known as Gregory Diggings, William H. Gregory discovered the first gold
       quartz mine in Colorado, May 6, 1859. This lode has produced $20,000,000
       in gold."

cover and hold the gold in a stern chemical lock." Simple crushing or milling
was insufficient. Gold-silver ore of this type could not be worked profitably without resort to metallurgical processes unknown to the miners, and the installation
of much new machinery. For this purpose capital was sought in the East, and
ore-treating plants were erected, sometimes unwisely and before the extent and
the character of ore bodies were investigated.

    This brief period of depression, during the shift of mining from oxidized
or weathered ore to the combined types, was experienced in other Colorado
mining centers at about the same time. The problem is well brought out in a
government publication of 1872 dealing with the Georgetown mining district.
It is pointed out that when the stamp mills of that district were made idle by
the exhaustion of the surface quartz,

. . . it was discovered that gold lodes had a market value in New York, and soon
the era of stock companies and speculation set in. Greenbacks and the " process
miners " took entire possession. The history of Empire in this respect is the history
of Colorado. Everything, from superheated steam to tobacco juice, was tried on
Empire ore. Disastrous failures followed glowing promises and the once constant

123 Buildings of the Medano estate, San Luis Valley, Colorado. View taken in 1927.

raising of wheat, oats, and potatoes in the small areas already settled. The northern part of the basin, beyond the drainage of the Rio Grande, was considered to be the least favorable, and was variously called San Luis Park, the Rincon Basin, and the Saguache (popularly pronounced Sa-watch') Basin. In this section, and especially toward the Sangre de Cristo Range on the eastern side, were a few large estates inherited from the time when this part of Colorado was in Mexico. The Medano and Luis Maria Baca estates spread over nearly 1,250,000 acres of the Trinchera, Culebra, and Costilla valleys of the Saguache Basin. (See Fig. 123.) The San Luis Valley proper — that is, the southern portion enveloping the Rio Grande — offered level surface and plenty of water for irrigation. Its only handicap for agriculture, in the opinion of the time, was its mile-high altitude.

AGRICULTURE IN THE PIEDMONT

The principal agricultural settlements of Territorial Colorado were along the piedmont, not in the high parks of the mountains. Ranching and farming grew out of the mining industry and as close to the mines as topography, soil, and climate permitted. A few farsighted gold-seekers had driven cattle on their way to the diggings, leaving them in the care of ranchmen who with equal forethought had established corrals along the main routes. As explained by Horace Greeley in 1859, " The miners leave or send back their cattle to herd [at $1.50 a head per month] on these prairies, while they prosecute their operations in the mountains where feed is scarce."

The mining camps, dependent on the outside world for food, stimulated agriculture as well as ranching in the piedmont. During the opening years of mining, most of the food was supplied by Midwestern farming regions that were 300 miles or more from the camps. As usual, the buyer bore the cost of transportation. Here were good markets where people expected to pay high prices and usually had money with which to back up their demands. Not unnaturally, therefore, farming started along the mountain front where small streams could be diverted for irrigation. From these small beginnings, agriculture expanded so rapidly that in 1869 the market value of farm products approached $3,500,000, nearly equaling the mining output of the same year.

The arrival of the first railroads in Denver in the summer of 1870 gave a new impetus to agricultural settlement. Northeastern Colorado was now linked to other parts of the country by two main lines, the Denver Pacific to Cheyenne, and the Kansas Pacific (later the Union Pacific), which approached Denver from the east. The Federal Government had awarded large land grants to both railroads as an inducement to the completion of their lines across unsettled country. The transfer of the granted land to private ownership became an immediate objective of the railroads for two leading reasons: 1. The sale of the land would provide immediate income. 2. The settlers along the rights of way would yield revenue for years to come.

Methods adopted by the railroads in the disposal of their alternate sections of land within the grant limits have been made familiar in earlier chapters. Subsidiary companies were set up to promote and handle the real-estate business. One of the more influential agents was the National Land Company, with offices in Chicago and other cities. This company, in preparation for its campaign, took cognizance of lingering doubts as to the possibilities of farming in the West, so recently known as the Great American Desert. They shaped their advertising accordingly, and directed it to the general public in the form of pamphlets, articles in magazines (including their own magazine, *The Star of Empire*), and editorials in newspapers.

Eastern readers were assured of the fertility of the soil, the dependability of irrigation from the many mountain streams, the existent markets in the mining towns, the probable rise in land values with continued settlement, the health-giving and health-restoring properties of the mile-high climate. Readers need not depend upon the self-interested word of the land company, its agents said, quoting at great length (and with evidence of much careful study) from the works of government surveyors and men of national reputation. They quoted from government men such as F. V. Hayden and John Pope, and from Samuel Bowles, the editor, who said in his book:

> The irrigated gardens of the upper parts of Denver fairly riot in growth of fat vegetables, while the bottom lands of the neighboring valleys are at least equally productive without irrigation. Think of cabbages weighing from 50 to 60 pounds each! And potatoes from 5 to 6 pounds, onions 1 to 2 pounds, and beets 6 to 10. Yet here they grow, and as excellent as big.

Typical of the National Land Company's advertising is this passage, which concludes a list of Colorado's resources and opportunities:

> In addition to these interests, we ever have the majestic hills, high above the wide world, pure and bracing atmosphere, picturesque scenery, to invite our attention.

It is to them America will go, as Europe to Switzerland, for rest and recreation, for new and exhilarating scenes, for pleasure and for health. We feel confident that the verdict has already been passed — that here along the range of the Rocky Mountains, within this wedded circle of majestic hill and majestic plain, under these skies of purity, and in this atmosphere of elixir, lies the pleasure-ground, the garden, and the health-home of the nation.

AGRICULTURAL COLONIES

Riding the crest of a wave of interest in Western colony promotion, the National Land Company was identified with a number of group settlements in the Colorado piedmont. The land company as well as many individuals reasoned that organized settlement, tried with varying success in other parts of the country, was well suited to this area, especially because of the requirement of irrigation. It seemed likely that a community would profit from unified action in the construction of dams and canals. Furthermore, the selection of the area to be settled was of fundamental importance. A locating committee charged with the responsibility of choosing a site might be expected to reach a sounder judgment than would an inexperienced individual. By group action, as in the case of the Mormons, irrigation water could soon be applied to the land, and the colonists would have the advantages of town facilities, such as schools and churches, from the very beginning.

The National Land Company indicated that through its relationships with the railroads special rates of travel to the colony site could doubtless be arranged. Neither the company nor other promoters were likely to enlarge upon disadvantages of colony settlement even if they had foreseen them. But the path followed by colonists was not always as easy as the idealists pictured it. There was always the possibility of poor management, and of dissension appearing among the colony members.

The Colorado colonies which originated in this brief period of planning and philanthropy have been grouped by the authorities into three main classes: co-operative, semi-co-operative, and non-co-operative. 1. The co-operative type bordered upon communism; indeed it was communism, with a time limit established by the organizers. The best example of this type was that of the German Colonization Society, organized in Chicago in 1869. 2. The semi-co-operative type, illustrated by the Greeley Union and the Chicago-Colorado colonies, exerted control over a limited range of undertakings, such as irrigation, but permitted individual action in other directions. 3. The non-co-operative type, of which the Fountain Colony at Colorado Springs is an example, was an informal group migration which did not involve the purchase or the development of the land. Others in this group were scarcely more than town companies.

The first two types will be briefly considered, remembering that individual settlement in Colorado as elsewhere was more important in the long run than colony projects. Altogether, the colonies had contributed about 5,000 inhabitants to the state by 1871, about as many as lived in Denver in the same year. On the other hand, the colonies were widely distributed, and national interest in them stimulated settlement in the state. (See Fig. 124.)

The German colony in Wet Mountain Valley.   The first colony to be settled in Colorado grew out of a plan by Carl Wulsten — a German-American who had served with the Union forces in the War between the States — " to ameliorate the physical condition of the poorer class of Germans, who were condemned by a cruel fate to work in greasy, ill-ventilated, and nerve-destroying factories in the great city of Chicago."

It was thought that somewhere west of the Mississippi River between the 35th and 42nd parallels a site could be found for about 250 colonists. A locating committee was dispatched, but as to its tour of inspection in Colorado little is actually known. Arriving at Canyon City, they investigated the broad, parklike mountain valley lying between the Wet Mountains and the Sangre de Cristo Range in present-day Fremont County. Land was selected in this area " on account of its agricultural, commercial, and mining possibilities." Perhaps the general resemblance of the valley — which varies in altitude from 7,500 to 9,000 feet above sea level — to certain areas in Switzerland played a part in the final selection. Although an agent of the National Land Company had aided the colony promoters, the chosen area was not included in the probable limits of railroad grants.

The German-American colonists reached the meadows of Wet Mountain Valley in March, 1870, and began at once to prepare the land for farming. Visitors to the colony during its brief existence gave conflicting views as to its progress, some saying that it was a fine example of industry and thrift, and others presenting an opposite view. At any rate, signs of disintegration soon appeared, for by September many of the colonists had departed and those who remained were unprepared for and dreading the approach of winter. Supplies sent them by Denver businessmen averted immediate disaster, but by the next spring the colony as such had come to an end. Some colonists remained on homesteads, and according to Professors James F. Willard and Colin B. Goodykoontz, " a few of the original colonists and many of their descendants are still [1926] to be found in the Wet Mountain Valley."

The failure of the German colony has been attributed to several causes, including impractical leadership, unfamiliarity with agriculture in general and especially in this setting, and dissatisfaction among the more industrious, who were placed on the same footing as the least skilled and capable.

Longmont, town of the Chicago-Colorado colony.   This project, organized by the National Land Company, proceeded logically through the various steps from promotion to successful completion. Colony organization started in Chicago in the fall of 1870 with the adoption of a charter fixing the terms and rights of membership. Only persons of " good moral character " were acceptable, and each was to pay fees totaling $155, a sum that was later found to be inadequate. Descriptive pamphlets were printed and circulated, with the result that nearly 400 members were enrolled by May, 1871. Many of the colonists were already resident in Colorado near the site of the colony, but the majority were Illinoisans.

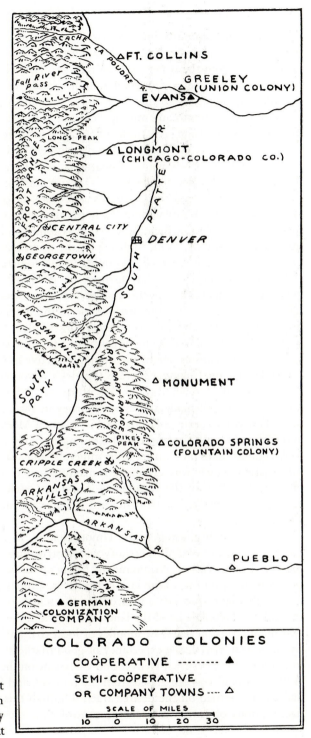

FT. COLLINS

GREELEY
(UNION COLONY)

EVANS

CACHE LA POUDRE

Fall River Pass

R.

Long's Peak

LONGMONT
(CHICAGO-COLORADO CO.)

PLATTE

CENTRAL CITY

DENVER

GEORGETOWN

SOUTH

KENOSHA HILLS

RAMPART RANGE

SOUTH PARK

MONUMENT

PIKES PEAK

COLORADO SPRINGS
(FOUNTAIN COLONY)

CRIPPLE CREEK

ARKANSAS HILLS

ARKANSAS R.

WET MTNS.

PUEBLO

GERMAN
COLONIZATION
COMPANY

COLORADO COLONIES

COÖPERATIVE ---------- ▲

SEMI-COÖPERATIVE
OR COMPANY TOWNS ---- △

SCALE OF MILES

10   0   10   20   30

124

The Colorado piedmont and adjacent mountain country, localizing colony towns discussed in the text

The locating committee journeyed to Colorado in the winter of 1871 and finally selected the area where the city of Longmont is now located, a region capable of irrigation from the waters of St. Vrain and Left Hand creeks. Reasons given for the selection were: (1) good soil that could be irrigated from perennial streams, (2) proximity to timber in the mountains, (3) availability of coal, (4) nearness to other towns and mining camps providing a market, and (5) adequate railroad transportation. All these advantages were actually present at the site, testifying to the honesty and the sound judgment of the committee.

The colony town was named Longmont from Longs Peak, which dominates the mountain sky line to the west. The site was divided into lots varying in size from 5 to 40 acres according to distance from the center of Longmont. Effort was made to unite beauty with utility in the checkerboard pattern; plans provided for an artificial lake, which, however, was found to be impractical because of limited water supply. With high hopes, the town planners reserved a lot for a prospective university, which also failed to materialize.

The Longmont colony was favored by geographical circumstance and by good management. Perhaps the most serious error was the inadequate provision for irrigation, a shortcoming attributable to the newness of the art among this group of planners and colonists. According to plan, the colony itself dissolved within a few years, but the town continued to grow substantially, and its tributary region remains as one of the more productive in Colorado.

Greeley Union Colony. Horace Greeley's advocacy of pioneering has been made generally known through his oft-quoted advice to young men to " go West." He himself made a Western journey in 1859, including Colorado in his tour. Ten years later a colleague of his, Nathan Meeker, also visited the West, and Colorado, with the purpose of forming a colony in an irrigable section. He took copious notes on climate, soils, minerals, and water supplies of likely sites, information which was evidently transmitted to Greeley in the early winter of 1869. As editor of the *New York Tribune,* Greeley editorialized on the advantages of organized settlement, and called a meeting of those interested for December 3, 1869.

This was the beginning of the Union Colony. In February, 1870, a locating party was sent to Colorado Territory with instructions to choose a location which measured up to various requirements. Many areas were visited before the selection was made on the Cache la Poudre River, 5 miles above its confluence with the South Platte. Reasons advanced for the selection concerned the fertility of the soil, the favorable lie of the land for irrigation, the availability of water from two main rivers, nearness to supplies of local coal and timber in the mountains 25 miles west, reasonable expectancy of good markets in the mining camps, and location midway between Denver and Cheyenne on the Denver Pacific Railroad. A block of land was purchased from the railroad, and from a few squatters who had already settled on the desired tract. Through this transaction, title to alternate sections of land was secured; control over the intervening sections that had not been granted to the railroad was gained, in effect, by the running of irrigation canals.

Colony organization took the form that was followed by the Longmont colony. A membership fee of $155 was charged, and the " good moral character " clause was rigidly observed. The land was to be equitably divided among the members, the sale of intoxicating liquors was prohibited, and members were assured of the early appearance in the community of schools, churches, and " good society." With these prospects, over 600 members paid full fees, providing the management with a working fund of close to $100,000.

Planning for the Greeley colony required preliminary thought as to the size of farm unit suitable for an irrigated region. Clearly, the farms should be smaller than in humid lands, but how much smaller? After consideration, the maximum unit was set at 40 acres, and such properties were to form the outer fringe of the occupied area. Advancing toward the center — the town of Greeley — units were to become smaller, some 20 acres, some 10, and those adjoining the town, 5 acres only. As an example of planning in advance of settlement, this does credit to managerial wisdom. A full section of land was reserved for the town, subdivided into lots of from 25 to 200 front feet. Lots were sold at moderate prices, and about 100 for school purposes were reserved for sale when prices had advanced.

Arrangements were made for reduced-rate transportation of the colonists, who originated in various cities, including New York, Boston, Buffalo, Cleveland, and Chicago. The colonists began to arrive early in May and were greeted with the normal cloudy and rainy weather of that season. With so much moisture about, many of them wondered why irrigation was thought to be necessary; to others, the Great Plains assumed a most forbidding appearance.

Some dissension arose from the inadequacy of housing at the time of arrival, explained by the failure of a contractor to deliver the lumber that had been ordered. Fortunately for these colonists, however, a similar venture had failed at a place called Evans, 5 miles from Greeley; many of the buildings of Evans were hauled by ox team to the new site. Another large building was purchased in Cheyenne and transported to Greeley in sections. The majority of the settlers took these difficulties in good part and credited the management with sincerity and diligence in its efforts to meet the emergency.

The progress made by the colonists was no less spectacular than that of the Mormons in Utah. Within a month water was flowing through ditches to planted fields. When the town of Greeley was only nine months old, an inventory of accomplishment showed the following: 40 miles of main irrigation canal capable of supplying 30,000 acres; 1,000 population with the majority affiliated with churches; 450 homes, 20 stores, 3 schools, a weekly newspaper — and no saloons or gambling houses. The success story continued, and within a few years Greeley had outgrown its colony management. As a productive region the Greeley area is outstanding among Colorado piedmont centers.

125

Mosca Pass across the Sangre de Cristo Range, looking west toward the San Luis Valley, Colorado. An early-day route across the range, it had become impassable in 1929, when the view was taken.

THE "BEAUTIFUL UNITY" OF THE MOUNTAINS

In one of his many reports, F. V. Hayden commented upon the "beautiful unity in the physical development of the western portion of our continent." Taken singly, he observed, the ridges and ranges seem to lack definite trends, "but when included in the aggregate, extend across the map in a direction nearly northwest and southeast."

The mountain ranges, reaching their greatest heights in Colorado, furnished plentiful supplies of water which fed the expanding irrigated areas along the piedmont. In this respect Colorado was more fortunate than Wyoming, but the very height of the mountains, as well as their continuity, increased their barrier effect on land travel. Thus it was that the main transcontinental routes to the Pacific coast swung around the Colorado Rockies. The importance of South Pass, representing a virtual break in the mountain wall, has already been shown.

The mountain passes of the central Rockies bear little resemblance to South Pass, for a pass in Colorado identifies the passage across a stream divide from the headwaters of one river to the upper branches of another. It is usually a short but difficult passage, often resorting to switchbacks in the final ascent. The majority of Colorado's passes are high, and are thus handicapped more by snow than are passes in many other mountains. In the final analysis, the valley approaches to a pass were of more importance than the absolute elevation above sea level in determining its early use.

Perhaps the most important Continental Divide pass in Colorado during the active mining and settlement period was Tennessee Pass, with an altitude of 10,876 feet. The valley approaches to it — those of the Arkansas River on the east and the Eagle River source of the Colorado on the west — provided a comparatively easy ascent. From this route, other passes and routes led to growing mining towns. It was a kind of trunk line, especially with the construction through it of the Denver, Rio Grande & Western Railroad (Royal Gorge Route).

The Tennessee Pass route, however, never attained the transcontinental importance of South Pass in Wyoming.

Many of the earlier routes from Denver and other mountain-front cities centered upon the parks earlier referred to, probably following pre-existent trails made by buffalo during their migrations. The fact that present-day Middle Park was at an early time called Bull Pen or Cow Lodge lends support to this view. At any rate, the Colorado passes were more significant for local travel for trappers, pioneers, and miners than for transcontinental travel. (See Fig. 125.)

The supremacy of Denver among Great Plains cities cannot be related to command over passes to the west of its site. Despite the high mountain barrier, Denver became the leading city at an early day and has maintained its position throughout the years. From a population of about 5,000 in 1870, the city grew to 36,000 in 1880, and doubled again in the next decade.

Part Six

FROM THE ROCKY MOUNTAINS
TO THE PACIFIC COAST,
TO 1870

The Oregon Country: Inland Empire and Coastal Valleys

OVERLAND TO COASTAL OREGON

ONE hundred and fifty miles beyond South Pass, at Soda Springs near the western flank of the Rocky Mountains, coast-bound emigrant trains came to a decisive fork in the trail. To the left lay the route to California; to the right was the " Oregon country." Before 1848 the Oregon Trail to the Columbia River carried most of the traffic, but thereafter the wagon ruts wore more deeply into the southwestern branch. This was greatly in contrast to the days before the gold discoveries; in 1844, 1,400 emigrants went over the trail to Oregon, and at least 5,000 the next year. But the Oregon Trail " bore no evidence of having been much traveled this year," wrote Major Osborne Cross in his journal upon reaching Soda Springs in 1849. (See map, Fig. 127, page 468.)

Fort Hall, gateway to Oregon. On guidebook maps, " Oregon " was lettered boldly across the space between the Northern Rockies and the Pacific, at the present time shared by three big states — Idaho, Washington, and Oregon. Most land-seekers following the trail to the Columbia River looked upon Fort Hall — near the junction of the Port Neuf River with the Snake and not far distant from present-day Pocatello, Idaho — as the entrance to the Oregon country; but Fort Hall and its environs gave little promise of the reputedly fertile lands of Oregon. In fact the Oregon which people sought was 650 weary miles farther on.

Like many Western trading stations which had acquired military functions and features, Fort Hall had seen varied service between 1832, when it was constructed, and 1848, the year that Oregon was named an official Territory. Occupied for many years by the Hudson's Bay Company, Fort Hall was a cluster of residences, offices, shops, and storehouses, with its needed food supplied in part by its own gardens and livestock. When the fort came into American hands, it fulfilled the functions of supply station and military outpost. A photographic view of Fort Hall in 1869 shows nothing of the enclosing adobe walls and bastions which are referred to in descriptions given during the emigrant period. (See Fig. 126, and for location see Fig. 127.)

126   Fort Hall, southeastern Idaho, in 1869. Photographed by W. H. Jackson. Courtesy of the U.S. Geological Survey.

Grand Ronde, Blue Mountains, and Umatilla Valley. From Fort Hall to Fort Boise, a distance of over 300 miles, the Oregon Trail struck across the Snake River plains, or " desert," as it was then known. At Boise, where gold was to be discovered in the 1860's, the trail bore northwest from the Snake River, avoiding its difficult northward course and heading directly for the Columbia over a less-dissected country that offered more abundant pasture and water for livestock.

A welcome sight to emigrants was the Blue Mountains, which rise high enough above the general level to cause greater rainfall. Among the streams on the Blue Mountains' eastern flank is the Grand Ronde River, which traverses a level plain more than 10 miles wide. " The prettiest place we have passed on the route," said Cross, and useful too, because of the good range land. The valley floor was observed to possess a dark, rich soil which, when irrigated at some future time, would support a thriving agriculture — if high altitude did not prevent. Records indicate that before the settlement period the Grand Ronde was a customary gathering place for Indian tribes. An agent for the Hudson's Bay Company noted in 1841 that

Kayouse and Walla Walla Indians had come thither to trade in horses with the Snake Indians. Their camp consists of twelve large lodges covered with boughs, each about 50 feet long. We pitched our camp alongside of the Indians. The plain had a very lovely appearance; more than a thousand horses were running about, and the Indians galloping to and fro

— historical precedent, if any is needed, for the nationally known Pendleton Roundup of that vicinity.

The Walla Walla and Umatilla valleys are also associated with the Blue Mountains. It was in the " Eumatilla " valley in 1850 that Major Cross " saw for the first time since leaving Fort Leavenworth, the signs of agriculture." These evidences were not altogether reassuring to people who were going to Oregon mainly to take up farm land. There were many remains of old fences and· previously cultivated fields, memorials to the efforts of missionaries who in the early 1830's zealously attempted to elevate the lives of the Indian peoples. Dr. Marcus Whitman, the best known of these missionaries, maintained a post named Waiilatpu near Walla Walla during the period when political control of the Oregon country was being contested between this country and Great Britain.

From Umatilla the Oregon Trail followed the south bank of the Columbia for 200 miles over dusty plains " sufficient to appal the stoutest heart." The river itself, gathering volume in its descent to the ocean, added a touch of majesty to the scene, particularly at the approach to the Cascade Mountains. The Dalles of the Columbia first appeared as little more than a rapid, then a dashing torrent as the river flowed in its constricted channel through the canyon.

Oregon west of the Cascades. At the Cascades, as if by the wand of a magician, the character of the country changed. To the west of the mountain barrier was a well-watered land, luxuriant in vegetation. Green forests and rich meadows replaced the dry and apparently sterile plains and plateaus of the interior. The fir trees clothing the mountain slopes and extending into the broad Willamette Valley and the narrower Cowlitz appeared particularly beautiful after a two-month journey through treeless plains. Viewing the heights of the trees and the closeness of the stand, newcomers indulged in estimates of the fabulous amount of cordwood they would produce — more than the ground could hold. The green beauty of the immediate landscape was framed in mountain ranges, with great peaks rising above. Enthusiastic Oregonians claimed for Mount Hood an 18,000-foot altitude; surveyors forced them to place it a mile lower, but could take nothing from its majesty thereby.

Oregon beyond the Cascades was the Oregon that people sought in the pioneer period. At the time Oregon Territory was formed, the settled area was an extremely small part of the total area. Nine-tenths of the people, of whom there were not more than 10,000 by 1850, were confined to the Willamette Valley, " the garden of Oregon," with detached settlements in smaller coastal lowlands such as the Rogue and the Umpqua. (See Fig. 127.)

OREGON, LAND OF INTERNATIONAL RIVALRY

Western Oregon was the Land of Promise and, in a special sense, of promises. Some of these predictions, made on the basis of inadequate information and in the heat of political campaigns, were not, and indeed in view of geographical conditions could not be, fulfilled.

To understand this situation, brief account must be taken of the rival interests of the United States and Great Britain, interests which involved ultimate control of the Oregon country. Both nations claimed Oregon on the basis of discovery. The United States pointed to the expedition of Lewis and Clark and to other discoveries of the mouth of the Columbia by sea; Great Britain countered with no less convincing discoveries by Mackenzie, Frazer, and others.

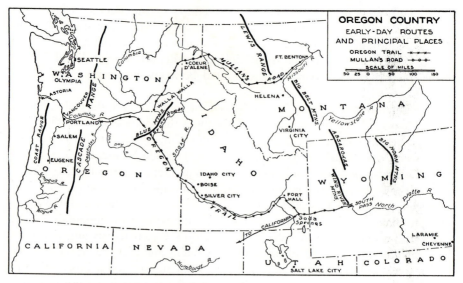

127   The Oregon country, a general map showing the principal roads to the Inland Empire and the lower Columbia

Commercial interests overlapped in the same area, with the Hudson's Bay Company and the American Fur Company playing leading roles. In 1812 the American merchants established a post, Astoria, at the mouth of the Columbia, while the more powerful Hudson's Bay Company extended its trading stations to numerous strategic points in the Columbia Basin. Among the latter were Forts Colville and Hall, and Fort Vancouver at the exit of the Columbia from the Dalles. To these, the British-controlled company added Fort George on the site of Astoria after the American firm had withdrawn.

The " Oregon question " became a diplomatic problem in 1818, with the United States urging the extension of the 49th parallel to the Pacific Coast and Great Britain holding out for the Columbia River as the boundary. In compromise, the two countries agreed to delay the final settlement of the boundary dispute for a ten-year period, thus initiating a " joint occupation " of the disputed territory. In the meantime Russia, by renouncing all claims to territory south of the parallel of 50° 40', did much to simplify the political geography of the Pacific Northwest.

The joint-occupation experiment was not wholly successful; at least no permanent settlement was made in the debatable land until 1834, when the missions already mentioned were established. American interests in the Pacific Northwest were growing, however. Proponents of settlement urged effective occupation of the land in order to give evidence of the right to ownership.

The Congress received numerous memorials urging immediate Territorial status and a prompt solution to the boundary question. An example was the memorial of J. Quinn Thornton to the Thirtieth Congress in 1847. Thornton pointed out that while the intricate diplomatic controversy was in progress and

. . . the Secretary of State was laboriously engaged with his pen in a masterly vindica tion of our title to Oregon, the hardy and enterprising emigrant, unaccustomed to the forms and distinctions of diplomacy . . . resolved upon terminating the dispute in his own way . . . by means of his rifle, axe, and ox goad; [furthermore,] our citizens were forming prosperous settlements in the rich and beautiful valley of the Willamette and were thus giving strength to our title resting upon occupancy.

In their enthusiasm the promoters often went beyond known facts and reasonable inferences, and permitted imagination to embellish their paeans of praise. Oregon was described as " one of the most favored portions of the globe." Unroll the map of Oregon, they said, and see that the Columbia River, greatest of all American streams, makes it accessible to the rest of the country. Note well, they pointed out, that Oregon faces the Orient, where teeming millions offer a rich trade. Moreover, Oregon had an abundance of fertile land under a health-giving climate which combined adequate rainfall with mild winters, a climate wholly different from that of corresponding latitudes on the East coast.

The Oregon question reached the public forum in the presidential campaign of 1844, during which the slogan " All Oregon or none! Fifty-four-forty or fight! " was widely heard. The meaning of " all of Oregon " was left undefined. The question of political control was settled diplomatically in 1846 by the extension of the 49th parallel as a boundary across the Rockies to the Pacific. This act set the stage for new migrations to Oregon, further stimulated in 1850 by the passage of the Oregon Donation Land Law. By the terms of this law, a married man was allowed 640 acres, one-half of which was to belong to the wife. This land law, applicable to all of Oregon but used for land selections mainly in the Willamette Valley, remained operative until 1855.

Country-wide attention was necessarily directed to Oregon during the protracted negotiations. Readers of newspapers and magazines could scarcely avoid reading accounts of the newly opened land, and for the most part the descriptions were on the favorable side. One might read, for example, that Oregon was " the finest grazing land in the world. Here there are no droughts as on the Pampas of Buenos Ayres or the plains of California, whilst the lands [of the Willamette] abound with rich grasses both winter and summer." The attractions of Oregon were advertised to such an extent that upon arrival in the Northwest many emigrants would have agreed with Major Cross that " The country on the Columbia, I think, has been much exaggerated, and that portion of it from the Dalles to the Pacific Ocean falls does not come up to my expectations."

Nevertheless, western Oregon could fall short of the roseate pictures drawn of it by misinformed enthusiasts and still be a most suitable region for pioneering. The great majority of settlers found the Willamette, the lower Columbia, the Rogue, the Umpqua, the Cowlitz, and many other regions to their liking.

WESTERN OREGON AS A FRONTIER

An old pattern in a new setting.   In the rainy climate of coastal Oregon (including Washington) irrigation was unnecessary — a most welcome circumstance to settlers from the East and the Midwest who were unfamiliar with this practice. No other Western region provided so large an area into which humid-land agriculture could be extended. Most of the crops grown in the East, and basic to a pioneering economy, were well suited to this environment. Occupancy of the land was thereby facilitated. The natural grasslands favored stock-raising, as did also the comparatively mild winters, which made elaborate housing unnecessary. Near at hand were sources of lumber which could be put to use in fencing and general building.

The log cabin became a feature of the landscape, remindful of earlier frontiers in the humid East. Jesse Applegate's thumbnail sketch of Oregon in 1852 as " a land but just emerging from a state of barbarism, where, in the settled portions, the recently and rudely constructed log cabin of the emigrant stands beside the ruder wigwam of the aborigines " could have fitted upstate New York or central Tennessee a half-century before. To some extent the forests were an encumbrance on the land, to be cut to make room for planting among the stumps until they in turn were removed. Of Olympia a visitor remarked as late as 1865 that there were " more stumps than houses within the city limits." Here was a repetition of the pattern of Eastern pioneer settlement, and here too were many Eastern place names — Portland, Salem, and Albany, to mention but a few.

Climatic characteristics and settlement.   Beneath these general resemblances to other frontiers were a number of differences which distinguished western-Oregon settlement from all other.

One difference was shown for all time in 1852 by Applegate. With his report on Oregon to the Commissioner of Agriculture he enclosed some wild flowers picked on December 8, which were received in Washington, D.C., when the outdoor temperature was 12° Fahrenheit. The mildness of the winters, at least of most winters, which had been stressed in the advertising, was borne out in the common experience. Snow, though abundant in the mountains, was a rarity in the lower lands, usually remaining on the ground no more than two or three days.

The best and the worst features of North Pacific winters were known by this time. In 1847 the January temperature dipped to —7° (in Oregon City), and snow lay deep in the Willamette Valley by mid-month. But this was considered to be unusual, as indeed it was, for not until the winter of 1861 did such frigid blasts from the north occur again. Despite occasional cold waves which caused all the more hardship because of the adjustment of housing to milder weather, intending settlers from the Eastern states were advised not to bring sleighs and sleds.

The mildness of the usual winter, remarkable for the high latitude, was correctly attributed to the tempering effect of the ocean. " The coastal winds so modify the climate," observed I. I. Stevens in the Pacific Railway report, " that the isothermal lines run nearly parallel to the coast, making the climate of Puget Sound nearly as mild, and in summer more agreeable, than at San Francisco, while it corresponds closely with that of the western coast of Europe in the same latitude, and especially that of the British islands." Climatic contrasts to the Atlantic coast were much as had been advertised, for " cultivation may be commenced some days earlier than at places several degrees farther south in the Atlantic states, and some weeks earlier than in places of the same latitude."

Although the Northwest climate provided a long frost-free season, favorable to many crops and to the grazing industry, the coolness of the summer was thought to prohibit the growing of corn. " Corn can never become a staple crop, owing to the climate," the Commissioner of Agriculture announced in 1851, phrasing the thought of many contemporaries. The belief that corn could not be grown in the Northwest except as a green vegetable virtually excluded this basic crop from the farm economy for a great many years. Corn was gradually introduced, especially as new varieties appeared, but the prediction of a century ago that this is not a " corn climate " remains essentially correct. However, if corn was not well suited to this region, experience soon showed that other crops were. Various kinds of fruits, berries, and grapes were found productive, and fall-planted wheat early became a principal crop.

Special importance was attached to two aspects of the rainfall: (1) its dependability from year to year, and (2) its concentration in the winter months. " No complaint of drought can be made of this climate," said Stevens in 1855, referring to the Puget Sound area. The truth of this statement has been confirmed by the years of weather records since that time. Many observers considered that it rained too much and too steadily, especially during the cooler months. " The winter is one long shower of six months," said a visitor, humorously and inaccurately.

Less pleasant were some of the remarks originating in California about the Northwest climate. In a vigorous competition for coast-bound emigrants, Californians pointed to the cloudy, " dreary " weather of Oregon, and characterized their Northwest neighbors as Webfeet. In actual fact the lowlands received only moderate rainfall, but the manner of its occurrence in the form of light, drizzly rains gave the impression of much larger amounts. The average summer was a time of many bright and sunny days, beneficial to pastures, the maturing of crops, and the harvest period. Unlike the southern Pacific coast, Oregon had no " drought period " in summer — a point emphasized by those favoring settlement there.

Isolation and inadequate markets. Western Oregon was a horn of plenty whose lavish abundance was not matched by adequate outlets for its products.

Nearest outlet was California's mining camps, booming by 1849 and demanding food products at almost any cost. Agricultural Oregon furnished many of these necessities until California valleys nearer the camps came into competition. The Willamette Valley, main center of Oregon settlement, was a long distance from the gold fields by water, and a route overland must necessarily negotiate the rugged Klamath Mountains which lay between. Somewhat nearer the gold fields were the valley lowlands in the coast ranges of Oregon, particularly the Rogue and the Umpqua. Their early settlement was stimulated by the profitable California market.

But the Oregon valleys could supply little that could not be produced as well in California once attention there was turned to farming. The climates of the two coastal regions were not sufficiently different to induce a coastwise trade comparable to that of the more diversified Atlantic coast. Wheat, fruits, vineyards, and stock-raising — these were typical alike of Oregon and of California. California, in fact, contributed greatly to the stocking of Oregon farms with cattle and sheep. A recorded drove of 630 cattle reached the Willamette from the San Francisco area in 1837 — a contribution, said the drover, " of Mexican California to the Oregon settlements."

The lure of gold was felt in the Willamette quite as much as in other parts of the country. Partly opened farms were vacated, and many persons intending to go to the Oregon country were diverted en route to the fabulous gold camps. Consequently, Oregon's rate of population growth was less rapid than would be expected in so favored a region. Joseph Schafer has pointed out that the Pacific Northwest grew in population at only one-fifth the rate of the states of Iowa, Minnesota, Nebraska, and Kansas at comparable periods. " All in all," he continues, " the Pacific Northwest has suffered in its agricultural development from the stupendous fact that nature had made the region tributary to the Pacific rather than to the Atlantic." A profitable trade with the Orient, fancied by early spokesmen, failed to materialize.

SLOW DEVELOPMENT OF OVERLAND TRANSPORT

The extent of Oregon's isolation from the rest of the country is emphatically brought out in the map showing overland mail routes from 1850 to 1859 (Fig. 128). During that period there were in fact no organized delivery routes to Oregon, nor were there any in all the country from Minnesota to the Pacific Coast. Within the next decade, Portland was connected by mail route with San Francisco, and Walla Walla-Umatilla was reached by a line extending from Salt Lake City. (See Fig. 129.) Routes of commerce were still wanting, however.

The beginning of a freighting route across the Northern Rockies took the form of a military road constructed under the direction of Captain John Mullan, between 1859 and 1862. It was not, however, intended as a connecting link with western Oregon, nor did it correspond in position to the track of Lewis and Clark. " Mullan's Road," following a circuitous route over the mountains from Fort Benton to Walla Walla, grew out of gold discoveries near Helena, Montana, and other strikes in Idaho across the Continental Divide. Passable at first only by pack trains, Mullan's Road was improved for use by 8-mule wagons which eventually carried Willamette-grown flour and meats to the mining camps. The

128   Overland mail routes, 1850 to 1859. Adapted, with permission, from C. O. Paullin's *Atlas of the Historical Geography of the United States,* published jointly by the Carnegie Institution of Washington and the American Geographical Society of New York.

Inland Empire thus furnished an additional, if limited, outlet for western Oregon products at this time. (See map, Fig. 127, page 468.)

Communications east of Helena and Fort Benton were very unsatisfactory, as may be recalled from the discussion of Missouri River navigation (Chapter 21). In an effort to speed connections with the East, in 1867 the Government let a contract for the delivery of mail by horse travel between Helena and Fort Abercrombie in eastern Dakota Territory. (See Fig. 129.) The route corresponded roughly to that followed by emigrants and gold-seekers in 1863 under the direction of Captain John Fisk. The territory was large and sparsely populated, with stations spaced at discouraging distances, and the mail service was ill-performed, scarcely adding to the glorious tradition of the pony express. The riders, it has been remarked, " found the fuel scarce and the newspapers heavy, and with a happy ingenuity got over both difficulties by burning the papers and, developing still further their inventive talents, made excellent cigar lighters of their mail sacks." For services so poorly rendered the Government refused payment, and the route was soon abandoned.

Early plans for a direct rail line to Oregon over a northern route proved to be entirely visionary. The Congress received the first proposal for such a line in 1845, when Asa Whitney, early exponent of transcontinental railroads, told of a project "which would have the whole world tributary to us — when the whole shall be tumbled in our laps." Whitney's enthusiasm for a rail line, not to mention his desire for a grant of land 60 miles in width along the right of way, evidently outdistanced his knowledge of Western geography; neither did he properly evaluate the amount of political pressure that would be aimed against

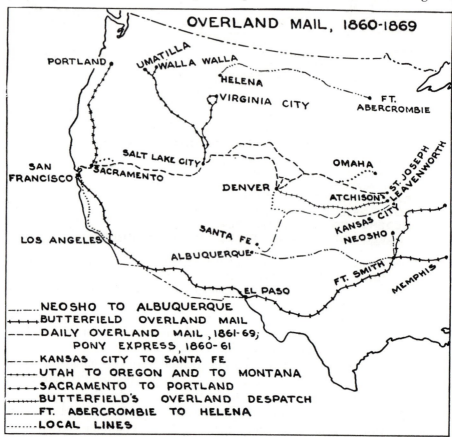

129   Overland mail routes, 1860 to 1869. Adapted, with permission, from C. O. Paul-lin's *Atlas of the Historical Geography of the United States,* published jointly by the Carnegie Institution of Washington and the American Geographical Society of New York.

his project. The proposal did show, however, that careful surveys of possible routes should in all cases precede the granting of land with a view to encouraging enterprises.

From the sketch of the Pacific Railway survey (Chapter 21) it will be seen that Governor I. I. Stevens of Washington Territory was entrusted with the route survey of the 47th parallel. When received in Washington, the Stevens report was found not altogether satisfactory, and was greatly revised and amended for publication. In final form, the proposed northern route corresponded roughly to the track of Lewis and Clark, approaching the mountains by way of the Missouri River, crossing the ridge at one of several possible passes, and from there following the Columbia drainage course to the ocean.

The northern route was seen to offer both advantages and disadvantages. On the favoring side were: (1) the comparatively short distance from the Missouri River to a seaport, with a possible western terminus in Puget Sound nearer to Asiatic ports than any other terminus in the United States; (2) the probability of coal supplies near Puget Sound; (3) the timber resources in the western part of the route to aid in rail construction; and (4) a relatively low profile, since the maximum altitudes are lower in the Montana Rockies than farther south. The latter consideration was believed all the more important because of the heavier snowfall in this northern country.

The low profile, however, gave a false impression of ease of construction in a distance of a thousand miles. Passes varied in altitude from 6,000 to 8,000 feet, low by comparison with the Colorado Rockies; nevertheless it was clear that they would have to be tunneled for railroad purposes. Glaciers, it was observed, appeared in the Montana Rockies despite the low altitudes. By tunneling, expected difficulties with heavy snowfall could be at least partially overcome. It was estimated that the Lewis and Clark Pass, 6,323 feet in altitude, would require a tunnel of 2½ miles. Other passes considered practicable for a transcontinental line were Marias, Cadotte's, Hell Gate, and St. Mary's.

Other disadvantages weighed heavily against the early completion of the northern route: (1) the long winters which would presumably interrupt construction and operations; (2) increased problems of engineering, seen in evidences of high floods in various rivers along which the tracks must be laid; and (3) the distance of the proposed Western terminus from San Francisco, "which will give the only large travel and business which may be counted upon with certainty." The last-named objection to the northern route was a bitter pill for the good and loyal citizens of Oregon.

The completion of the Union Pacific Railroad to California in 1869 stimulated new desires for a comparable line to the Northwest. Branch connections with the completed route, such as one corresponding to the old Oregon Trail, were not considered sufficient. Promoters appeared on the scene, first initiating rail lines around unnavigable stretches of the Columbia, and then connecting these links to form a rail route to the Inland Empire. On the other side of the Rockies the Northern Pacific Railroad, favored by liberal land grants, was being built across the sparsely inhabited Plains. And so in 1883, when these rails met, there was re-enacted in western Montana the ceremony of the golden spike which Utah had witnessed fourteen years before. A large gathering was on hand for the ceremony, including a pioneer who had made the overland journey by ox team in 1843. Fully three-fourths of a century had elapsed between the journey of Lewis and Clark and the completion of the transcontinental line over the northern route.

The role of Columbia River navigation. Tracing the accomplishment of the Northern Pacific Railroad has brought us ahead of the account of Oregon settlement. As elsewhere, the rail lines heralded a new era; but until the 1880's western Oregon was comparatively isolated, self-contained with its rich resources and varied agriculture, dependent for trade and travel on coasting vessels, local roads, and the waterways.

The Columbia River was an important avenue of communication, but it imposed some difficulties which were usually omitted from the early advertisements of the area. The Columbia was a great and powerful river, the only one to approach a major mountain system of the West and plunge through it on a direct passage to the sea. In early days called the Oregon, the river met the Pacific on a front over 4 miles in width. Here was an extensive sand bar, cut by deeper channels familiar only to experienced seamen. The ocean waves, dashing upon the bar, could be seen from Astoria as " flying sheets of foam, and the roaring may be heard for a much greater distance." Not an inviting approach from the sea, nor an easy entrance to find, as the name Cape Disappointment near the mouth seems to suggest.

Vessels that had successfully passed the bar could proceed up the Columbia for 120 miles to the junction of the Willamette. This river's natural depth of about 12 feet provided sufficient draught for coastwise vessels in common use during the 1850's, when Portland, 12 miles up the Willamette from the junction, was the recognized head of navigation.

The Columbia River above the Willamette junction was divided by natural barriers into several navigable sections. Steamboats of different sizes, most of them owned and operated by one company, plied within the various sections. Goods or passengers were transferred over portages around the falls; in the 1860's these portages were accomplished by short stretches of railroad. On a voyage up the Columbia from Portland, a traveler met the first interruption at the lower Cascades (where Bonneville Dam is now located). Here was a 5-mile rail line around the Cascades, at the head of which a second boat would proceed over the 45-mile stretch to the Dalles. A railroad 15 miles in length circumvented the Dalles, where raging water then, as now, impressed travelers by the " majestic, fearful intensity of its motion."

The third division of the Columbia was marked by arrival at Celilo near the junction of the Des Chutes River. Navigation above Celilo was unimpeded for boats then in use until the arrival at Priest Rapids in what is now southern Washington. During the peak of the gold-mining period in Idaho, navigation was extended to Lake Pend Oreille in the north fork of the Columbia. There were an estimated 2,000 miles of navigable water in the Columbia Basin — although, as has been noted, it could not all be undertaken in one commercial vessel.

Fishing. When settlers arrived in Oregon, remnant bands of once-powerful Indian tribes were living here and there west of the Cascades. Their dwellings of split cedar slabs roofed with bark were usually located within easy access to the river, from which much of their subsistence was derived. They spent much of their time fishing, on the water or from stagings jutting out from shore. They were expert boatbuilders. As described by a visitor in 1843, the Indian canoes were

. . . the finest ever seen, made of large white cedar, hewn out with great labor. They are constructed with a high prow and stern, which are separate from the main vessel, and are so neatly put on that the joints will not admit water. They are very light, and the edges are ornamented with Sea shells.

Artistic skill was also shown in their rush mats and grass baskets, the latter so closely woven as to be watertight.

The Indians were the the first fishermen of the lower Columbia River. Their seines, spears, and pole hooks were busy during the spring, when salmon came up from the sea. " The stench arising from the filth about their villages, in the fishing season, is almost insupportable," it was said. Scaffolds built near falls and rapids permitted small crews to operate advantageously, some of the natives spreading nets, others using spears. There were so many salmon that even at night the mere immersion of a hook fastened to a long pole was more than likely to bring out a good specimen.

The early settlers naturally followed the Indian example of fishing, and gradually improved on the methods. This supplementary source of food added to the suitability of the Northwest as a frontier region. A small export trade developed in smoked salmon, but it was not until comparatively recent times, with the development of reliable canning processes, that fish became a large item in the trade.

REGIONS OF SETTLEMENT IN WESTERN OREGON

The Willamette. The broad Willamette Valley combined most of the environmental factors which distinguished western Oregon as a whole. It became customary to refer to the Willamette as the heart of Oregon, or again as " Oregon itself." Actually it is a broad structural basin between the Cascades and the coastal ranges, a lowland through which the Willamette River follows a meandering course. When it was first described, the forest cover of the higher slopes descended in tongues to the basin floor, where extensive prairies or meadows lay ready for use. The soil was recognized as strong and clayey, adequately supplied with " vegetable loam " (humus), and of tolerable productivity.

The superior land was early set to orchards of cherry and apple, or to vineyards of Isabella and Catawba grapes; fall-sown wheat also took precedence over other crops. Pears, plums, and berries were found to do well in this environment. Cattle-grazing and sheep-grazing became increasingly important in this region of ample pastures and fairly certain rainfall.

The Willamette Valley was extensive, being some 150 miles long, and 75 in width. Although 50,000 people occupied the valley in 1865, only a tenth of the potential farm land had yet been plowed, and some of the better land could be purchased at prices ranging from $5 to $25 an acre. Many observers concluded that the farm units were too large for optimum farm economy, and wondered whether the Donation Land Law, permitting an entry of a square mile for a farm, had after all been beneficial.

Oregon City, laid out at the falls of the Willamette in 1842, soon lost its supremacy as the original capital of this region and of the whole of Oregon Territory. Portland rapidly forged ahead, with a population of 7,000 in 1865 and 27,000 in 1880. (Seattle, by comparison, was a city of 4,000 in 1880.) Even before the coming of railroads, Portland was the great entrepôt of the Northwest, even of British Columbia, with trade connections extending as far inland as Salt Lake City. Portland's seaborne trade was mainly in lumber — with California. When foreign trade became significant, commercial supremacy among Northwest ports passed from Portland to Seattle. Other growing towns of the Willamette were Salem, Albany, Corvallis, and Eugene City. As so often happens, the "City" was dropped from Eugene's name when urban status was actually reached by the turn of the century.

"Cross valleys" of the coast: Umpqua and Rogue. Interrupting Oregon's coastal ranges are several valley lowlands drained by smaller rivers emptying into the Pacific. Because of their direction more or less at right angles to the coast line they became known as "cross valleys," although the word "valley" is likely to convey here an incorrect impression. As one of the pioneers of the Umpqua remarked,

. . . the basin is very broken and when viewed from the enclosing mountains, seems to be merely a mass of hills and mountains, differing from its rim in being of less elevation, bald or timbered with oak, the evergreen only appearing in clumps on the loftiest summits, or lining the deep ravines.

Open land predominated over the forest-covered, the valley in this respect being a little Willamette. The Umpqua will serve for illustrative purposes, although it should be noted that each of the dozen coastal valleys presented individual features of settlement. In the Umpqua, for example, the settlers came into contact with a friendly Indian type, while the natives of the Rogue caused difficulties until 1856, when they were removed to reservations.

Although the Hudson's Bay Company maintained a post at the mouth of the Umpqua, the valley remained unsettled until 1850. Pioneer settlers then arrived, and followed a life remindful of earlier times on the Atlantic coast. The isolation of Oregon and of this valley on its Pacific coast was reflected in the high cost of farm machinery. Such laborsaving devices as were then in existence being unavailable, the land was turned with inferior plows and harrowed with " scragged treetops," and the grain was harvested with old-time cradles. Threshing was carried out on clay-packed floors on which

. . . the grain is laid regularly, the heads pointing obliquely upward. A wild, skittish band of horses is turned in and driven against the bristling heads of the grain, and by their scampering in a very short time the wheat is threshed from the straw. . . . Leaving the bottom undisturbed to the last, as it is sometimes dirty, the threshed grain is pushed to the centre, and another floor laid down, and so on until the crop is threshed.

With fanning mills difficult to obtain and costing $100 or more on Oregon's coast, frontier farmers depended much on the wind to separate the chaff from the grain.

The Umpqua profited somewhat and temporarily from the relative nearness to the California markets. A resident remarked that " a fine yield of both potatoes and gold may be dug from the same plot of ground in California," and pointed out that " when the mine market ceases, it is difficult to foresee what other market will be formed." Railroad connections finally brought the Umpqua into closer contact with markets.

Cowlitz Valley and Puget Sound. " Little attention is paid to the north side of the Columbia by American settlers," emigrants were informed in a guidebook of 1846. Uncertainties of political control delayed occupation of the region later to become the State of Washington, but the settlement of the boundary brought no immediate change. There was still plenty of room for expansion in the Willamette Valley and elsewhere south of the river; furthermore, western Washington was the more heavily timbered country. In the Cowlitz Valley, for example, topographically a continuation of the Willamette, only occasional " openings " were observed in 1865; for the most part one passed through forests in which " the very spirit of solitude reigned supreme." The size of the trees was astonishing. With girths of 6 feet, they shot up straight as an arrow for 200 feet or more.

The forests of western Washington, though delaying agricultural settlement, were the basis of a lumber industry already great in 1865. A dozen or more sawmills were already busy turning out 100,000 feet of lumber a day. Several of the present-day cities of western Washington originated as sawmill villages near the mouths of rivers entering Puget Sound — Olympia at the mouth of the Deschutes, and Seattle similarly located on the Duwamish. Their situation on Puget Sound gave the sawmill villages contact with a world market. Lumber was sent not only to California but to the Hawaiian Islands and around Cape Horn to the East coast of the United States. The lumber industry was in its infancy while the War between the States was being hotly contested in the opposite corner of the country. The business " will grow with the growth of the Pacific coast, and increasing dearth of lumber in other parts of the world," Samuel Bowles correctly predicted. Taking another look at the towering Douglas firs and other great trees, he remarked: " It is impossible to calculate the time when the supply will become exhausted."

The lumber industry continued to be the principal attraction of western Washington, although there was some agricultural settlement. Coal mining also provided some employment during the 1850's. Coal was discovered in 1851, with the aid of Indian informants, but the resources proved less abundant than was at first hoped. Gold strikes in British Columbia also drew people northward, and the prospecting which the strikes encouraged brought to light new farming opportunities in the Puget Sound area. (See Fig. 130.) Gold mining being a seasonal occupation in the coastal mountains, the miners sought work in the lumber towns during the winter season.

Western Washington's population was large enough by 1889 to warrant separation from Oregon as a state. Comparative growths of these two Northwestern states is reflected in their differing terms as Territories. Oregon emerged from its Territorial period within a decade, while Washington remained in that status for thirty-six years.

EASTWARD TO THE INLAND EMPIRE

Alder Gulch! Silver City! Boise! These were names sufficient to electrify the interest of farmers, lumberjacks, and town dwellers of western Oregon in the 1860's. They meant gold and silver in placers or lodes, discovered in the mountain fastnesses of the eastern rim of the Inland Empire. Distance and inaccessibility from the coast settlements seemed of little moment at such times. Alder Gulch lay east of the Continental Divide in Montana; Silver City, Boise,

130
A popular sketch map of the Northwest which appeared in *Leslie's Weekly,* August, 1858, soon after the reported gold discoveries in British Columbia

131   Hydraulic mining in Alder Gulch, near Virginia City, Montana, 1869. Photograph by W. H. Jackson. Courtesy of the U.S. Geological Survey.

and Idaho City were in the upper Snake River country not far from where the old Oregon Trail clipped the corner of Idaho. (See Fig. 127, page 468.)

Alder Gulch is better known by the name of the principal mining town to which it gave rise — Virginia City. Named for a minor tributary of the Madison River in the Bitterroot region, Alder Gulch was the theater of the original and the most extensive gold mining in early-day Montana. Within a half-dozen years Virginia City and other Alder Gulch camps together counted a population of about 14,000. People had flocked here from nearly all points of the compass — directly west from Minnesota and the Dakotas, from Wyoming over the Bozeman Trail, and eastward from Oregon and California. The placers of Alder Gulch were deep and extensive, and were worked over for many years by various methods. By 1869, hydraulic mining had developed, patterned after methods used earlier in California. In this process water under high pressure was forced against the alluvial deposits, thus freeing the gold more rapidly than was possible by hand processes. (See Fig. 131.)

Northward of Alder Gulch 150 miles, other gulches were found rich in precious metal. Helena was the chief mining town of this area, in which mining advanced rapidly from placering to lode workings. The city of Helena of 1869, shadeless and confined to the lower lands of its site, showed many characteristic features of an early mining town (Fig. 132). Although modern geographers would ordinarily not include Helena with the Inland Empire of the Northwest, yet a large share of the people who settled there, and during the mining period many of its supplies, came from Portland and other West coast cities.

The gold-silver camps of Idaho can be thought of as forming two widely separated groups. The northern cluster consisted of several towns in the Coeur

132   Helena, Montana, in 1869. Photograph by W. H. Jackson. Courtesy of the U.S. Geological Survey.

d'Alene Mountains in Idaho's " panhandle," to the east of present-day Spokane.

The mining region of southern Idaho included Boise (earlier known as Boise City) as well as Idaho City and the Owyhee mines some 60 miles to the south. Boise itself was less a mining town than the main center of an extensive mining region, a depot from which mining goods and supplies were distributed. With 1,200 inhabitants by 1865, Boise was the capital of Idaho Territory — a substantial, steadily growing town. Before minerals attracted a large number of gold-seekers, Boise was nearly self-supporting from the agriculture of its environs, but the demands of the influx of miners far exceeded local resources. Most of the food came from western Oregon by road and river; other supplies, such as salt and mining machinery, came from Salt Lake City.

Idaho City was the center of an important mining district in which 10,000 persons were living by 1865. As in many another mining town which grew with little planning or forethought, it was later discovered that Idaho City had expanded over some valuable deposits. Nothing daunted, the miners dug beneath the dwellings, propping them up sufficiently to permit work. South of Idaho City the placers and lodes thinned out, and became more silver-bearing. An important camp of the Owyhee district was appropriately named Silver City.

Mining, or prospects of mining, drew many people to the Inland Empire, where, in the course of time, minerals other than gold and silver were discovered. Not uncommonly, discouraged or disappointed miners turned to other activities in the same region, because they became attached to it. Perhaps they recalled pleasant valleys they had too hurriedly passed on their trip eastward to the mountains, places like the Grand Ronde, or Walla Walla. Thus settlement began in the interior country, the more modern development of which dates from the extension of railroads, and particularly from the beginnings of irrigation in the 1880's.

CHAPTER 26

The Great Basin and the Arid Southwest

THE existence of an inland sea somewhere in the mountainous West was vaguely known a century and a half before Great Salt Lake and related features appeared correctly placed on maps. Through the explorations of Frémont, Stansbury, and many others it was made clear that the great lake occupied an enclosed basin within an immense trough extending from the Rocky Mountains to the Sierra Nevada.

The continental trough was suitably named the Great Basin by Frémont in his second exploration of 1842–43. Frémont viewed this region as an " anomalous feature in our continent " because of its self-contained systems of lakes and rivers despite a relatively high altitude of from 4,000 to 5,000 feet above sea level. Shut in all around by high mountains and plateaus, this basin, he found, had no " connexion whatever with the sea." Even though troughlike as a whole, the predominating features of the Great Basin were sharp-sided, thinly forested mountain ranges whose north-south alignment conformed to the general direction of both the Rockies and the Sierras. Modern physiographers refer to the basin ranges as " block mountains."

The reports of explorers and travelers carried little encouragement to a reading public accustomed to the idea of a more or less mythical Great American Desert. Here it was at last, and no mistake about it. Little streams rising in the mountain ranges generally disappeared in the alluvial deposits at their bases, in salt swamps, or in temporary " playa " lakes farther out. Great rivers also met a like fate; the Humboldt River, after a 300-mile journey, found ignominious end in Carson Sink near the Sierra Nevada. Samuel Bowles, the editor and Western traveler who has often been quoted in earlier chapters, in 1865 viewed the Great Basin as " a region whose uses are unimaginable, unless to hold the rest of the globe together, or to teach patience to travelers, or to keep close-locked in its mountain ranges those rich mineral treasures that the world did not want or was not ready for until now."

Natural phenomena of the basin were of great interest, most of all the Great Salt Lake itself. East-west travelers over the central route could scarcely avoid its huge expanse, for it lay directly in their path. There were evidences on every hand of the former greater size of this inland sea. To the south as far as the eye could reach lay a plain of white sand which must have been lake bottom at no distant day. Many old shore lines could be traced, some elevated but a few feet above the water, " as distinct and well-defined and -preserved as its present beaches," said E. A. Beckwith of the railroad survey. Even the least-informed teamsters of the Beckwith party could distinguish these lower shore lines; but

. . . high above the diminutive banks of recent date, on the mountains to the east, south, and west, and on the islands of the Great Salt Lake, formations are seen, preserving a uniform elevation as far as the eye can extend — formations on a magnificent scale, which . . . seem no less unmistakable than the former to indicate their shore origin.

UTAH: TERRITORIAL EXTENT, AND CORE AREAS OF SETTLEMENT

" With great exceptions, many parts are fit for residence," wrote Frémont in 1847 when, as if to prove it, the advance wave of the Mormon migration was sweeping across the eastern rim of the Great Basin. Here the mountains reached their maximum altitudes, and thus the rivers flowing from them were larger and more permanent than elsewhere. This " basin within a basin " also provided an isolated sanctuary for the Mormon colonists, at least for a year or two before the discovery of California gold placed the Salt Lake Oasis on a main Western thoroughfare.

The leaders of the colony sought political control over the Great Basin as a means of maintaining their identity, and considered it desirable also to have a corridor to the sea in California. This ambition took form in the " State of Deseret " proposed in 1849 but never recognized by the United States. (See Fig. 133.) Instead, Utah Territory first appeared on the maps of 1850 within arbitrarily drawn boundaries which extended generously beyond the " core area " of Mormon settlements. Successive reductions of Utah's Territorial extent are shown in the map, as well as the settled area with which the following discussion is mainly concerned.

Broadly considered, inhabited Utah of the 1860's was a long and narrow belt along the base of the Wasatch Mountains and the High Plateaus. The most favored region was sometimes known as the Strait because of its extension along the Jordan River, the connecting link between fresh-water Lake Utah and Great Salt Lake. This area will be known here as the Salt Lake Oasis, and will be considered to include the Tooele (originally Tuilla) Valley just beyond the Oquirrh Mountains. South of the Oasis proper are the more restricted areas watered by the San Pitch and Sevier Rivers (earlier known as San Pete and Severo), which cut through portions of the High Plateaus. Shortly after the founding of Salt Lake City, these irrigable lands were brought within the scope of Mormon colonization.

Having previously considered other colony ventures in which much was accomplished in a short time, we are partly prepared to understand the rapid occupancy of the Utah oases. Here the co-operative effort was most pronounced and longest continued, and leaders spoke with a high degree of authority. As John W. Powell observed in 1878, "The greater number of people in the territory who engage in agriculture are organized into ecclesiastical bodies, trying the experiment of communal institutions." They were also experimenting with irrigation agriculture in a region which presented several limiting factors.

Settlement trials were often made in the name of the Mormon Church, whose custom it was "to send a number of people, organized as a community, to a town site on some stream to be used in the cultivation of the lands, and rarely has the first selection been final." Luxuriant vegetation often tempted the settlers to select lands at too great an altitude, where frosts prohibited successful agriculture, with the result that many towns were removed downstream. Again, selections were made too far away from stream sources, and as a means of ensuring a greater water supply, towns were moved upstream. Lands charged with alkali were often selected and later abandoned; it was, however, found that harmful salts could often be leached out by successive irrigations previous to the planting of crops.

A specific example of community experimentation is afforded by the village

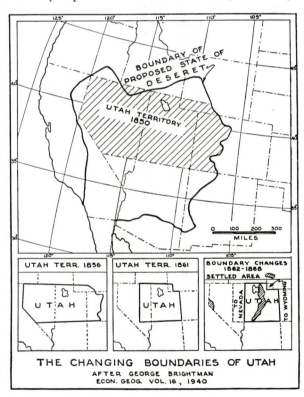

133
The changing boundaries
of Utah, 1850 to 1868

THE CHANGING BOUNDARIES OF UTAH
AFTER GEORGE BRIGHTMAN
ECON. GEOG. VOL. 16, 1940

of Panguitch in the Sevier Valley, at an altitude of 6,400 feet. In deciding to establish a village there, thought was no doubt given to the probability of frost, but who could tell whether it would severely limit farming? Panguitch was settled in 1860, but was soon abandoned because of crop failures. The authorities, still determined, re-established the settlement in 1867, but again it was abandoned, this time in consequence of Indian attacks. Panguitch was settled a third time in 1870 and with apparent success until August 1874, when frosts damaged the crops. However, the town survived its early trials, as is indicated by its present population of some 3,000.

Mobility, therefore, characterized the communal towns of the Utah oases. Swift advances were made into previously unsettled country, and not necessarily in the order in which they might be expected. As early as 1851, for example, Cedar City was established by a locating party 250 miles south of Salt Lake City, and others were formed at the base of the Sierras. By 1865 Mormon settlements extended nearly 700 miles from Idaho to Arizona, confined to a belt hardly more than 50 miles wide. Said Captain C. E. Dutton, an impartial observer, "Whatever the church deems best for the general welfare of its dependencies it dictates, and what it dictates is invariably done with promptitude, and none have yet [1878] been found to resist."

The Salt Lake Oasis. Within four years of the original settlement, the alluvial lands along the base of the Wasatch were described by Stansbury as " studded with flourishing farms, wherever a little stream flows down the mountain-side with sufficient water for irrigating purposes." Largest and most dependable of the rivers originating in the higher mountains were the Bear, the Weber, and the Provo, named from north to south. (See Fig. 134.) Since the principal sources of these rivers were in the high Uintas, where much of the precipitation was in the form of snow, they flowed perennially and carried adequate water in July and August, the " critical period " when water was most needed. The Provo, along with many other smaller streams, flowed into Lake Utah, a body of fresh water which, together with the sluggish Jordan River, provided additional sources of irrigation water. No serious engineering problems were involved in diverting water to the low-lying alluvial land which sloped, terracelike, to the mountain front. Visitors were impressed, even at this early date, by the contrast between the productive irrigated land and the barren plains of the Salt Lake desert just beyond the Jordan River.

Salt Lake City, in the approximate center of this narrow belt of verdure, was laid out on a magnificent scale. The site covered nearly 12 square miles, beautifully located in an amphitheater-like projection of the Wasatch Range. In the width of the streets and the provisions for public edifices, it was apparent that Salt Lake City was planned with vision. The main streets were 8 rods in width, and the 10-acre blocks were divided into 8 lots of 1¼ acres each, thus providing for ample garden plots for the residents. The consequent wide spacing of Salt Lake City houses, then constructed mostly of adobe, gave a " countrified " aspect to the city, as more than one visitor phrased it. The growth of Salt Lake

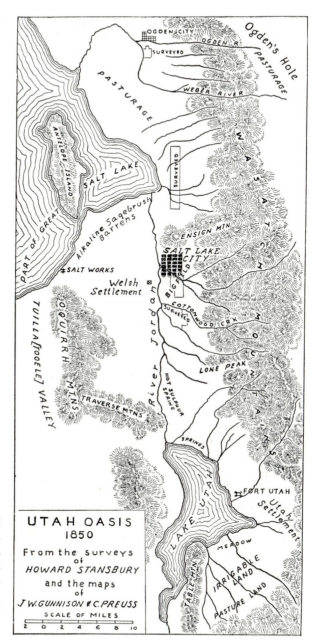

134

Salt Lake City area, adapted from the elaborate map accompanying Howard Stansbury's *Exploration and Survey of the Valley of the Great Salt Lake of Utah,* first published as a government document in 1851.

UTAH OASIS
1850

From the surveys
of
HOWARD STANSBURY
and the maps
of
J.W.GUNNISON & C.PREUSS

SCALE OF MILES

2   0   2   4   6   8   10

City reflected the expansion of the Mormon settlements. By 1865 the city's population was about 20,000; many great buildings had been constructed and the foundations of the famous temple were rising. During the earlier years, an enclosed area called the Bowery was used in summer for public gatherings.

By 1870 the greater part of the easily irrigable land of the Salt Lake Oasis had been taken up. The irrigators had found, according to Grove Karl Gilbert of the United States Geological Survey, " that many of the streams have increased in volume since the settlement of the country." Careful measurements of stream flow, carried out under Gilbert's direction, proved beyond a doubt that the popular impression was in this case the correct one. Many of the colonists believed this apparently desirable result to be clear proof of the old adage that " rainfall follows the plow." By improving and irrigating the land, they reasoned fallaciously, more water is evaporated into the air to be returned in increased precipitation. This same idea has prevailed in many of the irrigated districts of the West.

Careful inquiry by Gilbert into the possible causes of the increased stream flow into the Oasis and Great Salt Lake led to conclusions embracing two probable causes: (1) changes in the drainage basin brought about by man, and (2) a temporary increase in rainfall.

Surface Changes and Increased Stream Flow. During the twenty years of settlement in the Salt Lake Oasis, natural surface conditions were modified by cultivation of the soil, by the raising of herds, and by the cutting of trees. The destruction of beaver dams which originally ponded up the water of many of the mountain streams added considerably to the runoff, as did also the opening-up of springs which, originally contributing little to surface drainage, became linked to the irrigation canals.

The area in which grazing was carried on far exceeded the actual farmed land, and involved many of the headstreams in the higher country. Over large areas the grasses and bushes were destroyed or impoverished, with the result that runoff was increased. As Gilbert put it, " where once the snows of autumn were spread on a non-conducting mat of hay, and wasted by evaporation until the sunshine could melt them, they now fall upon naked earth and are melted at once by its warmth." It is also pointed out that the tramping of boggy ground by grazing animals tended to make the soil less pervious and thus to increase the proportion of runoff.

The cutting of trees for fencing and fuel also modified the original conditions of stream flow, especially during the period of normally high water. Snow beds that were formerly shaded became exposed more directly to the sun, with a consequent increased surface runoff. The cutting of trees in the upper river basins thus had a harmful effect in diminishing the regularity of stream flow.

Increased Rainfall during the 1860's. Another basic cause for the greater stream flow during this period was the above-average rainfall of the decade beginning with 1860. According to Signal Service data, the average rainfall for the nine years ending in 1869 was 24.81 inches, with every indication that it had been on the upswing for many years before. The long-time average rainfall for Salt Lake City, as derived from recent Weather Bureau reports, is 16.3 inches. The unusually heavy rainfall of the period in question was reflected not only in the greater volume of stream flow but in lake levels. Since it is an enclosed and shallow body of water, the level of Great Salt Lake is determined by the relation between evaporation and inflow. A succession of years of below-average rainfall causes a progressive fall in the lake, while a series of years of above-average rainfall results in a rise.

By 1870 it was found that the lake level was higher than it had been in the beginning days of settlement. Springs which had been used and mapped by Stansbury in 1851 were then under water. Important also as an indication was the more complete severing of islands from the main shore line. Antelope and Stansbury islands, which were originally accessible from the shore and had been used for herding, were now cut off by relatively deep water. Gilbert estimated that the area of Great Salt Lake in 1850 was 1,820 square miles and that in 1869 it was 2,125 square miles, an increase of 17 per cent. It should be added that during the years since 1870 similar long-period fluctuations in the lake have been observed.

The San Pitch-Sevier oases. If the Wasatch Range is " the eastern guard and parent of the Salt Lake Oasis," then the San Pitch-Sevier oases are the gift of the High Plateaus of southern Utah.

The Sevier River originates near the present Arizona line, with headwaters in the Paunsaugunt Plateau, where a lofty divide separates the drainage of the Colorado River from that of the Great Basin. Flowing northward for a distance of about 170 miles, the Sevier suddenly breaks through the Pavant Range, one of the mountain blocks of the Great Basin, and then turns southwest and empties into the salty Sevier Lake. Thus the Paunsaugunt Plateau furnishes much of the water which irrigates the lower lands. As described by C. E. Dutton, the canyon walls of the upper Sevier are

. . . crowned with vast precipices, 10, 20, and even 40 miles in length, which look down from snowy altitudes upon the broad and almost torrid expanses below. If the palisades of the Hudson had ten times their present altitudes and five or six times their present length, and if they had been battered, notched, and crumbled by an unequal erosion, they would offer much the same appearance as that presented by the wall of the Sevier Plateau which fronts the main valley of the Sevier.

Said Ebenezer Bryce, who gave his name to famous Bryce Canyon in the Sevier Plateau, " It's a terrible place to lose a cow in."

It was in this spectacular setting that Mormon settlements were established shortly after the founding of Salt Lake City. The chief limitation was that of water supply; there was more land suitable for irrigation than was naturally provided with the means for it, a shortcoming partially offset in more recent times by the storing of water in Sevier Reservoir, Sanpete County. Perhaps even more important in early-day settlement was the valley of the San Pitch, a tributary of the Sevier entering from the north. By 1870 more than 20,000 acres were under cultivation in the San Pitch Oasis, which was already known as the wheat-growing section of Utah. Despite losses from locust invasions from 1866 to 1868, the growing of apples and peaches was becoming increasingly important here, as it was elsewhere in the Territory.

MINING DEVELOPMENTS IN NEVADA

Among the widely scattered Mormon settlements, which always sought areas made " fit for residence " by living water, none were to have so unexpected an evolution as those at the base of the Sierra Nevada near present-day Carson City. A trading post (Beatie's) was established here in 1851, the beginning center for a communal development which, within a half-dozen years, gathered about it nearly 1,000 persons. Franktown, Genoa City, and Eagle Valley were the names of the Mormon communities; the two first-named can be located on a modern map near Lake Tahoe in the wide angle formed by Nevada's western boundary.

This was a likely place for trading and farming communities. Not only did the High Sierras provide water for irrigation, but the settlements lay on a natural route across the Great Basin from Salt Lake into the upper Sacramento or, alternatively, into the San Joaquin. The passes across the divide, such as Donner, Salmon Trout, and Walker, averaged about 7,000 feet in altitude but were less than half that above the Great Basin. No less important was the Humboldt River, whose course across the dry basin was mainly east-west, the presumed direction of travel and trade.

Frémont's belief that the Humboldt (earlier known as the Mary's or Ogden's River) presented qualities which " may give it both value and fame " was soon to be borne out. Only along its winding course could water and grass be found for a continuous journey of over 300 miles. The river also offered an easy-to-follow route across a country studded with numerous isolated mountains, among which opportunities for becoming lost were very great. In the words of the official wagon-road report delivered to the Congress in 1859:

The successive mountain ranges that extend from the rim of the Great Basin towards its centre are perforated by this river, thus making it a natural and easy road. Nearly the whole length of the stream is a fine, grassy bottom, whose rich alluvium invites the agriculturist and stock-grower, after a proper survey and assurances of protection from the Indians. It is well understood that the principal requirements of our emigrant road to California are water and grass; therefore, for large cattle trains, the occasional springs and patches of bunch grass in the mountains cannot be depended upon.

Emigrants unfamiliar with desert country were warned to prevent the animals from drinking the water in standing pools and to keep close to the Humboldt, which would lead them surely, if somewhat circuitously, in the desired direction. This greatest of Nevada rivers provided a link between the Mormon settlements on the eastern and western rims of the Great Basin, and was the main line for emigrant travel.

The Comstock Ledge and Virginia City. The Sierra outposts of Mormon colonization had scarcely been founded before prospectors searching for precious metal drifted across the mountains from the upper Sacramento. Placering yielded good returns, sufficient to encourage search for the mother lodes. They were found in 1859, high up on the mountainside, a great ledge that was soon traced for 3 miles, with a depth that was then incalculable.

Northeast of Carson City, and almost within sight of the neighboring Mormon communities, the Comstock Ledge, as it came to be known, began yielding its fabulous wealth. It was a black ore, saved at first for its gold, but soon mined principally for the silver it contained. The magnitude of operations here dwarfed that of other camps. Gould and Curry burrowed into the ledge to a depth of 600 feet along a $\frac{1}{4}$-mile front, excavating a million cubic feet of rock in a year. For the first six years the Gould and Curry take was reportedly $2,000,000 a year. The Ophir mine, another mammoth enterprise, rivaled that of the Savage Company, financed mainly by Californians, as were most of the Comstock mines.

Comstock ore was free-milling, requiring only crushing and amalgamation to yield a 60 per cent value, and for the first half-dozen years the ore was cheap to mine, lying near the surface. In 1865, there were more than 50 quartz mills noisily grinding Comstock ore; most of them were " custom mills," not company-owned, to which miners hauled their product. Many other quartz mills were already idle, representing as they did the period of speculation which blighted nearly every mining district. Overdevelopment and unsystematic workings here as elsewhere brought on a reaction which was particularly acute from 1865 to 1868. Depression settled over the mining towns. Many people concluded that the depression was a permanent one and pushed on to more inviting districts. Virginia City, the principal mining town, faithfully registered this depression in its shrinking population. From a high of perhaps 15,000 in 1863, Virginia City housed in 1868 not more than 10,000.

Appearances to the contrary, the great days of mining were just ahead. In 1873 the so-called Big Bonanza mine came into production, yielding $21,000,000 in value within twelve months. Production rose gradually to a reported $36,000,-000 in 1878, a memorable year, not only for the wealth raised to the surface, but because the Virginia City mines reached another stage in their meteoric career. Many of the tunnels were filling with water and yet, with surface ore dwindling fast, it was necessary to go deep into the ledge. The solution for the problem was believed to lie in a new master tunnel which would reach into deeper and presumably richer deposits, besides draining and uniting independent workings. This project took form in the Sutro Tunnel, which in 1882 struck an immense flow of hot water, driving mining operations once more to upper levels in worked-out veins. The final decline was then apparent except to the most optimistic, and the end was hastened by the repeal of the Silver Purchase Act.

In 1865, Virginia City was an exceptionally well-built mining city situated picturesquely along a mountain side "like the roof of a house, about half-way to the top." With Gold Hill, a separate town attached to it on the south, Virginia City was a big place of perhaps 15,000 persons, fully one-half the population of all of Nevada. By 1900 Virginia City-Gold Hill homes were mostly vacant, the mills in ruins, roads and streets in disrepair. The population of Nevada had similarly dwindled, reaching in 1900 its lowest figure of 42,335 — less than it had been thirty years before. This period of decline was brought to an end by new strikes in Tonopah and Goldfield, the discussion of which will not be attempted here.

Reese River ore, and Austin. The Reese River is one of the main southern tributaries of the Humboldt, but carries insufficient water to invite the irrigation of the many desert basins through which it flows. Austin, about midway of its length and located centrally in Nevada and the Great Basin, came into being as a mining town in 1863. (See Figs. 91, page 360, and 93, page 362.)

A typical boom town, Austin grew to a population of nearly 6,000 within two years; its houses were built, like those of Central City, anywhere and everywhere, and the streets were extended to reach them. The proved veins of the Austin belt extended for almost 5 miles, lying thick in "rotten quartz," a lean ore which at depth was compounded with sulphides. In the extraction of metal from Reese River quartz, stamp mills were commonly employed, each stamp in the batteries of 5 or 6 weighing about 500 pounds. Dropping at the rate of 60 times a minute, they crushed the quartz to a fine powder, which was then roasted and agitated over a flame for half a day. The next stage in extraction was that of amalgamation, accomplished in tubes or Freiburg barrels, about 75 pounds of quicksilver being allowed for each 1,000 pounds of pulp. Distillation of the amalgam yielded a product varying in value from $100 to $400 a ton.

Reese River ores were richer than those of Virginia City, but the supply was smaller and the mining costs greater, owing to the necessity of roasting the ore before amalgamation. Austin experienced alternating periods of growth and recession during the time of active mining, but after the richer ore was exhausted the decline was steady and inevitable. With no other basic industry for community support, Austin became, temporarily, a station on the Overland Mail Route. The transcontinental lines which were pushed across the Great Basin followed the route of the Humboldt, some 80 miles north of Austin.

SOUTHWESTERN INDIAN–LAND

The surveyors of the proposed southern railroad route to the Pacific estimated the total Indian population of New Mexico and Arizona in 1853 at less than 50,000. About half this number were village-living Indians concentrated in about 25 pueblos in New Mexico, the largest and westernmost of which was Zuñi. The Puebloans, said A. W. Whipple, "remain living in towns, irrigating and cultivating the soil, nearly in the same manner as was their custom previous to the period of the Spanish conquest." Their sedentary habits were considered the more remarkable because to the east and west of them were Indian groups of migratory habits. The eastern Apaches — "buffalo hunters" — were horse-riding Indians; by this time they were also raiders, their forays on pueblos alternating with depredations on wagon trains. The abandonment by 1840 of Pecos Pueblo, easternmost of the large villages of New Mexico and thus exposed to repeated attacks, has already been related (pages 80–81).

To the northwest of Zuñi, beyond the present New Mexico-Arizona boundary, was the homeland of the Navajo. Sometimes referred to as the Arabs or lords of the American Desert because they were seldom seen on foot, the Navajos had acquired an unenviable reputation among neighbors for their pillaging. After the establishment of Fort Defiance in 1852 on the eastern border of their land, the Navajos committed few depredations and turned to more peaceful ways of life. In 1857 they cultivated some 5,000 acres, and in the 15,000 square miles which they claimed, maintained sheep to the number of 200,000. In other respects, too, the brown-skinned Navajos were self-sufficing, for they wove blankets and other apparel, fashioned garments from buckskin, and made their own saddles and bits when these could not be obtained by less arduous means. For their 10,000 horses, nearly one per capita, they needed much equipment.

A third group of Indians, about 10,000 strong, inhabited the Gila River country, essentially the area acquired in the Gadsden Purchase from Mexico. These agricultural peoples included the Papago (4,000), the Pima (2,500), and the Coco-Maricopa (3,000?). Because they occupied a region of comparatively low altitude through which the projected railroad would very likely run, they were of special interest to the surveyors and other less-official travelers. The Gila River Indians were described as among the more highly civilized natives of the United States. Since their land was not particularly attractive to white people, their traditional ways of life had not been greatly altered.

The Indian groups thus identified — the Pueblos, the Navajos, and those of the Gila River — have been the subjects of extensive archaeological and anthropological study for a long period of time. Various "culture areas" have been outlined, occasionally with the definiteness required by a map, and different names have been applied to these areas. It may be helpful, by combining the recent work of A. L. Kroeber and Kirk Bryan, to recognize two spheres — the Puebloan and the Sonoran-Gila-Yuman. The Puebloan sphere, by far the larger in area, includes the true village-living Indians as well as the Inter-Puebloan, or transitional group, of which the Navajo is an example. The Sonoran-Gila-Yuman sphere to the southwest, sometimes called the Hohokam culture, was distinguished by a more mobile social organization, which was encouraged, in part, by a flora rich in edible plant foods. In the words of Bryan, " an individual or family was free to wander off and eke out a precarious but independent existence without complete reliance on farming or the aid of the farmer. The result was a social organization more diffuse than that of the Puebloan."

Both these realms were peripheral to the more highly civilized cultures of

Middle America. In this arid region of the Southwest, the natives had developed a more or less independent culture which utilized long-cultivated plants, supplemented by foods gathered or hunted in the surrounding country. To them, the land was far more friendly than it appeared to casual observers, who were likely to wonder, as did John W. Audubon in 1849, why any people lived in so desolate a land. As Bryan has recently pointed out, " One of the paradoxes of cultural development in the Old and New Worlds is the relatively high position of the early societies in arid lands."

Farming practices.   Agricultural methods of the Southwestern Indians had changed but little since the Colonial period (Chapter 5). Because of limited rainfall, planting fields were selected in situations which would be likely to receive water during flood stages or to which water could be directed in ditches. The practice of depending on natural floods to moisten the ground has been aptly called floodwater farming. It represents a step between dry farming — that is, the cultivating of crops in such manner as to conserve the limited rain that falls — and the art of irrigation, which implies systematic control of water.

In floodwater farming, the critical first step was the selection of a planting field at an arroyo mouth or along the flood plain. As explained by Herbert E. Gregory in his classic study of the Navajo country, the Indians came to know by experience or tradition the areas " liable to be flooded during occasional showers, as well as those annually inundated in July or August." Care was taken to choose a spot which would be flooded, but not to the extent of washing out the seeds or burying the crop under a heavy blanket of sediment. This was a precarious kind of farming, in which the Indian staked his shrewdness of observation and judgment against the vagaries of Nature. Perhaps the usual " thundershower floods " would not reach the selected field; or the annual inundation would be of unusual height and strength, sufficient to destroy the crop. In almost any flood plain of the Southwest, some sections would be eroded and others aggraded; a good deal of practical physiography was involved in the decision of what acre or two to select. As Gregory points out, " the portion of seeded ground remaining [at the end of the season] constitutes the irrigated field from which a crop is harvested."

By the erection of earthen dams, floodwater farmers often sought to direct the flow of water or to retard or prevent its runoff. Ridges a foot or two high were often sufficient to save a planted field from severe washing, while higher dams served to store water for the use of livestock. Since the dams were made of insubstantial material, it was necessary to renew them frequently.

Systematic irrigation, involving the layout of diversion ditches, was also practiced in the Southwest. This form of water control was most likely to be associated with perennial streams from which water could be taken when needed. Reports of Pima and Maricopa Indians show beyond a doubt that they were practicing fully developed irrigation in the 1850's, an art acquired possibly only a short time before. Their villages were along the Gila or its tributaries, westward of Tucson, which was then an adobe town of about 500 inhabitants, with a presidio (fort). Planting fields connected by canals with the Gila were used more permanently than were those which depended merely on floodwaters. As John R. Bartlett recorded in 1854, the bottom land occupied by these peoples extended for about 15 miles along the south bank of the Gila, a space 4 miles in width, " nearly the whole being occupied by their villages and cultivated fields . . . [and] the whole plain was intersected by irrigation canals from the Gila." For added protection from wandering stock, the permanently cultivated fields were usually fenced with stalks of the thorny mesquite, wattled with brush.

The agricultural methods of the Indians involved but slight disturbance of the soil. Planting of the common crops was simplicity itself: seeds were dropped into a hole punched into the alluvium with a sharp stick. To ensure protection from washing, as well as to provide for strong root systems, the holes were made several inches in depth. Simple tools came gradually into use as increasing contact was had with white men, but actual cultivation of the soil was a minor feature of Southwestern farming of that day. Light hoes were in use in 1854, and many of the Indians had wagons and carts which they had obtained from emigrants or salvaged from roadside dumps.

Farm products and their uses. *Zea mays,* the original multicolored corn of America, was the basic crop of the Southwest in the 1850's, just as it had been for untold generations before that time. Pink, blue, and white were the most common colors of the kernels, the blue variety being preferred for making the common bread. Some of the harvested corn was parched on stones or among coals before being eaten. The basis for more than one favorite dish was prepared by boiling the corn in a weak solution of limewater, then grinding it into a pulp; this was used for breadmaking, or mixed with chopped meat and dried for future use. A mixture of the pulp with pieces of meat and peppers, wrapped in soft cornhusks and boiled, produced a dish known as tamale. Some corn was combined with cactus-fruit syrup and fermented in deep holes in the ground, to form an intoxicating drink, the tiswin of the Apaches.

Wheat was introduced by the Spaniards into the country of the Pueblos at an unknown time in the past and was commonly grown by them as well as by Papago and Pima Indians. To a certain degree, wheat was a money crop among these peoples. Much was sold to traders and men of the Government, an official report stating that the million pounds of Indian-grown wheat produced in 1867 resulted in a " lively trade." The railroad surveyors passed through the Pima villages in February, 1853, finding corn, wheat, beans, and other foods, which the Indians " gladly traded for clothing." Wheat was ground in the primitive stone metate, or parched for added variety. Wheat flour mixed with the meal of mesquite beans yielded a food called pinole; this was also made into a gruel known as atole.

Beans and peppers were common crops of the Southwest. Also common were pumpkins, squashes, muskmelons, and watermelons; these were grown promiscuously in the same fields, and since they are allied by family, many hybrids were formed. Cotton was grown to some extent by the Pima and the Maricopa and possibly by other Indians. According to Philip St. George Cooke, who surveyed a military road through the Southwest in 1847:

They parch corn, wheat, etc., in a basket by throwing in live coals, and keep it in motion by throwing it into the air. They raise cotton, and spin and weave excellent blankets; their looms are rude and slow to work. They make good pumpkin molasses. They have plenty of horses which are in good order, and live on — what I cannot imagine, except dry-looking brush. I have seen only a bow or two and one or two guns amongst them all.

Other contemporary visitors casually remarked that some Indian villages had peaches of their own growing, and that quinces and pomegranates were occasionally to be found, possibly grown by Mexicans or mestizos.

Native plants for food and fiber. The Southwest Indian made full use of a flora rich in cacti, shrubby plants, vines, and coniferous trees which yielded a variety of fruits, seeds, berries, and leaves.

The various species occupied different habitats, and thus were not equally abundant in the same region. Perhaps the most varied and useful flora was the Sonoran, that of the more arid Southwest, which contributed to the less sedentary habits of the tribes inhabiting that area. In the Navajo country, with its greater range of altitude, five zones were recognized by Gregory as follows:

NAVAJO COUNTRY TREES

Zone	Trees	Altitude Range (in feet)
I	Cottonwood (alamo), cactus, yucca	3500–5000
II	Sagebrush and greasewood	5000–6000
III	Piñon pine and juniper	6000–7000
IV	Yellow pine	7000–8500
V	Engelmann spruce	8500–10,400

In the lowest and most accessible zone (I) various cactus fruits were picked according to the season and eaten fresh or cooked with other foods. One of the most important species was the famous giant or monumental cactus (*Coreus giganticus*) of the barren hills. Growing to heights of 50 feet, and recognizable by its deeply-ribbed trunk, the giant cactus bore a pear-shaped fruit which the Indians plucked with long sticks. The seedy pulp of the fruit was sometimes placed in soft inner husks of corn and exposed to the sun for preservation. A syrup made from this fruit, especially by the Papagoes, was sold in jugs of their own manufacture at prices varying from $2 to $5 a gallon. The smaller Thurber's cactus of the Papago country was used in similar ways. According to the Commissioner of Agriculture in 1870: " The Papago Indians, in transporting earthen vessels filled with syrup or preserves made of this fruit, cover their jars with a thick coating of mud, which renders them less liable to break in handling, and at the same time keeps the contents cool, and prevents evaporation, the crockery used being very porous."

The *Echinocactus Wislizeni,* more common in the higher plateau region of northern Arizona, was used in a different way. Sections of its thick stem often served as cooking-vessels, and its seeds, parched and pulverized, made a gruel or were mixed with other flours in breadmaking. The pulp of the fruit was rarely eaten in the villages, although travelers sometimes chewed it to quench thirst. A common sight along the roads and trails, it is said, was the punctured and discarded fruits of this cactus.

To this list of useful cacti may be added the prickly pear, and varieties of *Opuntia* which went under the common name " tuna." Great quantities of the latter's red-purplish fruit were dried and stored for winter; it was cooked with meat, or boiled to make a dish resembling applesauce. Tuna was probably cultivated for its fruit by both Indians and Mexicans; at least it was grown in hedgerows at Cucamonga, California, in the 1850's.

The mescal or American aloe (*Agave americana*) was a principal food article among the Indians from New Mexico to the Sonora. Its bulbous crown was cooked by a method resembling that of the New England clambake: heated stones were dropped into a pit, then the crowns were put in among layers of damp grass and tender agave leaves; over all was spread a thick coating of earth. After three days of baking, the product was a sweet, juicy food resembling the pear in taste. It was an article of trade eagerly bought by soldiers in the garrisons, not only because of its pleasant taste but also for its antiscorbutic properties. To make another favorite dish, the roasted heart and leaves were formed into thin cakes. But there were more uses for the agave than for food: the leaf was a substitute for tobacco; mescal spirit was made from the roasted heart by Papago and Apache; a black paint was made from the charred crown; and the leaves furnished a strong, coarse textile suitable for ropes and lariats. The Spanish bayonet (*Yucca baccata*) served also to produce a textile.

A close second to the mesquite, the utility of which has been discussed in Chapter 20, was the screw bean (*Prosopis pubescens*). Its pulverized beans, when mixed with water and kneaded, then baked in the sun, yielded a nutritious bread. The flour or meal was sometimes used for gruel, or made into a drink which it was said " was not to be refused by either red or white man." A molasses was also made from screw beans and this, in turn, entered the fermenting process from which tiswin emerged.

Least wild of the various native plants, since it was often grown in vineyards by the sedentary Puebloans, was the wild grape (*Vitis californica*). From the peculiar distribution of grapevines near ruined and abandoned pueblos, the railroad surveyors concluded that it had been cultivated for centuries before their arrival. Near Fort Whipple ancient vines were found, their arrangement in rows suggesting deliberate planting by some departed people. Among dense underbrush other vines were found, " different in many particulars from those native to the country." Large quantities of grapes were picked and consumed each year.

In altitudes above 6,000 feet, from the Pecos to the lower Colorado, the piñon (nut pine; *Pinus edulis*) was a common tree. The sweet and edible nuts of the small piñon tree became an article of trade throughout the Southwest. The berries of the local species of juniper, stored for winter use by the Indians, made a brownish-yellow flour. Poles of cedar and pine were used in various ways in the construction of the hogans, storage houses, and pueblos of the native people.

Variety in habitations. Greatest of the New Mexican pueblos of the 1850's was Zuñi, on a branch of the Little Colorado River (Fig. 135). Built in the usual setback style with three or four stories, Zuñi Pueblo had replaced earlier habitations whose ruins could be seen on the less accessible mesa top near by. Visitors were interested not only in Zuñi with its 1,500 or 2,000 inhabitants, but in Inscription Rock to the east of the village, on which were carved the names of early-day Spanish explorers. El Morro National Monument preserves this " mute but eloquent historian of the past."

The villages of the Pima and Maricopa, consisting of groups of from 20 to 50 inhabitants, were very unlike the substantial pueblos. A Maricopa dwelling was described thus by Cooke in 1847:

. . . rather above average in size and quality, [it was] 18 or 20 feet across, dug slightly below ground, only about five feet pitch inside, made of rank grass or reeds resting on props or cross-poles, and partially covered with earth; the door a simple hole about three feet high; the fire in the middle, the hole above very small; they are thus smoky and uncomfortable, and seemingly very ill suited to so warm a climate.

A slightly rounded roof was achieved by means of outside poles fixed to the ground and tied together at the top. The people lived out of doors much of the time, perhaps in the shade of a bower, which was usually festooned with gourd vines and, after harvesttime, with drying mesquite beans, ears of corn, and scarlet peppers. Cooking was also a common outdoor activity. Seen at a distance, a Maricopa village reminded Audubon of a collection of overlarge beehives not too well constructed. Storage bins, more carefully built than the houses, were symbols of a precarious life in which reserves of food were a stern necessity. The people gathered in winter in more compact communities on the higher lands, although their movements south of the Gila were limited by the Papagoes. The

135
Zuñi Pueblo during the buffalo dance, 1853. From Captain L. Sitgreaves, *Report of an Expedition Down the Zuñi and Colorado Rivers,* Doc. 59, 32nd Congress, 2nd Session, 1853.

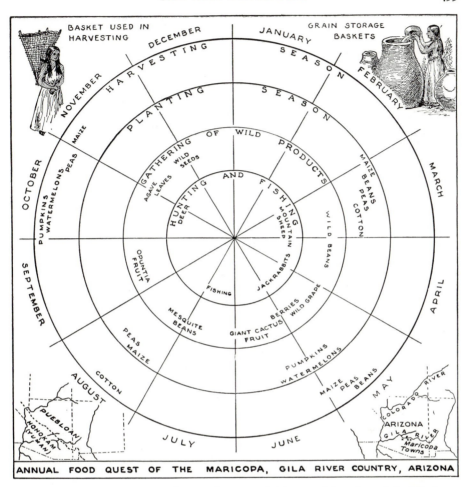

136   Annual cycle of food-gathering, hunting, fishing, and farming of the Maricopa Indians of southwestern Arizona

yearly round of activity among the Maricopa is suggested in diagrammatic form in Figure 136.

Surveyors and other visitors to the Gila River country speculated much on the origin of the Pima-Maricopa. Judging from outward appearances, they were much alike, and no sharp dividing line between their villages could be detected. They differed in language and in such customs as funeral rites, but both were evidently peace-loving. They were a friendly group, gathering quickly in large crowds at the approach of visitors.

Bartlett considered it probable that the Maricopa came to the middle Gila Valley about 1820 " from farther down on the Gila, where they were more exposed to attacks from the Yuma and Apache, which tribes, because of greater numbers, had nearly annihilated them." It was suggested that the Maricopa had drifted up from the Gila Bend for protection and alliance with the Pima (spelled Pimo in the 1850's), whose peaceful arts they adopted. Some modern students of the American Indian are in general agreement with this view. Leslie Spier, for example, believes that the Maricopa have lived on the Gila above Salt River junction since at least the year 1800, and that they may have moved upstream from the bend or slightly above. Among the Maricopa, says Spier, there is no tradition of having occupied the lower Colorado or the California area.

CHAPTER 27

Report on California:
I. San Francisco and Its Hinterland

Harper's Weekly in 1859 suggested that "perhaps the most significant, if not the most important event of the present century, connected with America, was the discovery of gold in California." Nearly a decade after the event, the furore created by it had subsided, though mining for the bright metal continued in unbelievably extensive deposits. While in 1848 scarcely 15,000 white persons lived in the land beyond the Sierras and south of Oregon, in 1857 there were a half-million Californians. Tent towns of gold-rush days had grown into substantial cities which marked an "astonishing progress of civilization."

Sacramento at the gateway to the gold region — a collection of shanties and tents in 1849 — was the promising capital of the new state. San Francisco, portal not merely to the mines but to all California, was much larger. Its population in 1857 was nearly 60,000, and no evidence remained of the tiny village of Yerba Buena which had preceded it on the same site. The effects of the gold rush had extended to all California cities and towns existent at the time — Monterey, Santa Barbara, Los Angeles, and San Diego, to mention but a few.

The markets created by the inrush of people from all corners of the nation stimulated agricultural settlement in the coastal valleys, such as the Napa and the Santa Clara, or San José. The Great Valley between the Coast Ranges and the Sierras, an area containing a few straggling Mexican ranchos in 1848, was also looked upon with favor after a decade of pardonable doubt. Some of the fortune-hunters who had come to California to prospect for minerals remained to enter the less spectacular business of farming; others drifted to likely mining regions and generated gold rushes into Colorado, Idaho, and Montana.

THE CALIFORNIA GOLD RUSH AND ITS CONSEQUENCES

In broad outline, the gold rush to California is a matter of common knowledge. The actual discovery occurred in January, 1848, when a few glittering particles were detected in the millrace at Sutter's Mill, now Coloma. The first effect of the news, in circulation a few weeks later, was to depopulate the towns and cities of California. For example, when Frémont reached San Francisco on June 20, 1848, he found that " all, or nearly all, its male inhabitants had gone to the mines. The town, which a few months before was so busy and thriving, was then almost deserted." Along Frémont's route to the diggings " mills were lying idle, fields of wheat were open to cattle and horses, houses vacant, and farms going to waste. At Sutter's there was more life and business. Launches were discharging cargoes at the river, and carts were hauling goods to the fort, where already were established several houses, a hotel, etc." This view of temporarily deserted towns and farms is confirmed by another traveler, E. Gould Buffum. Arriving at La Ciudad de los Angeles (The City of the Angels) in June, 1848, Buffum learned that in three days after hearing of gold discoveries " the city was deserted by its former inhabitants, departing with wagons laden with pans, crowbars, iron pots, shovels, etc."

By midsummer the sensational reports, repeated in newspapers with all manner of variations, had reached every section of the country. For a single example we may take the *Hartford* (Connecticut) *Daily Courant* of December 6, 1848, which said in an article entitled " The Gold Fever ":

The California gold fever is approaching its crisis. We are told that the new region that has just become a part of our possessions, is El Dorado after all. — Thither is now setting a tide that will not cease its flow until either untold wealth is amassed, or extended beggary is secured. By a sudden and accidental discovery, the ground is represented as one vast gold mine. — Gold is picked up in pure lumps, twenty-four carats fine. Soldiers are deserting their ranks, sailors their ships, and every body their employment, to speed to the region of the gold mines. In a moment, as it were, a desert country, that never deserved much notice from the world, has become the centre of universal attraction.

By land and sea to California.   Desert country or not, and distant though California was, people in all walks of life were on the move to the Sacramento. Large numbers, as many as 62,000 in 1854, went by land over routes which have been discussed elsewhere. Overland travel, suitable perhaps for land-seekers, was too slow for most fortune-hunters. Moreover, a crossing of the High Sierras in winter was a risky business. No meteorological stations were needed to prove that the Pacific slope of the Sierra Nevada received heavy snowfall. This was made familiar to the few who had read Frémont's reports and to the many who knew the tragic story of the Donner party, which attempted to cross the mountains in the winter of 1846. In summer, the best time for travel, emigrants were limited in the equipment they could carry, and even the novices knew that mining required at least some heavy machinery.

The alternative to an overland journey was a sea passage to California. It was a long, expensive, and perhaps perilous journey, but at least the emigrant could bring with him the physical equipment of civilization — furniture, printing presses, mining machinery, and small boats intended for use on the Sacramento River. Ocean craft of all kinds were pressed into service: side-wheel steamers, sailing brigs, and the newly perfected clipper ship. The usual sailing time from New York to San Francisco in 1850 was five months, obviously too slow for a race to gold mines. The clipper ship greatly reduced the time of travel, as is shown by the phenomenal coast-to-coast passage (1851) of the *Flying Cloud* around Cape Horn in eighty-nine days.

A shorter route was available by means of a double passage, with a land crossing at Panama or Nicaragua. By coincidence, the United States had in 1848 contracted with the Pacific Mail Steamship Company for the delivery of mail over the Panama route. Throngs of people sought the Isthmus route to California thus made available, or failing this, descended upon any likely stopping point for vessels on the Pacific coast. An idea of the importance of the Panama route may be gained from the notes of W. H. Emory, a member of the United States Boundary Commission, which met in California in 1849. The commissioners, like the gold-seekers, could reach their destination either by a long journey around Cape Horn or by the shorter one across the Isthmus. They chose the latter route, according to Emory, but

. . . it was with the greatest difficulty that passage to Chagres could be procured in the meanest craft. Every steamer and sailing vessel, without regard to sea-going qualities, that could be withdrawn from the regular channels, were put into commission. . . . Simultaneously with our arrival on the Isthmus, there was a precipitation upon it of all the odds and ends of the inhabitants of the Atlantic coast, South America, and Europe. It was estimated that as many as four thousand people were collected in Panama, awaiting transportation to California.

That these estimates were not exaggerated is indicated by other data. Professor John C. Parrish has found that on January 9, 1849, there were 450 impatient passengers on the Isthmus and by June 30, when a mail steamship arrived, there were hundreds more. He also states that on her voyage around Cape Horn in the winter of that year, the steamship *California* stopped at Callao, Peru, to take aboard as many as 75 passengers bound for San Francisco. Exorbitant rates were charged for passage on boats of only 10 or 15 tons capacity, some of which were wrecked before reaching the Golden Gate.

Busy San Francisco and the bay region. Ocean carriers bearing cargoes of people and their equipment to California converged principally on San Francisco Bay, one of the world's finest harbors. The bay, said Frémont in 1849,

. . . is not a mere indentation of the coast; it is a little sea to itself, connected with the ocean by a defensible gate, opening out between seventy and eighty miles to the right and left, upon a breadth ten or fifteen, deep enough for the largest ships, with bold shores suitable for towns and settlements, and fertile adjacent country for cultivation. The head of the bay is about forty miles from the sea, and there commences its connexion with the noble valleys of the San Joaquin and Sacramento.

Three bays rather than one formed this inland sea: Suisun Bay, which receives the waters of the interior rivers; San Pablo Bay to the north, and San Francisco Bay, which connects with the ocean through the mile-wide Golden Gate. (See Fig. 137.)

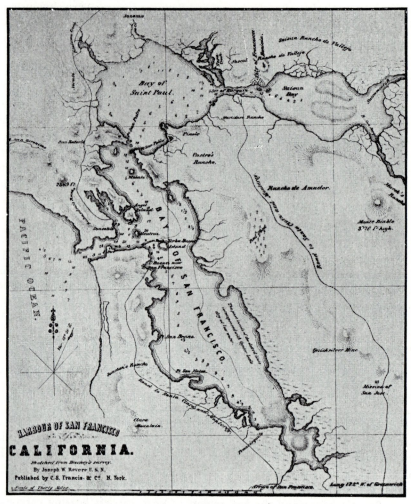

137   San Francisco and the bays as mapped at the time of the gold rush. From J. W.
Revere, *Tour of Duty,* New York, 1849.

On the hilly peninsula at the entrance to this series of bays was San Francisco,
with a population of 1,000 in 1848, 5,000 in 1849, and about 35,000 in 1850. Within
these few years the city was leveled by fire at least four times, only to suffer
another conflagration in May, 1851, when the business center of twenty blocks
was burned to the ground. After each disaster the city was rebuilt more solidly
than before, but it still presented in 1854 " a strange medley of buildings, from
the rudest hovel and canvas tent to the elegant mansion and the most substantial
warehouses." Lining the water front were local river boats as well as ships from
every quarter of the globe.

The bustle and confusion of San Francisco's streets, natural to a rapidly growing city, was increased by the "throng which moves to and fro from the city to the mines and the interior, and thence back again to the city." To one visitor with more than ordinary imagination, the gate city appeared "like an oriole balancing on the crest of his long pocket nest, peeking around the corner into the Pacific, but opening wide eyes north and south and east, and to the interior."

There are few reliable data on the extent of San Francisco's commerce during these early years, but a list of passenger arrivals and departures suggests that the " crisis " of the gold fever was reached about 1852.

PORT OF SAN FRANCISCO PASSENGER ARRIVALS AND DEPARTURES

	Arrivals	Departures
1849	91,415	
1850	36,462	
1851	27,182	
1852	66,988	22,946
1853	33,232	30,001
1854	47,531	23,508
1855	29,198	22,898
1856	28,119	22,747
1857	22,990	16,902
TOTALS	383,117	139,002

Sacramento was connected by waterway with the bay region, about 40 miles upstream from Contra Costa, as the coast opposite San Francisco was known. The capital-to-be grew to a canvas city of 1,000 inhabitants within three months, thriving on trade with the mining camps, and on the less tangible rumors of fabulous strikes. A very large proportion of the persons met with in Sacramento and the diggings were " in transitu," said a government report; upon inquiry it was usually learned that the place they had left was unproductive and they were bound for another, which they had *heard* was very rich; other parties were prospecting, or going to the " good diggings " they had heard of. Sacramento retained its position as distributing and outfitting center for the northern mines. Stockton, on the San Joaquin River, held a similar position with respect to the southern mines of Amador and Tuolumne counties.

Gold mining: Early phases. The diggings of '49 and '50 were some 50 miles east of Sacramento on the slopes and foothills of the Sierra Nevada. The principal rivers in whose deposits the diggings were first opened up may be traced on a modern map: American, Yuba, Cosumnes, and Mokelumne. Prospecting soon, however, embraced all the alluvial deposits of the San Joaquin and Sacramento rivers. Gold-bearing deposits were found to extend over a belt nearly 300 miles north and south and at depths varying from a thin veneer to 300 feet. Such quantities of alluvium ensured the continuation of placer-type mining for a great many years. Abundance of water favored the recovery of the gold known as " placer " — an Americanized Spanish-Mexican word originally pronounced " pla-thair'." Figure 138 shows mine locations at this time.

As in other gold-mining regions heretofore described, simple homemade methods sufficed for a brief period. Thus when Frémont surveyed the camps of the

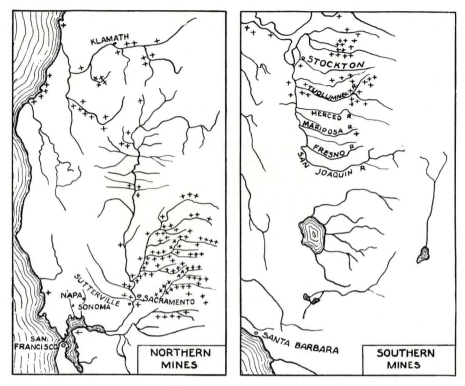

138   California mining camps, 1849–50

American River in 1849 he found the hillsides thickly strewn with canvas tents and bush arbors, with a few stores and the usual boardinghouses. About 200 men were at work at Mormon's Diggings, washing for gold in pans, cradles, and Indian-made baskets. According to Frémont's " moderate estimate " there were upward of 4,000 men digging for gold on the American River, with a daily yield of from $30,000 to $50,000.

The extent of workable deposits was so great that conflicts over claims were extremely rare. About one-half of the workers were Indians, and others of their race were commonly seen on the outskirts of the mining camps — " poor, miserable devils, dirty and half-clothed," said Audubon on his hasty tour of 1849. Shortly thereafter Chinese predominated in those diggings where simple panning methods were still adequate. Horace Greeley, who spent a week in the diggings of Eldorado, Placer, and Nevada counties in 1859, noticed that " every gully or ravine has been prospected, and have been dug to bed-rock," but did not see one white man engaged in pick-and-pan methods of gold recovery.

By 1860 most of the pickers-and-panners had drifted on to other regions in Idaho and Colorado, or had turned to other activities. Few indeed were the heavy nuggets described in Eastern newspapers. There was reasonable doubt that, by and large, gold mining paid common wages. Said a government report published in 1850, ". . . notwithstanding the disappointment of nine out of ten who came here, because of the large number of veins, diggers in the aggregate have produced much metal." Possibly from 50,000 to 80,000 persons had searched for gold by 1850; but " if only 10,000 had worked steadily for 300 days of every 600, and supposing each gathered an average of $3.00 per day, the aggregate would be $9,000,000, being very much more than the whole amount exported from California up to 1st December last, to all countries, Oregon included." Authorities emphasized the need of physical endurance for gold-seekers.

Hydraulic and lode mining. The California gold-mining region was the proving ground for mining methods that were later used, with necessary adaptations, in other mineralized regions of the West. The unusual depth of alluvial deposits in the California gold belt required the damming of rivers, or the sinking of shafts to reach bedrock, where pay dirt was often found. Such operations were called deep diggings or bedrock diggings. (See Fig. 139.)

Hydraulic mining, first used in California in 1852, permitted more rapid penetration to the deeper gold-bearing gravels than was possible by ordinary methods. As explained by one of its advocates, hydraulic mining washes away the deep overburden, " laying bare the more compact stone and rock, and loosens it from the bank. The strata containing gold may then be worked with the utmost efficiency and economy." Acceleration of the mining process, which was the essence of " hose-and-nozzle " methods, was reflected in a maximum gold output of $65,000,000 in 1853. The work of one man was multiplied ten or more times by the use of water under pressure, but this method required a large investment in aqueducts, pipes, and hose, and was thus unavailable to individual miners.

139 Mining operations in California. Courtesy of the Henry E. Huntington Library, from a unique original in E. Vischer, *Ein Ausflug nach der Californischen Minen-Region im Frühjahr, 1859.*

For example, one flume and aqueduct in the Tuolumne mining district was 70 miles long, required a year for its construction, and cost over $1,000,000.

Hydraulic mining was a destructive process. The waste water brought abnormal sediment loads into the rivers, causing many channels thus filled to be abandoned for new courses. The Sacramento River, said an eyewitness, became more muddy for its size than the Missouri. Thousands of fertile acres in the lower river valleys were ruined by the waste brought down from the hydraulic operations upstream. Ill feeling and outright antagonism developed between the farmers and the miners. An 1884 statute forbade hydraulic mining when in conflict with other interests, but by that time much damage had been done. In the view of the observant Samuel Bowles, a combination of tornado, flood, earthquake, and volcanic eruption could hardly have caused greater havoc than was to be seen anywhere in the path of the larger gold-washing operations.

During the 1860's, quartz mines were penetrating the mother lode, which had been traced for more than 60 miles, and other veins varying in width from a thread to 20 or 30 feet. Some of the more successful operations in hard-rock mining were in Grass Valley, Nevada County, and on the Frémont estate in Mariposa County. The stamp mill was one of several mining inventions of California that were later used with success in other gold regions.

Place names of the gold region. Place names in use during the quarter-century of active mining were a distinctive feature of this part of California. Only the major natural features, such as rivers, bore Spanish-Mexican names at the time of the gold rush, and the Indian nomenclature was difficult to pronounce even if it had been known. The miners were thus free to choose place names suited to new needs — American names of descriptive or homespun character, such as Quartzburg, Placerville, Placer County, Murphy's Diggings, Poor Man's Bar, Greenhorn Gulch, Grass Valley. A certain regard for the past is shown in the preservation of a few Indian names, such as Mokelumne; and of Mexican names, of which Amador and Mariposa may be taken as examples. In general, however, foreign names were unpopular, and if retained they were often translated: thus the Rio de los Americanos naturally became the American River. Professor Hallock F. Raup has found that in the more remote gold-mining districts of Trinity County, 83 per cent of the names were English-American, while in the more accessible Calaveras County the proportion was 77 per cent.

A great many of the gold-rush names were no more permanent than the camps or towns they identified. Only about 40 per cent of the original place names of the gold region are still current, often with changed spellings or renderings. Raup thus traces the successive forms of the present town of Murphys: Murphy's Diggings (1855), Murphy's Camp (1868), Murphy Camp (1888), Murphy (1897), and Murphys (1941). It is concluded that " in spite of the loss of many of the miners' earlier place names, enough remain in use today to lend a romantic atmosphere to the foothill and mountain areas of California and a distinction in its nomenclature." (See Fig. 140.)

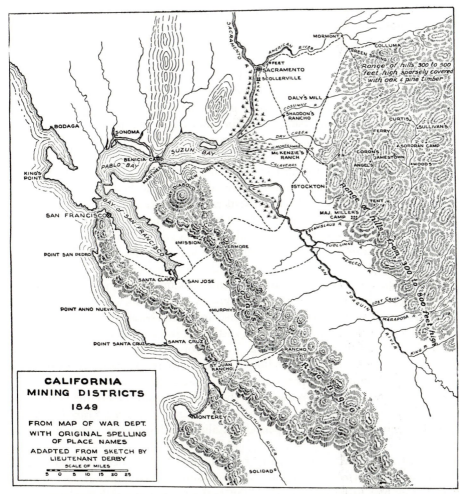

140   The gold region of California, from a map prepared by government surveyors
and explorers during the gold rush of 1849. The original map is in the Division
of Maps and Charts, the National Archives.

AGRICULTURAL DEVELOPMENT IN THE SACRAMENTO
VALLEY

Agriculture secured no permanent foothold in the Sacramento Valley until
years after the gold rush, this despite the high prices occasionally demanded for
food products in the near-by mining towns. It is well to say " occasionally demanded," because of short-period fluctuations in prices which registered the
fortunes of the miners and the abundance of staple products imported from
Oregon. It is reported, for example, that in March, 1848, flour in San Francisco

was selling for $5 a hundredweight; in December the price had risen to $200 in the mining camps. Such periods of inflation were often followed by sharp depressions, when products were disposed of as nearly worthless because of a glutted market.

For the slow growth of systematic farming in the Sacramento many reasons have been advanced. Two of the reasons may be inferred from the foregoing account: 1. Most of the adventurous people who came to the mining region had little if any farming background or interest. 2. The prospects of making a good strike made mining a relatively more attractive undertaking. Two other reasons, perhaps more fundamental and needing fuller explanation, are: (3) uncertainties of land titles arising from existent grants, and (4) the large extent of swamp and overflowed land in the lower Sacramento at the time.

Uncertain land titles as checks to settlement. A brief review of California's economy before its cession to the United States by Mexico is required to appreciate the delaying effect of existent land grants on new settlement.

One of the features of Mexican land policy had been the awarding of land to individuals and families as well as to the Church. Unfortunately for later developments — probably not foreseen at the time — many of the grants were loosely made, with indefinite boundaries. The grants were of varying sizes — at least so it appeared from later surveys — and the larger ones became ranches or ranchos mainly used for the raising of Spanish cattle and horses. Cattle-raising had long been the main activity of the Great Valley, of which the Sacramento is the northern part, with hides and tallow the chief exports. Distance from markets of course prevented the exportation of the more perishable products, although some meat was sold in the settlements and at the missions before the latter were disbanded. To those who have read the American classic *Two Years before the Mast* by Richard H. Dana, this period of California development should be clear enough.

When California became a part of the United States, there was no way of immediately confirming the grants. Time-consuming investigations of titles and boundaries had to be conducted. Many fictitious and fraudulent claims were made and, with increasing land values, grantees resorted to every means of delaying final settlement. The surveyors were often subjected to pressure to include the most valuable land that could possibly be interpreted as part of the original grant.

The results of the survey were not ready for publication, at least in map form, until September 15, 1860, when the General Land Office issued a magnificent map, of which Figure 141 is a greatly reduced version. Small though it is, the reproduced map suggests the extreme irregularities of the boundaries of the grants that were finally validated. The original map, it should be added, contains the names of the 340 grantees of as many parcels of land.

Clouded titles, many of them covering the more desirable agricultural land, delayed or prevented the normal settlement processes. The more cautious claimants, who seem to have been in the majority, preferred not to take up land and

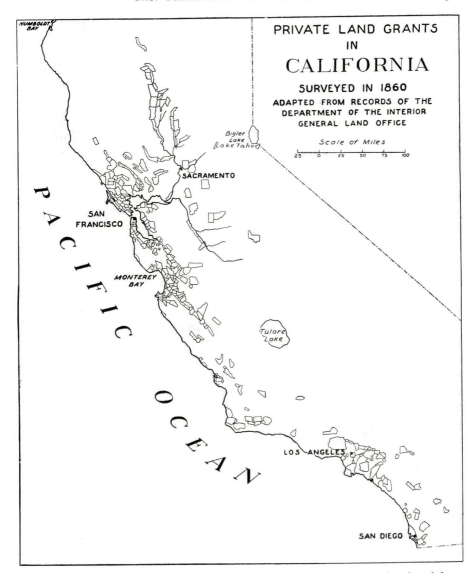

141   California land grants as finally surveyed in 1860. Adapted and reduced from an original Land Office map in the National Archives.

improve it, even if it lay beyond the assumed limits of valid grants. The Commissioner of Agriculture in 1866 estimated that these conditions " prevented the settlement of from five to twenty times the quantity of land that the terms of the grants call for." In the opinion of Horace Greeley in 1859, " Were the titles to land in California today as clear as in Ohio or Iowa, nothing could check the impetus with which California would bound forward in a career of unparalleled thrift and growth."

Tule marshes of the lower Sacramento. Of the 3,000,000 acres of swampland in California at the time of the gold rush, 500,000 lay about the lower Sacramento-San Joaquin rivers and Suisun Bay, an area early called the Delta of California. The ill-drained land went by the native name of " tule " or " tules " (two syllables), identifying the coarse, reedy grass which grew extensively in these as in similar soils elsewhere in the Great Valley.

To understand the tules of the delta, it is necessary to know that the lower Sacramento is a tidal river and that its bed has been elevated several feet above the flood plain. Tides working upstream from Suisun Bay caused periodic overflow of the lower lands. Salt-water tidal swamps thus developed around the bay and for some distance upstream; beyond these were equally extensive swamps inundated with fresh water. Above the tidal swamps, in turn, the tules were subject to seasonal floods from the combined effect of the melting snows of the Sierras and the winter rainfall typical of California. These floods became more severe with the development of hydraulic mining in the foothill tributaries. As an aggrading stream, the Sacramento flowed in a winding, island-strewn channel within natural levees elevated above the broad flood plain.

The term " natural levee " had not gained currency in 1872 when the Commissioner of Agriculture said: " According to recent geographical theory, the channels originally occupied the lowest points in the valleys. The annual overflows, by the deposit of sediment, gradually raised the immediate banks of the stream from 10 to 20 feet above the areas in their rear." Foothill streams, some of which do not reach the Sacramento during the dry summer season, constructed levees of their own. The lower Sacramento plain was thus virtually divided into a series of enclosed basins which were natural habitats for the reedy growths, as well as willows, live oaks, and vines. The Yolo Basin, on the west side of the Sacramento, may be cited as an example.

The dense stands of coarse grass added to the aggrading processes of the delta rivers. Their masses of roots and fibers tended to retard the flow of the sediment-carrying water, much as snow accumulates on the lee side of a fence. " For centuries past," it was said, " these tules have been burned off by the Indians in the dry season while in search of game, and the accretion formed by the roots mingled with the ashes, together with the deposits of soil carried down from the uplands, have gradually caused them to rise above the general level of the ordinary water-surface."

Beginnings of swamp reclamation and of rice culture. With a growing market near at hand and a climate favorable to the raising of varied products, early efforts were made to reclaim the tules by diking and ditching. Attention was first turned to the salt-water tidal lands near Suisun Bay, closest to the San Francisco market. Here the practice was to build dikes from 4 to 6 feet high; thus protected from flowage by salt water, the soil was gradually freshened by irrigation or by natural rainfall. Above the limit of salt water, dikes with self-regulating gates, not unlike those of South Carolina a century before, were constructed. Ditches supplied material for the dikes and aided in the drainage of the land. Manual labor during these earlier stages of reclamation was performed mainly by Chinese, but within a relatively few years ditching machinery was available. It is reported that many errors were made during the early days of the project, with dikes so unwisely placed that they forced water onto land not formerly subject to overflow. The work of reclaiming the river swamps above the tidal limit was not begun until the 1880's. Thus was opened on a small scale a project of reclamation which, under different auspices, has continued to the present time.

Rice cultivation in the Delta region commenced in the early 1870's, several years after the Commissioner of Agriculture had noted the suitability of the soil and the water supply for this crop. There was, moreover, a good market for rice, 20,000,000 pounds of which were imported to Pacific-coast ports in 1865. A Chinese population of some 60,000 was an additional inducement to its production. In 1872 " promising experiments " in rice culture initiated the growth of this crop, which has become of great importance.

Extension of agriculture in the Sacramento Valley. The Delta region, with its poorly drained soils, forms only a small part of the Sacramento Valley. With an area comparable in size to Maryland and Delaware combined, the valley between the Coast Ranges and the Sierras offered a wide field for agricultural development.

By the 1870's enough was known about the climate to permit intelligent experimentation with crops. Although warmer for its latitude than a corresponding position on the Atlantic coast, the Sacramento Valley experienced occasional low temperatures in winter which were thought to prohibit citrus-fruit culture. Two seasons, a wet and a dry, were recognized here, with the rainy season coinciding with the winter months. So great a departure from the climate of the Midwest and East, said the Commissioner of Agriculture, subjected " the culture of the soil to novel conditions, unsettling old traditions, and defying some of the most tenaciously held lessons of experience in the older parts of the country." No wonder, then, that farming was slow to advance in northern California, the more so because rainfall records compiled by 1874 showed wide departures from year to year. The extremes for several stations are listed below.

CALIFORNIA RAINFALL DATA, 1874

	Driest Year (in inches)	Rainiest Year (in inches)	Length of Record (in years)
Sacramento Valley			
Fort Reading	15.9	37.4	3
Sacramento	11.2	27.5	17
Benicia	11.8	20.0	12
Other stations			
Stockton	11.6	20.3	3
Monterey	8.2	21.6	5
San Diego	6.9	13.4	12
Fort Tejon (near pass)	9.8	34.2	5
Fort Millerton (in the Sierras)	9.7	49.3	

Offsetting the dry season of summer was the possibility of irrigation, particularly on the east side of the valley. " The great storehouse of moisture is the Sierra Nevada," it was said; the lower Coast Ranges also furnished a supply of water. Irrigation facilities would not only extend the growing season but would offer insurance against droughts such as occurred from 1868 to 1871. During these years, little rain fell during the normally moist winter months, a disaster to farmer and stock-raiser alike.

Despite the drought years, farming extended into the better soils of the Sacramento Valley, the chief crop being wheat, which could be planted in the winter and harvested in the dry summer; moreover, the grain could be exported to distant markets. This crop was grown on farms averaging 400 acres, although some holdings were of immense size. For example, one ranch on the west bank of the Sacramento had 50,000 acres under cultivation in 1880. Barley also became an important crop in this as in other California valleys. This grain was widely used as feed for draft animals and particularly for the pack trains which operated over long distances in California and the interior before the railroad era. " The extent of this business can hardly be realized by persons who have not seen it," said the Commissioner of Agriculture in 1866, " but they can form some idea when it is known that some of the routes traversed are from 500 to 1,000 miles long, and grain feed for animals must be carried almost the entire distance."

COASTAL VALLEYS OF THE BAY REGION

The coastal valleys contiguous to San Francisco Bay were of little interest to the thousands who streamed into Golden Gate bound for the mining region 200 miles inland. The valleys of the Napa, the Russian River (Santa Rosa), and the Santa Clara — in early days more commonly known as the San José — contained no precious metals so far as was known. There were, of course, the old missions of Santa Clara, San José, and Solano, which had been established by the Spanish-Mexicans three-fourths of a century before. And there were also the private land grants beyond the missions, nearly covering the floors of these narrow trenches between mountain ranges such as the Vaca, the Diablo, and the Santa Cruz. The grants were obstacles to new settlement, the more so when incomers set up claims of their own. In view of the confusion of land titles, a visitor in 1854 was led to the humorous remark that " for many years to come, the lawyers will doubtless derive the largest income."

The earlier period of occupancy had not been without its long-time benefits, however. Years of practical experience had shown the suitability of the wine grape and of prune plums and other tree crops to the coastal valleys. Frémont and others recognized the valleys as among the " most fruitful parts of California," productive of wheat and other cereals as well as fruits of both temperate and semitropical climates. About the then decadent mission of San José were vineyards and ancient fig and pear orchards. In 1849 the buildings of Santa Clara, in contrast with the " melancholy state " of the majority of the missions, were reported "in tolerable preservation," although its near-by gardens were neglected. The Indians for whose benefit the missionaries had labored were no longer here, having dispersed long before the mining people arrived. No "Christianos" were to be seen nearer than the mining camps.

Napa Valley: Sequence of settlement. Hemmed in by ranges of low, dark-hued mountains, the Napa Valley extends northward from San Pablo Bay for a distance of some 60 miles. A traveler going upriver from the bay in the early 1850's first met with unsightly tidal marshes, but beyond the village of Napa, up to which the river was then navigable, the 4-mile-wide valley presented a more attractive appearance. Wild oats covered the slopes of the enclosing hills; and the valley, said Bartlett in 1854,

. . . is now studded with gigantic oaks, some of them evergreen, although not so close together as to render it necessary to cut any away to prepare the land for cultivation. These magnificent oaks are found sometimes in long lines, and again in clusters of twenty or thirty, forming beautiful groves, and then again a space of ten or twenty acres will occur without a single tree. . . . It answers to the idea one has of the old and highly cultivated parks of England.

Although the Napa Valley was not the site of a mission, there were many evidences of its long-continued settlement. The absence of young trees and undergrowth among the full-grown oaks was attributed to years of grazing and repeated fires during the Spanish period of occupancy, and especially to burnings during the quarter-century of neglect following the secularization of the missions (see Chapter 5). A few orchards of pear and peach and an occasional old vineyard near the head of the valley also gave silent evidence of the earlier settlement period.

New settlement had only just begun in the Napa in 1854. Farms were spaced at intervals of about 5 miles along the main road, with buildings of the relatively poor and crude type to be expected in pioneer regions. The principal field crop was barley, capable of being raised without irrigation, and salable at good profits. Within the next few years development toward a horticultural economy was rapid, for in 1865 travelers made note of the many large and productive vineyards. The want of a steady market, said one, was all the Napa Valley suffered — a detriment soon to be corrected in the settlement of the surrounding area and the phenomenal growth of San Francisco.

Santa Clara (or San José) Valley. Extending more than 100 miles southward toward Monterey, the Santa Clara Valley resembled the Napa in its groves of spreading oaks, picturesquely disposed as if set out by a landscape gardener. Many visitors were reminded of the grassy plains of southeastern Texas, except that here rugged mountains limited the flat land on east and west. (See Fig. 140.)

Five miles from the bay was the old town of San José, approached by a tree-bordered road known as the Alameda. For a few months San José experienced a spurt of activity when it was tentatively chosen as the capital of the new state. Hotels and stores were hastily erected, but growth was immediately checked by announcement of the selection of Sacramento as the seat of government. At the time of the gold rush, several fine orchards and vineyards were attached to the vacant buildings of the Santa Clara mission, which was soon remodeled into a boys' school.

Few visitors expressed doubt that this fine valley would become one of the gardens of the state. By the 1860's wheat was the great crop, but orchards of plums and other fruits were being laid out — the beginning of the industry for which the Santa Clara is now widely known. At an early time, too, the valley experienced suburban development. In his visit of 1865, Bowles made note of many an " elegant country home which showed the overflow of San Francisco wealth."

Mining has been a distinguishing feature of Santa Clara Valley geography for nearly a century — not mining for gold but for quicksilver. The presence of outcroppings of cinnabar on the slopes of the Santa Cruz Range was a matter of common knowledge at the time of the Mexican War, and quicksilver was in production at least by 1849. The ore was known to the Indians, who used it as a source of vermilion pigment, but if the Spanish had worked the cinnabar, it must have been on a relatively small scale.

The mining village which developed in the vicinity of the ore became known as New Almaden, named for the town in Spain which until the development of the California mines was the world's chief source of quicksilver. New Almaden was a busy place in 1854. As described by Bartlett, the company-owned town embraced open-air furnaces — sheltered only by a roof because of the dangerous fumes — storehouses, shops, and dwellings for the 200 or more miners.

Cinnabar from the mountain outcrop was brought on muleback to the furnaces, which operated night and day owing to the demand for quicksilver in the mining camps. Vapors arising from the heated ore were precipitated in metal vats and the resulting quicksilver was prepared for shipment in iron flasks imported from England. The flasks, each containing 76 pounds of the mineral — the same unit as today — were transported by ox team to tidewater and from there shipped to San Francisco. Nearly 1,000,000 pounds of quicksilver were produced at New Almaden in 1854. The prediction commonly heard in the early days of mining camps that the ore was inexhaustible has in this case not yet proved to be false. New Almaden mines, continuously productive for nearly a century, experienced renewed activity during World War II.

Monterey, the Newport of San Francisco. Monterey, on Point Pinos overlooking broad Monterey Bay, was a pre-1848 rival of San Francisco. One of the older Spanish towns, Monterey became the capital when the Americans took possession of California, but this position was held only briefly. (See Fig. 142.) Naturally enough, the old presidio, built on a sightly point above the village, was taken over by Americans and was occupied by troops for many years following the annexation.

On the Carmel River, 4 miles from Monterey village, was the San Carlos mission, whose adobe buildings were tenantless and in partial ruin in 1854, when " not a human being was to be seen near, while the rank grass and weeds which

142   Monterey, selected as the capital at the time of the cession of California to the
United States. From J. W. Revere, *Tour of Duty,* New York, 1849.

monopolized the ground, showed that even curiosity did not often tempt visitors
to its deserted precincts." One corner of the church had begun to show the ravages
of time: its cornice had fallen and weeds had already taken root among its open
crevices. "The remains of an orchard and vineyard are still seen near, in a
decaying state . . . on the other side, the ocean rolls up its waves with a dull
monotonous sound, which adds to the solitary feeling of the place."

Monterey was the largest coastal town in California at the time of the annexation. During the Spanish period there had been some trade in cattle hides;
but its hinterland was restricted, and the harbor, exposed to winds and high
surf, was regarded as unsafe for large vessels. As a residential town, however,
Monterey afforded many advantages, and early visitors felt that in the future
it would bear the same relation to San Francisco that Newport did to New York:
a residential retreat for city people of wealth and quiet tastes.

CHAPTER 28

Report on California:
II. Southern Valleys and Sierras

THE maps of Frémont and contemporary surveyors were detailed enough to show that California's coast line between Monterey and San Diego was essentially harborless. They also showed a multitude of mountain ranges or sierras running parallel with the coast line, cutting off the interior from the sea. At only one point did a sizable lowland meet the coast, and that was opposite San Pedro Channel, as the roadstead formed by the Catalina Islands was and is known. Lest the observation lead to unwarranted optimism, the surveyors warned that this break in the coastal ramparts was far from the equivalent of San Francisco Bay. San Pedro was no harbor, only an anchorage where, in a favorable wind, coastal vessels could stop to discharge or take on cargo, or to obtain water and supplies. High surf driven by southerly winds forced vessels to seek the shelter of Catalina or induced them to proceed toward San Francisco through the Santa Barbara Channel. It was felt that Los Angeles, 20 miles from the coast, would remain an inland town with interests largely agricultural.

THE LOS ANGELES PLAIN

The Los Angeles Plain, in the restricted sense, is a triangular coastal lowland, bordered on the north by the Santa Monica Mountains and on the south by the Santa Anas. (See Fig. 143.) In a more general sense, however, the plain extends inland by way of embayments into and around the Coast Ranges, the Sierras of San Bernardino and Madre marking the interior limits. Through these mountain barriers, passes made the Los Angeles Plain accessible from the Mojave and Colorado deserts. Two passes, the Cajon and the San Gorgonio, were available for use during the prerailroad era. Both were relatively difficult passages even though the summit levels — 3,800 feet for Cajon and 2,500 for San Gorgonio — are not great. Cajon Pass is a breach in the San Bernardino and San Gabriel ranges; the ascent from the desert side is difficult, although the descent is quite gentle into the Los Angeles Plain. (Reference to Figure 145, page 523, will be useful here.)

Because of the ruggedness of the mountain country Cajon Pass was not greatly

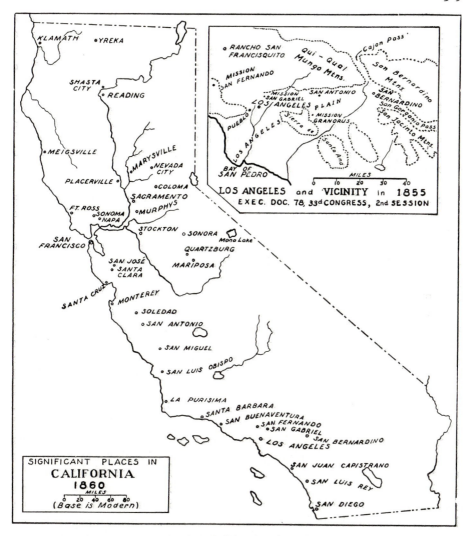

143   California, 1860

used, except by explorers and Indians, until the era of highway improvements
and of railroad extension. San Gorgonio Pass, though little used by wagon trains,
was thought by the surveyors to offer the better prospects for further development. It was relatively easy of ascent from both directions, but its eastern terminus
was reached through a valley in which water and other supplies were unavailable. For the purposes of a railroad, which would not be so dependent on roadside supplies as were the mule-drawn wagon trains, San Gorgonio Pass was
considered by the surveyors as " the best in the coast range."

The long-settled Los Angeles Plain presented a pleasant contrast to the desert
country east of the Sierras. " One of the finest agricultural regions in the state,"

so Bartlett described in 1854 the 80-mile stretch from Cajon Pass to San Pedro. Orchards and vineyards occupied much of the irrigated land (only a minute fraction of that available today); large haciendas and ranches extended toward the foothills. Grass and wild oats were abundant, said R. S. Williamson of the Pacific railroad survey:

> Nature has peculiarly favored this region, and has adapted it to grazing, by furnishing it with a succession of plants. The first crop is called pin-grass (*Erodium cicutarium*). . . . The next crop is of leguminous plants, such as medicago and several species of clover, which spring up one after another; then follow wild oats and other species of grass in great abundance.

In every direction " the eye fell upon large herds of cattle and horses luxuriating in the rich grass; so numerous were they that at any time there could not have been less than two thousand in sight."

Decadent missions and their contributions. The Los Angeles area was one of the principal theaters of Spanish settlement in California. Visible evidence of this activity were Los Angeles, which had started as a pueblo, and the near-by missions of San Juan Capistrano, San Gabriel, and San Fernando.

San Gabriel, 9 miles from Los Angeles, was " beautifully situated at the base of the mountains, surrounded by extensive gardens and vineyards," according to William P. Blake of the railroad survey party. This had been one of the richest of the missions, possessing in 1834 at the height of its development 105,000 head of cattle, 20,000 horses, and more than 40,000 sheep. Olives, oranges, and wine grapes were introduced at an early time, and each had been found well adapted to the environment. It is reported that 500 barrels of wine was an average yearly output of San Gabriel's vineyards. At least 3,000 Indians were attached to the mission before the secularization decree, and some of them were living in the vicinity in the early 1850's. A quarter-century of neglect was apparent in the overgrown orchards and the decaying mission walls. A visitor to San Gabriel in 1854 expressed the hope that the dilapidated mission would be " renovated, its broken walls be rebuilt, its roofless houses be covered, and its deserted halls be again filled with its ancient industrious, happy, and contented population."

San Fernando mission, in the valley of that name and similarly deserted in the 1850's, also gave evidence of the energy and enterprise of the founders. At the approach to the long arcade, the remains of a large fountain suggested to visitors something of the well-being of former days. Gardens within the crumbling walls contained groves of olive, lemon, and orange trees, an isolated spot of verdure in a desert plain. Figure 144 shows another of the missions, San Buenaventura, in 1846.

The contribution of the missions to California agriculture has been emphasized by all who have given thought and study to the subject. The suitability of several Mediterranean crops to the conditions of southern California was demonstrated through many years of growth and experimentation. Tracing the development of the raisin industry of the Fresno region, Professor Charles C. Colby points

144   Mission San Buenaventura as pictured in 1846 in *Life in California* [Alfred Davidson]

out that the Mediterranean type of grape was brought to San Diego mission in 1769 and from there its culture spread to other missions,

. . . and thus more than a century of pioneer cultivation preceded the development of the raisin industry. This was fortunate, because the Mediterranean grape is a highly specialized vine. Through centuries of careful cultivation it has been developed into an agricultural aristocrat demanding from the natural environment a combination of climate, water resources, and soil occurring in but few places in the world, and from the grower a thorough mastery of the practice and even the science of viticulture. . . . These able representatives of Mediterranean culture developed crops and practices which, after the gold rush of 1849, were capitalized by the ranchers who settled the state.

Los Angeles and its vineyards.   The town of Los Angeles experienced a better fate than did its mission neighbors. Five years after the gold rush, the town had grown to a population of about 5,000. It still presented the " sombre cast of a Spanish pueblo, relieved, as it were, by innovations of American comforts. There was the bustle and activity of a business place. Everywhere was indicated a thriving population and a land of intrinsic wealth."

The grape was of first importance in the agriculture of the environs of Los Angeles and the adjoining ranchos. Capable of being grown in naturally moist soil or requiring only light irrigations during the earlier years, the vine answered the needs of a region where water supplies were limited. Extensive vineyards contrasted with the barren fields roundabout, the fruit hanging in luxuriant purple, red, or pale-green clusters. Some vineyards contained as many as 25,000 vines in widely spaced rows. Close trimming produced a stem strong enough to provide support, for it was not customary to train the vines on framework or espaliers.

Until the development of the San Francisco market, most of the yield was turned into wine or brandy. In 1850, some 58,000 gallons of wine were produced in California, mostly in the Los Angeles region, thus exceeding the output of Indiana, where, the reader will recall, this industry had an earlier start under Swiss management. Some of the grapes were marketed fresh for table use, packed in redwood boxes of 60 pounds capacity. It may be inferred that this phase of the industry was profitable, for in 1853 grapes worth a few cents a pound at the vineyards sold in San Francisco for seven or eight times that figure.

EXAMPLES OF SOUTHERN CALIFORNIA SETTLEMENT

San Bernardino. Many of the early settlements in the Los Angeles region were made on the edges of the plain, near sources of water and wood in the mountains and in command of routes through them. Such a settlement was San Fernando on the piedmont slope of the San Gabriel Mountains and near Fremont Pass, an example from the Spanish period of occupancy. Fifty miles to the east of this ancient mission site is San Bernardino, occupying another corner of the plain, an alluvial-fan slope on the approach to Cajon Pass through the San Bernardinos. There was never a Spanish mission here, but a large, sprawling rancho occupied the site at the time of American settlement.

The selection of Rancho San Bernardino as the site of a civil community came about through planning by leaders of the Mormon Church in Salt Lake City. Envisioning the proposed State of Deseret, the Mormons' plans reached the Pacific in the Los Angeles region. It was thought desirable to establish on the route from Salt Lake City to the ocean port or ports a chain of settlements, each to become not only self-sufficient but capable of furnishing supplies for travelers and traders over the long desert miles. With this broad plan in mind, representatives of the Mormon Church were dispatched from Salt Lake City in January, 1850, to explore for likely settlement locations.

One of the sites selected by the Mormons was Rancho San Bernardino, on a main route across the southern mountain wall, and evidently well provided with irrigation water. Three streams, the Santa Ana River, Cajon Creek, and Lytle Creek, unite here to form the extensive alluvial fan of which the ranch and the present city occupy but a small portion. Irrigation had long been practiced before the period of American settlement, and it seemed evident to the locating party that the soil and climate, as well as the water supply, offered a secure foundation for agriculture. Apparently there was no knowledge of the abundant artesian water supplies on which local farming later came largely to depend. Nor could the locating party be expected to know that because of occasional freezes and unfavorable winds from the mountains, the orange would not thrive here as it did only a few miles away but nearer the coast. Such details were to

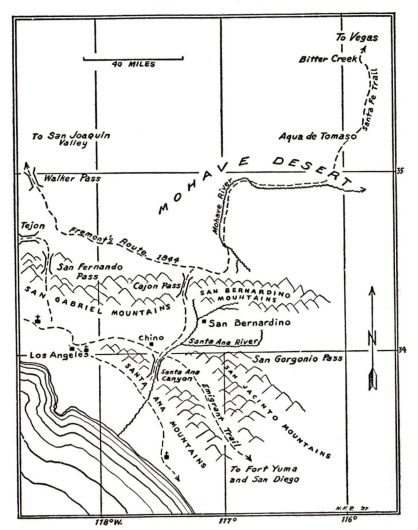

145 Southern California routes about 1851. Adapted from the official map of the state, 1854. Courtesy of H. F. Raup and the University of California Press.

be found out here, as in Utah, by the practical test of putting people on the land. The map (Fig. 145) shows San Bernardino and the surrounding area.

Resemblances between the chosen place and Salt Lake City were pointed out with the usual overemphasis by a member of the locating committee, who said, in part:

. . . in the rear we have the venerable snow-clad cap of the Sierra Nevada towering to the clouds; at the foot of which gush forth innumerable streams whose crystal waters can be dispersed throughout the city. . . . The site is upon an inclined plane at the foot of which for miles either way, extends a dense growth of willow, cottonwood, and sycamore, which affords an abundant supply of timber for fuel and fencing purposes. . . . Near the river we have our youthful vineyard of forty acres, which we purpose to increase to a more respectable size in time. . . . The hills as far as the eye can extend are covered with wild oats and mustard, and the valley with rich grass.

The Ranch Becomes a Mormon Colony. Setting out from Salt Lake City in March, 1851 (the more favorable season for travel across desert basins and mountains), the first contingent of Mormons reached the site in the following summer. They were greeted with unaccustomed warmth. Californians seem to have recognized the need for settlers on the land, and since the majority were themselves recent arrivals drawn from all parts of the country, if not of the world, they were the more inclined to view the newcomers with tolerance. Moreover, the Mormons had won a favorable reputation for industry and self-reliance. As viewed by a Los Angeles newspaper, these " wonderful people " had chosen the broad plains of southern California " for the triumphs of their skill and industry in agriculture." Their success in wresting the Salt Lake plain from the desert had already become an American classic.

With the dispatch which they had demonstrated in earlier ventures, the Mormon colonists set about converting the ranch lands into a community center. Temporary shelters of log and adobe were erected, and the work of surveying the land for cultivation promptly began. By January, 1852, a large wheat field had been planted and soon thereafter the first grapevines were brought in and transplanted; and plans were completed for the storage of crops and the erection of flour mills. Attention was then turned to the laying-out of the town, in which the general pattern of the earlier Mormon settlements in Utah was followed.

During the first two years the colonists learned by experience some of the hazards as well as the advantages of San Bernardino. The expected winter rains were delayed until December; when they arrived, water indeed " gushed forth from innumerable streams," but in a disastrous manner instead of that pleasantly pictured by the founders. The settlers also came to know the Santa Ana wind — the strong, drying blast which swept from the near-by desert down the Cajon Pass and then across the Los Angeles Plain. Some of the temporary dwellings were unroofed by a Santa Ana blow in the fall of 1851. This blow demonstrated not only the strength of the wind but also the inadequacy of the flimsy structures which then served as shelters.

The situation of San Bernardino on a major pass route exposed the colonists to danger from Indian attack, a menace from which California communities south of the gold region were, in general, immune. Friction developed between the new arrivals and the loosely organized Indians, numbering perhaps 1,500, who inhabited the mountain country. Apprehension of danger led to the erection of a blockhouse which gave a frontierlike appearance to the new community. " Among southern California settlements, San Bernardino was unique in its equipment for withstanding siege," says Professor Raup. " Certainly not the least of its uses was that of a fortified refuge in the event of attack. No other settlement could boast of a stockade for protection against Indians, although Anaheim, founded in 1857, erected a fence or hedge of willows to prevent destruction by herds of cattle."

Development of Agricultural and Forest Industries. When San Bernardino was visited by Blake of the railroad survey, the temporary dwellings had not yet been wholly replaced. " The city consists of an open square, surrounded by log houses and stout pickets, they having been obliged to bring their dwellings together in this way to be secure from the attacks of Indians." Beyond the town, however, new and neat buildings were " all over the valley "; the land was being brought rapidly under cultivation; a large flour mill was in operation and some of its product was being marketed in Los Angeles and San Pedro. " The valley is decked out with vineyards and cultivated fields," Blake continued. Above them rose the solid mass of the San Bernardinos, imposing enough to make one forget that from the other side the peaks were comparatively low hills.

By 1853 the settlers had extended their activities into the mountains where supplies of timber were available. Lumber companies were then in operation, and within a year thereafter 6 sawmills were feeding lumber to the valley settlement. The lumber industry soon became a winter occupation, complementing the summertime labor demands of the valley. The mills were kept busy until the late 1880's supplying local needs on a seasonal basis. However, forest resources in the San Bernardinos, now included in a national forest, were not extensive. The industry declined to such an extent, says Raup, that " for a quarter-century or more, no lumber of commercial importance has reached San Bernardino or Los Angeles from the San Bernardino mountains."

Disintegration of the Colony, and New Influences. The unity of action in the colony, which had evidently paid dividends, soon gave way to dissent and ill feeling, especially with the arrival of persons of other religious faiths. Many of the Mormons left San Bernardino in 1857 when a general call was issued for the return of members of the Mormon Church to Salt Lake City. The town became almost depopulated, and the end had come of the period of Mormon control.

Renewed growth came about 1870 with the accidental discovery of artesian water. With the multiplication of wells, new efforts were made to develop subtropical crops. Orchards of citrus fruits were set out over a period of a decade or more, but long-continued success was blocked by freezes, occasional snows, and cold or hot blasts from the mountains. The delicate balance of forces tipped in favor of viticulture, dairying, and general farming, eliminating the more sensitive tree crops except in protected sites.

Selection of Cajon Pass by the Santa Fe Railroad initiated another important phase of San Bernardino development. In more recent times than we have been considering, San Bernardino became known as a " railroad town," a main division point in southern California, the first sizable California city seen by tourists and others who enter the Los Angeles area from the Mojave Desert.

San Fernando. Railroads played the leading role in the modern development of San Fernando. Until the use of Fremont Pass by a main line of the Southern Pacific was assured, the San Fernando Valley retained the characteristics of a ranch country. Mission lands had passed into the ownership of Mexicans, whose cattle ranged over the valley floor and neighboring hills. As reported by Blake in 1853:

Herds of cattle were seen on parts of the broad plain, feeding on dried grass or the burrs of the California clover, which cover the ground in the latter part of the summer when all the grass has disappeared. This plain doubtless presents a beautifully green surface in the winter and early summer when watered by the rains. The road was bordered in some places by a low growth of shrubbery and cactaceae, which gave a peculiar aspect to the country. The distant ranges of mountains had a peculiar barren look.

There was plenty of grazing land in California; this particular " valley," however, differed from others in lying on a transmontane route. Exploratory and military expeditions had made use of the pass before the gold rush. After that event, emigrant parties in increasing numbers sought this way to the north. So considerable was the movement that a toll road was built over the pass and in 1858 this gave way to a stage route connecting St. Louis and San Francisco. For this new purpose it was found necessary to reduce the grade of the approaches and to lower the summit level by a deep cut. Nevertheless, efforts on the part of the Mexican landowners to develop a town site on their 117,000-acre estate were unavailing.

Anticipating a new era for San Fernando Valley once the railroad was in operation, a land company bought the northern half of the ranch for a reported sum of $115,000. This transaction led directly to the founding of the town of San Fernando near the site of the old mission town. Lots and farm land were placed on sale, but with other settlement opportunities available in the Los Angeles Plain there was no great rush to San Fernando. Settlement started on a modest scale, with the new town profiting from its position as a rail terminus during the three years of tunneling under the pass to complete the rail line. An enlivening activity during these formative years was the wagon-freighting business in lead, silver, and borax hauled over the pass from the Owens Lake district. But this business was lost to San Fernando when the railroad line was extended into the Mojave Desert, just as in more recent years great quantities of freight are hauled through the town rather than to it. Nevertheless, San Fernando gained materially from its pass site, the more so because heavy freight trains needed additional engines in the steep upgrade climb. The pusher service thus required gave San Fernando added importance as a rail station.

Agriculture had its beginnings in the valley long before even the most imaginative observer thought of steam locomotives puffing up the steep incline to Fremont Pass. At the time of the founding of the town, the two " gardens " of the mission, each containing 32 acres and irrigated by ditches and reservoirs constructed seventy years before, were in excellent condition. One garden contained

300 olive trees, 1,200 grapevines, and a large number of fig, pear, peach, walnut, almond, and pomegranate trees. The other garden held 7,000 grapevines and a similar assortment of olive and fruit trees. The first olive-oil refinery and soap factory were built in 1874 to process the olives secured from the old mission orchards. Continued agricultural extension was inevitable, not only through the efforts of the land company to dispose of their holdings, but also because of the valleys' evident proved suitability to Mediterranean-type products. Local water supplies from underground sources were found to be adequate. Its extending groves of olives, oranges, lemons, and deciduous fruits, and the green fields of vegetables, grain, and hay, made the San Fernando Valley a typical section of the Los Angeles Plain. With the completion of the Los Angeles aqueduct in 1913, bringing abundant water to the plain, the more modern development of agriculture began.

Anaheim: German home on the Ana. Like San Fernando, a number of southern-California settlements after 1850 grew out of land-selling schemes: Pomona, Santa Monica, and the many fancifully named suburbs of Los Angeles, which appeared first as blueprints of subdivisions. Here and there, however, were settlements which took original form as colony projects more or less centralized in authority, and thus had distinctive features during the early years of their growth.

A particularly striking instance of the colony project is Anaheim — remarkable not only because it followed closely the traditional steps of land settlement by organized groups elsewhere, but because the originators were Germans who, according to an oft-repeated generalization, were usually content to let other people do the pioneering. Anaheim, with a present-day population of some 12,000, lies 25 miles southeast of Los Angeles, 15 miles from the coast, on a small section of a gently sloping alluvial fan of the Santa Ana River. Before the gold rush and for many years thereafter, a large Mexican ranch known as Rancho San Juan Cajón de Santa Ana overspread much of the fan slope. The land was used mainly for cattle-grazing, but there were also some vineyards under the care of a Hanoverian German who was a member of the family holding title to the land.

Other Germans, emigrants from central and western Germany — possibly after temporary residence in other states in this country — were drawn to California by the prospects of gold mining. They shared the usual fates of gold-seekers of all nationalities: some were successful — indeed, were leaders in the development of hydraulic methods; others, not unnaturally, found themselves unfitted for the tough job of mining, or became dissatisfied with poor returns from their efforts.

Some of the latter group held meetings in San Francisco to decide upon a suitable line of future endeavor. The majority had farming backgrounds in their homeland or elsewhere, but not in regions with conditions similar to those met with in California. Only one of the Germans, evidently, had had previous experience in vineyard culture or wine-making. It appeared to the group that a profitable market was bound to develop in California — indeed had already developed, supplied mainly from Oregon, the west coast of South America, and the Eastern and Midwestern states. They took particular note of the wines being imported from great distances to the mining camps and boom towns.

Following the practice of other colonists, the German group sent a representative to southern California to prospect for a suitable site. Thus the two sides of this story converge: the locating party, favorably impressed with the vineyards on the lower Santa Ana River, recommended the purchase of 1,165 acres at a price of $2 an acre. The transaction completed, the community-owned land was systematically divided into 50 lots of 20 acres each and a smaller number of town lots. Irrigation canals were laid out; dams and weirs were constructed; a hedge was set out around the tract's boundaries; rude shelters were erected.

Even with all these improvements, Anaheim was no Hanover when the colonists came to their new home. It was probably with some dismay that the Germans who first arrived in 1858, as related by Professor Raup, " viewed the barren, sandy soil of Anaheim with its ditches, its inadequate willow fence, acres of tiny vine cuttings only slightly leafed out, and a few wooden shacks." The nearest center of trade, Los Angeles, was a day's journey away over roads dusty in summer and muddy in winter. Nevertheless, in the general opinion Anaheim had advantages for residence over the mining camps.

After a dozen years of unrecorded but doubtless patient experimentation with vineyard methods and wine-making, the Anaheim product won some repute on the market. The main route of outlet was by road, but some wine and other products were brought to a shallow harbor or landing for exportation. Occasional disasters befell Anaheim, particularly periods of drought and flood; and then in 1884 came the greatest calamity of all — the invasion of vine disease. Dead vines were torn out and burnt for fuel; investments in wineries were lost, and unemployment was widespread. By 1891, only 14 acres were in vineyard. Anaheim was no longer a German community; the foreign language had disappeared from general use, in fact had not been used in official records since 1871. Nevertheless, a community spirit prevailed in the face of the new catastrophe. Experiments made in new crops to replace the ruined vineyards were crowned by success in 1889, when Valencia oranges were found well suited to local conditions, as they were to other parts of southern California. The story of Anaheim after the introduction of the Valencia orange belongs to a modern geography.

THE GREAT VALLEY, SOUTHERN SECTION

The government surveyors of the gold-rush period would probably disapprove of the current tendency to apply the term Great Valley to all the lowland between the Sierra Nevada and the Coast Ranges in California. It is less a valley, they might say, than a longitudinal trough into which flow many streams, some to find their way out through the Sacramento and San Joaquin rivers, others to disappear in deposits of their own making or in enclosed basins which have no outlet to the sea. It is noteworthy that Frémont, who named the Great Basin, was less certain about the California lowland. Looking westward from the Sierra, said Frémont, "the main feature presented is the long, low, broad valley of the San Joaquin and Sacramento rivers — the two valleys forming one," the rivers together reaching the ocean through Suisun Bay. In a distant view, long dark lines of timber and tule outlined the streams, and the "bright spots" were the intervening plains.

The mountain-encircled trough extended southward for over 100 miles beyond the San Joaquin drainage. This was indeed a trough, the lowest points of which were occupied by swampy sloughs and sumps expanding and contracting with the yearly rainfall rhythm. They also shrank or enlarged over a longer cycle, for in some years the tule basins appeared as large, sparkling lakes, and in others as unsightly swamps or dry plains. They were fed by two main rivers, Kern and Kings, each comparable in size to the San Joaquin.

The basins of the south. The southern end of the so-called Great Valley is the drainage basin of Kern River, an area which has changed more through natural forces and human agencies than perhaps any other in California. When seen in 1849 by General Bennet Riley, the Kern Basin was "so barren as scarcely to afford subsistence for our animals, and can never be of much value for agricultural purposes." Aside from strips of natural pasture in soils permanently moistened by water seeping through the alluvial sands, there was evidently little arable land. The great handicap of this interior region was the lack of water for irrigation, although it was considered possible that artesian supplies could be developed from wells.

Kern River apparently could do no better than to form Buena Vista Lake, 10 miles long and 6 wide, and this seemed no great achievement. Of the lake, "Nothing can be considered more inappropriate than its name," said Lieutenant George Derby in 1852, "for no place can be imagined more forlorn and desolate of aspect." Droves of savage mosquitoes filled the hot summer air; reptiles, ground rats, and gophers darted about in the masses of tule — not a pleasant picture; nor is it applicable today, at least on the same scale.

The Tulare Basin, north of Buena Vista, was scarcely more attractive. To one person entering it from Tejon Pass in the summer of 1852, the basin's vegetation appeared "extremely sparse" except at the mouth of Kern River; here were swamps or ponds, or sloughs — their exact nature perhaps varying and uncertain — fed by water drained from the High Sierras. The deeper of the two main bodies of water was then known as Great Taché Lake; to the south of this was Ton Taché, which was "little more than a very extensive swamp, covering the plain for fifteen miles in width." Ton Taché, filled with sloughs and tule lakes, was seasonally variable in size, as could be inferred from the ridges of decayed weeds on the shore. There was much evidence that Ton Taché was gradually disappearing with the deposition of sediment and the encroachment of tule upon the sides.

Indian rancherias of the southern basins. Estimates of California's Indian population in the 1850's range from 45,000 to about 65,000. The larger figure was heard more commonly among people in the mining camps, who were probably inclined to overestimate the numbers of Indians. They had had some trouble with them, and many wandering bands were to be seen in the Sacramento and the northern mountains.

The Indian population appears to have decreased rapidly, not merely in imagination but in actuality, for contact with white men had brought new diseases. G. W. Barbour, who concluded treaties with Indian groups in California in 1852, has this to say of them: " They may be divided into three classes (which distinctions they themselves recognize), to wit: the Christian or Mission, Gentile, and Monos or Lost Tribes." Dispossessed of their former hunting and fishing grounds, the majority of the Indians had retreated to the interior valleys and the Sierra Nevada, where they maintained themselves largely on wild products and by means of occasional raids on wagon trains and settlements. Barbour states that the " whole number of Indians in San Joaquin and Tulare valleys, with whom treaties have been made, is about 25,000 to 30,000." The solution of California's Indian problem seemed to be to establish them on reservations or, to use the local term, rancherias. Most of the reservations were in the Tulare Basin and along the tributaries of the San Joaquin.

Slow agricultural settlement of the San Joaquin. That settlement was slow to spread into the southern part of the Great Valley is apparent from the general map of California for 1860 (Fig. 143, page 519). At that time there were no towns or cities beyond the coastal valleys and south of the mining areas of the San Joaquin.

Many factors combined to bring about this delay of settlement. Early reports, it has been noted, were quite unfavorable, sufficiently so to cause prospective land settlers to think twice before venturing into the interior. Unfavorable inferences could be drawn from the selection of sites of Indian reservations and the proposals to create others as necessity required — it was not very desirable land, probably, if such uses were contemplated. In the San Joaquin, as elsewhere, existent land grants proved an obstacle, but here it was a relatively minor one, since this interior country was peripheral to the main centers of Mexican colonization.

Professor Charles C. Colby has pointed out that progress of irrigation, on which white settlement depended, was handicapped by legal controversies and uncertainties. Two opposed legal rulings with respect to water prevailed in California. According to the common law or riparian doctrine, which was suitable to the more rainy parts of California, a landowner whose properties lay along a stream had a right to the unpolluted and undiminished flow of water through and past his land. Obviously, this doctrine prohibited the diversion of water for irrigation purposes. There also developed in California the " appropriation doctrine," which in essence recognized that the first person to use water for a beneficial purpose had a right to its continued use. This practice, which grew out of water

146
The Valley of the San Joaquin in the foothill belt
where the river leaves the
mountains and enters the
piedmont. The view over-
looks the site of old Fort
Millerton. Courtesy of
Charles C. Colby, from the
*Annals of the Association
of American Geographers,*
June 1924.

needs in the mining regions, was conducive to irrigation of the land. " California, therefore, from the very outset was saddled with irreconcilable laws in
regard to the utilization of its water resources," says Colby.

New surveys of water resources in the early 1870's tipped the scales in favor
of irrigation in the piedmont slope drained by the San Joaquin and Kings rivers.
These surveys took account of snow accumulation in the High Sierras, as well
as the underground water at shallow depths in the fan slope. (See Fig. 146.) Sum-
marizing many reports, the Commissioner of Agriculture in 1874 pointed out
that, contrary to earlier opinions, " The Great Valley is admirably adapted to
irrigation on the grandest scale. Its extreme length is about four hundred and
fifty miles, with an average breadth of fifty miles including the foothills."

The eastern declivity of the valley, it was observed, was twice as wide as the
western, the precipitation three or four times as great, and the valley was flanked
by a well-timbered mountain wall. The area susceptible of easy irrigation was
estimated at 7,650,000 acres, and by extension into the foothills this amount could
be increased to 12,000,000 acres. The many large tributary rivers, however, forbade the construction of a long line of canals. " The expense of bridging would
be enormous. The system in this part of the valley must, then, embrace numerous
short canals."

Modern irrigation in the Great Valley first developed in the Kings River and
Fresno districts, according to Colby. In this section there were fewer legal en-
tanglements than elsewhere, and a brief period of large-scale wheat farming in
unirrigated land had proved unsuccessful; the area was thus open to new development. A particular impetus to settlement in the Fresno district was the
selection of the area by colonies, " such as the Washington, Central, Fresno, and
Scandinavian colonies near Fresno," which divided their land " into small ranches
suitable to the intensive culture demanded by fruit growing. Moreover these
colonies provided the community of interest and the organized labor required
in building the irrigation dams and ditches."

After some experimentation, raisin grapes were found to be well adapted to
the Fresno district. Capable of thriving in a variety of soils, the deciduous grape

found here a winter climate cold enough to stimulate growth and yet lacking in severe freezes. The hot, dry summer was also found to have its advantages. Here was a favoring combination of intense sunlight, dry air, and moisture supplied by irrigation, which came very close to the ideal requirements of the vine. In a relatively few years the Fresno district advanced to first position in the output of raisins, and during the 1920's accounted for nearly one-half of the world's annual product. The principal development of the San Joaquin Valley, last of the lowlands of California to yield to settlement, is a matter of comparatively recent times and thus will not be summarized in these pages.

CHAPTER 29

Regional Settlement: A Panorama

A STUDY of the past geography of the United States is wide-ranging in time, space, and subject matter.

Inquiry into the Colonial period first draws attention to the closing years of the sixteenth century, when forces of expansionism among western-European people brought the shores of the new continent into their orbit. In the planting of colonies on the Atlantic seaboard, the British could draw but little from past experience. Overseas colonies were a new venture, especially in mid-latitude regions separated from the homeland by a wide and stormy sea across which the Gulf Stream set in an eastwardly course. It is true that the continents of North America and Europe are brought fairly close together in the Far North, especially if Iceland and Greenland be considered as steppingstones. Nevertheless, in terms of early-day transportation the agriculturally desirable part of the American Atlantic coast was remote from the British Isles and France.

On the western side of the American continent, the Pacific Ocean affords a less dangerous approach than that offered by the Atlantic. Both prevailing winds and ocean currents flow from Asia toward America, as Pacific-coast residents were unpleasantly reminded during World War II when Japanese bomb-carrying drift balloons descended in Oregon and California. The easier Pacific passage to America led Nathaniel Shaler to theorize that if the eastern shores of the Old World " had been occupied by an adventurous seafaring people sufficiently advanced in civilization to be impelled to great voyages, either from curiosity or from commercial ambition, this country would doubtless have been settled from that side, and Europe might have been discovered by America long before the Columbian time."

One is reminded, however, that a coasting voyage from China or Japan to our Pacific coast follows sterile peninsulas and islands for 5,000 miles. Oriental navigators would have been hardy indeed to have attempted such a voyage, supposing they knew of or suspected the existence of a continent subject to colonization, and would have arrived with inadequate supplies. Nor could ancient and primitive boats have supported a mass migration across a wind-swept ocean. Indeed, the increasing carrying capacity of ships played an important role in the founding of colonies during the opening years of the seventeenth century.

We need not speculate, however, on an America colonized from Oriental shores. The urge to expand came from Europeans, separated though they were from the desired lands by the inhospitable North Atlantic. The shock of colony-planting was measurably softened by two conditions only dimly realized at the time: (1) the general likenesses between Europe and America, and (2) the existence of native products and economic plants which helped to sustain the new settlements.

Similarities in climate enabled the transference to the New World of the ancestral products of the race. Rye, barley, and wheat, green vegetables, citrus and deciduous fruits, herbs for seasoning foods or for medicines, were found variously adapted or adaptable to New World conditions. America offered a wider range of climates and soils than did western Europe, encouraging the prompt importation of other food or commercial plants from various parts of the world. On some of these, such as rice and tobacco, the plantation economy developed. Leaf tobacco provided the earliest and most reliable basis for intercourse with the Old World.

The colonists levied upon a wide selection of native products, many of which were found to be allied botanically with species familiar to them in the homeland. Food plants were of immense importance; shortly medicinal herbs and commercial products were collected for home use or were prepared for trade. America had its own ancestral crop plants, headed by maize with its strong roots and long harvest period, which fitted it admirably for service as a frontier crop. The agricultural Indians of the East had cleared much land for gardening purposes, plots which often became the sites of white settlement, from Nova Scotia to Florida. It appears that the aboriginal contribution to colonization has been greatly underestimated.

The seaboard environment was originally deficient in some desirable resources. The absence of native grasses suitable for pasturage retarded the development of the grazing industry and delayed the rearing of livestock in a manner comparable with that of the homelands. Deterioration of cattle imported from Britain, the Netherlands, and Sweden was characteristic of the opening decades of the Colonial period, a situation not corrected until tame pastures replaced the tough and reedy growths native to the land. The North American Indian was not a herdsman; indeed he possessed no domestic animals save the dog until the Spanish introduced horses into Florida and the West. America as a whole was deficient in native animals capable of domestication for draft purposes. The largest of the native beasts, the bison, resisted subjugation to the will of man.

The Atlantic seaboard as a whole was less well adapted to frontier agriculture than interior regions proved to be at later times. The stony and hilly soils of New England tested the patience and industry of the Northern farmer, while the thin and sandy soils of the southern Coastal Plain proved easily exhaustible under the " robber economy " of the Southern planter. But to all rules there are exceptions. Area for area, there were no regions agriculturally superior to the Annapolis Valley of Nova Scotia, the Connecticut Valley of New England, the Narragansett country, or the Piedmont lowlands of eastern Pennsylvania.

The early colonists showed but little originality in their settlement forms. The English town and village was reproduced, with some variations, in New England, and property lines were run in metes and bounds in a confusing manner. The institution of common land influenced settlement to such an extent that it is still observable in many towns and cities of New England. Throughout the Midwest are villages of the New England type, usually in areas settled by emigrants from the Northeastern states. The Connecticut Reserve of Ohio contains many of them, while Princeton, Illinois, is a New England town in a prairie setting. The French displayed a strong preference for riparian landholdings (côtes). This distinctive feature has been observed in the St. Lawrence Valley, along the Detroit River, and in the central Mississippi Basin. Different still was the Spanish-Mexican settlement type, which emphasized the plaza and the landed estate.

One of the first policy-making acts of the United States as a country dealt with land surveys and property division. It was ordered that seven ranges of congressional townships be laid out in eastern Ohio according to systematic procedures. An ingenious solution to the problem of disposing of public lands, the "township and range" survey plan was extended, with minor variations, to all public-land states, and was also adopted by western Canada. Settlers came to think of farm properties in terms of sections, half-sections, quarter-sections, and "forties"; the rural pattern assumed angular characteristics; roads followed section lines, often in defiance of topographic conditions. In framing public-land laws, sectional divisions played leading roles, well displayed in the original Homestead Act permitting entry of 160 acres for a family farm. The rectangular survey was introduced into many regions for which it was ill suited. In the High Plains region, for example, the artificial boundaries of the survey often interfered with the maximum use of grazing land by depriving it of water supplies otherwise available. Recommendations that such lands be surveyed according to natural conditions were unavailing.

Soon after the formation of the Union, the United States became a power at sea. Ships based at Northern ports regularly visited the markets of Europe, Africa, and the Orient, pioneering new trade lanes under able leadership. The time was propitious for an American seaborne trade, and resources for shipbuilding were at hand. With nearly all of Europe at war, the United States as a neutral nation profited from an active carrying trade. But this epoch proved short-lived, for the United States became involved in difficulties with the warring countries, climaxed by the Embargo Acts, and the War of 1812 to 1814.

These upsetting or disastrous events led to the investment of capital in other directions. Manufacturing industries developed in the Eastern states, and new energies were unleashed for Western settlement. Until the introduction of steam-powered craft on the inland waterways and later on the Great Lakes, the Territory Northwest of the Ohio River remained comparatively unsettled. The new method of transportation made that region more accessible and permitted the marketing of its products in the East and the South. The region was also made more accessible to emigrants, not only from the older states but from European countries. When the first steamboat went down the Ohio in 1811, barely a million people lived in the trans-Appalachian country; within two decades their numbers were four times as great. " The settlement of the Mississippi Valley," said Shaler, " is the first instance in history of the reduction of a wilderness in a single lifetime."

The central trough of the continent was the experimental ground for many types of settlement. There were at first the ambitious land-company projects, illustrated by the operations of the Ohio Company of Associates, the Scioto Company, and the Connecticut Land Company. There were also the colony schemes, formally or informally organized, some communistic or socialistic, others depending more on national allegiance. Various centers of Welsh, Swiss, English, and German nationals grew out of colony projects, which were often viewed askance by earlier residents in the same areas.

" The people of this valley," said Timothy Flint of the Ohio-Mississippi country in 1832, " are as thorough a combination and mixture of the people of all nations, characters, language, conditions, and opinions as can well be imagined. Scarcely a State in the Union or a nation of Europe but what has furnished us immigrants." During the ensuing decades, Midwestern states made special efforts to attract foreign-born as well as " native " immigrants and in this actively competed with each other. Such efforts reached culminating points in Wisconsin and Minnesota, whose legislatures appropriated funds for distributing advertising matter in foreign languages under the direction of Boards of Immigration. At least one foreign country, Germany, envisioned an American state in which the German language, industries, and customs would become predominant. To this end German emigration societies were formed, such as those noted in Texas. From the evidence presented in various parts of this study it should no longer be considered safe to conclude that the German emigrants in this country settled well in the rear of the pioneer fringe. With remarkable frequency German settlers were found on the frontier, and doing very well.

From the Atlantic to the borders of the arid region, the advancing frontier of settlement may be traced on maps with some degree of accuracy. Beyond the 100th-meridian region a frontier line becomes fictitious, for settlement clung to travel lanes or appeared as islands in favored localities. In the West, travel routes assumed an even greater significance than they had in the humid East. This is shown by the rapidity with which ordinary trails became roads for emigrant travel or for freight or mail delivery, and then railroads of transcontinental importance.

An arid region was new to the experience of emigrants from the East and northern Europe. Irrigation was unknown to them, although it had long been practiced by the Indians and the Spanish-Mexicans of the Southwest and California. Furthermore, public-land laws which had been framed for the humid Midwest had not been adapted to fit the conditions now encountered. Many years were to elapse before irrigation settlements won a foothold in the High

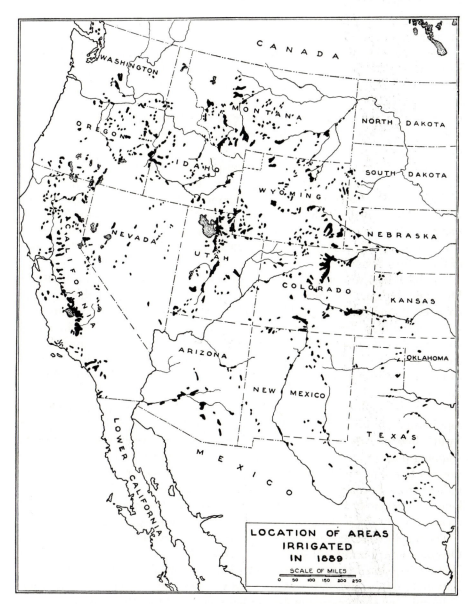

147 Irrigated areas of the western United States in 1889. From the *Census of the United States*, 1890, Plate 54.

Plains, and then it was in the piedmont regions of the Black Hills and the Rocky Mountains.

These schemes, promoted in part by railroad companies with land to sell, were the subjects of more optimistic reports than the actual facts warranted. Stories of the extraordinary yields of irrigated lands were widely circulated, and made more convincing by pictures of huge pumpkins, towering cornstalks, and enormous potatoes. It was pointed out that the Western soil was still rich, not having been " impoverished " by the " excessive rainfall " of the eastern part of the country.

Moreover, there were no anxieties about rainfall, sunshine was of daily occurrence, and weeds were practically unknown. The reader gathered that the life of the irrigation farmer was a round of pleasure and that success was guaranteed. Enthusiasm reached a high point in the publication of a book entitled *The Conquest of Arid America,* in which different chapters bore such lyrical titles as " The Blessing of Aridity," " The Miracle of Irrigation," and " The Better Half of the United States."

The Mormons were the first to demonstrate irrigation practice in the Rocky Mountain region. This was an organized effort, paralleled in the 1870's by colonies in the Colorado piedmont. Thereafter, irrigation developments were swift and widespread. Settlers on their own initiative or organized into stock companies placed large acreages under the ditch, with results shown on the irrigation map of 1889 (Fig. 147). An up-to-date map appears little different from this one except for the Federal projects that have been introduced in the present century.

The cattle-grazing industry of Texas and the High Plains passed through a rapid evolution. Following the War between the States, Texas became the great " cattle hive of America." Millions of longhorns were driven northward to rail shipping points; others were delivered to the Northern Plains for stocking purposes or to military posts and Indian agencies for butchering. But the open-range industry soon became livestock ranching supplemented by agriculture. National land laws generally favored the farmer over the stockman in this region which seemed to have been designed by Nature primarily for grazing purposes.

The mobility of the American people was well shown in the occupation of the Oregon country and California. The people who settled Oregon, as Professor Webb has pointed out, were seeking a land climatically similar to the humid East in its ample rainfall. It was gold and silver that drew people to Nevada and California, but the greater number of them remained for other reasons.

Many observers felt that the American people had done so well in the settling of a continent that it was to be regretted that no new lands were open to them. The withdrawal of the Russians from Alaska signalized the final step in the clearing-away of other than kindred people from North America. The United States was already a great country. In crossing it from ocean to ocean in the days when journeys were more leisurely than now, the traveler's wonder grew at the extent of the Republic and the unmistakable homogeneity of its people.

Bibliography

BOOKS FOR FURTHER READING,

AND CITATIONS TO SOURCES

W HEN this book was in its developmental stages, certain danger signals indicated that its context might become buried under a mass of *ibid.'s* and *op. cit.'s*, not to mention a number of other conventional insignia of the conscientious research worker. To avert this danger, it was finally decided to eliminate all footnotes and to confine a representative bibliography within a few pages at the end of the main text, where it would presumably disturb the smallest number of readers. In a further effort to reduce reader-annoyance, abbreviations have been avoided or used sparingly, even though their use would have permitted a greater number of citations. For example, *Sen. Ex. Doc. 47, 31 Cong., 1 Sess. (Ser. 558)* becomes *Senate Exec. Doc. 47, 31st Congress, 1st Session (Serial No. 558)*. The serial number is an added convenience, often omitted from citations to early congressional documents. It is all the information usually required on the call slip presented to the librarian.

The lists headed " Brief Notes on the Sources " fulfill some of the professional obligations an author assumes in venturing along a new route in the social sciences. The notes suggest the general range of source material which has been consulted. Citations are sufficiently explicit to permit the verification of data or the validity of conclusions drawn from them. The notes also show the extent to which the author has borrowed material from secondary writings, especially those published within the past quarter-century. More than this, they are keys to further research in the past geography of America.

In the briefer lists headed " References for Further Reading," the aim has been to refer to books on related themes likely to be found in even the smaller college or city libraries. Consequently, references are made to publications of the past few years, even though earlier ones might prove to be more important for a study of past geographical conditions. Many books equally good and available do not appear in these lists merely because of limitations of space. Most of the works referred to will suggest further profitable lines of inquiry, leading to the assurance that there is no shortage of literature touching upon the American past.

CHAPTER 1: Early Geography, Fact and Fancy

REFERENCES FOR FURTHER READING

Verner W. Crane, " The Promotion Literature of Georgia," in *Bibliographical Essays; A Tribute to Wilberforce Eames,* Yale University Press, 1924, pp. 281–98; also published separately by Harvard University Press, 1925

Fulmer Mood, " The English Geographers and the Anglo-American Frontier in the Seventeenth Century," in *University of California Publications in Geography,* Vol. 6 (1944), pp. 362–96

Lawrence C. Wroth, " The Maryland Colonization Tracts," in *Essays Offered to Herbert Putnam,* Yale University Press, 1929

CHAPTER 2: Taking Possession of the Land

REFERENCES FOR FURTHER READING

Charles M. Andrews, *Our Earliest Colonial Settlements,* New York University Press, 1933

Percy W. Bidwell and John I. Falconer, *History of Agriculture in the Northern United States,* Carnegie Institution of Washington, Publication No. 358, 1925

Jacques Cartier, *The Voyages of . . . Cartier, Published from the Originals with Translations, Notes, and Appendices,* ed. by H. P. Biggar, Publications of the Public Archives of Canada, No. 11, Ottawa, 1924

Samuel de Champlain, *Works,* ed. by H. P. Biggar, 6 vols., Champlain Society, Toronto, 1922

Ellsworth Huntington, *The Red Man's Continent: A Chronicle of Aboriginal America,* Yale University Press, 1919, Chap. 5 (Vol. I of the Chronicles of America Series)

Edna Kenton, *The Indians of North America,* 2 vols., Harcourt, Brace, 1927; and *The Jesuit Relations and Allied Documents,* 2 vols., Boni, 1925

Carl O. Sauer, " The Settlement of the Humid East," in U.S. Department of Agriculture, *Yearbook: Climate and Man,* 1941, pp. 157–66

Thomas J. Wertenbaker, *The Planters of Colonial Virginia,* Princeton University Press, 1922

BRIEF NOTES ON THE SOURCES (*Pages in bold-face type*)

7 Many explorers recognized the general similarities of western Europe and eastern North America, but perhaps the first American writer to stress their significance in colonization was Nathaniel S. Shaler in *The United States of America,* 3 vols., Appleton, 1894, Vol. I, pp. 23–30. A recent authoritative discussion of this theme is that of Carl O. Sauer, noted above.

8 The quotation beginning " Our transported Cattell . . ." is taken from a promotional pamphlet of 1610, reprinted in Vol. 3 of Peter Force, ed., *Tracts and Other Papers,* 4 vols., Washington, 1836–46. A contraction of the page-long title of this tract is: *A True Declaration of the Estate of the Colonie of Virginia.* References to New England by John Smith are from his *A Description of New England,* 1616; reprinted in Force, *Tracts,* Vol. 2. Possibly more readily available is *The Works of Captain John Smith,* Edward Arbor, Birmingham, 1884.

10 Champlain's conjecture as to the climate of the northeast coast is in Champlain, *Works*, Vol. I, pp. 329–30. This portion was translated by W. F. Ganong. The opening lines of Cartier's report are from *The Voyages of Jacques Cartier*, pp. 90–91.

10–11 The quotation referring to early unsuccessful attempts to occupy St. Croix is from Kenton, *The Indians of North America*, Vol. I, *Pierre Biard's Relation of New France, of Its Lands, Nature of the Country, and of Its Inhabitants*, Paris, 1616, pp. 28–47. The quotation from Fathers Paul Le Jeune and Jean Brébeuf is in the " Relation of What Occurred in New France in the Year 1635," *ibid.*, pp. 211–32.

11–12 Fuller estimates of aboriginal population can be found in James Mooney, *The Aboriginal Population of America North of Mexico*, Smithsonian Miscellaneous Collections, Vol. 80, No. 7 (1928); and Herbert J. Spinden, " The Population of Ancient America," *Geographical Review*, Vol. 18 (1928), pp. 641–60. Charles C. Willoughby in his *Antiquities of the New England Indians*, Peabody Museum, 1935, says in part (p. 282): " We are apt to picture the country when first seen by Europeans as thickly covered with primeval forests, and as having few open spaces and fields. This was probably true of the more remote uninhabited sections but does not apply to all tribal lands, especially those in the southern half of New England."

12 The Strachey description comes from his *History of Travails into Virginia Britannia* as quoted in David I. Bushnell, Jr., *Native Villages and Village Sites East of the Mississippi*, Smithsonian Institution, Bureau of American Ethnology, *Bulletin* 69, Washington, 1919, pp. 32–33.

13 Bidwell and Falconer give some attention to forest openings in their *History of Agriculture*, pp. 6–7.

Champlain's description of the Massachusetts coast is in his *Works*, Vol. I, Bk. I, p. 401.

15 Higginson's account is from his *New England's Plantation, or a Short and True Description of the Commodities and Discommodities of That Country*, Force, *Tracts*, Vol. 1.

17 This portion of the Champlain narrative is in his *Works*, Vol. II, pp. 77–93.

19 Indian clearings in Virginia are fully discussed by Hu Maxwell in " The Use and Abuse of Forests by the Virginia Indians," *William and Mary College Quarterly Historical Magazine*, Vol. 19 (1910), pp. 73–103; and more generally by Philip A. Bruce in *Economic History of Virginia*, P. Smith, New York, 1896.

CHAPTER 3: Making the Land and Sea Productive

REFERENCES FOR FURTHER READING

Percy W. Bidwell and John I. Falconer, *History of Agriculture in the Northern United States*, Carnegie Institution of Washington, Publication No. 358, 1925

Nicolas Denys, *Description, Geographical and Historical, of the Coasts of North America, with the Natural History of the Country* [1672], ed. and trans. by William F. Ganong, Champlain Society, Toronto, 1908

Lewis C. Gray, *History of Agriculture in the Southern United States to 1860*, 2 vols., Carnegie Institution of Washington, Publication No. 430, 1933, Vol. 1

Marc Lescarbot, *The History of New France*, ed. and trans. by W. L. Grant, 3 vols., Champlain Society, Toronto, 1911

Ralph G. Lounsbury, *The British Fisheries at Newfoundland, 1634–1762*, Yale University Press, 1934

Joseph Schafer, *The Social History of American Agriculture*, Macmillan, 1936

BRIEF NOTES ON THE SOURCES

24-25 This discussion of the fisheries is based mainly on Denys, *Description,* pp. 257–348, and Lounsbury, *British Fisheries,* supplemented by a number of studies, including Harold A. Innis, " The Rise and Fall of the Spanish Fishery in Newfoundland," *Transactions of the Royal Society of Canada,* Vol. 25 (1931), Sec. 2, pp. 51–70.

27-29 The description of Cape Breton in 1672 is from Denys, *Description,* pp. 182–87.

The section on Sable Island is a condensation derived from Champlain, *Works,* Vol. I, p. 225, and " Sable Island, Its History and Phenomena," by George Paterson, *Transactions of the Royal Society of Canada,* Vol. 12 (1894), Sec. 2, pp. 3–49.

29-31 The introduction of European crops and livestock to America is well summarized in Bidwell and Falconer's *History of Agriculture,* and in Gray's. The early *Reports of the Commissioner of Agriculture,* of which the present-day *Yearbook* is a lineal descendant, also contain numerous items. Particularly significant is " History of Agriculture of the United States," by Ben: Perley Poore, in the Commissioner's *Report* for 1866, pp. 498–527; and " A Hundred Years' Progress " by Charles L. Flint in the *Report* for 1872, pp. 274–304. The table of grasses introduced into England is from the Flint study, p. 277. The beginnings of agriculture in Canada are outlined by R. M. Saunders, " The First Introduction of European Plants and Animals in Canada," *Canadian Historical Review,* Vol. 16 (1935), pp. 388–406.

31-33 The section on the Narragansett country is a condensation of several studies, including Edward Channing, " The Narragansett Planters," in *Johns Hopkins University Studies in Historical and Political Science,* 1886, pp. 105–27; William G. Miller in *Proceedings of the American Antiquarian Society,* n.s., Vol. 43 (1933), pp. 49–115; and also in *State of Rhode Island and Providence Plantations at the End of the Century,* ed. by Edward Field, 2 vols., Mason Publishing Co., Boston, 1902, Vol. 1.

35 The quotation from Schoepf is from Johann David Schoepf, *Travels in the Confederation (1783–1784),* ed. and trans. by A. J. Morrison, 2 vols., W. J. Campbell, Philadelphia, 1911, Vol. 1, p. 45.

36 Accounts of the introduction of cotton are found in *De Bow's Review,* Vol. 1 (1846), pp. 289–300; and letters of W. W. Parrott and Thomas Spaulding in *Proceedings of the Massachusetts Historical Society,* 1855–58, pp. 221–25.

36-37 For a careful inquiry into the early history of rice in America see A. S. Salley, *The Introduction of Rice Culture into South Carolina, Bulletin of the Historical Commission of South Carolina,* No. 6, 1919.

38 The quotation from Oglethorpe is taken from *A Brief Account of the Establishment of the Colony of Georgia under General James Oglethorpe, February 1, 1733,* Force, *Tracts,* Vol. 1.

39 Among many references to the introduction and early cultivation of indigo is " The Culture of Indigo," *De Bow's Review,* Vol. 8 (1850), p. 495.

40-41 The section on sugar cane in Louisiana derives from Poore's paper (noted above) of 1866, pp. 510–11.

41-42 The Kaskaskia settlement is traced by John Reynolds, " Early Agricultural History of Illinois," *Report of the Commissioner of Agriculture,* 1857–58, pp. 130–33.

CHAPTER 4: French and English Settlements

REFERENCES FOR FURTHER READING

Carl Bridenbaugh, *Cities in the Wilderness*, Ronald Press Company, 1938
Charles C. Crittenden, *The Commerce of North Carolina, 1763–1789*, Yale University Press, 1936
Herman R. Friis, *A Series of Population Maps of the Colonies and the United States, 1625–1790*, Mimeographed Publication No. 3, American Geographical Society, 1940
Lewis C. Gray, *History of Agriculture in the Southern United States to 1860*, 2 vols., Carnegie Institution of Washington, Publication No. 430, 1933; Vol. I
Daniel Cobb Harvey, *The French Regime in Prince Edward Island*, Yale University Press, 1926
Joseph Schafer, *The Social History of American Agriculture*, Macmillan, 1936
Stella H. Sutherland, *Population Distribution in Colonial America*, Columbia University Press, 1936

BRIEF NOTES ON THE SOURCES

45-46 A contemporary source for Prince Edward Island is that of John Stewart, *An Account of Prince Edward Island*, London, 1806. In addition to D. C. Harvey's work cited above, one can refer to his shorter article in *Landmark*, Vol. 18 (1936), pp. 161–68. Population data for the island are given by Thomas Pichon in his *Genuine Letters and Memoirs . . . of Cape Breton and Saint John*, London, 1760.

47-48 The description of Isle d'Orléans is taken in part from Marius Barbeau, "An Early French Settlement on the St. Lawrence," *Bulletin of the Geographical Society of Philadelphia*, Vol. 30 (1932), p. 81.

48-49 The discussion of the seigniories comes in part from W. B. Munro, ed., *Documents Relating to the Seigniorial Tenure in Canada, 1598–1854*, Champlain Society, Toronto, 1908; and William Smith, *History of Canada*, 2 vols., Quebec, 1815. Ellen C. Semple, discussed the landholdings of the St. Lawrence in her paper "The Influence of Geographical Environment in the Lower St. Lawrence," *Bulletin of the American Geographical Society*, Vol. 36 (1904), pp. 449–66.

50 Population-growth curves as shown in Figure 12 come from Franklin B. Dexter, "Estimates of Population in the American Colonies," *Proceedings of the American Antiquarian Society*, n.s., Vol. 5 (1887–88), pp. 22–50.

54 The series of generalized population maps in Figure 14 is adapted from the detailed dot maps accompanying the article by Herman R. Friis, "A Series of Population Maps of the Colonies and the United States, 1625–1790," *Geographical Review*, Vol. 30 (1940), pp. 463–70. The maps of Figure 14 differ from those of Mr. Friis in that they do not show varying densities of population within the settled area.

54-55 The Londonderry description comes from *Old South Leaflets*, Vols. 1–9, Old South Meeting House, Boston; No. 93, Vol. 4.

55-56 Connecticut Valley towns have been discussed by Charles M. Andrews, "The River Towns of Connecticut," in *Johns Hopkins Studies in History and Political Science*, 1889; and by Martha K. Genthe, "The Valley Towns of Connecticut," *Bulletin of the American Geographical Society*, Vol. 39 (1907), pp. 513–44. The most recent interpretation of New England town patterns is that of Edna Scofield [Stone], "The Origin of Settlement Patterns in Rural New England," *Geographical Review*, Vol. 30 (1940), pp. 463–70.

58   The baronies of South Carolina are discussed at length by Henry A. M. Smith in *South Carolina Historical and Genealogical Magazine,* Vols. 11 (1910), 12 (1911), and 14 (1913).

61–63   Talcott Williams, in " The Surroundings and Site of Raleigh's Colony," *Annual Report of the American Historical Association,* 1895, pp. 47–61, presents much material on the North Carolina coast of this period.

65   Azilia is described by Charles C. Jones, *The History of Georgia,* 2 vols., Houghton Mifflin, 1883, Vol. 1, pp. 73–75; and in *American Colonial Tracts,* 2 vols., A. P. Humphrey, Rochester, 1897–98, Vol. I, 28 pp.; map opp. p. 10.

The quotation from the 1742 pamphlet is from Force, *Tracts,* Vol. 1, *An Account Shewing the Progress of the Colony of Georgia in America from Its First Settlement.* For an evaluation of the Georgia tracts see Verner W. Crane, *The Promotion Literature of Georgia,* Harvard University Press, 1925, or his *The Southern Frontier, 1670 to 1732,* Duke University Press, 1928, Chap. 12, " The Board of Trade and Southern Colonization," and Chap. 13, " The Philanthropists and the Genesis of Georgia."

CHAPTER 5: Spanish Settlement in Florida and the Far West

REFERENCES FOR FURTHER READING

Verne E. Chatelaine, *The Defenses of Spanish Florida, 1565–1763,* Carnegie Institu-
tion of Washington, Publication No. 511, 1941
Carita D. Corse, *The Key to the Golden Islands,* University of North Carolina Press,
1931
Le Roy R. Hafen and Carl C. Rister, *Western America: The Exploration, Settlement,
and Development of the Region beyond the Mississippi,* Prentice-Hall, 1941
George W. James, *The Old Franciscan Missions of California,* Little, Brown, 1913
John T. Lanning, *The Spanish Missions of Georgia,* University of North Carolina
Press, 1935
John B. Leighly, " Settlement and Cultivation in the Summer-Dry Climates," U.S.
Department of Agriculture, *Yearbook: Climate and Man,* 1941, pp. 197–204
Caroline C. Lovell, *The Golden Isles of Georgia,* Little, Brown, 1932
Woodbury Lowery, *The Spanish Settlements within the Present Limits of the United
States: Florida, 1562–1574,* Putnam, 1906

BRIEF NOTES ON THE SOURCES

68–69   Perhaps the clearest presentation of early Spanish expansion northward of St. Augustine is that of Herbert E. Bolton and Mary Ross, *The Debatable Land: A Sketch of the Anglo-Spanish Contest for the Georgia Country,* University of California Press, 1925. The authors point out therein (p. 1) that " The Georgia coast constituted the district of Guale, and was a part of the province of La Florida. Most of the Spanish establishments in Guale were in the islands, for these are *terra firma,* while the adja-cent mainland presents a wide strip of difficult swamp and salt-marsh, which even yet is uninhabited."

69   Motives for expansion are fully presented in Chatelaine, *The Defenses of Spanish Florida.*

69–70   The mission fields as here outlined are an adaptation of Maynard Geiger's *The Early Franciscans in Florida and Their Relations to Spain's Colonial Effort,* St. Anthony Guild Press, Paterson, N. J., 1936.

The nomenclature of the islands is derived from Lovell, *The Golden Isles,* p. 6 and map.

70–71   For the character of the missions and the Indians see Lanning, *The Spanish Missions;* and Mary Ross, " The Restoration of the Spanish Missions in Georgia, 1598–1606," *Georgia Historical Quarterly,* Vol. 10 (1926), pp. 171–99.

72–73   The quotation from David I. Bushnell, Jr., is from his *Native Villages and Village Sites East of the Mississippi,* Smithsonian Institution, Bureau of American Ethnology, *Bulletin* 69, 1919, p. 15.

73–75   For a recent discussion of the much-debated trans-Florida trail, see M. F. Boyd, " A Map of the Road from Pensacola to St. Augustine, 1778," *Florida Historical Quarterly,* Vol. 17 (1938), pp.15–25.

75–76   Trade with the Indians of the Southeast is well discussed by Verner W. Crane, *The Southern Frontier, 1670–1732,* Duke University Press, 1928, pp. 108–36.

76   References to Alexander von Humboldt in this and later chapters are to his *Political Essay on the Kingdom of New Spain,* 4 vols., London, 1811, especially Vols. 2 and 4. This quotation is from Vol. 2, p. 307.

The quotation from Herbert E. Bolton is from his " Spanish Activities on the Lower Trinity River, 1746–71," *Southwestern Quarterly,* Vol. 16 (1913), p. 339. Other valuable contributions to this theme by the same author are " The Spanish Occupation of Texas, 1519–1690," *ibid.,* Vol. 16 (1912), pp. 1–26; and *Texas in the Middle Eighteenth Century,* University of California Press, 1915.

78   The early importance of San Antonio is touched upon by William T. Chambers in " San Antonio, Texas," *Economic Geography,* Vol. 16 (1940), pp. 291–98.

79–80   Phases of the " conquest " of New Mexico are treated by C. W. Hackett, " The Retreat of the Spanish from Northern New Mexico in 1680," *Southwestern Quarterly,* Vol. 16 (1912), pp. 137–68.

80   The table of pueblo population of the Rio Grande in 1760 comes from Hubert H. Bancroft, *History of Arizona and New Mexico,* Highway Company, San Francisco, 1888, p. 279.

81–82   For an early discussion of missions and Indians in the Southwest, see John R. Bartlett, *Personal Narrative of Exploration & Incidents in Texas, New Mexico, California, Sonora, and Chihuahua,* 2 vols., Appleton, 1854, Vol. 2, pp. 161–83. A modern work is Earle R. Forrest, *Missions and Pueblos of the Southwest,* A. H. Clark Co., Cleveland, 1929, with special reference to San Xavier and Casa Grande.

83–85   The tables of California missions and attached Indian population and livestock come from Von Humboldt, *Political Essay,* Vol. 4, pp. 301–03.

CHAPTER 6: The Land: A General View

REFERENCES FOR FURTHER READING

Seymour Dunbar, *A History of Travel in America,* 4 vols., Bobbs-Merrill, 1915, especially Vols. 1 and 2

Alvin F. Harlow, *Old Towpaths: The Story of the American Canal Era,* Appleton, 1926

Archer B. Hulbert, *Historic Highways of America,* 16 vols., A. H. Clark Co., Cleveland, 1902–05; Vol. 9, *Waterways of Westward Expansion;* Vols. 11–12, *Pioneer Roads and Experiences of Travelers*

Rayner W. Kelsey, *Cazenove Journal, 1794,* Pennsylvania Historical Press, 1922 (Haverford College Historical Studies)

Reuben G. Thwaites, ed., *Early Western Travels:* Vol. 3, *Travels to the West of the Alleghany Mountains* by François André Michaux (reprinted from the London edition, 1805); Vol. 4, *Sketches of a Tour to the Western Country* by F. Cuming

BRIEF NOTES ON THE SOURCES

89–98   This sketch of the Atlantic-seaboard environment derives mainly from the opening chapters in Ralph H. Brown, *Mirror for Americans: Likeness of the Eastern Seaboard, 1810,* American Geographical Society, Special Publication 27, 1943, which, in turn, attempted to summarize geographical materials contemporary with the period. Only a few of the bibliographical items contained therein will be repeated here. Original sources are mainly to be found in special libraries or in the " treasure collections " of large institutions. Probably most accessible are copies of various editions of *The American Universal Geography* of Jedidiah Morse, 2 vols., London, 1792 and other editions, although Morse's volumes contained little that was not already available in another, and often better, form. Among the French and British travelers who left penetrative accounts of the American scene, mention may be made of Isaac Weld, Jr., Constantin F. C. Volney, François Michaux the younger, and François A. F. de La Rochefoucauld-Liancourt. Frequently mistaken or overcritical about the new United States, the foreigners' observations nevertheless serve to temper the enthusiasms of native Americans. From the purely scientific standpoint, the observations of contemporary geographers or geographical writers have been rendered obsolescent by their successors, but in a study of the historical geography of a given period, we must know what people thought about their environmental conditions.

92   The quotation beginning " This country possesses . . ." is from a review in the *Monthly Register,* Vol. 3 (1807), p. 96.

95   The quotation from Joseph B. Kincer is from his paper, " Is Our Climate Changing? A Study of Long-Time Temperature Trends," *Monthly Weather Review,* Vol. 61 (1933), pp. 251–59.

The quotation from the Salem physician is that of Edward A. Holyoke in " An Estimate of the Excess of Heat and Cold," *Memoirs of the American Academy of Arts and Sciences,* Vol. 2 (1793), p. 65.

96–98   The contemporary portrayal of physical features comes mainly from Constantin F. C. Volney, *A View of the Soil and Climate of the United States of America,* trans. by Charles Brockden Brown, London, 1804.

99   The full citation to the Gallatin report is " Report of the Secretary of the Treasury, on the Subject of Public Roads and Canals, Made in Pursuance of a Resolution of Senate, of March 2, 1807," included in *American State Papers, Miscellaneous,* Vol. I, pp. 724–921.

103   The table of toll rates in Connecticut was contained in a letter to Gallatin from Alexander Wolcott, and included in the Gallatin report, p. 873.

103–05   The Middlesex Canal has been discussed by Christopher Roberts, *The Middlesex Canal, 1793–1860,* Harvard University Press, 1938. A history of the Santee Canal by F. A. Porcher was published by the South Carolina Historical Society in 1903. General studies of transportation, such as Harlow's *Old Towpaths,* touch upon the origin of the Erie Canal.

106 Jefferson's advocacy of a national road to the Ohio country is to be found in his " Communication to Congress, February 19, 1808," *American State Papers, Miscellaneous*, Vol. I, p. 714.

CHAPTER 7: The Sea: Its Industries and Commerce

REFERENCES FOR FURTHER READING

Anna C. Clauder, *American Commerce as Affected by the Wars of the French Revolution and Napoleon, 1793–1812*, University of Pennsylvania Press, 1932

Charles C. Crittenden, *The Commerce of North Carolina, 1763–1789*, Yale University Press, 1936

Emory R. Johnson and others, *History of Domestic and Foreign Commerce of the United States*, 2 vols., Carnegie Institution of Washington, Publication 215A, 1915, especially Vol. 1

Walter S. Tower, *A History of the American Whale Fishery*, University of Pennsylvania Press, 1907

Arthur P. Whitaker, *Documents Relating to the Commercial Policy of Spain in Florida*, Florida State Historical Society, Deland, 1931

BRIEF NOTES ON THE SOURCES

111–17 Histories of the American whaling industry naturally stress the period of its greatest importance; that is, from 1825 to about the time of the War between the States. Logbooks and other records made by whalers on their cruises are extremely limited, for the reasons suggested in the text. In the next order of original data are various reports and tables in *American State Papers, Commerce and Navigation*, Vol. I, containing on pp. 8–22 Jefferson's " Report on the Fisheries " of February 4, 1791, of which liberal use has been made in this survey. The most authoritative summary of the whaling industry is Alexander Starbuck, " History of the American Whale Fishery from Its Earliest Inception to the Year 1876," U.S. Commission of Fish and Fisheries, *Report of 1875–76*, 1878, Pt. 4. The account of the whaling expedition to Chile in 1792 (page 115) is from a letter in the Jedidiah Morse collection at Yale University.

117–19 The section on practical knowledge of the fishing banks is based in part on extant maps of the period and scattered references in contemporary geographies, such as Constantin F. C. Volney — the French geographer mentioned — in his *A View of the Soil and Climate of the United States of America*, 1804. Among the travelers who wrote of the fishing banks from personal knowledge were the famous Robert Rogers, *A Concise Account of North America*, London, 1765; and George Heriot, *Travels Through the Canadas*, London, 1807. *American State Papers*, cited above, provide the statistical data for the graphs.

120 The recommended courses on the North Atlantic trade lane, and the Oriental routes referred to later, come mainly from maps of ocean currents and publications in explanation of them written by contemporary navigators. Also, use was made of manuscripts of Nathaniel Bowditch in the Boston Public Library, particularly his " Commonplace Books " in which he summarized some of the navigation literature of his period.

121 The log of the *President Adams* is in the American Antiquarian Society, Worcester, Mass.

The table of arrivals at Charleston in 1801 is from John Drayton, *A View of South-Carolina*, Charleston, 1802.

121–24 By reference to various logbooks kept on voyages to the Far East, an attempt has been made to give specific information on the Oriental trade, the general nature of which is well known. It would seem out of place to cite each one, but the reader may wish to know that such source materials do exist. The author is under obligation to the American Antiquarian Society, the Peabody Museum and the Essex Institute of Salem, Mass., the New Bedford Public Library, the Boston Public Library, and the Harvard College Library for privileges extended to him in the course of his investigation. The Canton trade, particularly as it involved the seal fisheries off the Chilean coast, has been discussed recently by Howard Corning in " Sullivan Doer, China Trader," *Rhode Island History*, Vol. 3 (1944), pp. 75–90, of which use has been made here.

125 The log of the *Retrieve* is in the Peabody Museum and that of the *Hannah* is in the Essex Institute.

126–29 Many contemporary geographies discuss various aspects of the coastwise domestic trade. Sailing times along the coast as well as to foreign lands have recently been itemized by Peter Oliver in *The American Neptune*, Vol. 3 (1943), pp. 292–313. The particular reference on the ice trade is in *Proceedings of the Massachusetts Historical Society*, 1855–58, pp. 52–60.

CHAPTER 8: Regional Studies: The South

REFERENCES FOR FURTHER READING

Avery Craven, " Soil Exhaustion as a Factor in the Agricultural History of Virginia and Maryland, 1606–1860," in *University of Illinois Studies in the Social Sciences*, Vol. 13, 1925
Archibald Henderson, *Washington's Southern Tour, 1791*, Houghton Mifflin, 1923
John B. McMaster, *A History of the People of the United States, from the Revolution to the Civil War*, 8 vols., Appleton, 1883–1913, Vol. 2
Ulrich B. Phillips, *American Negro Slavery: A Study of the Supply, Employment and Control of Negro Labor as Determined by the Plantation Regime*, Appleton, 1918

BRIEF NOTES ON THE SOURCES

130 The quotation, one of many of like character, is attributed to Elkanah Watson, an early advocate of plans for a canal across New York State, in Morse's *American Universal Geography*, London, 1792, Appendix.

131 The *Travels through the United States*, 2 vols., London, 1799, of François A. F. de La Rochefoucauld-Liancourt has been used extensively in this chapter. This quotation is in Vol. 1, p. 622.

133 The reference to sedimentation in Chesapeake Bay inlets is from L. C. Gottschalk, "Effects of Soil Erosion on Navigation in Upper Chesapeake Bay," *Geographical Review*, Vol. 35 (1945), p. 235. Mr. Gottschalk and the editor of the *Geographical Review* have permitted the reproduction of Figure 45.

134–36 This discussion of tobacco culture and marketing is based largely on William Tatham, *An Historical and Practical Essay on the Culture and Commerce of Tobacco*, London, 1800. Figures 46 and 47 come from this rare work.

140–43 This description derives mainly from works usually shelved in the rare-book collections in college libraries, including especially John Drayton, *A View of South-Carolina,* Charleston, 1802, and many contemporary travel records. See also F. L. Olmsted, *A Journey in the Seaboard Slave States,* London, 1856; quotation from pages 469–70.

143 The quotations on droughts in the rice country come from two widely spaced issues of the *Gentlemen's Magazine,* London: Vol. 12 (1752), p. 431; Vol. 54 (1784), p. 631.

147 Hopeton Plantation records are made available in Lovell, *The Golden Isles of Georgia,* 1932, pp. 214, 216. The Georgia traveler referred to was John Pope; quotation from pages 77–78 of his *A Tour through the Southern and Western Territories,* Richmond, 1888.

Marguerite B. Hamer, "The Foundation and Failure of the Silk Industry in Provincial Georgia," *North Carolina Historical Review,* Vol. 12 (1935), pages 125–48; reference on page 139.

147–48 The most readily available account of the "dead towns" of Georgia is that of Charles C. Jones, *History of Georgia,* 2 vols., Houghton Mifflin, 1883; but the subject was more fully treated by him in the *Morning News Press,* Morning News Steam Printing House, Savannah, 1878.

149 A basic work for Florida's early economic history is *Documents Relating to the Commercial Policy of Spain in the Floridas,* ed. by Arthur P. Whitaker, Florida State Historical Society, Deland, 1931; quotation from page xxii.

An accessible source on New Smyrna is Carita Doggett, *Dr. Andrew Turnbull and the New Smyrna Colony of Florida,* Drew Press, Fla., 1919; but original works can be found in the larger libraries.

150 The final quotation is from *The Journal of Andrew Ellicott,* Philadelphia, 1803, p. 274. As Commissioner of the United States, Ellicott spoke with some authority.

CHAPTER 9: Regional Studies: the North

REFERENCES FOR FURTHER READING

Albert P. Brigham, *Cape Cod and the Old Colony,* Putnam, 1920

Albert L. Burt, *A Short History of Canada for Americans,* University of Minnesota Press, 1944, Chap. 3

Victor S. Clark, *History of Manufacturing in the United States, 1607–1860,* Carnegie Institution of Washington, 1916

Marion I. Newbigin, *Canada: The Great River, the Lands, and the Men,* Harcourt, Brace, 1921

Derwent Whittlesey, "Coastland and Interior Mountain Valley: A Study of Two Typical Localities in Northern New England," in *New England's Prospect,* American Geographical Society, Special Publication 16, 1933

BRIEF NOTES ON THE SOURCES

151 Shifts in the population center of Massachusetts are discussed in Jesse Chickering, *A Statistical View of the Population of Massachusetts from 1765 to 1840,* Boston, 1846, p. 88.

152 Data on the sale of slaves in South Carolina are contained in Charles M. Wiltse, *John C. Calhoun, Nationalist, 1782–1828,* Bobbs-Merrill, 1944, p. 40.

The Yale president referred to was Timothy Dwight, whose four-volume work on *Travels in New-England and New-York* was published in London in 1823, a dozen years after the completion of his journeys. The quotation is from Vol. 1, p. 330.

153   Malcolm F. Keir has written many valuable works on economic geography; the source of the quotation here is "Some Responses to Environment in Massachusetts," *Bulletin of the Geographical Society of Philadelphia*, July–August, 1917, pp. 121–28 and 167–85.

155–57   This discussion of manufacturing industries in New Haven, Boston, and other centers derives mainly from contemporary geographies and gazetteers. For example, Lynn's shoe industry is described by Jacques Pierre Brissot de Warville in his *New Travels in the United States of America, Performed in 1788*, Boston, 1797.

157–60   Two excellent studies of New England communities provide the substance of this section: Adelbert K. Botts, "Northbridge, Massachusetts: A Town That Moved Down Hill," *Journal of Geography*, Vol. 33 (1934), pp. 249–60; and J. W. Goldthwait, "A Town That Has Gone Downhill," *Geographical Review*, Vol. 17 (1927), pp. 527–57. For a useful summary of seaboard settlement types, consult "Rural Settlement in Colonial America" by Glenn T. Trewartha, *Geographical Review*, Vol. 36 (1946), pp. 568–96.

160–62   Among the studies and early "travels" used in preparing this section are: Martha K. Genthe, "Valley Towns of Connecticut," *Bulletin of the American Geographical Society*, Vol. 39 (1907), pp. 513–44; E. A. Kendall, *Travels through the Northern Parts of the United States*, London, 1809; Robert Rogers, *A Concise Account of North America*, London, 1765; and Brissot de Warville, *op. cit.*

162–65   Details on the land uses and industries of the various towns derive mainly from a number of eyewitness accounts written by citizens of Cape Cod and included in early volumes of the *Collections of the Massachusetts Historical Society*, especially in those for 1794 and 1802.

166   The proposal for the separation of Maine was contained in *An Address to the Inhabitants of the District of Maine . . . by One of Their Own Citizens*, T. B. Wait, publisher, Portland, 1791; reference on p. 13.

166–68   Data on Ellsworth, Maine, come from "Land Grants in Maine, 1785 to Feb. 1, 1820," *Maine Historical Magazine*, Vol. 9 (1894–95), pp. 48–54; "Materials for a Study of Ellsworth," *ibid.*, Vol. 8 (1893), pp. 181–218; and Derwent Whittlesey's work noted in the general references above.

168–70   In addition to the general references to Lower Canada, two fundamental papers are available: Ellen C. Semple, "The Influence of Geographic Environment on the Lower St. Lawrence," *Bulletin of the American Geographical Society*, Vol. 36 (1904), pp. 449–66; and Roderick Peattie, "The Isolation of the Lower St. Lawrence," *Geographical Review*, February, 1918, pp. 102–18.

170–72   The regional description of Lower Canada comes mainly from an early-day work: Joseph Bouchette, *A Topographical Description of the Province of Lower Canada, with Remarks upon Upper Canada*, London, 1815. For example, Bouchette discusses the seigniories at length, and the Temiscouata route (pp. 537, 543). The quotation on Quebec is from Isaac Weld, *Travels through North America and . . . Canada*, London, 1799, pp. 196–97. Hugh Gray in his *Letters from Canada*, London, 1809, describes the compactness of settlement between Quebec and Montreal on page 129. Weld (pp. 177–78) presents the somewhat gloomy picture of Montreal, and the final quotation is from a travel book attributed to the Reverend

John C. Ogden, *A Tour through Upper and Lower Canada*, Litchfield (Conn.?), 1790, pp. 113–14.

CHAPTER 10: Frontiers — Seaboard States and St. Lawrence Valley

REFERENCES FOR FURTHER READING

Helen I. Cowan, *Charles Williamson, Genesee Promoter, Friend of Anglo-American Rapprochement*, Rochester Historical Society, Publication No. 19, 1941

Alexander C. Frick, ed., *History of the State of New York*, 10 vols., Columbia University Press, 1933–1937; see Vol. 5, pp. 141–75, " The Frontier Pushed Westward " by Paul D. Evans; and pp. 177–215, " The Settlement of the North Country " by Richard C. Ellsworth

Joseph Hadfield, *An Englishman in America, 1785: Being the Diary of Joseph Hadfield*, ed. by Douglas S. Robertson, Hunter-Rose Company, Toronto, 1933

Herbert B. Howe, *Jedediah Barber, 1787–1876: A Footnote to the History of the Military Tract of Central New York*, Columbia University Press, 1939

Harold R. Innis, *The Fur Trade in Canada: An Introduction to Canadian Economic History*, Yale University Press, 1933

Blake F. McKelvey, *Rochester, the Water Power City*, Harvard University Press, 1945

Ellen C. Semple, *American History and Its Geographic Conditions*, Revised by Clarence F. Jones, Houghton Mifflin, 1933, Chap. 4

Reuben G. Thwaites, ed., *Early Western Travels:* Vol. 3, *Journal of a Tour into the Territory Northwest of the Alleghany Mountains* [1805] by Thaddeus Harris

BRIEF NOTES ON THE SOURCES

174–75 References to Alexander Mackenzie here and elsewhere are to his *Voyage from Montreal, on the River St. Lawrence, through the Continent of North America . . . in the Years 1789 and 1793*, Philadelphia, 1802. The quotation from R. M. Lower is in " The Assault on the Laurentian Barrier, 1850–70," *Canadian Historical Review*, Vol. 10 (1929), pp. 294–307; reference on p. 294. Harold R. Innis is a leading authority on the economic history of Canada. The quotation is from one of his articles in the *Canadian Historical Review*, Vol. 8 (1927), pp. 308–16; reference on pp. 313–14.

175 The description of Michilimackinac is included in the journal of Charles C. Trowbridge, ed. by Ralph H. Brown and published in *Minnesota History* under the title " With Cass in the Northwest," Vol. 23 (1942), pp. 126–48; 233–52; 328–48; reference on pp. 142–43.

176 George Heriot, *Travels through the Canadas*, Philadelphia, 1807, pp. 233–34.

176–77 Among the rare works on the early fur trade is that of J. Long, *Voyages and Travels of an Interpreter and Trader*, London, 1791; quotation on p. 39.

178–79 Constantin F. C. Volney in his *View of the Climate and Soil of . . . America*, Philadelphia, 1804, gives the description of Niagara Falls (pp. 83–85), and Robert M'Causlin presents his data on their retreat in *Transactions of the American Philosophical Society*, Vol. 3 (1793), pp. 17–24; quotation on p. 24. Timothy Bigelow's *Journal of a Tour to Niagara Falls in the Year 1805* was published in Boston in 1876; quotation on pp. 49–50.

179–81 Eyewitness accounts of the Military Tract include John Maude, *A Visit to the Falls of Niagara, in 1800*, London, 1826, p. 38. For a full historical treatment, consult J. B. Sherwood, " The Military Tract," *Quarterly Journal of the New York State Historical Association*, Vol. 7 (1926), pp. 169–79.

181–82 The principal original work of Charles Williamson is *Description of the Settlement of the Genesee Country*, New York, 1799, available in *The Documentary History of the State of New-York*, 4 vols., Albany, 1849–1851: Vol. 2, pp. 1127–68.

182–83 Data on the Macomb Tract can be found in the *Documentary History* cited above, and in various studies, including C. H. Lette, " The St. Lawrence Ten Towns," *Quarterly Journal of the New York State Historical Association*, Vol. 10 (1929), pp. 318–27; and Frick, *History of the State of New York*, section by Richard C. Ellsworth (general references above). Washington Irving's *Journal of 1803* has been edited by S. T. Williams, Oxford University Press, 1934; quotation on pp. 13–16.

184–85 The quotation from Thaddeus M. Harris is in *Journal of a Tour into the Territory Northwest of the Alleghany Mountains*, Boston, 1805, p. 25, a rare work in the original but available in Reuben G. Thwaites, ed., *Early Western Travels*, Vol. 3.

188 Darrell H. Davis presents a full account of settlement in the Kentucky mountains in " A Study of the Succession of Human Activities in the Kentucky Mountains," in *Human Geography Studies*, ed. by G. J. Miller, McKnight & McKnight, Bloomington, Ill., 1935, pp. 71–86.

Excerpts here are from F. A. Michaux, *Travels to the West of the Alleghany Mountains in the States of Ohio, Kentucky, and Tennessee, . . . 1802*, London, 1805 (available also in Thwaites, ed., *Early Western Travels*, Vol. 3).

189–91 The western territories of Georgia are given much attention in the geographies of the 1790's, with a full summary in Jedidiah Morse, *Gazetteer of the Western Continent* (various editions). For an intimate account of the Creek Nations, consult Benjamin Hawkins, " Sketch of the Creek Country . . . 1798 and 1799," *Collections of the Georgia Historical Society*, Vol. 3 (1848). The Hawkins sketch was written fifty years before the date of publication.

CHAPTER 11: A General View of the Land

REFERENCES FOR FURTHER READING

Harlan H. Barrows, *Geography of the Middle Illinois Valley*, Illinois State Geological Survey, *Bulletin 15*, 1910
Reuben G. Thwaites, ed., *Early Western Travels*: Vol. 5, *Bradbury's Travels in the Interior of America, 1809–11*; Vols. 14–17, *James's Account of the S. H. Long Expedition, 1819–1820*

BRIEF NOTES ON THE SOURCES

Much of the material for the four chapters in Part III has come from original manuscripts for whose use the author is indebted to the Western Reserve Historical Society of Cleveland, the William L. Clements Library of the University of Michigan, and the Burton Historical Collections of the Detroit Public Library. Because it is unlikely that many would have the opportunity to make use of these valuable documents, only a few examples will be referred to, identified as to location by use of the initials WRHS, WLC, BHC.

195   The " Mr. Robinson " anecdote is from *Narrative of Richard Lee Mason in the Pioneer West, 1819,* printed for Charles F. Heartman, New York [1915] (160 copies).

197   The quotation from Amos Wheeler is in his manuscript diary, " Journal of a Tour in Ohio; and from Ohio to Missouri, May 21–July 28, 1816," WRHS.

199–201   Printed sources on the Kanawha salt industry include [William N. Blane] *An Excursion through the United States and Canada during the Years 1822–23,* London, 1824, pp. 99–100. A useful manuscript is " Journey of R. Ricks from Virginia to Ohio, September 12, 1807," WRHS. Comment on Yellow Springs is by Josiah Espy, in " Memorandum of a Tour in Ohio and Kentucky in 1805," *Ohio Valley Historical Series,* Cincinnati, 1871, pp. 4–5.

201   The quotation is from a letter written by Ephraim Brown of Trumbull County to O. Smith, October 30, 1816, WRHS.

202   Frequently referred to in this and later chapters is Daniel Drake's *Natural and Statistical View and Picture of Cincinnati,* Cincinnati, 1815.

203   *A Topographical Description of the State of Ohio, Indiana Territory, and Louisiana,* by a Late Officer of the U.S. Army, Boston, 1812, is attributed to Jervis (or Jervaise) Cutler, a son of the better-known Manasseh Cutler; quotation on p. 14.

The letter written by Thomas Hutchins to Captain Hamtramck " from Camp, 17 Miles on the East-West line " is one of a series in Harmar Papers, Vol. 4, WLC.

206   Conclusions reached here regarding the attitude of early settlers toward the prairie environment differ from those advanced by many other writers. For a summary of general thought on this subject see Glenn T. Trewartha, " Climate and Settlement of the Subhumid Lands," in U.S. Department of Agriculture, *Yearbook: Climate and Man,* 1941, pp. 167–76. Similar views are presented by William V. Pooley, " The Settlement of Illinois from 1830–1850," *Bulletin of the University of Wisconsin Historical Society,* Vol. 1 (1908), No. 4.

209   The quotation from Stanley D. Dodge is in his " Bureau and the Princeton Community," *Annals of the Association of American Geographers,* Vol. 22 (1932), pp. 159–200.

209–10   The Newberry quotation is from a typescript of " Henry Newberry's Tour in Ohio, 1822," WRHS.

CHAPTER 12: People in the Land: the State of Ohio

REFERENCES FOR FURTHER READING

James Truslow Adams, ed., *Atlas of American History,* Scribner's, 1943, maps 85–87
Reuben G. Thwaites, ed., *Early Western Travels:* Vol. 4, *Sketches of a Tour to the Western Country,* by F. Cuming; Vol. 8, *A Pedestrious Tour of Four Thousand Miles . . . 1818,* by Estwick Evans; Vol. 11, *Memorable Days in America, 1823,* by W. Faux
Alfred J. Wright, " Ohio Town Patterns," *Geographical Review,* Vol. 27 (1937), pp. 615–24

BRIEF NOTES ON THE SOURCES

212–13 The Ohio Company settlement is touched upon in " Military Journal of Major Ebenezer Denny, 1781–1795," in *Pennsylvania Historical Society Memoirs,* Vol. 7 (1860), pp. 237–409. Various letters and reports of General Harmar are in Harmar Papers, WLC.

218–20 Daniel J. Ryan has discussed certain phases of the Scioto Company in *Ohio Archaeological and Historical Publications,* Vol. 3 (1890), pp. 109–40; and in the same volume, pp. 45–81, John L. Vance considers " The French Settlement and Settlers of Gallipolis." Volney's visit to Gallipolis is recorded in his *View of the Soil and Climate,* [etc.] 1804, pp. 355–65.

220–27 This presentation of the Connecticut Reserve derives mainly from manuscripts in the Western Reserve Historical Society. A few of the more useful manuscripts are: the memoranda on the first survey by Amizi Atwater; " Diary of a Journey to Connecticut Reserve, 1806, by William Eldredge "; " History of Euclid," anon.; the account of Abraham Tappan, transcribed by Electra Tappan; " History of the Erie Land Company " in the Joseph Perkins scrapbook; and various letters of Ephraim Brown to correspondents in the East. The map and description of John Heckewelder is in *Tract 64,* Western Reserve and Northern Ohio Historical Society, 1884.

229–30 Newberry's description of Sandusky is taken from a typescript, " Henry Newberry's Tour to Ohio, 1822," WRHS. For Zane's Trace consult the paper of C. L. Martzolff in *Ohio Archaeological and Historical Society Publications,* Vol. 13 (1904), pp. 297–331.

231 The Licking Company is considered by F. W. Shepardson in *New England Magazine,* Vol. 20 (1899), pp. 97–117; and the Welsh settlements, in *Ohio Archaeological and Historical Society Publications,* Vol. 16 (1907), pp. 194–227.

235 Among the many firsthand descriptions of Cincinnati is that of Duke Karl-Bernhard in *Travels through North America during the Years 1825 and 1826,* 2 vols., Philadelphia, 1828, Vol. 1.

CHAPTER 13: People in the Land: Down River Country

REFERENCES FOR FURTHER READING

Solon J. Buck, *Illinois in 1818,* Illinois Centennial Publication, Introductory Volume, Springfield, 1917

Elias P. Fordham, *Personal Narrative of Travels in Virginia . . . and a Residence in Illinois Territory, 1817–1818,* ed. by Frederic A. Ogg, A. H. Clark Co., Cleveland, 1906

Walter B. Hendrickson, *David Dale Owen: Pioneer Geologist of the Middle West,* Indiana Historical Bureau, Indianapolis, 1943; Chaps. 2–5

Harlow Lindley, ed., " A Visit to the Colony of Harmony in Indiana [1825] by William Hebert," in his *Indiana as Seen by Travelers,* Indiana Historical Commission, 1916

Milo M. Quaife, *Pictures of Illinois One Hundred Years Ago,* Donnelly, Chicago, 1918, Lakeside Classics

Reuben G. Thwaites, ed., *Early Western Travels:* Vol. 10, *Flower's Letters from the Illinois, 1820–21* and *Woods's Two Years' Residence, 1820–21;* Vols. 11 and 12,

Parts I and II of *Memorable Days in America, 1819–20,* by W. Faux; Vol. 12, *Welby's Visit to North America, 1819–20*

BRIEF NOTES ON THE SOURCES

239-40 Various aspects of Vevay have been discussed by Peter Dufour in " The Swiss Settlement of Switzerland County, Indiana," Indiana Historical Commission, 1925, and by Julia Le C. Knox in *Indiana Magazine of History,* Vol. 11 (1915), pp. 216–30. The quotation from Edmund Dana is in his *Geographical Sketches of the Western Country,* Cincinnati, 1819.

240-44 The most important early work on Louisville is Henry McMurtrie, *Sketches of Louisville and Its Environs,* Louisville, 1819.

246-50 Notes on Harmony and New Harmony are found in a great number of travel records, too many to cite here. Of particular interest are the comments of George Flower in his " History of the English Settlements in Edwards County, Illinois," *Chicago Historical Society Collections,* Vol. 1 (1860). Julia Le C. Knox has discussed " The Unique Little Town of New Harmony " in *Indiana Magazine of History,* Vol. 32 (1936), pp. 52–58.

250-52 Equally scattered in a variety of contemporary sources are comments on the English Settlement. Fordham's narrative (noted above) is perhaps the most reliable of the many available.

253 The quotation from Professor Cutshall is in his recent study " Vincennes: Historic City on the Wabash," *Scientific Monthly,* Vol. 57 (1943), pp. 413–24.

CHAPTER 14: Travel and Trade on the Ohio River and Canals

REFERENCES FOR FURTHER READING

Seymour Dunbar, *A History of Travel in America,* 4 vols., Bobbs-Merrill, 1915; especially Vols. 1–2

Archer B. Hulbert, *Waterways of Westward Expansion,* 1904 (Vol. 9 of *Historic Highways of America,* 16 vols., A. H. Clark Co., Cleveland, 1902–05)

Almon E. Parkins, " Our Waterways and Their Utilization," Chap. 14 in *Our Natural Resources and Their Conservation,* ed. by Almon E. Parkins and J. R. Whitaker, 2d. ed., Wiley, 1939

BRIEF NOTES ON THE SOURCES

Manuscript sources for this chapter include several items from the Durrett Collection of the University of Chicago, and various letters in the Burton Historical Collections, Detroit Public Library. An unpublished thesis at the University of Chicago, " The Settlements at the Falls of the Ohio, 1819–1824 " by Etelka Holt, also contains material on this topic.

256 The account of the low water of 1819 is in [Jacob Burnet] *Notes on the Early Settlement of the North-Western Territory,* Cincinnati, 1847, p. 406.

256-58 Portions of James's account of the Long Expedition, cited previously, are especially valuable for data on navigation. Various editions of Zadok Cramer, *The Navigator,* Pittsburgh, 1806, contain detailed observations on navigable channels, types of river boats, and port facilities.

258-60 Ohio River boats are described in the first volume of Timothy Flint's *Condensed Geography and History of the Western States,* Cincinnati, 1828. If this rare source is not available, consult various articles in the *Ohio Archaeological and Historical Quarterly,* as follows: Archer B. Hulbert, " The Ohio River," Vol. 20 (1911), pp. 220–35; Richard T. Wiley, " Ship and Brig Building on the Ohio and Its Tributaries," Vol. 22 (1913), pp. 54–64; and Isaac F. King, " Flat Boating on the Ohio River," Vol. 26 (1917), pp. 78–81. The description of the keelboat journey from Pittsburgh to Portsmouth is included in the diary of Amos Wheeler, WRHS.

265 The quotation from Bloomfield, Ohio, is in a " letter from Ephraim Brown to Col. Brooks," September 4, 1817, WRHS. The letter from Vandalia was printed in the *Detroit Gazette,* Feb. 23, 1821.

266 Clinton's comment on the proposed Maumee-Wabash canal is included in the " Pictorial History of Fort Wayne," which ran in the *Fort Wayne Sentinel* beginning Jan. 3, 1914.

266–68 Modern studies which have touched upon the Ohio canals include: A. N. Doerschuk, " The Last Ohio Canal Boat," *Ohio Archaeological and Historical Quarterly,* Vol. 34 (1925), pp. 109–16; J. J. George, Jr., " The Miami Canal," *ibid.,* Vol. 36 (1927), pp. 92–115; and E. Willard Miller, " Cleveland — A Great Lakes Port," *Scientific Monthly,* Vol. 59 (1944), pp. 180–87.

269 Henry Schoolcraft's description of Chicago is in his *Narrative Journal of Travels through the Northwestern Regions of the United States,* Albany, 1821, pp. 283–85.

CHAPTER 15: Detroit and Southeastern Michigan

REFERENCES FOR FURTHER READING

George M. Fuller, *Economic and Social Beginnings of Michigan,* Michigan Historical Publications, Lansing, 1916

Almon E. Parkins, *The Historical Geography of Detroit,* Michigan Historical Commission, Chicago, 1918

BRIEF NOTES ON THE SOURCES

272 The letter from Woodbridge to Adams is in the Burton Historical Collections.

272–74 For a discussion of the Michigan-Ohio boundary dispute, see Charles O. Paullin, *Atlas of the Historical Geography of the United States,* American Geographical Society and Carnegie Institution, 1932; text, pp. 79–80; map, Plate 98 B. Summarized also by Milo M. Quaife in the *Dictionary of American History,* 5 vols., Scribner's, 1940, Vol. 3, pp. 390–92.

274–76 The Tiffin Report is in *American State Papers, Public Lands,* Vol. III, pp. 164–65.

277 The interpretation of Detroit's surface features by Jacob Lindley is in " Expedition to Detroit, 1793," *Michigan Historical Collections,* Vol. 17 (1892), p. 609. The favorable report of the three self-appointed explorers is recorded in the *Detroit Gazette* and also in Thomas J. Drake, " History of Oakland County," *Michigan Historical Collections,* Vol. 3 (1881), pp. 559–76.

279 The report on French agriculture by C. Jouett is in *American State Papers, Public Lands,* Vol. I, pp. 190–93, under " Description of the Lands and Settlers in the Vicinity of Detroit."

279–81 This description of Detroit comprises observations scattered in contemporary accounts: William Darby, *A Tour from New York . . . to Detroit*, New York, 1819, pp. 188–90; Daniel Blowe, *A Geographical View*, Liverpool [1820?], pp. 692–95; Henry Schoolcraft, *Narrative Journal*, Albany, 1821; also selections from *Burton Historical Leaflets*, Vol. 1 (1922), and a letter from Augustus B. Woodward to the Secretary of War, March 5, 1806, BHC.

284–86 Manuscript items in the Western Reserve Historical Society, especially the Quintus F. Atkins material, provide data on the Black Swamp road. The Catlin Papers are in the Burton Historical Collections. Parkins, *Historical Geography*, pp. 253–56, contains a good discussion.

CHAPTER 16: The Upper Lakes Country

REFERENCES FOR FURTHER READING

Walter Havighurst, *Upper Mississippi: A Wilderness Saga*, Farrar and Rinehart, 1937 (Rivers of America Series)

Grace Lee Nute, *The Voyageur's Highway: Minnesota's Border Lake Land*, Minnesota Historical Society, 1941; and *Lake Superior*, Bobbs-Merrill, 1944 (The American Lakes Series)

Chase S. Osborn and Stellanova Osborn, *The Conquest of a Continent*, Science Press, Lancaster, 1939

Milo M. Quaife, *Lake Michigan*, Bobbs-Merrill, 1944 (The American Lakes Series)

J. R. Whitaker, "Our Forests, Past and Present," Chapter 10 in *Our Natural Resources and Their Conservation*, ed. by Almon E. Parkins and J. R. Whitaker, 2d ed., Wiley, 1939

BRIEF NOTES ON THE SOURCES

294 Wesley discusses the Indian factory system in *Dictionary of American History*, Vol. 2, pp. 238–39.

295 The Sioux-Chippewa struggle, extending over a long period, is well summarized in William W. Folwell, *History of Minnesota*, 4 vols., Minnesota Historical Society, 1921–30; Vol. 1, pp. 80–88. The letter from Cass to Calhoun, dated February 2, 1821, is in the National Archives, Department of War, Letters Received.

295–96 This description of the Indians derives from a number of observations in exploratory journals, particularly those of the Cass expedition of 1820. Three members of the Cass party, Henry Schoolcraft, James Doty, and Charles C. Trowbridge, prepared journals of the tour. The version mainly used here is that of Trowbridge, noted above (Chap. 10). Unless otherwise cited, quotations come from the Trowbridge account. An excellent summary of the Indian peoples is available in Theodore C. Blegen, *Building Minnesota*, Heath, 1938, Chap. 2.

298–300 The Grand Portage of Fond du Lac (do not confuse with the better-known Grand Portage of the Pigeon River) has been treated exhaustively by Irving H. Hart in various papers in *Minnesota History;* for example, "The Old Savanna Portage," Vol. 8 (1927), pp. 117–39; and the Fox-Wisconsin route is given some attention by Lawrence Martin in *The Physical Geography of Wisconsin*, pub. by the State of Wisconsin, 1932, p. 21.

301–02 The conduct of the fur trade is described at length in the *Detroit Gazette*, Dec. 15, 1820, in an article possibly deriving from the American Fur Company and thus subject to some corrections for its overly approving attitude toward the trade. The note by "Hal" is in *Minnesota History,* Vol. 15 (1934), pp. 384–94, taken from a sports magazine, *Spirit of the Times.*

303–05 A convenient and authentic account of the early mining of copper and iron is found in *Geology of the Lake Superior Region,* Monograph 52, U.S. Geological Survey, from which the table of copper production has been taken.

305–08 The discussion of iron mining in the Marquette range comes mainly from J. R. Whitaker, *Negaunee, Michigan: An Urban Center Dominated by Iron Mining,* University of Chicago Libraries, Chicago, reprinted from *Bulletin of the Geographical Society of Philadelphia,* Vol. 29 (1931).

CHAPTER 17: From Mining to Farming in Southern Wisconsin

REFERENCES FOR FURTHER READING

William O. Blanchard, *The Geography of Southwestern Wisconsin,* Wisconsin Geological and Natural History Survey *Bulletin* 65, 1924

Joseph Schafer, "A History of Agriculture in Wisconsin," in *Wisconsin Domesday Book, General Studies,* Vol. 1, Madison, 1922; and "Four Wisconsin Counties," *ibid.,* Vol. 2, 1927

BRIEF NOTES ON THE SOURCES

311 Excellent for supplementary reading is the novel *The Bright Land,* by Janet Ayer Fairbank, Houghton Mifflin, 1932.

312–13 Original data on early lead mining in this region may be found in "Message Relating to the Lead Mines" in Senate Exec. Doc. 7, 19th Congress, 2d Session, 1826 (Serial No. 145). Excellent summaries occur in Guy-Harold Smith, "The Populating of Wisconsin," *Geographical Review,* Vol. 28 (1928), pp. 404–06; and Glenn T. Trewartha, "A Second Episode of Destructive Occupance in the Driftless Hill Land, 1760–1832," *Annals of the Association of American Geographers,* Vol. 30 (1940), pp. 100–42.

313–15 See Blanchard (general references) for data on smelting methods and the rise and decline of mining in Wisconsin.

316–19 The most comprehensive review of literature on the Driftless Area is to be found in Lawrence Martin, *The Physical Geography of Wisconsin,* first published in 1916, revised in 1932. The quotations from Keating and Daniels derive from this summary. David Dale Owen's "Report of a Geological Reconnaissance of the Chippewa Land District" is Senate Exec. Doc. 57, 30th Congress, 1st Session, 1848 (Serial No. 509). Settlement in southeastern Wisconsin is considered by Smith, *loc. cit.*

320–21 The Illinois-Wisconsin boundary dispute is mapped and discussed in the Charles O. Paullin *Atlas of the Historical Geography of the United States,* 1932, p. 82 and Plate 99C.

321–23 Schafer's work is noted in the general references above.

323–25 The basic study for Wisconsin's immigration policy is Theodore C. Blegen, "The Competition of the Northwestern States for Immigrants," *Wisconsin Magazine of History,* Vol. 3 (1919), pp. 1–29.

CHAPTER 18: Minnesota: Territory and State

REFERENCE FOR FURTHER READING

Theodore C. Blegen, *Building Minnesota,* Heath, 1938

BRIEF NOTES ON THE SOURCES

327–29 Perhaps the best summary of explorations in Minnesota is to be found in the opening pages of N. H. Winchell, *The Geology of Minnesota,* Vol. I of the *Final Report,* 6 vols., Pioneer Press Co., St. Paul, 1884–1901.

329–30 The Big Woods region, a critical area in Minnesota development, is carefully outlined by Rexford F. Daubenmire in *Ecological Monographs,* Duke University Press, Vol. 6 (1936).

331–32 Navigation on the Mississippi and Minnesota rivers, together with many other items of economic history, is discussed in Edward Van Dyke Robinson, *Early Economic Conditions and the Development of Agriculture in Minnesota,* University of Minnesota, 1915.

332 Details on Minnesota's roads can be found in Arthur J. Larsen, " Roads and Settlement in Minnesota," *Minnesota History,* Vol. 21 (1940), pp. 225–44.

334–36 Views concerning the climate of early-day Minnesota are summarized in Ralph H. Brown, " Fact and Fancy in Early Accounts of Minnesota's Climate," *Minnesota History,* Vol. 17 (1936), pp. 243–61.

337 The drought of 1862 is discussed, with other data, in *Report of the Commissioner of Agriculture,* Washington, 1863.

The valuable journal of " A New Yorker in the Great West " quoted here was edited by Bertha L. Heilbron and published in *Minnesota History,* Vol. 12 (1931), pp. 43–64.

Basic studies in German settlement by Hildegard Binder Johnson are " The Distribution of the German Pioneer Population in Minnesota," *Rural Sociology,* Vol. 6 (1941), pp. 16–34; and " Factors Influencing the Distribution of the German Pioneer Population in Minnesota," *Agricultural History,* Vol. 19 (1945), pp. 39–57.

342–44 For further material on railroad colonization, see Harold F. Peterson, " Some Colonization Projects of the Northern Pacific Railroad," *Minnesota History,* Vol. 10 (1929), pp. 127–44.

CHAPTER 19: The United States in 1870

BRIEF NOTES ON THE SOURCES

In the 1870's, geography was a subject for schoolchildren to plod through, along with the " three R's." The nature of the plodding can be quickly gathered by leafing through some of the books then in use — James Monteith's *Manual,* Sadlier's *Excelsior Geography* (for which the publishers borrowed Monteith's maps), and the *Eclectic Series* of A. von Steinwehr and D. G. Brinton. On a higher plane were the school texts of Arnold Guyot and Mathew F. Maury; both entitled *Physical Geography,* they reflected the trend away from humanized geography — and an unfortunate trend it proved to be. Guyot and Maury saved geography from total eclipse, but both men were probably known less as geographers than as earth scientists. Guyot, a Swiss immigrant and early-day glaciologist, was Blair Professor of Geography and Geology at the College of New Jersey (Princeton) from 1851 to 1884; Maury achieved lasting renown as an oceanographer.

Consequently, a brief geographical sketch of the country in the 1870's must be pieced together from basic sources rather than from a ready-made model. The Federal censuses are, of course, fundamental, especially Henry Gannett, *Statistical Atlas of the United States Based upon Results of the Eleventh Census,* Government Printing Office, Washington, 1898. Various maps in the Charles O. Paullin *Atlas of the Historical Geography of the United States,* 1932, frequently cited in earlier pages, are also important. Different portions of Nathaniel S. Shaler's *The United States of America,* Appleton, 1894, are also helpful, especially in Vol. 2, J. R. Soley, "The Maritime Industries of America," Chap. 10, and Edward Atkinson, "Productive Industry," Chap. 12. Scientific and popular magazines have also been resorted to; the Philadelphia Centennial, for example, was reported in *Frank Leslie's Illustrated Newspaper,* and in *Harper's Weekly.* Southern geography is well discussed by Almon E. Parkins, *The South, Its Economic-Geographic Development,* Wiley, 1938. For the Far West there are various government documents, reports of the Bureau of American Ethnology, and travelogues such as Horace Greeley, *An Overland Journey,* San Francisco, 1860, and Samuel Bowles, *Across the Continent,* Springfield, 1865, and *Our New West,* Hartford, 1869.

346 The table of territorial accessions is from Gannett, *Statistical Atlas,* 1898, Plate I and Diagram 3.

349–50 For more detail on railroad extension see T. M. Cooley and C. H. Cooley, in Shaler's text, Vol. 2, pp. 739–45. The prospectus of the Chesapeake and Ohio Railroad is from *Leslie's Newspaper,* Apr. 8, 1871, p. 62.

351–52 Various aspects of commerce are discussed by J. R. Soley in Shaler, Vol. 2, Chap. 10, "The Maritime Industries of America."

352–53 For a more adequate treatment of coastwise and Great Lakes trade, see Emory R. Johnson and others, *History of Domestic and Foreign Commerce,* 1915, Vol. 1, pp. 230–37, 348–51.

353–54 The account of the fishing industries is a condensation of "The Fisheries," *Statistics of the United States, 1860 (Eighth Census),* pp. 527–51.

Details on wages and hours of workers are from Atkinson, in Shaler's text, Vol. 2, pp. 715–21.

355 President Grant's remarks at the opening of the exposition were reported, evidently in full, in *Harper's Weekly,* May 27, 1876, p. 422.

356 The tables on manufacturing are computed from graphs in Gannett, *Statistical Atlas,* p. 58.

356–57 Data on city population and its ratio to total population are also from Gannett, *Statistical Atlas,* pp. 9 and 16.

357–59 Material relating to the South is a condensation of Almon E. Parkins, *The South,* pp. 317–25, and 471–80.

363–64 A basic source for Indian Reservations is "Indian Land Cessions in the United States," Bureau of American Ethnology, *Eighteenth Annual Report,* Washington, 1899, Part II. The speech of Bear Rib is taken from General W. F. Raynolds, "Report on the Exploration of the Yellowstone River, 1859–60," Senate Exec. Doc. 77, 40th Congress, 2d Session, 1866–67 (Serial No. 1317).

364   General John Pope is thus quoted in Raymond L. Welty, " The Indian Policy of the Army, 1860–70," *Cavalry Journal*, Vol. 36 (1927), p. 368.

366   The table of Upper Missouri Indian population is from Thaddeus Culbertson, " Journal of an Expedition to the Mauvaises Terres and the Upper Missouri in 1850," *Smithsonian Institution Report*, 1850, pp. 84–145; reference on pp. 141–45. The table of military strength is that of Raymond L. Welty in " The Army Forts of the Frontier (1860–70)," *North Dakota Historical Quarterly*, Vol. 2 (1928), pp. 155–67; reference on p. 156.

CHAPTER 20: The Great Plains Region

REFERENCES FOR FURTHER READING

Francis Parkman, *The Oregon Trail*, various editions, Little, Brown; especially Chaps. 1–7

Walter Prescott Webb, *The Great Plains*, Ginn, 1931, Chaps. 2 and 5

BRIEF NOTES ON THE SOURCES

370   The account of Queue de Bœuf comes from Maj. Osborne Cross, *Journey to Fort Kearny, 1850*, Senate Exec. Doc. 1, 31st Congress, 2d Session, 1850–51 (Serial No. 587), a reference to be used frequently in succeeding chapters.

The Great Plains were compared with the Russian steppes by I. I. Stevens in *Supplementary Report of Exploration for a Route for the Pacific Railroad*, Senate Exec. Doc. 46, 36th Congress, 2d Session, 1858–59 (Serial No. 992), p. 287.

371   F. V. Hayden wrote many reports on the West in his capacity as government geologist. This reference is from his *Preliminary Report of the U.S. Geological Survey of Wyoming and Portions of Contiguous Territories*, in *Fourth Annual Report*, 1871, p. 103.

372   The journals of Pike and Long and of Lewis and Clark have been edited and annotated so frequently that copies are likely to be available in college and large public libraries.

The quotation from Gouverneur K. Warren is in his *Explorations in Nebraska*, Nov. 24, 1858, Senate Exec. Doc. 1, 35th Congress, 2d Session, 1859 (Serial No. 975), pp. 620–70; reference on p. 644.

373   The description of Adolph Wislizenus, from *Memoir of a Tour to Northern Mexico, Connected with Col. Doniphan's Expedition, 1846 and 1847*, Senate Misc. Doc. 26, 30th Congress, 1st Session, 1848 (Serial No. 511), p. 7, should be better known than it apparently is.

375   One of the first scientific studies of the Black Hills was that of Walter P. Jenney, *Report of the Mineral Wealth, Climate, and Rain-fall, and Natural Resources of the Black Hills of South Dakota*, Senate Exec. Doc. 51, 44th Congress, 1st Session, 1876 (Serial No. 1664); references on pp. 57–63.

Randolph B. Marcy, leader of many surveys into the southern Plains and author of numerous reports, is one of the most reliable authorities. His comment here comes from *Explorations of the Big Wichita and Headwaters of the Brazos River, 1854*, Senate Exec. Doc. 60, 34th Congress, 1st Session (Serial No. 821), p. 5.

376   Year-round grazing in the Plains, as related here, is from the *Report of the Commissioner of Agriculture*, 1870, pp. 303–04.

377 Marcy describes the Cross Timbers in his *Exploration of the Red River of Louisiana in 1852*, Senate Exec. Doc. 54, 32d Congress, 2d Session, 1853 (Serial No. 666), pp. 84–85. Mesquite and its uses are detailed in "Food Products of the North American Indian," *Report of the Commissioner of Agriculture*, 1870, pp. 404–28; reference on p. 410.

378–83 The basic source for knowledge of the buffalo is J. A. Allen, "The American Bison, Living and Extinct," *Memoirs of the Museum of Comparative Zoology*, Vol. 4, No. 10, Harvard University Press, 1876. Nearly every documentary account of Western exploration, such as those already referred to, contains comment on the buffalo. The quotation from Howard Stansbury is in his *Exploration and Survey of the Valley of Great Salt Lake of Utah*, Senate Exec. Doc. 3, 32d Congress, Special Session, March, 1851 (Serial No. 609), pp. 34–37. The description of buffalo in the Yellowstone by W. F. Raynolds is in the report of his exploration, Senate Exec. Doc. 77, 40th Congress, 2d Session, 1866 (Serial No. 1317).

383 The Gilfillan family method of hunting antelope is related in *North Dakota Historical Quarterly*, Vol. 1 (1927), pp. 39–40.

384–86 The section on the locust is based mainly on "The Rocky Mountain Locust, or Grasshopper of the West," *Report of the Commissioner of Agriculture, 1877*, 1878. The description of the North Dakota flight of 1871 is in Mrs. H. E. Crofford, "Pioneer Days in North Dakota," *North Dakota Historical Quarterly*, Vol. 2 (1928), p. 131.

CHAPTER 21: Passage Across the Plains

REFERENCES FOR FURTHER READING

Hiram N. Crittenden, *History of Early Steamboat Navigation on the Missouri River*, 2 vols., Francis P. Harper, N.Y., 1903

Le Roy R. Hafen, *Fort Laramie and the Pageant of the West, 1834–1890*, Arthur H. Clark Co., Glendale, Calif., 1938

Ellen C. Semple, *American History and Its Geographical Conditions*, revised by Clarence F. Jones, Houghton Mifflin, 1933, Chaps. 10–11

For maps of the Western routes and forts, see James Truslow Adams, ed., *Atlas of American History*, Scribner's, 1943, pp. 100–101, 104, 112–19

BRIEF NOTES ON THE SOURCES

389 Santa Fe in the 1840's and 1850's is described by William W. H. Davis in *El Gringo; or, New Mexico and Her People*, New York, 1857; Adolph Wislizenus (citation in previous chapter); and Josiah Gregg, *Commerce of the Prairies*, 2 vols., Philadelphia, 1845, Vol. 1, pp. 143–45.

390–92 Particularly helpful in a detailed study of the Santa Fe Trail is James Josiah Webb, *Adventures in the Santa Fé Trade, 1844–1847*, ed. by Ralph P. Bieber, Arthur H. Clark Co., Glendale, Calif., 1931. The description of Council Grove, for example, comes from a footnote on p. 46 of this book.

392–93 The method of the Santa Fe trade and the products carried each way over it are touched upon in a great number of sources. Besides those mentioned there is "The Santa Fe Trail of Yesterday and Today," Florence E. Barnes, *Mentor*, Vol.

16, 1928, pp. 17–22, and Archer B. Hulbert, *Southwest on the Turquoise Trail,* Public Library, Denver, 1933.

394–95 The main dependence in this description of the Platte is Major Osborne Cross's narrative, cited in the notes on Chapter 20.

395 On the Laramie forts, see Hafen, cited above, various pages. Hafen also discusses the first emigrations over the Oregon Trail.

397 Among Hafen's contributions to the knowledge of the handcart migration is his paper " Hand Cart Migration across the Plains," Chap. 5 in *The Trans-Mississippi West,* University of Colorado Press, 1930.

398 Stansbury's narrative has been referred to in Chapter 20.

398–400 Details on the wagon roads in South Pass and the charges of ferries on approaching it are taken from *Report upon the Pacific Wagon Roads,* House Exec. Doc. 108, 35th Congress, 2d Session, 1859 (Serial No. 1008). The map of the pass roads (Figure 104) was adapted from this report. South Pass has been interestingly discussed by Edward W. Gilbert, " South Pass: A Study in the Historical Geography of the United States," *Scottish Geographical Magazine,* Vol. 45 (1929), pp. 144–54.

401 The full title of Marcy's book is *The Prairie Traveler, A Hand-Book for Overland Expeditions* [etc.], Harper, 1859.

401–04 The most comprehensive study of Missouri River navigation is Crittenden's book, noted above. Data concerning the length of navigation season and like matters come from the report of Gouverneur K. Warren, *Preliminary Report of Explorations in Nebraska,* Senate Exec. Doc. 1, 35th Congress, 2d Session, 1859 (Serial No. 975), pp. 651–52; and from *Reports of Explorations and Surveys to Ascertain the Most Practical and Economical Route for a Railroad from the Mississippi River to the Pacific Ocean . . . in 1853–[56],* 2 vols. in 13, U.S. War Department, 1855–80 (usually referred to as *Pacific Railway Surveys*), Vol. I, 1855, pp. 160–77 (John Lambert) and pp. 231–47 (A. J. Donelson). Use of the river by the military is considered by Raymond J. Welty in " The Frontier Army on the Missouri River, 1860–1870," *North Dakota Historical Quarterly,* Vol. 2 (1928), pp. 85–99.

406 A valuable study of the overland mail, providing the quotation used here, is Curtis Nettels, " The Overland Mail Issue during the Fifties," *Missouri Historical Review,* Vol. 18 (1924), pp. 521–34.

CHAPTER 22: Settlement in the Plains

REFERENCES FOR FURTHER READING

Edward E. Dale, *The Ranch Cattle Industry,* University of Oklahoma Press, 1930
Ernest S. Osgood, *The Day of the Cattleman,* University of Minnesota Press, 1929
Louis Pelzer, " Trails of the Trans-Mississippi Cattle Frontier," James F. Willard and Colin B. Goodykoontz, eds., *The Trans-Mississippi West,* University of Colorado Press, 1930, pp. 139–61
Stephen S. Visher, *The Geography of South Dakota,* South Dakota State Geological Survey, *Bulletin* 8, 1918, Chap. 7
Walter Prescott Webb, *The Great Plains,* Ginn, 1931, Chap. 6

BRIEF NOTES ON THE SOURCES

406 For the origin of the cattle industry of the Plains north of Texas see Osgood (above), Chap. 1, " The Cattleman's Frontier," pp. 1–23. According to

Osgood (p. 9): "The cattle industry of the High Plains began as a result of the necessities of the emigrants along the Oregon Trail."

408–09 The "discovery" of the winter-grazing possibilities of the Northern Plains is variously attributed. In the *Report of the Commissioner of Agriculture* for 1870, p. 303, it is stated that horses, oxen, and mules used in the 1849 emigration were wintered in Rocky Mountain valleys without hay or grain, and that "In the 1859 emigration winter grazing was also put to the test and found successful."

409 Louis Pelzer arrives at these conclusions regarding the trading companies in his chapter cited above, pp. 139–42.

410–11 Range rights are fully discussed by Osgood, *The Day of the Cattleman,* Chap. 5, "Organization," pp. 114–75.

414 The table of cattle droves is from Clarence Gordon, "Report on Cattle, Sheep, and Swine, Supplementary to Enumeration of Livestock on Farms in 1880," *Tenth Census,* Vol. 3, pp. 951–1110; reference on p. 975. This is one of the basic sources for studies of the Plains cattle industry.

415 A less temperate explanation for the decline of the open-range cattle industry was advanced by Owen Wister, famed for his Western novels. Writing in *Harper's New Monthly Magazine,* Vol. 91 (1895), pp. 602–17, Wister attributes the disappearance of the Western cowpuncher to three factors: the exhaustion of virgin grass, the coming of the wire fence, and "Mr. Armour of Chicago, who set the price of beef to suit himself" (p. 615).

417–20 The section on public land regulations is based in large part upon Benjamin H. Hibbard, *Public Land Policies,* Macmillan, 1924.

422–23 For a recent discussion of droughts in the Great Plains see James C. Malin, "Dust Storms, 1850–1900," *Kansas Historical Quarterly,* Vol. 14 (May, August, November, 1946).

424–25 The discussion of the settlement of South Dakota is largely based on the historical portions of Visher's study, noted above.

CHAPTER 23: Texas

REFERENCES FOR FURTHER READING

Grant Foreman, ed., *Marcy & the Gold Seekers: The Journal of Captain R. B. Marcy,* University of Oklahoma Press, 1939
John A. Hawgood, *The Tragedy of German-America,* Putnam, 1940, Chap. 5, "Germany in the Republic and State of Texas"
Almon E. Parkins, *The South, Its Economic-Geographic Development,* Wiley, 1938
Walter Prescott Webb, *The Great Plains,* Ginn, 1931

BRIEF NOTES ON THE SOURCES

427 The quotation on the Texas coast from John R. Bartlett is from his *Personal Narrative in Texas, New Mexico, California, Sonora, and Chihuahua, Connected with the United States and Mexican Boundary Commission during the Years 1850, '51, '52, and '53,* 2 vols., New York, 1854; reference in Vol. 2, p. 533. The quotation from William H. Emory is in his *Report on the United States and Mexican Boundary Survey, under the Direction of the Secretary of the Interior,* 1857, p. 56.

428 From John Pope comes the description of the upper Trinity country, in *Pacific Railway Surveys,* Vol. II, 1855, pp. 9–10.

429 Marcy's description of the "beautiful panorama" comes from one of his many journals, *Explorations of the Big Wichita and Headwaters of the Brazos Rivers* [1854], Senate Exec. Doc. 60, 34th Congress, 1st Session (Serial No. 821), p. 4.

430-31 Bartlett (above) describes Goliad, Vol. 1, pp. 26–27, and San Antonio, pp. 38–45. This is supplemented here by a *Report of the Secretary of War*, Senate Exec. Doc. 32, 31st Congress, 1st Session, 1849 (Serial No. 558), pp. 9–10.

433 Quotations from Solms-Braunfels come from a translation, *Texas, 1844–45*, by Karl, Prince of Solms-Braunfels, Anson Jones Press, Houston, 1936. Bartlett's account of Fredericksburg is in his *Personal Narrative*, Vol. 1, 59–60. Dr. Hawgood's excellent chapter in *The Tragedy of German-America* provides a background for this topic.

435-37 The earlier development of the cattle industry (to the 1840's) is derived mainly from the summary by Clarence Gordon, "Report on Cattle, Sheep and Swine," *Tenth Census*, 1880, Vol. 3, p. 965.

437 Data on the ranches specified come from "The Texas Cattle Trade," *Report of the Department of Agriculture* to the 41st Congress, 3d Session, 1870–71, pp. 346–49, 1871. Some of these data are corroborated in the paper by Cyrus Thomas, "Pastoral Lands and Stock Raising," in F. V. Hayden, *Preliminary Report of the U.S. Geological Survey of Wyoming*, 1870, pp. 248–57.

437-40 Cattle trails are discussed in many of the above sources and, in addition, by John Rossel, "The Chisholm Trail," *Kansas Historical Quarterly*, Vol. 5 (1936), pp. 3–14; and Charles M. Harger, "Cattle Trails of the Prairies," *Scribner's Magazine*, Vol. 11 (1892), pp. 732–42. The delivery of 25,000 steers to South Dakota is told by the drover, James H. Cook, in "Trailing Texas Long Horn Cattle through Nebraska," *Nebraska State Historical Society Publications*, Vol. 18 (1917), pp. 260–68.

442 Marcy's description of West Texas is found in his *Report and Map of the Route from Fort Smith, Ark., to Santa Fe, New Mexico, 1849*, Senate Exec. Doc. 12, 31st Congress, 1st Session, 1850 (Serial No. 554), p. 185. It was John Pope who corrected some of Marcy's observations in his railroad report, *loc. cit.*, p. 9.

442-43 Bartlett's El Paso account is in his *Personal Narrative*, Vol. 1, pp. 145–46, and that of William W. H. Davis in *El Gringo; or, New Mexico and Her People*, New York, 1857, pp. 379–84.

CHAPTER 24: Colorado

BRIEF NOTES ON THE SOURCES

There are several excellent books which deal briefly with the topics included in this chapter, but none are sufficiently accessible to justify a list of general sources. Comments in the source list below will suggest a few items which might be available in the average college or large public library.

444-46 The early growth of Denver is traced by Le Roy R. Hafen in his introduction to *Pike's Peak Gold Rush Guidebooks of 1859*, Arthur H. Clark Co., Glendale, Calif., 1942, pp. 21–80 (Southwest Historical Series, Vol. IX).

446-52 Field work by the author and two sources provide the basis for the Central City discussion: *U.S. Geological Exploration of the Fortieth Parallel*, Vol. III, James D. Hague, *Mining Industry* (Clarence King Survey), 1870; Rossiter W. Raymond, *Statistics of Mines and Mining in the States and Territories West of the Rocky*

Mountains, House Exec. Doc. 210, 42d Congress, 3d Session, 1872 (Serial No. 1567). Supplementary material was secured from other contemporary observations, such as Horace Greeley, *An Overland Journey, from New York to San Francisco, in the Summer of 1859,* San Francisco, 1860; Samuel Bowles, *Across the Continent: A Summer's Journey to the Rocky Mountains,* New York, 1865; Henry Villard, *The Past and Present of the Pike's Peak Gold Regions,* St. Louis, 1860 (which contains passages strangely resembling many in Greeley's account); C. M. Clark, *A Trip to Pike's Peak, and Notes on the Way,* Chicago, 1861; and Albert D. Richardson, *Beyond the Mississippi,* Hartford, 1867. Also helpful is Le Roy R. Hafen, *Overland Routes to the Gold Fields, 1859, from Contemporary Diaries,* Arthur H. Clark Co., Glendale, Calif., 1941 (Southwest Historical Series, Vol. XI). An excellent summary is provided by Harold A. Hoffmeister in " Central City Mining Area," *Economic Geography,* Vol. 16 (1940), pp. 96–104.

452   The quotation from Cyrus Thomas is from Part III, " Agriculture," p. 252, of F. V. Hayden, *Preliminary Report of the U.S. Geological Survey of Wyoming,* 1870.

455–58   The treatment of the German and Longmont colonies is a brief and inadequate summary of portions of " Experiments in Colorado Colonization," ed. by James F. Willard and Colin B. Goodykoontz, *University of Colorado Historical Collections,* Vol. 3 (1926).

458   The basic source for the Greeley colony is " Colonization" in *Report of the Commissioner of Agriculture,* 1870, pp. 569–72, and " Modes and Results of Irrigation," *ibid.,* p. 583.

460–61   The comment on Colorado passes is an abstract of portions of Ralph H. Brown's papers on that subject, including " Trans-Montane Routes of Colorado," *Economic Geography,* Vol. 4 (1930), pp. 412–24.

CHAPTER 25: The Oregon Country

REFERENCES FOR FURTHER READING

Otis W. Freeman and Howard H. Martin, eds., *The Pacific Northwest,* Wiley, 1942; especially Chaps. 1–2, 26–27
Joseph Schafer, *History of the Pacific Northwest,* Macmillan, 1928
Ellen C. Semple, *American History and Its Geographic Conditions,* revised by Clarence F. Jones, Houghton Mifflin, 1933; Chap. 11, " Expansion into the Far West by the Northern Trails "
Reuben G. Thwaites, ed., *Early Western Travels:* Vol. 7, *Adventures of the First Settlers on the Oregon or Columbia River* [1849] by Alexander Ross; Vol. 28, *Travels on the Great Western Prairies, the Anahuac and Rocky Mountains and in the Oregon Territory* [1843] by Thomas J. Farnham; Vol. 30, *Journal of Travels over the Rocky Mountains, to the Mouth of the Columbia River; Made during the Years 1845 and 1846,* by Joel Palmer

BRIEF NOTES ON THE SOURCES

465–67   Osborne Cross's *Journey to Fort Kearny, 1850* — Senate Exec. Doc. 1, 31st Congress, 2d Session (Serial No. 587) — has been referred to in other chapters; the reference here is on p. 159. Cross describes Grand Ronde on p. 212. The quotation from the Hudson's Bay agent is from Dr. Gairdner, " Notes on the Geography of the Columbia River," *Journal of the Royal Geographical Society*, Vol. 11 (1841), pp. 251–57.

467–69 The " Oregon question " is usually covered in American histories; especially useful treatments are in Schafer, and Freeman and Martin, both noted above. Thornton's memorial is printed in Senate Misc. Doc. 143, 30th Congress, 1st Session, 1847–48 (Serial No. 511).

470 Jesse Applegate's description is in his " Agricultural Report " in the *Report of the Commissioner of Patents, 1851*, Part II, 1852, p. 468. Comment on severe winters in the past comes from J. Orin Oliphant, " Winter Losses of Cattle in the Oregon Country, 1847–90," *Washington Historical Quarterly*, Vol. 23 (1932), pp. 3–17.

472 The particular cattle drive mentioned is narrated in *The Diary of Philip Leget Edwards, The Great Cattle Drive from California to Oregon in 1837*, Grabhorn Press, San Francisco, 1932.

472–73 An original source for Mullan's Road is W. M. Franklin, " The Geography, Topography, and Resources of the Northwestern Territories," an address before the American Geographical and Statistical Society, in his *Miners' and Travelers' Guide*, New York, 1865.

474 The humorous reference on mail delivery, or the lack of it, is from *Contributions to the Historical Society of Montana*, Vol. 2 (1896), p. 306.

476–77 Samuel Bowles describes Columbia River navigation in 1865 in his *Across the Continent*, New York, 1865, pp. 184–88.

477 Indian fishing methods are discussed by Overton Johnson and William Ware in *Route across the Rocky Mountains, 1846*, with notes by Carl L. Cannon, Princeton University Press, 1932, p. 60.

477–78 Agriculture in the Willamette is referred to in *Report of the Commissioner of Patents, 1850*, Part II, and by Bowles at a later time in *Across the Continent*, p. 179.

478–79 The Umpqua description is an abstract from Applegate, *loc. cit.*

480–82 Mining in the Northern Rockies is described by Bowles and other travelers; also by Judge F. H. Moody in " A Sketch of the Early History of Montana," *Contributions to the Historical Society of Montana*, Vol. 2 (1896), pp. 88–106, especially pp. 102–04.

CHAPTER 26: Great Basin and Arid Southwest

REFERENCE FOR FURTHER READING

Edmund W. Gilbert, *The Exploration of Western America, 1800–1850*, Cambridge University Press, 1933

BRIEF NOTES ON THE SOURCES

483 Frémont's basic work on the Great Basin is *Geographical Memoir upon Upper California*, Senate Exec. Doc. 148, 30th Congress, 1st Session, 1847–48 (Serial No. 511).

484–86 A significant article, dealing in part with the Mormon settlements, is George F. Brightman, " The Boundaries of Utah," *Economic Geography*, Vol. 16 (1940), pp. 87–95.

486 Panguitch as an example of the mobility of Mormon settlements is outlined in J. W. Powell, *Report on the Arid Regions of the United States*, Washington, 1879, p. 134.

486–89 If government documents are available, one could do no better for further study of the Salt Lake Oasis than to consult Howard Stansbury's *Exploration and Survey of the Valley of the Great Salt Lake of Utah*, Senate Exec. Doc. 3, 32d Congress, Special Session, 1851 (Serial No. 608), 1852. Gilbert contributed Chap. 7, " Irrigable Lands of the Salt Lake Drainage System," of which this is a summary, to Powell's treatise on the arid lands.

489 Similarly, the discussion of the Sevier Oasis comes mainly from Clarence E. Dutton's " Irrigable Lands of the Valley of the Sevier River," Chapter 8 in Powell's *Report*. Any student seriously interested in the arid West, not merely in the Utah region, should become familiar with Powell's classic.

492 The *Pacific Railway Survey* volumes applicable to the arid Southwest are Vols. 3 and 4, 1856 (surveys made in 1853–54), to which there were many contributors. First published as official documents, the reports were later issued by commercial companies. One of the documental accounts is House Exec. Doc. 91, 33rd Congress, 2d Session, 11 vols., 1855 (Serial Nos. 791–801). The *Report upon the Pacific Wagon Roads* appeared as House Exec. Doc. 108, 35th Congress, 2d Session, 1859 (Serial No. 1008).

493 Data on the agriculture of the Navajo Indians are included in William W. H. Davis, *El Gringo; or, New Mexico and Her People*, 1857, p. 395. Estimates of numbers of Indians are to be found in many of the official surveys, including the following three: Lt. Col. W. H. Emory, *Notes of a Military Reconnaissance from Fort Leavenworth to San Diego, 1848*, House Exec. Doc. 41, 30th Congress, 1st Session (Serial No. 517); *Journal of Lt. Col. Philip St. George Cooke, from Santa Fe to San Diego, 1849*, Senate Exec. Doc. 2, 31st Congress, Special Session (Serial No. 547); and *Pacific Railway Surveys*, Vol. 3, Pt. 3 by A. W. Whipple and others, p. 9 *et. seq.*

Both Alfred L. Kroeber and Kirk Bryan have written much and instructively on the Southwestern Indian and his land. Only two of their articles will be cited here: Kroeber outlines the " Cultural and Natural Areas of Native North America " in *University of California Publications in American Archaeology and Ethnology*, Vol. 38 (1939) — see especially pp. 32–43, 376, and Map 1a. Bryan proposes the two spheres (Puebloan and Hohokam) in " Pre-Columbian Agriculture in the Southwest, as Conditioned by Periods of Alluviation," *Annals of the Association of American Geographers*, Vol. 31 (1914), pp. 219–42.

494–95 An excellent study of Indian farming in the Southwest is provided by Kirk Bryan in " Flood Water Farming," *Geographical Review*, Vol. 19 (1929), pp. 444–56. The basic study of Herbert E. Gregory, *The Navajo Country*, U.S. Geological Survey, Water Supply Paper 380, 1916, should be consulted if available. Flood irrigation is discussed on p. 104. John R. Bartlett describes canal irrigation among the Maricopa Indians in his *Personal Narrative*, 1854, Vol. 2, p. 232.

496–98 Native food products of the Southwest are discussed exhaustively in " Food Products of the North American Indian," pp. 404–08 of *Report of the Commissioner of Agriculture*, 1870, of which these pages are, in part, a digest. George F. Carter in " The Role of Plants in Geography," *Geographical Review*, Vol. 36 (1946), pp. 121–31, presents new evidence of the spread of corn from Mexico into present-day United States.

498 Philip St. George Cooke's description of the Maricopa house is on page 53 of his *Journal*. Types of habitations are touched upon by the surveyors listed above. Reference to Audubon is from *Audubon's Western Journal*, ed. by F. H. Hodder, Arthur H. Clark Co., Cleveland, 1906, pp. 146–53.

500 The important study by Leslie Spier is *Yuman Tribes of the Gila River*, University of Chicago Press, 1933. The diagram of the Maricopa food quest derives mainly from data contained in Spier's work.

Supplementary Table

The question may well arise as to the number of Gila Indian peoples now on reservations or under jurisdiction in the Southwest. It will be noted that the reservations include the approximate areas occupied by these various groups in earlier days. The following table is abstracted from *Statistical Supplement to the Annual Report of the Commissioner of Indian Affairs for the Fiscal Year Ended June 30, 1943*, U.S. Department of the Interior.

GILA INDIANS

Reservations	Total	Residing at Jurisdiction	Residing at Another Jurisdiction or Elsewhere
Gila River			
Maricopa	284	270	14
Pima	4,531	4,349	182
Other tribes	280	247	33
Maricopa or Ak-Chin			
Papago	124	124	0
Salt River			
Maricopa	135	135	0
Pima	1,070	1,050	20
Other tribes	51	40	11
Gila Bend			
Papago	127	95	32
Papago			
Papago	5,645	5,217	428
Pima	27	27	0
Other tribes	12	10	2
San Xavier			
Papago	527	497	30

CHAPTER 27: California: San Francisco and Its Hinterland

REFERENCES FOR FURTHER READING

John B. Leighly, " Settlement and Cultivation in the Summer-Dry Climates," in U.S. Department of Agriculture, *Yearbook: Climate and Man*, 1941, pp. 197–204

John C. Parrish, " By Sea to California," in *The Trans-Mississippi West*, University of Colorado Press, 1930, pp. 125–38

BRIEF NOTES ON THE SOURCES

502 Frémont's comment on the effect of the gold rush is in *Frémont's Narrative, Exploring Expedition to the Rocky Mountains,* Buffalo, 1849, pp. 427–28. Buffum's journal was published as *Six Months in the Gold Mines,* Philadelphia, 1850; reference on p. 108.

503 The quotation from W. H. Emory is from p. 2 of his *Report on the United States and Mexican Boundary Survey,* Philadelphia, 1857; original source: House Exec. Doc. 135, 34th Congress, 1st Session (Serial No. 861).

505 Data on arrivals and departures at San Francisco come from Horace Greeley, *An Overland Journey,* New York, 1860, p. 368.

507 The quotation from the government report is in *Information in Relation to the Geology and Topography of California,* Senate Exec. Doc. 47, 31st Congress, 1st Session, 1849–50 (Serial No. 558), pp. 12–13.

507–08 Hydraulic mining is described in " A Trip to the Mining Regions in the Spring of 1859," translated in *California Historical Society Quarterly,* Vol. 11 (1932–33), pp. 224–46; 321–38; quotation on p. 237. The original is *Californischer Staats-Kalender* by Eduard Vischer.

508 Hallock F. Raup has contributed a paper in the *Geographical Review,* Vol. 35 (1945), pp. 653–58, " Place Names of the California Gold Rush," of which these paragraphs are a partial summary. Studies of the toponymy of California include Alfred L. Kroeber, " California Place Names of Indian Origin," *University of California Publications in American Archaeology and Ethnology,* Vol. 12 (1915), pp. 31–69.

509–13 The main sources used in this section are *Reports of the Commissioner of Agriculture* for 1866, 1872, and 1873, entitled respectively: *California — Her Agricultural Resources; Reclamation of Swamp and Overflowed Lands in California;* and *Note on Tule Lands.*

513 The climatic data come from the *Report of the Commissioner of Agriculture, 1874,* " Irrigation in California," p. 353.

515 John R. Bartlett, *Personal Narrative,* 1854, has been referred to in earlier chapters. He describes the Napa and Santa Clara valleys in Vol. 2, pp. 14–18 and 54–56.

516 Bartlett's discussion of the quicksilver mines is supplemented by Joseph W. Revere, *A Tour of Duty in California,* New York, 1849, p. 54.

CHAPTER 28: California: Southern Valleys and Sierras

BRIEF NOTES ON THE SOURCES

518–19 This summary of passes and routes comes in part from R. S. Williamson in Vol. 5 of *Pacific Railway Surveys,* p. 22. An excellent study of the same topic within recent years is that of John H. Kemler, " Railway Entrances and Exits to Los Angeles," *Economic Geography,* Vol. 16 (1940), pp. 312–14.

520 William P. Blake contributed to the Williamson volume (above), this quotation on San Gabriel being from p. 539.

521–22 Blake also describes vineyard control in the Los Angeles region, *loc cit.,* p. 77.

522–25 The discussion of San Bernardino derives mainly from H. F. Raup,

" San Bernardino, California, Settlement and Growth of a Pass-Site City," in *University of California Publications in Geography,* Vol. 8 (1940), 52 pp. and plates. Figure 141 is reproduced here through courtesy of Professor Raup and the University of California Press.

525-27 Similarly, the description of San Fernando depends chiefly on another excellent study of recent years: Clifford M. Zierer, " San Fernando — A Type of Southern California Town," *Annals of the Association of American Geographers,* Vol. 24 (1934), pp. 1–28.

527-28 Professor Raup is the authority on the Anaheim Colony, having published several papers on this and related topics; most recently, " Anaheim: A German Community of Frontier California," *American-German Review,* December, 1945, pp. 7–11.

529 Brigadier-General Bennet Riley gives his realistic view of Kern Basin in Senate Exec. Doc. 18, 31st Congress, 1st Session, 1849–50 (Serial No. 557), p. 672; and Lieutenant George H. Derby describes the Tulare Basin in his report published as Senate Exec. Doc. 110, 32d Congress, 1st Session, 1852 (Serial No. 621), p. 7. T. Butler King, Special Agent to California, reports on Indians in House Exec. Doc. 59, 31st Congress, 1st Session, 1849–50 (Serial No. 577). Testimony on the same subject is given by Adam Johnston, Redick McKee, W. M. Reyer, D. M. Wozencraft, and several others in Senate Exec. Doc. 4, 33rd Congress, Special Session, 1853 (Serial No. 688). Unfortunately for the modern student, their conclusions about the numbers and abilities of the California Indians are often contradictory.

530-32 The Commissioner of Agriculture discusses irrigation in the San Joaquin in his *Report* for 1874, pp. 352–62. The discussion of the San Joaquin is based primarily on a paper well known to professional geographers, Charles C. Colby, " The California Raisin Industry — A Study in Geographic Interpretation," *Annals of the Association of American Geographers,* Vol. 14 (1924), pp. 49–108.

Biographical Index

Note: See Bibliography (pp. 539–71) for other biographical references.

Subject Index